PSYCHOLOGY:

UNDERSTANDING HUMAN BEHAVIOR

PSYCHOLOGY

NEW YORK   TORONTO   LONDON

UNDERSTANDING HUMAN BEHAVIOR

Aaron Quinn Sartain

Alvin John North

Jack Roy Strange

Harold Martin Chapman

SOUTHERN METHODIST UNIVERSITY

McGRAW-HILL BOOK COMPANY, INC.   1958

This book is set in Caledonia, a typeface designed by the American artist and calligrapher D. A. Dwiggins. The chapter titles are set in Standard. Drawings are by Bob Gill. Technical illustrations are by Felix Cooper. Bea Danville was the picture editor.

PREFACE

We believe psychology can be effectively presented to the beginning student as a science and still be meaningfully related to his own experience. This has been our primary aim and constant guide throughout the writing of this book.

We have focused attention on material that is practical and useful to the general student. We have tried to shape this material to the student's interests. Our hope has been to produce an introductory text which would attract the student and lead him to continue his interest in and study of psychology after the course is over. We have recognized the danger of expounding solely in technical terms on the one hand, and the sin of oversimplification on the other. We have tried to chart a sensible course between these two extremes.

A preliminary edition of the present text has been used at Southern Methodist University for three years in a one-semester introductory course. The reception of this preliminary edition has convinced us that not only could psychology be presented in an interesting and meaningful way, but that the student could learn from it substantial facts and principles. Our experience led us to believe that students in the course were more interested than usual and that their achievement was higher.

The coverage of the present edition is complete and balanced while remaining within the scope of a one-semester course. Emphasis has been on understanding everyday human behavior; the areas of psychology which have to do with the abnormal or bizarre have received little emphasis. Since we have felt that the student must first understand the fundamentals of psychology before he can appreciate its specific applications, the space devoted to applied psychology has been kept at a minimum.

The plan of this book has been to treat as related topics motivation, emotion, the self, self-defense, and personality, including cultural and social influences. We have also included a survey of the physiological factors that provide the basis for these and other topics, such as perception, thinking, and learning. In a separate section we have discussed the instruments of evaluation of performance, ability, intelligence, etc. In addition we have made a determined effort to treat the relation between heredity and environment in a consistent and significant fashion.

References have been cited wherever the subject under discussion was controversial or where we felt the student would want to refer to the primary source. From experience, however, we have found that introductory students are not much impressed by citations of research. We feel it to be of greater importance to take the pertinent research into account in our own thinking. The material presented to these students has to stand or fall largely on the basis of its reasonableness, cogency, adherence to a systematic point of view, and relevance to their experience.

It is imperative to the student's understanding of the subject that he avail himself of the essential research data. To facilitate this and at the same time to provide material which stresses the importance of experimentation in psychology, we have interpolated into the text related research reports. These studies should impress upon the student that the theories of psychology are continually being modified and qualified by experimental research in the field.

It should be noted that we have raised many questions throughout the book: in the body of the text, in the Question sections at the end of each chapter, and in the captions for the illustrations. In answering these questions the student will soon realize that there is much in psychology that will demand his best thought and energy. Moreover, these questions will serve to remind him that he must constantly review his own acquired knowledge, not just the day before the test, but throughout the course.

Lastly, in order to assist the student to learn introductory psychology well enough to demonstrate objectively this learning, we have prepared a separate *Student's Guide*. This guide is designed to assist the student in studying the textual material and to check his understanding of the subject. It is not designed as a substitute for actual study; our purpose has been rather to provide material to help the student help himself.

As is always true in an undertaking of this sort, we are indebted to many people for criticism, encouragement, and direct assistance. Specifically, appreciation is expressed to Mrs. Dorothy Zook for her painstaking and efficient assistance in preparing the manuscript; to Mrs. Virginia Chancey who was most helpful in the development of the book and who has provided the supplementary materials; to Dr. Clifford T. Morgan, Consulting Editor of the McGraw-Hill Series in Psychology, who offered many valuable suggestions regarding style and content; and to our many students who used the book in its preliminary editions and who made many suggestions that have influenced its final form.

AARON Q. SARTAIN
ALVIN J. NORTH
JACK R. STRANGE
HAROLD M. CHAPMAN

RELATED FILMS

The 16mm sound films listed below are especially suitable for use in conjunction with this book:

COMMON FALLACIES ABOUT GROUP DIFFERENCES *The education of an uninformed but implacable exponent of all the usual group prejudices.* (Chapters 2 and 8.)
15 minutes

DEVELOPMENT OF INDIVIDUAL DIFFERENCES *Reviews and illustrates what is known and generally accepted about the relative influence of heredity and environment.* (Chapters 2 and 16.)
13 minutes

HEREDITY AND FAMILY ENVIRONMENT *Illustrates the roles of heredity and environment, how they mesh in actual living, voluntary and involuntary actions, and the physical effects of emotion.* (Chapter 2.)
9 minutes

TOWARD EMOTIONAL MATURITY *An eighteen-year-old girl remembers episodes from her early life in which love, fear, and hate were not always controlled, and is then able to make a decision which shows her emotional growth.* (Chapter 4.)
11 minutes

THE BRAIN AND BEHAVIOR *Describes the structure and function of the brain, especially its more complex areas, illustrated by case studies of persons with brain injuries.* (Chapters 9 and 10.)
22 minutes

HABIT PATTERNS *How habits are formed, and the social and personal advantages of the early formation of orderly and systematic daily habits.* (Chapter 9.)
15 minutes

PERCEPTION *Presents the theory that human perception is not merely a sensing of stimuli, but is a set of extremely elaborate processes through which we organize our sensory impressions.* (Chapter 11.)
17 minutes

FACING REALITY *How a high school boy, the victim of negative social attitudes, is helped by a sympathetic instructor who encourages him to talk over his problems.* (Chapter 13.)
12 minutes

CONFLICT *The decisions confronting a typical college student illustrate some basic conflicts created when social beings face opposing goals in everyday situations.* (Chapter 19.)
18 minutes

All of the above may be purchased from the Text-Film Department of the McGraw-Hill Book Company.

CONTENTS

PSYCHOLOGY:

UNDERSTANDING HUMAN BEHAVIOR

1 THE STUDY OF HUMAN BEHAVIOR

Interest in psychology has been increasing steadily in recent years. Psychologists are now found in the armed services, in government agencies, in mental hospitals, and in business and industry, and they are becoming more and more numerous. Articles are written by and about psychologists in the leading magazines of our country, and psychological themes underlie the plots of a great many books.

This development is not at all surprising, for all of us are concerned with human behavior, and this is the principal area of investigation for psychology. All of us have to adjust to the presence and the reactions of other people, and frequently our most important need is to understand them, to know what their intentions or motives are, and to anticipate and even control their responses. Under these circumstances we should expect a great deal of interest in psychology.

INTEREST IN HUMAN BEHAVIOR

Early in life we learn how important it is to each of us to get along satisfactorily with other people. We find that what others do to us and for us and how they feel about us make a great deal of difference. Our means of earning a livelihood and often our very existence depend on other people. Thus winning their approval—or at least avoiding their great displeasure—becomes a very important matter to each of us.

Besides, we all need companionship. Friendship and family life, by their very nature, depend on other people. Some of our greatest satisfactions come from cooperating with others in projects in which

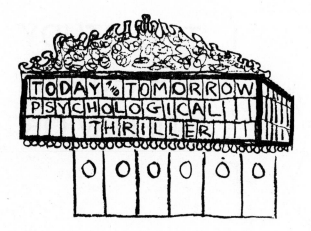

we are all interested, and some of our greatest disappointments stem from failure in such projects.

This matter takes on even greater importance if we happen to have responsibilities for leadership. Suppose we are officers in a club or some other group. If we take our responsibilities seriously, we are faced with the question of how to get people to work together to achieve a common purpose. How can we get the group to realize and adopt as their own the goals which they should set for themselves? How can we motivate the group—and the individual members of the group—to work enthusiastically for these goals? What can we do to interest Bill? Will the same approach work for Joe and Mary, or shall we need two or even three different methods here? How far can we afford to go in turning leadership over to the group itself rather than keeping the decision making entirely in our own hands? Needless to say, our answers to such questions as these will go a long way toward determining whether our group is successful or unsuccessful.

The leader of a business enterprise faces the same problems, and he plays for high stakes as he strives for cooperation among people. Indeed, the success of the business as a whole depends to a large extent on the skill with which the leaders at the various levels in the organization are able to bring this about.

The truth is that leaders in every aspect of our society—industry, government, the church, the school, and the multitude of small voluntary endeavors—must deal with such problems. Especially in a democracy like ours, where there are millions of "grassroots" leaders, such questions are of the greatest importance. In a dictatorship, the people would be forced to accept the judgment of a single individual and his assistants, but in a democracy, the people ultimately decide. To a large extent, the future of a democracy depends on the skill of the people in selecting their leaders and on the ability of the leaders to accomplish objectives through willing cooperation rather than through threat or force. Thus, it becomes essential that we concern ourselves with and try to understand what makes people "tick."

We are interested in understanding other people, however, even when we do not have the responsibilities of leadership. For example, we need to understand the behavior of our friends. Sometimes their actions are unexpected and unusual—sometimes even heroic. What makes a person act as he does, whether he is a hero, a coward, or just an ordinary fellow?

In addition to the behavior of others, we need and want to understand, and even to influence, our own behavior. From time to time, all of us behave unexpectedly and even harmfully. We may waste time, to the disappointment of our friends and ourselves. We may work too hard and injure our all-round development or even our health. We may even develop the symptoms of emotional disturbance or mental illness.

Of course, we may also behave admirably. We may work hard and achieve some worthwhile goal, or we may spend time and energy in helping a good cause. At times we may be truly outstanding in what we do and receive the praise of others and —what is often just as desirable—of ourselves. One of our problems is understanding why we behave as we do.

Thus, it is easy to understand why interest in psychology has been increasing. We have to know about people, and we hope psychologists can help us to understand them better.

WHAT PSYCHOLOGY IS

Let us look more closely at psychology and what it can contribute to understanding human behavior. What is psychology, and how does it go about accomplishing its objectives?

Human Behavior as the Chief Concern of Psychology. As we have already indicated, psychology is chiefly concerned with what makes people behave as they do. Thus, psychologists are interested in such topics as learning, emotion, intelligence, heredity and environment, differences between individuals, the nature and development of personality, how we influence groups and they influence us, and the body as it relates to and affects human behavior. Each of these topics, it will be noticed, relates to how and why people behave as they do.

Now it should be noted that the term "behavior," as we employ it in this book, is very broad. It includes what we think as well as what we do. It includes our feelings as well as our thoughts. It includes our "mental" responses as well as our "physical" ones. It includes the normal reactions in which we all engage, but it also includes our unusual, odd, or abnormal behavior.

The point should be made, however, that human behavior is not the only concern of psychology. Psychologists are also concerned with the behavior of lower animals, as will be seen later on in the discussion of various topics. When psychologists study the behavior of chimpanzees or white rats or other lower animals, this study is undertaken in large part for the light that it throws upon human behavior. From studies of lower animals, for example, we develop theories about the nature of learning that may be useful in understanding human beings. We also, incidentally, learn a good deal about the lower animals, and to some who are curious about nature that is satisfying in itself.

Psychology as a Science and an Art. One point that needs to be kept in mind is that psychology is a science. The next two sections of this chapter discuss in some detail the nature of science and specifically the nature of psychology as a science. Perhaps it would be sufficient here to say, first, that psychology tries to be objective in the sense that it tries to decide questions on the basis

Figure 1.1. Must all successful groups have a leader? If one is not formally chosen, will the group members choose one informally? How important to a leader is the willingness of each member to follow him?

of facts and not on the basis of wishes or desires; and second, that psychology gets its facts by observations rather than by "armchair" theorizing.

Psychology is an art and a profession as well as a science. Psychologists not only try to advance knowledge; they also attempt to apply it. Just as some chemists and physicists are engaged in research and others are making application of their knowledge, so some psychologists are engaged in research and some in practice. Certain psychologists, in other words, spend their lives getting more information about psychological problems, while others are using this knowledge, and skills derived from it, in areas where they are needed. Psychology as an art or a profession, that is, psychology as it is applied, is examined in greater detail later in this chapter.

Figure 1.2. While psychologists have a particular interest in the behavior of human beings, they are also concerned with the behavior of lower animals. Is it possible that things learned about white rats might enable us to understand more about human beings? Could one also simply become curious about how rats behave, and why? (Courtesy of Columbia University.)

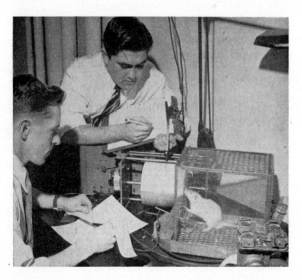

CHARACTERISTICS OF A SCIENCE

We hear a great deal today about science; most people respect and even admire it. Often, however, they do not understand just what science is and what it is not.

What do we mean when we use the term "science"? What do we mean when we say that psychology is a science? What are the distinctive features of a science? How is a science to be distinguished from "common sense"?

It is not easy to describe science in detail, nor is it practical at this point to attempt a complete explanation of the scientific method. But let us look at some of the most important ways in which science differs from ordinary, unscientific endeavors.

Dependence on Observation. One of the distinguishing features of a science is the extent to which it insists and depends upon *observation*. This is quite different from looking for ways to support our present beliefs. Yet it is a common human failing to start with the idea that a certain statement is true and then to consider only the evidence for it and overlook the facts that may be against it. In this way, nearly all of us, at one time or another, mistakenly bolster our cherished beliefs.

So far as the scientist is concerned, however, it is never sufficient simply to think or believe that something is true. A scientist insists on observing under many different circumstances; he insists on having many different individual cases observed and also on having more than one observer. He demands that records be kept of the observations that are made, and in general makes every effort to see that he is not misled by anybody's prejudices. This is what we mean when we say that science relies upon the method of observation.

It should be clear, of course, that observation is not the only method used by science, for if a scientist merely observes and never attempts to interpret or classify, then he can draw no conclusions. Scientists also must think about and reflect upon what they observe before they can reach conclusions. But the point is that such thinking is rooted in observation and goes beyond it only to the extent that is necessary. At times people may become unhappy with this conservative attitude of science, wishing that it would make very definite statements about controversial issues. But scientists have learned that it is better to be conservative than to outrun the evidence by any great degree.

It is worth noting that two kinds of observation are used by scientists. We call these *experiment* (or *experimental observation*) and *naturalistic observation*.

Experimental observation. In the first place, when we use the term "experiment," we imply *control of variables.* That is to say, if we do an experiment, we make an attempt to find as nearly as we can all the factors that might influence the event in question. We attempt to find where and how these influences exert themselves, and then we do whatever we can to control them—that is, all of them except one. Obviously, one of these influences must vary or change, or else nothing will happen at all. And so we allow, or even force, one of them to exert its effect, if any, in differing amounts.

Let us take an example from the field of physics, where the point can be demonstrated very easily. If we wanted to study the effect of pressure on the volume of a gas enclosed in a vessel, we should want to hold constant everything else (except pressure, that is) that might influence the volume of the gas. Thus, we should take special care to see that the temperature did not vary, because temperature might influence volume. We might also be concerned with humidity and with impurities that might get into the gas in question. We should, in a word, try to hold constant all these other factors not specifically con-

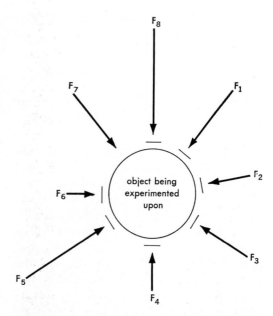

Figure 1.3. *The nature of an experiment. Suppose we let each of the F's represent forces that may influence the object being experimented upon. You will see that they are of different lengths (representing different amounts of force) and that they operate from various directions. If we let the line in front of the arrow serve as a means of blocking off or controlling the particular F, why is one F (F_7) not blocked off? What sort of a variable do we call F_7?*

cerned in our experiment. Then we should either allow pressure to vary, or else force it to change while we measured volume. By doing this a number of times with different amounts of pressure, we could observe the effect of pressure on volume.

Now, in such an experiment as this, the pressure is called the *independent variable* and the volume is called the *dependent variable.* The variable which we deliberately change, in other words, is the independent variable, and the variable which changes as a result of the changes in the independent variable is the dependent variable. This experiment, of course, could be turned around; we could force volume to change and note the resulting effect on pressure. In this case the volume would become the independent variable and pressure the dependent one.

How does all this apply in the field of psychology? Psychologists make considerable use of experiments. They attempt to control variables which would otherwise influence the outcome, in order to study a single variable independently of the others. This book includes a number of descriptions of experiments that have been carried out in the field of psychology. Some of these investigations are viewed as an integral part of the topic under discussion, and in that case they are simply described in the main body of the text. Others, however, serve as illustrations of the sort of research being discussed and in this case they are set in as special inserts. The first one of these immediately follows this discussion.

Since this arrangement is used from time to time throughout the book, it would probably be well to make some comments about it. For one thing, not all these inserts are experiments, since some do not involve the control of variables. (Most of the latter illustrate the method of naturalistic observation, described below.)

In the second place, they are included to give a clearer idea of what psychology is and how it proceeds. Actually becoming acquainted with such research is better than simply reading about general results obtained from many investigations.

In the third place, there is usually more to each of these studies than can be presented in the special inserts in this book. In a good many cases it will be worthwhile to go to the original article and read it. Furthermore, no attempt has been made to cover all significant investigations or even the most influential ones. Rather we have tried to find reports that are more or less typical of current research.

Each of these reports, whether in our abbreviated form or in the original, should be examined carefully. Just what does the particular research contribute to our understanding of human behavior? What important variables were controlled and which, if any, were not taken into account? Should there be other studies along this line? These are examples of the kinds of questions that it will be helpful to try to answer.

Naturalistic observation. Frankly, it would be ideal if we could get all our psychological knowledge from experiments, because obviously the experiment is relatively precise and definite. While no experiment is perfect, as a general rule experiments are very helpful in enabling us to conclude with considerable assurance about what we have observed.

Unfortunately, it is not possible to apply the experimental method in every situation. Some of our observations cannot be controlled. Rather we have to observe some things as they happen (even sometimes as

Figure 1.4. Clouds or "flying saucers"? One limitation of naturalistic observation is that we do not get a chance to see the effect of varying the forces that lead to a particular situation. If we are tense or upset, it is easy to interpret ambiguous stimuli in an entirely false way. Actually the photograph shows an unusual cloud formation over Marseilles, France. (Wide World Photos.)

This experiment * illustrates the meaning of dependent and independent variables in psychological experiments. It is one of many which have been done by psychologists to test the efficiency of *massed practice* (all the trials in succession without any rest between them) as opposed to *distributed practice* (a period of rest between each two trials or each group of trials). The task was to keep a pointer on a certain spot near the circumference of a revolving disk. The disk was 6 inches in diameter and was turning at the rate of 54 revolutions per minute.

The subjects were 100 college women each of whom was randomly assigned to one of five groups (20 in each group). Each subject had 21 trials

*Performance of five groups of college women on a pursuit-rotor task. Figures in upper left-hand corner represent the number of seconds of rest between trials. (*Journal of Experimental Psychology. *Courtesy of the publisher.*)*

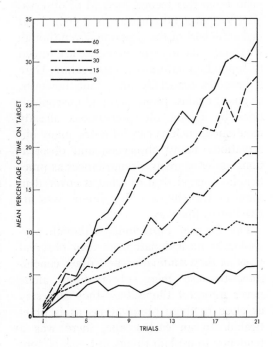

of 30 seconds each, with a record kept of the number of seconds (out of the 30) that the pointer was in contact with the designated spot. One group did all 21 trials successively. The second group rested 15 seconds between trials, the third rested 30 seconds between trials, and the fourth and fifth had 45 seconds and 60 seconds respectively of rest between trials.

It is clear that, *under these circumstances,* distributed practice (rest between trials) is better than massed practice (no rest between trials). The independent variable in this experiment was the amount of rest between successive trials; the dependent variable was the average of the percentage of the time that each girl was able to keep the pointer on the designated spot on the revolving disk.

* Lyle E. Bourne, Jr., and E. James Archer, "Time Continuously on Target as a Function of Distribution of Practice," *Journal of Experimental Psychology,* 1956, 51:25–33.

they *happen* to happen) and do the best we can to draw accurate conclusions. For example, how is an astronomer going to control all other variables while he studies the effect of Mars on the earth's orbit? He can do only one thing: observe the earth and Mars and all the other planets as they actually move, and draw his conclusions on that basis.

Likewise, in a good many situations encountered in psychology, we have to depend upon this second method of observation. We must take nature as it comes and make the best of the situation. Even though we should like to experiment, we are forced to depend on naturalistic observation. Here it becomes especially important, however, to guard against prejudices and misconceptions by taking the precautions already mentioned, such as careful notes, many observations, many observers, and observations under as many circumstances as practicable. A good deal of what is covered in some of the chapters that follow was arrived at in this way.

The Law of Parsimony. Although psychologists must depart from their observations as they summarize and draw conclusions—because mere observations alone never interpret themselves—they still stay as close to these observations as is practicable. In an earlier age, there was a tendency to explain things in terms of concepts, called "essences," that the thinker devised or found ready-made in his society. Thus, a great deal was said about things like "mind" or "will" or "conscience," all of which were used as explanatory terms. Today we are wary of using these terms, simply because they get a long way from the actual observations themselves. Rather, in our explanations, we make every effort to stay as close to the observations themselves as possible—and it is difficult, if not impossible, to observe a will or a mind or a conscience.

For example, we all realize that human beings make choices. They decide to do a certain thing and not to do something else. But how are these choices made? *What* does the choosing? It is easy to say that the choice is made by the "mind" or by the "will." Thus, we might say "My will chooses" or "My mind chooses." This statement may sound like an explanation, but it really is not, for it merely assumes an unobserved essence. It would be much closer to the observed facts simply to say, "I choose," or "The organism chooses." The point is that concepts like mind or will are essences far removed from actual observations; they have little value as explanations or answers to questions.

This brings us to an important principle of science, sometimes called *the law of parsimony* and formulated many years ago. The principle is that, when two possible explanations are both adequate, the simpler should be chosen. By "simpler" is meant, not the simpler to understand, but the simpler in terms of the number of unverified assumptions made. The theory of relativity, for example, is quite simple from the standpoint of its structure and the assumptions it makes, though its implications and consequences are so complex that few people fully understand them. In psychology, it may seem simple to explain behavior by appealing to "mind," "will," "instinct," or other assumed essences, but such explanations actually complicate the problem by interjecting essences which themselves need explanation and are difficult, if not impossible, to observe. Psychologists, as scientists, prefer explanations that involve the fewest possible assumptions, provided, of course, the explanations really explain.

Objectivity. Scientists also pride themselves on drawing from their observations conclusions that are unbiased by their own wishes or desires about the outcome. Of course, most of us think that we do this, but scientists have taken special steps to make reasonably sure that their conclusions are in fact objective and not based on feeling or prejudice.

For one thing, they deliberately cultivate objectivity or open-mindedness. They are willing to question any conclusion or any assumption, and they often take considerable pride in this willingness. This attitude can be carried too far, it is true, but most of us do not have enough of it.

For another thing, as we have already mentioned, they insist on trying—or observing—the same thing (or as near to it as possible) a number of times before reaching a definite conclusion. Certainly, they reason, if the conclusion is correct, it should continue to hold up in repeated tests.

Another factor involved in scientific objectivity is agreement in the observations made by different scientists. Science is not the opinion of a single individual. It is verifiable knowledge, and scientists would be most reluctant to accept an observation if only one individual found evidence for it.

Finally, there is the matter of carefully kept, accurate records. It is not sufficient to have a general impression of what has been discovered. The scientist must be as accurate as possible both in his observations and in the conclusions he draws, and this usually requires the keeping of careful records.

Thus, psychologists share the feeling of other scientists that conclusions must be based on facts, and so they do their best to lay feelings aside when they draw conclusions.

Knowing for the Sake of Knowing. It is easy to understand why science is interested in solving practical problems. These often make a lot of difference—obviously and immediately. What is not so generally recognized is that most of the world's great scientists, as well as many students of science, have been motivated by another aspect in science: the desire to know *for the sake of knowing.* In a good many instances, we pursue questions in science not because we expect useful results, but because we are curious about the answer. We want to know, without considering whether our knowledge will be useful or not.

There is nothing unnatural or even unusual about wanting to know simply for the sake of knowing. It is characteristic of some of us much of the time and of almost all of us some of the time. The subject may be the current major-league baseball race, or the geography of the South Sea Islands, or how a jet motor differs from one of the more conventional types, or something else. The point is that we want to know just because we want to know. And it can be very gratifying to find out.

The curiosity of a boy about motors is a good illustration. From some source—his father or his general science teacher or something he has seen on television—he learns about automobile engines and how they work. He tries to find out more and becomes acquainted with diesels. And then he hears about turbines and jets, and he just cannot rest until he knows a great deal more about all of them. As everybody knows, once such an interest is developed this boy may spend hours reading, tinkering, and experimenting—not for money or fame now or in the future, but just *because he wants to know.*

But why is this important for our purpose? Suppose the boy does know how the engines work—what difference does it make? Sometimes—maybe most of the time —it really makes no difference (though he goes right on wanting to know, just the same). But sometimes it does make a difference. In fact, it may make all the difference in the world.

The fact is that most of the significant discoveries of the last 300 to 500 years have been made by people who wanted to know merely for the sake of knowing. Somehow, when a person gets too "practical" in his outlook he may fail to see possibilities of great significance because he is too short-

Table 1.1   Three Methods of Studying Human Behavior

	"Armchair" theorizing	Naturalistic observation	Experiment (or experimental observation)
Distinctive feature of the method	Reasoning from conclusions already accepted (and not questioned)	Careful observation of events as they occur	Control of all variables except the independent one
When introduced into psychology	2,000–2,500 years ago	A.D. 1860–1880	A.D. 1860–1880
When used by scientific psychology	Never	When it is not practicable to use experiment	Whenever the situation permits control of significant variables
Characteristics of conclusions drawn	Sweeping generalizations; not close to experience or the facts; deals with broad and often indefinite issues; much use of "essences"	Avoids "essences"; follows law of parsimony; limited in scope	Same as for naturalistic observation
Provision for checking results	Examines reasoning for logical fallacies	Many observations by many observers; careful recording of results; consideration of alternative explanations	Repeated observations by different observers; making other variables the independent one and noting results; careful records; consideration of alternative explanations
Amount of time required	Very little; conclusions easy to draw	A great deal; involves hard work	Most of all; often time-consuming
Chief limitations of the method	Conclusions likely to be partly or wholly false; original assumption not examined in relation to observed facts	Time-consuming and expensive; conclusions often less sweeping and inclusive than we wish they were	Same as for naturalistic observation except often more time-consuming and expensive; difficult to control variables in many cases

sighted to appreciate them. When, on the other hand, he goes where curiosity leads him, he often comes upon ideas, principles, and discoveries of great practical consequence.

Many modern inventions, from the telegraph to the atom bomb, are based on discoveries of people who were not trying to invent anything at all. They were not trying to be practical. They were trying to satisfy their own curiosity. The whole electrical industry is an example. Volta, Galvani, Ohm, Ampère, and Faraday—to mention just a few—were not inventors trying to start a new industry and revolutionize sources of power or even to invent a telegraph. Rather they were "pure" scientists, men with great curiosity and the imagination and drive necessary to satisfy this curiosity. Their discoveries, however, were crucial to the electrical industry.

So we see, first, that it is not unnatural to be interested in knowing for the sake of knowing, and second, that such curiosity and attempts to satisfy it may ultimately have great practical value.

PSYCHOLOGY AS A SCIENCE

We cannot emphasize too strongly that observation and objectivity, as well as the desire to know for the sake of knowing, characterize psychology as well as the other sciences. The essential thing about a science is not its subject matter or even its findings and conclusions. The most distinguishing feature of a science is a spirit, an attitude, a set of values, and a group of methods for obtaining knowledge. Because psychology shares in the spirit, attitude, and values of science, and because it uses the methods of science, it must be classified as one of the sciences of the modern era.

Indeed, this is the principal way in which modern psychology differs from the psychology of a century or more ago. Among the Greeks, during medieval times, and

indeed until the latter half of the nineteenth century, the chief way of arriving at conclusions about human behavior was to think about what people did and to speculate about its meaning. "Armchair theorizing" and *a priori* reasoning were the principal tools employed in the task of understanding man's behavior.

These tools were dull and inept; they proved poorly suited for the job. All too often each theorist came to conclusions that disagreed with those of others. And there was no way to tell which one, if any, was correct.

This situation continued until men adopted a new method of "putting the question to nature," that is, the scientific method of carefully observing the facts and then interpreting them as cautiously as practicable, so that conclusions reached would stay as close to the facts as possible. Mere observations cannot interpret themselves, and so principles or theories have to be introduced as interpretations. The important point here is to be careful that the theories we develop represent not what we should like to believe or what might be true but rather what reasonably follows from what has been observed. This means that scientists, including psychologists, do not make as many broad assertions or sweeping generalizations as people did in the prescientific era.

It would not be fair to leave the impression that this new approach has solved all our problems. Surely there are many things as yet not understood about people. Still, progress has been made, and we feel that the future holds real promise for those who approach these problems as *scientists* using the *scientific method*.

PSYCHOLOGY AND OTHER SCIENCES

Before we look further into the nature of psychology as a science and as a profession, let us examine its relationship to some of

REMEMBERING FAVORABLE AND UNFAVORABLE MATERIAL

Here is another example of the application of the scientific method to the understanding of human behavior. One problem which has interested psychologists for the last fifty years or more is whether favorable or unfavorable material is remembered better. There are good arguments for each sort of material, and the many experiments done on the question have not always come to the same conclusion. This experiment * is another in the series.

Recalls Immediately after Hearing the Story

Type of item	Number of re- calls possible	Negro re- calls	White re- calls	Negro superi- ority, %	t
Favorable to Negroes	480	181	140	29	2.36 †
Unfavorable to Negroes	240	84	68	24	1.21
Ambiguous	150	76	57	33	1.12
Neutral	120	28	27	4	0.39
Total	990	369	292	26	3.70 ‡

† Significant at .05 level.
‡ Significant at .01 level.

A story was read to a group of 30 Negro boys and a group of 30 white boys. They were all in the same school, were matched in an earlier experiment for ability to recall, and had average mental ages (see Chapter 17) of 12 years 5 months and 12 years 7 months respectively.

The story was about a Negro baseball pitcher who was not allowed to play major-league baseball in the United States and who went to Brazil and achieved success, though he was still homesick for the United States. The story contained items that judges believed Negroes would find favorable,

* From Ronald Taft, "Selective Recall and Memory Distortion of Favorable and Unfavorable Material," *Journal of Abnormal and Social Psychology*, 1954, 49:23–28.

the other sciences, for there are others interested in human behavior. The truth is that all the social sciences and many of the biological sciences work in this field and have made significant contributions to it.

We are concerned primarily with the relationship between psychology and the three sciences closest to it in subject matter: anthropology, sociology, and physiology.

Psychology and Anthropology. Anthropology literally means "the study of man," and while this is descriptive to a degree, it actually takes in too much territory. More

specifically, anthropology studies man in groups, and ordinarily in large groups. One phase of anthropology, called *physical anthropology*, deals with the physical characteristics of the various peoples of the world. This certainly includes a study of the various races of mankind (so long as the term "race" continues to be a useful way of classifying people), their size, weight, and other physical characteristics, as well as their intellectual and emotional traits. Another branch of anthropology, called *cultural anthropology*, deals with various cultures, the others which would be unfavorable, and still others which would be neither favorable nor unfavorable. The story was broken down into the separate ideas or thoughts it contained (the "recalls" of the accompanying tables), and each was rated by three judges as to whether it was favorable to Negroes, unfavorable to Negroes, ambiguous, or neutral. The tables present the results obtained.

These tables involved some statistical concepts that we do not have time to go into here. But it is clear that Negroes recalled a significantly greater

Recalls Three Days after Hearing the Story

Type of item	Number of re- calls possible	Negro re- calls	White re- calls	Negro superi- ority, %	t
Favorable to Negroes	480	176	106	66	3.17 *
Unfavorable to Negroes	240	60	62	−3	0.28
Ambiguous	150	44	33	33	1.78
Neutral	120	16	12	33	0.65
Total	990	296	213	38	3.44 *

* Significant at .01 level.

number of items than did whites and also a significantly greater number of favorable (to Negro) items. This was true for recall immediately after the story was read and also for recall three days after it was read.

The authors conclude that *within the framework of this experiment* there is a tendency to recall more items, favorable and unfavorable, if a member of the person's own group (or a group with which he identifies) is involved and that this is especially true of items favorable to that group.

typical personalities to be found in each culture, the influence of culture on personality, and the like. If an anthropologist is interested in the various characteristics of a certain culture, he studies its institutions and the ways people behave in it, including their ways of meeting crises and celebrating joyous events. He is also concerned with how this culture or this people compares with others.

The principal distinction between psychology and anthropology lies in the emphasis of the former on the *individual* and of the latter on the *group*. Obviously, to understand an individual it is often necessary to understand his culture. And to understand a culture it is often necessary to understand how the people in it perceive and feel about it. Thus, psychology and anthropology have certain problems in common and areas of knowledge in which they supplement each other.

Psychology and Sociology. Sociology is another science directly concerned with human behavior. Like anthropology, it deals with people in groups, but ordinarily in smaller groups. Group behavior is the primary concern of sociologists, who also study the influence of groups on the individuals who comprise the groups. Sociologists also deal with social problems, including such things as crime and juvenile delinquency, divorce, the development of and changes in the family, war and other forms of group conflict, and similar topics. They too are concerned with the influence of social forces on personality and the ways in which these forces operate on the individual.

Again we see two sciences that have a great deal in common. The concern of psychology with the individual person and why he behaves as he does differs from the concern of sociology for the nature and behavior of the group. The two sciences have areas of overlapping, but the point of view and the emphasis are different.

Psychology and Physiology. A science that is not always thought of as dealing with human behavior—although it actually does—is physiology. This science studies the functions of the various organs (e.g., the stomach or the heart) of the body and its various systems (e.g., the digestive or circulatory system). This study, of course, involves not only the systems themselves but also the ways in which they interact. Hence, how the body functions, as well as how its parts or systems operate, is the domain of the physiologist. This is quite different from the concern of psychology

for the individual as a person, as a knowing, thinking, and otherwise reacting organism.

Differences in Emphasis among the Sciences. The distinction between related sciences is usually not a matter of hard and fast differences, with clear lines separating the sciences in question; rather it is one of varying emphasis. Thus, it is not possible to draw a line clearly dividing anthropology from sociology, or to separate sharply sociology from psychology or psychology from physiology. In each case, one of these spills over into the other (or perhaps into several others), and two or more sciences often study the same subject matter. For example, both physiology and psychology are interested in the functioning of the nervous system, though each from a somewhat different point of view. Psychology, sociology, and anthropology all concern themselves with the relationship of the group and the individual, but again the emphasis differs for each science. Incidentally, we have a similar situation in physics and chemistry, where the emphasis differs but no hard and fast boundaries can be drawn.

It is easy to get the idea that this is an unfortunate situation and that the various sciences should straighten out their titles to

Figure 1.5. Some of the relationships between psychology and other sciences. From the diagram would you conclude that (a) psychology studies human behavior and nothing else (b) other sciences also study human behavior (c) the various sciences overlap, that is, have areas of common interest? What other sciences or areas of study might be represented by circles in the above diagram? Where would you draw each?

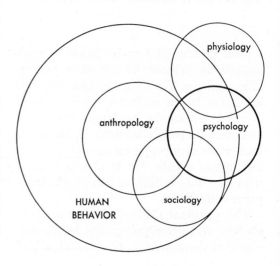

certain territories or areas of subject matter. Verbal battles have sometimes been fought over such issues, but fortunately for the welfare of science and society no permanent victories have been won. Areas of overlap in science can be opportunities for cooperation, and two groups of scientists, working together, have often attained insights denied to either group working alone. Human behavior is obviously a field that is complex and not so well understood as we should like it to be. No one has a monopoly on information about it or on methods of studying it. It is the concern of many sciences, including psychology.

APPLIED PSYCHOLOGY

One striking fact about modern psychology is, as we mentioned earlier, the increasing number of psychologists, especially since World War II. A great many more people are now earning a livelihood as psychologists than were doing so a few short years ago. This growth is largely due to the expansion of research and professional services concerned with the applications of psychology.

Until recently a majority of psychologists were engaged in teaching. Now teaching is still an important field of employment, but positions concerned with research and applying psychology to practical problems are the more numerous.

Psychology is now applied in a number of situations, varying from those that deal with children to those that deal with old people, and from those that deal with people who are in great difficulty to those that deal with people in positions of responsible leadership. Let us look at some of these fields in which psychologists are applying the findings of the science.

Clinical Psychology. The largest single group of professional psychologists are those who work in mental hospitals, mental health clinics, and the like. Clinical psy-

chologists, as the term implies, deal with people in difficulty. Some of these persons may have a serious mental illness, while others may have encountered more than their share of the problems we all face or may lack the skill that most of us have developed for dealing with such problems.

Here it might be wise to make a distinction between a clinical psychologist and a psychiatrist. Ordinarily a clinical psychologist has a Ph.D. in psychology. Having finished a bachelor of arts degree (and possibly a master of arts degree also) in psychology or a related field, he goes on to get the doctor's degree in psychology. In the course of earning this degree, he usually serves at least one year of internship, which gives practical experience in dealing with persons having psychological difficulties. This is a valuable supplement to classwork.

The psychiatrist, on the other hand, always has a medical degree. After completing his premedical training he usually spends four years in medical school, some time as an intern, and then some more as a resident. His area of specialty is the care and treatment of people with emotional and mental illness.

Another person who works with mentally disordered individuals, or with persons in difficulty, is the psychiatric social worker. He usually has a master's degree in social work and specializes in getting information about and understanding people who have emotional difficulties.

In many clinics and hospitals the *team approach* is used, the team consisting of a psychiatrist, a clinical psychologist, and a psychiatric social worker. To some extent each member of this team specializes in a particular area, but they combine their training and talents in investigating the problems of a particular patient and, after the diagnosis, in helping him regain his mental health. Many who work in this field feel that the team approach is proving its effectiveness and strengthening our efforts to combat problems in the area of mental health.

Counseling Psychology. Another field of professional specialization in psychology is known as *counseling psychology.* Though counseling and clinical psychology are closely related, they have two fairly distinct roles in the general scheme of psychological services.

We use the word "counseling" to refer to the function of psychologists whose principal job is to deal with people who are in need of help or advice but not primarily with people who have emotional difficulties. A typical example is to be found in the Veterans Administration, where the counselor acquaints an individual with vocational opportunities and gives him information designed to better his vocational adjustments. Since a person's vocation influences so many phases of his life, counseling psychologists often are called upon to deal with other problems which the individual may be facing.

Of course, not all counselors are psychologists. Other people do counseling— teachers, social workers, supervisors, ministers, lawyers, physicians, and so forth. But psychologists counsel too, and the point that needs to be emphasized is that one branch of psychology is concerned with the theory, as well as the practice and techniques, of counseling.

A branch of psychology closely related to counseling is to be found in the work of the school psychologist. School psycholgists often do educational and vocational counseling, but they also give advice and guidance on matters having to do with curriculum planning, teacher training, problems of parents, and the like.

Psychology in Business and Industry. Psychologists also practice professionally in business and industry. Human-relations problems in business and industry are often as important as any other sort, and the need for effective teamwork is probably nowhere greater than it is in this particular area.

Psychologists participate in the affairs of business and industry in at least three ways. In the first place, they have made some real contributions to business management by making it possible to do a better job of selecting, placing, and training employees. Here the first contribution that comes to mind is probably that of psychological tests, but while they have been important, they are not by any means the whole story. Interviews are also useful, and even observation of behavior over a period of time has proved worthwhile. Furthermore, psychologists have been able to improve methods of training people for their jobs.

In the second place, there are psychologists who specialize in counseling with the executives of a business and otherwise helping in their development. They are often the persons with whom the executive "talks out" his problems, and they help him gain insight into his own limitations and strengths and to improve his skill as an executive. The emphasis here is primarily on self-improvement, for in these matters as in many others, real development must come from within the individual.

This process of helping executives and supervisors to grow and develop is sometimes carried out with groups rather than with individuals. Through research, psychologists have uncovered some of the factors that distinguish successful leaders from those not so successful, and the industrial psychologist often has the opportunity to translate these findings into a form— and a set of skills—that will make them useful to the manager.

The third area in which psychology has played an increasing role in business and industry is often called *human engineering.* As the world of work becomes more complex and the machines and processes with which we have to deal become more involved, the problems of the control of the means of production or transportation be-

EFFICIENCY OF VARIOUS DIALS

▶ This experiment * throws some light on the work of the human engineer. The purpose was to determine which of several types of dials would give the most useful readings of an altimeter (instrument for measuring altitude). Each dial was presented to the subjects with twelve different settings. They were printed in a test booklet, with space provided in each case for indicating the correct reading. As far as possible, the printed designs were of the same size, with the same legibility of printing, the same number of gradations, etc. The order of presentation of the different dials was also varied systematically to reduce the practice effect. The subjects were 97 United States Air Force cadets and 79 college students without aircrew experience.

The accompanying figure presents the various types of dials used and also the results obtained. Dial A was one commonly in use at the time of the experiment, and, as can be seen, it showed up poorly both in errors and time for interpretation. It is interesting to note that at least in some cases the results of this study are quite different from what would be predicted by so-called "common sense."

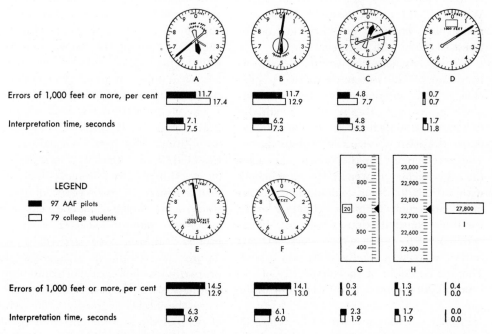

Speed and accuracy in reading altitude from different types of instruments. (Note that Instrument I proved most satisfactory under these conditions.) (W. F. Grether, Instrument Reading: I, The Design of Long-scale Indicators for Speed and Accuracy of Quantitative Readings, Journal of Applied Psychology, 33:365, 1949. Courtesy of the publisher.)

* W. F. Grether, "Instrument Reading: I. The Design of Long-scale Indicators for Speed and Accuracy of Quantitative Readings," *Journal of Applied Psychology*, 1949, 33:363–372.

come more difficult. Indeed, in many instances, more information can be given to the operator of a machine than he is able to perceive and use. Consider, for example, a large airplane. It has a number of engines, and each engine has a number of instruments reporting on its performance. Clearly, more information can be fed into the cockpit of the plane than any individual could ever assimilate in any reasonable length of time. Indeed, more information can be displayed in the cockpit than a crew of several men are able to assimilate. The problem is to make this information as usable as possible.

There is a question, for instance, as to what sort of design an instrument ought to have. Should it be black on white, or white on black? Should it be large or small? Where should it be located? These and many more complex questions are of interest to the human engineer.

Perhaps nowhere can we find a better illustration of the difference between psychology and "common sense." The common-sense approach to this problem would be to figure out which of these would seem to be the most serviceable and to use it. The psychologist, on the other hand, uses the experimental approach. He experiments with various kinds of cockpits and instruments and controls, and by holding other variables constant, determines not which one looks as though it would work best but rather which one really does work best. There is no doubt of the superiority of the psychologist's approach to this sort of problem.

Problems of this sort are to be found in many aspects of the world of work, and the contributions to their solution by psychologists may ultimately touch the lives of all of us.

Psychology and Attitude Measurement. Finally, among the applied fields we have chosen to discuss, there is the field in which the attitudes of individuals or groups are measured. Such attitude measurement has been used extensively in public-opinion polling (of which the so-called "Gallup poll" is an example) and in market research.

We are all familiar in a general way with polling procedures. Questions are carefully designed and studied and, when considered satisfactory, are asked of a great many people. Their responses are carefully noted, and conclusions are drawn concerning the attitudes of a larger group of people with regard to the matter being studied. This technique may be used to determine the feeling of people toward the several presidential hopefuls or toward a new brand of detergent.

Complexity of the Field of Psychology. By now it is apparent that modern psychology is not a simple field, with all psychologists having the same interests and skills. The various sorts of psychologists have a number of things in common, but they also have their own special interests.

The complexity of the field can be seen from a study of the American Psychological Association. This is the scientific and professional organization of American psychologists. Minimum requirements for associate membership are two years of graduate study in psychology (or one year of graduate study plus one year of experience in professional work that is psychological in nature) and employment in a job that is primarily psychological (or continuation of graduate study in psychology). More and more the Ph.D. degree is being required of people who are recognized as psychologists. In 1956 the association had about 15,000 members, in 1957 16,000.

At present the association is organized into seventeen divisions, some set up primarily on the basis of applied interests and others primarily on the basis of subject matter. These divisions are as follows:

General Psychology
The Teaching of Psychology
Experimental Psychology
Evaluation and Measurement
Developmental Psychology
Abnormal and Social Psychology
The Society for the Psychological Study of
   Social Issues
Esthetics
Clinical Psychology
Consulting Psychology
Industrial and Business Psychology
Educational Psychology
School Psychologists
Counseling Psychology
Psychologists in Public Service
Military Psychology
Maturity and Old Age

This list emphasizes the point made earlier that some psychologists are essentially research scientists, others are primarily teachers of psychology, and still others are practicing in various fields of applied psychology. Psychology is thus both a science and an art or a profession.

So far we have been talking about what psychology is and how it relates to science in general. Let us look now at some of the popular misconceptions of psychology and see wherein these are in error.

Psychology and the Mysterious. Many people imagine that psychology is something magical or mysterious and that somehow psychologists have a superior or almost superhuman way of looking into the thoughts and feelings of a person. The notion is, in other words, that there is a psychological method or approach, and that anyone who knows how to use this and uses it successfully has an advantage over anyone who lacks it.

Psychology, however, is no more myste-

Figure 1.6. Some people seem to think that psychologists have insight into human behavior that is little short of magical or mysterious. Others hold that we learn about human behavior only from experience and that psychologists really have nothing to contribute to our understanding of this subject. Neither of these extreme positions is correct.

rious than medicine or engineering or the other sciences. It is an ordinary, everyday, hard-working science. It has no magic, no mysterious ways, and no dark or hidden routes by which it gets its knowledge. Whatever psychologists have learned, they have learned through observation, through careful reflection upon what they have observed, and through the checking of their conclusions with other persons in this and other fields. Psychology is neither magical nor mysterious.

Psychology and "Common Sense." Some people go to the opposite extreme and assume that psychology is essentially nothing more than common sense. To them, psychology is simply what wise people have discovered from their experience, whether they have ever had formal training in the subject or not.

It would, of course, be overstating the case to say that psychologists have a monopoly of knowledge of human behavior. We have already acknowledged the role of the other sciences in studying human behavior, and we must further recognize that nonscientific endeavors, such as religion, literature, and the law, also have useful contributions to make to this understanding. We are not maintaining, in other words, that only psychologists understand anything about human behavior.

The fact nevertheless remains that scientific psychology and the "psychology" of common sense are often rather different. For one thing, there are statements that are accepted by common sense but not accepted by psychology. One example of this is the common notion that those who are insane or seriously mentally ill have "lost their minds." In other words, insane people are considered to be unable to reason adequately or accurately. This common-sense idea of insanity is far from the truth. Although intellectual abilities are sometimes disturbed in mental illness, a great many individuals who are insane are not suffering from lack of ability to reason. If given an intelligence test, they do as well on it as ever. In such cases, the difficulty is not in the intellectual realm at all but rather in the field of emotion. Thus, psychology must insist that insanity cannot be regarded as the "loss of mind."

On the other hand, a good many things that are accepted by psychology are not accepted by common sense. An example relates to the phenomenon of color. The common-sense view of color is that the color is in the object which we see. Thus, if we see yellow flowers and blue flowers in a vase on our desk, common sense says the yellowness and the blueness are actually in the flowers themselves. From the standpoint of modern science this view is entirely unacceptable. We have every reason at present to believe that the color is not in the object but rather in the perceiver. The object reflects to our eyes light waves of a certain length, and the color which we see depends upon the length of the particular light waves. Thus, if long light waves strike our eyes we get a sensation which we call red, while if short light waves strike our eyes we get a sensation which we call violet. Light waves of intermediate length may lead to blue or green or yellow. But there is no serious reason to believe that the flowers themselves are colored. Color is our response to light waves which they reflect.

Thus, it can be seen that psychology, while it sometimes agrees with common sense, is not *just* common sense. It does not agree with all that common sense holds, and common sense sometimes mistakenly holds to what psychology has shown to be untrue.

Psychology and the Pseudo Sciences. People sometimes confuse psychology with a whole group of endeavors which have come to be known as *pseudo sciences.* (These are called pseudo sciences because the term *pseudo* means "false.") Among these pseudo sciences are phrenology, physiognomy, numerology, palmistry, and astrology.

Why do we call them false sciences? In the first place, as will be clear when we examine them in some detail, the claims made by them simply do not fit with the other established facts about the nature of the world and of man. In the second place, they are untrue to, or inconsistent with, the spirit of science and the scientific method. In other words, they do not stick close to the facts but rather rely on essences for their explanations. They do not depend primarily on observation but rather on *a priori* reasoning and predetermined conclusions and prejudices. Instead of being objective they select evidence supporting their positions, while overlooking, neglecting, or even denying the facts that do not fit their preconceptions.

Let us look more closely at some of these endeavors. Phrenology goes back about 150 to 175 years. A celebrated anatomist by the name of Gall got the idea that he could relate the contours of the brain to the mental life of the individual. He further believed that the contour of the skull reflects accurately the contour of the brain. He went on to map out the brain area, finding thirty-nine "propensities" and "faculties," as he called them, each with its own localized area. Thus, he concluded that the intellectual faculties are mainly concentrated in the forehead and that emotional factors are located toward the back part of the head. Gall believed that the size of an area was a measure of the strength of the particular faculty, and hence he advocated careful mapping of these areas.

We now know that Gall's suppositions were without foundation, although different parts of the brain and even of the cerebrum do have different functions. There is no reason to believe that we actually have the faculties which he designated (or any faculties, for that matter) or that they were

located as he thought they were. Furthermore, the contours of the brain cannot be inferred from the shape of the skull, nor is the size of a brain area correlated with the strength of a faculty. All Gall's major assumptions are false. Hence, phrenology is a pseudo science.

Much the same remarks can be made about physiognomy. This pseudo science did not restrict itself to the shape of the skull but considered facial features and the shape of the body as a whole. For example, one physiognomist held that a person with a misshapen or a deformed body is also likely to have a personality similarly warped. More specifically, it has been held by some physiognomists that a square jaw means determination, a high forehead means intelligence (a view which they might share with the phrenologists), and so forth. Now, the truth is that the claims of physiognomy, like those of phrenology, do not stand up when carefully investigated. There is no serious reason to believe that any of the teachings of physiognomy correspond to the facts.

Likewise, numerology attempts to determine the character of the individual (and sometimes his future) from the combinations of numbers connected with his name or other things in his life. Palmistry attempts to predict his character and his future from the lines on the palm. And finally, astrology makes predictions about him from the stars under which he was born. The claims made by these endeavors are false almost without exception. There is no trustworthy evidence that the numbers really influence a person's life or that the life line on a palm has anything to do with how long he will live. Likewise, the stars under which he was born have no real influence on his personality. Psychologists have had a great deal to do with showing through experiment and other careful study how these claims have no basis in fact. They involve *a priori* reasoning and "essences."

It is easy to understand that psychologists do not like to be classed with these pseudo sciences. This is partly because the conclusions of the pseudo sciences are false, but it is even more because they violate the fundamental spirit of science in their ways of investigation and their methods of arriving at conclusions.

SUMMARY

All of us have an interest in human behavior. Part of this interest comes from the fact that we need to understand, predict, and control the actions of other people. Part of it comes from our need for self-understanding and self-control.

Psychology is the scientific study of the behavior of living organisms, with especial attention given to human behavior. It is to be distinguished from anthropology and sociology in that they focus their attention largely on the group, while psychology studies primarily the individual. It is to be distinguished from physiology in that physiology emphasizes the various systems of the body and how they interact and also how the organism adjusts to its physical environment, whereas psychology studies the individual as a person, as a thinking, remembering, imagining, feeling, and reacting individual.

Actually all these sciences overlap in subject matter. No hard and fast lines can be drawn to separate psychology from any of the others, but there are differences in degree and in emphasis. This makes it possible for scientists from several areas to concentrate on the same problem.

When we say that a certain endeavor is a science, we refer primarily not to a set of facts or a body of knowledge but to a set of attitudes and values and, in particular, to certain methods for acquiring knowledge. A science proceeds from observations, carefully checked, recorded, and confirmed. It insists on objectivity, on drawing conclusions on the basis of what is observed and not on the basis of what the scientist wants to find or believe. It stays as close to the actual observations as practicable, though it is admitted that observations never interpret themselves and the scientist has to go at least somewhat beyond them to interpret them. Finally, though a scientist may be interested in information that can be used, another important motive is a desire to know simply for the sake of knowing.

Scientists customarily use two kinds of observation: (1) the experiment, which involves control of all the relevant conditions except the independent variable, which is allowed to change or forced to change; and (2) naturalistic observation, which is the observing of events as they occur. If it were practicable, scientists would use experiments in all their observations, because they permit better control of variables, but since this is often impossible, they must make use of naturalistic observation.

Psychology is both a science and a profession. As a science, it is interested in understanding more and more about the behavior of the organism. As a profession, it is concerned with applications of this knowledge to the prediction and control of behavior.

It is easy to believe that psychology is magical or mysterious, or, on the other hand, that it is nothing more than ordinary common sense. Likewise, psychology is sometimes associated with pseudo sciences like phrenology. All these are false conceptions, as psychologists have been able to demonstrate.

QUESTIONS

1. What is a science? In what ways does it differ from nonscientific endeavors?

2. What do we mean by saying that a scientist often wants to know for the sake of knowing?

3. What is an experiment? How does it differ from other types of observation?

4. Compare and contrast (*a*) "armchair" theorizing and experiment; (*b*) "armchair" theorizing and naturalistic observation.

5. What is the law of parsimony, and what is its importance?

6. Just what is psychology? Name several problems that are distinctively psychological in character.

7. In what applied areas are psychologists found today? Describe the principal work of each area.

8. What is anthropology? On what kinds of problems would both psychologists and anthropologists work?

9. What is sociology? On what kinds of problems would both psychologists and sociologists work?

10. What is physiology? On what kinds of problems would both psychologists and physiologists work?

11. In the experiment on remembering favorable and unfavorable material, what was the independent variable? What was the dependent one? What other variables did the experimenters attempt to control?

12. Do the same for the experiment on the efficiency of various dials.

13. What arguments can you give to prove that psychology is not just "common sense"?

14. How would you demonstrate the inaccuracy of the claims of phrenology? What are the chief differences between psychology and phrenology? (Consider both conclusions and methods of arriving at conclusions.)

SUGGESTED READINGS

Britt, Steuart Henderson: *Social Psychology of Modern Life*, rev. ed., Rinehart, New York, 1949, chap. 2.
(An interesting and informative treatment of the scientific method in psychology.)

Brown, C. W., and E. E. Ghiselli: *Scientific Method in Psychology*, McGraw-Hill, New York, 1955.
(Application of the scientific method to many psychological problems.)

Chapanis, A., W. R. Garner, and C. T. Morgan: *Applied Experimental Psychology*, Wiley, New York, 1949.
(A discussion of the scientific design of equipment for human use.)

Daniel, R. S., and C. M. Louttit: *Professional Problems in Psychology*, Prentice-Hall, Englewood Cliffs, N. J., 1953.
(The nature and growth of the profession of psychology.)

Gray, J. Stanley: *Psychology Applied to Human Affairs*, 2d ed., McGraw-Hill, New York, 1954.
(Application of psychology to contemporary problems.)

Marcuse, F. L.: *Areas of Psychology*, Harper, New York, 1954.
(An introduction to the various fields or branches of psychology.)

Ogg, Elizabeth: "Psychologists in Action," Public Affairs Pamphlet 229, 1955.
(A survey of the activities of the professional psychologist.)

Watson, Robert I.: *Psychology as a Profession*, Studies in Psychology series, Random House, New York, 1954.
(Applications of psychology to the problems of today; the nature of the profession of psychologist.)

2 HEREDITY AND ENVIRONMENT

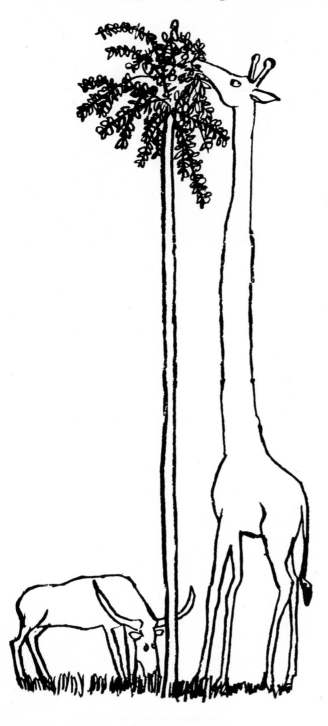

In order to study behavior more efficiently, the psychologist often separates the biological and cultural factors. In his separation of these factors, he does not mean to imply that some characteristics are biologically inherited and that others are acquired by living in a certain society. Rather, our traits and characteristics are the products of the *interaction* of our heredity and our environment.

In this chapter we shall discover why the emphasis is to be put on the word "interaction." We shall see what the facts are that make it incorrect to think that any trait of a living creature is entirely hereditary or completely environmental. On the contrary, it is more correct to say that all traits and characteristics are *both* hereditary and environmental.

HEREDITY VERSUS ENVIRONMENT

During the nineteenth century biology emerged and took its place among the sciences. By the end of the century, both the facts and theories of biology were having considerable impact on the thinking of scientists about human nature. Of particular importance was Darwin's theory of evolution, which stressed the survival of those inherited characteristics through which animals adapted to their environments. The Darwinian emphasis on heredity led biologists, physicians, and even people generally to consider heredity as the most important factor in determining human traits and characteristics. By the close of the nineteenth century, too much emphasis (as we see it now) had been placed on man's heredity as the molder of his character and personality.

In time, opinion began to shift away from this view. Many scientists, especially the sociologists, came to feel that too much emphasis had been placed on heredity. Gradually, during the early decades of the twentieth century, a case was made for environment as the more influential factor in growth and development. By the time of World War I, many sociologists were expressing the belief that heredity is relatively unimportant in the elaboration of character and personality. They admitted, however, that for some physical traits, such as eye color and shape of face, heredity had some importance.

As so often is the case, the full swing of the pendulum put too much emphasis on environment, just as heredity had been accorded too much importance by biologists and physicians. Caught in the middle were several groups to whom the issue was of some practical significance. The educators were one such group. They did not know whether to go along with the emphasis of physicians and biologists on heredity, or whether to join those sociologists who stressed environment. To seek a resolution of the problem, one group of educators set up a study committee.[1] The purpose of the committee was to determine which is more important—heredity or environment. At least they wanted to find out which traits and characteristics of the human being are accounted for by heredity and which are accounted for by environment.

When the committee got into the problem, assembling and organizing the relevant scientific facts, it became apparent to them, as it had to some biologists and some sociologists, that it is impossible to separate the influences of heredity from those of environment. Rather, the two always go along together.

[1] *Intelligence: Its Nature and Nurture,* Thirty-ninth Yearbook of the National Society for the Study of Education, 1940.

Figure 2.1. Julian Huxley, the noted biologist, is the grandson of the distinguished nineteenth century biologist Thomas Huxley. His brother is Aldous Huxley, noted critic and novelist. Does this illustrious family tend to show the greater significance of heredity in the production of genius? Can a case be made here for the interaction of heredity and environment? (International News Photos.)

HEREDITARY AND ENVIRONMENTAL INFLUENCES ON TRAITS

Today we know that all traits—the social, the psychological, and the physical—are a product of the interaction and the interrelation of heredity and environment. Certainly, no trait can develop without some inheritance, nor, on the other hand, can any trait or characteristic develop unless the proper environment is provided. It is obvious that the hereditary factors present in the egg of a chicken cannot produce a human being. It should also be obvious that, if the right environment is not provided, these same factors *cannot* be made to produce a chicken.

It is correct to think of every organism

and also of each part of every organism as a joint function of three factors: heredity, environment, and time. Each of these factors is indispensable. If there is no heredity, all the time and environment in the world cannot produce a living organism. On the other hand, if there is no place (environment) in which to grow and develop, no amount of time and heredity can bring forth a living organism. Likewise, in addition to the other two factors, a life span (time) is necessary for the very existence of every living plant and animal.

In order to clarify our thinking, let us set up a concise expression for the interaction of these factors.

$$P = f(H,E,T)$$

P is the individual person who is some function (f) or product of the three factors heredity (H), environment (E), and time (T). This is a way of saying that all three factors are essential and must work together for an organism to survive and develop. Note in the formula that if any one of the three (H, or E, or T) is reduced to zero (is nonexistent), the result is zero, which means that there will be no person. Also, we can think of P as the whole person or as any part of the person, i.e., any trait or characteristic.

In order to understand some of the important implications of this formula, we must now see what is technically meant by the terms *heredity* and *environment*.

HEREDITY

A human body is composed of many small cells, each of which has a nucleus. Within each nucleus are a number of small rodlike or threadlike objects named *chromosomes*. Particularly important for our discussion is the fact that in these chromosomes are some tiny submicroscopic particles called *genes*. These genes are the unit carriers of heredity. They are the units that largely direct the growth and development of the human being. Biologists have good reason to believe that the genes are giant organic molecules, which somehow act as the blueprints for the building of the organism. Under their influence and given the proper environment, a fertilized egg (one cell) can divide and grow into a human being composed of billions of cells. Furthermore, these billions of cells are formed into tissues and organs which have definite places and functions in the life of the organism. How the minute genes manage to do what they do is still one of nature's closely guarded secrets. In any case, what we mean by the word "hereditary" is *gene-directed*.

Let us consider now the role of the genes in human heredity. For a human being to be conceived, an egg from the mother must be fertilized by a sperm cell from the father. Once the egg has been fertilized, a brand-new individual is begun. From the mother comes half the number of genes needed and from the father the other half. Hence, both mother and father contribute an equal amount of heredity to the new individual. If these genes are to direct the growth of this new individual, a specific, proper environment must be present. In the case of the human being, the proper place is the mother's uterus. If the fertilized egg is left in a normal uterus for seven to nine months, an infant more or less ready to take its place in the outside environment will develop. Were we to remove the egg from the uterus at the time of conception and place it in a test tube, it would soon die. Even our common sense tells us that a test tube is not the proper place for an egg to develop. So we see that we must have both the necessary genes and also the proper environment for the development of a new individual.

Chromosomes. As a rule, each of the billions of cells in the human body has a nucleus containing 48 chromosomes. In each chromosome are something like 1,000 genes.

Actually, it is better to speak of the 48 chromosomes as 24 pairs, because they are found in pairs and also because there are a few cells in the body that contain 24 chromosomes (one from each pair) instead of the full 48.[2] These cells, which prove to be the exceptions to the rule of 48, are the egg cells in the female and the sperm cells in the male. But nature has provided well. When the sperm cell fertilizes the egg cell, its 24 chromosomes pair up with the egg's 24 and form the 48 needed by the new individual. Thus, nature gains variety by letting two different lines of heredity contribute equally to the new offspring. The baby will be somewhat like both its mother and father and yet not exactly like either of them.

Reductive cell division. How does it come about that the egg and sperm each contain only 24 chromosomes rather than the typical 48? In the female *ovaries*, where eggs are produced, and in the male *testes*, where sperm cells are made, mother cells with 48 chromosomes each divide into daughter cells that have only 24. This process is called *reductive cell division.* During this division the 48 chromosomes of the mother cell line up in 24 pairs. One member of each pair goes to each daughter cell. However, for each individual pair it is a matter of pure chance as to which member of the pair goes to which of the two daughter cells. Because of this random process, millions of different combinations of chromosomes are possible. It is unlikely that any two eggs produced by the same woman would have exactly the same 24 chromosomes.

With the exception of one pair, each chromosome in a pair carries genes which match the genes on the other member of the pair. That is to say, each member of a given pair has genes controlling the growth

[2] For many years, biologists have set the number of chromosomes at 48. A very recent count, however, has found 46 (23 pairs). With either number, genetic theory and principles are the same.

Every cell in our body has
48 chromosomes (or 24 pairs)

(A pair of chromosomes showing genes; each chromosome has about 1,000 genes)

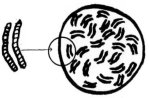

except the egg cell

and the sperm cell,

each of which has only 24
(1 from each pair)

and development of the same specific set of features and characteristics as the other member of the pair. Biologists have sorted out these 24 pairs and designated them by the first 24 letters of the alphabet, A through X. Thus, either member of any woman's A pair can match up with either member of any man's A pair and the developing child that receives this new A pair (along with the other pairs) will be assured of those human features that are transmitted by the A pair.

The one exception to the simple matching of pairs occurs in the twenty-fourth pair. Where both of the A's, B's, C's, etc., are the same in shape and size, the two members of the last pair may be different. Biologists note this fact by labeling this pair

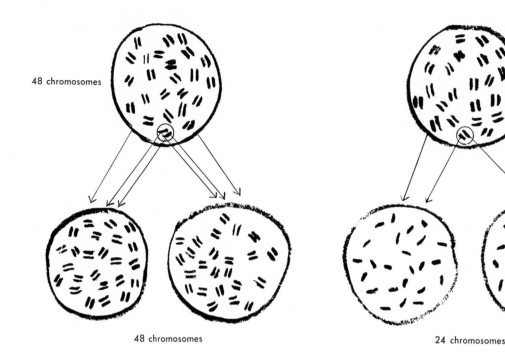

48 chromosomes

48 chromosomes

48 chromosomes

24 chromosomes

ORDINARY CELL DIVISION

REDUCTIVE CELL DIVISION

XX when the two members are alike and XY when they are different. The X chromosome is a full-sized chromosome, but the Y is dwarfed.

This pair of chromosomes is important because the sex of the offspring depends on it. If a child receives an X from its mother and an X from its father so that it has a matched XX pair, the child is a girl. If it receives an X from the mother and a Y from the father, it is a boy. Every woman and girl has two X's, and every man and boy has an X and a Y. We see, then, that we always receive an X from our mother and either an X or a Y from our father. Hence, any complaints about our sex should be made to our father, not our mother.

Ordinary cell division. One egg and one sperm cell unite to begin one new human being. This fertilized egg divides by what is called *ordinary cell division* into two cells. Each of these cells has its own nucleus with 48 chromosomes. Moreover, these cells, usu-

ally stick together. The process of cell division continues, and with each new division the number of cells is doubled. Before long, billions of cells have been produced. Under the direction of the genes and in the ideal environment of the uterus, these cells form a human infant.

Twins. Most of the time the fertilization of one egg by one sperm cell produces one offspring. Once in a while, however, the first two cells into which the fertilized egg divides do not stick together. Instead, each of these two cells then multiplies independently and produces an infant. These two infants are *identical twins.* The important point is that they come from one egg and one sperm cell and are, therefore, two individuals with exactly the same heredity (genes). Identical twins (triplets, etc.) are, in fact, the only cases known where two (or more) people have identical heredity. Since they are identical in heredity, they are always of the same sex. We shall see later that these facts are valuable to the psychologist who is trying to study experimentally the influences of heredity and environment.

Occasionally two eggs instead of one are ready at the same time for fertilization within the mother. In this case two different sperm cells may fertilize these two eggs and two infants result. These twins are called *fraternal twins* and may be two boys or two girls or a boy and a girl. Moreover, these twins are not of the same heredity. They are no more related than any other two brothers and sisters born at different times.

The relatedness of relatives. On the average, brothers and sisters are related to each other in heredity about as much as they are to either parent; that is, on the average, *siblings* (all the children of the same parents) have 24 chromosomes in common. Some siblings have more than 24 in common, and some less than 24. Since kinship depends upon the possession of common chromosomes, some siblings are more (or less) related than others. One of the extremes in relationship is, of course, the case of identical twins (all 48 chromosomes in common). The other extreme, which probably never occurs (but is theoretically possible), is the case of a brother and a sister who have no chromosomes in common. Biologically speaking, these two siblings would not be akin to each other at all. This remarkable state of affairs might arise if, by chance, 24 of the mother's chromosomes went to the boy and a different set entirely went to the girl *and* if the father's chromosomes were similarly divided. In the usual case, however, the girl receives one or more of the chromosomes that also went to the boy. Consequently, our best bet is what our common sense tells us, that brothers and sisters are related. Or to emphasize the point in another way, we may say that there is no known case of siblings who are not related, even though it is possible genetically for them not to be related.

We have presented these extremes simply to set the limits of kinship. We may now say that, biologically speaking, we are related to only those people who share with us at least one chromosome. We have also seen that we receive 24 chromosomes from our mother and 24 from our father. Thus, we are always related half and half to our two parents—there are no exceptions. Our parents, of course, received their chromosomes from their parents, which means that our chromosomes came to us (through our parents) from our four grandparents. On the average, then, we received 12 from each of our grandparents. However, because which chromosomes are passed on is a matter of chance, some of us received more than 12 from a particular grandparent (e.g., our mother's father) and some received fewer. Thus we may be more or less related to a particular grandparent, just as we are to our siblings. Moreover, as in the case of siblings, it is theoretically possible for us to have received as many as 24 or as few as none from any one of our grandparents. Again it is not very likely that we possess no kinship at all to one of our grandparents, and even less likely that we are unrelated to two of them.

The likelihood of no kinship increases as we trace our lineage back through more and more generations. From each of our 8 great-grandparents we receive, on the average, 6 chromosomes. This far back, the possibility of our not being related to one of them is not so remote. From our great-great-grandparents we receive on the average 3 from each. From the next generation back, we average only $1\frac{1}{2}$ from each. And from our ancestors six generations back, we are given on the average only $\frac{3}{4}$ chromosome from each. Since a chromosome is usually transmitted all in one piece, we have at last come to a generation of ancestors in which some of the individuals are definitely not akin to us. These facts make highly questionable our attempt to trace our family trees back very far. Many

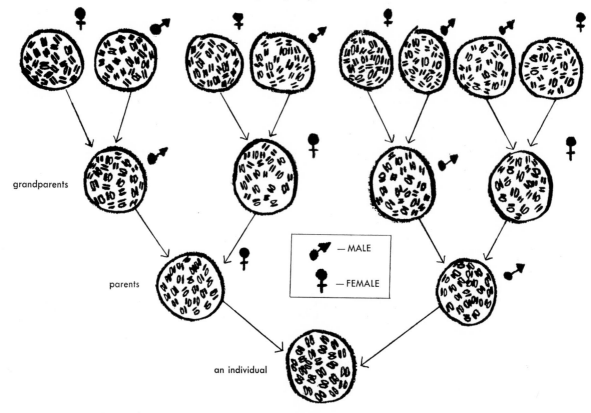

Figure 2.2. On the average, how many chromosomes does a person receive from each generation of his ancestors? In this drawing the chromosomes are represented as ovals and may be traced back for three generations. A count will show that the typical individual represented received 24 from each of his parents, 12 from each grandparent, and 6 from each great-grandparent.

people who glory in a supposed kinship with some historic personage are only fooling themselves. The possibility that they have a chromosome in common with that person is too remote to consider seriously.

Dominant and Recessive Genes. *Genetics* is the name biologists give to the special study of heredity. As the name indicates, genetics is the science that deals with the genes. The first laws of heredity were formulated about a hundred years ago by an Austrian monk, Gregor Johann Mendel [3]

[3] V. Grant, "The Development of a Theory of Heredity," *American Scientist*, 44(2):158–179.

(1822–1884). He learned about inheritance by growing and crossing several varieties of garden peas. His work was neglected until about 1900, when his laws were rediscovered and the science of genetics began to flourish.

One of the most important findings of genetics is that some genes are *dominant* and some are *recessive*. To illustrate the meaning of these terms, let us first take a classical example from Mendel's work with the color of pea flowers. Some of these flowers are white and some are red. If the flower contains only the genes for red, it is called *pure* red. If it has only genes for white, it is called *pure* white. If it contains genes for both red and white, it is called a *hybrid*.

In Figure 2.4 we see that the crossing (mating) of a pure red flower and a pure white produces offspring that are all red in color and that are designated as hybrid red.

In Figure 2.5 we observe that, if two of these hybrid reds are crossed, the result, on the average, is three red and one white offspring out of every four. Further, by subsequent breeding experiments, we can show that one of these reds is pure red like its

red grandparent and the one white flower is pure white like the other grandparent. The other two reds, however, are hybrids like their parents.

The foregoing illustrations show that, though the hybrid red looks like the pure red, it breeds differently. It must carry a gene for white because, when cross-bred, it has white offspring. Because the gene for white is not expressed when paired with the gene for red, it is called "recessive."

The fact that the hybrid is red indicates that the gene for red dominates the gene for white. For that reason, it is called "domi-

Figure 2.3. What is peculiar about the heredity of this individual? By counting the chromosomes, drawn as ovals, we discover that this individual received 24 from each parent, just as we all do. However, from his paternal grandmother he received 15 and from his paternal grandfather only 9, making up the 24 from his father. Even more unusual, he received 24 chromosomes from his maternal grandfather and none at all from his maternal grandmother. Thus, he is not genetically related to his own mother's mother! Such an occurrence as this is very unlikely, but it does illustrate one remote possibility in heredity.

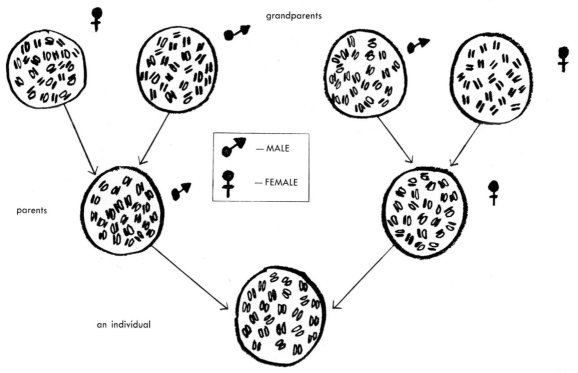

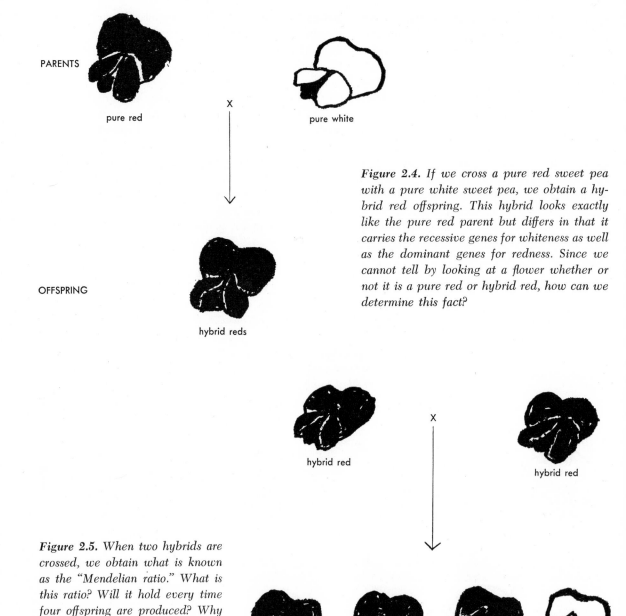

PARENTS

pure red

X

pure white

OFFSPRING

hybrid reds

Figure 2.4. If we cross a pure red sweet pea with a pure white sweet pea, we obtain a hybrid red offspring. This hybrid looks exactly like the pure red parent but differs in that it carries the recessive genes for whiteness as well as the dominant genes for redness. Since we cannot tell by looking at a flower whether or not it is a pure red or hybrid red, how can we determine this fact?

hybrid red

X

hybrid red

Figure 2.5. When two hybrids are crossed, we obtain what is known as the "Mendelian ratio." What is this ratio? Will it hold every time four offspring are produced? Why was the discovery of this ratio important for the science of genetics? (For further discussion of this ratio, see Figure 2.6.)

pure red

hybrid red

hybrid red

pure white

nant." A dominant gene is one that, when paired with a recessive gene, dominates; i.e., its character shows up in the offspring. It dominates but does not eliminate the recessive gene. Whenever in later generations two recessive genes come together, the recessive characteristic again appears.

If we let R stand for the dominant red gene in our pea and w for the recessive white, we have in Figure 2.6 a picture of hcw the genes pair off. Figure 2.6 is a combination of the facts of Figures 2.4 and 2.5. In this figure one R and one w have been enclosed in parentheses simply to allow us to follow them more easily from generation to generation.

This same rule of dominants and recessives holds for human genes as well as for those of the pea plant. Human characteristics, however, are seldom determined by a single pair of genes. Rather, we must think in terms of complex groups of genes pairing with each other. This is the reason that simple human examples are hard to find. It would be convenient, for example, if we could say simply that brown eyes are con-

trolled by a single dominant gene and blue eyes by a single recessive one. Such a statement would allow us to follow Figures 2.4, 2.5, and 2.6, changing only "pure red flower" to "pure brown eyes" and "pure white flower" to "pure blue eyes." Unhappily, such a statement is not true. Although brown eyes are usually dominant and blue eyes usually recessive, eye color in the human being is so complex that we need further genetic laws to handle them. Some of these laws exist, but we must leave their study to the course in genetics.

It is sufficient for us in this introduction to genetics to see that human heredity follows definite patterns and laws. Furthermore, these principles hold generally for all living organisms, plants and animals alike.

The So-called "Purely" Hereditary Traits. In the last section we seemed to ignore the part environment plays in the determination of the characteristics of redness and whiteness in pea plants or brownness and blueness in human eyes. Actually we merely considered environment to be held constant. This is not to say, however, that environment is unimportant. If E and T in the formula $P = f(H,E,T)$ are held constant between two individuals, they nevertheless influence the growth and development of both individuals. However, any difference between these two people will be attrib-

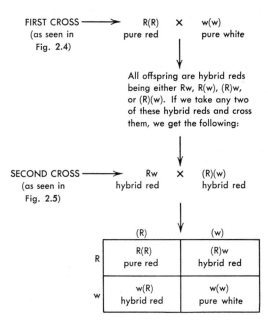

Figure 2.6. A first cross between a pure red and a pure white pea plant. All offspring of this cross are hybrid reds. A second cross between two of these hybrids shows the Mendelian ratio of 1-2-1; i.e., one pure dominant, two hybrids, and one pure recessive. With only a few second-cross offspring this ratio may show chance variations. However, with large numbers of offspring the ratio holds. This ratio was discovered by Gregor Mendel. (The parentheses are used simply to identify one of the R's and one of the w's.)

utable to *H* which has varied (i.e., *H* is different for each of them). In identical twins we have it the other way around; *H* and *T* are constant (they have exactly the same genes and age), while only *E* can vary and be different for each of them.

In the example of the pea plants we are assuming that all the plants are grown in the same soil, with the same climate, etc. Also we are comparing them after the same lapse of time in each case. In a later section, we give a number of examples that show how changes in environment can affect traits ordinarily called "hereditary." For the time being we shall simply reaffirm that all traits and characteristics are both hereditary and environmental.

ENVIRONMENT

Each of us realizes that he lives in an environment. Whenever the word is mentioned, we probably think of the house we live in, of the school we attend, of all the objects we own, of the grass and the trees in our yard, and even of the air we breathe. All these elements, and many more, are a part of our external, physical environment. But it would be a great mistake if we were to limit our use of the word to only this sort of environment.

The most useful way for us to define the word "environment" is to say that it includes all the conditions in the world that influence in any way our behavior, growth, development, or life processes—except the genes (and even genes can be considered to provide environment for other genes). According to this broad definition, not only are there a multitude of factors in our environment at any one time, but there are also a great number of other factors that are potentially capable of influencing us. However, our actual environment consists in only those factors in the world around us which do exert their influence. In order to examine more closely the composition of

our environment, let us divide it into three parts: the external, physical environment; the internal environment; and the social environment.

The External, Physical Environment. We have already listed a few of the elements that make up our external, physical environment—houses, trees, air, etc. It would take a list almost without end to exhaust everything that could possibly become a part of this environment. We get around this difficulty by using the general term *external stimuli.* Since we take up the topic of stimuli in a later chapter, it is enough to say here that a stimulus is anything which is able to stimulate or excite the receptors in any one of the several sense organs (eye, ear, skin, etc.). It is through our sense organs that the external world ordinarily influences us.

To some extent our every action is determined by what we see, hear, or feel. Life is a continual and continuous responding to stimulation. We change and mold and shape our external environment at the same time that it molds and shapes and changes us. Moreover, certain external factors must be in the environment if genes are to exert their influence on human characteristics. For example, in Europe during World War II some children could not find enough food and were permanently stunted in growth. Although a boy might have inherited the genes that with the right environment (a better diet) would have allowed him to be 6 feet tall, under wartime conditions he might stop growing at a height of barely 5 feet.

The Internal Environment. We have mentioned food as a part of our external environment. We see food, taste it, and respond to it by eating it. Once it is in our stomachs and intestines, it is in between our external and internal environments. We say "in between" because until it is digested and absorbed into our blood stream it is not properly spoken of as internal environment.

If it were not for the fact that it is inside our digestive tract, it would be best to consider it as an external stimulus.

Once food and water are in the blood stream (and in the lymph fluids), they affect every cell in the body and are definitely part of the internal environment. The same thing can be said for the vitamins we eat and the hormones produced by the glands. This aspect of our internal environment is treated more fully in Chapter 9.

If we accept the concept of inter~~¹ environment, we must be prepared to admit that it is nearly impossible to tell where our environment leaves off and we begin. Or to put it another way, we must say that we cannot draw a sharp line between ourselves and our environment.

The Social Environment. Psychologists generally recognize our social environment to be extremely important in shaping our individual behavior and personality. In using the word "social" we mean to include all the other human beings who in any way influence us. Some people influence us by direct, daily contact—our families, our friends, our school and business acquaintances, etc. Other people have as much or more influence through indirect contact—over radio and television, in books and other publications, and in many other ways.

Especially in personality is each of us a result of the interaction of our genes and our social environment. Because of this interaction, each of us is unique. Even in the cases of individuals who have some genes in common or similar social environments,

the interaction produces wide variations in personality. Siblings, who have both similar social environment and some genes in common, also show this wide variation. Even where heredity is the same (identical twins), and the social environment is allowed to vary, personalities show remarkable differences.

The reason we ordinarily think of identical twins as having inherited the same personality is that they most often have very nearly the same social environment as well as the same genes. However, on close analysis such identical twins show consistent individual differences in personality (note the case of twin T and twin C on page 36). In the rare instances where identical twins have been separated at birth and reared in extremely different social environments, their adult personalities have been quite different (note the case of Mabel and Mary on page 37). In the next section we shall examine several more examples of interaction, some of which show the effect on the total personality and some the effect on one or two characteristics.

Figure 2.7. Which aspects of this scene can be considered as the external environment of these students? What things are actually stimulating them at the moment and what are potential stimuli? Can you describe the social environment as it is depicted here? (Standard Oil Company, New Jersey.)

These babies are identical twins, 38 weeks old. Since they have exactly the same heredity and have been reared together, they are about as much alike as two human beings can be. It is not surprising that they are responding quite similarly in the test situation. However, one infant is reaching with its right hand and the other with its left. The reason is that they are "mirror-image" twins—the left side of one twin is identical with the right side of the other one. (Courtesy of Dr. Arnold Gesell.)

IDENTICAL TWINS REARED TOGETHER— TWIN T AND TWIN C

Because they have exactly the same heredity, identical twins reared together can be expected to show great similarity in nearly all respects. On the other hand, since there are at least small differences in their environment, we can also expect to see some individual differences between them. Such similarities and differences are shown in the study of twin T and twin C.* These identical twin girls were studied for fourteen years by the Yale Clinic of Child Development.

From time to time in this study the method of co-twin control was used. Twin T would be given training in such activities as stair climbing, manual coordination, block building, and vocabulary, while twin C was left untrained as a control. At first in each task twin T would tend to excel, but as C reached the proper level of maturation, she soon equaled T's performance.

As would be expected, these twins were very much alike in physical growth and appearance, in intelligence, and in many other characteristics. However, closer study showed a number of persistent and durable differences. T was quicker, C more deliberate. In drawing a picture T preferred to use straight lines and angles, while C preferred curved lines. T appeared a little brighter, C was a bit better in a social situation. T was more prompt in attention, while C was more alert.

Although these differences were slight, they added up to a distinctive personality for each of the two girls. Certainly they were not so unlike as most people, but each had her unique personality. Of interest is the fact that some of their differences showed up in infancy. This fact points up the importance of the prenatal environment in the development of temperament. Other of the differences showed up later.

We should remember that interaction of heredity and environment produced everything about these twins, including both their differences *and* their similarities. However, since their heredity was identical, we must con-

* A. Gesell and H. Thompson, "Learning and Growth in Identical Infant Twins: An Experimental Study by the Method of Co-twin Control," *Genetic Psychology Monograph*, 6:1–124, 1929.

clude the environmental variations accounted for the differences they possessed. Certainly such differences exist, for since two people cannot occupy the same identical space at the same time, they must have at least slightly different environments. In the mother's uterus, for example, if one twin is on the left side the other must be on the right side. Also, in growing up even twins will receive, at least occasionally, different treatment. Very important in the case of twin T and twin C were the co-twin control observations. The training that twin T received constituted environmental stimulation which twin C did not have.

We can conclude from this study that even identical twins reared together can be expected to show small differences in addition to a great amount of similarity.

▶

IDENTICAL TWINS REARED APART— MABEL AND MARY

Mabel and Mary * were identical twins separated early in life. Mabel lived in the country and participated in all the rural activities, including hard farm chores. She was permitted to finish only eight grades in the small country school near her home. Mary grew up in a medium-sized city, where her main interest was the study of music. She attended three years of high school in this city and then finished her fourth year in a large-city school. After graduation she became a music teacher. Both girls had the advantage of living in relatively prosperous homes.

At the age of twenty-nine Mabel and Mary were studied by a psychologist. In intelligence they were separated by 17 IQ points on the Stanford-Binet Test (see Chapter 17 for information about this test). Mary was rated as high average in intelligence and Mabel was low average. In personality Mabel, who was still a farm woman, was slow and phlegmatic, and yet was considered an aggressive leader in her community. Mary was excitable, nearly neurotic. In manner Mabel was almost masculine, while the music teacher Mary was quite ladylike. This difference in manner showed up in their walk— Mabel had a firm, manlike stride, Mary a very feminine step.

Even in physical appearance these twins differed. Mabel had hard muscles and weighed 138 pounds. Mary's muscles were soft and not well developed, and she weighed 110 pounds.

Over-all, they were unlike in behavior and appeared to be as strikingly dissimilar in personality as the psychological tests had indicated. They did not seem to be identical twins at all, although undoubtedly there was a family resemblance.

Mabel and Mary illustrate how widely two persons, even with heredity constant between them, can vary in personality and appearance if reared separately. We have already seen in the study of twin T and twin C how identical heredity and rather small variations in environment can produce small but real differences in personality.

In these studies we again see proof that a person is a result of the interaction of both heredity and environment. These twins were alike because of identical heredity, yet dissimilar because of environmental differences.

* H. H. Newman, *Multiple Human Births*, Doubleday, New York, 1940.

Most of us have learned somewhere in our education that eye color is inherited. This is true, but it is also true that eye color is partly determined by environment—a statement which may at first seem a little surprising, since we are likely to think that "inherited" means "completely inherited." How can environment in any way affect the development of eye color?

When a human individual is conceived, he has the proper genes present to determine the production of eyes, eye color, hair, face, limbs, and all the other features of a human being. We must remember, however, that he also had present the proper environment, his mother's uterus, in which to develop. If he had not had that proper environment, a number of features might have turned out differently. We know this from experiments in lower animals.

Fruit-fly Experiments. It has been said that geneticists know more about the heredity of the fruit fly, *Drosophila*, than they do about any other living organism. Why this preoccupation with the fruit fly? The reason lies in the facts that *Drosophila* has in its salivary glands giant chromosomes, which are easy to study, and that it can be bred rapidly under laboratory conditions.

In one experiment it was shown that fruit flies whose heredity did not contain a gene for yellow body color could be caused to have yellow bodies by an environmental change. This was done by including a chemical, *silver nitrate*, in the food on which the larvae fed. These flies were not different in appearance from flies that have the gene for yellowness. However, when these flies which had been fed silver nitrate were bred, their offspring were not yellow but were, as they should be by the laws of genetics, the dark-brown color of their grandparents and other ancestors. Of course, these dark-brown offspring had not had their environment changed by the ad-

dition of silver nitrate to the food they ate.

Bearing directly on our interest in environmental influences on eye color are a number of other experiments with *Drosophila*. Some of these experiments show that even such relatively simple environmental factors as changes in temperature during the incubation of the eggs can affect the adult fly's eye color. In one experiment fruit flies with genes that normally produce rust-colored eyes were made to have red eyes by adding a certain chemical, *kynurenine*, to the fruit flies' environment during eye development. Since the interaction of genes and environment in *Drosophila* is not basically different from that in human beings, we must conclude that similar changes could be effected in human eye-color development.

It is within the realm of possibility that chemical changes in a human mother's uterus could cause an eye color to develop that would not have been predictable from a knowledge of the child's heredity. Although actual human examples pertaining to eye color are not available, we do have examples that illustrate the importance of prenatal environment in the development of other so-called "hereditary" characteristics. Let us consider two of them.

Human Examples of Interaction. One example of interaction in human development is sometimes seen in German measles in the pregnant woman. German measles, of course, is a rather mild disease so far as most adults are concerned. It is also a mild disease so far as the pregnant woman herself is concerned, but it can be injurious to the unborn child. As the mother's body fights the disease, toxic substances are built up in her blood stream. These substances reach the developing embryo. If the embryo is at the stage when the eyes are developing, there may be a defect in the structure of the eyes. If it is at the stage when the ears are developing, the ears may be defective. Thus, the child may be born blind, or deaf, or with any of a number of other defects. A proper environment is therefore just as important as the genes in the development of such organs as eyes and ears. Furthermore, if a child blinded in this way grows up, marries, and has children, they will have normal sight; for the toxic environment has affected only the developing organs, not the genes that partly direct their development.

Another somewhat similar example is so-called *Mongolian* feeble-mindedness. This is a type of feeble-mindedness in which the child has peculiar-appearing eyes, a long pointed tongue, and certain other distinctive physical characteristics. The misfortune of being feeble-minded, or at least dull in intellect, is, of course, the most important part of the defective condition. It has been discovered only recently that certain toxic substances built up in the mother's blood stream at about the eighth week of pregnancy may be the cause of this malforming of various organs and parts of the body, resulting in Mongolian feeble-mindedness.[4]

Both these examples illustrate the fact that the human being can have its environment changed in its early days of life just as the fruit fly can in the laboratory. Most important, they show that such environmental changes result in serious consequences. Both structurally and functionally the organism is different from what it would have been had not the environment been altered.

Thus, we see that heredity and environment are inseparable. It is a hopeless task to try to separate the various human traits and characteristics into those which are hereditary and those which are environmental. The only correct statement is that

Figure 2.8. This unfortunate child is an example of Mongolian feeble-mindedness. At the present time it is thought that chemical changes in his mother's uterus denied him a normal prenatal environment. (From Dr. Theodore H. Ingalls, "Mongolism," Scientific American, February, 1952, pp. 60–62, by courtesy of the author and publisher.)

all traits and all characteristics are produced by the joint action, interaction, and interrelation of both heredity and environment. To say that one is more important than the other is like saying that either the ball or the bat is more important in playing baseball. Without both a bat and a ball a baseball game is impossible.

It may seem, at this point, that only extreme changes in environment or very abnormal conditions will in any way affect the action of the genes. It may seem further that in an ordinary or normal situation environment is a neutral factor and that genes alone direct growth and development. The facts are, however, that environment is just as important in normal development as in abnormal (see the two twin studies).

[4] This hypothesis about the cause of Mongolian feeble-mindedness has not yet been conclusively proved. However, it does illustrate the fact that scientists are searching for causes based on the interaction of heredity and environment.

MATURATION

Many people confuse the terms "heredity" and "maturation." The two words do not, however, mean the same. We have seen that heredity is the direction given by the genes to growth and development. *Maturation* is the completion of growth and development within the organism.

Every organ and every system within the body must mature over a period of time before it is ready to function. Most organs are capable of functioning at birth, but some of the organs and systems are farther along than others. The heart, for example, is already capable of pumping blood, and the digestive system can handle milk. The nervous system is functioning at its lower levels, but many years must pass before the higher levels of the brain are completely developed and fully functioning.

In the process of maturation we see the interaction of heredity and environment over the course of time. For example, a girl's ovaries are not mature enough to produce fully ripened eggs until she reaches puberty, which comes ordinarily between the years of eleven and fifteen. However, a number of environmental changes and conditions can affect the onset of puberty. Malnutrition, chronic illness, serious emotional unbalance, etc., can all slow this maturation process. A girl in a war-torn country without sufficient food may not reach puberty until she is twenty years old.

Motor Maturation and Development. At the time of birth the various muscles of the body are capable of functioning, but they are far from being completely mature. As the muscles develop and the nervous system matures, more and more complex sequences of motor behavior become possible. That such behavior depends upon the prior maturation of the underlying organs and systems is a logical, but not necessarily obvious, fact. For proof that it is not so obvious to some people, we need

only witness a parent pushing a child to do things far beyond its level of maturation. What a foolish waste of effort is a mother's attempt to teach her six-month-old baby to walk!

In Figure 2.9 we see the sequence of motor maturation and development in an average child. Individual children may be somewhat slower or faster in going through this sequence and still be within the normal range. Also, some children do not follow precisely the order of the sequence, or some may even drop out parts of it. Parents who are not familiar with the sequence of maturation often worry unnecessarily about the progress of their babies.

In Figure 2.9 we can see that children learn to walk at an average age of fifteen months. Of course, some children walk earlier and some later than this. We say "learn to walk," yet we must remember that such learning depends upon a sufficient level of maturation in the muscles and nervous system of the child.

Most of us would assume that unless a child were allowed enough freedom of movement to follow the several steps in the motor sequence his walking would be delayed. Such is not necessarily the case, as has been pointed out in a number of Indian tribes (note the example of the Hopi Indian children on page 42). In these tribes, young infants spend the first several months (up to a year) of their lives tied to a cradle board unable to move. Yet, they walk at an average age of fifteen months, the same as children permitted unlimited freedom of movement.

It is interesting to watch the motor development of identical twins. Since they have exactly the same heredity and since they are most often reared in the same environment, they tend to follow very much the same pattern of maturation. This fact is illustrated in the study of twin T and twin C.

Maturation and Learning. Behavior of all types must wait until the maturation of

0 mo. FETAL POSTURE

1 mo. CHIN UP

2 mo. CHEST UP

3 mo. REACH AND MISS

4 mo. SIT WITH SUPPORT

5 mo. SIT ON LAP GRASP OBJECT

6 mo. SIT ON HIGH CHAIR

7 mo. GRASP DANGLING OBJECT

8 mo. STAND WITH HELP

9 mo. STAND HOLDING FURNITURE

10 mo. CREEP

11 mo. WALK WHEN LED

12 mo. PULL TO STAND BY FURNITURE

13 mo. CLIMB STAIR STEPS

14 mo. STAND ALONE

15 mo. WALK ALONE

Figure 2.9. During the maturation and development of locomotion, the typical infant goes through the sequence shown in these drawings. The ages given are averages computed from the observation of many children. Thus, an individual child may progress somewhat faster or slower and still be considered normal—he may walk at a year or even earlier, or he may begin standing alone at 16 months or even later. Although generally followed, the sequence itself may be changed slightly in individual cases. Can you suggest which parts of the sequence are most often transposed and which seldom are?

AGE OF WALKING
AMONG HOPI
CHILDREN

▶ From the time a Hopi Indian baby is born until it is six months to a year old it spends nearly all the hours of the day and night tied to a cradle board.* It leaves the board only to be cleaned or bathed. It even nurses while tied to the cradle board. The baby is tied so tightly that little leg or arm movement is possible.

Contrary to what might be expected, this enforced inactivity does not slow the child's maturational processes so far as walking is concerned. When compared with other children, the Hopi child is shown not to be inferior at all in learning to walk. Among a group of Hopi who followed the old, traditional way of life (including cradling), walking began, on the average, at 14.98 months. In a group of Hopi who followed modern ways and did not use the cradle board, age of walking was 15.05 months. Thus, there was practically no difference between the groups.

We should note that this study is an excellent example of naturalistic observation. The scientists were able to obtain information in this manner that would have been very difficult to obtain experimentally. There is a limit to what we are willing to do to a human being, child or adult, in order to have a controlled experiment.

* W. Dennis and M. G. Dennis, "The Effect of Cradling Practices upon the Onset of Walking in Hopi Children," *Journal of Genetic Psychology*, 56:77–86, 1940.

organs and systems has proceeded far enough to make the behavior possible. Behavior which is learned is no exception to this rule. For example, if a person is to learn to dance or to ice-skate, he must have muscles and nerves matured considerably beyond the point required for walking. Even walking behavior in a baby must be delayed until the muscles and nerves have matured for about fifteen months. Nearly all learned behavior requires that a vast amount of maturation precede it.

Learning to talk. Learning to speak a language is one of a human being's most difficult tasks. No other animal is able to accomplish this task, although some, like the dog and horse, may learn to respond to a few spoken commands. Others, like the parrot or parakeet, are able to speak a few words, but without knowing the meaning of them—and without meaning there is no true language.

At birth the infant's respiratory and vocal apparatus has matured only enough to allow it to cry. After the baby has matured for a month and has gained some control of its breathing, it learns to make different sounds for hunger, pain, and discomfort. Between two and four months it begins to coo and babble and learns to look in the direction of a human voice.

From six to nine months the infant matures enough to repeat syllables ("Da-da-da-da," "Ma-ma-ma-ma," etc.) and will vocalize in response to a human voice. By one year of age the baby can understand simple commands (e.g., "Look at Mama!" or "Hold the toy dog!") and speak its first word. However, the first word may not appear until fifteen months or even later.

When the baby is eighteen months old, it is likely to have a vocabulary of three to five words. Also by this time it can understand and respond to the admonition "Don't." By the age of two the child is able to name objects (doll, doggy, ball, etc.) and begins to combine words ("Where dolly?" "Give me cooky!"). From this time on, there is continual progress in phrase and sentence building.

During these first two years there has been a constant maturation of breathing control, of vocal cords, and—very important —of brain centers that control speech and understanding of language. This same period is also used by the baby to develop a whole language of gestures and expressions (of face, hands, and body). As in learning to walk, an infant must await the proper level of maturation before a given level of speech or gesture can be attained.

CONCLUSION

Human traits and characteristics are complexly determined through the interaction of heredity and environment. We cannot say that the shape of our friend's nose was determined entirely by the genes he received from his father. Nor can we say that his trait of generosity resulted wholly from his having a generous mother from whom to learn. We must say that both his nose and his generosity are functions of the interaction and interplay of his heredity and his environment.

Furthermore, human heredity is so complicated a study that we know only its general rules and principles and have difficulty explaining specific details. Exactly which group of our friend's 48,000 genes is partly responsible for his nose, we do not know. And we are even less sure about the environmental factors that are essential to the molding of such a nose. In the case of his generosity, we feel that we can isolate a few of the environmental elements that are necessary. About the group of genes involved in generosity, however, the science of genetics cannot yet offer us anything, although constant progress is being made.

As genetics makes progress, we, who are primarily interested in the personality of the individual, hope to comprehend more fully the interaction of heredity and environment. At least, we now have a general frame of reference for understanding the interaction; it is concisely summarized in the expression $P = f(H,E,T)$. We must leave to the future the expansion of this formula to the point where individual traits and characteristics can be explained.

SUMMARY

Although in the past many biologists were pure hereditarians and many sociologists were strict environmentalists, today both groups agree that a person is a result of the interaction of both heredity and environment.

Heredity can be defined best as that which is contributed to a person by his genes. The genes are located in the chromosomes, which are in the nucleus of each cell of the body. The genes direct and guide the growth and development of the organism. They are often called the unit carriers of heredity.

Genetic kinship can vary all the way from that of identical twins, who have all 48 chromosomes in common, to that of individuals who have only a single chromosome alike. If two individuals do not have any chromosomes in common, they are not genetically related, regardless of what their genealogical chart says.

Some genes are dominant and some recessive. When a dominant gene is paired with a recessive gene, the dominant gene directs the development of the characteristic in question. In order for a recessive gene to direct development, it must be paired with another recessive gene.

Environment includes everything in the world (with the exception of the genes) that influences in any way our behavior, growth, or development. We ordinarily divide environment into three parts: the external (air, trees, houses, etc.), the internal (blood and lymph), and the social (other people). The social environment is important in shaping our personalities.

All our traits, features, and characteristics are a function of the interaction of heredity and environment. Examples of this interaction range all the way from eye color to ice-skating ability.

Maturation is the process of completing growth and development within the organism. Our organs, systems, and behavior sequences must all mature over a period of time if they are to function properly.

QUESTIONS

1. Explain the formula $P = f(H,E,T)$.

2. Define briefly the following terms: (*a*) chromosomes, (*b*) genes, (*c*) dominant, (*d*) recessive.

3. What is reductive cell division? What cells result from reductive division?

4. How and why are studies of identical twins useful to a psychologist?

5. *Must* we be related (genetically) to (*a*) our parents, (*b*) our siblings, (*c*) our grandparents, (*d*) our uncles and aunts? Explain your answers.

6. What is meant by "the Mendelian ratio"?

Give an example of this ratio.

7. What is meant by the term "environment"?

8. Explain why eye color is as much a function of environment as it is of heredity.

9. How does the word "maturation" differ in meaning from the phrase "effects of heredity"?

10. Of what importance for psychology is the study of walking among Hopi children?

11. Trace the development and maturation of speech and language in babies.

12. Substantiate the following statement: Learning to speak English is an example of the interaction of heredity, environment, and time.

SUGGESTED READINGS

Baldwin, A. L.: *Behavior and Development in Childhood,* Dryden, New York, 1955.
> (A recent child-psychology textbook written from the developmental point of view.)

Carmichael, L. (ed.): *Manual of Child Psychology,* Wiley, New York, 1946.
> (An encyclopedic anthology of all aspects of child development and growth.)

Scheinfeld, A.: *You and Heredity,* Lippincott, Philadelphia, 1950.
> (A popular account of the facts of heredity.)

Sinnott, E. W., et al.: *Principles of Genetics,* 4th ed., McGraw-Hill, New York, 1950.
> (A standard textbook on genetics, with a good summary of the work on *Drosophila.*)

Zubec, J. P., and P. A. Solberg: *Human Development,* McGraw-Hill, New York, 1954.
> (A good technical account of human development from conception on through life.)

3 MOTIVATION

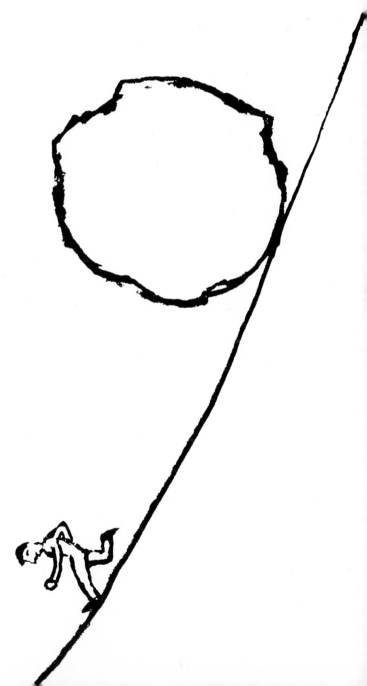

Master Sergeant Harold E. Wilson, U.S.M.C.R., received the Congressional Medal of Honor for courageous action in Korea.

Out of the spring night, the Red banzai attack hit like a thunderstorm. The darkness exploded into a nightmare of flaming confusion. But Sergeant Wilson went into action at once, rallying his hard-pressed men. Bullets wounded his head and leg; disabled both arms. Refusing aid, he crawled, bleeding, from man to man, supplying ammunition, directing fire, helping the wounded. As the attack grew fiercer, a mortar shell blew him off his feet. Still, dazed and weakened, he held on, leading the fight all night till the last Red assault was beaten off. At dawn the Sergeant had saved not only his position, but the precious lives of his men.

Whenever we read about men like Sergeant Wilson, nearly all of us pause and ask ourselves, "Why does any man do what he did?" In terms of what we are going to study in this chapter, our question is best expressed as, "What were Sergeant Wilson's *motives?*"

So long as things go smoothly, we have little occasion to wonder about motives. However, nearly every day someone around us—some fellow worker or neighbor—does something that we did not expect. Again the question "Why did he do it?" Again we are asking, "What were his motives?" Only on rare occasions do we sit down and wonder about our friends' everyday actions and more ordinary behavior. Happily, on these occasions we feel that we know the motives and there is little need to wonder for long.

When Mr. Brown rushes into a restaurant at noon and eats a hearty lunch, it does not take a lot of analysis for us to reach the conclusion that he is hungry. Hunger is a motive that we feel we understand, although we may be mistaken. When the body needs food in order to stay alive, we become hungry and seek food. As soon as we find food and eat it, our need is satisfied. But some actions are harder to understand; when one day the respectable Mr. Smith embezzles money from his firm, both we and the police begin to wonder about the motive.

Not only do we wonder about the motives of Sergeant Wilson and Mr. Smith, but we also at times wonder about our own motives. How many times have we all had the sad experience of having to say to ourselves, "Why did I do that? It's not like me; I don't do things like that!" We may have been unaccountably rude to the bus driver on the way to town; we may have spent some of our savings foolishly; or maybe, as we came in the front door after a hard day, the cat got in our way and we kicked it. We realize that we must have been motivated to act as we did, but what were our motives and why? In this chapter we shall examine some of the facts about motivation that psychologists have been able to uncover. These facts will not allow us to answer all the questions that we have raised, for motivation is one of the most complex topics in psychology. However, we can expect to gain some additional insight into why we behave as we do.

SOME DEFINITIONS

Without becoming involved in theory, we shall define a number of terms that will be used in this chapter. For our present purposes we shall consider *motive* and *drive* as much the same in meaning. In general, a motive or a drive is a complex state within an organism that directs behavior toward a *goal* or *incentive*. The goal is what the organism appears to be seeking; or, more objectively, the goal is what terminates the organism's behavior. If we wish to empha-

size the fact that such *goal-objects* attract or repel the organism, we use the term "incentive."

It is true that many psychologists confine the use of the word "drive" to such states as hunger, thirst, and sex. These and similar states are referred to collectively as the *physiological drives*. The same psychologists then use the term "motive" to refer to all the others. Since such a distinction between the two words is not especially useful, we shall use "motive" and "drive" more or less interchangeably.

Sometimes the word *need* is given a special definition in the study of motivation. However, we shall use "need" only as a term that describes a certain lack within an organism. An animal that needs something is simply one which lacks something.

These terms will become more meaningful as they are encountered in context. Any difficulties as to definition arise only when different theories of motivation are being compared.

Useful Ways of Classifying Motives. A number of years ago, many psychologists divided motives into the *primary appetites and aversions* and the *secondary or higher-order motives*. Through learning and socialization, the higher-order motives were supposed to have grown directly out of the more basic appetites and aversions. We cannot prove that this is the origin of the higher-order motives; however, this scheme remains a useful way to classify our motives. In this system, the appetites include not only such drives as food-hunger, sex-hunger, rest-hunger, etc., but also such drives as contact-hunger (the desire to touch and be touched) and play-hunger. The aversions are usually listed as the drive to injury-avoidance (the wish to keep away from objects that cause pain) and the drive to interference-avoidance (the desire not to have our behavior stopped or thwarted by outside factors).

Another useful way of classifying motives is to divide them into the physiological

Figure 3.1. How do these two situations differ in respect to motives and goals? In what respect are they similar? Can the goal-objects be considered the same merely because the actions are similar? In what ways can the motives of the spectators be compared? (Wide World Photos.)

drives and the *social motives*. Again, the unprovable assumption is that the latter grow out of the former. Without accepting this connection between them, we still may use the two categories as simply a handy way of grouping the many motives that have been studied. As a matter of convenience, we shall use this system of classsification in our study of some of the facts of motivation.

THE PHYSIOLOGICAL DRIVES

When we study biology, we discover that living cells are very complex. Further, we learn that every living cell is involved in a constant and continual series of chemical reactions. These reactions are the basis for all the life processes: growth, repair, reproduction, etc. Some of the chemical substances needed by the cell include oxygen, water, salt and other minerals, food (fats, proteins, and carbohydrates), and vitamins. When these materials are available, each living cell uses them to maintain a state of biochemical equilibrium. To keep them available, a complex organism must use a number of systems: digestive, circulatory, respiratory, excretory, nervous, etc. In addition, the body has many regulatory mechanisms that coordinate and control the working of these systems. Such mechanisms help in the maintenance of temperature, of the pH (acidity-alkalinity balance) of the blood, and of the biochemical equilibrium generally. In physiology these regulations carried out by the whole organism are referred to by the term *homeostasis* or *homeostatic mechanisms.*

Many psychologists feel that the physiological drives are a part of the homeostatic regulatory mechanism. If the cell is to live, the organism must be motivated toward the goal-objects of food, water, salt, and all the other essential chemical sources. The belief is that, when certain substances are needed to maintain the equilibrium, a state of tension occurs in the organism. This tension continues until the needed chemicals are obtained. Thus, for example, the thirst drive is viewed as the result of the tension arising in an organism which has a need for water. We shall now examine a number of these physiological drives or motives.

Figure 3.2. Correlation between hunger pangs and stomach contractions is demonstrated by this technique. Each time the stomach contracts, the swallowed balloon is squeezed, marking the graph. And each time the subject feels a hunger pang, he presses the key. The resulting graph shows that hunger pangs occur simultaneously with stomach contractions. (After Cannon, W. B., "Hunger and Thirst," in C. Murchison, ed., Handbook of General Experimental Psychology, *Clark University Press, Worchester, Mass., 1934, p. 250.)*

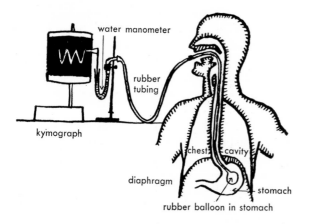

Hunger and Thirst. Until recently, hunger for food was thought to result from the stomach contractions, which in turn had resulted from the animal's need for food (see Figure 3.2). Today, we think that these contractions themselves are simply one of the results of the general tension arising from this need. Some biologists are convinced that, when the cells need food, they secrete a *hormone,* a special chemical substance (see Chapter 9), into the blood stream. This hormone is supposed to initiate the general tension. Unfortunately, if this hormone does exist, it has not yet been isolated. However, hormones are not needed to explain hunger. Any number of different chemical reactions in the body are able to stimulate the central nervous system, resulting in a general tension.

In a similar fashion thirst was thought to arise from a dryness of the mouth and throat. Today, we believe that the dryness accompanies the general tension state and is a result, not the cause, of thirst. As in the case of hunger, no specific hormone for thirst has been found.

Our study of hunger and thirst is complicated by the fact that the two must be considered together. The physiologist can show us that it is impossible to find any creature that is only hungry or only thirsty. Rather, in all cases the need for food goes along with that for water, because solid food must be put into solution. Furthermore, all natural foods contain large quantities of water, so that some of our thirst is quenched as we eat. Most animals find it impossible to eat more than a very small amount of completely dehydrated food unless ample water is available. Less well known is the fact that even people dying of thirst on the desert are unable to quench that thirst by drinking water unless they have food to eat with it. Later we shall see that our study of all motives is complicated by the fact that every motive is interrelated with other motives.

SPECIFIC HUNGERS IN BABIES

▶ In an experiment * sometimes referred to as the "cafeteria-feeding experiment" young children were allowed to select their own diets. These children began the experiment at the age of weaning, which varied from six to eleven months of age. The study continued for six years.

At every meal, each child was permitted to choose what he wanted to eat from an array of many foods. Every day he was allowed to select from the following: water, sweet and sour milk, sea salt, ten vegetables, five fruits, ten varieties of meat, and five cereals. All these foods were prepared without artificial flavoring or spices, so that they had only their natural flavors. Some were presented cooked and some raw.

It was discovered that, over a period of time, even young infants are able to choose for themselves a diet that is as well balanced as any that could be prepared by an expert dietitian. It was noted that the babies began their selection by a process of trial and error, but soon they learned by taste and smell which of the foods satisfied their needs. We can conclude that it was their specific hungers that made it possible for them to succeed in their diet selection.

* C. M. Davis, "Results of the Self-selection of Diets by Young Children," *Canadian Medical Association Journal*, 41:257–261, 1939.

Hunger and thirst differ from some other drives in that they cannot be left unsatisfied for very long if we are to continue to live. We are not at all surprised when we read about people in a famine-stricken country rioting wildly in an attempt to get food. We might even be convinced that for all people everywhere hunger and thirst are the main motives in their daily lives. However, we have only to pause and consider our own lives in America to realize that, for all practical purposes, we hardly know that we have the motives of hunger and thirst. As soon as we become aware of them (often even before we do!), we eat and drink heartily, removing both.

In this connection, it is useful to conclude that the whole mechanism of motivation has evolved in such a way that it seldom intrudes itself upon our consciousness. However, this is true only so long as our motivated behavior leads us quickly and efficiently to the goals that satisfy our needs. We become conscious of a motive like hunger only if our behavior does *not* lead us to food without causing us too much trouble. Our whole civilization has progressed to its present complexity by seeing to it that a large number of motives like hunger and thirst are kept out of the way, for in the order of urgency hunger and thirst ordinarily have a high place unless they are regularly satisfied. Of course, a large segment of our population must devote their lives to work which guarantees that food and water will be readily available for all of us. On the whole, our civilization has adequately provided for our motives of hunger and thirst, thus leaving room for other motives to play more prominent roles in our daily lives.

We have been considering hunger and thirst as they relate to actual needs of the body for food and water; many times what appears to be hunger or thirst may be some entirely different motive. For example, a person who is greatly overweight from what he describes as an "insatiable hunger" is often discovered to be motivated in his overeating, not by actual need of food, but by a need for affection and love or by feelings of insecurity.

Specific hungers. All animals, of course, have a hunger for food, but often it is for certain specific foods, not for just any food. We know, for example, that horses eat grass, and lions and tigers eat the flesh of other animals, not because they have been taught to do so, but simply because it is their *nature*—this, at least, is the popular explanation. Through its specific hungers, each animal automatically chooses a balanced diet that satisfies its total food needs. Human beings, like the other animals, also have specific hungers and, as the "cafeteria-feeding experiment" illustrates, these enable even infants to select the proper foods.

At first thought this experiment seems astounding—how, we may ask, can babies know what to eat?—but it becomes less surprising when we stop to realize that the human species lived and evolved for many centuries before we had dieticians, or even civilization. Just as the horse, by nature, has specific hungers for certain grasses and herbs, the human being naturally craves the types of food needed to keep him alive and healthy.

A great deal of research on specific hungers is now in progress, and a number of experiments have shown that changes in diet and nutrition will produce or satisfy certain specific hungers. It will be some time, however, before we can determine the many neural and chemical factors underlying this important type of motivation.

Air-hunger. Some of our physiological drives are so readily and consistently satisfied that we seldom realize we have them. Air-hunger, or our drive to breathe, is such a drive. If we seriously doubt that we have this drive, we have only to let someone hold us under water. Before many seconds pass, we shall be struggling desperately to get back up to the air.

Air-hunger results from the need of the cells for oxygen. When we take a breath of air, our lungs are filled and our red blood cells take up the needed oxygen. As we use up the oxygen in the cells of the body, we release carbon dioxide to the blood stream. The carbon dioxide is carried to the lungs and breathed out. It is the presence of carbon dioxide in the blood that keeps us breathing. When an excess of carbon dioxide is there, our breathing increases in proportion to the excess.

A peculiarity of air-hunger is demonstrated when we are very gradually deprived of oxygen. For example, when we climb a mountain or ascend in an airplane, we are hardly aware of our need for more oxygen. When the scarcity of oxygen passes a certain crucial point, we do have a reaction, but it is not the expected one. Pilots often report a false sense of well-being. Although their plane may be out of control, they feel that everything is all right and that they know what they are doing. Apparently, many pilots have lost their lives because of this strange phenomenon. Presumably in our evolution we did not take sudden ascents; therefore, we did not evolve protective mechanisms which would save us.

Rest and Sleep Drives. As we use our muscles to move us about, we are aware of the fact that they gradually become fatigued. If we perform strenuous exercises, we hasten the fatigue effects. In addition, there is a gradual but temporary decline in strength that accompanies the accumulation of a substance called *lactic acid* in the muscles as they repeatedly contract. However, there seems to be little correlation between this accumulation of lactic acid and feelings of fatigue. It is true that during rest the lactic acid is removed by the blood stream and the muscles recover their strength. This picture of the rest drive is further complicated by the fact that many neurotic individuals feel fatigued all the time, regardless of whether they use their muscles or rest them.

The sleep drive is certainly related to the rest drive but is not identical with it. We may rest without sleeping, but we seldom sleep without resting. At one time it was thought that sleep came when certain chemical substances built up in the muscles and blood stream. In Figure 3.3 we see evidence that it is not something in the blood that causes sleep. It is now known that sleep is largely controlled by the central nervous system. A center for wakefulness and a center for sleep have been located in the *hypothalamus* (see Chapter 9) of the brain. However, conditions in the muscles and in the blood stream probably have considerable effect on these centers, without being the crucial factors in their operation.

Pain Avoidance. The drive to avoid pain is another one which we all share. Anything which tends to harm or destroy the tissues of the body can be a stimulus for pain. At the instant pain is felt, we react quickly to move away from its source. This reaction is known as a *reflex* (see Chapter 9)—the withdrawal reflex. Through experience with the various sources of pain, we learn to avoid them. In time the very sight of such an object brings out our avoidance motive. The drive itself is an unlearned one, but just as we must learn the goals for hunger, we must learn what things to avoid. Of course, there are wide individual differences in such learning. Furthermore, it is not possible to know all the many sources of pain in the world around us.

The Drive to Void the Bowel and Bladder. As waste products accumulate in the bowel and bladder, pressure builds up in these two organs. It is this distension or pressure that seems to be the starting point for the drive to void or empty these organs. Like all the other physiological drives, these are basically unlearned but are modifiable. We see such modification in action when we witness the toilet training of a small child or the housebreaking of a pet.

The Sex Drive. In the narrowest sense, the sex drive originates in the hormones secreted into the blood stream by the *gonads* or sex glands (the *ovaries* in the female and the *testes* in the male). In most

Figure 3.3. One head of this two-headed infant is awake while the other one sleeps. This indicates that sleep is controlled by the brain rather than by factors in the blood, since both heads share the same blood supply. (Courtesy of Life Magazine, © Time, Inc.)

female animals, the secretion of these hormones is cyclic in nature. In all mammals except the human being, the female periodically comes into *estrus* (or heat), at which time she is receptive to the male and much more active than usual (see Figure 3.4). In most mammals, including the human, the male is sexually excitable more or less continuously. The human female is unique among the mammals in that she, like the male, tends to be continuous rather than cyclic in her sexual receptivity.

Unlike the other physiological drives which we have been considering, the sex drive can be ignored and denied satisfaction for indefinite periods of time without fatal results. It is very likely that prehistoric man, like most other animals, satisfied this drive as it arose and attached no greater importance to it than to the others. Civilized man, as Freud pointed out, is often unable to satisfy this drive immediately. For example, marriage often is not permitted until many years after sexual maturity is reached. Since sex is one of the motives most frequently blocked or thwarted, it is very commonly involved in neurotic conflict and frustration. However, there is no reason to think that it is by nature any stronger than, if indeed as strong as, the air, water, or food

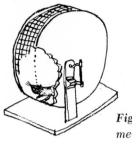

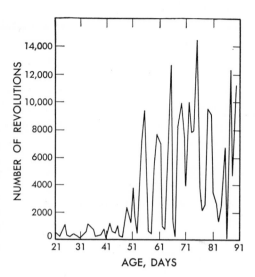

Figure 3.4. The activity-wheel experiment demonstrates that the sex drive produces increased activity in the female rat. As the graph shows, the degree of activity rose sharply at fifty-one days, the onset of puberty. Activity was then heightened at four-day intervals when the female rat was in heat. (From Wang, 1923, and Richter, 1927.)

hungers, which are usually more quickly and easily satisfied.

The Maternal Drive. We find that all mammal mothers take care of their young. The basic source of the maternal motive is found in certain hormones put into the mother's blood stream by the pituitary gland[1] at the time of the birth of the offspring and for a period thereafter. A mother rat will wash her babies, retrieve them if they wander from the nest, nurse them, and generally take good care of them. If we counteract her hormones by injection of other hormones, she will stop her motherly chores and desert her babies. This is not the case, of course, in human mothers.

In nearly all animals, parental attention depends upon the presence of the proper hormones. In man, however, social learning has come to play an important role. It is true that the human mother has the proper hormones for taking care of her baby. Yet the human offspring is helpless for a longer period than the hormone is secreted. As we know, the human mother continues to take care of her child—and, more frequently than

---

[1] *Prolactin* is one such hormone. Its primary function is the stimulation of milk secretion. Secondarily, it seems to influence a number of other aspects of maternal behavior.

not, increases her loving attention—long after the specific hormones have disappeared from her blood. Thus it seems that the very existence of our species depends upon social living and education.

So important is social learning for human beings that today in America the majority of fathers show a "paternal" motive, which in some cases is stronger than the typical maternal drive. This fact is quite impressive when we consider that we know of no specific hormones in man for this motive, although some male animals do have such hormones. Always in our study of motivation we must keep in mind that all the basic urges in human beings are modifiable by social learning. Furthermore, it seems that motives can be learned which have little or no known connection with any of these urges.

Other Physiological Drives. We do not have time to examine in detail all the known physiological drives and motives. We have glanced at those which seem the most important and which have been studied the most thoroughly. A number of the others are also interesting, although less has been discovered about them.

Many animals, including man, seem to have an exploratory drive. Although the source of this drive is not known, it appears to be fairly strong and very persistent in some animals. Anyone who has ever worked with the rat knows that it possesses this drive. In the past, some psychologists have attempted to explain the drive as resulting from hunger or thirst or some of the others, but recent research has established an independent exploratory drive. The least we can say (and maybe the most) is that the exploratory drive is definitely a distinct drive, although, like the others, modifiable and modified by learning.

It seems too that there are activity drives (see Figure 3.4), sensory drives, warmth and cold drives, and a host of others. Research on these is going on, but it will probably be a few years at least before there is a great deal to say about them.

The Strength of the Physiological Drives. We have already mentioned the fact that there is an order of urgency among all our drives and motives. A simpler way of stat-

ing this fact is to say that there is an order of strength among motives, ascending from the weakest to the strongest. Certainly the main physiological drives are among the most powerful motives we have. In the rat experiment using the obstruction box, it was found that the maternal drive is strongest and is followed in order by the thirst, hunger, sex, and exploratory drives.

Although it is impossible to make a direct comparison between drive strength in rats and in human beings, we can guess that about the same ranking of drives would occur if we were put into the obstruction box. With the maternal drive at a maximum, human mothers have been known to give their lives for their babies. It is also a fact that most human beings who have experienced deprivation of both food and water report that thirst seems to be a more intense drive than hunger. Even the relative weakness of the sex drive is demonstrated in the reports of people who spent time in

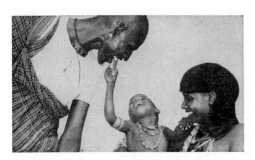

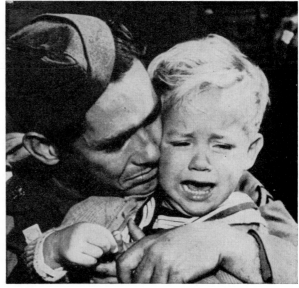

Figure 3.5. Widely different cultural patterns may produce similar modifications of basic drives. The paternal drive is developed entirely by social learning, there being no known hormonal basis for it. Even the maternal drive is to a large extent a product of social learning, since this drive continues long after the hormonal balance returns to normal. (British Information Services and Los Angeles Times News Bureau.)

OBSTRUCTION-BOX EXPERIMENT

▶ A classic rat experiment * which has been repeated many times gives us a comparison of the relative strength of several physiological drives. The method used in this experiment is called the *obstruction-box method*. In the procedure followed, each animal was placed in the entrance chamber of the box which opens into the obstruction compartment. The obstruction is a grid floor that is wired so that an electric shock can be given to an animal standing on it or crossing it. From this compartment the animal went into the incentive chamber, which contains a place for the goal-object or incentive. For instance, a hungry animal was put into the entrance chamber and food was put into the incentive chamber. Each time the animal crossed the obstruction in order to get to the food, it received a shock. As soon as the

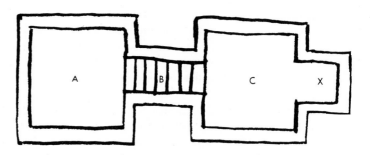

food was reached, the animal was returned to the entrance. The object of the experiment was to see how many times in twenty minutes the animal would suffer a shock to get to the food.

Twenty different rats were tested in the obstruction box for each of the following drives: sex, hunger, thirst, maternal, and exploratory. Each rat

* C. J. Warden, *Animal Motivation Studies*, Columbia University Press, New York, 1931.

concentration camps during World War II. Those prisoners who were fairly well fed reported only minor concern about the lack of a mate, while those who were starved reported that in fact the sex drive seemed to disappear and was consequently of no concern. This last fact is very likely another example of the interaction that probably occurs among all drives and motives.

SOCIAL MOTIVES

As basic as any of the so-called "basic" or physiological drives is the tendency for all human beings (even infants) to respond to other human beings. In the old days

when everyone spoke of instincts, this tendency was referred to as the *gregarious* instinct. Many other, but not all, animals show this tendency. Undoubtedly horses and cattle are highly gregarious. Apes and monkeys are also gregarious, but to a somewhat lesser extent, while cats are much less so. Occasionally in nature we find the truly solitary animal, which meets with its own kind only to mate.

We cannot say that all the many and varied social motives spring from and are based solely upon the tendency to respond to others. Without experimental and scientific facts to back us up, we should fail just as all the others have failed in trying to remained in the box for twenty minutes. During each twenty-minute period the appropriate incentive was present. As a control, twenty other rats, satiated for all these drives, were put into the box for a control period of twenty minutes with no incentive of any kind present.

Relative Strength of Drives

Drive	Crossings	Incentive
Maternal	22.4	Offspring of female
Thirst	20.4	Water
Hunger	18.2	Food
Sex (males)	13.8	Receptive member of opposite sex
Sex (females)	13.8	Receptive member of opposite sex
Exploratory	6.0	Blocks, sawdust, etc.
(Control)	3.5	None

The accompanying table shows the result of this experiment. Some of us are surprised at first that the maternal drive was the strongest. On second thought, it is common knowledge that mammalian mothers are highly motivated to retrieve and protect their babies. An interesting finding of this experiment is that the sex drive does not seem to rank with maternal, thirst, or hunger in strength. However, this does fit in with what we have already studied about these drives. The exploratory drive was the weakest one studied, as might have been expected. It is also interesting to note that even when no incentive was present, it took the animals an average of 3.5 trials presumably to learn that the obstruction compartment was what hurt them, or that nothing interesting was over there.

trace all complex human motives back to a few basic ones. We shall simply assume that our tendency to respond to our own kind has played some part in the building of our social motives. Certainly a more gregarious animal has more scope for building social motives than one limited to its family group.

Probably more important than this tendency is the tremendous capacity of the human species for learning to adjust to its environment. The more complex adjustments can be made only by a cooperating group of people and not by a single individual alone. Thus, many of our motives are learned in order that we may better adapt to our environment. Accordingly, different peoples in different places and at different times in history have developed somewhat different motives. In America today, we take it for granted that nearly everyone will have a motive to excel his fellows in whatever they are doing whenever he can. To many of us this may seem like a natural, inborn motive, yet anthropologists [2] tell us about a group of primitive people in the wilds of New Guinea who have no such motive. In fact, these people have just the opposite one. They have learned in their society to be motivated not to excel and not

[2] M. Mead, Sex and Temperament in Three Primitive Societies, Morrow, New York, 1935.

Figure 3.6. *Different animal species vary in their tendency to be gregarious.*

to compete with their fellows. A person with our motive to excel seems to them to be abnormal and odd.

Some Common Social Motives. Some of the social motives which we in America possess are also common to many other peoples in various parts of the world. To illustrate, let us look at some of the motives that seem to be a part of a general desire for social acceptance and approval. Obviously, if we are to succeed in group living, we must gain at least some measure of group approval.

Most of us can find in ourselves a *need for recognition*. It is not enough to be an ignored part of the group. We are motivated to do things which will bring us recognition from the other members of our group. It is partly through this recognition that we know we are accepted and approved. Recognition dispels our doubts and gives us a feeling of security. Sometimes, when recognition is slow in coming, we do ridiculous things to gain attention. Unhappily, these actions most often bring us only momentary attention but not lasting recognition. They may even backfire, resulting in social disapproval and rejection—the very opposite of what we really want.

Most of us also can find in ourselves a *need to be needed.*[3] We have a great longing to feel and believe that among our friends and relatives there are those who

[3] W. W. Finlay, A. Q. Sartain, and W. M. Tate, *Human Behavior in Industry*, McGraw-Hill, New York, 1954, pp. 27–30.

really need us. We do not want to stop with just recognition; we are further motivated to do things which are essential to the group. We wish to feel that the group actually needs us and knows that it needs us. We want to feel that, were we to leave the group, it would make a real difference to every member of the group. Undoubtedly one reason a large number of workers in America are dissatisfied with their jobs is that they can gain neither recognition nor a feeling of being needed in the work group. A painful frustration comes with the realization that, were they never to return to the group, no one would ever miss them.

Many other motives fit into this pattern or family of motives. Our purpose has been to illustrate how complex and how far from the physiological drives some of our everyday motives are. Rather than attempt a catalogue of social motives, we shall now study some of the motive systems which include most of our specific motives.

Human Value Systems. Probably the most important lesson taught us as we grow up in the group is what to value. In order for a number of people to live together in harmony, they must reach some agreement concerning what is to be valued to the point of veneration, what is to be despised, and where everything else comes in between. This does not mean that each individual in the group must value everything exactly as everyone else does, but only that everyone must agree in general to a system of values.

Each of us was born into a group in which the adults had reached some consensus about what to value. In growing up, we found that we had to learn these values and abide by the system or become a delinquent and outcast. Our specific motives and goals were also learned, but we discovered that a certain amount of leeway was permitted in motives and goals so long as the new ones fitted into the accepted value system.

In America, as in most complex cultures and societies, we have a great many value systems. To list all of them would be nearly impossible, but we can group them into a small number of categories, which are rough but useful. One such grouping [4] includes the following values: the theoretical, the religious, the social, the political, the economic, and the esthetic.

All of us in America participate in all these values, but enough freedom usually exists to allow each of us to emphasize one category or another. Psychological tests have been constructed that try to determine which values an individual tends to emphasize. This is not an attempt to type people; rather, these tests give us a rough measure of some of our values, or at least show their relative strength. The person who emphasizes the *theoretical* is one who values theories which try to explain the nature of things; most scientists lean in this direction. The *religious* person values the attempt to explain the why of the universe. *Social* values are important to the person who considers other people to be of great value; the man or woman who loves social service work is a good example here. The *political* category is highly valued by those

[4] E. Spranger, *Types of Men*, Stechert, New York, 1928.

Figure 3.7. Most of us find in ourselves a need to be accepted and needed by others.

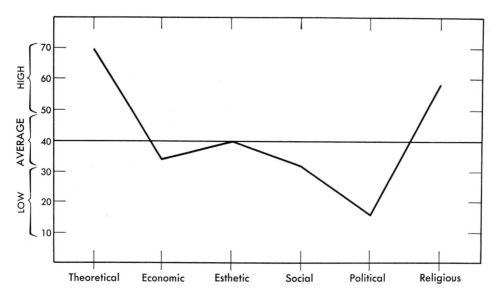

Figure 3.8. An example of a profile of scores on the Allport-Vernon-Lindzey Study of Values.

who consider important the shrewd manipulation of people and things in order to gain power in the group. The person who emphasizes the *economic* category values not only money and material wealth but also all the intricate relations of gain and loss in our society. The person with *esthetic* values enjoys and often works with the relations between sensory objects and the manipulation of these objects; the artist is a good example of this type of person.

In Figure 3.8 we show a profile of one individual who took the Allport-Vernon-Lindzey Test of Values.[5] This test consists of statements concerning the six value categories listed above. The person whose profile is shown is high in theoretical and religious, average in social, economic, and esthetic, and low in political values. It is possible for different people to have entirely different profiles, having many different combinations of highs, lows, and averages. Some people are average in

[5] G. Allport, P. Vernon, and G. Lindzey, *A Study of Values,* Houghton Mifflin, Boston, 1951.

nearly all the categories we have just listed.

The person who is high in theoretical values presumably will learn the motives and their goals which fit into his high valuation of the theoretical. Even in childhood he probably sought scientific explanations, desired a toy chemistry set, and read books and stories about science and scientists. In school he very likely elected science courses and began to aim toward a life devoted to science. The reason he wanted a paper route may have been to save money so that he could go to college and major in physics. Thus, his whole life and the most important of his motives may have derived from his early acceptance of the value of the theoretical. In this same way, all of us have learned and built our many specific motives so that they would serve what we consider valuable.

HABIT AND FUNCTIONAL AUTONOMY OF MOTIVES

Habit refers to the whole framework of our consistent, repeated, habitual ways of behaving. Since we are motivated to behave as we do, habit is a sort of crystallization of our everyday motives into a regular pattern. We get up in the morning, dress and eat, catch the bus and go to school or work, attend to the same details as always, eat lunch at the same restaurant, and so on, day after day.

After these many everyday motives have been fitted into the framework of habit, they may continue to operate even after the original causes for them have disappeared. A man who learns a particular trade simply because no other work is available at the time and it is a matter of taking a job or starving may nevertheless find, when he retires thirty years later, that he still wants to go to work every day. The motive to work at his trade has become so habitual that he still has it, although there is no longer any necessity for him to work. We can say that this motive has become *functionally autonomous;* that is, it continues in strength long after the original set of circumstances in which it was learned has ceased to exist.

Gordon W. Allport,[6] of Harvard University, has used the concept of functional au-

[6] G. Allport, *Personality: A Psychological Interpretation,* New York, 1937, chap. 7.

tonomy to explain such everyday motives as the retired sailor's desire to return to the sea, the successful city businessman's longing for the farm life of his youth, and even the miser's desire for more gold. Allport points out that in the beginning each of these motives served a definite purpose and did not exist for itself alone. The sailor may have been forced to go to sea by his poverty-stricken parents. At first he may have hated it, but since it provided him a living, he learned to like it. The farm meant a great deal to the businessman in his youth simply because all his loved ones lived there. Now, even after they are gone, he persists in his habitual longing to go back. And who knows what good reasons the miser may have had in the beginning for his thrift?

Another example of functional autonomy is seen in many cases of adult nail biting. Let us examine such a case and see what has happened. An otherwise normal, well-adjusted man of thirty bites his fingernails excessively. Looking back into his childhood, we may discover that as a small boy in an orphans' home, he had feelings of rejection and suffered from lack of affection. He built up general tensions which were relieved by his nail biting. At the age of ten he was adopted by a couple who gave him

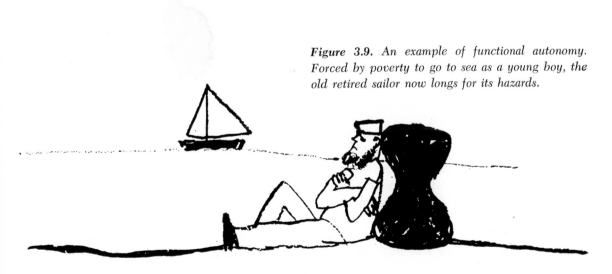

Figure 3.9. An example of functional autonomy. Forced by poverty to go to sea as a young boy, the old retired sailor now longs for its hazards.

the love and security he needed. Soon he no longer felt rejected. His general tension subsided and he became a normal, healthy boy. However, the nail biting continued. The motive became a habit, and we can say that the man now bites his nails simply to be biting them, and it will be very difficult to get him to stop.

Even in animal experiments we have some evidence of this sort of phenomenon. Young rats that have never been used in an experiment before will run a maze for a food reward if they are hungry. After a few trials they will learn the shortest path to the food and learn to avoid the blind alleys. After the maze has been thoroughly learned, the rats can now be put into another maze. However, it is no longer necessary to make the rats hungry, nor is it necessary to have food in the maze. The rats will run through the new maze, learning to avoid the blind alleys, simply because they have the habit of maze running. In the rat experiment, this phenomenon has been called *externalization* of drive. In other words, we may say that the motive of maze running has become functionally autonomous, just as the motive of nail biting had in the previous example.

CONFLICT OF MOTIVES

We have pointed out a number of times that motives interact with each other. We can seldom study, or even speak of, a single motive in isolation. We must expect, then, that often our motives will interfere with each other. Sometimes one motive will get in the way of the satisfaction of another motive. When this occurs, we call it a conflict of motives. There are at least three different ways in which motives can conflict: *approach-avoidance, approach-approach,* and *avoidance-avoidance* conflicts.[7]

[7] K. Lewin, *A Dynamic Theory of Personality,* McGraw-Hill, New York, 1935, pp. 104, 123.

Approach-Avoidance Conflict. In approach-avoidance conflict, there is one goal and two incompatible motives. One of the motives leads us to approach the goal-object, and the other motive leads us to avoid this same object. A good example of this type of conflict is seen in the small child who wants to play with an ash tray on the coffee table and who also wants to leave it alone because his hand has been slapped for touching it on previous occasions. His conflict is easily visible, for he alternately reaches and withdraws his hand, not able to decide which impulse to follow. He may resolve his conflict by leaving the room, by grabbing the ash tray and throwing it on the floor, or by falling to the floor in a temper tantrum.

We adults, too, have our approach-avoidance conflicts. A familiar type of *guilt*, in fact, is a special case of this type of conflict. We have a desire to do a particular thing, but we also have a motive not to do it because it is forbidden. Whenever we are tempted to do it, or even whenever we think of the act, we feel guilty. Many neurotic personalities are so burdened with such conflict-based guilt that they are unable to adjust to everyday life. (See Figure 3.10 for a diagram of this conflict.)

Approach-Approach Conflict. Approach-approach conflict (also see Figure 3.10), a second type of conflict, may take one of two entirely different forms. One form is called *convergent* and the other *divergent.* In convergent approach-approach conflict, there are two incompatible motives to approach the same goal, with the result that neither can be satisfied. An example is seen in the case of the boy who loves his brother and is motivated to pat him on the back and at the same time hates his brother and wants to punch him in the nose. In both motives we see approach, but the satisfaction of either motive blocks satisfaction of the other.

In divergent approach-approach conflict,

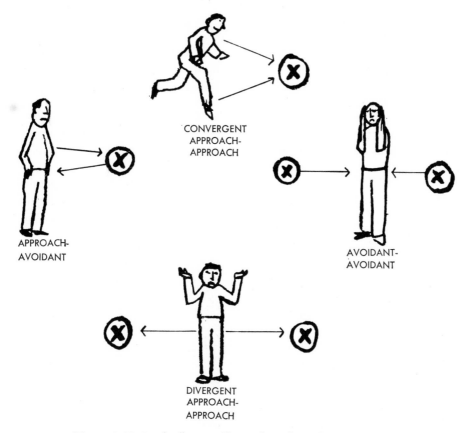

CONVERGENT
APPROACH-
APPROACH

APPROACH-
AVOIDANT

AVOIDANT-
AVOIDANT

DIVERGENT
APPROACH-
APPROACH

Figure 3.10. In the "approach-avoidance" conflict, one of the motives leads us to approach the goal-object while the other motive leads us to avoid it.

In the convergent "approach-approach" conflict, there are two incompatible motives leading us to the same goal-object. In the divergent approach-approach conflict, there may be two goals and one motive or two goals and two motives.

In the "avoidance-avoidance" conflict, there are two goal-objects, neither of which is desired but one of which must be chosen.

we have two motives and two goals competing with each other at the same moment. For instance, a girl wants to go to church on Sunday morning at eleven, and she also wants to go on a picnic set for the same hour. Sometimes we have only one motive which is directed toward two different but conflicting goals at the same time. Imagine a boy who wants to get married and who has narrowed the field down to two pretty girls, both of whom are equally attractive to him!

Avoidance-Avoidance Conflict. In avoidance-avoidance conflict, the third type of conflict, there are two goals, neither of which is desired but one of which must be chosen. We are in such conflict when we are motivated to avoid both the "devil and the deep blue sea" but must choose one. Hamlet was deep in this kind of conflict

when he said, "To be or not to be . . ."
He did not want to live and he did not
want to die, but he had to do one or the
other. The soldier is in this conflict when he
wants to avoid the dangers of the front line
and also wants to avoid being labeled a
coward (again, see Figure 3.10).

During the course of a single day we
may be momentarily in one conflict situation
after another. The normal person resolves
these conflicts quickly and is not especially
troubled by them. On occasion we may
even be in a multiple conflict which combines all three types. Usually even this situation is soon resolved and we forget that it
occurred. On the other hand, the neurotic
person is in continual conflict and may never
resolve it without outside help. When such
help is needed, it is unwise to seek it from
the amateur psychologists among our
friends. We may, however, seek the guidance of a competent counselor.

UNCONSCIOUS MOTIVES

Whether or not we are conscious of our
motives has little to do with their importance. All of us are conscious, of course, of
many of our motives; we know some of the
goals we seek and why we seek them. Often,
however, we are not even aware of our
goals, and, consequently, we are unable to
explain why we seek them.

Certainly all of us realize that many processes go on within our bodies without our
conscious awareness. We seldom know just
what our internal organs are doing at a
given moment. It does not worry us that
most of the time the beating of our hearts
and the digestion of our food go on without
our conscious knowledge. By the same
token we should be neither surprised nor
worried that some of our motives direct our
behavior without our being aware of the
process.

Repressed Unconscious Motivation.
Sometimes we remain unaware of very
strong motives because of a process called
repression. Freud introduced this term to explain the "active forgetting" of unpleasant
memories (see Chapter 6 for a fuller treatment of repression). Through repression
these unpleasant memories may be kept
from consciousness, yet these memories may
continue to motivate us strongly. The clinical psychologist and the psychiatrist discover such repressed unconscious motivation in many of their patients.

*Figure 3.11. Sigmund Freud (1856–1939)
was the founder of psychoanalysis. He was
one of the greatest of the pioneers in modern
psychology. Freud was especially interested in
unconscious motivation. His contributions to
the study and understanding of human motivation rank among the most fruitful that have
ever been made. (International News Photos.)*

A clinical example. During the last war, psychiatrists had an especially good opportunity to study many cases of repression. For instance, many pilots in the Air Force went through horrible experiences, which they quickly repressed. One of these pilots was flying a bombing mission over enemy territory when an enemy fighter strafed his plane. Before his very eyes, he saw his co-pilot blown to bits. It was only by an extraordinary stroke of luck that he was able to bring his plane back.

As soon as he returned to his base, he was questioned by the Intelligence Section. They were amazed to find that, although he had been completely uninjured, he had no conscious memory that anything had happened to the copilot. For a while, he seemed dazed and violently resisted any discussion about the copilot. Later, when he appeared to have returned to normal, he steadfastly maintained that the copilot had missed the flight at the last minute and that he had gone on alone. Because of terrible nightmares, he was unable to leave the hospital and rejoin his unit. After a few weeks, he was transferred to a psychiatric ward.

Even after weeks of psychiatric interviewing, the pilot was unable to remember the dreadful incident and continued to have night "terrors." The psychiatrist then decided to use a drug in his interviews. He gave the pilot injections of *sodium pentothal* (popularly referred to as a "truth serum"), which put him into a semiconscious state. Gradually the physician got him to relive his repressed experience. The pilot slowly began to readmit to consciousness the emotional memories of his battle experience. Finally, he was able to remember every little detail of the enemy plane's attack and of his friend's death. He would scream in horror during these interviews just as he had when the event actually occurred.

Certainly he proved during these interviews that he had not forgotten much of his terrifying experience, but he had immediately repressed this memory and had resisted for months attempts to bring it back into consciousness. The memory was simply too horrible and too unpleasant to face consciously. At the unconscious level, the memory had continued vivid and active, motivating his terrifying nightmares.

Many other examples could be given to show that repression does occur and must be taken into account in explaining some of our unconscious motivation.

Unconscious, Unrepressed Drives or Motives. We must not take the view that all unconscious motivation stems from repression; many basic motives remain unconscious because they have no way of entering our awareness.

For example, there have been many times when each of us has been thirsty and there was no doubt about it. On other occasions, we have found ourselves taking a long drink at the water fountain in the hall and only after we started drinking were we conscious of our thirst. Or, how often do we light up a cigarette without being aware of the motive to do so? Most of us who are smokers will admit that it happens quite often. Another instance of an unrepressed, unconscious motive occurs each time we put on our glasses to read, without consciously thinking about it.

Perhaps the best example of this kind of motive is seen in our specific hungers. They can be classed as a basic part of our store of unconscious motives. Until we have eaten the food in question, we seldom have an inkling that it is the food that we crave. There is no doubt that the babies in the "cafeteria-feeding experiment" were unaware of their motivation. Sometimes, of course, when we are presented with a large array of foods (as in a cafeteria), the moment our eye falls on a certain food, we know that it is exactly what we want. However, it is only on rare occasions that we are conscious of a craving for a specific food.

For an animal in the jungle, it is undoubtedly better for survival that specific hungers remain unconscious. For civilized man, the case is more complicated. Through our great learning ability and through the cultural heritage which that learning ability has helped accumulate, we adult human beings are often able to modify motives that in lower animals remain unconscious and are little affected by experience. Where specific hungers are concerned, many of us have learned to avoid the very foods that would satisfy our natural specific hungers. In fact, we may learn to prefer foods that eventually lead to ill health and death. An example is the refusal of many Oriental peoples to eat unpolished rice, which is rich in the vitamins of the B complex. Instead they insist upon eating polished white rice and so develop beriberi, a vitamin-deficiency disease.

Nevertheless, the point is that specific hungers are another unconscious aspect of our lives.

Experimental Hypnosis and Unconscious Motives. It is commonly thought that hypnotism is a mysterious power possessed by only a few unusual individuals. Unfortunately, this belief is fostered by many stage hypnotists, who are all too often quacks or charlatans. Actually, hypnosis is a natural phenomenon, no more mysterious than sleep or digestion. Certainly, it is not to be classed with the occult or esoteric; it is not mind reading or fortunetelling, nor is it any sort of magic power over someone else.

Psychologists generally describe hypnosis as a state of increased suggestibility; that is, the hypnotized person receives and follows suggestions more readily than he would ordinarily. The hypnotized person is intensely motivated to do just one thing: follow the directions of the hypnotist.

What concerns us at this point is how experiments in hypnosis illustrate the way unconscious motives work. The best examples come from what is called *posthypnotic suggestion.* While the subject is still hypnotized, the hypnotist gives a sugges-

tion that is not to be carried out until later. After the subject is no longer in the hypnotic state, he will usually perform the suggested action, at whatever time he has been directed to do so—whether a few minutes later or months later. He does it with no other motive than that the hypnotist told him to do it; yet he has no conscious memory of what the hypnotist said. The important point is that a person in a perfectly normal state does something without being aware of his own motive. A simple example will clarify what we mean by posthypnotic suggestion.

During a demonstration of hypnosis the psychologist may say to the hypnotized subject, "When I count to ten and snap my fingers, you will be wide-awake and no longer hypnotized." Before he snaps his fingers, he says further, "After you are out from under the hypnosis and have returned to your seat, I will light a cigarette. When you see me light the cigarette, you will come back to the front of the room, take the cigarette from my hand, drop it to the floor, and step on it. You will do all these things for no other reason than that I am now telling you to do them. Furthermore, you will not remember, consciously, that I have told you." The hypnotist then counts to ten, snaps his fingers, and the subject awakens from the hypnotized state. The subject returns to his seat and participates in the general conversation about what has gone on.

After a few minutes, the psychologist takes out a cigarette and lights it. The former subject is seen to be watching this action closely. After a moment of hesitation he gets up, returns to the front of the room, takes the cigarette from the psychologist's hand, drops it to the floor, and steps on it. One of the other members of the group, acting on previous instructions, asks, "Why on earth did you do such a rude thing to our guest, who has been kind enough to give us this demonstration?" This puts the former subject on the spot and he

Figure 3.12. At Nürnberg after World War II, these two German generals were tried for war crimes. They had commanded troops that executed tens of thousands of civilians. According to the defendants, these civilians were "hostages" killed in "reprisal" for the death of German soldiers. Do you think they were deliberately lying about their motives? How would you distinguish their motives from those of the men who prosecuted them? (Wide World Photos.)

must give an answer. Since he does not know consciously why he did it, he must resort to rationalization [8] (see Chapter 6). The only real motive for his action was the suggestion of the hypnotist, which he does not remember. He is in the same predicament that we all are in when we do something for an unconscious motive and are asked to give our reasons.

He stammers for a moment, but being adept at rationalization, just as we all are, he soon thinks up some logical-sounding reasons. He says, "Well, you see, it's this way: even though I am a chain smoker myself, the smoke from your cigarette nauseated me. If I hadn't put it out when I did, I would have vomited before I could have left this room. I think the reason for it is my having missed breakfast this morning—I overslept. So, if you will excuse my rude action. . . ." By this time he has convinced himself that these are the true reasons for his actions. Also by this time the rest of the group can no longer restrain themselves and peals of laughter surprise the former subject. When the real story is later explained to him the subject finds it hard to believe what has happened.

We have seen in this example of hypnosis how a person can do something because of an unconscious reason or motive. The example is a good one, for we know why he did what he did—the only reason

[8] Rationalization is the giving of false reasons for some action, without being aware that the reasons are false.

was that the hypnotist told him to. But we also see how he rationalized in order to explain his action to himself. What is shown here in an experimental situation is what presumably happens every time unconscious motives encourage us to rationalize.

CONCLUSION

Not only can we say that practically all behavior is motivated, but also we can come to two further conclusions. First, different people may perform the same act for entirely different motives, and second, in a given person a single act is most often the result of several motives.

For example, we have already seen that the act of eating can be motivated by food-hunger or by desire for affection (love). Of two students who work equally hard on their college courses, one wants to learn the subjects, and the other works to earn the convertible promised him if he makes all A's. Such examples could be multiplied endlessly, since nearly every human act can be instigated by a variety of motives.

These same examples also serve to illustrate the point about a single act resulting from a set of motives. The person who eats mainly because of need for affection also has food-hunger. And the student who works hard mainly for the gift of a convertible may also be motivated to learn something. Furthermore, he may also enjoy the prospect of making Phi Beta Kappa and of graduating *cum laude*. In addition, either of the two students may or may not have a neurotic compulsion to be perfect in whatever he does. In fact, any student motivated to make A's is likely to have a long list of pertinent motives. And thus it is with nearly everything we do—there are usually many motives, not just one motive.

SUMMARY

A motive, or drive, is defined as a complex state in a person that directs his behavior toward a goal. For purposes of classification and study, nearly all motives can be regarded either as physiological drives or as social motives.

The physiological drives are part of the homeostatic regulatory mechanisms. These drives include hunger, thirst, sex, pain-avoidance, rest and sleep, and a number of others.

The social motives include the many motives we learn in group living. As gregarious organisms, we acquire a large number of such motives. In every society and culture the individual's social motives fit into certain value systems. In America, some of these value systems are the economic, the political, the religious, and the theoretical.

Functional autonomy is a condition in which motives have become habitual and outlast the original set of circumstances under which they were learned.

At times our motives interfere or conflict with each other. Such conflicts are often classified as approach-avoidance, approach-approach, and avoidance-avoidance.

Many of our motives are unconscious; that is, we are not aware of them. These unconscious motives may be either physiological drives or social motives. In experimental hypnosis, posthypnotic suggestions are often used to demonstrate the existence of unconscious motives. The subject in such experiments must rationalize in order to account for these motives.

QUESTIONS

1. Is it possible that the physiological drives originate in homeostasis?

2. Is it probable that our social motives are derived from homeostasis?

3. Can you make a case for the assertion that hunger and thirst are a single motive?

4. Why is it that air-hunger does not seem ordinarily to be as strong as food-hunger?

5. How does the paternal motive in human beings differ from the maternal motive?

6. Which value systems explain the motives of a candidate for public office?

7. Give several examples of functional autonomy other than those given in this chapter.

8. Describe a case in which a person is involved at one time in more than one type of conflict.

9. How is hypnosis used to demonstrate unconscious motivation?

10. What is the meaning of (*a*) motivation, (*b*) motive, (*c*) drive, (*d*) need, (*e*) incentive?

11. Describe the obstruction-box technique for measuring the strength of the various drives of the rat.

12. How are young children able to select a balanced diet for themselves?

SUGGESTED READINGS

Cannon, W. B.: *Bodily Changes in Pain, Hunger, Fear, and Rage,* 2d ed., Appleton-Century-Crofts, New York, 1929.

(A classic on both motivation and emotion.)

Ford, C. S., and F. A. Beach: *Patterns of Sexual Behavior,* Hoeber, New York, 1951.

(An interesting, informative book for the beginner by an anthropologist and a psychologist.)

McCrary, J. L.: *Psychology of Personality,* Logos Press, New York, 1956.

(Motivation as a fundamental aspect of personality.)

Morgan, C. T., and E. Stellar: *Physiological Psychology,* 2d ed., McGraw-Hill, New York, 1950, chaps. 17–20.

(The physiological aspects of motivation.)

Young, P. T.: *Motivation of Behavior,* Wiley, New York, 1936.

(An older textbook on motivation, still worth reading.)

4 EMOTION

Our emotions give color to our lives. A person incapable of feeling emotion would strike us as drab and uninteresting. We could throw mud in his face, and he would not become angry. We could hold a revolver to his head, and he would feel no fear. Nor could he love or hate anyone or anything. We could not possibly accept him as a real, live human being, for we all recognize that to be human is—in part, at least—to feel emotion.

Because of our personal experiences with them, we all know what the emotions are. Fear, anger, love, grief, joy, and all the others are thoroughly familiar. Moreover, we are all aware of the importance of such feelings. How we feel about the world situation, about racial conflict, or about a national election greatly influences our actions. Even our everyday behavior at home or with our associates is closely tuned to our emotions.

Furthermore, human emotions are as varied and complex as they are important; consequently, a large amount of psychological research has been devoted to their study. In this chapter we shall follow two main approaches: first, we shall acquaint ourselves with several of the aspects that define an emotion, and second, we shall examine in some detail the nature of the emotion.

FOUR ASPECTS OF EMOTION

All emotions have at least four aspects which may be analyzed and investigated. The first aspect is *personal emotional experience*—those characteristics of the emotion which the person consciously feels, knows, and can describe verbally. The second is the physiological or *bodily changes*

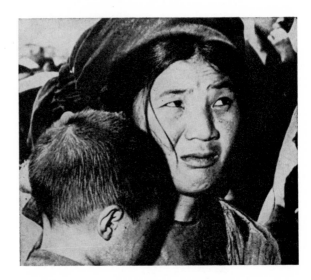

Figure 4.1. Emotions are so vital a part of our lives that we cannot even witness emotion in another without being somewhat affected ourselves. What emotions would you imagine this homeless Korean mother feels? What emotions, if any, do you feel while viewing this picture? (*Courtesy of CARE.*)

that occur during the emotion, such as changes in blood pressure, pulse, or breathing. The third aspect is the *behavior* of the emotional person—how he acts and what he does. The fourth aspect is that of *motivation*, for an emotional organism is also a goal-directed one.

Emotional Experience. At one time psychologists made a greater distinction between the terms "feeling" and "emotion" than they do today. Feelings were supposed to be such states as unpleasantness, pleasantness, tension, relaxation, excitement, or quiet. It was thought that the emotions were more complex states that grew out of various combinations of these feelings. Today, we most often use the word "feeling" simply to describe our personal emotional experiences. According to the emotion being experienced, we may say that we feel dejected, elated, afraid, happy, sad, or pleasant.

These subjective feelings of emotion add color and warmth to our lives. They are the basis of our preferences and our annoyances. We enjoy associating with certain people because we like the way we feel when we are with them. We avoid some situations because of the unpleasant feelings they arouse in us. In fact, in most of our undertakings we tend to follow our feelings, even if we must rationalize (see Chapter 6) in order to do so.

We know our own feelings through the process of *introspection*. We look into our emotional experience, so to speak, and are able to feel and know it consciously. If we like, we may report our feelings to someone else, and our report may be taken as data to be studied scientifically. As we shall see in the following sections, some of the other aspects of emotion yield data that may be more easily verified. No other person can check the truthfulness of our verbal report. Nevertheless, much of what psychologists know about emotion has resulted from the fact that, while studying the other aspects of emotion objectively, they also feel and know their own personal *affective* [1] states.

Since we are so often aware of our feelings, we tend to jump to the conclusion that emotions are always conscious. However, just as we discover through insight that many of our motives are unconscious, so do we also discover that we can and do have feelings and other affective states of which we have little or no conscious awareness. As a dramatic illustration of this point,

[1] The word "affective" is a psychological term used to refer to emotion.

Freud has shown that children sometimes have an intense but unconscious hatred for their parents. He demonstrated this fact in adult patients by using psychoanalysis to bring to their consciousness these feelings, which often were so strong that the patient wept with emotion. Another example is the man who is afraid of his employer but is not aware of his own fear. If we observe his actions when his employer is present, we see overt signs of his fear. However, until he gains insight, he is unable to know this fear consciously and admit it. We can say, then, that many times we are unaware of our true feelings.

There are other times when we know our emotion but prefer to keep others from knowing it. All of us have developed a certain skill in masking the overt expression of how we feel. There are times of great sorrow when we hold back our tears and force a smile. There are other times when we should like to lash out in anger, but instead we stand immobile and try to appear calm.

Bodily Changes in Emotion. Physiologists have shown that during the states which we call "emotion" a number of bodily changes take place. Not all these changes occur at the same time, nor do they occur in all people who experience similar emotional states. In fact, it may be that even when the same person is angry, for instance, significantly different bodily states occur on different occasions.

Heart rate and blood pressure. In strong emotion (for example, anger, fear, or sexual arousal) the heart rate usually increases. This increase is accompanied by more vigorous contractions of the heart. As a result of these changes, the amount of blood pumped by the heart is considerably raised.

Blood pressure also changes. However, even in the same emotion (as in anger), it is difficult to predict the direction of change. There may be either a rise or a fall

in the blood pressure. In sexual arousal in the male, however, a rise in pressure is consistently observed.

Changes in breathing. Respiration, or breathing, may change in a variety of ways during emotion. The rate may change; that is, breathing may speed up or slow down. It may become deeper or more shallow. Or, even more dramatic, a change may occur in the ratio of inspiration to expiration, i.e., the length of time taken to inhale a breath divided by the length of time it takes to exhale. For instance, in fright the breath may be inhaled more slowly than usual.

These various changes in respiration during emotion may be interrupted by such things as sneezing, yawning, coughing, and sighing. At best, breathing is a very complex indicator of emotion. Yet, if properly measured, changes in breathing can serve as a very sensitive sign of even subtle emotion.

The GSR and other skin responses. The skin, like most parts of the body, will conduct an electric current. If a weak current is applied to the skin by attaching electrodes, changes in skin resistance to such a current can be recorded on a galvanometer. A drop in skin resistance usually accompanies a sudden increase in sweatgland activity. Since perspiration increases during emotional excitement, the drop in skin resistance can be used to indicate the onset of an affective state. This change in resistance is known as the *galvanic skin response* (GSR). However, the GSR may also arise from other causes, such as the contraction of skeletal muscles. Thus, caution must be exercised in its use as an indicator of emotion. When properly used, the GSR is a very sensitive indicator. It is useful as an indicator of emotion when the subject (or patient) might have reason to hide the external manifestations of emotion, for it is virtually impossible to control the GSR consciously.

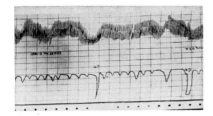

Although not connected with the GSR, another skin change during emotion is a rise or drop in skin temperature. Emotional stress is supposed to cause a drop in skin temperature, while emotional security results in a rise. Unfortunately, it is difficult to measure skin-temperature change, and consequently it is not used so much as some of the other indicators of emotion.

Other bodily changes during emotion. A host of other bodily changes occur with some regularity during emotion. Salivary-gland secretion may change, as in the dryness of the mouth observed in fear. The little muscles that control the erection of hairs on the body may contract during emotion, so that we literally bristle with anger. Metabolism (the body's rate of oxygen consumption) is usually increased during emotion. Skeletal muscles may be tensed involuntarily, and also a tremor may be detected in them.

Although many more bodily changes can and do occur during emotion (some of which we shall discuss later), we have listed enough of them at this point to give an idea of what can be expected. These bodily changes are spoken of as "indicators" of emotion. More properly, they are an integral part of the total emotional response of the organism. In addition to—or, more correctly, *along with*—the bodily responses go the feeling and knowing of the emotion.

In Figure 4.2 we can observe a *polygraph recorder* (often called a "lie detector") in

Figure 4.2. What two bodily changes are being recorded by this lie detector? What other changes might be used as indicators? Can you determine in the graph the places that show significant changes? Is it possible for the lie detector itself to lie? What safeguards can be used to avoid misusing such an apparatus as this? (International News Photos.)

action. Such a polygraph makes a graph of each of a number of bodily changes that occur during emotion, such as GSR, blood pressure, and breathing. Police departments use this device as a "lie detector" by noting which answers given by the subject during interrogation are accompanied by signs of emotion. Needless to say, the results of the "lie detector" must be interpreted by an expert, for the machine itself is not foolproof.

Bodily changes in anger and fear. We have seen how, in general, various bodily changes can be expected in an emotional state. Let us now examine and compare two specific states: *anger* and *fear*. We shall see that some of the changes that we have listed occur. In addition, however, a number of others not already mentioned will be discussed.

During both anger and fear the heart rate increases and the pulse is stronger than usual. Sometimes the heart pounds hard enough to be quite noticeable. This harder,

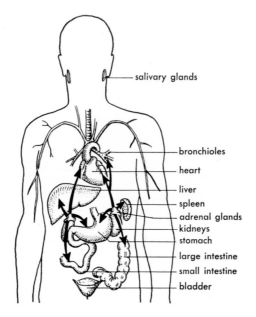

salivary glands

bronchioles
heart
liver
spleen
adrenal glands
kidneys
stomach
large intestine
small intestine
bladder

Figure 4.3. Under the stimulus of fear the adrenal glands send adrenalin in various directions (shown by the arrows) throughout the body; salivary glands secrete less saliva, causing dryness of the mouth; while the bronchioles become dilated, causing the depth and rate of breathing to increase. Other parts of the body are affected too; the heart pumps blood faster, the liver liberates more sugar, the spleen discharges red cells, kidneys and bladder become more active, and the stomach and intestines are drained. What do these body changes accomplish for the individual under a stimulus of fear?

more vigorous beating allows the heart to pump much greater amounts of blood than it ordinarily does.

Breathing also increases in anger or fear, at least in most cases. Breathing becomes not only more rapid but also deeper, allowing more oxygen to be brought into the lungs and transferred to the red blood cells.

Also in anger and fear, there may be a flushing, or reddening of the skin; on the other hand, there may be pallor, or whitening of the skin. The flushing is caused by a dilation of the surface blood vessels, bringing more blood to the skin. The pallor is caused by a constriction of the blood vessels so that the skin is left short of blood supply. In anger or in fear there is sometimes a flushing and sometimes a pallor, even in the same individual.

Another bodily change that occurs in both anger and fear is a release of *glycogen* from the liver. The minute this substance enters the blood stream, it is converted into usable sugar.

Also, red blood cells are released from storage and are added to the blood stream. These cells allow more oxygen to be carried to all the cells of the body. Again, if the oxygen and blood sugar are to be used as fuel, the blood needs to circulate rapidly, taking this fuel to the various cells in the muscles and other parts of the body.

The galvanic skin response (GSR) is still another bodily change that occurs in both anger and fear.

Perhaps the most important bodily change in anger or fear is the secretion of *adrenalin* by the adrenal glands. For adrenalin not only reduces bleeding by constricting blood vessels if a wound occurs, but it also helps stimulate other organs into activity. Adrenalin can work both alone and in conjunction with the nervous system. Sometimes the physiologists speak of this joint action as the *adrenal–nervous system reaction* in anger and fear. The various bodily changes that occur in these two emotions are maintained longer than would otherwise be possible by this adrenal–nervous system cooperation. We shall explore this reaction more fully in the section on the autonomic nervous system.

Some bodily changes accompanying a pleasant emotion. We have looked at many of the changes that occur in anger and fear. Let us look now at some of the bodily changes that take place in a pleasant emotion, such as that accompanying courtship and mating. We find some of the same changes occurring during the mating response that we found in anger and fear. For instance, we find a blushing reaction which is very similar to the flushing we found in anger and fear. We find that there is also a pounding of the heart and an increase in breathing. On the other hand, there are certain bodily changes during the mating response that are not found regularly in anger and fear. It would be logical to assume that blood pressure would always rise in anger and fear, but there is no set pattern; in some people there is a rise and in others a lowering. But in the male during mating there is nearly always a rise in blood pressure.

We might point out that from the bodily changes alone it is difficult to distinguish among anger, fear, and the mating response. This should not disturb us, because we define and classify emotions not by their bodily states alone but by the general behavior tendencies and feelings that the organism has. We might add that, whether or not we label it emotion, whenever we have a feeling of pleasantness or unpleasantness or tension, some of these bodily changes are probably occurring.

The autonomic nervous system. A good many of the bodily changes in emotion are under the control of the autonomic nervous system. Hence, a large part of the understanding of the physiological side of emotion comes from the study of the anatomy and function of the autonomic system. This system is connected with the central system but is in many ways independent of it. As the name "autonomic" implies, physiologists once thought that it was completely independent of the rest of the nervous system. However, it has been discovered that there are control centers for this system in the *hypothalamus* (see Chapter 9) of the brain. The role of the hypothalamus in emotion is discussed later in this chapter.

The autonomic nervous system is composed of two principal divisions, the *sympathetic* division and the *parasympathetic* division. The sympathetic division is located along each side of the spinal column (see Figure 4.4). It is composed of a chain of *ganglia,* each ganglion being a cluster of nerve cells. These ganglia send out motor fibers to various organs in the body. The parasympathetic division is itself divided into two parts, the *cranial* and the *sacral.* The cranial part consists of nerves from the brain (inside the cranium) and the sacral consists of nerves that leave the lowest part of the spinal cord (in the region of the sacrum).

Most of our internal organs and smooth (involuntary) muscles are served by nerve fibers from both the sympathetic and the parasympathetic divisions. In general, the sympathetic division seems to take over in times of emergency or stress, when we are experiencing an emotion such as fear or rage. Most of the bodily changes mentioned in the section on anger and fear are the result of nerve impulses from the sympathetic division. On the other hand, the parasympathetic division is more active during relatively calm periods in which the body is vegetating, for example, while sleeping, relaxing, or digesting and storing nutriments.

Actually, it is better to say that at all times, in calm and in stress, the two divisions work together in a balanced manner. For example, the heart muscle is innervated by fibers from both. The sympathetic nerve impulses cause the heart to speed up, and the parasympathetic impulses cause it to slow down. The balanced action of the two divisions allows the heart quickly and smoothly to change rhythm so as to correspond to the varying situations in which we find ourselves.

In the sketch (Figure 4.4) we see the autonomic nervous system and its location relative to the central nervous system. Notice that most organs of the body receive

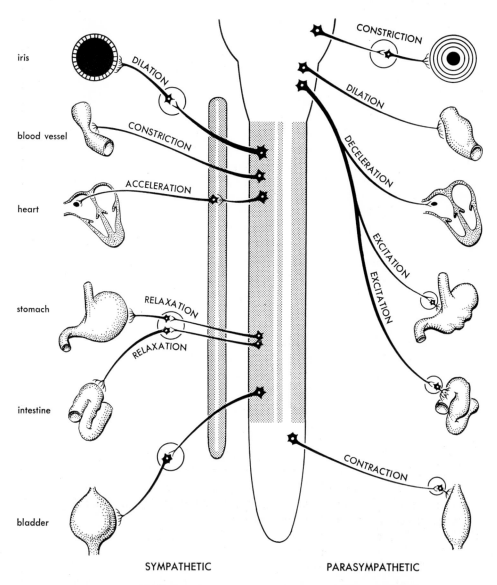

iris

blood vessel

heart

stomach

intestine

bladder

DILATION

CONSTRICTION

ACCELERATION

RELAXATION

RELAXATION

CONSTRICTION

DILATION

DECELERATION

EXCITATION

EXCITATION

CONTRACTION

SYMPATHETIC   PARASYMPATHETIC

*Figure 4.4. Most of our body organs are innervated by both the
sympathetic and parasympathetic divisions of the autonomic nervous
system. For example, the sympathetic fibers speed up and strengthen
heart action, while the parasympathetic fibers slow down the heart. In
general the sympathetic division readies an organ for strenuous or
emergency activity, and the parasympathetic is concerned with con-
servation, or the vegetative functions of the organism. Can you predict
how each division will affect the various organs shown? (From Paul
B. Weisz, Biology, McGraw-Hill, New York, 1954. Courtesy of the
publisher.)*

stimulation from both the sympathetic and the parasympathetic divisions. For example, the iris muscle of the eye receives cranial-nerve stimulation and also sympathetic. The bladder receives sacral and sympathetic stimulation. The large intestine is rather unique in that it receives both cranial and sacral stimulation as well as sympathetic.

While discussing the role of the adrenal gland in anger and fear, we mentioned the interaction of the hormone adrenalin and the nervous system. This reaction is referred to as the *adrenosympathetic* reaction. The sympathetic stimulation of the adrenals causes adrenalin to be secreted. Then, as the adrenalin circulates in the blood stream, it in return stimulates the

sympathetic system to continue its neural outflow. The end result of this reaction is a prolongation of the emotional state (anger, fear, etc.).

The Behavioral Expression of Emotion. A person experiencing an emotion nearly always expresses it in some way in his overt behavior.

Facial expressions. Most people expect emotion to be expressed in a person's face. To a lesser extent, the average person also expects hand and body movements and gestures to express and signify the emotion, but he pays more attention to the face. Sometimes, as in this case, scientific investigation tends to follow the lead of common sense. Quite a bit of work in psychology has been done on facial expression in emotion,

Figure 4.5. These card players are attempting to hide their facial expressions of emotion in order to prevent the other players from guessing what cards they drew. Although these men may in time develop completely enigmatic poker faces, might they unconsciously show their emotions with other expressions which their opponents can read? (Black Star.)

Figure 4.6. What emotions are portrayed in these two photographs? In the one on the left, is the young woman frightened or merely surprised, or is she acting out an emotional experience? What about the man below? Is his emotion best described as a mixture of satisfaction and restrained joy? (Turn to page 87 for the key to answers.)

while hand and body gestures have been relatively neglected.

Psychologists have studied the problem of whether or not there are typical facial expressions for each emotion. Most studies have concluded that there are definitely cultural differences in the expression of emotion (note the study concerning Chinese emotional expression). However, as in everything else that is human, we find that both heredity and environment must be considered in emotional expressions. In other words, emotional behavior is a result of both maturation and learning.

From studies of blind children we have discovered that a number of facial expressions do not depend upon a person's having seen these movements in others.[2] To a certain extent happiness, anger and fear,

[2] J. Thompson, "Development of Facial Expression of Emotion in Blind and Seeing Children," *Archives of Psychology,* no. 264, 1941.

startle, and a few others are distinguishable in the blind child. When compared with normal children, however, blind children do not develop so many subtle shadings of expression. The older the children, the more marked are the differences between the normal and the blind. The reason for this is that the blind child has difficulty learning expressions he cannot see.

Among normal children and adults, the same facial patterns may accompany a number of different emotions. For instance, anger and fear often have a similar pattern. Likewise, happiness and surprise are sometimes very similar.

In tests in which the subject is asked to name the emotion expressed in a photograph of a face, a certain amount of error is always found. On the other hand, agreement about certain photographs can be remarkably good.

In Figure 4.6 are photographs showing faces portraying different emotions. See if you can name the emotions in each photograph. This little experiment will reveal some of the ambiguity that exists in the patterns of facial expression of emotion.

Vocal expression of emotion. We are all aware that we sometimes judge emotion by listening to the sound of a person's voice. The sound of laughter nearly always indicates happiness. Crying, however, may accompany sorrow, fear, anger, or a number of other emotions.

Many cues may be detected in a voice. Its loudness may indicate a certain emotion.

THE CULTURAL PATTERNING OF EMOTIONAL EXPRESSION

The social environment can be very important in helping to determine the behavioral expression of an emotion. We find as great cultural variations in emotional expression as we do variations among individuals. For example, among the Maori of New Zealand, when friends meet after an absence, they are expected to shed tears. On the other hand, in Japan a person is supposed to smile while being reprimanded by his teacher, or even when announcing the death of his child.

In one study * a psychologist read a number of works of Chinese literature. In these stories he noted the descriptions of emotional behavior. In some instances the expressions were the same as those in the United States. For example, "Everyone trembled . . .," "His hairs stood on end . . .," and "Pimples arose all over the body" describe expressions of fear in both countries, and "He gnashed his teeth" can be recognized as anger.

However, in many other instances, an American could hardly be expected to recognize the emotion from the Chinese description. For example, "Her eyes grew round and opened wide" would suggest surprise to us but indicates anger to the Chinese. Also, "He laughed a great ho-ho" describes anger to the Chinese but would not to an American. To us the statement, "They stretched out their tongues" might imply hatred or derision, but certainly not surprise as it does to the Chinese.

In this study a check was made to see whether or not the literature reflected the actual Chinese expressions of emotion in everyday situations. It was found that the stories accurately portray Chinese life in this respect.

It would be interesting and useful if studies like this one were made in all the different cultures.

* O. Klineberg, "Emotional Expression in Chinese Literature," *Journal of Abnormal and Social Psychology*, 33:517–520, 1938.

Its pitch, or even a change in its pitch, may be a cue as to the emotion. Whatever the many cues used, most people do about as well or as poorly in judging recordings of voices portraying different emotions as they do in judging photographs.

Judging a situation. Many studies have pointed out that most of us can judge emotion best when allowed to view a total situation. The whole situation, of course, adds many cues to those obtained from face and voice. For example, a man's facial expression may seem to be a reflection of either anger or fear. However, when we are allowed to see that the man is cornered by a hungry lion, we know the emotion to be fear.

Certainly, in everyday life we most often judge what the emotion is while viewing the total situation. Nevertheless, it is important for the scientist to analyze the total situation into the various separate behavior patterns which make it up. Only in this way can he later fit these expressions into the scheme of emotions that also must include the other aspects.

Emotions as Motives. In the chapter on motivation we saw that motives direct behavior toward goals. Since most emotions also orient the individual toward goals, they too must be considered as motives. For example, an angry person strives to strike or even to destroy the object of his anger, a man gripped by fear seeks a place of safety, and a woman in love desires to be near her beloved.

In any situation in which a person feels emotion, he is not likely to be a disinterested bystander. There is always something that he wants or something that he wishes to do. Of course, he may not be able to attain his goal, in which case his emotion and motivation increase. In conflict situations like those discussed in the previous chapter, intense emotion is almost always found. A frustrated person often becomes very aggressive. If he is not able to attack

the obstacle that thwarts him, he may turn in fury upon an innocent scapegoat. In such an event we say that he has *displaced* his aggression (this mechanism is treated in more detail in Chapter 6).

Generally, we find that in pleasant emotions a person is motivated toward whatever it is that gives the pleasure. Moreover, he aspires to maintain or, at least, prolong his contact with the desired goal-object. In the unpleasant emotions, he seeks either to escape from the situation or to change it as quickly as possible. In the latter case, he may attack the object that causes his displeasure and attempt to destroy it.

Not only do we find motives in emotion, but we also find feeling and emotion in practically all motivation. For example, hunger and thirst are considered unpleasant by most of us, while the sex motive is experienced as pleasant. A good case can be made for the study of motivation and emotion as a single topic. In this connection it is interesting to note that both words come from similar Latin roots, *movere*, which means "to move," and *emovere*, "to move out of" or "to stir up or agitate."

THE NATURE OF EMOTION

In order to understand the nature of emotion, we must know something of its evolution in the species and its development in the individual. We must also know something of the theories that attempt to explain it.

Emotional Evolution. The famous biologist Charles Darwin stated that, like everything else about an organism, the emotions evolved and have persisted because of their survival value. Their purpose, he held, was to deal with emergency situations. If an organism found that it was being attacked, it had to be motivated either to fight or to run away. The emotions of anger and fear, according to Darwin, evolved side by side with these motives.

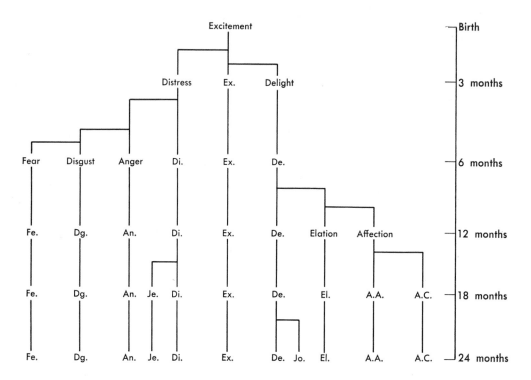

				Excitement					Birth
			Distress	Ex.	Delight				3 months
Fear	Disgust	Anger	Di.	Ex.	De.				6 months
Fe.	Dg.	An.	Di.	Ex.	De.	Elation	Affection		12 months
Fe.	Dg.	An. Je.	Di.	Ex.	De.	El.	A.A.	A.C.	18 months
Fe.	Dg.	An. Je.	Di.	Ex.	De. Jo.	El.	A.A.	A.C.	24 months

A.A. affection for adults
A.C. affection for children
Je.   jealousy
Jo.   joy

Figure 4.7. Are any of the primary emotions left out of this scheme of development and differentiation? Would you change the placement of any of the emotions in this chart? Why is it useful to know the developmental relations among the emotions?

In more recent years, Cannon, who was a physiologist at Harvard University, enlarged on Darwin's ideas about emotions, calling his own approach an "emergency theory of emotion." His examples also were taken mainly from the states of anger and fear. Cannon attempted to show that anger and fear are useful to an organism, mainly in getting it ready to fight or to run away, so that the emergency function is part feeling and part motive.

A good deal of the evolutionary explanation of emotions makes sense. There is little doubt that, like many other bodily mechanisms (digestion, etc.), the physical changes that occur during emotion evolved. Obviously, any creature that is not emotionally prepared to cope with an emergency will find survival difficult, if not impossible. Thus, one fact about the nature of emotions is that they evolved and were perfected because of their survival value to the organism.

Emotional Development of the Individual. The section on maturation in Chapter 2 points up the fact that nearly all an organism's structures, systems, and behavior patterns must undergo a process of development before they are ready for use. Emotional behavior in all its aspects is no exception to this rule. In the young infant there appears to be only one emotion, a general excitement. No matter what strong stimulation—loud noises, loss of support, pain, or caresses—the baby receives, its response pattern is the same. There seems to be an over-all discharge of motor (muscle) activity.

One logical conclusion from these facts is that all later and more specific emotions stem from this general excitement. The process involved in this development is called *differentiation*. Gradually, from this initial and diffuse state of excitement, the various other emotions grow and become distinguished.

Figure 4.7 shows schematically how a number of emotions may develop from infantile excitement.[3] We see that, in the three-month-old baby, distress and delight have become differentiated. Then, with excitement continuing as an emotion, both distress and delight begin to differentiate into still other emotions. By the time the child is twenty-four months old, from delight have sprung elation, affection, and joy. From distress have come anger, disgust, fear, and jealousy.

We must remember that both heredity and environment are involved in such a differentiation. It would be a mistake to think of the process as being dependent upon the genes alone. Of necessity, both maturation and learning would be involved.

Although this particular scheme of differentiation (Figure 4.7) is admitted to be a tentative one, there is considerable agreement among psychologists that emotions do differentiate in the baby. It is possible that future studies will suggest changes in this scheme, but it is unlikely that the concept of differentiation will be discarded.

[3] K. Bridges, "Emotional Development in Early Infancy," *Child Development*, 1932, 3:324–341.

The Sequence in Emotions. Part of the nature of an emotion is that it does not occur instantaneously. It is an event in the organism that requires a certain minimum duration of time—although, of course, the emotion may be prolonged considerably beyond this minimum. A number of steps must occur if we are to experience an emotion. These occurrences follow a sequence.

The sequence usually starts with the fact that the organism must in some way *perceive* an emotional situation. In order to have the emotion of fear, the organism must perceive the situation as one that is fearsome. In order to be angry, the organism must perceive some object or situation that arouses anger. To have the emotion of love, something must be perceived in the situation that calls forth this emotion. Nearly everyone is agreed about this first step; however, there are several different views

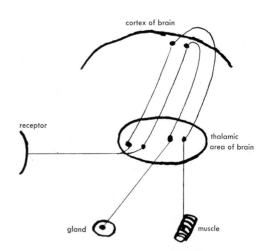

Figure 4.8. *Although the layman is not likely to express it in such technical terms, the popular view of emotion assumes that impulses arising in a receptor or sense organ go through the thalamus to the cortex of the brain, where we then experience the emotion. Next, impulses go out from the cortex through the thalamus to our glands and muscles, setting them in action.*

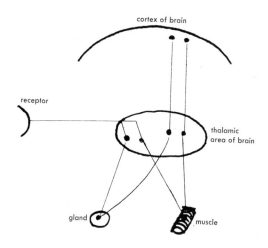

Figure 4.9. The James-Lange view of emotion assumes that the impulses arising in the receptors go first to the muscles and glands and then to the cortex, at which time emotion is experienced.

concerning the order of the sequence following this initial step. Let us examine some of these views.

The common-sense view. If we ask the average person to describe what goes on in emotion, we get the following picture. He says that, first, a person perceives a situation as fearsome; for instance, that he is in a crowded theater when a fire breaks out. Immediately this person knows and feels fear. This knowing and feeling of fear is the second step after the perception of the fire as dangerous. The third step is the person's running out of the theater and all the other physical activities involved in escape (heart beats faster, etc.).

Looking over these steps again, we find that to the average person emotions proceed in the following manner: first, there is a perception of an emotion-producing situation; second, there is the awareness and the feeling of the emotion; and third, there is the action that follows, the pounding of the heart as well as the running away. The average person would give, in

support of his view, all sorts of examples in which he himself has noted this supposed sequence of events in his own behavior. He will tell us, "I was once in a building and saw that it was on fire. I knew first that I was afraid, and then my heart began to pound as I ran for the fire escape." This type of example could be multiplied endlessly from all our own experiences.

The James-Lange view. The famous American philosopher and psychologist William James proposed a strikingly different view of the sequence of events in emotion. Soon after, independently and without knowledge of the James theory, the Danish physiologist C. Lange also brought out substantially the same view. In a fear situation, according to James and Lange, we first perceive the situation. Second, we react—our hearts pound and we find ourselves running away. Third, and last, we know that we are afraid and feel afraid. Thus, the knowing and the feeling come after and result from the action of the heart

Figure 4.10. The Cannon-Bard view assumes that the impulses arising in the receptors arrive simultaneously at the cortex and the muscles and glands by way of the thalamus. Thus, the experiencing of the emotion coincides with the bodily manifestations.

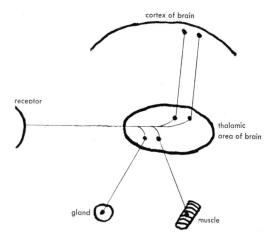

WILLIAM JAMES

William James * (1842–1910) has often been called the father of American psychology. In 1875, at Harvard University, he introduced the first course in scientific psychology ever to be taught in this country.

In 1884, his theory of emotion appeared in an article in the British journal *Mind*. This article later became a chapter in his book *Principles of Psychology*, published in 1890. James' book remained for many years the best book on modern psychology available in English. It is now considered to be a classic.

In evaluation of James' work, it can be said that he foreshadowed most of the trends that were to follow in American psychology. There is little that we have today that cannot be traced back to one of the chapters in his *Principles*.

In later life, James left psychology for philosophy. In this area he also became one of America's foremost. He is to be credited with much of the promotion and popularization of the concept of *pragmatism*, which has been called the most typically American philosophy.

* R. B. Perry, *The Thought and Character of William James* (Briefer Version). George Braziller Publisher, New York, 1954.

(*Culver Service*)

and the other bodily changes and after the external behavior, such as running away.

James put it very dramatically. He said that according to common sense a person sees a bear, knows fear, and runs away. He turned this around and said that we see the bear, run away, and are then, last of all, afraid. Or, in another dramatic example from James: we do not weep because we are sad; *we are sad because we weep.* If we think about this for a minute, we can see how it does follow from his sequence. While he mentioned only weeping, James meant to include all bodily changes that occur in the emotion of sorrow.

To the average person the James-Lange theory seems to be one that is completely groundless. On the other hand, James was able to give as many examples to support his view as there are to support the common-sense view. James gave this sort of example: we are crossing the street; a speeding vehicle comes by, missing us by only a hair; we rush to the curb and sit down; and only then do we know fear. James would say we perceived the fear situation, we acted (ran to the curb), and only

then did we know and feel fear. Obviously this type of example could be multiplied manyfold to support the James-Lange sequence.

We cannot say that either one of these two views is right or wrong. They are both simply descriptions of what seems to occur, at least in some instances. The James-Lange view is especially important because of the emphasis it places upon the bodily changes that occur in emotion. Before this view had been presented, these bodily changes had been considered only a result of emotion, not a vital aspect of it.

The hypothalamic view. Physiologists have discovered that the part of the brain called the *hypothalamus* is the control center for the complex neural activity in emotion. It has been suggested by some (mainly Cannon) that the best theory to describe what happens in emotion is a central or hypothalamic theory. It is central in the sense that it is the central nervous system that is in control and in charge of the emotion.

According to this view, the emotional sequence is as follows. First, the organism perceives a situation to be a fearsome one. Second, the hypothalamus takes over, and at one and the same time impulses go out from this central portion of the brain both to the upper parts of the brain and to the various other parts of the body. Thus, we have the knowing and feeling of fear at the same time that we have the bodily changes and the action of running away. Some research workers have claimed that this hypothalamic or central theory settles the conflict that exists between the common-sense theory and the James-Lange theory. The central theory states that both conscious awareness and bodily changes occur together as soon as the hypothalamus takes over.

As we look back on the emotional experience, however, we may emphasize either the knowing and the feeling of the emotion or the bodily expressions of it. If we stress in our memory the conscious aspects of the experience, we tend to agree with the common-sense explanation. On the other hand, if we remember best the bodily changes and activity, we are likely to accept the James-Lange theory. According to the central view of the sequence, both these aspects of emotions occur simultaneously. Thus, it is simply a trick of memory as to whether we interpret the experience according to the James-Lange explanation or the common-sense one.

The main contribution of the central theory is the fact that a control center for emotion is located in the hypothalamus of the brain. Our best general conclusion concerning all three views is that no one of them is completely correct and that each of them contributes to our understanding of emotion.

An Activation Theory of Emotion. Lindsley [4] in 1951 formulated an activation theory of emotion. We shall omit the details

[4] D. Lindsley, "Emotion," in S. S. Stevens (ed.), *Handbook of Experimental Psychology*, Wiley, New York, 1951, chap. 14.

of this theory (which require extensive neuroanatomical knowledge) and emphasize only its broad outlines. The main concept is that emotion is a heightened state of activity of the nervous system, particularly the cerebral cortex. By "heightened activity" is meant an increased rate of discharge of neural impulses. Specifically, the reticular formation in the brain stem (see Chapter 9) arouses or activates the cortex.

By means of sensory feedback from the muscles to the central nervous system, activation of the nervous system is further increased. For example, when an organism is fast asleep, it is at a very low level of activation. The cortex is relatively inactive, the sympathetic nervous system is discharging very little, and the muscles are relaxed, resulting in very little feedback. But the minute the organism is awakened by a strong stimulus, such as an alarm bell, the

Figure 4.11. Some of these alerted jet pilots were probably asleep; some were playing cards; all were at a very low level of activation. The alert signal immediately increased their level of activation. What neural changes are responsible for this increase? What emotions might be felt by these men at a time like this? What motives lie behind their behavior? (U.S. Air Force.)

nervous system slowly begins to be activated.

After a person awakens in the morning and begins his daily routine, he increases the activation of the nervous system continually by muscular movement and all his other activities (glandular, etc.). If his motives are blocked and he becomes frustrated, his sympathetic nervous system will discharge more impulses and adrenalin will be secreted. The hypothalamus must coordinate these activities, and its increased discharge will in turn increase the activation of the cortex. What we call "emotion," this theory says, is really a rather high level of activation.

This theory also attempts to show the relation of motives and emotions. Like the emotion, the motive too occurs at a certain level of activation. In this theory motives and emotions are hardly separable. Their separation in experience is accounted for by custom and convention. We learn to label various levels of activation (and the feelings that go with them) with such words as "anger," "fear," "hunger," and "sex."

Certainly we must admit that this theory does not yet have enough evidence behind it to convince us that in fact its main hypotheses do hold up. Furthermore, since Lindsley is more concerned with the neuro-

THE NEW "TRANQUILIZER" DRUGS

During periods of prolonged stress such as occur in war or high-pressure business competition, many people tend to become more and more tense According to the activation theory of emotion, the reticular formation in the brain of the tense person extends and intensifies the arousal of the cortex of the brain (see page 179 for a more detailed account of the reticular activating system). The person often seems to lose control of his emotions very easily and to be high-strung and overemotional.

In recent years medical research has produced a number of drugs which tend to reduce the tension in many of these people. The patients very often report that after taking the tranquilizer they are less anxious, more relaxed, and feel fine. Experiments have shown that even the psychotic (insane) person may sometimes find a temporary relief from his symptoms by taking these drugs. This temporary respite allows the psychiatrist or clinical psychologist a chance at psychotherapy. (See Chapter 6 for a discussion of psychoses.)

Two of the most widely used of these drugs are chlorpromazine and reserpine. Reserpine is a natural chemical substance extracted from the snakeroot plant, which has been used in India for centuries as a remedy for mental and nervous disorders. On the other hand, chlorpromazine is a new synthetic chemical. Recent experiments have shown that small doses of chlorpromazine block the activating system and produce a calming effect on the patient. Although small doses of reserpine stimulate the arousal mechanism, the same general calming effect is produced by depressing certain centers in the hypothalamus. Thus, we see that the two drugs work differently on the nervous system but have the same over-all effect on the patient.

As a caution, it must be emphasized that not all tense or psychotic people are helped by the tranquilizers. In some cases, harmful side-effects are produced in the patient. Certainly, a person should never take such drugs without a proper medical diagnosis and prescription.

ALBERT AND
THE WHITE RAT

Albert * was an eleven-month-old baby who had been reared in a hospital environment. When first presented with a tame white rat, he showed no fear reaction. Rather, he reached for the rat and touched it with his fingers. Nor was he afraid of rabbits, dogs, cotton, furs, and the like.

At the age of eleven months, three days, as Albert was being handed the white rat, a heavy metal bar was suddenly struck with a hammer, making a loud noise. At the sound, the baby fell forward, burying his face in the mattress. After several such pairings of the noise and the rat, Albert would begin to cry as soon as the rat appeared.

Any baby will show an emotional reaction to a sudden loud sound. Thus, Albert learned to fear the rat because it was paired with a stimulus that caused a fear reaction in him. (In Chapter 12 of this book we see that this kind of learning is called *conditioning*.)

Albert next was presented with a rabbit, cotton, and a fur muff. Although he had not been afraid of these things before, he now whimpered at their appearance. We can say that his learned fear of the rat had *generalized* (see Chapter 12) to other similar objects. We must emphasize the word "similar," for this fear did not generalize to his blocks or other toys that were dissimilar to the rat.

Like Albert, most of us have learned to fear a number of harmless things. What can be done to remove such fears? Psychologists have discovered several ways in which a person can unlearn these responses. One way is to present the fear-provoking object at a distance while the person is engaged in some pleasant activity such as eating candy. Day by day, the object is gradually brought closer until fear is no longer manifested.

Another practical way to remove this unwanted behavior is to allow the person to be around the feared object while in a congenial group. Of course, the other members of the group must be completely unafraid of the object in question.

* J. B. Watson and R. Rayner, "Conditioned Emotional Reactions," *Journal of Experimental Psychology*, 3:1–14, 1920.

anatomical problem than with general emotional phenomena, it is difficult to evaluate this theory at the present time. Nevertheless, this theory is a new approach to the study of emotion which may prove fruitful in the future.

Learning and Emotion. In an earlier section, we saw how learning plays a part in the acquisition of emotional expressions. Learning is also very important in our perception of objects and situations which arouse our emotions. A child must learn that a busy street is dangerous or that his aunt from Chicago is a lovable person. Unfortunately, the child may also learn to climb happily into a car with any stranger who offers candy or to scream in terror at the sight of a harmless white rabbit (note the case of Albert and the white rat in the above insert).

The important topic of learning is taken up in Chapter 12. It is sufficient to note here that learning enters into all human behavior.

SUMMARY

Our emotions (anger, love, etc.) are what give warmth and color to our lives. Emotions may be felt and known consciously, or they may be unconscious.

Certain facts about emotions are well established. First, there is the personal emotional experience. This aspect includes our subjective feelings and knowledge of the emotion.

Second, there are the bodily changes which occur in emotion, such as in heart rate, breathing, blood pressure, and galvanic skin response (GSR). Many of these changes are mediated by the autonomic nervous system. Sometimes, similar bodily changes may accompany different emotions, for example, anger and fear.

Third, there is the behavioral expression of emotion. This aspect is concerned with the facial expressions and other bodily movements that can be observed in emotion and used as cues to determine what emotion is being experienced. Since the same expression may accompany a number of different emotions, no observer is completely accurate in the use of these cues. We find both individual and cultural variations in emotional expression, because such expressions develop through the interaction of heredity and environment.

Fourth, emotions act as motives, for an emotional organism is also a goal-directed one. There is even some logic in considering motivation and emotion as a single topic.

In the study of the nature of emotion we discover that the emotions evolved to serve the organism in times of emergency.

Excitement is the first emotion to appear in the development of the child. Later it differentiates into other emotions, such as joy, fear, and jealousy.

A number of investigators have studied the sequence of events that occur in emotion. Most of them agree that the sequence begins with the perception of an emotion-arousing situation. As for what happens after this perception, the common-sense view is that the conscious awareness of the emotion comes next and is followed by the bodily changes and activities. The James-Lange theory holds just the opposite: that the bodily changes and behavior are followed by the knowing and feeling of the emotion. The central view is that the hypothalamic brain center instigates both these aspects simultaneously.

One of the more recent theories of emotion is Lindsley's activation theory. In his view, emotions are high levels of neural activation, especially of the cerebral cortex.

As it does in all aspects of human behavior, learning plays an important role in the acquisition of emotional responses.

QUESTIONS

1. What would human life be like if no one had any emotion?

2. What are the four main aspects that define an emotion?

3. Describe several different bodily changes that regularly occur during emotion.

4. Compare and contrast anger and fear in terms of bodily changes, feeling, and facial expression.

5. What is the importance, in relation to emotion, of each of the following terms: sympathetic, parasympathetic, hypothalamus, adrenalin, and glycogen?

6. What is meant by "personal emotional experience"? Describe such experiences as they might occur in rage, love, and hatred.

7. What is the reason for studying the facial expressions of blind children?

8. List the cues afforded by emotional expressions that might be found in a real-life situation. (First describe the situation, and then list the cues.)

9. Compare the common-sense, James-Lange, and hypothalamic views of the sequence of events in emotion.

10. Trace the development of emotion in the infant.

11. Briefly describe and evaluate Lindsley's activation theory of emotion.

12. How is it possible both to learn and to unlearn emotional responses?

SUGGESTED READINGS

Cannon, W. B.: *Bodily Changes in Pain, Hunger, Fear, and Rage,* 2d ed., Appleton-Century-Crofts, New York, 1929.

> (A classic in the study of emotion, emphasizing the various physiological changes that occur in emotion.)

Inbau, F.: *Lie Detection and Criminal Investigation,* Williams & Wilkins, Baltimore, 1942, part I.

> (The method and practice of scientific lie detection.)

Lindsley, D.: "Emotion," in S. S. Stevens (ed.), *Handbook of Experimental Psychology,* Wiley, New York, 1951, chap. 14.

> (A summary which includes the best account of the activation theory.)

Morgan, C. T., and E. Stellar: *Physiological Psychology,* 2d ed., McGraw-Hill, New York, 1950.

> (An up-to-date picture of the bodily changes in emotion and also of the autonomic nervous system.)

Reymert, M. L. (ed.): *Feelings and Emotions,* McGraw-Hill, New York, 1950.

> (A symposium of experts summarizing what is known today about this topic.)

Ruckmick, C.: *The Psychology of Feeling and Emotion,* McGraw-Hill, New York, 1936.

> (An informative, historical approach to emotion.)

Woodworth, R. S., and H. Schlosberg: *Experimental Psychology,* rev. ed., Holt, New York, 1954, chaps. 5, 6, 7.

> (An excellent account of experimental work on emotion.)

Young, P. T.: *Emotion in Man and Animal,* Wiley, New York, 1943.

> (A useful general source of information on emotion.)

Key to Figure 4.6, page 76. The photo on the left shows Margaret Truman registering surprise at something said to her on a TV panel show, while Steve Allen is amused at her reaction. On the right is the photo of an Air Force colonel who has just landed his plane after shooting down his first Russian-built MIG in Korea. (Wide World Photos and U.S. Air Force.)

5 THE SELF AND BEHAVIOR

As has been pointed out earlier, human beings are influenced by both external and internal forces (see Chapter 3), and their behavior is definitely changed as a result of emotional factors (see Chapter 4). In this chapter we want to look somewhat more closely at some of these forces, emphasizing particularly some internal ones in which feelings and emotions often play a large part. More specifically, we want to examine the opinions and sentiments that a person has about himself.

THE SELF-PICTURE

It is obvious, but significant, that everyone does have ideas and feelings about himself, which, furthermore, are of great interest and importance to him. To cite just a few examples, a college boy may feel that he is a good football player, a coed that she is one of the most popular girls on campus, and a businessman that he is successful.

The individual's ideas, thoughts, and beliefs about the kind of person he is (and also about the kind of person he is not) may be called his *self-picture*. Whether or not this picture is accurate, it often has a decided influence on how the person reacts to other people and to his own plans, hopes, and ambitions.

Some Questions about the Self-picture. Perhaps all this will be more understandable in terms of our day-to-day experience if we raise some questions about ourselves. We shall find that these questions overlap and that answering one helps answer another, but they help us to explain what we mean by the self-picture.

"Who am I?" One of the ways to examine the self-picture is to ask the question "Who

am I?" Of course, one reply is to give our name: "Who am I? Well, I am John Jones." A little reflection, however, will make us realize that we do not value the name for itself. The name is a mere label, although we may have strong feelings about it. It is not the name itself that is important, or the words themselves, but rather the association of these words with ourselves.

This becomes apparent when somebody begins to make slurring or genuinely uncomplimentary remarks about our name. Our impulse is to come to our own defense. We may struggle against this impulse and manage to hold it back, but it will be there nevertheless. So one answer to the question "Who am I?" is, "I am John Jones and I demand a certain amount of consideration and respect for that name."

We demand respectful treatment, however, for more than our name. For one thing, we want to be thought of as valuable *in and of ourselves*. We are not content to be treated merely *as a means to an end;* we are not satisfied to be simply a cog in a machine or a name on a payroll. We insist on respect for our personal worth.

Let us take an example. Suppose someone who is sitting next to us accidentally bumps into us. The contact may have been a very slight one, so slight that by no stretch of the imagination could it have hurt us, but the other person knows what etiquette demands under these circumstances, so he says, "Excuse me." If he finds it necessary to walk in front of us, again he excuses himself. Why does he ask our pardon for such harmless acts?

The answer seems to be that as individuals we demand respect for the "living space" that we occupy. For the moment it is ours, and when another person intrudes upon it he should do so with our permission. He may not *have* to get our permission, but we expect him to do so.

And so—"I am John Jones. I do not want you making fun of my name. I demand that

Where am I?
What am I?
Who am I?

Figure 5.1.

you show consideration for my personal worth. I am not content if you treat me merely as a means to an end, and I strongly desire that you respect the space in which I live." This is part of the story of *who* we are.

"What am I?" This question represents another approach to the self-picture and, though it overlaps the previous one, it enables us to emphasize characteristics that we believe we have (or some, especially of the undesirable sort, that we feel we do not have). For example, nearly all of us believe that we are good sports. Furthermore, many of us would say, "I am handsome, or at least not ugly," "I am intelligent," or "I am a good citizen." Actually, there are an almost unlimited number of illustrations. "I am a campus beauty," "I am popular," "I am one who knows how to enjoy life"—all such statements throw some light on the self-picture of the individual involved. Thus, if we can discover who and

what a person really thinks he is, we greatly increase our understanding of him.

"*Where am I?*" It may appear a little unusual at first to raise this question in connection with the self-picture. It is clear, of course, that our geographical location may be a part of our self-picture, but that is not what we have in mind. Rather, in asking, "Where am I?" we are thinking of our *prestige* as individuals and how we fit into the social groups of which we are a part. Let us consider some answers to this question: "I am a doctor," "I am a supervisor," "I am president of the senior class," "I am a student assistant," "I am captain of the football team." These are all examples of positions that give us rank or prestige or status in a group, and they become an important part of the self-picture as well.

Status symbols associated with these or other positions often become very real and significant parts of the self-picture. The letter (or other award) which an athlete gets for making the football team is an example.

It is not, of course, the monetary value of the award, though it may have some, that really counts. It is the fact that the award represents a mark of *where he is* in the group or in several groups.

Likewise, the size of an executive's office, the kind of desk he has, whether he has a rug on the floor, and his title—all these symbols and many others have probably become for him important parts of the self-picture. When people make fun of them or take them lightly, the executive usually feels hurt whether he shows his feelings or not.

Clearly, there are other questions that we could ask about the self-picture. We might examine the religious values of a person or his commitment to the American way of life. We could inquire into his plans and hopes for the future and the degree to which he feels that he has made progress in achieving the goals. We could examine his conceptions of his failures and shortcomings, for these too may be a part of the self-picture.

It is apparent, then, that everyone has a self-picture, beliefs about who and what and where he is. Furthermore, the chances are that these beliefs are more elaborate and go into more detail than people are often inclined to believe.

Importance of the Self-picture. One interesting thing about human beings is how strongly each individual feels about his self-picture. As an illustration, let us consider a person's statement, "I am a good sport." What happens if somebody seriously questions this? We all know what usually happens; it *hurts*. How the person visibly reacts depends, of course, on the circumstances. It might be diplomatic to do nothing or say nothing, but we all know that his

Figure 5.2. It is disappointing to be merely a cog in a machine, to be simply a means to an end for someone else. We want to be valued for what we are, not just for what we can do.

impulse would be to defend himself against the aspersion.

There are other examples of this sort of reaction. Suppose a list is made of people who have attained something significant—it may be the honor roll in school, or a list of those who have won letters in football, or an announcement of those who have been promoted to better jobs. Suppose, furthermore, that a certain person's name should be on the list but that somehow his name has been left off. Again it is impossible for anyone to say in advance what he would do, but it is possible to say with considerable certainty what his *impulse* would be. His impulse would be to rush to the person who had made this list and protest the omission of his name. Now, if someone questions him as to why he did this he is likely to say, "It's not simply that I was left off the list—I can understand how that might happen—but it's the *principle* of the thing. This list should be complete, and these mistakes should not be made." Of course, it is not really the principle of the thing. Rather, it is the offense to the person's feelings about himself that is most likely to cause him to protest the mistake. When he argues on principle, he is merely rationalizing to cover up his hurt feelings.

Another interesting thing about these ideas which make up the self-picture is how far they may be from the truth. As we have said, "I am a good sport" is a part of the self-picture of practically everyone in our society. But a striking fact here is that people who are not good sports seem to believe this about themselves as strongly as those who are. Here is an individual, let us say, who is not a good sport at all. He "can't take it," as we say, and is very sensitive and very difficult to get along with. If we question that individual about his beliefs and feelings concerning himself, however, we shall be likely to find that "I am a good sport" is a rather important part of his self-picture.

The same remarks can be made about

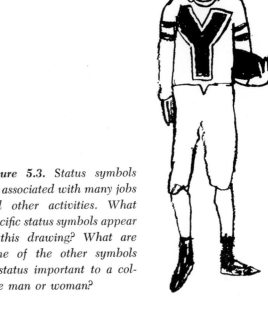

Figure 5.3. Status symbols are associated with many jobs and other activities. What specific status symbols appear in this drawing? What are some of the other symbols of status important to a college man or woman?

the statements "I am intelligent" and "I am handsome." Some people who believe they are intelligent actually are, but some people who believe they are intelligent are definitely below average. There are some handsome people who know they are handsome and frankly admit it—just as there are people who are not handsome and recognize that fact—but, on the other hand, there are people who believe they are handsome who are not handsome at all.

Thus, it turns out that these beliefs which people hold about themselves may be quite incorrect. Indeed, there may be no evidence for them at all, but they may go right along holding them just the same.

Another illustration: Here is a man who had taught for a while in college but who had not been at all successful in college teaching. When he had an opportunity to go into the business world at a salary about the same that he had been making in teaching, he took that opportunity. It was interesting as the years passed to hear him

Figure 5.4. What factors enter into the motivation of these men? Why have they driven themselves almost to the point of exhaustion—for self, team, school, family, or something else? Might they have difficulty in answering these questions accurately? (Wide World Photos.)

talk about his teaching experience. He believed all along—or perhaps came to believe—that he had been a very successful college teacher. There was no evidence to support this position; indeed, all the evidence was to the contrary. The truth is that most teachers believe they are good teachers, most lawyers believe they are good lawyers, and most doctors believe they are good doctors. In each case this number includes many who are *not* good teachers, or good lawyers, or good doctors. And certainly the same thing is true of people in other occupations. Whether the self-picture is close to the truth or far from it does not seem to be a matter of the intelligence or education of an individual. We can find about as many instances of unconscious distortion in individuals who are well educated and of high intelligence as we can in other people.

We have made two points in this section. The first is that the self-picture contains elements about which we feel very strongly—indeed, so strongly that we may be greatly upset when they are questioned. The second is that some elements in the self-picture may be very far from the truth.

UNCONSCIOUS ASPECTS OF THE SELF

So far we have been discussing the self-picture. We have defined the self-picture as the ideas and beliefs which a person has about himself. As we have discussed it, we have been dealing with things of which the individual is aware. It is based on what he knows about or has contact with. The self-picture is therefore the more or less conscious aspect of the self. But the self also has unconscious but very real aspects.

Here is a youngster, for example, who has a little brother. The two are within a couple of years of each other in age, and they quarrel and fight a great deal. What, now, if someone from outside the family begins to make slurring remarks about the younger brother and even to attack him? How does the older brother react? Quite likely, past feelings will be laid aside, and the older boy will rush to the defense of the younger. On the other hand, if, prior to this incident, the older boy had been questioned about his love and affection for the younger, he would probably have denied that he had any. Asked what he thought about his younger brother, he might have had nothing good to say about him. Apparently, then, there is a devotion, a regard, between these two youngsters of which both, and perhaps especially the older brother, are unaware.

Or to take another illustration: Suppose a young man grew up in a small town and later moved to the city. After he has been in the city for a while and considers himself a sophisticated city dweller, somebody makes a disparaging remark about his old home town, maybe without knowing that he is from that town. He may hold his tongue, because he may not want people to know where he is from or how he feels about the old home town. But there is not much question about what his impulse is. His first tendency is to rush to the defense of the old home town. Though he may think he has lost all affection and regard for it,

"I am kind to animals."

the way he feels when it is attacked shows that it is still a part of his real self.

Thus it is clear that there are elements in the self of which we are not aware. If asked about some of these things we would deny them and do so in good conscience. Indeed, we are sometimes surprised at our own reaction to some of these situations. Often we have no inkling of their existence unless they are challenged or forcibly called to our attention. Even then, of course, we may not frankly admit them.

To make clear the distinction between the self-picture (the conscious aspects of the self) and the unconscious aspects of the self, let us take a person who tends to be miserly. His tendency to save money has long since passed the point of mere saving

"I am a good marksman."

Figure 5.5. What we think and feel we are and what we actually are may be quite different. It is surprising how different the self-picture may sometimes be from reality.

Barrymore in Tolstoi's play Redemption.

The actor's sketch of himself in the same play.

The actor as sketched by an artist friend.

Studio photograph of John Barrymore.

Figure 5.6. Which one of these pictures of John Barrymore would you suppose reveals most closely the true self? Do you think the camera, being objective, is more accurate in depicting the self than the artist? Why? (Courtesy New York Public Library and Culver Service.)

and has become an unreasonable compulsion to hoard money. It is unlikely that he knows all the impulses of this sort that he has. In other words, when a person tends to be miserly, it is relatively rare that he consciously knows or admits this tendency. Although being miserly may actually be a part of the self, *it might not be a part of the self-picture*. It may be a part of him, but he may be unaware of its existence, especially if it is an unworthy motive. If it is not consistent with the picture which he has built up for himself, he is likely to put it "out of mind" and refuse to admit its existence, even though to all his friends and to everyone else who knows him its presence is obvious.

Thus we see that there is an unconscious aspect of the self and that it comes from at least three sources. In the first place, the unconscious elements may be unconscious simply because we have not had occasion to think of them. They may never have been challenged or attacked, so that up to the present we have accepted them without questioning. Since we are not aware that

they are there, we have not incorporated them into the self-picture. In the second place, they may develop because we refuse to face them; we may forcibly put out of mind the unworthy impulses and deny them simply because we do not want to admit that we have them. In other words, they have been repressed. (The process of repression is discussed in some detail in the next chapter.) Finally, that there are some occasions when we do not recognize very favorable facts about ourselves, simply because they seem improbable to us. We may actually be more charitable or more handsome or more capable than we give ourselves credit for being.

Meaning of the Term "Self." We use the word "self" (as opposed to "self-picture") to refer to all the beliefs, ideas, attitudes, and feelings, whether conscious or unconscious, which an individual has concerning himself. The self-picture, on the other hand, includes only those of which he is conscious. The self-picture is thus a part, but only the conscious part, of the self.

To state the matter another way, the self

is the *individual as known to and felt about by the individual.*[1] The term "known to" is used to indicate the conscious aspects of the self (and hence the self-picture) and the term "felt about by" is here used to refer to the unconscious aspects of the self.

The self, then, is the individual's self-picture plus the unconscious feelings and ideas that he has about himself. The self is the individual as known to and felt about by the individual, whether this knowing and feeling are conscious or unconscious.

CONSCIOUS AND UNCONSCIOUS IN PSYCHOLOGY

Let us discuss at somewhat greater length the terms *conscious* and *unconscious* as they are used in modern psychology. It is easy to surround these words with an air of mystery, but they are really not difficult to understand. When we say "unconscious," we simply mean "unaware" or "unperceived." Thus if we have some unconscious feelings and attitudes about ourselves, these are simply feelings and attitudes of which we are not aware.

Furthermore, there are different degrees of awareness of the events going on around us and within us. Of some events we may be completely aware (or conscious); of others we may be totally unaware (or unconscious); but of many others—perhaps of most—we may be *partially aware* (or *conscious to a degree*). Perhaps an illustration will help make this point clear.

[1] For this definition we are indebted to Gardner Murphy, who defines self as "the individual as known to the individual" (see his *Personality: A Biosocial Approach to Origins and Structure*, Harper, New York, 1947, p. 148). Murphy obviously emphasizes the known or conscious aspects of the self, though he probably intends to include unconscious aspects as well.

One of the first scientific psychologists to pay particular attention to the self was M. W. Calkins. An example of her writing along this line is "The Self in Scientific Psychology," *American Journal of Psychology*, 26:495–524, 1915.

Suppose a person is driving west in the late afternoon with the sun directly in front of him. The chances are that most of the time he is highly conscious (aware) of the sun shining in his eyes. If he has driven an hour or two, he also may be conscious (aware) of feelings of fatigue, but unless he is quite tired these feelings probably will not get as much of his attention as the sun does. So far as the hum of the motor is concerned, he is probably aware of it only if something goes wrong, though, of course, he can "bring it into consciousness" whenever he wishes. Some of his bodily processes he might easily become aware of (e.g., breathing). Others may go on without awareness even being possible (e.g., secretion of the pancreas).

Hence our needs, feelings, and other experiences vary in degree of consciousness or awareness all the way from those at the center of attention to those of which we cannot—or will not—become aware at all. Likewise some of our beliefs about ourselves may be at the "center of consciousness," as we say, and hence be part of the self-picture. Others—for example, aspects of the self of which we are ashamed, or those too flattering to believe—may actually be a part of us though we may be unaware of them. They are part of the self but not of the self-picture. Many other aspects of the self are in between, so far as awareness goes, and may or may not be a part of the self-picture, depending on degree of awareness and how we classify them. In any case, however, they are a part of the self, and perhaps of the self-picture.

IDENTIFICATION AND EGO-INVOLVEMENT

One point that should be clear from our previous discussion is that the self often includes more than just the body. This may not be true of the infant, for when self-awareness is just beginning the body is probably the central or even the only part

This research * was designed to study the stability of the self. The subjects of the study were 62 members of two cooperative houses at the University of Michigan. Each had been in his particular cooperative house for at least five months and therefore presumably was acquainted with all its other members.

A self-rating inventory was developed especially for use in this research. It required the individual to rate himself on 25 traits, including such things as intelligence, neatness, generosity, sportsmanship, and over-all adjustment. On one occasion he was asked to do this rating in such a way as to give himself the benefit of every reasonable doubt (but still trying to be truthful). On another he was asked to do the rating so as to deny himself the benefit of every reasonable doubt. The difference between these two ratings was taken as measure of the stability of the self-concept. Each subject was also asked to rate 16 other members of the group on substantially the same 25 traits, and in addition, to take a standardized personality test by Guilford and Martin known as the *GAMIN* test. Finally, each person was asked to take a "test" for tendencies to hold authoritarian or fascist attitudes (known as the F-scale).

The top 15 people on the F-scale were eliminated from the study, for reasons we need not go into here. From the remaining 47 men two groups were selected on the basis of a stability index (the amount of change between the two conditions of self-rating). These two groups consisted of the 15 men showing the greatest amount of stability (least change when not instructed to give themselves the benefit of the doubt) and the 15 showing the least stability. These two groups did not differ significantly in age, years in school, membership in the armed services, etc., although the less stable had a higher grade-point average.

The following conclusions were drawn from the study: The men with the more stable self-concepts rated themselves higher than did the men with the less stable ones. Furthermore, this higher rating was for the traits in general and not for only a few. The more stable men were found to be better liked and considered more popular by their peers, and to see themselves more nearly as their associates saw them. They were better known to the rest of the group, and showed less of nervousness and feelings of inferiority, according to the GAMIN scale.

The study indicates that under conditions such as these stability of the self-concept goes with being more popular and better liked and with showing less defensive behavior.

* John J. Brownfain, "Stability of the Self-concept as a Dimension of Personality," *Journal of Abnormal and Social Psychology*, 47:597–606, 1952.

of the self. Even for the adult the body is an important part of the self—there is no disagreement with that point—but there is much more to the self than just the body.

Expansion or Broadening of the Self. The self, for example, includes the clothes which we wear—and, incidentally, the clothes that we own but are not wearing at the moment. And it also includes our other possessions. The best way to prove this is to see what sort of feeling wells up in us when someone damages or steals our clothes or threatens our other possessions. Our possessions are a part of us (or a part of the self of each of us).

Our families, also, are a part of us. It makes no difference whether we are living at home with our mothers and fathers, or whether we have families of our own; in any case, our families nearly always become a part of us. How do we feel when a member of the family is ill or is threatened with disaster? There may be quarrels within a family—indeed, a certain amount of quarreling may be thought of as normal rather than unusual—but when a member of our family is threatened, frequently the quarrels are laid aside and we rush to his defense.

Then, our fraternity (or sorority) may become a part of us. Again the best way to prove that this is true is for us to be in a group where fraternities are being discussed and for our particular fraternity to come in for slurring remarks or be treated lightly. As we have already said, there is no way to be sure what we will do under those circumstances. We may even keep silent, but we certainly *want* to defend that fraternity.

It is significant that, if we are fraternity or sorority members, we often come to feel that our particular group is the best that there is. At times this may be a matter of pretense or of trying to impress other people, including prospective pledges. On the other hand, this is frequently a deep and sincere conviction about the excellence of the group. Needless to say, this phenomenon is not restricted to fraternities and sororities.

The labor movement may become a part of us. We may come to respect and feel affection for the union to which we belong and to the organization with which this union is affiliated. We may believe that the hope of the workingman lies in the labor movement and be willing to do a great deal more than the minimum for the cause.

It is important to note that the feelings

Figure 5.7. To what extent do you think the British people identify with the royal family? Does this identification influence what happens in Great Britain? (Courtesy British Information Services.)

we have about any one of these groups, as well as the ideas that we use to support these feelings, often develop considerably *after* we have accepted the group itself. For example, if we believe our fraternity is the finest in the world, we can find a good many arguments to support that position, but very often these arguments do not occur to us until after we have pledged the fraternity. We *could* come to the conclusion as a result of the arguments, but the chances are that we come to the arguments after having accepted the conclusion.

Meaning of Identification or Ego-involvement. It is clear, of course, that we have been dealing here with the principle that a person may make something outside of himself a part of himself and that, having made it a part of himself, he may defend it or work hard for it. This process is called *identification with* or *ego-involvement in* the object or person or cause. Thus, if we identify with or become ego-involved in the objectives of our employer, we make those objectives our own, and to whatever extent the business organization fails to achieve these objectives, we are personally hurt. In other words, we have made the organization a part of us, a part of our selves.

Or here is the football team from our

your state

the old home town

free enterprise

union

other possessions

team

clothes

family

church

lodge

club

fraternity

younger brother

SELF

at a certain
stage in life

school. Perhaps we have not bet on the football game, and from the standpoint of our future success or failure it makes no difference whether the team wins or loses. Yet it may still make a great deal of difference to us, and if we were given the opportunity of serving or sacrificing for that team, we might very well be willing to do so. We have become ego-involved in that team or have identified with it.

Thus it is easy to see that identification and ego-involvement are important concepts in understanding human behavior. While a distinction can be made between the two, on the basis that ego-involvement actually implies a stronger degree of feeling than does identification, in this book it is convenient to treat them as meaning the same thing.

We should note here, however, that the term "identification" is also used later in this book in a somewhat different sense. In Chapter 6, identification is mentioned as one of the defense mechanisms. Even in this case it implies making something (usually another person) outside the self a part of the self, but when it is used defensively it enables the person to avoid facing life as it really is. All this will be clearer after reading the next chapter.

Thus, we see that the self includes not only beliefs, ideas, and feelings that we have about our body and our own personal future and welfare, but also everything with which we have identified or in which we have become ego-involved. It includes

Figure 5.8. Early in life the self is necessarily narrow and restricted. As we grow older, however, it expands and grows by identifying with things not originally a part of it. Can you think of other things that an adult in our culture usually makes a part of the self?

everything that we really care about: our team, our family, our fraternity, our possessions, and our home town. All these become a part of the self to whatever extent we really feel strongly about them and identify with them.

Goals Other than Pleasure and Self-interest. Here, of course, is the great weakness of the theory of *psychological hedonism,* a theory which holds that always and under all circumstances a person tries to increase his own personal pleasure (or to avoid his own discomfort). This view was once widely defended by certain philosophers and has had its influence on the thinking of a good many people. In addition, there are related views which simply hold that everyone is seeking his own self-interest, without specifying, as the psychological hedonists

do, that such self-interest is properly thought of as pleasure.

The weakness of all these views lies in the fact that they do not recognize that we may become ego-involved in another person or another thing. They do not recognize, in other words, that when we make something outside ourselves a part of ourselves we may serve and sacrifice for that as completely as we would for our own personal pleasure and welfare. The self, in other words, is not simply the individual. It is the individual as *known to and felt about by* the individual, and when the individual says "I am a Catholic," or "I am an American," or "I am an alumnus of X College," he is then describing the self. Our attempts to defend and enhance the self include attempts to defend and enhance all that with

RELATION BETWEEN ATTITUDES TOWARD THE SELF AND TOWARD OTHERS

To what extent do people who have a favorable attitude toward themselves also have a favorable attitude toward other people? This study * should be thought of as a preliminary investigation of that problem.

To that end, 50 statements expressing attitudes were devised. Of these, 25 referred to attitudes toward the self, e.g., "I feel that I have very little to contribute to the welfare of others," and "I think I would be happier if I didn't have certain limitations." The other 25 referred to attitudes toward others, e.g., "One soon learns to expect very little of other people," and "Some people are always trying to get more than their share of the good things in life."

Each person was asked to indicate, for each of the fifty statements, the degree to which he agreed with it: "Rarely or almost never true for me," "Sometimes but infrequently true for me," "Occasionally true for me," "Very often true for me," or "True for me all or most of the time." The people were asked not to sign their names. Two groups of college students (125 in all) and two groups of high school students (86 in all) responded to the statements.

The results show a positive, although a moderate, relationship between attitudes toward the self and attitudes toward others. The coefficients of correlation (explained in Chapter 16) ranged from .51 to .74. This means that, generally speaking, people who had a favorable opinion about themselves tended to have favorable opinions about others (and vice versa), though there were a great many exceptions.

* E. Lakin Phillips, "Attitudes toward Self and Others: A Brief Questionnaire Report," *Journal of Consulting Psychology,* 15:79–81, 1951.

which we identify or in which we have become ego-involved.

Of course, when we define the self so as to include all that with which we identify we are using the word in a very different sense from that in which it is employed ordinarily. Usually, when we say that a person is selfish, we mean that he is striving for himself in the narrow sense of the term. He is trying to advance his own interests or his own pleasures. But in the present sense of the term he may be working for someone else, even to his own injury, because he has identified with this other person.

Let us consider the case of a loyal and devoted member of a church. The church calls upon him for financial contributions and he makes them. The church asks him to render other service—to engage in a campaign for soliciting members, or to teach a church-school class, or to serve as an usher or in some other capacity—and he does these too. The older point of view, that everybody is out for himself, would have to assert that he engages in these activities either because he enjoys them, or because he expects to gain from them financially or otherwise, or else because he fears the consequences of omitting them. He might, for example, be afraid that if he does not engage in them he will lose business or will slip in the esteem of others or that he will be bothered by his conscience. Such motives may, of course, sometimes be at work. The point, though, is that there is another class of motives operating in him which may be in every respect as powerful and as influential as the more "selfish" motives. The church worker, in other words, may make the church a part of himself and serve and sacrifice for the church, do things beyond the minimum and beyond what he has to do or even can be expected to do, *because he loves the church.*

Sometimes we work hard for another person or a cause because we are forced to do so. But when we identify with it we probably work hard for it because we want to. Here it is easy to get the idea that, since we do this because we want to, it is as selfish and self-centered as any other act. But the point is that, as a result of strong identification, we may expend energy and even

Table 5.1 Psychological Hedonism versus Identification or Ego-involvement

	Psychological hedonism	Identification or ego-involvement
Is everything done for our own personal pleasure (or to avoid pain)?	Yes	No
Are our voluntary actions primarily (or usually) rational?	Yes	May be or may not be
Is real sacrifice for another possible?	No	Yes
Will we cooperate with others?	Yes, if we think we will gain by doing so	Yes, if we have identified with them; sometimes also for personal gain
Do we ever make another a part of the self?	No, this possibility is not recognized	Yes, this may—and often does—occur

risk our lives for another—and do this either without counting the cost to us personally or even in spite of the cost. Psychological hedonism may seem quite logical and accurate as an account of human behavior, but it is not.

It is, of course, often true that in these sacrifices for others we often reach our greatest usefulness and eventually our greatest happiness. This is related to what the philosophers of an earlier age called the *hedonistic paradox*, the fact that if we seek for pleasure in narrow, selfish sense we usually miss it, whereas if we identify with something outside ourselves and really work for it, we often find the greatest satisfactions of life.

WHAT WE ARE AND WHAT WE APPEAR TO BE

Let us consider the self in relation to what we really are and in relation to what we appear to others to be.

The Self and Reality. It should be noted that nothing has been said so far in this chapter to indicate that the self is what we really are. We have said it is the individual as known to and felt about by the individual. But it may very well be that what a person feels and thinks he knows about himself is, as we have already indicated, quite different from what he really is.

As a matter of fact, this is usually true to some degree. It is doubtful whether many people in the world completely understand themselves, knowing fully what they are and what they are not. Certainly the average individual is under some misconceptions. We have already seen that, although the individual who says "I am intelligent" or "I am handsome" may be right, he may just as well be wrong and be unaware that he is wrong. In other words, he may have some notions about himself quite contrary to the real situation.

In some cases of mental illness, we see this much more clearly than we do in normal individuals. Here is a person, for example, who believes that he is President of the United States. If we check into his background, however, we shall probably find that he is one who has amounted to very little so far as status and achievement go. His belief that he is the President comes not from evidence but rather from a need to believe it. And the interesting thing is how tenaciously and sincerely he holds to his belief. This is certainly an instance of the self's being far from reality.

As a matter of fact, self-understanding is hard to achieve. Indeed, it is sometimes easier to understand another person's motives, the real causes of his behavior, than it is to understand our own. Most people recognize the need for self-understanding, but this does not guarantee that they have achieved it.

Why is it that, though we live more intimately with ourselves than with any other individual, accurate self-understanding is still hard to get? In the first place, we may not have self-understanding because we simply lack knowledge, and this may come about largely because we are complex and have many hidden or unconscious motives.

A second and more important reason for our not understanding our selves well is that we have a great concern for the self and find it difficult to believe about the self anything that is unworthy or that reflects upon it. Of course, it is not impossible to believe unpleasant or unfavorable facts about ourselves, but it is difficult to do so.

The fact is, then, that the conception which we have of our selves comes from two sources. It comes, first, from our experience and the evidence from those experiences. It comes, second, from a need to hold certain beliefs about our selves, and this need to believe has a great deal of influence on what we actually do believe.

Hence, the self is not the individual as he is. It is rather the individual as he appears to and feels about himself. This self may be far from reality in the case of some seriously maladjusted individuals, or it may be close to reality in the case of some other individuals. (This subject is discussed further in the chapter on personality.)

The Self and What We Appear to Be. It is also obvious that the self is not the same as what we appear to others to be. We have a tendency to wear a front or a veneer and to keep others from knowing how things really are with us. We often attempt to appear more generous, more laudable, or more likable than the facts warrant. What we are and what we appear to be may be quite different.

Here, for example, is an individual who appears to be the very essence of security and self-possession. Apparently he is never at a loss in any situation that arises, and he shows self-confidence at every turn. The interesting point about him is that inwardly he may be a very insecure person. The apparent security in which he clothes himself is simply a front to cover up a feeling of insecurity.

It is not hard to find others who illustrate this point. Here is a blustering individual who apparently is very courageous, who never seems to fear anything that comes along. When we get to know him well, we may find that his real feelings are just the contrary. Or here is a person who appears to feel very superior to others. He appears to look down upon them, to feel that they do not count for much, and to act as though he alone is of real importance. A clearer

EMOTIONAL ADJUSTMENT AND THE PERCEPTION OF THE SELF

The question investigated in this study * was, "Will a well-adjusted child accept as true a larger number of derogatory statements about himself than will a poorly adjusted one?"

The research employed two instruments. One was the California Test of Personality, a paper-and-pencil questionnaire designed to measure the degree of adjustment or maladjustment. The other was a list of 20 statements judged to be true of most children but not at all complimentary. Three examples were "I sometimes say bad words or swear," "I sometimes am lazy and won't do my work," and "I sometimes talk back to my mother."

The subjects of the investigation were 180 sixth-grade children from consolidated rural schools in Pennsylvania. The California Test of Personality was used to break the group up into two subgroups, one consisting of those who scored above the group average in the direction of good adjustment and the other consisting of those scoring below the average. Two weeks later the 20 statements were presented in mimeographed form, and the children were asked to indicate any that were true of them.

The results showed clearly that children who were above average on the personality test accepted (or agreed with) a significantly larger number of threatening statements than did the below-average group. The authors conclude from this that the better-adjusted children are better able to recognize and accept uncomplimentary facts about themselves than are the less well adjusted ones.

One interesting problem discussed by the authors is the value of a paper-and-pencil personality test in measuring maladjustment. That question is taken up later in this book (see Chapter 18).

* Charles Taylor and Arthur W. Combs, "Self-acceptance and Adjustment," *Journal of Consulting Psychology,* 16:89–91, 1954.

look, however, may reveal again exactly the opposite of what we see on the surface. Actually he may be a person who is struggling desperately against overwhelming feelings of inferiority and who has adopted superior attitudes as a "front."

The self may therefore be very different from what the individual appears to others to be. It is the individual as really known to and felt about by himself and not necessarily what others judge him to be, though it certainly includes what *he thinks* others judge him to be.

SELF-REJECTION

All through this discussion we have talked about admiring the self and placing a high value on it. Certainly, a great deal of our time and energy is used in this sort of activity, and nearly everyone engages in it. It would be misleading, however, if we did not also call attention to the fact of *self-rejection*.

Some people do in fact reject the self. They find it anything but lovely or praiseworthy, and they simply refuse to defend it. Self-inflicted punishment, ridicule, and even suicide are possible symptoms—and results—of self-rejection. Obviously, such behavior is unusual or at least relatively infrequent.

It should be noted that much that appears to be self-rejection is really something quite different. Often, when we make uncomplimentary remarks about ourselves, we are looking for reassurance or even a compliment. Thus if we say, "I certainly am stupid this morning" usually we do not want anyone to reply, "Yes, I know that. In fact, I've noticed that you are stupid a good deal of the time." What we really want is for someone to disagree—and thus help us in self-enhancement and self-defense. Nevertheless, to understand people we must recognize that real self-rejection does occur.

DEGREE OF CONSISTENCY OF THE SELF

Thus far we have spoken about the self-picture and the self as though there were only one for each individual. Indeed it would be convenient, though perhaps a little boring, if the self were unvarying, unchanging, and consistent from one time to the other. As a matter of fact, it is very easy to oversimplify our concept of the self and to see it in a degree of consistency that it actually does not have.

It is necessary to recognize, however, that we have different beliefs and feelings about ourselves—and different ways of responding—in many of the various social situations in which we find ourselves. Suppose, for example, that we are dealing with people who are younger than we are, or with people of our own age but of lower social status. Here it is easy to act in a superior manner and to feel ourselves genuinely superior to most other people. On the other hand, we may act in the opposite way and have feelings of considerable inferiority in the presence of persons of superior status. How we feel about ourselves, therefore, is determined in part by our surroundings.

The same may be true of our ethical values and other standards of conduct. When we are with people who believe in

Figure 5.9. What would you guess about this man's feelings of self-regard? While most of us hold ourselves in moderate or high self-esteem, some people feel that they are unworthy and of little or no value. (Photo by Fritz Henle, Monkmeyer Press Photo Service.)

service to others or in equal treatment for all people, regardless of race, religion, or status, it is easy to believe that these are our values, too. But when we are in a self-centered, self-seeking, or prejudiced group we are likely to shift in the direction of their values, and to some extent not only to act as they wish but actually to identify with their values.

Thus, an important point emerges: the self is not always consistent from one situation to the other. In other words, we may view ourselves differently at times from what we do at other times. We may have different ideas and feelings in one situation from what we do in another. We must recognize, then, that the self is not always the same. It is interesting to note, though, that our behavior nearly always appears more consistent to us than it does to people who observe it. This is particularly true if we hold apparently opposing or inconsistent views. To an outsider these views may appear completely inconsistent, but the chances are that we have found some way of rationalizing or reconciling them. The self, then, is not neat, consistent, and logically ordered.

On the other hand, it would be a mistake to carry this point too far. Despite changes with situations and certain inconsistencies, the self is relatively continuous and stable. Indeed, if we know a person well, the chances are that we can make some rather accurate predictions as to how he will behave under many circumstances. Thus there is consistency in behavior and a continuity in the self, even though it is possible to overemphasize these.

SUMMARY

The self is the individual as known to and felt about by the individual. It includes (1) the self-picture, those ideas and feelings which a person has about himself and of which he is aware; and (2) unconscious feelings and attitudes that a person may have about himself.

These ideas and feelings that a person has about himself are usually very valuable to him. When they are attacked or treated lightly he is hurt, whether he shows it outwardly or not. And when they are admired or otherwise enhanced he is well pleased. Indeed, the majority of people spend a great deal of their time defending and enhancing the self, even though there are people who reject the self.

Unconscious aspects of the self are those which we do not perceive, of which we are not aware. The feelings we have about the self vary all the way from those that are fully conscious to those totally unconscious, with many degrees of awareness in between.

There are at least three reasons why we have unconscious feelings about ourselves. In the first place, we have simply failed, or perhaps been unable, to become aware of some of them. In the second place, some facts about us may be so complimentary to us that we find them difficult or impossible to believe. And in the third place, some facts about us are unworthy of our self-picture or are out of keeping with what we want to believe, and so we repress them.

It is possible to make something outside of the self a part of the self. This process occurs through identification or ego-involvement. After we have identified with or become ego-involved in something outside our selves, we may serve and sacrifice for it fully as much as we might for our selves (in the narrow sense of the latter term).

The self is not what we are but only what we think and feel that we are. Likewise, it is not what we appear to others to be but what we appear to ourselves to be. And while it is far from wholly consistent and unitary (since it varies with changing circumstances), on the whole it is fairly dependable.

QUESTIONS

1. Just what is the self? How is it related to the self-picture?

2. What else (other than the self-picture) is included in the self?

3. Is the self an essence or entity such as we were warned against in Chapter 1? Defend your answer.

4. Discuss the importance to the individual of status and status symbols.

5. Are all aspects of the self either conscious or unconscious? Explain.

6. What is meant by (a) defending the self, (b) enhancing the self?

7. How does it happen that there are parts or aspects of the self of which we are not aware?

Why is it often difficult to achieve clear self-understanding?

8. What is meant by (a) ego-involvement, (b) identification?

9. What is psychological hedonism? What are the principal arguments against it?

10. Wherein does the self differ from (a) what we are, (b) what others think we are?

11. What is meant by self-rejection? How often does it occur? Are all instances of apparent self-rejection real or genuine self-rejection? Explain.

12. Is the self always consistent? To what extent is it dependable? Explain.

SUGGESTED READINGS

Hilgard, Ernest R.: "Human Motives and the Concept of the Self," *The American Psychologist*, 1949, 4:374–382.

(The self from the standpoint of an experimental psychologist.)

McClelland, David C.: *Personality*, Sloane, New York, 1951, chap. 14.

(Summary of representative experimental and other scientific investigations of the self.)

Murphy, Gardner: *An Introduction to Psychology*, Harper, 1951, chap. 21.

(A simple, effective presentation of the nature of the self.)

Murphy, Gardner: *Personality: A Biosocial Approach to Origins and Structure*, Harper, New York, 1947, chaps. 20, 21, 22.

(A rather detailed explanation of the meaning of "self"; considerable emphasis on how the self develops.)

Rogers, Carl R.: *Client-centered Therapy*, Houghton Mifflin, Boston, 1951, pp. 136–141, 494–524.

(The role of the self in counseling and psychotherapy.)

Sherif, M., and H. Cantril: *Psychology of Ego-involvements*, Wiley, New York, 1947.

(A thorough discussion of the concept of ego-involvement.)

Stagner, Ross: *Psychology of Personality*, 2d ed., McGraw-Hill, New York, 1948, chap. 9.

(A discussion of the self in motivation and personality development; on pages 170 to 172, a good presentation of its consistency and inconsistency.)

6 DEFENSE AND ENHANCEMENT OF SELF

In the previous chapter we saw how the self grows through identification and ego-involvement, and how the great majority of people are seriously concerned with it, especially when it is threatened. This chapter will explore the self further and describe the person's efforts to enhance the self and to defend it when it is threatened.

Self-defense and Self-enhancement. Most of us can recall some instances of self-defense in our own behavior. Suppose that an acquaintance of ours has just been elected to an office that we thought was going to be ours, one which we wanted very much. Under these conditions, how easy it is to say, "It's all right, but I'd hate to do what he did to get that office!"

Or we see a person who is financially successful while we have not done nearly as well. Again, how easy it is to say, "Money isn't everything, or even the most important thing in the world!" Of course we are implying by that statement that we have at least been successful, perhaps as successful as he has been, even though people may not recognize us as much as they recognize him.

Or here is a football coach who is "building character" this year. His team has lost all its games so far, and character training suddenly takes on a new importance at this institution.

We do not mean to imply that every time we object to someone who has been successful we are being defensive. Sometimes we have reasonable, factual grounds for our objections, but often we are being defensive, and we need to understand that.

Let us take another example. Suppose we have made a serious mistake. We were trying to make a sale or to get a highly rated man to pledge our fraternity; because we did and said exactly the wrong things, we failed completely in our efforts. What do we do under these circumstances? Confronted with the fact of failure, we are likely to say, "Sure, I did it, *but. . . .*" And it is interesting what follows the word "but." It is nearly always some form of self-justification.

It is easy to say of another person, "He is a failure," or even, "He is stupid," but it is very difficult to make such statements about ourselves. About the *worst* we will say is, "I may sometimes appear to be stupid, *but. . . .*" And the implication is, "I am not so stupid!"

Not all our self-oriented efforts, however, are defensive. The other side of the coin is self-enhancement. Sometimes we say, "See, I'm pretty good!" or, "Gee, I'm really good-looking and attractive!" or, "Boy, I won that game all by myself!" Again, these statements may be completely true; on the other hand, we may make them even if we are not very good, or not particularly good-looking, or did no more than our share— and maybe not that much—to win the game. The point is that in our desire to enhance the self we may go considerably beyond the facts, and do so unintentionally and unknowingly.

There is no way to measure how much of our time and energy is expended in defending and enhancing the self, but it must be a great deal. Sometimes, when we try to defend or enhance the self, we know full well what we are doing. At other times we realize after we have done it that we have been defending or enhancing the self. Very frequently, however, we do not understand this process either while it is going on or afterward. Altogether, then, a lot of our time and energy goes into these processes.

WAYS IN WHICH WE DEFEND THE SELF

What are the ways in which we attempt to defend (and sometimes to enhance) the self? This is a hard question to answer definitely, for the relevant facts are complex, and they have been classified in a number of different ways. We have chosen to consider them under four headings: (1) defense by attack, (2) defense by withdrawing, (3) defense by restructuring the world, and (4) defense by restructuring the self. Though the process of restructuring is essentially the same whether it is the world or the self that is restructured, we shall discuss the two methods separately.

By Attack. One of the ways in which we attempt to defend and enhance the self is by aggressive behavior. If there is a block in our path, we can attack it head on and do so again and again. If we eliminate the block or get over or around it, fine. If we do not succeed in dislodging it, at least we may get satisfaction from trying.

We may attack, of course, a little less obviously and directly. Suppose another fraternity has beaten ours in touch football or in securing a larger number of pledges. Even if we cannot beat them in football or cannot outrush them, we can make uncomplimentary remarks about them, or even throw rocks at their fraternity house—and get some satisfaction from these flank attacks.

Or here is a fellow who is smarter than we are. If we are stronger than he, we may be able to dominate and ridicule him. We may actually do so, not because of anything he has done, but because of the humiliation which we suffer as he shows us up in intellectual matters.

Aggressive behavior may be even less obvious. It is easy for us to take out our feelings of aggression on someone who has little or nothing to do with causing them. Thus, a child who has been punished at home may, as a result, show hostile reactions toward his teacher. Or a man who has been reprimanded by his boss may take it out on his wife and children at home. Often there is not so much satisfaction from

Figure 6.1. Three ways of defending the self are attack, withdrawal, and restructuring.

this kind of behavior as there would be from evening the score with the source of the difficulty, but it is partly satisfying.

By Withdrawing. Another way to defend the self is to retreat from the threatening situation. For example, if a boy wants to play football but finds his best efforts so poor as to make any real success unlikely, he can give up this activity completely. Or if a girl wants to make an outstanding record in college but finds that the best she can do is average or below, she can forget about trying to make good grades. Except that it is difficult to leave a goal and forget it completely, especially if we really want it! So we are more likely to retreat into the realm of imagination, where we have more complete control over what happens. We may even take on behavior patterns which we found satisfying in an earlier and happier period. We shall have more to say about this sort of behavior before we finish this chapter.

By Restructuring the World. A third way to defend the self is to remake the world in which we live. Sometimes we actually go to work and bring about some real changes in the world, but this is not what we mean. Rather, in restructuring the world, we change the world *only in our imagination, thinking, and perception of the world.*

In order to explain and develop this point, we had better first introduce a concept that has proved useful in understanding human behavior. The concept is *autism;* [1] it refers to *the influence of motives* —or needs or desires or drives or urges or any other of the so-called affective processes—*on the intellectual processes.* It refers, in other words, to the tendency to see what

[1] This term has been developed by Gardner Murphy, *Personality: A Biosocial Approach to Origins and Structures,* Harper, New York, 1947, chaps. 14 and 15. We have also followed Murphy closely in this account of the main ways in which we defend the self.

Figure 6.2. We all tend *to see what we want or need to see.*

we want to see and to believe what we want to believe.

It should be made clear that autistic response is not deliberate misrepresentation. Autism occurs unconsciously; that is, we are influenced by our needs to believe something even though the facts do not support this belief. We do not realize what has happened; we believe because we *want to believe.* We see the thing that is not there because *we want to see it.* In both cases, we think that we draw our conclusions on the basis of the evidence. Autism, then, is not a deliberate or intentional process.

Let us illustrate. We go to see our team play a baseball game. It is a hotly contested game for the championship of the league. Each time our team gets a rally started, it is wiped out by a close decision by the umpire. Everybody knows that umpires make mistakes, but the strange thing about this game is that *all* the mistakes favor the other team! Our team just "can't get a break" with the umpires. In actual fact, of course, the umpire is not ego-involved with either team and is calling the plays as he sees them. We tend, however, to see in the situation what we need to see. One of our batters may be out by a step or two at first base, but it is easy for us to see him safe by that margin. Or one of their batters may be safe by a step or two

but we can easily see him out by that much or more.

There are many other illustrations of the same point. A labor union looks different to one of its ardent members from what it does to a member of management, especially to an executive who has had trouble with it. And management looks different to a member of management from what it does to a person in a controversy with management. The member of each group, in other words, *tends* to see in that group—and also in opposing groups—what he needs to see or wants to see.

Perhaps one of the best illustrations of our point is to be found in the way in which parents praise their children. It is obvious, of course, to any parent that his children are smarter than the average, and better looking too. The interesting thing is that somewhere there must be some average children and some below-average children, but it just happens that the average and below-average children are not *his* children. They are our children, or the children of someone else. Again our point is that parents *tend* to see in the characteristics and behavior of their children what they need or want to see.

We do not mean to imply that our desire to see or believe something is the only thing that influences what we see or believe. Unquestionably, we sometimes see what we do not want to see and accept conclusions that are most unpleasant. Sometimes the other team does win the game simply by outplaying ours. Sometimes, too, we have to admit that one of our children really is below average in appearance or intelligence. The point is, however, that we *tend* to see and believe what we want to see and believe, especially when our desires are very strong and when the facts are ambiguous enough to permit some differences in interpretation. Indeed, it is amazing at times how much our needs shape our perception of situations!

But let us return to the relation between autism and self-defense. Autism operates in the defense of the self by helping us to see in the self or in the external world whatever we need to see. In fact, there is hardly anything that we cannot believe if we need to believe it badly enough, and one of the factors that gives special force to a belief is the need to hold it or accept it in order to defend or enhance the self.

But what about restructuring the world? What we are here implying is that we remake our conception of the world so that it is more acceptable to us and more in line with our conceptions of—or perhaps our wishes about—ourselves. Here is a man who goes from one job to another, never quite succeeding on any job; yet he is one of the most optimistic persons we have ever met. In his view, right around the corner are a great many prospects, not only for moderate success but for riches. All his life he has felt this way, but hard luck (he tells himself) is always plaguing him. This is an example of restructuring the world. The man sees in the external world what he needs to see, and it is certainly easier for him to live with his failures if he can be-

lieve that these failures are not actually his fault. It is often easier to believe that the world, and not we ourselves, is responsible for our lack of success.

Many of our beliefs about the old home town or our high school or our state fall into the same class. We have all known people who are intensely proud of the town in which they grew up and who really believe it is the finest, most progressive, and prettiest town anywhere, when, in fact, it is not outstanding in any sense. This is a fine example of autistic restructuring, that is, of seeing in the world what we want or need to see when the facts are against us.

We must not leave the impression that all restructuring of the world makes it seem better than it is. Sometimes it does the opposite, making the world seem worse than it is. For example, if a person can believe that other people are untrustworthy or always out for themselves, then it is not so bad if he has these tendencies. Undoubtedly there are people who restructure the world, including the human beings around them, so as to make it less damaging when compared to their own none-too-trustworthy or none-too-admirable selves. Thus, if we

THE TENDENCY TO OVERVALUE OURSELVES

▶ An interesting study that throws light on several aspects of this chapter and the preceding one was done by Torrance.* He asked a group of 1,215 college freshmen to estimate what they would do on entrance examinations just before the examinations were taken and what they thought they had done just after the tests were finished. Each person estimated how he would rank relative to the rest of the group on general scholastic ability, number ability, verbal ability, English usage, spelling, vocabulary, reading speed, and reading comprehension.

An analysis of the results showed that there was little relationship between self-estimates and scores made. For example, 65 per cent of the total group estimated that they were in the top quarter of the class, and 95 per cent put themselves in the top half. Of those who actually were in the lowest quarter, 62 per cent thought they would be in the upper quarter and 92 per cent thought they would be in the upper half. Estimates were more realistic after taking the tests than they were before. Women were more accurate in their evaluations than were men, and also furnished a larger percentage of those who undervalued themselves.

The students were also given an opportunity to offer excuses or rationalizations for their performance. About one-fourth of the group did so. Study of this group revealed that women who rationalize their performance overevaluate themselves definitely more than women who do not. (The results for men were in the same direction but not statistically significant.)

So far as the kinds of rationalizations are concerned, it was found that 90 per cent of those giving headaches as a reason for poor performance overestimated themselves. For nervousness the figure was 75 per cent. Results for other rationalizations were not so clear-cut and definite.

* Paul Torrance, "Rationalizations about Test Performance as a Function of Self-concepts," *Journal of Social Psychology*, 39:211–217, 1954.

can see the world as not too good and if we are not too good ourselves, then we are better by comparison. Thus we are saved from embarrassment.

To sum up, we have said that one way of defending the self is to remake the world and the people in it. If we can remake the world into a more satisfying form from our point of view, we may have gone a long way toward defending or enhancing the self.

By Restructuring the Self. We have earlier called attention to the fact that we sometimes make ourselves appear to ourselves to be smarter, more open-minded, or better looking than we actually are. We often give ourselves desirable characteristics which we really do not have. As has already been indicated, we may be completely deceived by this reevaluation of ourselves. We believe it, however, not because the evidence supports it, but because we want or need to believe it. Having accepted it, we feel that we are in better position to defend the self and also to enhance it.

We have seen some of the ways in which we attempt to defend and enhance the self. Others might be added to this list, or the same list might be classified differently. As a matter of fact, in the section to follow, we shall discuss these same processes from a different point of view.

We have been discussing the defense and enhancement of the self in rather general terms. In speaking of defense by attack, by withdrawing, and by autistic restructuring, we have necessarily grouped together many different reactions which, in a finer analysis, can be distinguished from each other. In this section we shall examine these various reactions in more detail.

The specific reactions that may be used to defend the self against threats of various kinds have been called *defense mechanisms.* The term "defense mechanisms," as well as a description of such mechanisms, was supplied by Sigmund Freud in the course of his practice of psychoanalysis with mentally disturbed patients. Since psychoanalytic ideas have been widely popularized in recent years, most people are familiar with some of the defense mechanisms. Many people, however, do not know them all and have not had them clearly explained.

From the descriptions of the defense mechanisms below, it is clear that many of them could be classified under one of the four general headings of the last section. On the other hand, some defense mechanisms might fit under two or more of these headings. Hence there is no simple means of relating the two ways of classifying defenses of the self, and it is better to consider the defense mechanisms as a different, more specific scheme for understanding human habits of self-defense.

But first, let us be more specific about the nature of these reactions. By the term "defense mechanism" or "mechanism of self-defense" we mean a habit which a person develops for defending and at times enhancing his regard for himself. Defense mechanisms have at least two general characteristics. First, they are called mechanisms of self-defense simply because they defend the self. The self (or self-picture) is threatened, not necessarily with annihilation but at least with serious injury. It is

about to be made to appear less admirable, less worthy, or less successful than we want it to be. The mechanisms of self-defense are used to bolster the self in this sort of situation. It goes without saying that this process may also work in a positive direction. We may wish to see the self as more admirable, more worthy, or more successful than it is, and thus we may call upon the defense mechanisms in order to *enhance* the self.

In the second place, the defense mechanisms are unconscious or at least partly so; they are not used deliberately. While we are using a defense mechanism, we do not understand it or its purpose. We may or may not become aware of it later. Indeed, we usually deny the purpose for which it was used, if we are confronted with it. Incidentally, the nearer the purpose comes to being obvious to an outsider, the more we may struggle to deny it! Thus, the mechanisms of self-defense become one of our best illustrations of autism and autistic reaction.

Rationalization. We sometimes say that *rationalization* means giving acceptable reasons instead of the real ones or making excuses, which we accept as true, for our actions or beliefs. When we emphasize the defensive nature of the mechanism, however, we prefer to say that rationalization is unconsciously false self-justification.

About the only part of this definition likely to cause any difficulty, so far as understanding it is concerned, is "unconsciously false." It is particularly important to notice that "unconsciously" modifies "false" and not "justification." Rationalization is *not* unconscious self-justification. It is self-justification in which the person is unaware (or unconscious) of the fact that he is using false reasoning (or false reasons) to defend or enhance the self. Let us consider some examples of rationalization.

Suppose a girl comes to college intent on pledging a certain sorority. When she gets to college, she is not rushed by that sorority and gets no bid to join it. It is interesting to note how the girl's attitude toward that sorority changes as time passes. By the end of the first year she may convince herself that it was a fine thing she did not pledge that sorority. By the end of the second year she may come to believe that she never seriously wanted to pledge it at all. It is not impossible that before the end of her college career she may have come to the conclusion that, of all the sororities on the campus, this is the worst and that no one in her right mind would consider joining it.

Some people do not react this way. Nor do all people who decide a certain sorority is not worth joining come to their conclusion as a means of defending themselves. In some cases the conclusions may be justified by the facts, but often they are not.

If this girl had been pledged and later initiated by the sorority in question she probably would have become an enthusiastic member. But it is difficult to say, "I am not attractive enough, I do not have the personality that is required." It is much easier to say, "I didn't want to pledge anyway, and besides, that sorority is not worth joining." Clearly, this is defensive.

Everyday language has a word for such an attitude as this. It is often called *sour grapes*. This term comes from the story about the fox who tried for a long time to get a particularly attractive bunch of grapes hanging just out of reach and who, finding that he could not get the grapes, turned away with the remark, "Well, I didn't want the grapes anyway, because they are sour."

There is also a *sweet-lemon* mechanism, which may not be quite so familiar. In the "sweet-lemon" response a person has to accept something that he really does not want; or perhaps he gets what he has worked hard to get, only to find it less pleasant than he had expected it to be. However, because he is ego-involved and cannot admit to himself, "I am wrong, I

Figure 6.3. When a person rationalizes about a mistake in judgment, he is more concerned with defending his own good opinion of himself than with convincing others that he is right.

made a mistake," he may contend to his dying day that the lemon was sweet.

It should be stressed here that when we rationalize we are *primarily* concerned with keeping our own good opinion of ourselves, or with not allowing this opinion to be damaged any more than is necessary. In other words, we are not so concerned with convincing other people as we are with convincing ourselves. Of course, it helps if others are convinced too, because if others do not believe the story it is harder for us to believe it. Rationalization, however, is directed primarily toward the rationalizer. We are trying to justify ourselves in our own eyes.

Projection. Another defense mechanism is known as *projection*. Projection, used defensively, is a habit of *attributing our own unworthy impulses or motives to other people.* We see in other people the undesirable traits or tendencies or feelings that we actually have ourselves. "People are not to be trusted," "Every man is a wolf in sheep's clothing," "Every man has his price"—these often represent attempts to disguise our own questionable motives by projecting them to other people.

It should be noted that projection is sometimes used to cover up traits that we do not actually have but are tempted to have. We may not actually be selfish or untrustworthy, but if we project these traits to others we probably have inclinations to be. When we fear that we may be the kind of person we cannot admire, there is considerable comfort in believing that most other people are that kind.

It should be noted in passing that projection is not always defensive; sometimes we project onto the world and the people in it our admirable motives and our pleasant feelings. "God's in his heaven, and all's right with the world" represents projection but not *projection used defensively*—not if the statement represents how we really feel, both consciously and unconsciously.

Regression. In defending the self, we may revert to an earlier or happier period in our lives and adopt the behavior patterns, including the patterns of thinking and feeling, of this earlier period. Here is an illustration: A child of eighteen months acquires a new baby brother or sister. Perhaps by this age the older child has well-established habits of toilet training, has learned to keep his crying under reasonable control, and feeds himself fairly well. It is not at all unlikely, however, that with the coming of the new youngster the older one will show a great deal of *regression*. He may forget his habits of toilet training, he may cry and have temper tantrums, and he may insist on being fed by his parents as completely as he was six or twelve months before. It is easy to see how this sort of reaction is defensive. The new baby

represents a threat to the security and affection of the older child, and the regressive behavior is an attempt to regain his own previously secure position and the affection he has lost.

Incidentally, this is a fine illustration of the unconscious nature of defensive behavior. We know that a child of eighteen months does not adopt this behavior as a result of conscious planning. Even if he had a sufficiently large vocabulary he could not tell us exactly how his reactions have changed or why they changed. He adopts the behavior, nevertheless, and it is defensive even if he is in the dark as to what has happened and why.

Other instances of regressive behavior are to be found in old people. A certain amount of childish behavior in old people

Figure 6.4. The child who "throws" a temper tantrum is often defending the self in a threatening situation by withdrawing to a behavior pattern that was effective in an earlier period. (Courtesy of Giorgina Reid.)

is due to physical deterioration, limiting what they can do and reducing their ability to reason and remember. Some of the childishness of old age, however, is regressive; the individual retreats to an earlier, happier period and lives partly in the realm of fantasy. The older person too may be completely unaware both of the behavior and of the reasons for it.

It must not be overlooked that people other than infants and the aged also regress. Every one of us understands the appeal, "Make me a child again, just for tonight!" There is something attractive about the day when we had few problems and worries and when there was someone to look after us. Regardless of our age or education, we sometimes succumb to that temptation.

Compensation. From time to time we all face situations in which, because of some weakness or limitation in ourselves, we cannot get what we dearly want. Thus, we may want to excel in scholarship, athletics, or social acceptance and yet find ourselves unable to do so. At times the frustration may seriously disturb us, while at other times it may be of small concern, the difference being primarily in the extent to which the desired but unattainable goal is an important part of the self.

Under these circumstances we often make a direct attack upon the cause of the thwarting. If we want to make better grades, we may study harder and work longer at our assignments and suggested readings. If we want to make the basketball team, we may train better, practice longer, and spend more time in studying the game. And if we want to be more popular, we may examine our techniques for getting along with others and try to find ways to become more friendly and more worthy of respect.

Clearly, these are often very healthy reactions and should not be considered defensive. Sometimes, though, our best efforts along any or all of these lines do not succeed. Try as we may, we still make poor grades, do poorly in basketball, or fail to achieve popularity. Sometimes, in other words, merely working hard at the job accomplishes nothing except to increase our feelings of anxiety and tension.

It is here that *compensation* is likely to occur. If our best efforts to overcome the handicap end in failure, we are likely to look around for some other reasonably satisfying goal and to adopt it instead of what we would really like to have. Thus, basketball may be a compensation for scholarship (or the reverse), or either might be used to take the place of popularity. Obviously, popularity can also be a second best.

There is nothing wrong in itself with this compensatory activity. The problem lies in the fact that so often it really is a *second best,* actually and psychologically. In other words, no matter how much we work at our new tasks and no matter how successful we become in them, there is the danger that we shall always feel, unconsciously if not consciously, that the new achievements are not really satisfying.

The term "compensation" is used to describe such a situation as this. We have adopted our second choice and have worked hard at developing it, but in spite of our successes the accomplishments are not basically satisfying so far as our own self-respect is concerned. (Of course, activity that is originally compensatory may through long practice and repeated success become satisfying in itself and thus lose its compensatory character.)

The fact is that the second best may be overplayed and overdeveloped until it becomes obvious to everyone (except the person himself) that it is a compensation. Thus we may have chosen some activity that is not widely engaged in or admired, perhaps not even socially approved, and have carried it to such extreme that we become obnoxious with it. For example, a boy who is weak and effeminate while young may grow up to become a criminal who desires publicity or a dictator who tries to conquer the world. These are cases of *overcompensation*.

One may, of course, overcompensate in less spectacular ways and in activities generally approved. Thus a girl who wants to be a campus beauty but is much too homely may develop such an interest in scholarly pursuits, and so thoroughly condemn beauty contests and social events generally, that all her friends realize she is compensating—and overcompensating—for her own inadequacies. A young man may develop such an interest in sports and so much contempt for intellectual activities that his fellow students suspect the same of him.

It is important to realize that not all instances—not even *most* instances—of real or intense interest in activity represent compensation in any form. A great interest in a certain activity may have developed in normal ways that are discussed elsewhere in this book (see Chapters 3 and 12 especially). This activity may be a natural first choice, and yet the interest may be just as intense as it could ever be if it arose from compensation. Nevertheless, some of our important interests and values represent second-best choices and are compensatory in character.

Another term often used in this connection is *sublimation*. Sigmund Freud, who was mentioned earlier, made much use of the term. As Freud employed it, the term referred to a situation in which we take the energy of an antisocial or disapproved urge and redirect it into socially approved channels. Thus the energy of the sex urge may be sublimated into vigorous athletic competition or even into welfare work, to mention two possibilities.

Reaction Formation. Somewhat like overcompensation is a mechanism which we call *reaction formation*. In reaction formation, we show—and, at the conscious level, think we have—tendencies or feelings toward another person or object that are exactly the opposite of what we unconsciously feel. Suppose a mother unconsciously hates one of her children, wishing that she did not have this child and the burdens that he imposes. Under such circumstances, the mother may make a greater display of love and affection and may even consciously believe that she has greater love and affection for this child than does the ordinary parent. The hatred of the child is thus overcome, at least at the conscious level, and the opposite tendency developed. This is reaction formation.

Repression. Repression is another defense mechanism. By *repression* we mean a forcible "putting out of mind." When we use it we are attempting to forget, and we succeed. Indeed, this process is sometimes referred to as "active forgetting." It is interesting, incidentally, that in repression, feelings of guilt are usually connected with the forgotten event or habit. It is also interesting that, even though the event may be forgotten and the memories repressed, the effects linger on.

For instance, a young woman had a fear of running water. She reacted normally to water in a basin or a container, but to hear water drawn or to see it running in a stream terrified her. Investigation revealed that when this young woman was a small girl she had been forbidden by her mother to go near a stream close to her house. One day she disobeyed her mother and fell into the stream. She was helped back into the house by a visitor and found some dry clothes, so her mother never knew about the disobedience. For days, however, the little girl lived in terror lest her mother should learn of it. Time passed and the incident seemed to have been forgotten, but it had merely been repressed. Though the memories faded, the effects continued, and the *phobia* (or abnormal fear) of running water appeared. This phobia seems to have arisen directly from this earlier experience. Thus, in repression experiences are forcibly put out of mind, but their effects may live on.

Fantasy. Another mechanism we all use

Figure 6.5. One defense mechanism we all use from time to time is the daydream. In the "conquering hero" type, we temporarily make up for real-life deficiencies by constructing victories in the realm of the imagination.

from time to time is to retreat into the realm of imagination. The daydream, of course, is a good example of this mechanism, and perhaps the best example of daydreams is the so-called "conquering hero" daydream. Suppose a boy has been very unsuccessful in playing baseball. He dreams of being a major-league star, but the prospects of his ever playing baseball with distinction are remote indeed. There is, however, nothing to keep him from imagining that he is at bat in the world series. It is the last half of the ninth inning, the series is tied at three games each, and the home team is three runs behind, with two men out and three on base. Of course he hits a home run and thus wins the world series. He obviously enjoys the daydream immensely, and for the moment he forgets his deficiencies as a baseball player.

A similar mechanism is called the "suffering hero" daydream. Here the situation is reversed; the child—or adult—imagines that he has been mistreated and goes away to a distant country. Misfortune overtakes him, and he is brought home seriously ill or even dead. As he imagines the weeping and sorrow of those who mistreated him before he went away, he has the satisfaction of feeling that they are sorry for what

they did. The daydream serves as a defense because it helps him forget his present limitations and makes him feel that things are not so bad as they appear.

Identification. The term *identification* was introduced in the preceding chapter to refer to our making a person or object outside ourselves a part of the self. Used as a defense mechanism, identification not only makes the other person a part of the self but permits us *to live our life and gain our satisfactions through the experiences of the other person.* In other words, the accomplishments and satisfactions of the person with whom we identify become a substitute for our own.

A familiar example of identification is the mother who was unhappy during her girlhood and who identifies with her daughter. She tries to shape her daughter's life to follow the patterns which the mother wishes hers had followed. She thinks for her child and is extremely interested in all that the child is doing; she gets her satisfaction through the accomplishments of the child. Another case in point was the many poor, weak Germans who hitherto had amounted to nothing but who identified with Hitler and gloried in his triumphs. Perhaps every well-known leader, especially every authoritarian one, intentionally or unintentionally encourages this mechanism.

It is interesting to note that it is the weak and not the strong who typically use the method of identification. Hence, used in this sense, identification is primarily a defensive process.

Introjection. We all have to get along with the world in which we live and to observe standards imposed upon our conduct. People insist that we behave in certain ways and that we not behave in others. Sometimes these standards become rather difficult to meet and unpleasant to follow. If we go through life regarding these standards as imposed upon us from outside, we may be resentful and unhappy. There is one way, however, for us to come to grips with these standards and make a better adjust-

ment to them (or at least a more comfortable one), and that is to impose them upon ourselves. We *introject* them, as we say, making them our own. We are then able to give orders to ourselves.

Here is a little girl about two years of age. Her mother and father are trying to convince her that a new coffee table is out of bounds for her and that the ash trays on the table should be left alone. Every time she goes near the table, her parents say, "Don't . . . , don't. . . ." After a few days, whenever the little girl starts toward the table, and while she is four or five steps away, she starts saying to herself, "Don't, don't, don't!" Actually, her saying this makes no difference. She goes right on to the table and picks up the ash trays, but this is an interesting process, for she is tell-

RELATION OF FANTASY AGGRESSION AND OVERT AGGRESSION

Aggressive behavior may be an open and direct attack on a person or other object, or it may be simply aggressive thoughts and feelings about others. One question in this research * was the extent to which these two go together. That is, do people with a relatively large amount of fantasy aggression tend to engage in more acts of actual aggression? Another question was the effect of fear of punishment on the overt expression of aggression.

The subjects were 29 boys from the lower social class. (For an introduction to the social classes, see Chapter 8.) Their feelings of aggression were ascertained through the use of the Thematic Apperception Test, a projective device discussed in Chapter 18. Their actual or overt aggression was checked by six observers who lived with the boys for two weeks. Careful definitions of aggressive fantasies and aggressive acts were worked out, for both the test administrators and the observers.

The results indicate that, for lower-class adolescent and preadolescent boys in this particular setting, (1) there is a decided and positive relationship between the amount of aggressive thoughts and feelings and the actual acts of aggression, and (2) there is the expected tendency among such boys for a fear of punishment to restrain the expression of overt aggression.

The authors feel that it would be a mistake to hold that these conclusions necessarily apply to people of other age groups. They also caution against the assumption that they necessarily apply to middle-class and upper-class boys, since attitudes toward aggression are probably different among the various social classes (see Chapter 8).

* Paul H. Mussen and H. Kelly Naylor, "The Relationship between Overt and Fantasy Aggression," *Journal of Abnormal and Social Psychology*, 49:235–240, 1954.

RELATION OF ATTITUDES TOWARD OTHERS AND TOWARD OURSELVES

▶ As an example of the kind of research that is conducted in the area of projection, identification, and the like let us cite a recent investigation by Omwake.* She administered to 113 women college students three personality inventories, each containing items relating to (1) acceptance of the self and (2) acceptance of others. These were administered under circumstances which made it easy for the woman to answer as she really felt, since names were not put on the inventories.

Since there were three different inventories, each measuring two different attitudes, it was possible to determine how consistently the attitudes were measured and also to what extent the two attitudes were related to each other. Acceptance of self was measured quite consistently, the coefficients of correlation (explained in Chapter 16) being from .49 to .73. Acceptance of others was measured less consistently, the coefficients of correlation being .13 to .60. The relationship between acceptance of self and of others was positive, though moderate, and at the same time too high to be accounted for by chance, the coefficients of correlation being from .18 to .41.

The author concludes that there is a definite relationship between the way in which we perceive ourselves and the way in which we perceive others. Those of us who accept ourselves tend to accept others, and the reverse is also true. Thus we tend to see others in somewhat the same way in which we perceive ourselves.

* Katharine T. Omwake, "The Relation between Acceptance of Self and Acceptance of Others Shown by Three Personality Inventories," *Journal of Consulting Psychology*, 18: 443–446, 1954.

ing herself what her parents have been telling her. A week or two later, this little girl is saying "Don't, don't" and actually stopping before she reaches the table itself. Apparently, though she still finds the ash trays most attractive, she has found the prohibitions of her mother and father even more difficult to bear. She has finally succeeded in introjecting this standard and thus imposing it upon herself.

It may be difficult to see how this is defensive. It is defensive because it avoids the tension and the loss of self-respect that come from being "ordered around." It is defensive in the sense that it lets us impose our standards on ourselves. If we have to follow these standards, we might as well make them our own.

It would, of course, be a serious mistake to suppose that all our moral and ethical standards are achieved in this fashion. Un-

doubtedly, some develop through the process of introjection, but others emerge from an intelligent understanding of a situation. Such ethical insights represent some of the highest achievements of human beings. Introjection, however, is one way of acquiring ethical and moral standards, though it is certainly not the only way.

Introjection can also be seen in regard to the attitudes toward us that we find others holding. It is hard to believe ourselves admirable, superior, or even good, if all around us people believe the opposite. We are likely to discover—and introject—some of their feelings toward us. Perhaps one reason why immigrants often feel inferior to the native-born is that they have introjected some contemporary beliefs about them!

Displaced Aggression. Another mechanism for self-defense is to be found in *dis-*

placed aggression. Displaced aggression means *aggressive behavior directed against some object other than the one actually causing the feelings.* A little girl, for example, is spanked by her mother. Perhaps she would like to spank her mother, but since under most circumstances that is impractical, she may simply go to her room and spank her doll. The doll is the object of displaced aggression.

Or a certain man is continually bossed and ordered around at the office. He has to do what he is told and is in fear of losing his job if he makes a mistake. One of the things he may do, though, is take out his feelings on his wife and children when he gets home. Of course, the mechanism could work the other way; he might have very little freedom at home and take out his resentment on his subordinates on the job.

A fine example of displaced aggression is to be found in the process of *scapegoating.* A scapegoat, of course, is something that is blamed for trouble for which it actually has no responsibility. For example, Hitler made the Jews into scapegoats in Germany. He must have known that the charges he made against the Jews were false. But the Germans, who were frustrated by defeat in World War I and by its aftermath, including the economic depression, found it convenient to take out their feelings on the Jews, often being completely unaware of the underlying mechanism.

Displaced aggression is common in everyday affairs. It is a defense that lets us release our pent-up feelings on people or objects that are close at hand and cannot retaliate. Taking out our aggression on someone makes it easier to live with ourselves and our emotions. Incidentally, such behavior is often supported by an elaborate system of rationalization.

Dissociation. One example of *dissociation* is having two or more inconsistent phases of personality at one and the same time and never letting them get together.

Here, for example, is a man who claims he believes in the Declaration of Independence and asserts that "all men are created equal." In the next breath, however, he maintains that the members of a minority group must stay in their places and not get ideas of equality into their heads. Here is another who says that service to others is the only really worthwhile goal in life and everyone should be committed to that goal. At the same time his business philosophy is "Get your competitor before he gets you." Both these men, provided they do not see their inconsistencies, are using dissociation.

Still another example of dissociation is to be found in a rare phenomenon, *dual personality.* Here a single individual may shift his sense of identity from one personality to another (or from one time to another) and act quite differently in these two personalities or at these different times. The difference may consist only in being carefree and happy in one personality and

Figure 6.6. A public meeting of the Ku Klux Klan draws a crowd. What defense mechanisms might these people be unconsciously employing? How would you explain the Klansman's use of a disguise? (Wide World Photos.)

Figure 6.7. Loss of effective contact with reality is one manifestation of a psychosis. These four cats, drawn by a once famous English painter of cats, were part of an exhibition illustrating some of the ways in which a psychosis may affect the capacity for self-expression in art. The pictures are arranged from left to right in the order in which they were painted, as disintegration of the painter's personality increased. (Wide World Photos.)

serious and sedate in the other, but the personalities are usually quite unlike. The individual apparently expresses in each dissociated state some feelings that he is unable to express in the other or an integrated personality.

SELF-DEFENSE AND MENTAL ILLNESS

Mental illness is a subject of great interest to most people. Many plays and novels have had this as their theme, and news items concerning it are often widely read. In addition many books have been written on the subject.

This interest is easily understood and is on the whole good, for mental illness is one of our pressing social problems and should be widely understood. Unfortunately, however, people sometimes get the impression that the mentally ill are the chief or almost the only concern of psychology, and that is far from the actual situation. This problem needs to be evaluated in the light of the psychology of the normal individual, and that is the way we treat it in this section.

The Nature of Mental Illness. Mental illness is usually divided into two general classes. We may think of these as the major (or more severe) mental illnesses and the minor (or less severe) ones. No one should get the impression, however, that a so-called minor mental illness is of no real importance, for it may be serious and disabling. A major mental illness is usually called a *psychosis*, while a minor one is referred to as a *neurosis* (or *psychoneurosis*). A psychosis is often called *insanity* by the man in the street and usually requires treatment in a mental hospital, whereas a neurosis is often sufficiently mild to be treated successfully without entering a hospital. People with neuroses sometimes work out a fairly good adjustment without any formal treatment at all.

Another way of classifying mental illnesses is to divide them into those that are *functional* and those that are *organic* in origin. In functional illness, no physical basis for the illness can be found, whereas in organic illness something is definitely wrong with one of the organs or systems of the body. Typically, though not always, this is the nervous system.

Functional mental illness is of a special interest to us as we discuss the defense of the self. In such illness, nothing is wrong, so far as we can discover, with the brain or the heart or any other organ of the body. Nevertheless, in many instances, the individual is as disturbed and maladjusted as if there were organic disease. It is interesting to note, incidentally, that, of all psychotics, half or more of the cases are functional rather than organic. The percentage among neurotics is even higher; in fact, some would say that all neuroses are functional.

The present conception of the individual with a functional mental illness is that he is making poor use of good physical equipment, because he is carrying some of the mechanisms of self-defense to an extreme.

The Overuse of Defense Mechanisms. It must be obvious that not all attempts at defending and enhancing the self are successful. Some of them fail, just as any human effort toward a goal may be wide or short of the mark. In the case of defense mechanisms, however, the situation is often more complicated, for defense mechanisms often *fail because they succeed.*

What does such a paradoxical statement mean? It means that the defense mechanism may *reduce tension in the short run only to increase it in the long run.* It may temporarily help a person to forget his troubles or even give him feelings of accomplishment and success. We all know, for example, what happens to people who drink to excess over a long period; they may at times drown their troubles with drink, but instead of solving their problems, they only add to them.

A similar situation may arise in connection with rationalization. A person may convince himself that he is better looking or more generally successful than he really is. Temporarily this may lead to tension reduction. But in the long run, if he *seriously* distorts the facts, either there will be a day of rude awakening to the realities of life, or one rationalization will call for another until the person loses effective contact with

reality. Something like this is apparently what has happened to many psychotics and neurotics, though neurotics may make reasonably satisfactory adjustments to life, often at a cost of considerable extra effort and energy.

Two important precautions: In the first place, we must not oversimplify problems of mental illness. Unquestionably, there is more involved in psychosis than overuse of the defense mechanisms, for there must be some reason for the overuse. Something causes the individual to need to defend himself to an excessive degree, and this cause, along with the defensive behavior itself, must be carefully examined and appraised. In the second place, mental illness

Figure 6.8. Victims of certain types of insanity are often restored to society by use of the electric shock treatment. For the patient shown in this photograph shocks of an average of 600 milliamperes (about the same current drawn by a 75-watt light bulb) lasting two-tenths of a second were applied twice a week for five weeks. Such a shock produces immediate unconsciousness, followed by a convulsion lasting about a minute and a half. Within five minutes the patient emerges from the shock and unconsciousness without remembering either. (Wide World Photos.)

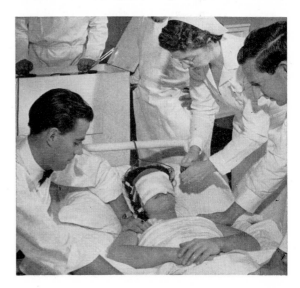

is related to the *overuse* (and not simply to the use as such) of defense mechanisms. If we find ourselves using one or more of the mechanisms of self-defense, in other words, that does not mean that we are developing a psychosis or a neurosis, for everybody engages in such behavior. On the other hand, extensive use of defensive reactions is usually evidence of serious maladjustment.

Some Symptoms of Functional Illness. Let us look first at some of the symptoms of psychoneurosis. One of them is likely to be *a great deal of anxiety.* A psychoneurotic may worry constantly and show it in many of his actions. It goes without saying that we are not talking about normal worries and anxiety but about a degree of anxiety exaggerated beyond anything that the situation actually justifies.

Another symptom that often appears is *dissociation.* This might present a picture of dual personality, mentioned earlier. A more likely possibility is for the person to convert his emotional tensions into physical symptoms. Thus, he may have a functional appendicitis or a functional disturbance in the digestive system or functional heart trouble, when nothing at all is organically wrong. The term *conversion hysteria* is often applied to this kind of dissociation.

A third and not infrequent symptom of psychoneurosis is *compulsive behavior;* the individual performs certain actions without knowing why, and often in spite of his desire not to perform them. In *kleptomania,* for example, a person steals not because he wants the object he takes or for any sort of financial gain. He steals compulsively, without being able to resist the temptation to steal.

A final symptom of psychoneurosis, so far as this discussion goes, is *undue fatigue.* The person may be more irritable and tired than he has reason to be. Such fatigue is neurotic and not the result of hard work.

As we have already said, these symptoms

can be explained at least in part by unwise uses of the mechanisms of self-defense. In an attempt to defend and enhance the self, the person may have fallen upon a tension-reducing mechanism, which he continues to use more and more, in spite of its long-run bad, or even disastrous, effects. Thus, neurosis and the self may be closely related.

Now let us look for a moment at some of the symptoms psychotics often show. One of these is *delusions.* When a person has a *delusion of grandeur,* he thinks of himself as someone much more important than he actually is; in the *delusion of persecution* he feels that a certain individual, people, or perhaps the whole world, is conspiring to harm him. It should be noted that some, but not all, psychotics develop delusions. The same statement can be made about the other symptoms to be discussed.

Another symptom shown by some psychotics is *extreme withdrawal.* The withdrawal in this case is far more complete and extreme than we ordinarily encounter in people. The patient may sit for hours apparently oblivious to any of his surroundings. He may even be so withdrawn that he refuses to eat and may literally starve to death unless fed artificially.

Still another symptom of psychosis is *disorientation,* in which the patient is unable to locate himself in time or space. He may not know who or where he is and may not have any idea of what day, month, or even year it is.

Finally, in this brief treatment we mention extreme *ups and downs in mood,* which occur in certain psychotics. At one moment the patient may be very happy, and a few days (or even a few hours) later he may be in the depths of depression. This cycle of happiness and depression may continue for a long time, sometimes for the remainder of the patient's life.

It is easy to overlook the fact that the use of defense mechanisms is not confined to patients with functional mental illness.

Those suffering from organic psychoses also use them. Thus a person who is psychotic as a result of the prolonged overuse of alcohol still has his problems of self-respect, self-defense, and self-enhancement. He too, in other words, must face questions like, "Who am I?" "What am I?" and "Where am I?" For him to deal with them satisfactorily is often far from easy under the circumstances. Similar remarks could be made about a person who has a severe brain tumor or who has been the victim of lead poisoning. Everyone, including the organically psychotic, must learn to adjust and to live with his feelings and fears concerning his own self-regard. An important aspect of organic mental illness is the effort of the individual to defend and enhance the self.

Thus, the concepts of self-enhancement and self-defense not only help us understand the behavior of many normal people whom we know, but they are also useful in helping us understand the behavior of those less well adjusted.

CONCLUSION

It is important not to overstate the point made in this chapter; not all problems of human beings deal with the self. Not all their difficulties come from attempts at self-defense or self-enhancement. Indeed, as is pointed out in the preceding chapter, some people reject, and hence do not defend, the self. Some others may get along so well that they have little or no need to protect it. Not all problems, therefore, are self problems. However, it is difficult, if not impossible, to understand certain important aspects of human behavior if we are not familiar with the concepts of self, self-defense, self-enhancement, and the defense mechanisms.

SUMMARY

A great deal of our time and energy is spent in defending and enhancing the self. We try to protect ourselves from loss of esteem in our own eyes and to make ourselves admirable and worthy.

There are four general ways in which we attempt to defend (and often to enhance) the self: by attack on the source of frustration, by withdrawing from the situation, by restructuring the world around us, and by restructuring the self. Sometimes these methods take a form that makes them difficult to recognize without careful examination. An important concept here is autism, the tendency of our feelings and emotions to distort our intellectual processes.

We also employ defense mechanisms, devices used at least to some extent unconsciously but nevertheless for the purpose of self-defense. Some of these are rationalization, projection, reaction formation, fantasy, regression, repression, displaced aggression, compensation, introjection, identification, and dissociation. Sublimation may also be added to the list.

Attempts to defend and enhance the self may lead to mental illness. One kind of mental illness is the psychosis, which is severe, and another is the psychoneurosis, which is relatively less severe. A mental illness may also be either organic (having a known physical cause) or functional (related to the overuse of defense reactions).

Among the most common features of mental illness are anxiety, dissociation, compulsion, fatigue, delusion, withdrawal, disorientation, and swings in emotion. At times some of these symptoms appear in normal people; in mental illness they are likely to be present to a much greater degree.

QUESTIONS

1. Just what is meant by defending the self? Wherein does this differ from enhancing the self?

2. How frequently do we engage in self-defense and self-enhancement? How important are such activities?

3. What is meant by "autism"? How is it related to self-defense and self-enhancement?

4. What is the meaning of "defense mechanism"? In what sense is a defense mechanism unconscious?

5. In defense by attack, is it necessary for the thwarted individual actually to attack physically the source of thwarting? Explain.

6. What are some of the forms or kinds of withdrawal that a person may show (e.g., fantasy)?

7. What is the meaning of "autistic restructuring"? Just what is restructured? Explain and give examples.

8. State the meaning and give an example of each of the defense mechanisms discussed in this chapter.

9. What is meant by (*a*) the "sour-grapes" and the "sweet-lemon" reactions, (*b*) the "conquering-hero" and "suffering-hero" responses?

10. What is the relationship between defense mechanisms and mental illness? Is mental illness nothing more than the overuse or improper use of defense mechanisms? Explain.

11. What is the difference (*a*) between a psychosis and a psychoneurosis, (*b*) between a functional and an organic mental illness? How is defensive behavior related to any or all of these?

12. What are some of the frequent symptoms of (*a*) psychosis, (*b*) psychoneurosis?

13. The text makes the point that defense mechanisms may fail because they succeed. Explain what is meant by this statement.

SUGGESTED READINGS

Britt, Steuart Henderson: *Social Psychology of Modern Life,* rev. ed., Rinehart, New York, 1949, pp. 239–251.

    (The defense mechanisms as unconscious factors influencing our relations with others.)

Hall, Calvin S.: *A Primer of Freudian Psychology,* World Publishing, Cleveland, 1954.

    (A detailed examination of the assumptions of Sigmund Freud, including an examination of his conceptions of the mechanisms of self-defense.)

Lehner, George F. J., and Ella Kube: *The Dynamics of Personal Adjustment,* Prentice-Hall, Englewood Cliffs, N. J., 1955.

    (A recent book dealing more extensively with self-defense and attempting to classify the defense mechanisms under some general headings.)

McClelland, David C.: *Personality,* Sloane, New York, 1951, pp. 501–524.

    (An account of the defense mechanisms which stresses their function in reducing anxiety.)

Murphy, Gardner: *An Introduction to Psychology,* Harper, New York, 1951, chaps. 22, 23.

    (A discussion of the defense of the self, and also of self-assertion, closely related to what in this book is called self-enhancement.)

Murphy, Gardner: *Personality: A Biosocial Approach to Origins and Structure,* Harper, New York, 1947, chaps. 22, 23.

    (A critical examination of various ways in which the self is defended and enhanced and of the Freudian account of these processes.)

Shaffer, Laurence Frederic, and Edward Joseph Shoben, Jr.: *The Psychology of Adjustment*, 2d ed., Houghton Mifflin, Boston, 1956.

(A revision of a text that has been popular for a number of years in courses on adjustment, mental health, and similar subjects.)

Stagner, Ross: *Psychology of Personality*, 2d ed., McGraw-Hill, New York, 1948, pp. 120–138.

(The defense mechanisms considered from the point of view of how they are learned.)

White, R. W.: *The Abnormal Personality*, Ronald, New York, 1948.

(An introduction to the nature and the dynamics of mental illness. This book helps us to understand how such illness may be real and disabling even though not organic in nature.)

7 PERSONALITY

In everyday speech, much is said about having "a lot of personality" or "no personality." Let us see what is meant by these expressions. "A lot of personality" usually refers to the attractiveness of the individual, especially on initial contact. It implies a nice appearance, a pleasant manner, and a considerate attitude toward others—the characteristics that make a good first impression. "No personality" is usually used to describe an individual lacking these traits, one who makes no strong impression, appears to be "run of the mill," seems neither vigorous nor vivacious, and is easily forgotten.

Actually these two characterizations leave much to be desired so far as understanding personality is concerned. The first stresses the *positive* aspects of the individual and the second, more or less *indifferent* ones. It must never be forgotten, however, that some personality characteristics are *negative*. Individuals may be domineering, overly aggressive, or otherwise unattractive. Any adequate conception of personality must consider these aspects too.

There are other limitations to this popular approach to personality. One is the importance of qualities other than those that make an individual seem attractive or colorless on first meeting. How we evaluate a person a week or a month later is often more important than our first impressions. Some people, as we all know too well, turn out to be "flashes in the pan"; they start well but wear poorly. Other people do not appear to be much when we first see them, but they grow on us as we know them better. In the long run we may come to respect them as sincere, capable individuals. First impressions indeed are often misleading.

Figure 7.1. If we assume that personality is altogether a matter of superficial attractiveness, there would be no question about which of the two men shown here has the "better personality." In reality, however, many things have to be considered in judging personality.

Another limitation of the popular approach is that it is superficial. It is content with what appears on the surface, with what is easily observed, and does not attempt to get behind this to the underlying causes. Thus, a person may be relatively quiet and even withdrawn, but why he behaves this way is at least as important as what he does. If, for example, he is retiring because he wants other members of the group to take over leadership roles, that is one thing. It is quite another, of course, if he is retiring because he is genuinely afraid of people. This fear in turn would need to be analyzed, for it may have various causes.

Likewise, if a person is outgoing and friendly, that is significant, but it is also important to know why he has these traits. Does he behave this way because he has had pleasant experiences with people in the past and really likes to be with them, or does he only appear to have such an interest in order to gain something at their expense?

The point is that the basic reasons for the individual's reactions are often more important than the impression they create. What appears on the surface may sometimes reflect what lies beneath, but frequently it is misleading.

It is apparent that if we are to understand people thoroughly we need more than this ordinary approach to personality. Superficial characteristics should be noted, of course, but we are interested in much more than that. And so we think of personality in a much broader sense, one that includes not only appearance and attractiveness but also *dynamics,* the mechanisms that lead the individual to behave as he does.

WHAT PERSONALITY IS

Almost any term closely related to human behavior has been defined in different ways. Sometimes these definitions agree in substance and differ only in the ways in which they are expressed. Sometimes they represent differences in point of view. Let us see how personality can be defined to serve us best in our attempt to understand why a person behaves as he does.

History of the Term. The word "personality" probably came from two Latin words, *per* and *sonare.* The term *per sonare* literally means "to sound through." The word *persona* apparently came from these two words and originally meant an actor's mask, through which the sound of his voice was projected. Since traditionally the actors of the period wore these masks in the theater, it is easy to understand why this term *persona* later was used to mean not the mask itself but the false appearance which the mask created. Still later it came to mean the qualities of the character in the drama.

It is interesting that the term *persona* once meant nearly the opposite of what "personality" means at present. Once *persona* meant what the individual was not but only appeared to be, whereas psychologists now use the word "personality" to

Figure 7.2. The persona *or theatrical mask.*

refer to something real and dependable about the individual.[1]

Misconceptions of Personality. Another way to approach a subject or a term is to look at various misconceptions of it. From mistaken views about personality we can come to some conclusions about what it really means. Incidentally, at the end of each of these statements of misconceptions we shall have something positive to say about the subject.

That it is exclusively the product of culture. It is easy to believe that the personality of an individual is exclusively the product of his social environment. As we all know, the people in any one region are often very much alike. Their ethical and moral standards are much the same, and their customary ways of behaving and indeed even their ways of thinking and feeling and evaluating their experiences differ very little. It is not surprising, then, that some people think we learn our personalities from our social groups and indeed that there can be no such thing as personality apart from the group.

In evaluating this view, let us admit that culture has a great deal of influence on personality, so much so that the next chapter of the book deals exclusively with this subject. Undoubtedly, we should be different if we had grown up in a different environment. But there is another side to this story. Even those of us who have grown up in the same culture may differ from each other. Members of the same family, and even brothers or sisters of practically the same age, may also be different from each other. Evidently some factor is operating here besides our culture and background.

It is sometimes argued that no two backgrounds are the same, and hence we should not expect two personalities to be identical. Culture is not the same for everyone, it is contended, and we should therefore expect personalities to differ because of these differences in culture and background. However, as we see in Chapter 8, there is good reason to believe that the differences between people in personality are too great to be accounted for exclusively by the differences in social background. There is more to the matter of difference of personality than simply differences in culture.

And so our conclusion from this section is twofold. In the first place, personality is in part, *but only in part,* a social product, and in the second place, personality is unique, with each person differing from all other people.

That it is determined solely by heredity. The misconception that personality is determined solely by heredity is the other side of the same coin. Persons who argue for the hereditary determination of personality point to the similarity of personality from generation to generation. "Like father, like son" is an expression which we have heard many times—and which, incidentally, contains a great deal of truth.

One interesting example of this belief that personality is largely, if not exclusively, a product of heredity is to be found in a story of about fifty years ago, one which was widely read and quite influential.[2] The story is about a certain family

---

[1] The history of the term "personality" is thoroughly discussed in Gordon W. Allport, *Personality: A Psychological Interpretation,* Holt, New York, 1937, pp. 24–29.

[2] Henry Herbert Goddard, *The Kallikak Family,* Macmillan, New York, 1912.

in the eastern part of the United States that had two branches. These two branches had descended from a common ancestor about 150 years before, and there had been almost 500 descendants in each branch. In one branch of the family there were lawyers, judges, college presidents, and successful businessmen in large numbers; with practically no exceptions, the people were good citizens and fine, respectable people. In the other branch of the family, there were poverty, crime, and feeblemindedness; again, the record was rather uniform.

Now the interesting point is that, while each branch of the family had the same father, the mother of one branch was a normal, intelligent woman, and the mother of the other branch was a feeble-minded woman. The conclusion drawn was that heredity has a tremendous influence in determining the personality of the individual.

This contention is dealt with in Chapter 2 of this book. It is sufficient here to say that nothing is ever exclusively hereditary and nothing is ever exclusively environmental. Each factor is necessary at all times, and each is an important influence on a person. It is therefore imperative that we not overlook the point that was over-looked in this study: that the inferior side of the family also had an inferior environment, while the good side of the family had a good environment. What should have been concluded is not "Look at the bad effects of inferior heredity," but rather "Look at the bad effects of inferior heredity and inferior environment."

So our conclusion is that personality is influenced by heredity but certainly not exclusively determined by it.

That it is determined by physiological factors. All around us we see evidence of how profoundly people are influenced by the systems of the body. We know something of what happens when the brain fails to function properly. Likewise we are aware of some of the effects of heart trouble or difficulties with digestion or with the ductless or endocrine glands.

Now it is easy from evidence of this sort to conclude that personality is solely a function of physiological factors. William James half humorously suggested many years ago that a person's temperament depends primarily on his digestion. A person with good digestion, he said, is an optimist, while one with poor digestion is a pessimist.

It is interesting to notice that those who

Figure 7.3. "Like father, like son." The man on the left is the father of the other man and the grandfather of the boy. How much of this resemblance is due to heredity and how much to environment? (International News Photos.)

deal with the physiological determination of personality usually give special consideration to the endocrine glands. They list these glands, as we do in Chapter 9, and then attempt to show the effects of poor functioning of each of them. The conclusion is often drawn that these glands regulate personality. So strong was this opinion some years ago that a whole book was written in an attempt to show that personality is almost exclusively the product of the endocrine glands.[3] To be sure, this point of view never gained wide acceptance, but it is one that sometimes appeals to people.

Now, what is the evidence on this question? The evidence is definitely against such a view. True, the endocrine glands may, and do, influence personality, sometimes in a profound way, but other things influence personality too. Among them, as we have already said, are the other physiological systems of the body and also the physical environment. In addition, we should have to include the person's feelings of self-respect or self-regard, discussed in Chapters 5 and 6, and the social groups with which he has contact, which are dealt with in Chapters 8, 15, and 19 especially.

So our conclusion is that, although physiological factors influence personality, many other forces, such as culture and the physical environment, are also very important.

That it is the sum of the personality traits. One term that is very popular in the study of personality is "trait." When we speak of a personality trait we mean a dependable way of thinking, feeling, and responding—or, as Stagner has put it,[4] "A generalized tendency to evaluate situations in a predictable manner and to act accordingly."

It is not possible to say just how many personality traits there are, for our generalized tendencies overlap, and lists of them are therefore frequently not the same from one author to another. However, when personality traits are mentioned we think of such aspects of behavior as objectivity, agreeableness, neurotic tendency, dominance-submission, introversion-extroversion, optimism, sociability, self-confidence, and aggressiveness.

One question often raised in the study of personality is whether we can fully understand personality by understanding these traits. Is it true that personality is simply the sum of the personality traits? Obviously, if it is, our task is simplified, for we can then concentrate on a study of traits and pay little attention to other factors in the individual. Unfortunately, however, the trait approach to personality has at least two serious limitations: first, it neglects the fact that the various personality traits (and other aspects of personality) interact to comprise a system or a totality; and second, it leads at best to a fair *description* of personality but does not help much so far as understanding *why* the particular response is made or what the individual will do in the future. Let us look at both of these points in more detail.

It is evident that one personality trait seldom exists in isolation from the others. The presence of one trait may influence all the others, and the system which is personality will differ as a result. It may be good to be optimistic, but an optimistic psychotic is quite different from a successful and optimistic leader of people. Likewise, an aggressive criminal is very different from an aggressive champion of the values of his religion or the American way of life. A trait, then, is seldom meaningful when considered in isolation. It is the whole of which the trait is a part—a whole which is different from the parts which make it up —that is our main concern.

Furthermore, even the traits themselves are often far from simple. Being optimistic or aggressive may itself be a system made

[3] Louis Berman, *The Glands Regulating Personality,* Macmillan, New York, 1921.

[4] Ross Stagner, *Psychology of Personality,* 2d ed., McGraw-Hill, New York, 1948, p. 143.

Figure 7.4. An automobile is not just the sum of its various parts. . . .

It is the parts in certain relationships to each other.

up of more elementary sorts of motives and responses. Thus personality, instead of being the sum of the personality traits, is more than its parts. It is a system of systems, much more complex than the trait approach would lead us to believe.

If it seems strange to say that the whole is more than the sum of its parts, it might be well to mention that this is frequently true in human behavior and in other aspects of life as well. Certainly, an automobile is not simply the sum of the parts which make it up. It is these parts in organized form; it is a system of the parts of which it is made. The same is true of a chemical compound, as distinguished from a mixture. Water, for example, is not simply hydrogen plus oxygen. It is these elements in a certain relationship to each other. And water certainly has properties or characteristics not possessed by either hydrogen or oxygen. We should not be surprised, therefore, to find much the same to be true of personality.

The second limitation of the trait approach is that it is descriptive of what has happened but not useful in prediction of what will happen. Often it is more important to know why a person has neurotic tendencies than it is to know simply that he has them. If we know why certain tendencies exist, it may be quite meaningful so far as estimating his future behavior is concerned. Ultimately, of course, that is our main concern.

We conclude, therefore, that personality is not simply the sum of the personality traits but that it involves these traits, and

perhaps other phases of personality, in an interacting, patterned whole.

That a person actually has a personality. One of the temptations, when we begin to work in a field as complex as that of human personality, is to believe that personality is a real "thing," something that actually exists. Once we get that notion, of course, we are likely to start looking for it and speculating on its nature. We begin to ask questions like "Where is personality?" "How much space does it occupy?" and "What is the ultimate reality of which personality is made?"

As we use the term "personality," however, we do not mean to imply anything of this sort. "Personality" is a term referring to certain aspects of behavior, overt and mental. It helps us understand how and why people react—how and why they think and feel as they do—but personality is not an entity existing alongside the body. It is not something which may be found with a microscope or a telescope or an X-ray machine—or in any extrasensory fashion, either.

And so we are concluding that, in the sense in which we are using the term in this book, we do not *have* a personality. "Personality" is only a term or a concept for certain features of human motivation and behavior. It is necessary for us to realize this and to use the term accordingly.

Meaning of the Term. When we use the term "personality" in this book we refer primarily to the organization of the interrelated traits and other aspects of the be-

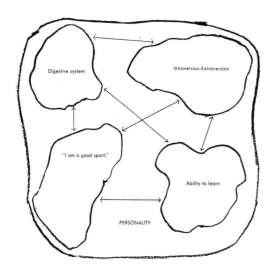

Figure 7.5. Personality is the organization of many traits, aspects, and systems, each having some relationship with the others. What are some of the many things that go to make up personality?

havior of an individual. These traits and aspects are psychophysical; they cause the individual to do as he characteristically does and also set him apart from everyone else as a unique individual. They include his attitudes and beliefs, his values and ideals, his knowledge and skills, the various ways in which his body functions, and the like. We say more about them in the next section of this chapter.

Personality is relatively stable; we do much the same thing each time the same set of circumstances appears. Yet it is constantly changing, for we do not remain the same regardless of our age, station, and achievements. These changes usually occur in at least a fairly predictable fashion. This predictability, of course, is basic to our feeling that we really know a person.

PERSONALITY AND THE SELF

As we discussed the self earlier in this book, it was probably easy to get the im-

pression that the self is the focus of everything important in psychology. We said so much about the self-picture and the self, and about attempts to defend and enhance the self, that it would be easy to come to this conclusion.

Actually this is far from the truth. The self influences our behavior, and to understand the self is to understand a good deal about human behavior. But other parts of personality are also important, and we should point out what some of them are.

The Self as an Aspect of Personality. Self, it will be recalled, was defined as the individual as known to and felt about by the individual. It consists in the self-picture, the conscious aspects of the individual's conception of himself, and also the unconscious beliefs and feelings about oneself. The self, in a word, is the individual's appraisal of and feelings about who, what, and where he is. Personality, on the other hand, includes more than this. It is the dynamic organization of the individual's psychophysical systems which determine his

Figure 7.6. The self is only one aspect of personality. In addition to the four aspects shown here, there are many others.

► **PERSONALITY FACTORS IN FRIENDSHIPS**

What are the factors in personality that lead two people to choose each other as "best friends"? Is this a matter of certain personality traits, or is it a question of the total effect of the interacting forces that constitute personality? This study * is thought of by its authors as a preliminary investigation of these problems.

Thirty-two pairs of women between the ages of fifteen and twenty-five years were the subjects of the study. For each pair each person had chosen the other as her "best friend." Five so-called "personality tests" were given to each person. (The nature of these tests is explained in Chapters 16 and 18.) The tests are designed to measure such things as ascendancy-submission, values, and social adjustment. A control group of "nonfriends" was also used.

The following conclusions were drawn from the results of the study: Friends are more similar in the factors measured than are nonfriends. However, no one area of personality showed more similarity than other areas. The length of time that the friendship had persisted had no effect on the amount of similarity shown by the tests.

The authors of the study interpret their results to show that friendship is not based on the possession (or lack) of certain personality traits as much as it is on the effects of the personality as a whole. They suggest as the principal determinants of friendship the mutual satisfaction of needs and the availability of social contacts.

* Natalie Reader and Horace B. English, "Personality Factors in Adolescent Female Friendships," *Journal of Consulting Psychology*, 11:212–220, 1947.

unique adjustments to his environment.[5] Let us look at several parts of this definition.

First of all, personality is dynamic; this means changing, but changing in an orderly fashion as a result of inner forces, motives, and other needs of the individual. As has been said earlier, it is an *organization of systems*, and not simply an addition of separate parts. It is also psychophysical, that is, both psychical (or mental) and physical and not either of these to the exclusion of the other. And finally, it is unique, there being no two personalities in the world that are exactly alike.

As we look at these two concepts, personality and self, it is easy to see that personality includes the self and also much

[5] This is a slight modification of a definition given by Allport, *op. cit.*, p. 48.

more. Personality includes not only what the individual thinks and feels that he is but also his behavior and tendencies toward certain behavior, whether or not he accepts these as part of himself. The self includes his body as he knows and feels about it, but personality includes his body as it is, regardless of how he—or other people, for that matter—may evaluate it. The self includes his intellectual ability, his achievement, and his motives as he views them, but personality includes these same things as they actually are, again without regard to what he or others judge them to be. The self is thus only one part—even if a very important part—of personality.

Other Aspects of Personality. Personality is complex; it consists of many aspects, and it includes the self but is more than the self. To attempt to list and discuss all the as-

Sir Winston Churchill

Actress Grace Kelly

Artist Salvador Dali

pects of personality would be a long and tedious task. Let us therefore list and comment on a few of them, primarily to emphasize aspects of personality other than the self.

Personality traits. We might start with the personality traits already discussed, our various generalized tendencies to evaluate situations in a certain way and to act in accordance with these evaluations. Obviously these tendencies are a part of personality.

Intelligence. Personality also includes alertness, ability to learn, speed in seeing relationships, ability to make good judgments, and ability to bring together many facts or inferences into a conclusion—characteristics we usually imply by the term "intelligence." This is clearly a part of personality.

Appearance and impression. As has already been pointed out, appearance is another factor in personality. Obviously, there are differences of opinion as to what constitutes pleasing appearance. But since other aspects of personality may also be difficult—or, at times, even impossible—to judge with accuracy, this in no way detracts from the importance of appearance.

Health. Unquestionably our health is a factor in personality. Its importance is so obvious that further comment is probably not necessary.

Figure 7.7. Personalities are often identified with physical things that are external to the self. A cigar, a pair of sunglasses, a moustache— to what extent do these things enhance the personality? Do you think these people feel such things are important parts of their personality? Do you know anyone who is identified in your mind with something that is different or a mannerism that is peculiar? (Courtesy of British Information Services and Wide World Photos.)

▶ A total of 140 sorority girls volunteered to participate in leaderless group discussions and were divided into 20 groups of seven girls each.* In general the girls were strangers to each other. Two trained observers studied each group in action and ranked all seven members. Nine of the girls who were ranked highest and nine of the ones ranked lowest in the groups of seven were selected for a nondirective interview calculated to get at attitudes toward the self and others. (Incidentally, the two observers showed a high degree of consistency in their ranking of the girls.)

An analysis of the results showed that the "leaders" (those ranked highest) produced one and a half times as many "thought units" as the "non-leaders" (those ranked lowest). The "leaders" sized up the situation, gave it meaningful structure, and "took command" early. Furthermore, in the subsequent interviews they made twice as many favorable statements about how they felt about themselves as they did negative ones, whereas "non-leaders" made about the same number of each. "Leaders" also tended to perceive others as having a more positive feeling toward them, and they also perceived the world in a less negative fashion. "Nonleaders" in general expressed more negative feelings, and were more restricted in the subjects they discussed.

This study indicates that in leaderless group discussion the person who has confidence in the self and who sees others as favorable and not as threatening is more likely to emerge as the leader.

* Arnold S. Gebel, "Self Perception and Leaderless Group Discussion Status," *Journal of Social Psychology*, 40:309–318, 1954.

Size, weight, and body build. Size, weight, and body build are closely related to appearance, although two people may be the same in these respects and yet be different in appearance. Any one of the three may be a significant aspect of personality.

Attitudes toward others. Here is still another significant aspect of personality. Some of the attitudes which we have toward others unquestionably represent projections of our own attitudes toward ourselves and may be defensive in nature. We must not suppose, however, that every attitude we have toward another person comes from attempts at self-defense or self-enhancement. Personality includes all our attitudes.

Knowledge. How much we know is a factor of considerable importance in our personality. Knowledge varies in many ways. It may extend all the way from a knowledge of ice hockey to information about nuclear fission. There is no neat way of classifying the various kinds of knowledge, but undoubtedly what we know plays an important role in our vocation, our social acceptability, our recreational interests, etc.

Skills. Another phase of personality which may have a great deal of influence on our reactions is our skill in various sorts of muscular activity. Such skills may include ability in athletics, competence as a craftsman, excellence in driving an automobile or baking a cake, and many others. Obviously, all these may influence how other people feel about us—and, what is often more important, how we feel about ourselves.

Values. In studying personality we cannot afford to overlook our values and ideals. These values may run all the way from a sincere belief that a certain major-league team ought to win the pennant and the world series to the most important conceptions of ethics and religion. Any value, attitude, or belief that we hold may have a far-reaching effect on our personality. A term frequently used in connection with this aspect of personality is *character*. Character can be defined in much the same way as personality, except that it is restricted to matters having to do with right and wrong. Character, in other words, is the aspect of personality having to do with ethics and morals.

Emotional tone and control. We differ from each other in our emotional outlook on life. Some of us are pessimistic, while others are optimistic. Some have a chip on the shoulder, while others find everything rosy. This matter of emotional tone has also been recognized as a special aspect of personality, and the term *temperament* has been used to describe the prevailing emotional tone of the individual. However, we are not always consistent or dependable in the emotions that we feel and show. Some of us are easily upset or show great extremes in emotion, while others are relatively uniform in this regard.

Roles. Later in this book (see Chapter 15) we deal with the fact that each of us has a particular place or position in each of the social groups to which we belong. Along with this position go certain duties and responsibilities. These duties and responsibilities comprise the role that we have in any particular group. Since each of us is a member of several groups, we have a number of different positions and different roles.

It goes without saying that our roles significantly affect our personality. If we are physicians, we act differently from what we would if we were priests. If we have responsibility for recruiting new members for our club, we act differently from

what we would if we were simply members. Illustrations of the significance for personality of the roles that a person occupies are almost limitless.

CLASSIFYING PEOPLE

Everyone is familiar with attempts to classify people into kinds or types. We do this in many of our activities. In business we talk about executives, salesmen, clerks, and so on. In college we sometimes speak of the athletic type, the social type, or the studious type.

The truth is that we continually classify people into types or kinds. No doubt we shall always do that, because we all have a limited number of categories for classifying people, and we try to put each person in one of them. Besides, it is impossible to deal with each individual as entirely separate from others. Each person is unique, as we have said, but in relating ourselves to others we often have to overlook some of these differences.

Theories of Inherited Psychological Types. However, there is a type theory that goes considerably beyond the kind we have just mentioned. From the days of the Greeks and perhaps even before, there have been those who believed that by inheritance people fall into certain types. There really are *kinds* of people, according to this view, and the hope is that if we understand the characteristics of a particular kind of person we can understand and deal effectively with at least most of the people of that particular kind or type.

It is certainly easy to see why such a belief has wide appeal. It would be of the greatest practical significance if we could discover what the true personality types are, what their important characteristics are, and how we should deal with them.

The theory of Jung. Let us look at one set of proposed types of personality in

The subjects of this research * were seventeen male transfer students in the University of Michigan. At the beginning, each man was a stranger to all the others. The men lived in the same house and were assigned roommates on a chance basis. From time to time they were interviewed, and each man filled out questionnaires about himself and the other sixteen men.

One of the chief findings of the study was that there was a strong correlation between a man's report of his liking for the other members of the group and their reports of their liking of him. As a closely related result, it was also found that an even stronger relationship obtained between a man's liking for another person and his estimate of how well the other person liked him.

It was also found that men whose status in the group rose during the period of the study were more accurate in their perception of how well they were liked than were men whose status declined. This result seems to arise primarily from the need of the lower-status men to keep a favorable opinion of themselves in spite of some evidence leading to the opposite conclusion. Furthermore, when the men were asked to describe their "ideal self" and then themselves as they really thought they were, those who described themselves as closest to the "ideal self" were found to be better liked. Moreover, those pairs of men who agreed most closely in describing the other 15 men tended to be attracted more closely toward each other. Finally, men who were attracted toward each other also were similar in their attitudes toward nonperson objects. (An example is scores on a test of values, such as economic, political, religious, etc.)

* Theodore M. Newcomb, "The Prediction of Interpersonal Attraction," *The American Psychologist*, 11:575–586, 1956.

order to see what the types are supposed to be and what characteristics each is supposed to have. Since space is limited we shall let this theory serve as representative of a number of such theories that might be discussed. This theory of personality types, which is fairly generally known, is that of a Swiss psychiatrist named Carl Jung. Jung has proposed that all people, or at least practically all, may be divided into two types, the *extrovert* and the *introvert*. What are the characteristics ascribed to each of these types?

In the extrovert, according to Jung, we have an individual whose decisions and actions are determined primarily by objective relationships and not by subjective values. His attention and interest are centered on the immediate environment, and he may have—indeed, usually does have—difficulty in adjusting to the long-run environment. The extrovert's inner needs and inner life tend to succumb to external necessity. He is an objective, reality-oriented individual, who may, however, go so far in the direction of objectivity as to deny many of his own inner needs and aspirations.

The introvert, on the other hand, is governed primarily by subjective factors or subjective values. What he does tends to be guided by his own ideas, by absolute standards. He tends to lack flexibility and to adjust to his own inner values. Thus the

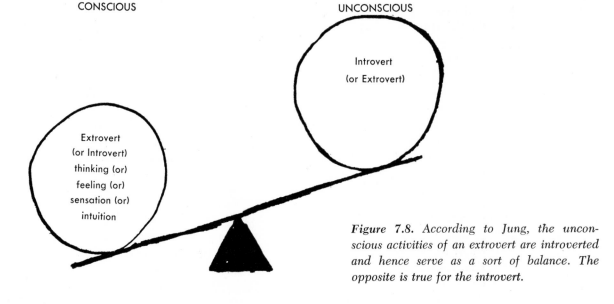

CONSCIOUS   UNCONSCIOUS

Introvert
(or Extrovert)

Extrovert
(or Introvert)
thinking (or)
feeling (or)
sensation (or)
intuition

Figure 7.8. According to Jung, the unconscious activities of an extrovert are introverted and hence serve as a sort of balance. The opposite is true for the introvert.

introvert tends to be subjectively, instead of objectively, oriented. This, of course, is the opposite of the extrovert.

While what we have just said about Jung is true as far as it goes, it oversimplifies his theory. He has also proposed that all of us have four different ways of approaching the universe (or four different "basic functions") and that in each of us one of the four tends to be emphasized or to be predominant.

One of these functions is *thinking*, in which the individual tries to understand the world by reasoning, that is, in terms of facts and logical relationships. Another is the *feeling* function, in which he attempts to understand in terms of the pleasant or unpleasant feelings aroused by his experiences. The third function is *sensation*, in which he deals with perceptions themselves, with things as they are perceived, without interpretation or evaluation. Finally, the *intuition* function, which cannot really be understood without knowing more about Jung's ideas concerning the unconscious, is much like the sensation function except it is based on an "uncon-

scious 'inner perception' of the potentialities in things." [6]

The important point for our purpose is that for Jung, each of us tends to be extroverted or introverted and also to excel in one of these four functions. Thus, there is an extroverted thinking type, an extroverted feeling type, an extroverted sensation type, and an extroverted intuition type. Likewise there are four more types, with the word "introverted" replacing "extroverted" in each of the four.

Jung's theory gives a great deal of weight to the unconscious. It is thought to be very influential in our lives, even to the point of furnishing us with our best understanding of ourselves and the universe. It is also thought to serve as a sort of balance wheel. Thus, if a person is an extrovert in his unconscious, he is introverted in the conscious realm.

Evaluation of belief in inherited types. One difficulty with Jung's theory and with the others which hold that there are a

[6] Jolande Jacobi, *The Psychology of C. G. Jung,* rev. ed., Yale University Press, New Haven, Conn., 1951, p. 15.

certain number of inherited psychological types is the inevitable borderline case. Let us take the introvert-extrovert classification as an example. As we have already said, not everyone is an extrovert or an introvert. Some of us are partly one and partly the other. Actually, borderline cases usually cause us no great difficulty provided there are only a few of them. Thus, there are human beings whose sex is difficult to determine, but unquestionably the great majority of us are clearly either male or female. In the matter of personality, however, the borderline case seems to be the rule rather than the exception. For example, most of us are probably partly introvert and partly extrovert. Indeed, there are so many borderline cases that type theories are open to serious doubt because they account for only a few people and not for the great majority. Any theory which purports to represent *the* types of human personality certainly must take into account the great majority of human beings and be able to deal with them successfully.

The truth is that we seem to vary with regard to most aspects of personality in such fashion that only a few of us are at either extreme of the trait, while most of us are to be found between—often close to halfway between—these extremes (see Chapter 16). There are only a few of us who are very weak, very short, or very thin, and likewise only a few of us who

are very strong, very tall, or very fat. Most of us are in between. All this means that theories holding that there are true psychological types are open to serious question.

Another difficulty with type theories is the very complexity of people. Again we may use Jung's theory to illustrate. Even with all his subtypes, Jung deals with only a few aspects of personality and fails to consider many others. Thus, Jung has nothing to say about a number of the personality aspects discussed earlier in this chapter, in spite of the fact that our list was not intended to be anything like exhaustive. This is a fundamental limitation with practically all theories of psychological types; they are so limited in scope as to be of little usefulness in understanding the whole person.

From what has just been said it follows

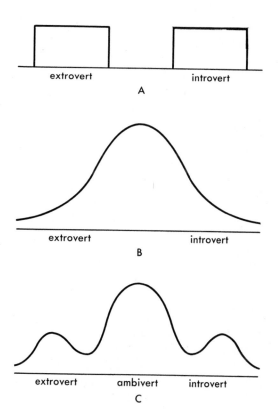

extrovert   introvert

A

extrovert   introvert

B

extrovert   ambivert   introvert

C

Figure 7.9. Jung's theory would be essentially correct if people were distributed as shown in A. Even if they were distributed as in C he might defend his theory, though he would need a third main type, the ambivert. However, if people are actually distributed as in B—and this seems most likely—his theory is not correct. (From R. Stagner, Psychology of Personality, *2d ed., McGraw-Hill, New York, 1948, p. 242. By permission of the publisher.)*

that personality types, like personality traits, have limited predictive value. Types may help us *describe* what a person does; they do not help much in understanding why he does it or what he will do in the future. Thus a belief in inherited psychological types, however attractive it may be, cannot be accepted.

Theories of Relationship between Physique and Temperament. A belief that goes back to Hippocrates is that there is a relationship between the shape and size of a person's body and his emotional and intellectual activities. This view has persisted and has its adherents today. Again we shall examine one theory and let it stand for the others.

The theory of Sheldon. The best-known contemporary theory of this kind is that of Sheldon, who believes that there are three important ways in which people differ in body build and a corresponding three ways in which they differ in prevailing temperament. One sort of person, from the standpoint of body build, he calls an *endomorph.* Such an individual is one in whom the internal organs of the body are well developed; he tends to be rather thick, or even fat, in proportion to his height. A second kind of individual he calls a *mesomorph.* This person is strong, tough, and athletic. He tends to be well built and well proportioned. The third type of individual he calls an *ectomorph.* The ectomorph tends to be long, thin, and poorly developed, and on the whole he is rather weak physically. Those with some knowledge of embryology will realize that Sheldon bases his type theory on tissues present in the embryo.

We have already stated that Sheldon believes that there are also three ways in which one's temperament varies. If a person shows a preponderance of endomorphy Sheldon holds that he will be likely to show a good deal of *viscerotonia.* Such a person seeks comfort, loves fine food and eats too much of it, and is greatly interested in se-curing affection. Corresponding to mesomorphy is *somatotonia.* This sort of person is fond of muscular activity and tends to be aggressive and self-assertive. Finally, corresponding to ectomorphy is *cerebrotonia,* which is characterized by excessive restraint, inhibition, and avoidance of social contacts.

An important point in understanding Sheldon, however, is that he looks upon each of these three aspects of both physique and temperament as components of the personality of each of us. Thus we all possess something of endomorphy, as well as a certain amount of mesomorphy and ectomorphy. In any individual the first of these may predominate and the other two be present only to a limited degree, or the second or the third may predominate and the others exercise little influence. Another possibility is an even balance of all three. As we have just indicated, the same statements can be made for the related temperaments —viscerotonia, somatotonia, and cerebrotonia.

Evaluation of physique-temperament theories. In certain respects Sheldon's theory encounters the difficulties of Jung's. There is, for example, the possibility of oversimplifying personality. Sheldon has dealt with some significant aspects of personality—whether correctly or not we shall consider presently—but many are left untouched. This is not a fatal objection to the physique-temperament theories unless their adherents use these theories as *the* key to understanding human nature. Sheldon has avoided this error, at least in the main.

Since he believes in components which may be present in varying amounts, Sheldon has taken care of the borderline case satisfactorily, but of course, the real difficulty with his theory and the others like it is the serious doubt that exists about the accuracy of the fundamental proposition. Is it true that the shape and other characteristics of the body and the temperament are actually tied together by heredity? Are we actually endomorphs, mesomorphs, or ectomorphs by nature? Or, on the other hand, are we dealing with a theory not proved by the evidence? The latter seems to be the case. Sheldon did examine many individuals, carefully determining body build by measurements and having judges rate them so far as temperament was concerned. He found that physique as measured and temperament as rated were actually correlated to a considerable degree, but to what extent did the predispositions of the judges unconsciously influence their ratings? In other words, did the judges already believe that there were certain connections between physique and temperament, and were they unintentionally influenced by these beliefs? Not enough research has yet been done for this question to be conclusively answered, but the chances are that the relationship is nonexistent, or at least by no means as close as Sheldon believes.

This whole question obviously relates to the topics of heredity and environment discussed in Chapter 2. The conclusion in that chapter is that heredity never operates alone, nor does environment. What we are saying, then, is that any connection between physique and temperament can never be due to heredity alone but always depends on both heredity and environment. This principle certainly has implications for most type theories.

Culture and Differences in Social Groups. We have just seen that the theories of inherited psychological types and inherited components of physique and temperament do not offer much promise for understanding people. There is, however, another possibility: it may very well be that there are different sorts of individuals as a result of different social backgrounds. Society may encourage people in certain occupational, religious, or minority groups, for

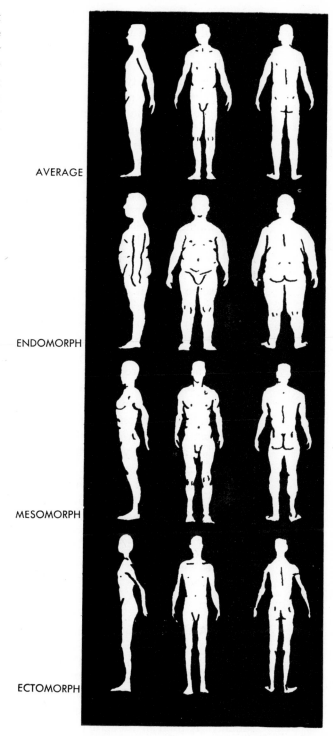

AVERAGE

ENDOMORPH

MESOMORPH

ECTOMORPH

Figure 7.10. Sheldon's conception of the kinds of body build.

example, to develop certain behavior patterns and characteristic ways of thinking and feeling. There may be a medical type, a legal type, and an engineer type; there may be a Protestant type, a Catholic type, and a Jewish type; and there may be a Polish type, a Chinese type, and an American type.[7] It is difficult to say to what extent this "typing" has occurred for various groups, though it has obviously taken place to an appreciable degree in some. Reliable information in this area can be quite useful for understanding and influencing people.

One might even classify people with regard to their attitude toward the self. As has already been said, most people accept the self and attempt to defend and enhance it, but some reject it. Since probably very few people are neutral on this point, there may actually be two types of people with regard to attitude toward the self, those who accept it and those who reject it.[8] Even here we must be careful, for people may reject the self at one time and not at another or in one situation and not in another. However, this hypothesis, like the one mentioned just above, is worthy of further investigation and may yield valuable information.

Thus, we see that there may be social types of personality, types based on the experiences of the individual rather than exclusively on his genes. These types, however, would vary from society to society and even from generation to generation in a single society. That fact does not discount their usefulness, but it certainly does not argue that people are by nature sorted into types.

Present Status of These Theories. The theories that have been proposed for classifying people have served a useful purpose. They have prompted extensive evaluation of people, they have instigated research which otherwise would not have been done, and they have called our attention to significant ways in which people differ from each other. We should have less understanding of personality if such theories had not been proposed.

These theories tend to oversimplify personality, however, and consequently to mislead. Certainly anyone who attempts to hire on the basis of the types of people will frequently be misled, and anyone who attempts to predict or control the actions of people on the same basis will meet with little success.

Finally, there is serious doubt whether types have any hereditary basis. They may exist on what is primarily a social basis, but even that has not been conclusively established.

We shall no doubt continue to classify people into types, because such classifications are useful and convenient, but it is quite another matter to say that there really are true types of people.

[7] Gardner Murphy, *Personality: A Biosocial Approach to Origins and Structure,* Harper, New York, 1947, pp. 752–760.

[8] *Ibid.,* pp. 741–742.

SUMMARY

Personality is often thought of in terms of superficial attractiveness. This limited conception overlooks many important facts about an individual. When the term "personality" is used in modern psychology it refers to a person's tendencies to act or think or feel in a certain way. These tendencies are organized in a dynamic system, which is unique or different for each individual.

Personality is neither mental nor physical but both; it is the result of neither heredity nor environment but of both; it is the product neither of the social environment nor of the body and its functions but of both of these sets of forces—and others—acting together. And it is more than simply the sum of the traits or processes included in it. Personality also includes everything with which we identify.

Personality is distinguished from the self in that it refers to characteristics, motives, and reactions actually possessed or shown by a person, whereas the self represents the individual as he thinks and feels he is. Thus the self is a part or an aspect of personality. There are many other aspects of personality, among them being intelligence, health, knowledge, skills, values, emotional control, social roles, and the personality traits.

There has long been an interest in classifying people, and many type theories have been proposed. One of the more popular is that of Jung, who sees people as either introverts or extroverts, and subdivides both introverts and extroverts into the thinking, feeling, sensation, and intuition subtypes. A related theory is that of Sheldon, who believes he has evidence for a close relationship between the shape and development of the body, on the one hand, and the temperament of the individual, on the other. Sheldon's scheme provides for three components of physique and three closely related components of temperament. Everyone is thought to possess some of each component for both physique and temperament, though one usually predominates over the other two.

Most type theories assume that types depend on heredity. There is actually little evidence for, and much against, this belief. There may, however, be types that are determined primarily by the expectations of social groups or by a person's attitude toward the self.

QUESTIONS

1. What are the chief limitations of using personality to mean the attractiveness of a person?

2. Discuss the history of the term "personality."

3. Just what is personality, as the psychologist uses the term?

4. Evaluate the belief that (a) personality is determined solely by the social environment; (b) personality is exclusively the result of the endocrine glands; (c) personality is simply the sum of its various parts; and (d) personality is an agent or an entity existing alongside the body.

5. In what sense do we have a personality and in what sense do we not have one?

6. What is a personality trait? How many personality traits do we have? What is the relation of personality and personality traits?

7. What is the relation between personality and the self? Are there personality problems that are not self problems? Explain.

8. What are some of the aspects of personality (in addition to the self)?

9. Explain and evaluate the type theory of Jung.

10. Explain and evaluate the theory of Sheldon.

11. Why does psychology look with suspicion on the theory that there are genuine types of personality?

12. Explain and evaluate the belief that (a) there are social types of personality; (b) there are types of people with regard to attitudes toward the self.

SUGGESTED READINGS

Allport, Gordon W.: *Personality: A Psychological Interpretation,* Holt, New York, 1937.

(The pioneer book in the psychology of personality; the source of our definition of personality and of many of the concepts of this book.)

Harsh, Charles M., and H. G. Schrickel: *Personality: Development and Assessment,* Ronald, New York, 1950.

(Special emphasis on how personality develops through the various ages of life; theories on the nature of personality and findings on how personality is accurately evaluated.)

Jacobi, Jolande: *The Psychology of C. G. Jung,* rev. ed., Yale University Press, New Haven, Conn., 1951.

(A discussion of Jung's theories about psychological types and other important phases of his psychology.)

Jung, Carl G.: *Psychological Types,* Harcourt, Brace, New York, 1926.

(Jung's theories concerning types explained and evaluated by the author.)

May, Rollo: *Man's Search for Himself,* Norton, New York, 1953.

(A popularly written, interesting treatment of the problems of man in the present society, with suggestions as to how these problems may be solved.)

McClelland, David C.: *Personality,* Sloane, New York, 1951.

(Another text for psychology of personality; emphasizes theory and research findings.)

Murphy, Gardner: *Personality: A Biosocial Approach to Origins and Structure,* Harper, New York, 1947.

(A thorough treatment of personality and important related topics; difficult to read but rewarding when read carefully; has greatly influenced especially Chapters 5, 6, and 7 of this book.)

Patty, William L., and Louise Snyder Johnson: *Personality and Adjustment,* McGraw-Hill, New York, 1953.

(A discussion of the nature of personality in relation to adjustment; attention to the growth of personality and some social situations directly influencing it, as well as to several of the topics of this chapter.)

Sheldon, W. H., and S. S. Stevens: *The Varieties of Temperament,* Harper, New York, 1942.

(A presentation of Sheldon's theories concerning physique and temperament.)

8 CULTURE AND PERSONALITY

In the previous chapter we touched briefly on the relationship between personality and culture. It was pointed out that while culture influences personality, so do other factors, such as the physical environment and the biology of the individual. These factors, as well as the cultural ones, affect the way in which we contact our surroundings and respond to them.

In this chapter we shall examine the influence of culture more closely. In particular, we shall discuss the nature of culture and how it exerts its effects on the individual. Also there is the question of how differently people behave in different cultures. Finally, we shall examine some of the characteristics of the American personality and the forces that shape it.

WHAT CULTURE IS

When we speak of *culture* we refer to *the principal ways of behaving, the values, and the material possessions of a people.* Ordinarily a large (or at least a distinctive) group is intended when we say a "people" in this sense. Thus, we might speak of an American culture (or more properly, perhaps, of a *Western* culture), but we should hardly speak of California culture or St. Louis culture. For some of the smaller or less distinctive groups we sometimes use the term *subculture.*

Material Possessions. As we have just said, the definition of culture includes the material objects which a people owns and uses. Thus, our various means of transportation, communication, and production are a part of our culture. So also are our homes, our church buildings, our government buildings, our stores and warehouses, our schools,

Figure 8.1. Navajo woman weaving a rug in her hogan. Would your ideas and attitudes in regard to education, recreation, group life, and the world of work be the same as they now are if you lived in such a cultural setting? (Courtesy of the American Museum of Natural History.)

and the like. Of course, if an object is really to be considered a part of a culture, it must be characteristic of that culture or found frequently in it. Thus the hogan (a round earthen house) of the Navajo is found in America, but it is not a part of American culture, though it is, of course, a part of Indian culture or at least of Navajo sub-culture.

The physical objects of a culture are not so important in themselves as are our attitudes toward them. Certain physical objects (for example, an idol) may be of great concern in one culture and have slight or even no value in another. Furthermore, material possessions in the form of wealth or property may have greater significance in one culture than they have in others. Clearly, these objects and attitudes influence the personality of a person who is a member of the cultural group.

Knowledge and Skills. What our associates know (or think they know) also greatly

influences us. In our culture, such knowledge may be rather elementary or extremely complex—from the fact, for example, that water flows downhill to a complicated discovery about nuclear fission. Both these facts and many others have influenced our lives, often profoundly.

Likewise, the skills of a people are a part of their culture. Among such skills, of course, are those that have to do with production and distribution. We should be very different individuals if it were not for these means of producing goods and putting them in the hands of consumers. But of course there are many other skills too, such as those involved in teaching, surgery, making a speech, etc.

It might be pointed out in passing that what a people knows, or thinks it knows, about the nature of the universe and man's place in it may have far-reaching significance for how this same culture evaluates human beings and how human beings are dealt with in that culture.

Language. One of the distinctive characteristics of a culture is its language. Language is important, first, because we use it in order to communicate, and second, because much of our thinking employs language symbols.

A language nearly always reflects the discriminations regarded as important in

Figure 8.2. All societies are greatly influenced by and even dependent on the skills of the workers.

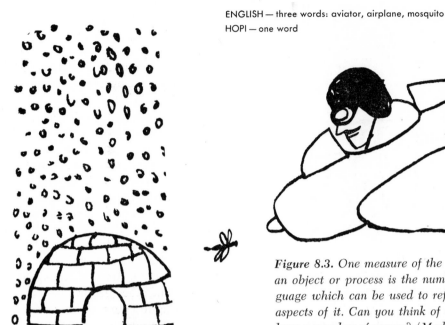

ENGLISH — three words: aviator, airplane, mosquito
HOPI — one word

ENGLISH — one word: snow   ESKIMO — three words

Figure 8.3. One measure of the importance to a people of an object or process is the number of words in their language which can be used to refer to different varieties or aspects of it. Can you think of other things for which we have a number of names? (Modified from S. I. Hayakawa: Language in Action, Harcourt, Brace, New York, 1941. Used by permission.)

a given society because our language represents our way of thinking.[1] The world in which we live can be split up or divided in many ways in our thinking processes, so that we can group and classify as suits our purposes. Our language often reflects the distinctions and groupings which we find useful or even necessary in our thinking. Thus, in an elaborate kinship system, in which food, shelter, property, and obligations of many types are involved, each status and relationship has a distinctive name. Likewise, in a highly elaborate system of commercial credit, such as ours, each type of negotiable instrument has a particular designation. Arabs have many different words for camels, distinguishing different stages of pregnancy, functions, ownership, and the like. And Eskimos, for whom snow is important, have many different names for various conditions of snow and ice.

[1] See B. L. Whorf, "Science and Linguistics," *Technology Review*, 44:229-231, 247-280, 1940.

Our world has a rich symbol system. We learn the shared meanings for its symbols and how to use them in reaching our goals. Through language, other people influence our attitudes, give us useful information, reward and punish us, and provide esthetic experiences. Also important is the fact that our thought processes have to a large extent been molded in the pattern of the language we speak, and this, in turn, profoundly affects the way we interpret our experience.

Institutions. Another important part of a culture is its institutions. Broadly defined, an institution is a patterned way of behaving. For example, the family is an institution that appears in some form in every society. The family may consist of a husband and wife, together with their children who have not reached adulthood, or some-

Figure 8.4. *The framework of institutions within which a person seeks his goals is like a network of roads. Like roads, institutions provide certain routes to goals and also limit movement in certain directions. Culture, of course, is much more complex and changing than our analogy might suggest.*

times it may be an extended kinship system, consisting, for example, of a patriarch together with his various wives and their children and grandchildren. To the people in each society its own family institution seems the only right and proper one. And of course it has a great deal of influence on the experience of the person as he grows up and on the ways in which he is himself permitted or encouraged to behave.

Another institution is the school. A person in a school soon learns that there are students, teachers, and administrators. He also finds that the school (or the people in it or in charge of it) has goals which he must take into account and that many activities center around the school. As an institution the school is part of his environment, shaping his experiences, affecting his goals, and blocking or fostering satisfaction.

There are many other important institutions: churches, banking practices, military organizations, factory systems, and social-class systems. In each of these are certain

more or less standardized ways of behaving. A person usually has to learn these ways of interacting with others, if he is to satisfy his needs.

Mores and Folkways. Also of interest in this connection are the expected or required ways of behaving in the society of which we are a part. Here, for convenience, we usually distinguish between folkways and mores. *Folkways* are *expected or "correct" ways of behaving,* whereas *mores* are *required ways of behaving.* Thus, our folkways are such that we would not wear a sport shirt and slacks to a formal dance or eat peas with a spoon, but our mores require that on a crowded two-lane highway we stay on the right side of the road, and also that we refrain from violating the property rights of other people.

It is interesting to note the differences in punishment that are accorded violations of the folkways and of mores. The infringement of folkways usually leads to some disapproval. If we violate one of them, we shall probably be thought odd, uncouth, or ignorant, and people may let us know about it, but ordinarily they will not put us in jail. The violation of mores, on the other hand, is serious. It practically always evokes strong social disapproval; and breaking the most important mores may be punished by

Figure 8.5. *How many folkways and mores do you see illustrated in this picture? (Courtesy of Ewing Galloway.)*

Figure 8.6. Kamba dances in Kenya. The cultural patterns of a people are both an expression and a cause of personality differences. In any culture, personality is influenced by many conditions—whether children are indulged or deprived, whether man is perceived as good or corrupt, whether authoritarianism or permissiveness exists in the family and the state, etc. These and many other factors affect personality. (Courtesy of British Information Services.)

death in the electric chair. People expect us to follow the folkways; they require us to follow the mores.

It is a mistake to think there is just one set of folkways and one set of mores in our culture. Folkways and mores differ from one group to another, so that different people may grow up under different customs even in the same society. Under these circumstances we should expect—and we usually find—different personalities. One way to tell where one culture stops and another begins is to find out where the folkways and especially the important mores undergo *decided* changes. Thus, folkways and mores are not alike in all parts of our culture, but they have much in common throughout it.

It is also a mistake to look upon the average person as a rebel at heart, dragged along relentlessly by an autocratic, dictatorial society. At times, of course, mores and folkways are imposed on us by the group without our consent and even against our wishes, but typically we impose these customs on ourselves. The mores and folkways, in other words, become a part of the self (see Chapter 5), and generally we follow them—at least in adulthood—because we want to and not because we have to.

Other Values. No short discussion of culture can do justice to its variety and complexity, and so we shall simply say that in addition to the values underlying and growing out of our material possessions, our language, our institutions, our knowledge, and our mores and folkways there are many others. We can mention, for example, those relating to religion and the church, or to the home, or to recreation, or to the state. Our attitudes toward various social groups and our beliefs about what seem to us to be the important social issues are also important.

PERSONALITY AND CULTURE IN OTHER SOCIETIES

One way to appreciate the influence of culture on personality is to look at other societies and the personality patterns that develop in them. Particularly in the years since World War I, social scientists have become interested in and made extensive studies of other peoples and their ways of behaving. These have usually been of small groups of people with a culture quite unlike our own, though there has also been some interest among anthropologists in studies of Western culture and particularly of unusual groups in that culture.

Some Other Societies. Let us examine three of these societies in some detail and then make some general comments about others. A number of years ago, Ruth Benedict,[2] a cultural anthropologist, made a study of the Kwakiutl Indians and also of the Dobuans and the Zuñi. Most of what

[2] Ruth Benedict, *Patterns of Culture*, Houghton Mifflin, Boston, 1934.

we have to report about these peoples comes from her studies and reports.

Kwakiutl society. Like several other Indian tribes in the Pacific Northwest region, the Kwakiutl had a highly differentiated status system. Each clan had a position in a prestige hierarchy, and within each clan each individual had some rank. The whole society, in fact, was intensely rank-conscious. Each person had many symbols of rank, such as his name, the position he could take in ritual affairs, the age and honor of the shield which he took into battle, his position in the battle and the hunt, the prestige of his wife's family, and his worldly possessions.

There were a number of ways in which an individual could change his position in the status hierarchy. He could perform an act of unusual bravery, such as swimming on a dark night in a stream inhabited by an evil spirit. Or he could marry the daughter of a clan having higher rank than his own, providing he could be accepted by such a clan. Possibly he could perform successfully a daring exploit in battle, such as saving the life of a high-ranking person. Or he could resort to the *potlatch*.

The potlatch was an institutionalized device for changing status. A Kwakiutl seeking to enhance his social position invited a rival to a feast. According to Kwakiutl norms, the one invited might decline only if to accept would lower his own prestige. But he was obligated to accept the invitation of any genuine rival. In the host's lodge a very hot fire was built, and the rival was so placed that he would be extremely uncomfortable. In the meantime he was artfully abused and insulted. The high point came when the host began giving the rival large numbers of blankets. The ultimate was for the host to show how rich he was by throwing blankets upon the fire, thus destroying his possessions.

The rival was supposed to be awed by the power and riches of his host, and to be humiliated by his own relative weakness and poverty. Within a reasonable time the rival had to return the potlatch feast on an even grander scale, or else lose face.

Now are these merely strange customs, or is the person really a different personality for having lived in such a culture? It is highly probable that a Kwakiutl perceived his social world as a highly competitive place; that he placed a high value on prestige in this system; that he felt humiliated and guilty if he failed to support others in his clan; and in general that his conception of himself was closely tied to the customs and values of this sort of society. Certainly growing up among the Kwakiutls had a decided influence on personality.

Dobuan society. Another society fostering unusual personality development was that of the Dobu, who lived on an island off eastern New Guinea. Benedict tells us that the Dobuans were a very jealous, resentful, and suspicious people. They saw success as coming from a struggle with an evil world, and hence things which we would consider highly unethical, such as cheating, stealing, and hurting others, were considered entirely legitimate for the good man in that culture. Indeed, to do these things might add considerably to his status so they were done frequently.

Among the Dobu there was also much hostility between husband and wife. In alternate years each lived in the other's village and there was subjected to humiliation and exploitation. Each individual suspected all others of evil intent. He felt that he needed sorcery and magic to protect himself and to attack others.

If Benedict's conclusions about the Dobuan personality are valid, here is another society in which a person's values, his goals, his views about others, and his conception of himself were radically different from what we know in our society. A normal personality in Dobu would be highly abnormal here, and vice versa. Like the typical person in any society, the Dobuan tried to enhance his self-esteem and defend his self-

Anthropologists study many different phases of group life. Since personality formation involves learning, they are especially interested in child-training practices. Anthropologists study these practices in two principal ways: (1) by observing the behavior of members of the society in question, and (2) by interviewing informants, who are members of the society. The following data on child-training practices among the Apache Indians were obtained by interviewing: *

> When a child is mischievous, they call an old man who looks fierce. He is no relative. The old man limps in with a sack or blanket in his hand. He acts angry and shouts, "What's the matter?"
>
> The father and the mother sit there. They say, "This boy won't obey. He is always fighting. You can take him and do what you wish with him. You can cut off his head or sit on him. We don't care. We aren't going to put up with him any longer." The boy begins to cry.
>
> The old man says, "So, you won't obey? I'm going to check you off right now." The boy cries louder.
>
> "Now stop that! Listen to me. Come over to me or I'm going to get you." The child is frightened. He tries to crawl behind his father, his mother, or his grandmother. But they act as if they have given the old man the privilege to do what he wants with the boy, and they push the boy forward. The old man grabs him and struggles with him. He puts him in the sack and says, "Are you going to behave?"
>
> After that the boy is prompt and behaves. If he won't get wood, his mother says, "All right, I'll call the old man." Then he goes for the wood at once. After the old man works on him like this two or three times, he comes to be a good boy.

The Apache employed many other methods in training their children. The foregoing example shows that they were willing to resort to frightening a child in order to get him to conform and that they believed that parents have a right to exercise authority. Eventually almost every boy became a "good boy" according to the norms of Apache society.

* M. E. Opler, *An Apache Life-way*, University of Chicago Press, Chicago, 1941, p. 31.

picture, but for this he chose methods that seem to us strange and inadequate.

Zuñi society. The Zuñi, who are Pueblo Indians of the Southwest, present a contrast with the Kwakiutl and the Dobuans. Here the goal of life was anything but personal domination and power over others. Leadership positions were sincerely avoided, and a man who strove for one was likely to be looked down upon or otherwise punished by the group.

An ideal man among the Zuñi was a person who was friendly and dignified but who did not call attention to himself. Even in contests of skill, if a person really excelled he was soon prevented from competing, for the Zuñi liked contests where the odds were even and no outstanding competitor could dominate the scene.

According to Benedict, the Zuñi were not emotionally expressive. Emotional excess in anything—religion, death, marriage, or personal relations—was distrusted. Mildness in manner was the rule. The contrast with the fierce competitiveness of the Kwakiutl and the harsh hostility of the Dobuans is dramatic. Nowhere is the contrast in personality more striking than in religion. Whereas the Kwakiutl sought spiritual exultation and power through fasting, self-torture, frenzied dancing, and even such acts as eating filth, the Zuñi sought orderliness

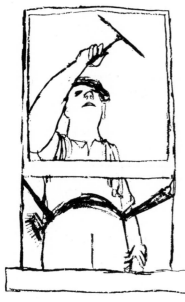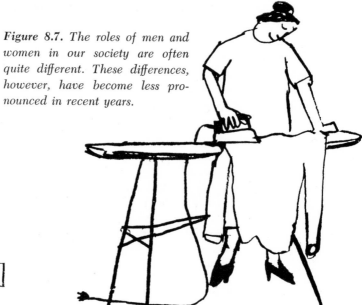

Figure 8.7. The roles of men and women in our society are often quite different. These differences, however, have become less pronounced in recent years.

and stability through elaborate formal dances and prayers. By contrast, the Dobuan used magic and sorcery to please evil spirits and to vent his hostility upon others.

Personality as a Function of Culture. There is a wealth of other material of the kind we have been discussing, but the conclusion in all instances is substantially the same: personality is much influenced by social institutions, language, attitudes, values, and the ideals of a culture. Thus, our personality is in no small degree (*but not exclusively*) a function of the culture in which we grow up, and the anthropologists have given us some appreciation of how profound and extensive these differences may become in various cultures.

THE AMERICAN PERSONALITY

The purpose of this section is to show how growing up and living in America affects our personalities. The fact that we are Americans makes us different persons from

what we should have been if we had grown up in another society.

There are a number of ways in which growing up in America has influenced us. For one thing, it has affected our beliefs and values. It is no accident that many of us believe that a free-enterprise economic system is the best. And like other Americans, we probably feel very strongly that every one of us ought to have as much opportunity as possible to develop his capacities. The fact that we are Americans has also influenced our motives. For example, it has made many of us want to get an education and to work for success in some form distinctively American. Being an American has created problems for us, too. For instance, we must compete with others for prestige and at the same time try to obtain affection from them. In all these ways and more, being an American has had an effect on our personalities.

A Typical Example. In order to see such influences at work, let us look at a particular

American, John Hawes. John lives in Harmon City, a Middle Western town of 15,000 in the midst of a farming region. John, who is now thirty-two years old, has operated a drugstore at the corner of Main and Elm for the past five years. Mary Hawes, whom he married eight years before, while he was still in training as a pharmacist at State College, takes care of the house and their two children, Mike, who is seven, and David, who is four.

Recently John went to visit his mother and father, an experience which always makes him think of his childhood. John's parents are small-town folks, people who own a modest house on the edge of town. John's father has a job as clerk in a feed mill. Often John remembers how he and his older brother had various jobs to do around the house and yard. His mother was regarded as a good housekeeper. She prepared excellent meals, kept the house clean, mended the children's clothes, and saw to it that they learned good manners. John's father believed in the value of thrift and hard work. Although he enjoyed his contacts with his neighbors, he had little sense of affairs beyond his immediate circle. The larger world was something described in the newspapers from Chicago. John remembers his parents' ambition that he "make something" of himself. Through considerable sacrifice, they sent him to State College, where he studied pharmacy. John's parents are proud of the fact that he owns his own drugstore and is in the Harmon City Chamber of Commerce.

John and Mary Hawes are also ambitious for their children. Often Mary tells seven-year-old Mike that if he studies hard and learns a lot, maybe he can become a medical doctor like Dr. Peterson, or a lawyer like Mr. Payne. "You can become anything you want, if you are only willing to work hard enough," she tells Mike.

Mary is a good housekeeper, just like John's mother. When they first were married, John sometimes teased Mary about her cooking, but he soon learned that wasn't wise. Really, John feels proud of Mary for the way she cares for the children and the house. It does bother him a little that Mary is going to a lot of club meetings and even political functions, but then so are Mrs. Peterson and Mrs. Payne.

All in all, John Hawes feels that he is making a success of life. He has a good wife and two fine boys. The drugstore is bringing in a good income and the mortgage on the house is being paid off. Of course, it would be nice to have a new station wagon, but then you can't have everything all at once. Most likely he will come up soon for an office in the Chamber of Commerce. And people often ask his opinion about civic and political affairs.

It just doesn't seem right to John that some people get ahead without working as hard as he has worked, but he feels that his boys will have an opportunity second to none. Sometimes it is disturbing to him that so many changes are taking place. A lot of people are moving into hastily built shacks on the other side of the tracks. Most of them go to work in the new factory. John doesn't know whether he wants his children to associate with the factory workers' children. Of course, he thinks, those people are just as good as everyone else—they just haven't had a chance up to now. Another thing, all these taxes and regulations and the national debt—things are just getting out of hand. John doesn't like to think of it, but there is always the threat of war— you never can tell what those Communists will do.

John Hawes is much like the rest of us. He believes a lot of things that we believe. His values—his notions of what ought to be and what is right and wrong—are familiar to all of us. It is easy to see that he is a product of the family in which he grew up. We can see how much his interests are centered in his family and how ambitious he is for his children. We can appreciate, too, how much his work means to him—certainly more than just the money he gets out of it. We too live in a complex, changing world. Perhaps, like John, we do not always understand it very well, but it has a strong influence upon us.

American Beliefs and Values. As was mentioned before, there are some more or less typical American beliefs and values. These are ways of looking at things and feeling about them which we share with others. It is true, of course, that we do not all feel exactly the same about everything, but by and large we tend to agree on many things. Let us look at some typical American beliefs and values, so that we can better understand the American personality.

Worth of the person. One important cluster of American beliefs and values has to do with the worth or value of a person. The important idea here is that a human being is valuable for his own sake. We believe that a person has worth simply because he is a human being—not merely for what he can do or even for how much he contributes to society. Just because he is a human being, we feel, his welfare is important.

Suppose a baby needs a transfusion of a rare type of blood. Once his need is brought to their attention, even strangers are likely to become concerned. The saving of this child's life becomes supremely important. But if we were to be purely practical, it is doubtful that the baby's life would be thought worth all this effort and expense. In fact, he is a burden to others. It must be that we value the child's life for its own sake.

In some circumstances, hardly any sacrifice is felt to be too great for the welfare of a person. Suppose that a miner has been trapped as a result of a cave-in. People will work feverishly to save him. Some of those who work the hardest may not even like him. Perhaps in order to reach him it may become necessary to destroy a productive tunnel. Do we stop to ask whether it costs more to save him than he is worth in dollars and cents? Not usually. If we do, we are likely to feel little and mean. In making a sacrifice in effort and money, we feel that we are working for something important—the welfare of a human being. It is a feeling which is tremendously gratifying to Americans.

Or here is a criminal. Do we feel that he too has worth as a person? Probably we have mixed feelings. We disapprove of his actions, and we may even feel hostile toward him. Yet we do not knowingly let him be cruelly abused. Nor, except in the gravest offenses, do we want to see him put to death. More and more, we recognize that criminals are human beings who are entitled to everything we can do to help them be useful and happy members of society.

Most of our examples have dealt with extreme cases, such as those where a life is at stake. But our attitudes toward personal worth go further than just valuing life. We value a human being for what he might become. We feel that it is our obligation to foster his development. Especially do we think this about children. We feel that a child is entitled to the best that his parents and society can offer him and that he should be helped to develop as far as he is able.

As a people, we Americans are easily aroused by appeals for human welfare. Many times we have responded generously to the needs of victims of flood and famine, not only in our own country but in far parts of the world. Of course these needs have to be made real to us, but once they are, we often contribute liberally.

Tied to this central value regarding personal worth are a number of related ones. We feel that each person's welfare ought to be as important as that of any other. We say that we are equal before the law and in the eyes of God. The more helpless a person is (such as the crippled and the mentally disturbed), the more strongly we feel that he needs to be protected. Moreover, we believe that as persons we are entitled to dignity and freedom from degrading or humiliating experiences. Slavery and prejudice have had to reckon with this value. If we violate it, we must rationalize, project, and in other ways defend the self-picture and the self. In industry the attitude is growing that a worker has worth beyond his productivity and that an employer should regard his employees as more than just tools.

Another part of this cluster of values is the ideal of service to others. We have a sense of obligation to be useful to others, to promote their welfare. This feeling shows itself in various ways. We need to believe that our work makes a contribution to others. Certain occupations, such as medicine, the ministry, and education, carry with them an air of dedication. It is usually easy for people in these professions to feel that they are contributing to the welfare of others. Those who produce and distribute goods, especially quality merchandise, can feel this way too, although the relationship may be a bit more indirect. Actually, nearly every occupation makes its contribution to the social good.

So the worth of a person is a powerful value in America, and nearly all of us are profoundly affected by it. We may not always live by it, but when we do not, we are likely to feel guilty and to resort to ways of defending the self. When we do live up to it, we have a better regard for ourselves.[3]

Individualism. Closely related to this idea of the worth of a person is the American emphasis on individual achievement and initiative. We have a conviction that it is good to compete with others, to strive to come out on top or in the top group, and to excel others.

Some of these attitudes of individualism and competition no doubt were fostered by

[3] An interesting statement of the "American Creed" appears in G. Myrdal, *An American Dilemma,* Harper, New York, 1944.

Figure 8.8. These two persons have just been rescued from the ill-fated liner Andrea Doria *after its collision with the* Stockholm. *What is our reaction when we learn of the grief of others, even strangers in remote places?* (*Courtesy of American Red Cross.*)

the conditions of frontier living. Certainly the life of the pioneer put a premium on individual performance and success. His neighbors were often helpful, but there was no state to take care of him in his old age or in times of unemployment and no Community Chest or United Fund to fall back upon. To a large extent he succeeded as an individual or failed as an individual.

The traditions of our ancestors before they came to America may very well have been the starting point for these beliefs. Many of these people left their native lands because of a desire to be independent, to think and to act for themselves. They wanted to avoid the domination of an autocratic ruler or a political or social institution. They desired freedom to express themselves in their own way—to be individuals, free and independent.

It is obvious that in some quarters this desire was carried too far. At times on the frontier a strong man would impose his will on his fellows and even run roughshod over their rights. And there were industrialists in a later period who were ruthless in competition and far from benevolent employers. Though often feared and even hated, however, such people were frequently also admired.

From such a background came our present more moderate philosophy of individualism. We still admire the person who competes successfully, but there are more rules about how we ought to compete. We have to fight within the rules. We may still struggle for success in the sense of besting others, but there are more limitations on how we can do it.

Our conception of success may still emphasize the externals—the achievements that stand out in other people's eyes. It is often said that we have a materialistic culture, and there seems to be some truth in this statement. We *do* tend to stress the value of material possessions; after all, they are visible and tangible. We can see and admire a huge estate, with a palatial home and landscaped grounds, but it takes imagination and contemplation to value music and noble character. In our country, people move about so much and have so many different, casual contacts that it is hard to appreciate anything in others that is not highly visible. At times we still tend to value a person more for what he can do than for qualities that are within him, such as his kindness, wisdom, and decency.

The search for prestige is a part of the individualistic cluster of values. In our country prestige is not, as it tends to be in some parts of the world, largely hereditary. It is true, of course, that the family connections have *something* to do with it. More important, perhaps, are family resources that help in the competition for prestige. Mainly, we have to acquire prestige through our own efforts.

It is possible to overemphasize this matter of individualism. It is sometimes implied that we are as individualistic as any people in the world, but that is not true. Americans have never stood for the sort of freedom that means license, the right to do as we wish even if others are hurt by it. We have always believed, and we still believe, that freedom should be accompanied by a sense of responsibility. Besides, we like to be with people and work with them. We are individualists, then, but not anarchists.

Social Class in America. In America we like to talk about the equality of all people. Although at times our actions are quite inconsistent with this belief, we have certainly taken it seriously and attempted to put it into practice. Not all Americans, of course, are equal. Some of us are taller, older, or better informed than others. Some of us have wealth and prestige, and others have little or none of either. In the sense of being valuable in and of ourselves, however, we Americans are equal. Otherwise, we are all different.

We have heard a good deal of discussion in recent years about "social classes" in America. If the term is to have any real meaning, Americans must be divided (or divisible) into groups in each of which their status, income, actions, beliefs, attitudes, values, etc., are very much alike and also different from those in other social classes.

Identifying social classes. Social classes in America are not so rigidly defined as in some parts of the world. There is a lot of overlapping. Any division into social classes is somewhat arbitrary.

There are a number of schemes for labeling social classes. One is the division into *upper*, *middle*, and *lower* classes (with an upper and lower subdivision of each). Thus, according to this classification, there is an upper-upper class and also a lower-upper one. Likewise there is an upper-middle and a lower-middle group, and an upper-lower and a lower-lower. This scheme has proved to be helpful, so let us look at it a bit more closely.

How do we tell to what class a person

Need a personal loan? **It happens to everyone!**

Get yours from the
Personal Loan Department

MANUFACTURERS TRUST COMPANY

MORE THAN 100 OFFICES IN GREATER NEW YORK

Figure 8.9. What class attitudes and beliefs are assumed in this advertisement? To what social class do you think this advertisement is directed to appeal most? Would you have any reservations about asking to borrow money from a bank? From a friend? (Courtesy of Manufacturers Trust Co.)

belongs? Obviously, there is no single mark that determines it. We have to look at a lot of different signs. Where does he live? In the better part of town or across the tracks? How important are his parents and ancestors? Are they "old aristocracy," reaching back to Jamestown, or are they poor immigrant workers? What is his occupation? Is he a professional person, such as a lawyer, or a common laborer? How much wealth does he have, and if he has a lot, did he acquire it in a respectable way? We should also need to look at the social standing of his closest friends, the organizations to which he belongs, and many other signs.

Many psychologists consider the most important mark of a person's social class to be his attitudes and beliefs. In other words, what he believes and how he feels—real parts of personality—are the fundamental marks of his class status. To this should be added his appreciations and enjoyments. Thus, there are upper-class values, middle-

class values, and lower-class values, and these are most important in understanding social classes.

Training in class behavior. Where do we learn the attitudes and beliefs that are so much a part at once of our personalities and of our class position? Where do we learn the expected ways of acting in different situations? Much of this learning—indeed, the most important part of it—normally takes place in the family. Most of us have ideas of right and wrong, ideas of the proper way to act, and ideas of what people are like that are quite similar to those of our parents. If we understand our parents' class behavior, we shall understand a lot about our own, even where our behavior is different from theirs. Of course, all of us have been exposed to many influences outside the home, but even in those our class position plays a part. The people with whom we associate tend to be from our own class level, as do the organizations to which

CLASS DIFFERENCES IN COMMUNITY ATTITUDES AND STATUS ASPIRATION

▶ Subjects of the study * were 100 men in Evanston, Illinois. They were all married, were native-born whites, and were chosen in such way as to be representative of the married, male, native-born, white population of the city. They were then interviewed to determine the degree to which each participated in group activities, the extent to which they were leaders in such activities, and the extent to which they wished to move up in the class structure and had a realistic understanding of how this could be done.

The group was then divided on the basis of income, education, and the prestige of the occupation in which they worked. In each case the mid-point was used as a dividing point, and the larger group broken into two subgroups on the basis of whether they were above or below the middle.

The principal findings of the study were as follows: First, whether income, education, or occupation was used to put the men into the "high" and "low" groups, the "high" showed a greater degree of involvement and participation in community activities. They read more books, attended church more frequently, belonged to more organizations, and held more offices in the organizations.

Second, the "high" group was more realistic in appraising the requirements for moving upward in the occupational hierarchy. A larger proportion reported themselves as willing to learn a new routine, work harder than they were then working, leave their families for some time, take on more responsibility, and give up leisure time.

The authors conclude that for this sort of population differences in income, education, and occupational status go along with—if, indeed, they do not cause—differences in participation in group activities and in behavior designed to enable one to increase his occupational level.

* Leonard Reissman, "Class, Leisure, and Social Participation," *American Sociological Review*, 19:76–84, 1954.

we belong. Even our perceptions may be selective, so that we react to whatever fits in with our existing ways of believing and feeling—which were influenced by our family and our associates.

What is it like to grow up in a middle-class family? In a lower-class or upper-class one? Of course, no simple word picture can do full justice to the situation or allow fully for the wide differences among different families within the same social class. But we can note some of their more typical features.

There are certain things that middle-class families tend to emphasize. If we grew up in such a family, probably our mother and father stressed *achievement*. They told us

that it is important to do everything well, particularly in school. They probably took a lot of interest in our development, seeing to it that we had a chance to learn music and anything else that would help us to excel. Most likely, they were proud if we talked or walked unusually early. If we grew up in such a home, it probably is important for us to succeed, to be recognized for superiority in one or more things. In other words, we have a strong need for achievement, and what is related to it, a fear of failure if we do not succeed.

If we grew up in such a home, there is a good chance that our parents were always thinking of the future. They saw our childhood as a preparation for adulthood, and a lot of planning went into our development. As a matter of fact, they saw (and perhaps still see) anything which we did, not so much for its present consequences as for its future implications. Suppose we quit something that we had begun enthusiastically. "What if he quits everything that he begins after he grows up?" they probably asked themselves. In other words, there was a lot of *future orientation*. They saw things in relation to a long time span, extending into the future. And, in their position, it was often realistic for them to do so. If we grew up in such a home, probably we too have future orientation, and probably we too shall feel this way about our children.

If we grew up in a middle-class home, our parents were probably also very much concerned about *what other people thought*, especially the "people who counted." How many times we have heard our parents say, "What will people think?" Many students of class behavior have pointed out the conventionality of middle-class standards—how much conformity there is, with "everybody watching everybody else" to find out what is proper. If we developed in a middle-class environment, probably we too are sensitive to—even anxious about—other people's evaluations.

Another thing which we learned if we grew up in a middle-class family is to *control our aggression*. No doubt our parents (and teachers, who come largely from the middle class) told us not to be mean or unkind to those weaker than ourselves. They also told us that we must always be respectful to those who are proper authorities, such as our parents, teachers, and officials. Not only were we punished for aggression, but we probably learned to feel guilty if we expressed it, and even if we felt angry. Probably we learned to channel our aggression into competitive sports and competition of all kinds. (This is an example of sublimation, discussed in Chapter 6.)

Hence, if we grew up in a middle-class family, we learned a whole pattern of beliefs and values which are now a part of our personalities. We probably feel, at least to some degree, a need for achievement but without clear, final goals to be reached; a need to be different but an anxiety about nonconformity; and a fear of failure coupled with pride about our successes. It is in this middle class that both humanitarian ideals and the competitive drive for power, gain, and prestige are the strongest.

The behavior and value patterns of the lower and the upper classes have been studied less extensively than those of the middle class, but a good deal of information is available nevertheless. In lower-class families there is usually less emphasis on achievement, less concern with status, more of a tendency to live in the present and not to be concerned with the future, more likelihood of the open expression of aggression, and, especially in the lower-lower groups, less strict adherence to social and moral standards.

On the other hand, if we grew up in an upper-class family, the chances are that our family had power, wealth, and prestige, or that our ancestors had them. Indeed, in the highest classes a sense of tradition is deeply rooted—the present is seen as an extension of the past. Our parents probably exhorted us to live up to our family traditions. They were able, of course, to provide us with the material luxuries and the proper training for our position in society. In particular, it was important to them that we should have the kinds of enjoyments and appreciations typical of their class. We were taught that snobbishness is taboo; that self-display is vulgar; that scenes and boorish conduct are to be avoided; and that a casual manner is desirable. We learned that upper-class men should play a part in practical affairs, but not in a strenuous, labored way, and that upper-class women should excel in the social and recreational activities of their class. If such was our training, it is likely

Figure 8.10. Both advertisements imply the value of material possessions as the way to the good life. To which class level does each advertisement appeal? What are the different values involved? (Courtesy of Ford Motor Co.)

that by such standards we perceive and evaluate ourselves and others.

Moving in the class hierarchy. Many people rise, and some fall, in their class position. How do we try to change our class position, and what personal problems do we encounter in trying to do so?

There are a number of ways in which a person can raise his class status, although each has some practical limit. Education is one of the most important, especially for lower- and middle-class people. Another way is to marry someone from a higher class—but not too much higher. If we do so, we must be able to meet the requirements of this higher class. Another way is to come into money, particularly in a high-prestige occupation. Wealth alone is not enough, however, for higher-class behavior must also be mastered and the old lower-class habits and friends must be discarded. There are other ways, but these are some of the most important.

But it often takes more than just external changes to adjust to a higher class and be accepted by it. We may have to change some of our lifelong ways of acting and feeling. We may have to learn somewhat different interests and appreciations. Yet these very lessons can be learned most readily only in the family, and they are hard to learn without intimate contact with the very people whose acceptance we seek.

Going up the class ladder may create personal conflicts. We may feel guilty in being disloyal to our former friends. It may be necessary to abandon some of the beliefs and values of our parents. Indeed, some people find their lower-class parents a liability, and then feel guilty in rejecting them. Changing what we enjoy in the way of amusements is not easy, either. These are only a few of the problems that we meet if we try to raise our class status.

Other Aspects of the American Personality. There are some other aspects of the American personality and its problems at which we should look if we are to under-

SOCIAL CLASS
MEMBERSHIP AND
RELATIONS TO
OTHER PEOPLE

▶ This is a study * of ten clubs of adolescents in the San Francisco area. The members were between twelve and sixteen years of age, and for each club they were either all boys or all girls. The average total attendance at club meetings was 126. Each club had a president and an adult leader and held weekly meetings. The meetings studied were discussions relating to program planning.

Each group was classified, primarily on the basis of the average occupational level of the fathers, into lower or middle social class. Groups were then paired (a lower- and a middle-class one in each case) with the following factors equal or nearly so in each group: average age, range in age, and sex (boys' groups paired against boys' groups, and girls' groups against girls'). Each group was observed by two independent adult observers, who were found to agree rather closely in their reports of what took place in the groups.

The conclusions related to the sort of behavior shown toward the adult leader, the president of the group, and the other members. The principal findings were as follows: First, the lower-class members directed more collaborative behavior toward the adult leader than did the middle-class members. (Collaborative behavior means showing respect, making suggestions, yielding, etc.) Second, the middle-class members directed more collaborative and also more aggressive behavior toward the president than the lower-class members did. And third, the lower-class members were more aggressive toward other members than the middle-class members were.

The author concludes that these findings are consistent with the way in which each class *perceives* the roles in question. Thus, according to this view, the lower class finds the adult leader a more significant and important figure. Furthermore, different attitudes toward the president and toward other members are held to be consistent with the background of the social class.

* Henry S. Maas, "The Role of Member in Clubs of Lower-class and Middle-class Adolescents," *Child Development*, 25:241–251, 1954.

stand ourselves. They are masculinity or femininity, our work, and our group relationships.

Masculinity and femininity. One of the most important facts about us is that we are male or female. But at least as important as this biological fact is the social fact that our society expects different things of men and women and of boys and girls. It provides them with different experiences. Masculinity and femininity are roles (see Chapter 15).

Let us look at some of the differences between masculinity and femininity in our country. We should understand at the outset that these roles have been and are chang-

ing, and also that different social classes define them somewhat differently. However, the differences that we shall consider are more or less typical of our country.

One difference is that men tend to have higher prestige than do women (other things being equal). This attitude shows itself in many ways. We think of men as knowing more about the political and economic world. We consider them more practical. We speak of the man as the head of the household. The important positions in government and industry usually go to men. Unfair as it seems, there is sometimes a double standard in industry, with women earning less for the same job than do men.

These differences once were greater than they now are, but they still exist to a degree.

Another difference is in dominance and submissiveness. Women are not expected to be aggressive. Even as little girls they are taught not to fight, while a father may take pride in his son's prowess as a fighter. The ideal is for women to be sweet-tempered and even submissive. A man, on the other hand, is expected to be more assertive or dominant. In view of these standards, you can see why it is so important in the self-esteem of men that they take a dominant role, especially with respect to women. This is why it is often hard for a man to work under the supervision of a woman. This is why a man is uncomfortable when he depends on a woman for his status, as when a lower-class man marries a higher-class woman. It is easy to see, too, why women often feel ambivalence (mixed attitudes) about their roles. In our prestige system, it is a man's world, and it is easy for women to resent the dependent role accorded them by society.

Men and women are expected to have different interests. A man, we feel, should be interested in his work. He should enjoy sports and the more virile forms of entertainment. But a women, we think, should be interested in the home and children. She is expected to devote a lot of attention to cultivating her appearance. What would we think of a man who spent many hours in beauty shops and in shopping for clothes? Such behavior is not only permitted but expected of women.

In our society, the ideal woman is young, attractive, and marriageable. The matron is not usually the object of admiration. We feel differently about men. A man is admired if he has maturity. This can be seen in our motion-picture idols. The women nearly always have to look young and pretty. The men may be older in years; sometimes they even gain in appeal as the years go by. We can understand, then, why women are so concerned with preserving their youth and beauty and why they are so threatened when they see it slipping away. Usually the threat to self involved in aging hits men somewhat later, when attractiveness to women and status in the field of work are threatened. We can see how intimately a thing as private as the the self depends on social factors.

Occupation. In America we feel that a person ought to make a useful contribution. Doing work is the most usual way of doing this. Actually, we find it hard to accept someone who does not work, whether hobo or playboy. If this really is a group standard, then all those who do not work have to defend the self against this shortcoming. Truly, our work is one of the most significant ways in which we perceive and evaluate ourselves.[4]

An important fact about the world of work is that different occupations have different levels of prestige. Being a professional person gives more prestige than being an unskilled laborer. And our place in this prestige system is likely to affect our evaluation of ourselves.

[4] E. C. Hughes, "Work and the Self," in J. H. Rohrer and M. Sherif (eds.), *Social Psychology at the Crossroads,* Harper, New York, 1951.

It is harder to become deeply ego-involved in (or identified with) some jobs than others. A lot of jobs nowadays deal with only a part of a total product. A worker may install a tail pipe, which he does not know how to make, on a car which he will probably never see again. It is difficult for us to have much sense of importance if our work is like this. If our job is like that of a physician, however, it is easier to see the meaning of our work as a whole.

Or suppose that our work is useful but not regarded as having high prestige. It is more difficult for a garbage collector or a janitor, for example, to identify fully with his work than it is for a lawyer or the owner of a business. And of course, it is easier to get great satisfaction from our work if we see it contributing importantly to people's welfare. An educator, or anyone in a similar occupation, usually finds that his work has great meaning to him. Those whose occupations exploit or degrade the public must have more serious problems in enhancing and defending the self.

So deeply do we tend to become involved in our working roles (and perceive ourselves in terms of them) that retirement often comes as a threat. As yet, in America, we have done little to help people to make the change from work to retirement. It will help in understanding the American personality if we realize that our work is a vital part of us.

It is a mistake to think that our job is just something that we do, like operating a lathe or fixing shoes. A job is also a relationship with others. If our family is the primary group with which we identify, our work group is second in line. Our job includes our relations with our supervisor and our fellow workers. Their esteem and their acceptance usually are vital in our lives. A person who does not feel close to his fellow workers, who is not interested in them or who withdraws from them, is missing some truly satisfying experiences.

Group relationships. Each of us is a member of many groups. For most of us, one of the most important of these is our family. It certainly was important in our childhood. Just think of how much our childhood experience depended on what our mother and father were like as persons. If they loved us, we probably learned to trust others and feel secure in their approval. Thus, we found it possible to regard ourselves as worthy, as deserving love. If they were rejecting—cold, distant, or punishing—then we tended to build up other attitudes, to perceive ourselves as unworthy and not lovable by others. Consequently, much of our present personality is likely to depend on these affective relationships in the home.

Normally, the family is the primary group with which we identify. We like to feel that in the family we are valued *for ourselves* and not for how superior we are in competition with others. We like to think of the home as an emotional haven from the pressures of the outer world. All of us know that this picture is not entirely realistic. There are often tensions in American families—conflict between husband and wife, and conflict between parents and children. We know, too, that today less and less of our important experiences and interests are centered in the home. More and more activities which were once in the home are now outside the family: work, recreation, religious worship, education, and many others. In most families a lot of our personal experiences outside the home are not even known to the other members of the family.

In addition to the family group, we have already mentioned the work group. But there are many other groups with which we are affiliated. Just think of how many clubs, honoraries, and social groups there are on the campus, and how many of them some people we know belong to. The situation outside the campus is not essentially different in this regard. Sometimes it seems that there is no limit to how many groups we could find to join if we had the time, money, and inclination.

A person can get a lot of satisfactions from joining such groups. Many of them have enjoyable and worthwhile activities, and besides, they have some interesting people in them. They are not, however, without their limitations, particularly for someone who belongs to very many of them. For one thing, it is often difficult to get real emotional satisfaction from a group. Our contacts with it are often slight, and we may never become seriously ego-involved with either the members or the objectives of the group. Along this line, a modern author has spoken of "the lonely crowd." [5]

A second limitation, growing directly out of the first, is that a certain superficiality in human relations tends to be encouraged. We establish contacts quickly and try to make a good impression. And often we talk about unimportant things and get involved in "busy work" without developing real intimacy with or understanding of our fellow members.

Finally, the fact that we encounter so many varied points of view is likely to make us less sure about what we believe and value. How different it would be to live in only one major group, such as a primitive tribe, where only one major set of beliefs and values is expressed! No wonder the members of such a society are usually so

[5] David Riesman, *The Lonely Crowd: A Study of the Changing American Character,* Yale University Press, New Haven, Conn., 1950.

certain about right and wrong, fact and fiction. The uncertainty and lack of deep conviction arising out of contact with many points of view sometimes place us as individuals at the mercy of group opinion, though at times it can be very stimulating.

CONCLUSION

By now it should be clear that knowing about culture (group-shared ways of behaving, believing, and feeling) is important in understanding human behavior. It might even look as though culture were all-important, but such a view would be extreme and unrealistic.

As we pointed out earlier, a person is what he is, not only because of social influences, but also because of his heredity. Furthermore, we do not all contact the culture in the same way. Every one of us has had a uniquely different set of experiences in the world of people. Our parents were unique as personalities. Our social class, the geographical area we grew up in, whether we lived in the city or country —these and many other factors determined our particular experience. Furthermore, as our personalities developed, we began to *select* our experiences. That is, we chose certain friends, certain organizations to belong to, and certain careers, and these factors in turn further influenced us.

Thus it is easy to see why we conclude both that culture is important in influencing our personalities and that each of us is a unique person.

SUMMARY

Culture represents the principal values and the chief ways of feeling and behaving of a group of individuals. Subcultures are significant differences in valuing, feeling, and behaving as these appear within the larger group.

Culture consists of many components, including knowledge and skills, language, institutions, and mores and folkways. The mores are the required or demanded ways of behaving, and the folkways are the expected or "correct" ways of behaving.

The cultural anthropologists help us to understand how culture influences personality. Growing up in a society quite unlike our own develops a personality quite unlike that of the typical American. Our own individual heredity and environment, however, also shape personality and account for the fact that, in the last analysis, each of us is unique.

When we examine the American personality we find at least two important values: a belief in the worth of every person, and an emphasis on the achievement and recognition of the individual.

Also in America, as in practically every other society in the world, we find social classes. Among the most important values of the middle class in America are achievement, future orientation, and control of aggression. Lower-class goals stress these values less, and especially the lower-lower groups characteristically show different social and moral standards. Upper-class values, on the other hand, emphasize a person's position as a bearer of tradition, the importance of the social graces, and re-sponsibility to take part in community leadership and development.

In America also, the male is expected to be more dominant and practical, as well as to show little emotion. Women are valued more than men for their attractiveness, and thus being young and beautiful is more important to women.

Americans are work-oriented. Our jobs frequently become a part of the self, and anyone who does not work is likely to face his own self-reproach as well as the disfavor of his associates.

Finally, Americans join a great many, and often widely varied, groups. This leads to many pleasant and profitable social contacts, but it also introduces problems. Often being in the group affords no real satisfaction and encourages superficiality in relationships. It places a premium on conformity, but since the groups are so numerous and so different it often subjects the individual to widely different standards for valuing and behaving. Needless to say, for some people, this can engender emotional conflict.

QUESTIONS

1. What is meant by culture? What is a subculture? Illustrate.

2. Discuss some of the most important parts or components of a culture, e.g., knowledge and skills.

3. Distinguish between mores and folkways. Give three examples of each in our culture.

4. Can you think of something that is not clearly one of the mores or the folkways but in between? Explain.

5. Describe the sort of personality that you would expect to find among (a) the Kwakiutl; (b) the Dobuans; and (c) the Zuñi.

6. Discuss the American belief in the worth of a person. Do you find evidences of this belief (a) in the Declaration of Independence; (b) in any other important American documents?

7. What is meant by saying that Americans believe in individualism? Does this belief ever lead to conflict with our belief in the worth of a person? Explain.

8. What is meant by a social class? Are there social classes in America? Defend your answer.

9. Compare and contrast the chief values of the middle class in the United States with those of (a) the upper class; (b) the lower class.

10. Do Americans ever change from one social class to another? How does a person move to a higher social class?

11. What problems are caused when a person moves into a higher social class?

12. Is it easier to change social classes in America than in most other parts of the world? Why do you say so?

SUGGESTED READINGS

Benedict, Ruth: *Patterns of Culture,* Houghton Mifflin, Boston, 1934.

(A fascinating account by an anthropologist of a number of cultures in different parts of the world; dramatizes the unity of a culture and how it influences personality.)

Eaton, Joseph W., and Robert J. Weil: *Culture and Mental Disorders: A Comparative Study of the Hutterites and Other Populations,* Free Press, Glencoe, Ill., 1955.

(A study of the effects of culture on the personality patterns of contemporary American groups; particular attention given to the problem of mental disease.)

Kluckhohn, C., and H. A. Murray (eds.): *Personality in Nature, Society, and Culture,* Knopf, New York, 1949.

(A comprehensive treatment of personality; under the joint editorship of an anthropologist and a psychologist.)

Mead, Margaret: *Sex and Temperament in Three Primitive Societies,* Morrow, New York, 1935.

(An attempt by an anthropologist to answer the question, "Are masculinity and femininity, as we know them in the United States, inherently linked to maleness and femaleness?"; presents results from three quite different societies.)

Murphy, Gardner: *Personality: A Biosocial Approach to Origins and Structure,* Harper, New York, 1947, chaps. 32–41.

(A critical analysis of the influence of cultural factors on personality development.)

Newcomb, T. M.: *Social Psychology,* Dryden, New York, 1950.

(A text with numerous chapters dealing with social influences on personality.)

Riesman, D.: *Individualism Reconsidered, and Other Essays,* Free Press, Glencoe, Ill., 1954.

(A series of thought-provoking essays on the subject of the American personality.)

Sherif, M., and C. W. Sherif: *An Outline of Social Psychology,* rev. ed., Harper, New York, 1956.

(A text with a clear theoretical treatment of cultural and social influences on individual and group behavior.)

Warner, W. L., M. Meeker, and K. Ells: *Social Class in America,* Science Research, Chicago, 1949.

(An authoritative analysis of social class structure in the United States, with extensive supporting evidence.)

9 PHYSIOLOGICAL FACTORS IN BEHAVIOR

There is a biology of psychology, just as there is a chemistry of biology. The modern biologist must often turn to the chemist for help in understanding the structure and the function of the many organs, processes, and systems that make up a living organism. The process of breathing, for example, cannot be comprehended unless something is known of the ways in which oxygen mixes and combines with other elements.

Important to note, however, is the fact that chemists and biologists no longer believe (as they once did) that someday advances in chemistry and physics will make the study of biology, as such, obsolete. At the time this belief was held, the reasoning ran something like this: psychology will be swallowed by biology, which in turn will be taken over by chemistry, which in the final analysis will itself disappear into physics. This argument has been thought through and criticized by the great American psychologist R. S. Woodworth. In his autobiography [1] he says:

> The different sciences will employ different techniques, and in particular, one science will go into finer detail than the other. . . .
>
> Let me take a . . . concrete example. Cellular physiology reveals something of the "fundamental" or "underlying" processes that go on in the heart muscle; but, if we want to understand the heart as a pump, we must study its action in another, less minute way. Both approaches are needed, and neither makes the other superfluous.
>
> In the same way, the psychologist describing a conditioned reflex in terms of stimulus and response, and the physiologist describing

[1] C. Murchison (ed.), *History of Psychology in Autobiography,* Clark University Press, Worcester, Mass., 1932, vol. 2, pp. 378–379.

it, as far as possible, in terms of nerve currents, etc., are describing the same identical process, the physiologist in more detail, the psychologist with more breadth. The chemist would demand still finer analysis than the physiologist gives, and the sociologist might wish to include the conditioning of the individual in a still broader view than is taken by the psychologist.

Woodworth realized that in order to understand the individual we must study him as a whole person (psychology) and at the same time study the physiological processes (biology) going on within him.

In this chapter we shall take up a few of the most important topics in the biology of psychology. We shall touch, however, on only some aspects of the large field called *physiological psychology,* which encompasses much more than we shall have time to mention.

THE MIND AND THE BRAIN

The part of biology that is of greatest interest to the psychologist is the anatomy and physiology of the nervous system. The man in the street will confidently explain this relation by saying that "the mind is located in the brain." Is this really the rea-

son? Most psychologists will reply that, so far as scientific psychology is concerned, there is no evidence of "mind." How can we explain this difference between the popular view and the scientific one? The solution lies in the definition of the word "mind."

A Definition of Mind. As defined centuries ago by some philosophers and as understood by most people today, "mind" means the *place* in which thought, reason, imagination, and all the other "mental" activities exist, and in this sense it is one of the essences mentioned in Chapter 1. Traditionally, many other philosophers have defined the mind as being made of no material, as needing no space in which to exist, and, in a word, as being pure "spirit." Such a definition as this is closely related to the commonly accepted definition of the word "soul." The truth is that philosophers have often used the two words "mind" and "soul" interchangeably. With this definition, mind is legitimately studied in the fields of philosophy and theology. Certainly such study is valuable to all of us. However, it does not come within the scope of the science of psychology.

Psychology the Science of Behavior. Science studies only those aspects of the world about us that are observable. It can study only things that can be seen, heard, smelled, touched, etc., either directly by the sense organs or indirectly through such instruments as telescopes, microscopes, Geiger counters, and cloud chambers. So long as psychology (in Greek the word *psyche* means "soul") was a branch of phi-

Figure 9.1. Would this tribal witch doctor be likely to make use of any of the facts of physiological psychology? Of psychology? How would his approach to the control of human behavior differ from the scientist's? (Courtesy of the American Museum of Natural History.)

losophy, it could be a study of "mind" defined as "soul." However, when psychology became a natural science in the latter part of the nineteenth century, it became apparent that a new word was needed to express what psychology studies. At first, the word "consciousness" replaced the word "mind," and it in turn was replaced by the word "behavior."

Most psychologists today define psychology (as we do in Chapter 1) as the science that studies behavior. Behavior is defined as what the organism does; all the activities of the organism that are directly or indirectly observable are legitimately admitted for scientific study. This is why the scientific psychologist says that in his science there is no such word as "mind." However, the psychologist most assuredly does study the various "mental" activities such as thinking, reasoning, imagining, and feeling, because these activities can be observed either directly or indirectly in the behavior of the individual. Also, through introspection each of us knows some of our own mental activities, which we can report to others.

At this point, the conclusion of the layman is that, if not the mind, then at least all mental activity must be identified with the brain. The fact is, however, that modern psychology does not try to locate the mind anywhere in the body. Rather we say that certain bodily activities are correlated with our mental activity. It is true that the functioning of the brain seems always to be involved in such activity, but other parts of the body are also involved.

Neural Correlates of Thinking. Mental activity involves not only the brain but also those two parts of the nervous system responsible for feeding impulses into the brain and spinal cord and carrying impulses out from them:

1. A *sensory* nervous network brings information to the central nervous system (the brain and spinal cord) by means of impulses from the various receptor cells throughout the body. These receptor cells are located in the sense organs: eyes, ears, nose, tongue, skin, muscles and joints, etc.

2. A *motor* nervous network carries impulses away from the brain and spinal cord, taking these impulses to the muscles and glands. These motor impulses cause muscles to contract and glands to secrete.

Mental activity, then, is correlated with neural activity in all three of the major systems: sensory, central, and motor. Furthermore, the sensory system can work only if its receptor organs are stimulated by things external to themselves (either within or outside the body). Likewise, the central system depends upon stimulation from sensory channels. At the end of the chain is the motor system, which is of the utmost importance in the survival of the organism and in its adjustment to the environment.

To reiterate, all mental activity must be correlated with the activity in all three systems. For example, in order for us to think, receptor organs must be stimulated and must send sensory impulses into the brain. The brain must connect and interconnect these impulses, and finally, motor impulses must be sent out. These motor impulses cause the muscles to contract and the glands to secrete. What we call "thinking" is thus correlated with this whole process.

The importance of the brain, therefore, lies in its function of coordinating nearly all body activity and behavior. A main part of this work is to classify and store information for future use. To provide a basis for understanding the role of the brain in behavior, the next several sections of this chapter give some of the anatomical and physiological facts of the nervous system, including the brain.

NERVE CELLS

The basic structural unit or building block of the nervous system is the *neuron*

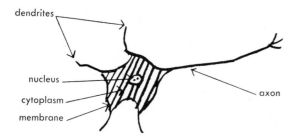

Figure 9.2. *A neuron or nerve cell.*

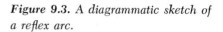

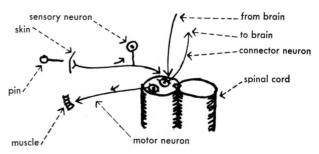

Figure 9.3. A *diagrammatic sketch of a reflex arc.*

or nerve cell. The typical nerve cell consists of several parts. Like all cells, it is filled with *cytoplasm*, which is the living material forming the body of the cell. The cell is enclosed within a membrane, and it contains a nucleus. Like most cells, it has certain parts that have become specialized. The membrane of the neuron has greater irritability and conductivity than that of other cells. In addition, each nerve cell has long fibers called *axons* and shorter fibers called *dendrites* which allow the neurons to communicate from one part of the body to another. Figure 9.2 is a diagrammatic sketch of a neuron.

When a nerve cell is sufficiently stimulated, a nerve impulse is aroused. This impulse usually passes down the cell from dendrites to cell body to axon. This being the case, different neurons bring sensory impulses into the central nervous system and carry the motor impulses away from it.

The Reflex Arc. The neuron is called the structural unit of the nervous system because it is the one and only building block used to construct all the various parts and structures of the total nervous system. A functional unit of the nervous system is the

reflex arc. The reflex arc consists of sensory neurons connected in the central nervous system with motor neurons through other intervening neurons, sometimes called *association neurons.* For the sake of simplicity, we diagram the reflex arc using the minimum number of nerve cells—one sensory, one central, and one motor. Figure 9.3 is a sketch of a reflex arc.

To understand how a reflex arc works, let us trace one while looking at Figure 9.3. A pin sticks into our skin, slightly injuring the dendrite endings of a sensory neuron. We can call the pin a *stimulus* because it arouses the sensory neuron to activity. This activity takes the form of a neural impulse carried into the central nervous system where the sensory neuron's axon meets the dendrites of an association neuron. Such a place, where the axon of one neuron meets the dendrites of other neurons, is called a *synapse.* At this synapse, the dendrites of a central neuron are stimulated, resulting in another neural impulse. This central nerve cell connects with other central cells in the spinal cord and brain and with a motor neuron, which sends an impulse out to the muscle fibers lying near the skin, causing them to contract and pull the skin away from the pin. By the time a number of these peripheral and central nerve impulses have occurred, we are conscious of having been stuck by a pin.

The foregoing example is a simplification of what goes on in even the simplest reflex arc. In reality, large numbers of sensory, central, and motor nerve cells are stimulated in even a simple "pin-sticking" reflex. Moreover, the muscle response in this reflex would consist of the contraction of many fibers in many different muscle groups. The way we presented it, a pin stuck into the skin of our arm would cause a slight muscle twitch in the arm, pulling the skin away from the pin. We all know what does happen: we are stuck with the pin and, the next thing we know, the muscles in the arms, in the legs, and in the back and abdomen all contract so that we move the whole body away from the painful stimulus. At the same time, or immediately afterward, we are also *conscious* of the fact that we have been stuck by a pin and that it hurts.

Another oversimplification in our example is the implication that a reflex has a simple stimulus—in this case, the pin. We must remember that, at the same time that the pin sticks us, a number of other external and internal stimuli are impinging upon various of our sense organs. The response that we give is not to the pin alone but to all the concurrent stimuli. We have described how we jump and move our whole body away from the pin, yet this does not invariably happen. If our physician had just told us that he had to give us a "shot," would we jump and react to the needle exactly as before? No, our muscular responses would be, as they always are, those demanded by the total situation (including the physician) and not by just a part (the needle) of the stimulus complex.

Thus we see that we must not take too simple a view of the reflex arc. Nearly always the stimulus is complex. Activity in the central nervous system is vast and varied, and any particular response involves many muscles and glands.

Conduction of the Nerve Impulse. We have had occasion to mention several times the nerve impulse that passes over the neuron. What is this impulse? We can best describe it as an electrochemical event in the cell itself. (For more information on these impulses, see the material on electrical potentials in nerve fibers on page 174.) When a nerve cell is at rest waiting to receive stimulation, it is in a state of chemical equilibrium. The stimulus is an object or state that is capable of disturbing this equilibrium. Once the cell is stimulated, this chemical disturbance travels the length of the cell. Thus, a nerve cell (neuron) can communicate "information" from one of its ends (dendrites) to the other (axon). An important feature of this chemical reaction is the production of electrical "side-effects" which are capable of acting as a stimulus to the dendrites of another neuron at a synapse. These electrical side-effects are produced by the chemical changes in the cell (similar to the action of a dry-cell battery); they do not pass from one cell to another. The "information," however, passes from one neuron to another at synapses and so reaches all parts of the nervous system.

Whenever anything stimulates a resting nerve cell just barely enough to upset the equilibrium, we say that the *threshold* of stimulation has been reached. If a stimulus is strong enough to reach this threshold of the cell, a nerve impulse occurs. However, we cannot say, "The stronger the stimulus the stronger the impulse." The stimulus is nothing more than the "trigger" mechanism for the "firing" of the impulse. Because a rifle shell has its power (gun powder) self-contained in the cartridge, the bullet does not travel faster or hit harder when we pull the rifle trigger quicker and harder. We can think of the nerve cell in the same way; it has its "power" (its internal chemical state) self-contained, and its chem-

The nerve impulse is an electrochemical event in the neuron and its fibers. By means of a voltmeter, we are able to record changes in electrical potential as they occur in the axons and dendrites. In the accompanying figure, we see a voltmeter attached to a nerve fiber.

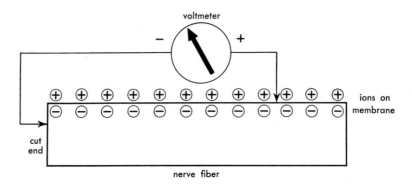

In this figure, the fiber is represented as *polarized*; that is, chemical ions * are arranged along the membrane of the fiber with a balance of positive ions on the outside and negative ions on the inside. So long as the cell is at rest, the state of polarization continues. However, when the fiber is stimulated to the threshold point, a wave of *depolarization* sweeps along the length of the fiber. Depolarization is a recombination of the positive and negative ions. This wave of depolarization is picked up by the voltmeter and is what we call the nerve impulse. As soon as the impulse passes along the fiber, the ions again separate and the state of polarization is restored.

The electrical side-effects that accompany depolarization in a fiber (axon) of one neuron may act as a stimulus to set off a nerve impulse in a fiber (dendrite) of another neuron.

*Many chemical compounds separate into positive and negative parts when dissolved in water or certain other liquids. For example, common table salt (NaCl) breaks into positive (+) ions and negative (−) ions.

ical reaction depends on internal conditions, not on the external stimulus. This fact is referred to in biology as the *all-or-none law* of the nerve impulse. The law states that a stimulus, if it is at or above threshold strength, will cause the nerve impulse. It further says that the stimulus acts only as a "trigger" for the chemical disturbance in the cell proper and that *no* energy from the stimulus is used by the cell.

It is true that a stronger stimulus will stimulate more individual fibers to have impulses. Also, a longer-lasting stimulus will cause the same fiber to send impulses over and over again. For example, if we push a pin into the skin very hard, we stimulate a larger number of nerve fibers. And if we leave the pin sticking in the skin, the fibers will continue to send impulses for a time.

THE NERVOUS SYSTEM

Structurally, the *nervous system* is a complex combination of many billions of individual neurons. In the human being, by far the largest number of these nerve cells are found in the brain and spinal cord. The other parts of the nervous system contain the rest of the cells. For purposes of classification, we divide the nervous system into these two main divisions: the *central nervous system,* which consists of the brain and the spinal cord; and the *peripheral nervous system,* or all the parts that lie outside the central system.

The Peripheral Nervous System. The peripheral nervous system is composed of two parts: the *autonomic nervous system* (which is discussed in Chapter 4, "Emotion") and the *somatic nervous system.* The autonomic system is mainly a motor system, supplying impulses to most of the internal organs and smooth muscles of the body. It is an *involuntary* system, over which we have little conscious control. The somatic system is composed of the sensory neurons and the motor nerve-cell fibers serving the skeletal muscles. On the motor side this system is a *voluntary* one. For example, we can move our arms and legs as we will.

In the peripheral system the term *nerve* is used to denote a bundle of nerve-cell fibers (axons or dendrites). A nerve is usually covered with a white protective substance called *myelin.* Some nerves contain primarily sensory fibers and other nerves mainly motor axons. A large number of nerves are of the mixed variety, containing both sensory and motor fibers.

In the somatic system the sensory nerve-cell bodies are collected in ganglia located outside the central system. The fibers leading to and from these sensory neurons are bundled together into nerves. The sensory dendrites bring impulses from receptor organs, while sensory axons send impulses into the central nervous system.

The motor axons of the somatic system have their nerve-cell bodies inside the spinal cord. Thus, only the axons are a part of the peripheral system. The rest of the motor neuron (cell body and dendrites) is a part of the central nervous system.

The Central Nervous System. As we have seen, all the neurons of the brain and spinal cord make up the central nervous system. These nerve cells connect with each other and with the peripheral nerve fibers. *Tracts* or *pathways* of fibers run between the various levels of the spinal cord and brain. These tracts are comparable to the peripheral nerves, even to the extent of the myelin covering of the fibers. Because myelin is white, nerves or pathways are visually distinct. Hence, the term *white matter* is used to refer to the parts of the nervous system where fibers predominate. In contrast, clumps of nerve-cell bodies appear gray in color. Thus, *gray matter* denotes the parts of the nervous system where cell bodies are in abundance, such as the ganglia in the peripheral and the brain centers in the central nervous system.

In the next section we shall examine in some detail the anatomy and functioning of the brain. There we shall note a few of the more important parts and centers.

FUNCTION OF THE BRAIN

When we use the word "brain," we are ordinarily referring to that part of the *forebrain* called the *cerebral hemispheres.* In addition to the forebrain, there are also parts called the *midbrain* and the *hindbrain.* There are a great number of anatomical parts and areas in the brain, but for us it will be enough to consider the cerebral hemispheres, the *thalamus* and *hypothalamus* of the forebrain, and the *cerebellum* and the *medulla* in the hindbrain.

Figure 9.4 shows a schematic representation of the brain. We see in this drawing that the spinal cord connects with the medulla. This part of the hindbrain is sometimes called the "bulb" or the "vital knot" because it contains the reflex centers for such vital functions as breathing and heartbeat. *Bulbar* ("bulb") *poliomyelitis* is a form of the disease in which the virus attacks the medulla, often resulting in the death of the patient or at least necessitating an "iron lung" to help him breathe. The

BRAIN WAVES IN ADULTS AND CHILDREN

We have seen that neural activity is accompanied by electrical side-effects. One way of studying these electrical phenomena is by recording them through electrodes attached to the scalp. When recorded in this way, they are popularly called "brain waves." The process of recording these waves goes by the long scientific name of *electroencephalography*; the record itself is an *electroencephalogram*. Fortunately, both are usually abbreviated as EEG.

In an interesting EEG study, Lindsley * recorded and compared the brain waves of several hundred subjects, ranging in age from one month to sixty-four years.

He found several types of waves in his subjects. Other experimenters had previously recorded these same types but had not made the developmental study that Lindsley did. He found a number of changes that occur as age increases. For example, the alpha rhythm (wave), which is prominent in most EEG records, was not found in children under three months of age. However, at four months the alpha waves appear and show greater amplitude (height) in children than in adults. Occasionally in some recordings, the alpha waves temporarily disappear.

Lindsley gave his subjects intelligence tests and personality inventories (see Chapters 17 and 18). He then sought to see what relationship exists between such tests and the alpha and other brain waves. He was not able to find any significant relationships between the personality measures and the EEG records. It is still possible that such relationships exist but have not yet been established. We may need more refined instruments and techniques than now are available.

Electroencephalography, however, does have some important uses at the present time. For instance, in certain kinds of brain tumors and in most forms of epilepsy the diagnosis can be made by examining the brain-wave record.

* D. B. Lindsley, "Electrical Potentials of the Brain in Children and Adults," *Journal of General Psychology,* 19:285–306, 1938.

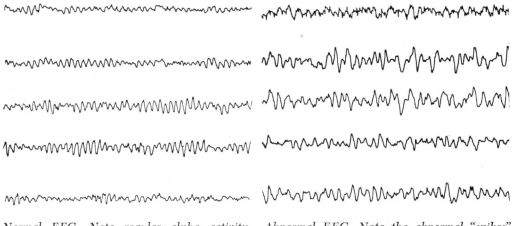

Normal EEG. Note regular alpha activity (regular 8–10 per second waves), especially in the 2d, 3d, and 4th leads from bottom.

Abnormal EEG. Note the abnormal "spikes" and slow waves, visible in all leads. (Courtesy New York University.)

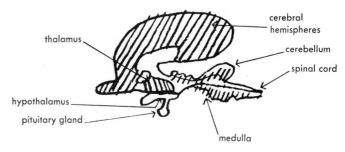

Figure 9.4. This drawing shows the brain pulled apart so that all the main parts can be seen. The pituitary gland is not a part of the brain although it is closely connected with the hypothalamus both anatomically and functionally. The stalk that holds the gland is called the infundibulum, and the hypothalamus is just above it.

cerebellum is also in the hindbrain and is often referred to as the "organ of motor coordination." It is the cerebellum that helps to smooth out complex muscular acts.

The thalamus contains many relay centers and neural pathways that connect the rest of the nervous system with the cerebral *cortex* (outer layer). In the hypothalamus are located the control centers for emotions, sleep, activity, temperature, etc. Psychologists are most interested in a study of the cerebral hemispheres, however, because activity there seems to be correlated with much of the coordination of such activities as thinking, imagining, and reasoning.

The cerebral hemispheres are divided for study into several *lobes:* the *frontal,* the *parietal,* the *temporal,* and the *occipital.* Each of the two hemispheres has all these lobes, so this important part of the brain exists in duplicate. Figure 9.5 shows these lobes and also the location of some important centers.

Some Important Cerebral Centers. In the frontal lobes is an area containing the control centers for voluntary motor (muscle) activity. When we want to raise our arm, for example, it is activity in this area that is correlated with the initiation of this action. In the parietal lobe is located the *somesthetic* or "body-sense" area. It is this area that receives the impulses bringing information of sensory stimulation throughout the body, including pain receptors in the skin and other parts of the body and the kinesthetic or "movement" sense receptors in the muscles and joints.

In the occipital lobe we find the *primary visual center* and next to it an association area for *visual recognition.* Adjacent to this area is the *visual reading association area,* which coordinates reading activity. An association area is one that does not send or receive impulses directly to or from the peripheral parts of the body; its function is to integrate and coordinate such impulses as they are received by the primary areas. This visual recognition area is involved whenever visual cues are used to recognize a person or object.

Notice that, like the visual areas, side by side are the primary *somesthetic area* and the *tactual recognition area,* which is also an association area. We have seen that the somesthetic area is the "body-sense" area. The tactual recognition area works with the somesthetic and allows us to recognize what we touch. Note likewise that next to the primary motor area is the motor writing area, an association one; also near the

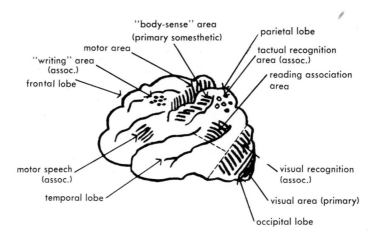

Figure 9.5. Side view of cortex.

primary motor area is the association area for speech. The first of these controls handwriting and the other controls oral speech.

In addition to the many primary and association areas (only a few of which we show in Figure 9.5), there are many so-called "silent" areas in the cerebral hemispheres. These areas are supposed to be used for a general integration and coordination of behavior. Unfortunately, not enough is known about these silent areas. Since all the areas we have briefly pointed out need to be studied much more intensively, it behooves us to remember that we are here noting progress on the frontier of physiological psychology. In the near future we may hear of discoveries that change somewhat the present picture.

Sometimes an injury to one of these specific primary or association areas is followed by a specific loss of function. For example, if the motor speech area is destroyed, the patient will have most of his other mental and physical abilities but will no longer be able to speak. A fuller treatment of these specific losses of function can be found in an advanced textbook on the subject.[2]

Most often, injuries to the brain involve

[2] C. T. Morgan and E. Stellar, *Physiological Psychology*, 2d ed., McGraw-Hill, New York, 1950, chap. 24.

parts of several adjacent areas. In these cases we do not see clear-cut loss of a specific function. However, impairment may be shown in some broad area of behavior, such as learning. For example, in rats a correlation has been found between the amount of cerebral cortex destroyed and difficulty in learning. The human study on some effects of brain injury on learning is another good example (see page 183).

THE INTERNAL ENVIRONMENT

In our study of motivation earlier in this book, we referred to the process of *homeostasis* in the body—the tendency of the body to maintain a biochemical equilibrium. In a complex organism like man, the various cells of the body depend upon the blood stream as a source of the materials needed to maintain the equilibrium. The blood stream not only brings the necessary chemical substances to the cells but also takes away the waste products and unwanted materials. Some writers have referred to the blood stream as the "internal environment." But in a broader sense every cell in the body is an environment for other cells.

The blood stream and the *lymph* system bathe and connect all the cells in the body

▶ In Chapter 4, we learned that Lindsley's emotion theory was based on neural activation and that the primary activator is the reticular formation. Now we shall examine the location and function of this nerve network in the central nervous system.

The reticular activating system (RAS for short) is situated in the central portion of the brain stem and is no larger than the little finger. Yet without this system we would probably never be conscious of anything, for its task is to awaken the cortex of the brain and keep it awake. The RAS accomplishes this task by screening all incoming sensory impulses and acting as a general alarm system. No matter which sense organ (eyes, ears, etc.) is involved, the response is the same—the arousal of the cortex.

Thus, the RAS is a vital part of the nervous system. Injury to it nearly always results in a condition of coma, which cannot be remedied unless the RAS can be made to function again. Moreover, as might be guessed from our discussion of tranquilizers in Chapter 4, anesthetics and sedatives block the nerve flow from the RAS to the cortex and do not affect the direct sensory flow of impulses. Also, various stimulants enhance the outflow from the reticular formation.

More unexpected is the influence of the RAS on motor nerve impulses. Certain reflex action, for example, can be increased or inhibited by RAS stimulation. Using the method of electrical stimulation, experiments have shown that stimulation of the upper portion of the RAS can exaggerate the knee-jerk reflex in a monkey, while stimulation of the lower portion can decrease the jerk.

Information about the RAS is far from complete, for research is no more than well under way. Therefore, we must not accept the present findings as final or absolute. However, an important contribution to physiological psychology has already been made, and further contributions appear to be on the way.

and are a part of our internal environment, just as the air and everything else surrounding us make up our external or outside environment. This internal environment is the one in which the physiological regulation of homeostasis takes place. Let us look at some of these reactions which underlie all the behavior that the psychologist studies (see also Chapter 3).

In order to do their jobs in the body, all the cells must have fuel to burn. They obtain this fuel from the blood stream; then, through the process called *metabolism*, they use the energy that it supplies. Simply stated, the cells take food and oxygen out of the blood stream and burn (oxidize) the food with the oxygen. As a result of this oxidation, energy is made available for the cell to use and certain waste products are returned to the blood stream.

In order for living cells to function, they must have, in addition to ordinary food and oxygen, a number of other chemical substances. These substances include small quantities of certain minerals, *vitamins, enzymes,* and the various *hormones* produced by the *endocrine* glands. The action of many of these substances is *catalytic;* that is, these chemicals often speed up or slow down other chemical reactions without themselves being expended. The minerals and vitamins must be taken into the body

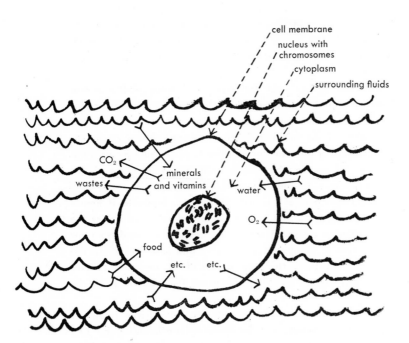

cell membrane
nucleus with chromosomes
cytoplasm
surrounding fluids

CO_2

wastes

minerals and vitamins

water

food

O_2

etc.   etc.

Figure 9.6. This sketch illustrates a cell in its fluid environment. Only a few of the products exchanged between the cell and the fluid are depicted. What are other chemicals used or discarded by living cells?

from the outside, while the hormones are internally produced.

The Endocrine Glands and Their Hormones. In the body are many glands, whose function is to secrete various substances. Some glands pour out their secretion through tubes; these are called *duct* glands. Examples are the mammary glands (milk), the salivary glands (saliva), and the various glands that secrete digestive juices. Other glands secrete their substances (hormones) directly into the blood stream; these are called *ductless* glands.

The study of the action of the hormones is important to the psychologist because much of human behavior cannot be understood without taking them into account. Figure 9.7 shows the approximate location of the various endocrine glands.

The pituitary. The pituitary gland [3] is often called the "master gland" because it secretes a number of hormones whose main function is to stimulate other endocrine glands. The pituitary has a hand in many of

[3] A more recent name for this gland is *hypophysis*. The older name is retained in this book because of its greater familiarity.

the most vital processes of the body; for example, it provides hormones to help the ovaries regulate the production and ripening of egg cells.

The pituitary also sends special hormones to the thyroid, adrenals, testes, etc., stimulating these other glands to secrete certain hormones of their own. These glands in turn pour out secretions that affect the pituitary. Some years ago it was thought that the pituitary controlled only growth. It does control growth, and an excess of its growth hormone results in giants, while a deficit produces midgets. In addition, however, it has many other important functions that justify our calling it the "master gland."

The thyroid. The thyroid gland in the neck produces a hormone that is necessary for proper metabolism. The person who has an undersecretion of thyroid hormones (*hypothyroidism*) is likely to be both mentally and physically sluggish. The person with too much thyroid secretion (*hyperthyroidism*) is just the opposite—overly active in his behavior. Hypothyroidism is often accompanied by a *goiter* in the neck. Goiter is a swelling of the thyroid gland

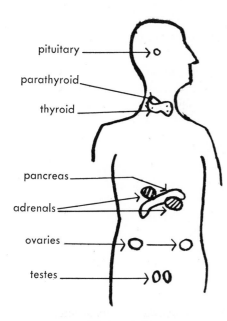

pituitary

parathyroid

thyroid

pancreas

adrenals

ovaries

testes

Figure 9.7.

substance controlling the balance of various minerals in the blood stream. If this balance is not maintained, the organism cannot survive for long.

A part of the *pancreas* produces *insulin,* which is needed in the regulation of blood sugar by the cells. Inability of the pancreas to produce enough insulin causes the disease known as *sugar diabetes.* The *gonads* —*ovaries* in the female, *testes* in the male— produce hormones controlling the appearance of the secondary sex characteristics in the body, along with primary sexual maturity. The adolescent boy's changing voice is one of the many changes effected by the hormones of the gonads.

Endocrine imbalance. Several previous chapters refer to the influence of hormones on human personality. It is true that any marked endocrine imbalance is likely to affect our total functioning and behavior. Moreover, the malfunctioning of a single gland can affect certain aspects of our behavior more than others. For example, we have seen that hypothyroidism causes mental and physical sluggishness. However, even in these cases of disturbance in a single gland, other glands are also involved. For instance, in the hypothyroid woman, the ovaries are affected and the cycle of egg production will be slowed. This malfunctioning has both specific and general effects on behavior.

Vitamins and Enzymes. In a single year, millions of Americans consume literally tons of vitamin pills. Each of them sincerely believes that he is greatly improving his health. However, if he has not consulted a physician about his need for such pills, he is very likely to be wasting his time and money. In rare cases, he may even be endangering his health.

Vitamins are powerful catalysts, essential to good health, needed ordinarily in minute quantities. According to biochemical research, vitamins probably aid other chemicals in the body to produce enzymes.

occasioned by the gland's overworking to secrete enough hormones. A lack of iodine in the diet is a contributing factor in many goiters.

In children, the effects of hypothyroidism can be serious. An infant who is severely hypothyroid from birth onward develops as a feeble-minded child, known as a *cretin.* Fortunately, we can now partially correct hypothyroidism by daily administration of thyroid extract and thereby overcome to a considerable extent the deleterious effects of the deficiency.

The adrenals. On the kidneys are located the adrenal glands, which produce a number of hormones, including *adrenalin,* the uses of which are discussed in the chapter on emotions. The other hormones, which include *cortisone,* seem to be necessary if the organism is to respond successfully to stressful situations. They are used by physicians in the treatment of *rheumatoid arthritis,* a disease that causes the joints of the body to become stiff and useless.

Other glands. Adjacent to the thyroid gland are the *parathyroids,* which secrete a

Enzymes and metabolism. We have observed the role of some of the hormones in the regulation of metabolism. The hormones probably do their work by partially controlling the supply of enzymes in the body. The enzymes are specific catalytic agents that help regulate each step in the biochemical process of metabolism. Therefore, a great many different enzymes are needed in the metabolic "machinery" of the body. Even in a small part of the process, such as the metabolism of sugar in the brain, several enzymes are involved. If a single one of these enzymes is lacking, the consequences are quite serious.

The importance of a specific enzyme is seen in a certain hereditary type of feeble-mindedness.[4] This condition results from a single defective gene. Because of this gene, the enzyme needed to remove *phenylpyruvic acid* from the brain is missing. Since this acid accumulates in brain metabolism, failure to remove it prevents the brain from functioning normally.

COMPARATIVE PSYCHOLOGY

When Charles Darwin introduced his theory of evolution in the middle of the nineteenth century, we human beings were forced for the first time to view ourselves as part of the animal kingdom. We discovered that by studying the anatomy, physiology, and the behavior of the lower animals we could learn more about ourselves as organisms. Out of Darwin's work developed the comparative approach. By comparing the development of other animals with that of man, we are able to understand more fully the function and use of the various parts of our bodies. Also stemming from Darwin and similar in approach to comparative biology is *comparative psychology* (often called *animal psychology*). As comparative psychology has developed, it has

Figure 9.8. Glandular malfunctioning can produce freaks. Which gland is responsible for this giant and this midget? Is it possible that more than one gland is involved? Could anything have been done to prevent their abnormal growth? (International News Photos.)

[4] This type of feeble-mindedness is known by the jawbreaking term *phenylpyruvic oligophrenia.*

A recent study * was made of a group of war veterans with various brain injuries. All of them had unilateral lesions, i.e., only one of the cerebral hemispheres had been injured. Half the group had right-side injuries and the other half had lesions in the left side. Some of the men had only one cerebral lobe involved, while others had two or three. It was not possible to determine the exact brain centers affected in each of the subjects. However, this information was not needed, since the object of the study was to note the effects of unspecified unilateral brain lesions on the learning of a tactual discrimination.

The subjects learned to distinguish by touch alone six different patterns made of metal strips. A control group of veterans without brain injuries showed significant and equal amounts of learning for both hands on this task. The experimental group was equivalent in learning to the control group for the hand on the same side as the brain injury. However, for the hand opposite the side of the lesion, the subjects showed no significant learning or improvement. This was the case regardless of the lobe or lobes involved in the injury.

It has been known for a long time that the main sensory projections from each side of the body go to the opposite cerebral hemisphere. Although the sensations arising in the fingers project to only a small area of the hemisphere, injury to any part of this hemisphere interferes with learning. Thus, this study emphasizes the importance for learning of the health of the whole cerebral hemisphere involved.

* L. Ghent et al., "Effect of Unilateral Brain Injury in Man on Learning of a Tactual Discrimination," *Journal of Comparative and Physiological Psychology*, 6:478–481, 1955.

kept a close relationship with both comparative anatomy and physiology. We are interested not only in comparing behavior but also in comparing the biological activities correlated with and underlying behavior.

Much of the information in this chapter was contributed by a working partnership of comparative and physiological psychologists. It is much easier and safer to study the brains and nervous systems of rats than those of human beings. Moreover, by using the comparative approach, research with the rat can be made to shed light on the working of the human brain and nervous system. Likewise, the study of the endocrine glands in lower animals throws light on the endocrine system in man.

The Team Approach. In order to understand man best in all his facets, the psychologist must team up with experts and specialists in other fields. The sociologist, the biologist, the anthropologist, the chemist, the physicist, and just about all the other natural and social scientists have something valuable to contribute to our understanding of human behavior. The best approach for the psychologist is the one that accepts willingly from these different disciplines the knowledge they have accumulated. This constitutes the *interdisciplinary* or team approach.

This approach has resulted in the formation of a number of special sciences that have developed to fill the gaps between the old traditional limits of the sciences. Examples of these new sciences are biochemistry, biophysics, social psychology, physiological psychology, and physical chemistry. Basic to our understanding of the biology

EXPERIMENTALLY PRODUCED INSANITY

We see in Chapter 6 that the psychoses are divided into two groups—the organic and the functional. The organic psychoses are characterized by some neural or chemical disturbance within the body, while the functional psychoses are supposed to be produced by environmental stress. In recent years evidence has been found to indicate that some of the psychoses classified as functional might be placed more appropriately in the organic category. Of interest are a number of experiments in which psychotic symptoms are induced in normal subjects by the administration of certain chemicals.

From left to right: The first two sketches were drawn by subject before experiment, the next two while under LSD. In describing his feelings to experimenter, subject said: "I'm up in the universe . . . I talk to a person and their face escapes away."

A series of such experiments has been in progress at the Boston Psychopathic Hospital since 1949.* The chemical used in this research is prepared from a fungus that grows on rye and is called LSD (short for d-lysergic acid diethylamide tartrate). Through the years more than 100 healthy subjects have been given this drug and their resulting symptoms observed and recorded.

* Six Staff Members of Boston Psychopathic Hospital, "Experimental Psychoses," *Scientific American*, 192 (6):34–39, June, 1955.

of psychology is some knowledge of these special sciences. Of particular value, however, are the sciences of biophysics and biochemistry, which are contributing facts about the mechanism of the nerve impulse, the chemistry of homeostasis, etc.

CONCLUSION

A great many years must pass before biologists and psychologists will have gathered enough facts to let us say that we know the biological correlates of complex behavior. For instance, at the present time we can only guess at exactly what goes on in the brain when we think. How the central nervous system classifies and retains information is another mystery. We do not have enough data yet to explain the "physiology" of memory. And so it is with most of the other mental and physical aspects of behavior. We are sure that physiology and behavior correlate, but we cannot yet say exactly how.

Psychology must work closely with biology, for the "person" that psychology studies is also the person whose organs are studied by the biologist. A person with a weak heart is a different person because of that weakness. A living, pumping, heart is part of a person and is vitally affected by changes in his over-all functioning. As facts accumulate we shall know this relationship better. The result will be a rewarding increase in our understanding of human behavior.

When given a standard dose of LSD, a normal person shows both physical and mental effects which last for six hours. There is a muscular tremor, restlessness, sweating, weakness, and sensations of hot and cold. These physical symptoms begin within the first hour and persist without much change during the whole experimental period. Of more importance, however, are the mental symptoms, which show a definite progression.

During the first hour, the normal responses to stress are shown—anxiety, apprehension, irritation, and hostility. The first truly psychotic symptoms appear in the second hour. The subject becomes confused and apathetic and gradually loses touch with reality. Everything seems strange and different, and he may experience visual hallucinations. He laughs and smiles without provocation, even while feeling depressed. His emotions are shallow and unreal. The subject has great difficulty communicating with others; he cannot find words to express his new and startling experiences. By the fourth hour the psychotic symptoms begin to disappear, and by the sixth hour only the initial symptoms of irritation, anxiety, and hostility are present. After a time the effects of the drug are completely dissipated and the subject is again normal.

In the accompanying figure are drawings made by a male subject before and during an LSD experiment. Such drawings are very similar to those produced by schizophrenic and other psychotic hospital patients.

These and other experiments being performed at the present time may force us to reclassify several of the "functional" psychoses as organic. Thus, joint work in medicine and physiological psychology enables us to gain a new and better picture of some of the behavior disorders.

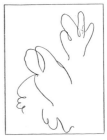

Top picture was drawn by subject to show that his head was most important part of self. One minute later drew bottom picture to show his hand had become biggest part. The investigator then asked: "What about your feet?" Subject replied: "Feet are not important. They are pretty pedestrian."

SUMMARY

There is a biology of psychology just as there is a chemistry of biology. Although these sciences are related, each is distinct and has its special contributions to make to the understanding of human behavior.

We cannot say that the mind is the brain, nor can we say that the mind is located in the brain. What we can say is that there are a number of neural correlates of mental activity. Whenever we think, feel, or imagine, there is activity in sensory, central, and motor nerve cells.

The basic structural unit of the nervous system is the neuron or nerve cell. One of the simplest functional units is the reflex arc.

The nerve impulse is best described as an electrochemical event within the cell itself. This impulse occurs when the threshold of stimulation is reached in the neuron.

The nervous system is divided into the central nervous system and the peripheral nervous system. The central system is composed of the brain and spinal cord, while the peripheral system contains all the other neural structures of the body.

When we use the word "brain," we are ordinarily referring to that part of the forebrain called the *cerebral hemispheres.* In the lobes of these hemispheres are located many brain centers, controlling such activities as vision, hearing, speech, and walking.

The blood and lymph systems of the body are sometimes called the *internal environment* because of the important substances they carry to all the cells.

The hormones secreted by the endocrine glands are vital components of the internal environment. Hormones act as catalytic agents in various biochemical reactions. Examples of endocrine glands are the pituitary, the thyroid, the adrenals, and the gonads. Their hormones help regulate such bodily activities as growth, metabolism, and reaction to stress.

Vitamins and enzymes are other essential constituents of the internal environment. The vitamins help in the production of enzymes which regulate each step in the process of metabolism. Like hormones, enzymes and vitamins are chemical catalysts.

Charles Darwin introduced the comparative approach to both biology and psychology. This approach allows us to study lower animals in order to understand the human organism better.

The interdisciplinary approach to the study of man consists in the cooperation of all the sciences, both the natural and the social. Because of this approach such sciences as physiological psychology and biophysics have been developed.

QUESTIONS

1. What does Woodworth mean by the terms "finer detail" and "finer analysis"? Does he imply that one type of analysis is better than another?

2. Why is it incorrect to say that the mind is in the brain?

3. What are the neural correlates of thinking?

4. Why is the reflex arc called a basic functional unit of the nervous system?

5. What is the nerve impulse and how is it conducted?

6. Define the following: neuron, nerve, ganglia, peripheral nervous system, myelin.

7. Name the main parts of the forebrain, midbrain, and hindbrain.

8. Explain the function of the following brain centers: primary visual area, motor speech area, and the somesthetic area.

9. What is the internal environment and what does it contain?

10. List the endocrine glands and describe the functions of each.

11. Why should psychologists study rats?

12. What do we mean by the interdisciplinary approach?

SUGGESTED READINGS

Beach, F.: *Hormones and Behavior,* Hoeber, New York, 1948.
> (An excellent but difficult book concerning the relationship of the glands and behavior.)

Gardner, E.: *Fundamentals of Neurology,* rev. ed., Saunders, Philadelphia, 1952.

> (A well-illustrated book on the nervous system, covering both structure and function.)

Marcuse, F. L.: *Areas of Psychology,* Harper, New York, 1954, chap. 11.
> (A good short introduction to physiological psychology.)

Morgan, C. T., and E. Stellar: *Physiological Psychology,* 2d ed., McGraw-Hill, New York, 1950.

(A comprehensive textbook on the subject which, however, a beginning student without a background in biology may find difficult.)

Stevens, S. S. (ed.): *Handbook of Experimental Psychology,* Wiley, New York, 1951.

(Difficult but authoritative chapters on the physiology, biophysics, and biochemistry of the nervous system.)

Wenger, M. A., et al.: *Physiological Psychology,* Holt, New York, 1956.

(A more elementary approach to physiological psychology than Morgan and Stellar.)

10 THE SENSES

As Robert Louis Stevenson said, "The world is so full of a number of things." In this chapter, we shall learn how we come to know of all these things. We shall study the several senses that we use to explore and learn about the world. We have already seen that when we are motivated we seek goals. Through our senses, we are able to identify and to know these goals. In order to identify them, we must be able to distinguish them from everything else in the world. Our senses are the starting point for such discrimination.

Over two thousand years ago the great Greek philosopher Aristotle listed what he called "our five senses": vision, hearing, touch, taste, and smell. To this day, most of us still believe that we have only five senses. The reason for our error (and Aristotle's) is the fact that we are not conscious of the working of some of our most important senses. For example, the sense of balance is essential to walking and moving about with reasonable skill. However, since the organ for this sense is hidden within the bony structure of the skull, we are often unaware of it and its operation. We shall see too that there are other senses of which we are unaware.

AN OVER-ALL VIEW OF OUR SENSES

Later in this chapter we shall consider the specific uses of the different senses. At this point, however, we are concerned with the similarities among them. First, all our senses are sensitive to *stimuli* in the environment. Second, for each sense, there is a sense organ or *receptor* in the body connected by nerve fibers with the central

nervous system. Third, the functioning or working of each sense organ enables us to have *sensations* and *perceptions* of the world around us. Let us consider each of these points in detail.

Stimuli. A stimulus (the plural is stimuli) is any physical energy in the environment capable of exciting or arousing a receptor. We must remember that our total environment includes internal conditions as well as external ones. Some of our receptors are stimulated externally and some internally. For example, external light energy stimulates our eyes, while the internal pressure of liquid in semicircular canals in our skulls stimulates the sense of balance. External stimulation is observed also in sound waves exciting the ear, odors reaching the nose, liquids stimulating the tongue, and objects touching the skin. Internal stimulation occurs not only in the sense of balance but also in the movement or *kinesthetic* sense, which responds to the movement of our muscles and joints, and in the *organic* sensitivity, which is stimulated by various changes inside our abdominal and other body cavities.

Receptors. Each sense has its own sense organ or receptor. Some of these organs are familiar to everyone—the eye, the ear, the nose, the tongue, and the skin. Others are not so well known—the *semicircular canals* (sense of balance), the kinesthetic endings in the muscles and joints, and the many unspecialized nerve fibers scattered throughout the body. In each case, the receptor is connected with the central nervous system. When the sense organ is stimulated, nerve impulses travel from the organ to the spinal cord and brain. The brain sorts and distributes these incoming impulses, meanwhile decoding them so that we can learn about the world we live in.

Functioning of the Sense Organs. As our sense organs function, we experience sensations. For example, redness is a visual sensation, loudness is an auditory sensation, sweetness is a taste sensation, and pungency is a sensation of smell. We often speak of the *perception* of sensations. By "perception" we mean the interpretation of what we sense—the fitting of our sense data into frames of reference. Another way to put it is to say that we have sensations of lights and sounds and odors, while we perceive objects such as the moon, a melody, and the scent of a rose.

VISION

Now let us look at some of our senses in more detail. A good starting place is vision. For most of us, vision is the most precious of our senses. It is disturbing even to think of not being able to see the forms, colors, and other sights of the world around us. Certainly vision is one of our valuable senses; however, we shall learn that some of the others are just as valuable and may be even more important.

Figure 10.1. Since the lamp bulb produces light, it is seen directly as a luminous object. On the other hand, the flowers, vase, table, and all other nonluminous objects are seen by reflected light. In this illustration the light bulb is the source of the reflected light.

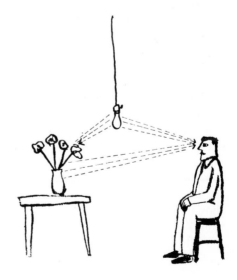

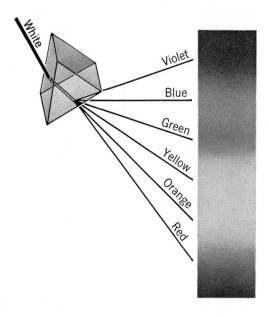

Figure 10.2. White light is composed of a number of different wavelengths of light. Each of these wavelengths is perceived as a different color (hue). When a beam of white light is put through a prism, it is separated into its component wavelengths, forming a "rainbow" of hues. An actual rainbow in the sky is formed by sunlight passing through raindrops, which act as prisms. In both cases, the order of the hues is the same. (Morgan, Introduction to Psychology, McGraw-Hill, New York, 1956, p. 451. By permission of the publisher.)

The Stimulus for Vision. Light rays are the external stimuli for vision. We can see directly any object which emits light, such as the sun or an incandescent light bulb. All other objects are seen by reflected light. For example, we see the moon at night because its surface reflects light from the sun. We see this book because it reflects light from some source to our eyes, but we see the flame of a match directly. Figure 10.1 shows these two ways of receiving light stimulation.

Visible white light, such as that emitted by the sun, is composed of a number of dif-ferent wavelengths. Each of these wavelengths is seen as a distinct color or *hue*. This can be demonstrated by sending light through a glass prism, thereby breaking it up into its component wavelengths and forming a "rainbow." Figure 10.2 shows this phenomenon. It is interesting to note that drops of water in the atmosphere can act as prisms and thus form the "real" rainbow in the sky. In both cases, the colors are always in the same order: violet, blue, green, yellow, orange, and red.

These visible wavelengths are a part of a series of electromagnetic waves that range from X rays and ultraviolet rays, which are shorter, to infrared rays and the various radio waves, which are longer. We might say that our eyes are tuned to be sensitive to the same *kind* of wavelengths as are our radios and television sets. One way these wavelengths are measured by physicists is in terms of *millimicrons*. A millimicron is defined as a length or distance equal to a billionth of a meter. The spectrum of light that we see stretches from 390 millimicrons (violet) to 760 millimicrons (red).

The Eye. The receptor or sense organ for vision is, quite obviously, the eye. Our eyes are ball-shaped and are set into sockets in the head, with only a small part visible. Both the structure and the functioning of the eye have been compared to those of a camera. In Figure 10.3 we see that both eye and camera have an opening (*pupil* of the eye, aperture of the camera) which admits light, a *lens* which focuses light, and a back wall upon which the light image is cast (*retina* of the eye, film of the camera).

However, we must realize that there are as many differences as there are similarities between our eye and a camera. The differences between the two are disclosed only when we examine them in some detail. The camera is filled with air; the eye, with liquids called the *aqueous* and *vitreous humors*. The iris muscles which form the

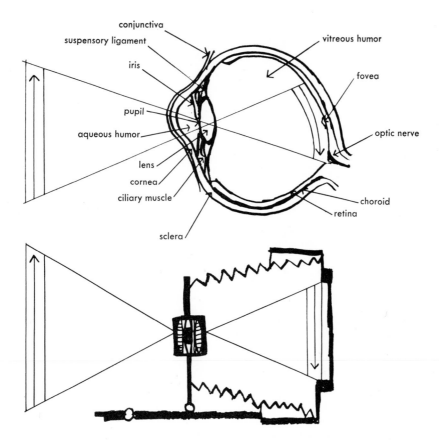

Figure 10.3. The parts of the human eye have been labeled. What are the comparable parts of the camera? Are there structures in the eye that have no counterpart in the camera? In what ways are the eye and the camera similar? In what respects are they different? Which is more efficient, the eye or an expensive camera?

pupil are controlled by the amount of light on the retina, while the camera aperture is manually set. The lens of the camera is made of several glass elements, and focusing is a matter of moving the lens nearer to or farther from the film. The lens of the eye is a transparent bag filled with a half-fluid, half-solid crystalline substance; light is focused on the retina by changes in the shape of the lens. Incidentally, the finest camera lenses are much better in resolving power than the lens of the eye. But overall, the eye is better than the best camera, with the superiority lying in the excellence of the retina over the best film. Composed as it is of living cells, the retina not only is very sensitive to light but also is capable of continuous operation throughout our waking hours. A piece of film can take only one picture; the retina can record thousands upon thousands of images and still be ready for another.

Rods and cones. Viewing the retina through a microscope, we discover that its sensitive cells are the millions of rods and cones. Although they are named for their appearance, rods and cones are now defined in terms of their function. The cones

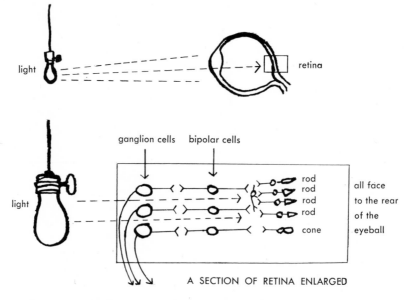

Figure 10.4. *Light entering the eye is focused on the retina. To reach the rods and cones, the light must filter through a mass of neural and vascular tissues. Yet the rods and cones are very sensitive to even small amounts of light. A light stimulus causes a photochemical response in the rods and cones that sets off nerve impulses that travel through the bipolar cells to the ganglion cells. The long fibers (axons) of the ganglion cells leave the retina and form the optic nerve, which goes directly to the visual centers in the brain.*

are sensitive to the various different wavelengths and are used in color vision. They are closely packed in the *fovea,* which is the central area of the retina. For this reason, and because they have a better connection to the brain, the cones are used for detailed vision and for most daylight seeing. The rods are more numerous and more sensitive to light than the cones, but they are not centrally located nor do they have a one-to-one connection to the brain as the cones often do. The rods are used for twilight or dim-light viewing and are not sensitive to colors; they "see" everything in terms of white, black, and gray (see Figure 10.4).

Functioning of the Eye. Light enters the eye and is focused upon the retina, where the rods and cones are stimulated by it.

The rods and cones have a chemical composition which changes when stimulated by light. This change trips off nerve impulses which travel to the brain. When the visual centers in the brain are stimulated, we become aware of such sensations as light, color, and form. We then perceive these sensations as objects in our environment. In this way we see the world.

Visual Acuity. Our eye is well constructed to pick out and differentiate many of the details of objects around us. It possesses excellent *acuity;* that is, we are able to see clearly and distinctly objects that are quite small. Furthermore, we can rank these small objects according to their relative size and can separate them as to shape or form.

In Figure 10.5 we see a *Snellen-type eye*

chart which is used to test visual acuity. Many people have been tested on this chart, so we know what the normal or average eye should see at a given distance. We also discover that some eyes are better than the average and some are worse. Usually the subject is asked to stand 20 feet away from the chart and read it. If he is able to read what the average person can read at 20 feet, he is rated as 20/20 in acuity. If at 20 feet he can read only what the average person is still able to read at 200 feet, he is rated 20/200, which indicates that he has relatively poor acuity. If, on the other hand, he is able to read at 20 feet what the average eye can read only at 10 feet, he has above-average acuity and is rated 20/10.

In order for us to see an object, it must stand out from or *contrast* with its background. Also it must be sufficiently illuminated. For example, the Snellen eye chart has black letters which contrast greatly with the white background when properly lighted. In a darkroom from which all light is excluded, we should not be able to see either the letters or the background. Or, were we to fill in the background with the same black ink used in the letters, we should see only a solid black chart even under the strongest spotlight.

Sensitivity to Light. Sometimes it comes as a surprise to us to realize that there can be light in our surroundings which is too dim to be seen. The physicist can prove this fact by using a very sensitive photometer (light meter). We must therefore determine exactly how little light must strike the retina in order for us to be aware of it. This lowest level of stimulation is called the *absolute threshold* of light sensitivity. The absolute threshold is the amount of light that we are barely aware of.

It is also of value, sometimes, to determine the *differential threshold* of light sensitivity. This threshold is the smallest detectable difference between two lights. If the difference is below threshold, the two

lights will appear to be equal in brightness. We determine the differential threshold in much the same way as we do the absolute threshold. The value of the differential threshold is sometimes called the *j.n.d.*, which means the "just noticeable difference." The size of such a difference is relative to the intensity of the two stimuli being compared. We can distinguish a smaller difference in illumination between two relatively dim lights than between two bright lights.

It was discovered nearly a hundred years ago that the ratio of the j.n.d. to the level of the stimulus intensity is a relatively constant fraction. For example, if we are barely able to notice the difference between the brightness of a 100-watt light and a 101-watt light, our j.n.d. is 1 watt and our ratio is 1:100. We then discover that we can barely tell the difference between a 200-watt light and one of 202 watts; again, the ratio is 2:200 or 1:100. Similarly, we find that we can tell the difference between a light of 25 watts and one of 25¼, between one of 400 and of 404, etc. In each case the

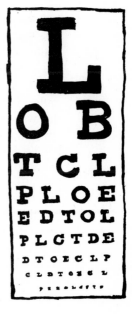

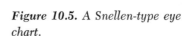
Figure 10.5. A Snellen-type eye chart.

ratio of the j.n.d. to the stimulus intensity is 1:100. If we were to continue, we should find that this fraction holds for most comparisons except those between very dim lights and those between very bright lights.

This principle is called the *Weber-Fechner* law and is named in honor of the two men who discovered it and perfected its use. We should note that it holds fairly well not only for vision but also for hearing and all the other senses. However, each of the several senses has a different fraction.

Seeing Color. For most of us the world of color is both beautiful and useful. Colors are useful in allowing us better to distinguish and identify the many objects around us. At the same time, most of us derive some esthetic satisfaction from the harmonious combination of colors, as experienced in art or in nature. Psychologists recognize and study three aspects of what we ordinarily call "color": hue, saturation, and brightness.

Hue refers to the distinctive quality of the color, as red, blue, green, or yellow. We have seen that the experience of hue corresponds closely with the wavelength of light striking the retina. A "red" ball, for example, is one which reflects a light of about 650 millimicrons into our eyes. The redness, therefore, is in our experiencing this reflection, not in the ball. The ball itself is not red; it simply has certain absorption properties that allow it to reflect light of specific wavelengths. If we look at the ball under a light that does not contain any of the wavelengths above 650, we shall discover that the ball does not look red any longer. Under a sodium vapor lamp, such as those yellow lamps used at highway intersections, the ball looks brown.

Saturation is the amount of the color or hue that is present in proportion to the gray or white present. A completely saturated color is one that has the maximum amount of the hue. A *red* red is one that is highly saturated. This same hue of red may be seen relatively unsaturated in a light pink.

Brightness refers to the relative lightness or darkness of the stimulus. Brightness is determined by comparing the lightness or darkness of the color with a gray that has the same darkness or lightness. Sometimes we speak of the grays, which run from white to black, as the *achromatic series,* meaning that they do not have hue.

Color Blindness. Fortunately, very few people are totally color-blind. However, about 4 per cent of the population has some measurable degree of color weakness. We refer to them as *partially color-blind.* These people, it is thought, have cones that are in some way different from those of most of us. They are able to see many colors (hues) but are not able to see and distinguish all that we do.

Not all the partially color-blind have the same defect. Some see all the hues that the normal person does with the exception of very light pinks, greens, tans, and browns, which are confused. These people are known as the *anomalous color-weak*. A fairly large group are known as *dichromats,* because their color vision is limited to only two hues. In most cases, the hues are blue and yellow, and the various shades or tints of these two. They tend to confuse the various reds and greens and traditionally have been known as the "red-green color-blind." Some of them also have difficulty in telling the brightness of the various reds. A relatively small group of dichromats have trouble with blue also.

Seeing in Three Dimensions. Since our retina is a two-dimensional surface and since we see only what is projected upon that surface, how do we see depth, which is the third dimension? This question puzzled scientists for many centuries, because the answer is quite complex. There are a great many cues which we use to see depth. Some of the visual cues are called *monocular* (one-eye) and some *binocular* (two-eye). Other cues are not visual at all but rather are *kinesthetic* (muscle-sense) cues.

Figure 10.6. In viewing the photograph of Paris (left) we perceive a three-dimensional or depth effect. What are the cues that we use in this perception? Are they primarily monocular or binocular cues? (Courtesy of the French Government Tourist Office.)

What is the smaller photograph (above) a picture of? Turn it over. What cues give us the perception of depth? Why do we perceive the picture differently when the photograph is held upside down? (Courtesy of the American Museum of Natural History.)

Monocular cues are those which allow a single eye to see some depth. One of these cues is *overlap;* if one object blocks part of the view of another object, the blocked object appears to be farther away. Another cue is *linear perspective;* the farther away an object is, the smaller will be its image on the retina. A midget a block away seems even farther away if we mistake him for a full-sized man. The reason is that an average man would have to be farther away to cast the same size image on our retina as the midget does at one block.

There are a number of other monocular cues, of which two are *haziness* and *shadows.* We all know that distant mountains appear hazy. Thus, if a common object cannot be seen clearly, we assume that it is farther away than similar objects that appear clear. Shadows make an object appear to have depth.

Artists must be very skillful in the use of shadows and all the other monocular cues. After all, a sketch or painting has only two dimensions but must give the appearance of three. How many of these cues are illustrated in Figure 10.6?

Binocular cues are those that arise in looking at the same object with both eyes at once. Each of our eyes views the object from a slightly different angle. Therefore, the image of this object on the retina is slightly different for the two eyes. We call this cue *retinal disparity.* The famous painter Leonardo da Vinci was the first person to diagram this effect, and his diagram, given in Figure 10.7, is still a good way of portraying the situation. Although each eye does not see a part of the background, together they see it all. The impression is that we see around the ball; hence, it appears to have roundness or depth. With only a little help from the monocular cues and other binocular cues, retinal disparity adds the third dimension to what we see.

Kinesthetic cues come from the muscles that control the eyes. One such cue comes from the muscle that pulls the ligaments attached to the lens of the eye; this cue is called *accommodation.* To view objects closer than 20 feet, our lens must change shape. Thus, it is entirely possible that we get some assistance in perceiving depth from the movement sense organ in the muscle that pulls the lens.

Figure 10.7. The famous Renaissance painter Leonardo da Vinci was the first person to diagram binocular vision and thus to show, in part, how the effect of the third dimension is given. The two eyes are focused on the object. Both left and right eyes can see everything from A to F except what is blocked by the object. Yet, the left eye can see what the right eye cannot, i.e., B to C. Together the two eyes can see around the object, taking in almost the whole background from A to F.

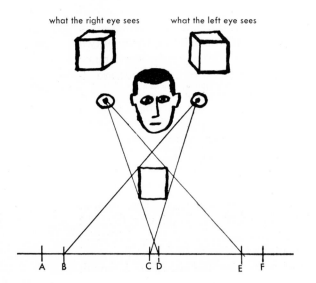

what the right eye sees   what the left eye sees

A B   C D   E F

Convergence is another possible cue for seeing depth. In convergence it is the muscles that move the two eyes in together which aid us in seeing the third dimension. To see an object nearer than 25 yards, our two eyes must move in and converge on the object. Beyond 25 yards the lines of sight of our two eyes are virtually parallel and no further cues are possible.

HEARING (AUDITION)

A totally blind person may still participate normally in most social and business conversations. But a totally deaf person, even if he reads lips quite well, is at a loss in trying to follow a conversation with more than one or two persons. We shall now examine in some detail the sense of hearing or *audition,* as it is more technically termed.

The Stimulus for Hearing. Mechanical disturbance can cause the molecules in solids, liquids, and gases to vibrate. These vibrations can be felt or seen in the shaking of our automobiles or steam pipes or in the circular waves set up when a pebble is thrown into the water of a placid lake. These mechanical vibrations can range in frequency from less than 1 per second to millions per second. When the frequency is between about 20 and 20,000 per second, we can hear the vibrations as sounds if they reach our ears.

The vibrations we hear are usually in the form of wave motion in the air. Most sounds have very complex wave motions. However, it has been discovered that these complex waves can be analyzed or broken down into a number of simple *sine* waves. A simple sine wave is a pure tone, such as the tone of a tuning fork. The wave shown in part A of Figure 10.8 is a typical sine wave. Each hill and valley, taken together, form what is called a *cycle.* The *frequency* of a sine wave is the number of these cycles of vibrations that occur in 1 second.

The height of the hills and the depth of the valleys are related to the amount of force or pressure in the wave. In fact, the physical energy or *intensity* of a sound wave is simply the amount of the pressure squared. To understand any sound wave, we must know its frequency and its intensity.

In this day of jets and rockets, most of us have come to know the velocity or speed of sound in air; at sea level it is about 760 miles per hour, or 1,100 feet per second. Sound waves travel about four times as fast in water and about ten times as fast in steel.

The Ear. Our ear is divided into three parts: the *external ear*, the *middle ear*, and the *inner ear*. The only visible part is the external ear or *pinna*. In man, the pinna has little to do with hearing, though it is useful as a knob to hook our glasses on. In addition to the pinna, the external ear contains the *external auditory canal*. This canal funnels sound waves from the pinna to the eardrum, or *tympanum*. The tympanum is a membrane which separates the external ear from the middle ear.

In the middle ear are three small bones called the *ossicles*. When the eardrum vibrates, the ossicles vibrate and allow the sound waves to enter the *oval window*. This window consists of a membrane in the bone of the head and separates the middle ear from the inner ear.

The inner ear is encased in the *cochlea*, which is a spiraled bony structure. The

Figure 10.8. (A) A tuning fork produces a relatively simple sound wave, sometimes called a sine wave. (B) and (C) Several tuning forks struck at the same time will form a more complex sound wave. (D) A simple musical instrument like a flute produces a sound wave that is not too complex, while a note played on a clarinet (E) is quite complex. Yet both instruments produce a regular wave that is composed of a fundamental sine wave to which several overtones are added. The clarinet adds more overtones than does the flute. If we had a large enough set of tuning forks, we could reproduce or duplicate the tones of both these and other musical instruments by combining several sine waves.

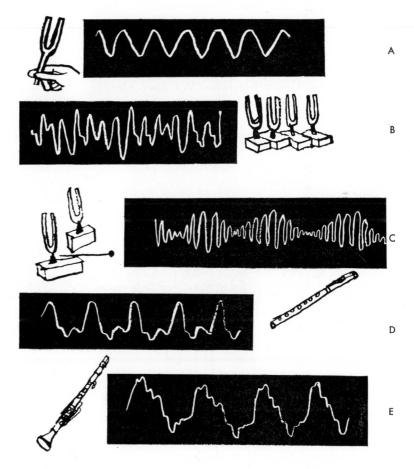

word "cochlea" means "snail shell" and this organ bears a marked resemblance to one. The cochlea is filled with fluid and contains a number of structures. Those of importance to us are the *basilar membrane* and the *organ of Corti*. On the organ of Corti are many little *hair cells*. When stimulated by sound waves, these hair cells set up nerve impulses which travel in the *auditory nerve* to the brain.

Functioning of the Ear. Thus we see that sound waves travel through the air to the head where they are collected by the pinna and funnel down the external auditory canal. Arriving at the eardrum, the sound travels through it and through the ossicles to the oval window. As the sound waves enter the cochlea, the fluid begins to vibrate and in turn the various structures vibrate. When the vibrations reach the basilar membrane and the organ of Corti, they set in motion the hair cells, thus arousing nerve impulses which travel to the brain. It is at this point that we hear the sound.

Pitch and Loudness. We have already noted that, for our purposes, the two important physical aspects of sound are frequency and intensity. Related to, but not identical with, these physical dimensions are two psychological aspects of hearing, *loudness* and *pitch*. Pitch varies mainly with the frequency or cycles per second of the tone, but it also varies to a small extent with the intensity or energy of the tone. For example, the highest note on the piano has a frequency of over 4,000 cycles per second, while the lowest note has about 30. If a high note is made very intense, it seems a little higher in pitch, although the frequency remains the same. On the other hand, a low note sounds lower in pitch if its intensity is increased.

Loudness, as we all know, varies most with the intensity of a sound, but it is also affected by changes in frequency. Thus we can say that both loudness and pitch are functions of both intensity and frequency.[1] The following illustration will help emphasize the fact that loudness is a psychological aspect of hearing.

If we sit in the middle of a large auditorium and listen to an orchestra that sounds comfortably loud, we can determine with a sound-pressure meter the exact physical intensities of the music from moment to moment. On returning home, if we play a tape recording of this orchestra in our living room and tune it in to sound exactly as loud as it did in the auditorium, we shall be surprised to discover on the sound-pressure meter that we have much less intensity than we did in the auditorium. If we turn up the sound until the physical intensity is the same as it was in the auditorium, we shall find the music unpleasantly loud and shall not want to stay in the living room with it. The difference in surroundings has made a great deal of difference in the perceived loudness of a particular intensity.

In hearing, just as in vision, we may determine our absolute and differential thresholds for both pitch and loudness. Figure 10.10 pictures a subject making one such measurement on an *audiometer*. This

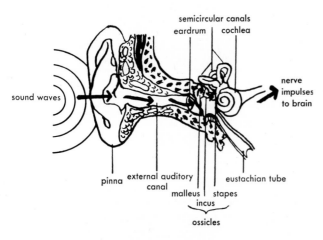

Figure 10.9.

[1] S. S. Stevens and H. Davis, *Hearing*, Wiley, New York, 1947, p. 70.

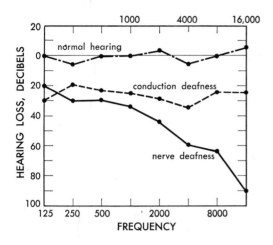

Figure 10.10. Graph shows three typical audiograms.

This boy (right) is having his hearing tested on an audiometer. When he hears a tone in the earphone he will raise his hand. Tones of various frequencies and intensities are used in the test. (Black Star.)

is an instrument for determining our absolute thresholds of loudness for tones of various frequencies. Also in this figure is a graph showing three audiometric records. The upper one is for normal hearing. The lower record indicates deafness for tones of the higher frequencies. The middle one shows conduction deafness.

High-tone deafness ordinarily follows injury or disease of the nerve fibers in the inner ear. *Nerve deafness* is very serious, because nothing can be done to cure it. *Conduction deafness* results most often from some disorder in the middle ear. In this condition, sounds are not conducted normally through the middle ear. This kind of deafness can sometimes be cured by an operation and can be partially corrected by the wearing of a hearing aid.

Sound Localization. To a certain extent we can tell where a sound comes from by listening to it. When a sound comes from

directly overhead, however, it is extremely difficult to locate. Indeed, we tend to confuse all the sounds that come from directly in front of us, directly behind us, or directly overhead. That is to say, we tend to confuse all sounds in a plane cutting through the center of the head exactly between the two ears. We can localize best of all those sounds located straight out from the right or the left ear.

A number of physical cues are used in sound localization. For instance, a sound coming from the right side gets to the right ear more quickly than to the left ear. It also sounds slightly louder in the right ear than in the left. Thus, both time of arrival and intensity are useful cues in localization. A number of other cues are also helpful.

We use our eyes and ears together to locate objects in our environment. Notice how disconcerting it is to watch a sound motion picture when the loud-speaker is off to one side instead of behind or in front of the screen.

There is a piece of apparatus (see Figure 10.11) which permits the sounds from our right to come into the left ear and the sounds from our left to come into the right

Figure 10.11. This instrument is called a pseudophone. Sounds from each side are heard by the ear on the opposite side of the head. What effect will this instrument have on the subject's ability to locate the direction from which the sound is coming? If he were to wear these earphones for several days or weeks, could he learn to locate sounds correctly?

ear. When this *pseudophone,* as it is called, is first put on, we are utterly confused in our localization of sounds. After a time, however, we become accustomed to the reversal of cues and are able to point out correctly the various sound sources. Thus, we see that so long as sensory cues are consistent, our brains are able to interpret the incoming impulses. The impulses from each sense organ are like a complex code, and the job of the brain is to decode them.

THE OTHER SENSES

In reflecting on the senses, people have long emphasized the importance of the eye and the ear. In this tradition, scientists have studied these two senses intensively and have tended to neglect the others. For this reason we shall not be able to treat the others so fully as we have vision and hearing.

In the introduction we stated that there are more senses than the five mentioned by Aristotle. In this section we shall look at six more senses, bringing our total to eight. Many physiologists prefer to distinguish and name even more senses than we do here. Instead of only five, we have eight or more senses, according to how we classify them.

The Sense of Taste. The sense of taste, or *gustation* as it is more technically called, is excited by liquids in the mouth. Some liquids, such as pure water, have little or no taste, while others are extremely effective stimuli. No one has yet been able to classify all the various chemicals that are capable of being taste stimuli. However, we do know about certain ones. For example, we know that the presence of the hydrogen ion in a liquid causes us to say that it is sour in taste. Also, as we might have suspected, most inorganic salt compounds taste salty. On the other hand, a large number of different chemicals are capable of tasting sweet (sugar, saccharine, and even some poisons). Bitter, like sweet, is a taste produced by a number of complex stimuli, although we can say that most alkaloids (such as quinine) taste bitter.

The *tongue* is the sense organ for taste. On the tongue are many small holes or depressions ringed by supporting cells. At the bottom of these holes are certain other cells that are sensitive to the taste stimuli. These *taste cells* are connected to nerve cells, so that when they are stimulated a nerve impulse is sent to the brain. (For knowledge of what happens when these impulses reach the brain, read the study on gustatory nerve impulses.) It is only when liquids enter these holes that stimulation can occur. If we dry our tongue with a piece of cotton and place a lump of dry sugar on the tongue, we find that, so long as we keep both tongue and sugar

GUSTATORY NERVE IMPULSES

One of the most interesting experiments * on taste used a cat as the subject. The cat's gustatory (taste) nerve was dissected, and individual fibers were isolated. Very small electrodes were then placed on each of these nerve fibers. By stimulating various spots on the tongue, the experimenter soon discovered which spots were connected with the several isolated fibers. This connection was shown in each case by the neural response of the fiber, picked up by the electrode.

Next, each of these spots was stimulated by four substances: a mild acid, salt, sugar, and quinine. These stimuli were used to elicit the four basic taste qualities: sour, salt, sweet, and bitter. An unexpected finding was that all the spots responded to the acid (sour). However, some of these fibers fired an impulse to acid only, while others responded to acid and to quinine, and still others to acid and to salt. Thus, there were three types of fibers: for sour only, for sour and bitter, and for sour and salt. The experimenter was unable to find any fibers for sweet. This may mean that the cat is unable to taste sugar or that the experimenter was not lucky enough to isolate the right fibers.

The most important finding in this experiment is the fact that even a simple taste quality depends on a pattern of neural discharges and not on the response of a single fiber. In the table given below, we see the patterns determined in this experiment. Presumably, the central nervous system must sort out or "decode" these patterns.

The Three Types of Fibers Found in the Gustatory Nerve of the Cat

| | *Response* | | |
	Sour	*Salt*	*Bitter*
Fiber A	X		
Fiber B	X	X	
Fiber C	X		X

It is likely that this patterning of nerve impulses is a general principle in the functioning of all sensory receptors. According to this principle, sensory quality does not depend on specific fiber responses but rather on the pattern of responses from all active fibers.

* C. Pfaffmann, "Gustatory Afferent Impulses," *Journal of Cellular and Comparative Physiology,* 17:243–258, 1941.

dry, we do not taste anything. If we dissolve the sugar in the saliva of the mouth, then it can be tasted.

There are only four different qualities of taste: *sour, salt, sweet,* and *bitter.* In Figure 10.12 we see the areas on the tongue that are most sensitive to these four tastes. The tip is most sensitive to sweet and salt, the sides to sour, the back to bitter, and the center to none of them. It is ironical to note that, in the old days of bitter medicines, the patient was often told to put the

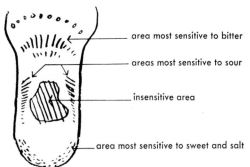

area most sensitive to bitter

areas most sensitive to sour

insensitive area

area most sensitive to sweet and salt

Figure 10.12. A human tongue.

medicine far back on the tongue so that he would not taste it!

We might protest that we taste a lot of flavors in addition to the above four tastes. The point is that we *smell* these flavors, not taste them. The so-called distinct "taste" of vanilla ice cream comes from the smell of the vanilla extract. In fact, the word "taste" in everyday usage often refers to more sensations than just that of taste. For instance, part of the "taste" of celery is the sound of the crunch; part of the "taste" of strawberry ice cream is the sight of the pink color; and part of the "taste" of any ice cream is the feeling of cold on the mucous membrane that lines the mouth.

The Sense of Smell. The stimuli for the sense of smell, or *olfaction* as it is called, are gases that enter the nose. Not all gases can be smelled, only those that in some way affect the organ of smell, the *olfactory epithelium*. The olfactory epithelium is located in the upper reaches of the nose. As we inhale, small eddy currents waft air to the epithelium. If it contains an odorous gas, certain reactions occur in the cells of the epithelium, causing nerve impulses to go brainward. Unfortunately, the chemists and physiologists have not as yet discovered the details of this process. Also unfortunate is the fact that we have not been able yet to determine the basic qualities of smell comparable to the four for taste.

(For a group of experiments on the basic qualities of smell, see the study on the classification of odors on pages 204–205.)

The sense of smell is extremely sensitive; only a few molecules of gas need enter the nose to be smelled. This extreme sensitivity might be a nuisance if it were not for the fact that our sense of smell adapts very readily. *Adaptation* is a process in which a sense organ gradually ceases to respond to a constant stimulus. When, for example, we first enter a pine forest, we find the odor of pine very strong. Within a short time, we no longer notice the odor; our sense of smell has become adapted. All our senses are capable of such adaptation, but smell is especially so.

The Skin Senses. The skin, or *cutaneous*, senses are four in number. For this reason, many physiologists would insist that we have four separate skin senses, not just one. Were we to use their classification, we should have eleven senses altogether instead of eight. These four cutaneous senses are *pressure* (touch), *pain, warmth*, and *coolness*. Aristotle listed all four of these under the heading "touch."

The stimuli for pressure are all those objects and forces that depress the skin. These stimuli may be solids, liquids, or gases (as a strong wind). The stimuli for pain are all those objects and forces that injure the skin, even slightly (pins, fire, chemicals, etc.). The stimuli for warmth and coolness are objects that are warm or cool, respectively. By "warm or cool" we mean warmer or cooler than the skin itself. Since the skin temperature continually changes with the environment, an object of a given temperature may feel cool or warm according to whether we have been standing by the fire or have just come in out of the cold.

The sense organs for the cutaneous senses are very small free nerve endings in the skin, or sometimes more specialized structures. For pressure, the most common specialized structure is a nerve fiber entwined

**DISTRIBUTION OF
SKIN RECEPTORS**

▶ The receptors for the four basic skin qualities are not distributed evenly over the whole area of the human skin. Explorations * of the skin surface have given us the relative concentrations of the several skin receptors in the various parts of the body. The skin is explored by using stimuli appropriate for the four cutaneous sensations: pressure, pain, warmth, and coolness.

Thus, the receptors are located indirectly by their correlation with the sensitive spots found on the surface of the skin. From a number of studies we are able to compile the accompanying table. It is to be noted that pain

The Number of Sensitive Spots Found in Several Skin Areas of the Body

	Number of spots per square centimeter			
	Pain	*Touch*	*Coolness*	*Warmth*
Inner side of forearm	203.0	15.0	6.0	0.4
Chest	196.0	29.0	9.0	0.3
Back of hand	188.0	14.0	7.0	0.5
Forehead	184.0	15.0	8.0	0.6
Tip of nose	44.0	100.0	13.0	1.0

spots are most numerous generally in the skin. Next most numerous are the pressure spots. A much smaller number of spots for coolness have been found, while the least numerous of all are the warmth spots.

This indirect evidence gives us a good picture of the relative distribution of skin receptors. However, direct studies of the skin by means of dissection do not always find a receptor for each sensitive spot. This fact can be explained, at least in part, by the discovery that simple free nerve endings (dendrites) may act as receptors for any of the four qualities. Another finding that is hard to explain is the fact that the sensitive spots do not seem to be stable. A later remapping of the same area gives a slightly different distribution of spots. One reason for this finding is the difficulty encountered in stimulating a second time exactly the same small spot that was touched before.

We may safely conclude, however, that different areas of the skin are differentially sensitive to the four basic qualities of pain, pressure, coolness, and warmth.

* E. von Skramlik, "Psychophysiologie der Tastsinne," *Archiv für die gesamte Psychologie*, Erganzungsbd. 4, 1937.

in the *follicle* at the base of a hair. Whenever the hair moves, impulses are aroused and sent to the spinal cord and brain. The same is true for the free nerve endings or for other specialized structures: when they are stimulated, nerve impulses are tripped off and travel to the spinal cord and brain. These receptor organs are not equally distributed in the skin. (The report on the distribution of skin receptors gives their differential placement in the skin.)

It has often been said that our cutaneous

▶ Although no final agreement has yet been reached as to the basic qualities of smell, a number of investigators have studied the problem. One of the classic attempts to settle the issue was Henning's * series of experiments on the classification of odors.

Henning's approach was to have subjects smell various substances and describe the similarities and differences among the odors. He used as stimuli over 400 different odorous substances. He tested a large number of subjects and selected the six who appeared to be the most reliable. Since these six could handle only about twenty stimuli a day, the experiment proved to be a long one.

After a while the subjects reached some agreement in classifying the odors

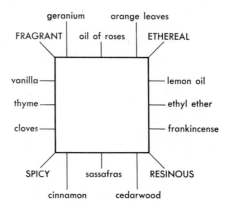

into several distinct groups. With Henning's help, the subjects agreed on a four-way system of classification. They determined what they believed to be the four distinctive odors: *fragrant, ethereal, resinous,* and *spicy.* Then, they made an odor square with the four corners corresponding with the above four salient odors (FERS).

* H. Henning, *Der Geruch,* Barth, Leipzig, Germany, 1924.

senses are our reality senses. When we feel something with our skin, we are convinced that it is really there. Which would seem more real, an invisible man that we could feel with our two hands, or a visible man that we could not feel? Most of us would agree that the man we could see and could not feel would be only an apparition or hallucination or maybe "done with mirrors," but not really there. On the other hand, the invisible man that we could feel would seem real if puzzling.

Like all our other senses, the skin senses contribute to our adjustment to the environment. We rely on the skin to help us survive in changing temperatures. Our pain receptors are sentinels that warn us of harmful objects around us. And we have seen that what we can feel with our skin seems more real to us than nearly anything else in the world.

Kinesthesis. Earlier in this chapter we referred to the kinesthetic or movement sense. Deep in our muscles and joints are little

Next, they placed all the substances used in the experiment on the sides of the square. For example, between fragrant and ethereal they put geranium, oil of roses, and orange leaves. In the figure showing the FERS odor square, we see other examples of their placement.

In a later experiment, Henning added two more salient odors (*putrid* and *burned*) and made what he called the smell prism (see the figure). He now believed that all odors could be placed somewhere in this prism.

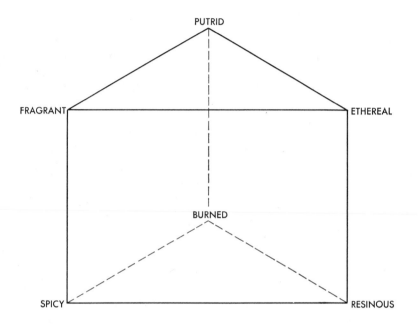

Although these experiments are very interesting, later ones have disagreed somewhat both with the idea of a prism and with what are the salient odors. However, no really better system has been devised to replace Henning's. We can only hope that in the near future the problem of the basic smell qualities will be solved.

capsules (similar to those in the skin) whose function is to respond to the movement of the muscles or joints. For example, when a muscle stretches, one of these receptors sends a nerve impulse to the central nervous system, though we are seldom aware of it. One reason Aristotle did not know of this sense is that we are not often conscious of its working.

Information from the kinesthetic sense, however, causes us to make various responses and muscular adjustments. Indeed,

if it were not for kinesthetic impulses, we could not perform any coordinated actions or movements. Coordinated behavior calls for a feedback system, which is provided by kinesthesis. When a muscle moves, it reports in, so to speak, that it has moved. Unless the central nervous system has this information, it cannot sensibly stop or continue the movement of that muscle.

Walking, for instance, would be impossible were it not for our kinesthetic feedback. When we started our leg out, either it would go too far, so that we should fall, or it would not move enough to do us any good. If we were completely without kinesthetic sense, we should be helpless, bedridden invalids. We could not even depend upon our vision, for the focusing of our eyes depends on the eye muscles, which in turn must be coordinated through kinesthesis. Fortunately, no person is ever completely lacking in kinesthesis.

The Sense of Balance. Most of us as children had the experience of being twirled around and around until we became so dizzy that we fell down. What happened was that as we accelerated or decelerated in our twirling we stimulated some of the sense organs of balance (often called the *vestibular sense organs*). Near the cochlea (see Figure 10.9) in the inner ear are three canals called the *semicircular canals*. In these canals is a fluid which moves whenever we turn or rotate our heads. Lining these canals are some small hair cells that respond with a nerve impulse when the fluid pushes against them. These impulses, when they reach the central nervous system, participate in maintaining equilibrium. In addition to these canals the sense organs for balance include two other cavities in the bone near the cochlea. These cavities are filled with small crystals that respond to gravity (the *static sense*). These receptors respond to the position or tilt of the head.

As with kinesthesis, we are seldom aware of our sense of balance. Yet, when something disturbs it even momentarily, we are handicapped in moving about. For example, alcohol may interfere with nerve connections in the central nervous system and cause a loss of equilibrium. Even after only a few drinks we may have an uncomfortable feeling of unsteadiness. Seasickness, also, is in part a result of the peculiar motions set up in the fluids of these canals by the motion of the ship. After all, we evolved as an animal that confined its ac-

tivities more or less to dry land. One of the most amazing results of this fact is that pilots in a fog sometimes fly their airplanes along upside down without knowing it. The reason is that once they are upside down and the fluid in the semicircular canals stops moving, they do not have any more impulses and the central nervous system assumes that everything is normal. Furthermore, everything they see inside the airplane is in proper relation.

Organic Sensitivity. Throughout our bodies, wherever blood vessels go, there are free nerve endings that act as receptors. Some of these are for pain reception and others are for various other kinds of sensations. We all know what it means to feel nauseated or to have an upset stomach. In fact there are a number of different feelings that seem to come from inside us. All these sensations are grouped together and called *organic sensitivity*. Not much is known either about the receptors or about their connections in the central nervous system.

INTERRELATION OF THE SENSES

In our discussion of the confusion about the use of the word "taste," we noted how odors, temperatures, sights, and sounds can all contribute to what we commonly call taste. This is but one example of the interrelation of our senses. In order for us to adjust to our environments, we need all the information we can get. All our sense organs send information to the central nervous system, where it is coordinated and used. Because we are not conscious that this coordination is going on, we are able to concentrate on meeting the whole situation at hand.

Perception. As we perceive (interpret) sense data we coordinate the working of all our senses. For instance, we perceive our pet dog not only by sight but also by sound (his bark), by smell (his doggy odor), and by touch (his shaggy coat and his wet nose and tongue). Furthermore, the pet is known by all these perceptions rolled into one. If any of these aspects are missing, we note the difference. If too many are lacking, we may not recognize the dog. It is not easy to recognize a shaggy, smelly poodle after he has been bathed, clipped, trimmed, and perfumed.

The next chapter takes up the topic of perception in further detail.

SUMMARY

We have eight or more senses that we use to explore and learn about the world.

Each of our senses has a specific sense organ or receptor, and each sense organ is sensitive to certain stimuli in the environment.

The eye is the receptor for the sense of vision and is sensitive to light energy. Sometimes the eye is compared to a camera because each has a lens which focuses light images on a sensitive surface. This surface in the eye is the retina, which is composed of rods and cones.

The cones allow us to see the different wavelengths of visible light as different hues or colors. We can also distinguish differences in brightness and in saturation of colors.

The rods do not distinguish colors but are more sensitive to light than are the cones. The rods are better in dim light, and the cones in bright light. Visual acuity is better with the cones than with the rods.

We measure the sensitivity of the rods and cones in terms of absolute and differential thresholds. The absolute threshold is the smallest amount of light that will stimulate the receptor. The differential threshold is the smallest increase in light that will allow us to say that one light is brighter than another.

We see depth and the third dimension because of a number of monocular and binocular cues. The most important cue is a binocular one, retinal disparity, in which the retina of each eye receives a slightly different image of the object being viewed.

The ear is the sense organ for hearing and is sensitive to sound waves, which are mechanical vibrations in the air. The ear has three parts: the outer ear, the middle ear, and the inner ear. The first two parts are concerned with the conduction of sound waves. The inner ear contains the sensitive hair cells which have neural connections to the brain.

The two main sensations in hearing are those of pitch and loudness. Both these are a function of the physical dimensions of sound: frequency and intensity.

Deafness can result either from injury to nerves or from interference with conduction through the middle ear.

A number of cues aid in sound localization. Among these cues are differences in time of arrival and intensity of sound at the two ears.

The tongue contains receptors for taste. There are four taste qualities: sweet, sour, salt, and bitter.

The sense organ for smell is located in the nose and is sensitive to certain gases.

The skin, or cutaneous, senses are four in number: pressure, pain, warmth, and coolness.

Kinesthesis is the movement sense. Its receptors are found in the muscles and joints. It provides a feedback system, which aids coordination.

The semicircular canals are organs used for the sense of balance, and they are stimulated by movements of the head. There are also crystal-filled cavities near these canals that act as positional or static sense organs of balance.

Free nerve endings within our bodies appear to be the receptors for what is called organic sensitivity.

All our senses are interrelated, and the information they send to the brain is used to help us better to adjust to our changing environment.

QUESTIONS

1. Why did Aristotle believe that we have only five senses?

2. In what ways are all our senses similar?

3. In what ways might it be misleading to say that our eye is like a camera?

4. What are the rods and cones? How are they alike? How different?

5. Explain the following: threshold, j.n.d., and Weber-Fechner law.

6. What are the main cues for depth perception?

7. Trace the path of sound from the pinna to the hair cells.

8. What is meant by "sound localization"? How does it take place?

9. What are the other senses besides vision and hearing? List the sense organ and stimulus for each.

10. How is kinesthesis of importance to an organism?

11. Of what use to us are our senses?

12. What is the connection between perception and the senses?

SUGGESTED READINGS

Chapanis, A., et al.: *Applied Experimental Psychology*, Wiley, New York, 1949.
> (Facts about the senses for engineering and industry.)

Davis, H. (ed.): *Hearing and Deafness*, Rinehart, New York, 1947.
> (An interesting book for the layman about audition and the problem of deafness.)

Geldard, F. A.: *The Human Senses*, Wiley, New York, 1953.
> (A complete treatise on the senses.)

Morgan, C. T., and E. Stellar: *Physiological Psychology*, 2d ed., McGraw-Hill, New York, 1950, chaps. 6–12.
> (The physiology of the sense organs.)

Stevens, S. S., and H. Davis: *Hearing*, Wiley, New York, 1938.
> (A classic on the sense of hearing.)

11 ⓅERCEPTION

Suppose that, as we are sitting indoors, we suddenly hear a high-pitched squealing sound, followed by a crashing noise, then by the sound of shouting. Although we had not seen two cars skidding and crashing into one another and people running to the scene of the accident, this is what the sounds we heard would probably mean to us. It is this meaningfulness in our experiences that is the central feature of perception. We define *perception* as the process of interpreting stimuli, that is, of finding or constructing their meanings.

Let us see what is involved in perceiving. As is pointed out in Chapter 10, various physical energies in our environment act on sensitive receptors from which nerve impulses go to the brain. There these impulses give rise to sensory experiences and to perceptions of objects and events. This sequence of events is shown in Figure 11.1. As goal-seeking organisms, we seldom take any interest in sensations for their own sake. Indeed, it is somewhat difficult for us to pay attention to sensations as such, apart from their meanings. Normally we find, search for, and even invent meanings for our sensory experiences.

MEANING IN PERCEPTION

We shall now examine somewhat more closely the characteristics of perception and how the perceptual process takes place. Our emphasis will be on how we try to make sense of our experience, that is, on how we interpret the stimuli which act on our sense receptors. In the example given in our opening paragraph, sounds furnished the basis for the interpretation that a car accident had occurred. The sounds functioned as *signs* of the total situation.

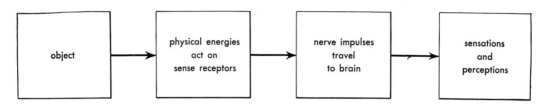

Figure 11.1. The sequence of events in perception.

Functional View of Perception. To perceive a meaningful world helps us to adjust. From a minimum of information—sounds, lights, etc.—we are able to know a great deal about our environment. We must continually digest and interpret this information if we are going to adjust to a changing world. In order to satisfy our motives, we need to know what resources are available in our environment, and we need to know the dangers that threaten us and the barriers that block off the paths to our goals. Thus, to satisfy motives, we are continually striving to make sense out of our world. Perception therefore serves a useful function.

Perceiving Objects. Our world of experience appears to us to consist of many more or less separate objects, such as buildings, cars, and people. These objects seem to have a more or less enduring existence and to be relatively detached from each other. The interesting thing is that nearly all people perceive these objects as being independent of the perceiver. Somewhat naïvely, perhaps, we tend to regard them as having a reality and as having properties which do not depend on how we view them. The fact, however, is that we can know objects only through perception. All that we can observe is a pattern of stimulation—lights, sounds, smells, etc. Perception is as much a function of the perceiver as it is of the thing perceived.

How do we come to perceive our world as made up of objects? This difficult problem has concerned psychologists (and philosophers) for many years—in fact, for cen-

turies. Suppose, for example, that we see an airplane overhead. The fact that we can distinguish this object from its background probably does not depend entirely, or even mainly, upon learning. Someone totally unfamiliar with airplanes would presumably be able to perceive the same bounded area, although he might not know what it meant or might interpret it differently from us. Even though unlearned factors may play a part in perceiving something as a whole and relatively independent from its background, learning also may play a part. Being familiar with airplanes helps us to see the object in the sky as an airplane with all that being an airplane implies. It is a meaningful object in our culture. In another culture (or at an earlier time), it might have appeared as a big bird. We might say that the meaning of airplane includes the various expectations which are aroused by whatever accounts for the pattern of stimulation. These expectations would include such things as the fact that the airplane has a motor, that it has a pilot (even though we cannot see him at the moment), that it may have passengers and a payload, and that it may be on a scheduled, prescribed course of flight. Having identified something as an object of a given kind enables us to anticipate the various characteristics which we have learned to expect from objects of this kind.

Our expectations enter at two points: First, if we expect a certain object, we are more likely to perceive something as being this object than if we do not. If we are expecting to meet our friend at the station, we may mistake a stranger for our friend. Secondly, once we have identified an object, this brings into play our various expectations (anticipations) about it. Once we have identified our friend, we expect that he will answer to his name, know of various common experiences, and so on. Since these expectations are learned, it is obvious that learning plays an important part in perception.

Perceptual Constancy. We may notice that an object looks much the same on different occasions even though as a stimulus pattern it may have varied considerably. For example, under most conditions snow looks white, even though its brightness under dim illumination may be less than that of coal under bright illumination. Our friend usually looks like the same person even though we see him from various points of view and in different settings.

The phenomenon illustrated by these examples is called *perceptual* constancy, which is the tendency of a stimulus situation to be perceived in the same way under varying circumstances. Some of the factors accounting for perceptual constancy are known. One factor is that a stimulus may bear a constant *relationship* to its background.

For example, in the case of the brightness constancy of snow and coal, this brightness is perceived in relation to the brightness of the background. Snow in dim light *is* brighter than most other objects in such light. Many characteristics such as brightness are relative to background conditions.

A second factor is that we learn to *select* as a basis for perception those aspects of a stimulus situation which are most *dependable* for purposes of object identification. These dependable aspects are those that remain relatively constant under changing circumstances. On the other hand, the undependable, variable features of a stimulus situation tend to be ignored. For example, the angularity (sharp nose, outthrust

jaw, etc.) of our friend's face, together with other relatively constant features, help us to recognize him. We see him as being the same person at various times despite variations in his clothes, the background, and other details. Moreover, once we have identified our friend a whole set of expectations regarding him are aroused, and these expectations are a part of the percept. There are, however, limits to how much variation in a stimulus pattern may occur before an object looks markedly different.

Search for Meaning. Sometimes we do not immediately find a meaning for a stimulus situation. Suppose that outside the room we hear a series of loud sounds, irregularly spaced. We do not know what caused

Figure 11.2. What are these things for? Until a frame of reference is provided, the picture is ambiguously perceived. Actually these objects are used in connection with oil-well drilling. In order for the objects to become fully significant detailed knowledge of oil-drilling methods would be necessary. (Standard Oil Company, New Jersey.)

them, but we search for their meaning. Is it dynamiting? Not likely in this part of town. Is it gunshots? Probably not. And then we think of the answer: shock waves from passing jets. There has been a search for meaning. This is what we normally do. If we cannot immediately find the meaning of a stimulus situation, we search for it.

We need to make sense out of our experiences, to see them in relationship. This is especially true if what is happening affects our welfare, as in times of danger. Then there is a desperate need to find the meaning of events, that is, how they fit together and what is likely to happen next.

Reduced Cues. The strength of the tendency to find meaning in our experiences is exemplified in our reactions to *reduced cues.* We hear a roaring sound and catch a glimpse of something going down the street. What we perceive is a car passing. This time we have perceived a car on the basis of far fewer signs than might ordinarily be available. We are responding to reduced cues. Perhaps there is a tickling sensation on our neck, and we perceive it as a crawling bug or as a loose thread. Upon hearing some scraping and clicking sounds coming from the kitchen, we perceive that someone is getting ready to set the table. Such perceptions on the basis of reduced cues are commonplace in our lives.

We depend on reduced cues to a great extent. The more reduced they are, the less they point to any given object. Indeed, they may be used to make interpretations of conditions that are not even observable—of *abstractions,* such as other people's attitudes. Someone smiles and extends his hand; we perceive an attitude of friendship. Likewise we perceive a smirk as contempt, or a scowl as disagreement. It may be useful to rely on reduced cues to perceive abstractions. But abstractions are double-edged—powerful if critically arrived at and properly used, but dangerous, or at least misleading, if invalid.

On the other hand, it is very economical to be able to perceive objects from reduced cues. It would be impossible to make an exhaustive check of everything—or of anything, for that matter—to be sure of what it is. By reacting to a few signs, we can get an enormous amount of useful and fairly reliable information about our world.

Perception and Probabilities. All this ties in with another facet of perception. We perceive in terms of probabilities. No sign by itself tells us the whole story, but it, together with others, points in a certain

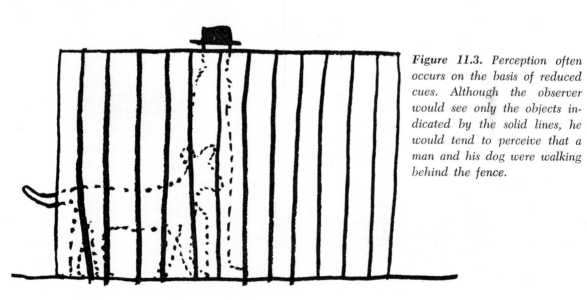

Figure 11.3. Perception often occurs on the basis of reduced cues. Although the observer would see only the objects indicated by the solid lines, he would tend to perceive that a man and his dog were walking behind the fence.

direction. Our experience teaches us that certain objects or events go together—or follow one another—with a high degree of probability. When we see something that looks like a chair, we expect that it can be sat upon. It would be very unexpected, and disturbing, to find that it was a fake made from sponge rubber. In other words, this reacting to signs in terms of probabilities helps us in getting information rapidly and continuously enough for it to be of use.

Errors in Perception. Sometimes, however, we make mistakes in perception. We may be horrified to see a child pick up a knife and stab another, only to find that it was just a rubber knife. Magicians are adept at taking advantage of our normal expectations by performing highly improbable actions. In cases such as the foregoing the errors do not matter—they may even be fun. But there are situations in which errors in perception have practical, even life-and-death, consequences. In battle, for example, it makes a big difference whether the approaching aircraft is one of the enemy's or one of ours.

Under certain stimulus conditions, certain errors of perception occur in nearly everybody. Such errors, which depend on stimulus conditions and occur in normal people, are called *illusions*. A familiar example is the "bent-stick" illusion which is seen when a fishing pole is stuck into the water at an angle. Other illusions are discussed and illustrated later in this chapter.

Hallucinations, on the other hand, are false perceptions that occur under abnormal conditions. For example, under the influence of certain drugs a person may see visions and hear voices which bear no relation to reality. People with severe personality disturbances may also hallucinate events which do not exist or which are extreme distortions of reality. Incidentally, hallucinations are distinguished from *delusions*, which are systems of false beliefs about reality (see Chapter 6).

There are many different reasons for errors in perception. The opportunity to observe may be poor, as in dim light or with obstacles partially blocking our view. Then, too, events may take place so rapidly that we fall behind in interpreting them. Witnesses at accidents often are baffled by the rapidity of the action.

Expectations can also distort our perception. Sometimes we so strongly expect a certain event to happen that nearly anything that happens will be interpreted as that event. Most of us have been embarrassed at one time or another by "recognizing" the wrong person as a friend for whom we had been waiting.

Finally, as is discussed later in this chapter, our needs and attitudes can cause us to perceive wrongly.

If it is very important not to make errors, then we can take precautions. We can try to get more complete information. We can check our evaluations against those of other people. We can deliberately look for other possible interpretations, and then see if the evidence is for or against them. We can try to be aware of some of our attitudes, especially prejudices, to make allowance for them. In other words, we can try to be like the scientist at his best when he systematically records data, analyzes them objectively, considers various possible explanations, and then arrives at a tentative conclusion.

STIMULUS FACTORS IN PERCEPTION

We have looked at perception as the meaningful interpretation of our sensory experiences. On the other hand, the objects and events which are experienced impose some limits on how they are likely to be perceived. Different stimulus patterns—a cow, a building, a book—provide different raw materials for the organizing process of perception. On the other hand, as we have seen, our expectations and our needs have much to do with what and how we perceive.

All this leads to an important conclusion: Perception is determined jointly by outer (stimulus) and inner (personal) factors.[1] This statement is opposed to the "common-sense" idea that we directly perceive what is "out there." What is perceived depends as much on the perceiver as on that which is to be perceived. The two factors working together determine perception.

It is not possible, however, to separate completely inner from outer factors in perception. The two classes of determinants are highly interdependent, but for convenience in analysis we treat them one at a time. In this section we shall consider the part played by the stimulus, and, in the rest of the chapter, the part played by the person.

Attention and Stimulus Conditions. We do not perceive everything at once; rather, we select certain objects to perceive while ignoring others. The direction of perception toward certain selected objects is called *attention*. Attention is determined partly by personal factors, such as interests, which are discussed later in this chapter. In addition, there are a number of

[1] G. Murphy, *Personality: A Biosocial Approach to Origins and Structure*, Harper, New York, 1947, pp. 331–361.

stimulus conditions that help to determine the direction of attention.

First, an intense stimulus is more likely to be noticed than one that is less intense. For example, a brightly colored page of advertising matter is more likely to be noticed than one that is not so vivid.

Second, a changing stimulus is more likely to be noticed than one that does not change. Most of us have observed that a flickering light is more attention-getting than a steady one. Something that moves is more likely to attract our attention than something which is stationary.

Third, a repeated stimulus is more likely to be noticed than one that is not repeated. For instance, we may have to call someone's name several times in a crowd before he hears us. In more controlled experiments, too, such an effect of repetition has been demonstrated.

Fourth, a contrasting stimulus is more likely to attract attention than one that is not contrasting. One black sheep among a flock of white ones stands out from the rest.

Stimulus Factors Favoring Organization. The most extensive studies of stimulus characteristics favoring perceptual organization have been made by the gestalt psy-

Figure 11.4. Striped-paper chamber used to test the visual perception of an infant chimpanzee raised from birth in total darkness. The test was made by rotating the chamber and observing whether the animal's eyes followed the moving stripes. The results of this and other tests show that the development of visual perception during the first few months of life depends upon learning through experience. (From George W. Gray, "The Yerkes Laboratories," Scientific American, February, 1955, p. 71, by courtesy of the publisher.)

Figure 11.5. The simplest level of perceptual organization is a simple figure on a simple ground. Notice that the boundary between the black and white areas is perceived as belonging to the black figure.

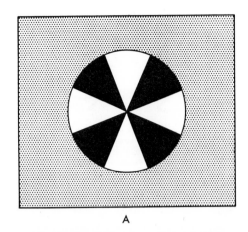

A

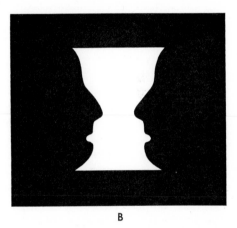

B

Figure 11.6. Look at each picture for about 30 seconds. Can you see each picture in more than one way? To what extent are the different ways of perceiving these objects subject to conscious control?

chologists. The term *Gestalt* means "form" (or "organized pattern") in German. The gestalt psychologists discovered that all perceptions have an organized character. The parts of a stimulus situation depend on the whole of which they are a part. For example, a melody sounds essentially the same in different keys. Even though the individual notes are changed, the melody as a whole remains unchanged, and the different notes are high or low in relation to the melody as a whole.

Figure and ground. When we perceive an object, usually one part tends to stand out while the rest seems to remain in the background. For example, the letters on this page stand out against the background of the page as a whole. The part which stands out is called the *figure,* and the rest of the stimulus pattern is called the *ground.* The concept of figure and ground is not restricted to visual perception alone. The ticking of a clock may be the figure against the ground of other sounds, such as the singing of birds and the rustling of leaves.

The gestalt psychologists have studied a number of conditions affecting the tendency to perceive certain parts of a stimulus situation as figure and others as ground. Among them are all the factors in attention which we have discussed—intensity, change, repetition, and contrast. Some-times, however, figure and ground relationships are ambiguous, that is, reversible. Figure 11.6 illustrates this effect. Both parts of the illustration have the unusual feature that figure and ground are interchangeable. *A* may be perceived either as a black cross or a white cross. *B* may be perceived either as two black faces or as a white vase. As we look at a diagram, it may change suddenly without any intention on our part. See if you can see these patterns either

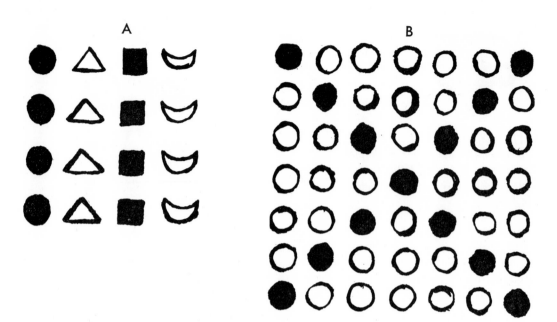

Figure 11.7. Which is the easier way to see the left-hand part (A) of the figure, as rows or as columns? What gestalt factor accounts for the X which you see in the right-hand part (B)?

way at will. It will be observed that these perceptions are mutually exclusive—B can be perceived either as a pair of faces or as a vase, but not as both simultaneously.

In many cases it is possible to perceive different parts of the same stimulus situation as figure. For example, at a football game, the star quarterback may stand out for a moment as the figure; at another time, the whole backfield; then the band or the cheering section. The interesting thing about these different organizations of the stimulus situation is that the various perceptions are so different from one another even though they may contain many elements in common.

Law of similarity. Gestalt psychologists have pointed out a number of factors favoring the organization of part of a stimulus pattern into figure. One of these is the factor of similarity. Stimuli which are similar tend to be perceived as forming a group, that is, a figure. Figure 11.7 illus-

trates the law of similarity. In the A part of the illustration the items are more readily perceived as forming columns than as forming rows, since each column has similar, in fact identical, figures. The B part of the illustration shows that the similarity among the filled in circles helps us to perceive an X. Can you perceive the open circles as forming a four-leaf-clover figure? This may be harder to perceive than seeing an X.

On the basis of similarity we are likely to perceive as figure a group of pine trees scattered among other trees; a series of whistle blasts interspersed among other sounds; a small number of dissenters among those who agree. There are many other examples of the same tendency to perceive as figure stimuli which are similar to one another.

Law of proximity. Stimuli which are close together (proximate) in space and time tend to be perceived as forming a figure. This law is illustrated in Figure 11.8. In the *A* part of the illustration the lines which are close together readily form pairs. See if you can perceive as pairs the lines which are more widely separated. It is certainly difficult to do so. In constellations of stars (see Figure 11.8*B*, below) we can see the same tendency for stimuli which are close together to form a whole in perception. The law of proximity is further illustrated in both written and printed material. The words on this page stand out as units because the letters are grouped closely together and spaces separate the words and lines.

Stimuli which follow each other closely in time are also likely to be grouped as figure. The codes used by telegraphers employ this principle of grouping dots and dashes together according to the time intervals between them. Groups of drumbeats are readily perceived as such. In our speech we make use of rhythm and other devices to indicate the appropriate group-ing of the words so as to form meaningful units of thought.

It seems likely that the tendency to organize as a unit stimuli which occur in immediate sequence is a sort of unlearned perception of cause and effect. A bright flash of lightning immediately followed by a loud rumble of thunder is likely to be perceived as a causal succession—as the lightning causing the thunder. The events would seem to be interdependent parts of the same perceptual whole.

Suppose that just as (or immediately after) we switch on a light a loud explosion occurs. It probably would seem to us that turning on the light somehow caused the explosion. The causal perception would occur to us immediately, although we might reject it after critical thought. There are many examples in children's behavior of naïve perception of causality in what adults have learned to regard as chance coincidences. The point, however, is that we all tend to perceive a causal relation-

B

Figure 11.8. Notice how the lines appear as pairs and how the stars appear to form clusters. What stimulus factors are responsible for this effect? (Courtesy of the Yerkes Observatories.)

A

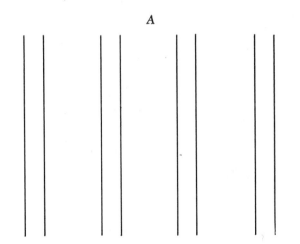

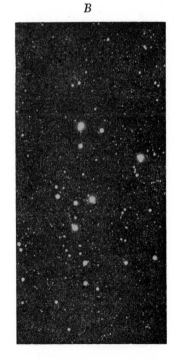

▶ Max Wertheimer, the man who founded gestalt psychology, was born in 1880 in Germany. After obtaining his doctor's degree at the University of Würzburg, he taught at a number of German universities. Wertheimer became interested in the perception of movement. In 1912 he published a report of his experiments in this area, using the term "Phi phenomenon" to refer to the apparent movement which is perceived when one stimulus light goes off and another nearby comes on. Wertheimer, together with Kurt Koffka and Wolfgang Kohler, played a major part in the development of gestalt psychology. In more recent years all three of these men came to the United States, where they continued their research and writing. One of Wertheimer's later contributions was a book, *Productive Thinking*, which applies the principles of gestalt psychology to thinking and problem solving. This little volume includes many interesting examples of creative thinking by children. It also includes accounts of problem solving by Einstein, who devised the theory of relativity, and Gauss, a famous mathematician.

Figure 11.9. According to the law of Prägnanz, "poor" forms tend to be perceived (and remembered) as being like the corresponding "good" forms. Why do you think this effect occurs? Would knowledge of this effect be of any advantage in dealing with our world?

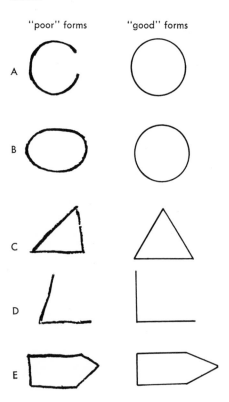

"poor" forms   "good" forms

A

B

C

D

E

ship between stimuli that change together or closely follow one another, at least until further learning or a reasoned understanding make us think otherwise.

Law of Prägnanz. One of the most general principles of perception has been called "the law of *Prägnanz*" by the gestalt psychologists. This law says that we tend to perceive a stimulus as a "good" form—or at least as "good" as the stimulus conditions permit. There are certain stable, normal forms toward which our perceptions (and memories) tend. These are so-called "good" forms. In general, "good" forms tend to be symmetrical, balanced, and complete. These are not very objective criteria, but they can be illustrated in Figure 11.9, which shows a number of so-called "poor" forms and some corresponding "good" forms. There is a tendency to perceive (and remember) the "poor" forms as though they were "good" forms. For example, broken circles tend to be perceived as complete circles, as shown in *A*, and ellipses which are near circles (*B*) tend to be seen as more nearly circular. In *C* the left-hand triangle, which is not symmetrical, tends to be modified in perception so as to be more nearly symmetrical, like the equilateral triangle on the right. The "poor" form in *D*, which might be regarded as an "imperfect" right angle, tends to be perceived as a normal right angle. Finally, in *E* the pointed object on the left may be perceived as being even more pointed (or, possibly, as blunted). Note that these changes do not occur every time we perceive, but there is a *tendency* for perceptions to approximate a so-called good form.

The law of *Prägnanz* also refers to the tendency to fill in the gaps perceptually when the stimulus is incomplete. The black patches of Figure 11.10 become organized as a picture of a kitten, a meaningful whole. In the same way many very incomplete and sketchy cartoon drawings are "improved" in perception by filling in the gaps, smoothing out irregularities, and in other ways approximating a "good" form.

Illusions. Under some circumstances our perceptions tend to be misleading. They give us erroneous pictures of our environment. Some well-known illusions are shown in Figure 11.11. In part *A* the two vertical lines are actually straight, although they appear to be bent inward, and in part *B* the straight vertical lines appear to be bent outward, to bulge away from each other. The two central circles in part *C* are actually of the same size, even if they look different. Are the two slanting lines of part *D* part of the same straight line? They do not appear to be, but actually they are. In part *E* the two figures are actually of the same size, although they appear to be markedly different. Even when we know about these illusions, the figures still tend to look as they did before. If, however, we needed to react to these figures over and over again and attainment of our goals depended on making accurate judgments about them, we should eventually be able to react correctly and the figures might even look different to us.

Perception of the part depends upon the whole. In each of these illusions the way

Figure 11.10. *What gestalt principle is illustrated in this picture?*

in which a part is judged depends upon the setting of the other parts. Although illusions demonstrate this fact quite dramatically, this same principle—the organized nature of perception—holds also in our usual, nonillusory perceptions.

Perception of Motion. The active, organizing character of perception is shown in the perception of motion. We *put* motion into some of the things we observe. One demonstration of this is what the gestalt psychologists have named the *Phi phenomenon:* If two light sources (not too far apart) are switched on and off in close succession, a light appears to *move* from one place to the other. Advertisers make use of this effect in signs consisting of lights that appear to move, when all that happens is that lights are going on and off in some particular order.

The same effect is perceived when we look at motion pictures. The pictures flashed upon the screen are merely a series

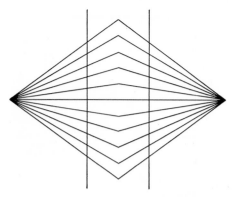

A. Are the vertical lines bent or straight?

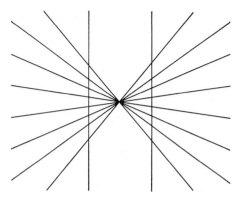

B. Are these vertical lines parallel?

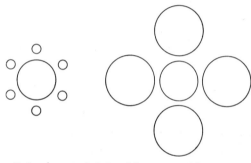

C. Are the central circles of the same or different sizes?

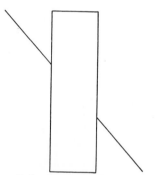

D. Are the two lines part of the same slanting line?

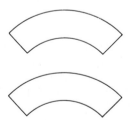

E. Which of the above is larger?

Figure 11.11. Some familiar illusions.

**THE DISTORTED
ROOM ILLUSION**

A fascinating series of experiments in perception has been carried out at Princeton University. When objects are seen in a special room at the Perception Demonstration Center, they undergo some dramatic changes in appearance (see the figure below). When the observer looks at this room through a hole and with one eye, it looks like a normal room with rectangular walls, floor, and ceiling. But the apparent size of the objects in this room depends on their location. Two objects of the same size look much different in size if one is on the right and the other on the left. This illusion is experienced by everybody. Actually, the room is distorted (see figure on page 222). Since the room, which appears to be rectangular, provides the dominant frame of reference, the apparent size of objects depends on where they are located in the room. Even after a person knows about the nature of the distorted room, he still experiences the illusion when he views the room with one eye and from the right position. This demonstration is important in showing how stimulus conditions and our assumptions (for example, our assumption that all rooms are rectangular) influence perception.

Things are not always what they seem. Actually, the two men are about the same size. For an explanation of how this effect was produced, see the next figure and the text. (Courtesy of Perception Demonstration Center, Princeton University.)

of stills, as is shown in Figure 11.12. If they follow one another rapidly enough, they appear to move smoothly. Animated cartoons also use this same device—a series of stills differing slightly from frame to frame, projected in rapid sequence. The motion is not in the pictures, obviously, although the characteristics of the pictures and their manner of presentation play their part. The motion is an illusion. We fill in the gaps and thus have the perception of motion.

Even when we look at a moving object, unless our eyes successively fixate the object in different positions, we see only a blur. Each fixation is like a still picture, and a succession of these stills gives us the impression of motion.

HOW OUR NEEDS AFFECT PERCEPTION

The way in which we perceive is determined not only by the nature of the stimulus but also by personal factors. It has already been noted that the direction of attention—what we notice—is affected by our interests. We may want a new suit, for example, and so find our attention turning to suits in display windows. But although these factors may attract our attention,

they are not necessarily sufficient to hold it. Motivation usually is essential for attention to persist in reading, in watching a game, and in many other activities. We tend to perceive objects which are relevant to our motives—both those that are potentially satisfying and those that are potentially threatening.

Ambiguous Stimuli. The more ambiguous or indefinite the stimulus situation, the more our motives are likely to influence the way we perceive it. In the so-called projective tests of personality, the stimuli (ink blots, pictures, incomplete sentences, etc.) are intentionally made ambiguous, thus giving personal factors a greater chance of asserting themselves.

The influence of needs (and expectations) is especially apparent in times of crisis. If two people have had a quarrel and consequently are unsure of their attitudes toward one another, the meanings of each one's acts become uncertain to the other. Hostile feelings, anxiety, or a desire for reassurance are likely to influence how they perceive one another's behavior. In situations of danger, too, such as a soldier's experiences on the battlefield, where his survival is often uncertain, projections of anxieties and other feelings are highly likely.

Effect of Strong Tensions. Although the influence of needs is more apparent when the stimuli are ambiguous, our perception of even relatively unambiguous stimuli can be affected when we are subjected to unusual stress and tension. Indeed, under intense motivation our perception may be grossly distorted. For example, a man was driving home in a great hurry at the end of the day. As he approached an intersec-

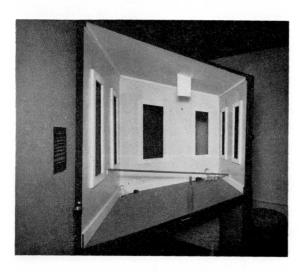

This is how the room shown in the preceding illustration looks when viewed with both eyes and at a distance. (Courtesy of Perception Demonstration Center, Princeton University.)

tion where he usually turned left, he noticed that a new traffic signal light had been put up. As he approached the intersection, the light turned red, but the car just ahead turned left anyway. At the same time he caught a glimpse of a sign under the light which he interpreted as reading "Left turn on red." Actually, the sign read "*Right* turn on red." His desire to get home quickly, coupled with a hasty glance at the sign, autistically distorted his perception—he read the sign as he wanted it to read.

In our discussion of the enhancement and defense of the self (Chapter 6), it is pointed out that we tend to perceive ourselves and our experiences in ways that are self-enhancing and lessen threat. This does not mean that we always close our eyes to threat. An extremely anxious person may perceive threats everywhere—in other people's remarks, in the news, in traffic situations, or in mysterious noises in the night.

There is considerable research pertaining to the effects of threat on perception. One view is that we tend not to perceive those stimuli which are threatening to the self, or else to misperceive them. The idea is an interesting one—that at an unconscious level we perceive something as a threat and somehow block it off from reaching awareness at a conscious level. Others have pointed out that at least some people are threat-oriented; they tend to perceive threats nearly everywhere. We often perceive in accordance with prevailing emotion. Thus people who are afraid tend to perceive fear-producing stimuli. Although the concept of "perceptual defense" is controversial, it has stimulated a considerable amount of research and theory.[2]

Really extreme cases of perceptual distortion prompted by needs occur in *para-*

Figure 11.12. Motion pictures do not move, as this strip of film shows. What is the explanation for the motion we see when film is projected? What happens when the successive frames are shown too slowly? When they are speeded up beyond the speed at which they were taken? (McGraw-Hill Text Films.)

[2] A reference that will help in following up this subject is an article by C. W. Eriksen, "The Case for Perceptual Defense," *Psychological Review,* 61:175–182, 1954.

noid delusions, in which, for example, hidden threats may be read into innocent remarks, or a person in humble circumstances may perceive himself as a great industrialist.

It has been said that people believe what they want to believe, and there is truth in the assertion. But it is easy to exaggerate the point. Normally our perceptions are not wholly at the mercy of our wishes. If we completely distorted all our interpretations in line with our wishes, even survival would be impossible. There are some limits to autistic distortion. After all, the recognition of realities, no matter how unpleasant, may lead to behavior which in the long run is more adaptive and satisfying. Indeed, a part of being a mature personality is realism in perception. But autism operates in all of us nevertheless.

FRAMES OF REFERENCE AND PERCEPTION

Among the inner (personal) factors that determine perception jointly with outer (stimulus) factors, we have already considered one class—our needs. A second class of inner factors consists of our frames of reference.

Where are we now? In order to answer this question, we must employ some frame of reference. We can give our street address, which has meaning in terms of a city map. We can give our direction and distance from some reference point, which implies some system of directions. Another such question is *who* we are. "I am a student" implies an academic institution as a frame of reference. "I am a twenty-one-year-old enlisted man in the Marine Corps" has meaning in terms of a complex social frame of reference.

A frame of reference, then, is a set of dimensions and reference points in terms of which one perceives. The dimensions may be any kind—spatial, rank systems, scales of judgment for weight, time, prestige, or beauty. The reference points are standards to which we refer in judging or locating objects.

All our perceptions involve frames of reference. Objects are perceived in relationship to the larger setting in which they occur. Sometimes these frames of reference may be present as part of the stimulus sit-

Figure 11.13. How tall is "tall"? What does this illustration tell us about perception and judgment? Can we judge anything in nature absolutely, or must we necessarily compare it, either directly or indirectly, with other things?

uation, as in the case of the grid coordinates of a map. In other cases we bring them to the situation ourselves, as when we judge someone to be tall in comparison with other people whom we have known. In either case, our frames of reference influence or perceptions.

How We Acquire Our Frames of Reference. Our frames of reference are acquired through learning. We form concepts of classes of objects such as dogs, people, occupations, diseases, negotiable instruments, and psychological processes. Such concepts are like pigeonholes into which we fit our various experiences. These concepts provide ready-made interpretations of experience and, often, formulas for action. Where do these concepts come from? Most of them are acquired through communication. Some are unique to us as individuals and derive from our particular experience. The processes of learning concepts are the same as those of any other social learning.

Not only do we form concepts of classes of objects, but we also learn what are significant variations among the instances of each class. For example, we learn what are the significant ways in which people vary —age, sex, occupation, class position, personality traits, and so on. When we perceive a person, we have available numerous such frames of reference. Whenever we perceive something, we perceive it in terms of those scales of judgment which we have learned to apply to the class of object in question, whether athletes, entertainers, husbands and wives, or criminals.

We judge in terms of scales and standards. If we lift a series of weights varying from 1 ounce to 10 ounces, one at a time, we tend to form a scale of judgment as to what is light, medium, or heavy (or some other scale categories). Afterward we judge a new weight in terms of this scale, even though we are not aware of the particular weights on which our scale is based. This same tendency to form scales in terms

of experienced variations holds generally. We may have established scales relating to prestige of occupations, rates of promotion, grades in school, and what is a fair day's work. It is obvious that different people's experience will result in learning somewhat different scales of judgment. Consequently our evaluations will vary to some degree.

The introduction of an unusually light or heavy weight outside the range we have previously experienced (if it does not deviate too much) will alter the weight scale. This tendency of an extreme "anchorage point" to alter the scale is characteristic of all scales of judgment. For example, when a salesman sets a new sales record, former top levels of performance no longer look so impressive.

Judging and Evaluating. As has been stated before, we judge and evaluate in terms of frames of reference. There are a number of points which should be emphasized in this connection.

In the first place, we are not necessarily aware of our scales of judgment and standards of reference when we evaluate. If we judge someone's action as "dishonest," we do not necessarily have in mind specific points of demarcation along the range of honesty-dishonesty. Nor can we necessarily describe the standards in terms of which we judge.

A second point is that, within limits, we can select our reference points. And apparently our needs play a part in this process. For example, a businessman who has been accused of dishonesty can compare himself with others who have been intensely competitive. A student who is doing poorly in college may compare himself with others who are not outstanding. In other words, we may be motivated to select reference standards which lessen threat and enhance gratification.

Third, our evaluation of a situation depends on which frame of reference we select. An act of delinquency, for example, may be evaluated in a *moral* frame of ref-

The perception of a stimulus depends on the frame of reference in which it occurs. This principle has been demonstrated many times and in many ways. It remained for Sherif * to demonstrate what happens to perception when there is no external frame of reference. What he did was to place a person in a dark room, thus eliminating any visual frame of reference. Then he presented a single point source of light for a brief time and asked the subject to signal when he saw it move and to report how far it had moved. Actually, however, the light was fixed in position—it only appeared to move. This illusion, which is called the *autokinetic effect*, is experienced by practically everybody under these conditions.

Sherif was interested in determining the influence of other people on an individual's judgments. In one of his experiments, half the subjects were tested alone first. Each person developed a characteristic average and range for his judgments, and individual differences were considerable. Then they were tested together in three-man groups, each person hearing the others announce their judgments. As is shown in the upper part of the figure, their judgments tended to become more alike. In other words, the members of a group established a group standard as to how much the light appeared to move.

Thus far we have considered what happened when subjects were tested first alone and then together. The lower part of the figure illustrates the results for the other half of the subjects. These judged *initially* in three-man groups. Note that their judgments were quite similar. Afterwards they were tested alone. The group standard which had been established under the group condition still influenced them. Their judgments continued to be relatively alike, although individual differences increased somewhat.

This experiment strikingly demonstrates the influence of other people's judgments on an individual's perception when the stimulus situation is ambiguous. It also shows that this influence tends to persist after the individual is by himself.

* M. Sherif, "A Study of Some Social Factors in Perception," *Archives of Psychology,* no. 187, 1935.

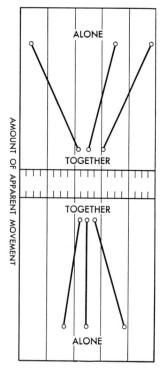

This graph illustrates the results of an experiment on the influence of the group on individual judgment. Sherif found that the individual's judgment about the amount of movement of a fixed-point source of light in a darkened room (the autokinetic effect) was influenced by other people's announced judgments. Half the subjects first judged individually and then in three-man groups. The other half first judged in three-man groups and then individually. The figure shows how individual judgment was changed in two such three-man groups.

erence as "bad" or "sinful." On the other hand, the same act may be evaluated in a *psychological* frame of reference, as a way of enhancing self-esteem by winning approval from the gang, or as an act of hostility against a rejecting parent. Notice that it makes a great practical difference which of these frames of reference is applied. The former evaluation may imply punishment; the latter, therapy. One of the major factors in human disagreements is the fact that different people apply different frames of reference. When they agree on frames of reference, they usually can also agree on the "facts" and on courses of action.

Finally, when frames of reference are rigid and stereotyped, perception is likely to be distorted and insensitive to new experience. A person with a stereotype about Jews in which they are assigned traits of shrewdness, hostility, and greediness is likely to perceive these characteristics in a Jew's behavior. Behaviors which do not fit in with such a stereotype tend to be dismissed—they just have no meaning. The perception tends to be selective, emphasizing features which agree with the stereotype, playing down those which do not.

CONCLUSION

In analyzing human behavior we have frequently made use of the concepts of motivation, learning, and perception. These are fundamental psychological processes. But they are not separate processes; they are interdependent in the whole person.

This interdependence is shown in many ways. We learn goals which will satisfy our drives, and we learn ways of attaining these goals. We also learn to be motivated in certain ways, such as to desire other people's approval. In this chapter, we have seen how needs influence perception. On the other hand, the way a situation is perceived may also arouse needs. For example, what is perceived as imminent failure may arouse a need to avoid failure. We have seen that we learn the frames of reference in terms of which we perceive. It is also true that learned ways of perceiving can affect further learning. For example, knowing how to perceive mathematical notation aids further learning of mathematics. It is apparent, therefore, that we cannot fully understand any one of these basic psychological processes without understanding the others.

SUMMARY

Perceiving is defined as the interpretation of stimuli. It involves finding meaningful interpretations of our experiences.

Perception is functional in that it gives us information about our environment which may be useful in the pursuit of our goals and in avoiding threats.

In perceiving, we interpret the total situation on the basis of a limited number of signs. Although the use of a limited number of signs is an economical way of getting information, it may also result in errors in perceiving.

Perception is a joint function of the stimulus situation and of the perceiver with his needs and frames of reference.

The characteristics of the stimulus situation influence perception. Conditions such as intensity, change, repetition, and contrast influence attention. Various factors leading to the perception of organized wholes have been pointed out by the gestalt psychologists. These include the factors of similarity, proximity, and *Prägnanz*.

Illusions depend on the frame of reference provided by other parts of the stimulus situation and illustrate the organized nature of perception. The perception of motion is an interpretation of the perceiver. It depends as much on the perceiver as on the conditions of stimulation.

Our needs influence our perceptions, this effect being more marked when the stimulus situation is ambiguous and our tensions are strong.

Perception is influenced by frames of reference, which are sets of dimensions and points of comparison, most of which are learned. Frames of reference are important in judging and evaluating. A change in frame of reference will change the way in which a stimulus is perceived.

QUESTIONS

1. What is meant by perception? How is it related to sensation?

2. What is meant by putting meaning into our sensory experiences?

3. What are some of the causes of errors in perception?

4. Distinguish illusions, hallucinations, and delusions.

5. What are some of the gestalt factors in perceptual organization?

6. How do we explain (*a*) illusions, (*b*) perception of motion?

7. What is perceptual constancy? How may it be explained?

8. Under what conditions are our needs especially likely to influence perception?

9. What are frames of reference? What is their role in perception?

10. If perception depends in part on the perceiver, how is it possible to obtain agreement among different observers?

11. What are some of the important frames of reference in terms of which you evaluate yourself?

SUGGESTED READINGS

Blake, R. R., and G. V. Ramsey (eds.): *Perception: An Approach to Personality,* Ronald, New York, 1951.
    (A symposium dealing with the perceptual aspects of personality.)

Boring, E. G.: *Sensation and Perception in the History of Experimental Psychology,* Appleton-Century-Crofts, New York, 1942.
    (A technical and authoritative discussion of theories and experiments in the area of perception and sensation.)

Gibson, J. J.: *The Perception of the Visual World,* Houghton Mifflin, Boston, 1950.
    (A well-illustrated analysis of visual perception.)

Hebb, D. O.: *The Organization of Behavior:*

A Neuropsychological Theory, Wiley, New York, 1949.
    (An account of perception in terms of neurophysiological and learning principles.)

Kohler, W.: *Gestalt Psychology,* 2d ed., Liveright, New York, 1947.
    (An authoritative and well-illustrated presentation of the gestalt view of perception and related aspects of behavior.)

Osgood, C. E.: *Method and Theory in Experimental Psychology,* Oxford, New York, 1953.
    (Selected chapters on perception and problem solving, including a thoroughgoing attempt to apply learning theory to these aspects of behavior.)

12 LEARNING AND REMEMBERING

Learning and remembering are very important in human behavior. Just how important they are is easy to see if we imagine how helpless a person would be if he could not learn and remember. He could not walk, or talk, or understand others, or know what was going on around him. He would not profit from his experience or remember any of it. Indeed, he would hardly seem to us to be a person. (In Chapter 17 we see that such a condition can actually exist.)

Learning may be defined as a change in behavior as a result of experience. The term is used to include such widely differing changes as responding differently to a signal, acquiring a skill, altering the way in which something is perceived, coming to know a fact, and developing an attitude toward something.

How do learning processes take place? What conditions affect them? How can we improve learning and remembering? All these are practical questions, since the answers will help us to understand human behavior.

CONDITIONED-RESPONSE LEARNING

Any classification of learning processes is bound to be somewhat arbitrary. It will be helpful, nevertheless, to begin with one kind of learning about which much is known, *conditioned-response* learning.

Conditioning. Learning by conditioned response was first studied by the Russian physiologist Pavlov.[1] An apparatus which he used is shown schematically in Figure 12.1. The purpose of the training was to

[1] I. P. Pavlov, *Conditioned Reflexes* (translated by G. V. Anrep), Oxford, New York, 1927.

Figure 12.1. Schematic diagram of Pavlov's apparatus for conditioning salivary responses. For explanation see text. (After I. P. Pavlov, Lectures on Conditioned Reflexes, International Publishers, New York, 1928, p. 271. Courtesy of the publishers.)

observe changes in the dog's salivation as a result of various conditions of training. A salivary duct had been brought to the outer surface of the dog's cheek by a simple operation. A tube running from the duct led to a device which measured the number of drops of saliva secreted. The dog was held by a harness which restrained his movements. The stimuli (tones, lights, etc.) and the food reward, which was located on the pan at the end of a pivoting shaft, were remotely controlled from the experimenter's booth. The experimenter, who was screened from the dog, watched him in a mirror. This procedure permitted careful control of the stimuli and measurement of the response.

At the outset of the experiment Pavlov observed that the sight or taste of food caused the dog to salivate but that a tone did not have this effect. After the tone had been paired with food for a number of trials, the tone alone caused saliva to flow. The salivary response was then said to be *conditioned* to the tone stimulus.

There are a number of terms which are used to specify different aspects of the conditioning process. An *unconditioned stimulus* is a stimulus which is adequate at the outset of training to produce the response in question. The response to such a stimulus

is termed an *unconditioned response.* In Pavlov's experiment, the sight or taste of food was an unconditioned stimulus for the unconditioned response of salivating. A *conditioned stimulus* is one which is initially inadequate to evoke the response in question but becomes able to do so as a result of being paired with the unconditioned stimulus. The learned response to such a stimulus is then called a *conditioned response.* In Pavlov's experiment, the tone was the conditioned stimulus for the conditioned response of salivating. Finally, there is *reinforcement,* which is the strengthening of the association between a conditioned stimulus and a conditioned response as a result of pairing an unconditioned stimulus with the conditioned stimulus. In Pavlov's experiment the sight or taste of food acted as a reinforcement; that is, pairing the food with the tone resulted in the tone's becoming more adequate as a stimulus for salivation. The different aspects of the conditioning process are shown schematically in Figure 12.2.

Many different responses can be conditioned, depending on the situation. A conditioned eyeblink can be established by pairing a tone with a puff of air directed against the cornea. This pairing must take place a number of times before any conditioning can be observed. Even an emotional response, such as fear, may be conditioned to the sight of a dentist's drill if painful experiences are paired with seeing the drill.

It is said that the burned child fears the flame. This fear may be acquired by a conditioning process. Being burned by the flame acts as an unconditioned stimulus for fear (and withdrawal). Pairing the painful stimulus with the sight of his hand near the flame reinforces fear as a response to the conditioned stimulus of hand-near-flame. Indeed, the fear may be conditioned to other stimuli, such as the room in which the painful experience occurred.

Conditioning may occur without awareness being involved. For example, we may learn to salivate at the sight of a dinner table without knowing that we are making this response.

Extinction. What happens to a conditioned response if it is no longer reinforced? In other words, what happens if the conditioned response occurs in the absence of an unconditioned stimulus, that is, in the absence of reinforcement? Pavlov tried this very thing. After fully conditioning a dog, he changed the procedure by repeatedly sounding the tone without accompanying it with food. In other words, he stopped reinforcing the response. At first, of course, the dog salivated as usual, but after a number of such nonreinforced trials, the response became weaker and weaker until no saliva at all was secreted when the tone sounded. Thus the conditioned response was *extinguished* by not reinforcing it when it occurred.

A conditioned eyeblink, too, can be extinguished, by repeatedly sounding the tone (conditioned stimulus) without blowing air against the eye (nonreinforcement). A child can lose a conditioned fear of a doctor, if on future visits to the doctor's office his fear is not reinforced with further unpleasant experiences.

The extinction of a fear response, how-ever, is often a very slow process, especially where the response leads us to avoid the situation in which it was acquired. When we avoid what seems to be a threatening situation, we have little or no chance to learn where the real dangers, if any, lie. Indeed, the circumstances that led up to the original pain and fear may have been purely accidental, as when a little child learns to fear, and avoid, a certain playground because he happened to have been stung there by a bee. The learned avoidance of anxiety-arousing situations has great importance for personal adjustment. If we avoid situations in which we might develop new skills, we limit our satisfactions in life. Repression (see Chapter 6) has been conceived as a learned avoidance response to anxiety-arousing memory or motive.[2]

Partial Reinforcement. Suppose that the conditioned stimulus (which occurs on every trial) is followed by reinforcement on only *part* of the trials. The response is said to be *partially reinforced.* Suppose

[2] J. Dollard and N. Miller, *Personality and Psychotherapy*, McGraw-Hill, New York, 1950, pp. 198–221.

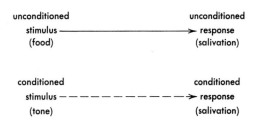

Figure 12.2. In this diagram of the conditioning process, the solid-line arrow indicates that the connection between the unconditioned stimulus and the unconditioned response existed at the outset of training. The dashed-line arrow from the conditioned stimulus to the conditioned response indicates the learned relationship acquired through reinforcement (pairing the unconditioned stimulus with the conditioned stimulus).

Figure 12.3. How might we account for this child's reaction in terms of conditioning principles? How might the concepts of partial reinforcement, extinction, and generalization be applied in this situation? (Wide World Photos.)

that the response in question is a conditioned eyeblink in human beings, with a tone as the conditioned stimulus, and a puff of air directed against the eye as the reinforcing stimulus. Suppose we compare the effects of 100 per cent reinforcement (a puff of air directed against the eye every time the tone is sounded) with those of 50 per cent reinforcement (a puff of air directed against the eye on only 50 per cent of the trials). Not only is the rate of conditioning almost the same under the two conditions, but also the *resistance to extinction* is much greater for the partially reinforced responses; that is, it requires a larger number of trials without reinforcement to eliminate the eyeblink response when it has been learned under conditions of partial reinforcement. Parents also see the practical

results of partial reinforcement—though they may be unaware of the principle— when they make occasional exceptions to rules and then find that children are remarkably persistent in requesting further exceptions. As another illustration, a fear response which has been partially reinforced may endure for years or even for a lifetime.

Generalization of Conditioned Responses. If a dog has learned a response to one stimulus, another somewhat like it will also cause the response. For instance, if a tone of one pitch has been used in training, then later a tone of another pitch will also evoke the response. This tendency for a stimulus similar to the conditioned stimulus to elicit the conditioned response is known as *generalization*. The response generalizes to a stimulus similar to the one used in training. The more similar the stimuli, the greater will be the degree of generalization. Usually the response to a similar stimulus is somewhat weaker than the response to the stimulus used in training.

There are many examples of generalization of conditioned responses in everyday life. Suppose a child has been frightened by a wildly barking dog. The fear response may generalize to other dogs, even those which are not barking. The more similar these other dogs are to the original one, the stronger the fear reaction is likely to be. Attitudes and prejudices often arise in this way, that is, through generalization of conditioned responses. A person who has had an unfavorable experience with one member of a profession may generalize his unfavorable reaction to the whole profession.

The tendency to generalize can be very adaptive. We can learn what one member of a class is like and transfer this knowledge to new instances. On the other hand, generalizing may get us into difficulty. Treating a skunk as a cat is a well-known example. Even though some of our generalizations may turn out to be misleading or trivial, on

One of the best illustrations of generalization of a conditioned response is furnished by an experiment by Hovland,* who used human beings as subjects. An electric shock or nearly any other strong stimulus tends to be followed by a momentary drop in the electrical resistance of the skin, largely as a result of increased secretion by the sweat glands. This reaction is the galvanic skin reaction, or GSR (see Chapter 4). First the GSR was conditioned to a tone of a certain frequency (stimulus 1 in the figure shown below). After this response had been conditioned, the investigator measured its amplitude in response to three other frequencies (stimuli 2, 3, and 4) differing by progressively greater degrees from the frequency of the tone used in training. As shown by the graph, the GSR was strongest in the case of the conditioned stimulus and progressively decreased in amplitude as the stimuli differed more and more from this conditioned stimulus. Thus Hovland demonstrated a gradient of generalization along a pitch dimension. Other experiments have demonstrated gradients of generalization along other sensory dimensions and also along more abstract dimensions.

* C. I. Hovland, "The Generalization of Conditioned Responses: I. The Sensory Generalization of Conditioned Responses with Varying Frequencies of Tone," *Journal of General Psychology,* 17:125–148, 1937.

Generalization of a conditioned galvanic skin response (GSR).

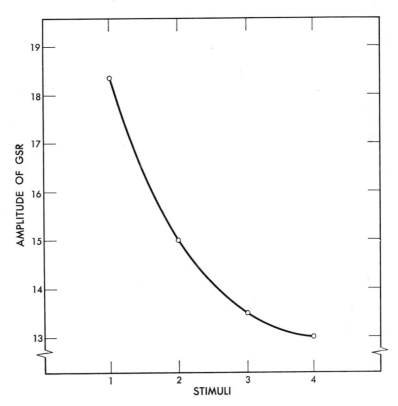

'the whole there is no doubt about the usefulness of the generalizing process.

Discrimination. Suppose Pavlov's dog has learned to salivate to tone A and generalizes this response to tone B. What will happen if he is rewarded every time tone A occurs but not rewarded when tone B occurs? If the difference between the two tones is not too small, he will continue to salivate to tone A, but not to tone B. The response to tone B becomes extinguished. The dog is now *discriminating* between the two stimuli. The evidence that he discriminates the two tones is that he responds differently to them.

In our example, we have considered discrimination in the sense of responding to one stimulus and *not* responding to another stimulus that is somewhat like it. Pavlov's dog has learned to salivate to tone A, but not to tone B. The dog is doing more, however, than just *not* making the response in question—salivating; he *is* making a lot of other responses when tone B occurs such as scratching himself, stretching, etc. This means that he is responding to other stimuli, that tone B does not control his behavior.

There are many familiar examples of discrimination that is learned in the same way as in our example. Suppose that a child has learned to call all men "Daddy." But when he does this, he finds that only one man responds to him, that the others do not. He then learns to discriminate his father from other men.

Experimental Neurosis. After a dog has learned to discriminate two stimuli, what happens if the difference between the stimuli is gradually reduced to such a degree that the animal can no longer distinguish the stimuli? What happens is interesting: the dog becomes nervous, irritable, and upset. Indeed, his earlier ability to discriminate even coarse differences breaks down. This disturbed behavior is called *experimental neurosis.*

We, too, can become highly disturbed if we are pressed to make discriminations which are too difficult for us. Suppose that our supervisor on one occasion approves and the next disapproves what to us appears to be the very same behavior. Most of us would find it very hard to get along in such a situation. In fact, many of us would become quite disturbed, especially if we were afraid of losing our jobs. Our supervisor might be perfectly consistent from the point of view of his standards, but we do not know what they are, and the situation may be too complicated for us to figure them out. Another possibility, of course, is that the supervisor really is not consistent, which makes our problem even harder.

Child psychologists have pointed out a similar difficulty for the child in trying to learn the complex distinctions that his parents make. What to parents may look like perfect consistency on their part may be utterly confusing to a child who has not yet learned the abstract basis on which the parents discriminate. Not being able to make the fine distinctions that the parents do, the child may become disturbed.

LEARNING INSTRUMENTAL RESPONSES

In our survey of conditioned-response learning there was comparatively little emphasis upon learning as a goal-oriented activity. The terminology and methods for the study of conditioning are somewhat difficult to apply to situations in which we learn a series of responses leading to some goal, such as learning the skills necessary for driving a car. The learning of responses which attain goals is often termed *instrumental learning*. The responses are called "instrumental" because they are a means of attaining a goal, that is, of satisfying a motive. How does such learning take place?

Learning by Trial and Error. It is often said that we learn by *trial and error*. For example, we may try to learn how to shoot with a bow and arrow. At first we miss the target completely, except by accident.

When the arrow falls short, we may try aiming higher; when it flies off to the right, we aim farther to the left, and so on. As we try various responses, some of them fail and are gradually eliminated. Others succeed and are retained.

During the first third of the present century Thorndike,[3] a psychologist at Columbia University, studied learning both in animals and in human beings. His views of learning as a trial-and-error process have remained influential down to the present day. In one of his experiments, a cat is placed in a so-called puzzle box, a sort of cage. Inside it hangs a loop of string which if pulled raises a door and lets the cat out to eat a morsel of salmon in a nearby dish. When first placed in the cage, the cat does many different things, such as squeezing his head between the bars, scratching at the box, and pawing at the door, but all without effect. Sometime, in his exploratory behavior, the cat pulls the string, the door comes open, and he goes out and eats the food. The second time the cat is put in the box, much the same thing happens, although the string may be pulled a little sooner. Gradually, in repeated trials, more and more of the ineffective responses are eliminated, and the correct one occurs more and more promptly.

Thorndike's line of reasoning in explaining these results was as follows. The cat was motivated to get out, but this motive was blocked (frustrated). When a motive becomes frustrated there is an increase in the variability of responses. Some of these responses have a greater probability of occurring than do others, depending on the motive, the stimulus conditions, the past experience of the individual, and other factors. In other words, the behavior is not random, though it may appear so. A number of the cat's responses might reasonably be conceived as escape attempts. Responses

[3] E. L. Thorndike, *The Fundamentals of Learning*, Teachers College, Columbia University, New York, 1932.

which are followed by reward tend to be strengthened; that is, they are more likely to occur (and after less delay) on later occasions. Thorndike's explanation was that the responses that are followed closely by reward are strengthened more than those that are temporally more remote from reward. Since the correct response leads to reward, it is strengthened more than are earlier ineffective responses; responses not followed by reward tend to become weakened. Consequently the correct response eventually dominates competing unsuccessful responses, and learning is said to have occurred.

Thorndike viewed the whole process of learning as being purely automatic: connections between stimuli and responses are strengthened as a result of being followed by reward and weakened as a result of not being followed by reward. This principle is known as the *law of effect*. That is, the effect or result of a response—reward or nonreward—determines whether it will be strengthened or weakened. If a response is followed by reward (even if this happens by chance), the response is strengthened. On future occasions it is more likely to occur and will tend to happen sooner. It is also likely to be greater in amplitude; for example, the cat may pull more vigorously at the string. If the response is not followed by reward, it becomes weakened.

According to Thorndike's view, it is not necessary for the learner to *perceive* a relationship between his responses and their effects; all that is necessary is for a response to be followed by reward. For example, the cat does not have to know how and why pulling the string results in opening the door. The fact that he pulls the string does not imply that he understands the relationship between this act and the door's opening. Thorndike even set up one experiment in which the experimenter opened the door whenever the cat licked himself. Since the response of licking was thus closely followed by reward, it was strengthened rela-

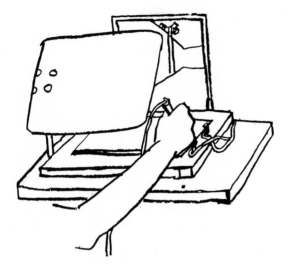

Figure 12.4. This is a mirror-drawing apparatus. The task of the subject is to move the stylus around a star-shaped pattern without touching its sides. If the stylus touches the sides, an electric clock records the duration of the contact. The screen blocks the subject from directly viewing his hand, the stylus, and the pattern, so that he can see them only in the mirror. Because of the mirror the subject must learn to move his hand differently in response to the visual stimuli. (Refer to page 248 for further details.)

tive to other possible responses. Presumably the cat had no insight into this arbitrarily imposed relationship between his response and reward. Insight into *why* a response works or does not work is not necessary for this response to be strengthened or weakened. All that matters is whether or not the response is followed by reward—a purely automatic kind of learning process.

We have discussed Thorndike's views because they have strongly influenced a number of more recent learning theorists such as Hull and Guthrie (references at the end of this chapter) and their followers. Each of these theorists attempts to explain learning as the formation of stimulus-response connections. Each of them makes little systematic use of the concepts of purpose and insight into relationships. Presently we shall examine other views of learning which, by contrast, emphasize these very factors.

The trial-and-error conception has been applied to human learning, too. For example, we may try to solve a complicated mechanical puzzle. Most of our attempts fail, and some of the failures may be repeated. Sometimes certain parts go together without our knowing why. Like the cat, we gradually eliminate errors and become faster and more accurate. Some of us im-

prove gradually, without knowing what we do that works, and why. Or we may improve for a while, then spend a long time on one trial, and suddenly show marked improvement. (In the latter case, we are said to have gained *insight*—we see a relationship or principle that helps. Trial-and-error conceptions of learning do not have much to say about insight.)

Figure 12.4 shows a typical mirror-drawing apparatus, one of several devices that have been useful in studying a trial-and-error process in human learning. The results obtained on this type of apparatus are comparable to those obtained with animals in trial-and-error situations.

Returning to the law of effect, the effects or consequences of responses are believed to control learning. This principle would suggest that the more closely a response is followed by its effect, the more rapid the learning ought to be; that is, an immediate effect strengthens or weakens responses more than a deferred one. If we were trying to learn to aim a rifle, we should learn faster if we knew the results after each shot than if we had to wait a few minutes to find out how we had scored. A related idea is that the more information about the effects of our responses we get, the faster we learn.

Insight in Learning. Some psychologists feel that the trial-and-error description of learning is of relatively limited usefulness. Those who stress this point most strongly are the gestalt psychologists. Their ideas about perception are examined in Chapter 11. They also have contributed to our understanding of learning.

What do they have to add to the trial-and-error conception? They say that we often solve a problem by getting *insight* into a principle or relationship. This idea can be made clear by an example. During World War I Köhler,[4] a leader in gestalt psychology, was on the island of Teneriffe off the coast of Africa. He became interested in how chimpanzees solve problems and conducted several experiments on their problem solving. In one typical experiment a bunch of bananas was tied to the end of a rope so that it was out of the chimp's reach. Nearby were some wooden boxes. The chimp at first tried to reach the bananas by jumping. After trying over and over again, he finally sat down and looked around. He saw the boxes. Quickly he seized one of the boxes, put it under the bananas, and climbed up to get them.

Now it should be clear that this was not just a random response. It makes more sense to say that the chimp had insight—he perceived the box as something that can be climbed upon in order to seize something high. What happened does not look much like the gradual elimination of errors and the gradual strengthening of a correct response hit upon by chance. It has the earmarks, rather, of insight into what leads to what. And once the insight has been attained, the problem is mastered. It can be solved immediately the next time. After the principle is understood, quite a few changes in the situation can be made without causing any difficulty. Then it matters little whether the lure is banana or orange, or

[4] W. Köhler, *The Mentality of Apes,* Harcourt, Brace, New York, 1925.

just where the box is located, or its shape or size. (Of course, there are limits to how big the changes can be without causing trouble.) In other words, the learning generalizes (or transfers) widely, once the principle is understood. This is one of the important characteristics of insight in learning.

Köhler also found that some chimpanzees were able to solve more complicated problems, like stacking boxes so as to get bananas placed even higher or fitting two sticks together to make a rake long enough to reach food placed outside their cage. Typically the solution came rather suddenly, usually after a quiet period in which the chimp looked over the situation.

In the gestalt view, we solve a problem in this way. We have various hunches (hypotheses) about what to do. Practically never do we fumble blindly, although some of our hunches may be very poor ones. What we try helps us to know which

Figure 12.5. Could you solve this jigsaw puzzle by getting insight into a single principle? When problems are complex, trial-and-error manipulations coupled with numerous partial insights are characteristic of the learning process.

hunches will not work. It is as though we are testing our hunches, although we usually are not very systematic in doing so. Merely by thinking, we may perceive some possibilities and their probable effects without our doing anything overtly. Finally, either all at once or piecemeal, we get insight into the principle or relationship needed to solve the problem. Once we know the principle, we can use it to solve not only this problem but many others like it.

Certain factors may make it easier or harder to get insight into a problem. For one thing, past experience with similar problems may be helpful. A person with an engineering background, for example, is more likely to get insight into an engineering problem than someone without such a background.

It can also make a difference whether or not the various parts of the problem are open to view. The cat in the puzzle box is handicapped in that the mechanism is largely hidden. Therefore, the insight into the relationship between pulling the string and the opening of the door is not possible. That is why his learning must be a fumbling, trial-and-error process.

Another factor having bearing on insight is strong preconceptions. We can feel so strongly that the solution lies in a particular direction that we are blind to other possibilities. All our efforts go into the wrong channel, and all our ingenuity may be wasted in trying to make the wrong idea work. For instance, so long as we think that the way to get a stuck door open is to force it, then all that we can think about is how to bring enough force to bear. We might end with an ingenious arrangement of jacks and levers that finally breaks the door down, when *unlocking* it would have done the job! Even in our stupidity, however, our behavior is not random or automatic. The lesson for all of us is clear: we should not get stuck on a premature hunch but should look over the problem in order to get a *variety* of hunches. Then we shall be less likely to waste our time in a blind alley.

Conditions of Trial and Error and Insight. Instrumental-learning tasks vary in the degree to which their solution is a matter of trial and error or a matter of insight. Actually, solving most novel problems entails both insight and trial and error. Learning therefore seems to vary all the way from insight to trial and error, when these terms are used descriptively. In this sense, "trial and error" refers to a learning process characterized by (1) the gradual elimination of errors, and (2) relatively limited generalization of the solution when the conditions are changed. "Insight," on the other hand, refers to a learning process characterized by (1) the mastery of a principle or relationship, usually fairly suddenly, and (2) considerable amount of transfer when the conditions are changed.

The level on which we attempt to solve a problem depends on a number of factors. One is the nature of the problem or task itself. Some problems *can* be solved by finding a single principle; others cannot. Some mechanical puzzles, for instance, cannot be solved by a single principle; a lot of learning is needed about the separate parts, how they fit together, and the order in which to assemble them. Hence the nature of the problem has something to do with the level on which we can solve it.

Another factor is our previous experience with problems like the one we are trying to solve. After all, it would be very difficult to have insight into an electronics problem without knowing a lot of physics and mathematics. If we do not have the necessary background knowledge, we are forced to approach the problem in a piecemeal, trial-and-error way. We call the effect of previous experience upon new learning *transfer of training*. If this effect of earlier learning helps in solving the new problem, the transfer is *positive*. If it interferes, the transfer is *negative*. Both kinds are encountered in practical situations. Our earlier experience with similar problems may therefore be a help or a hindrance in getting insight.

Finally, differences in intellectual capacities affect the level at which a problem is attacked. A bright child may be able to solve by insight a problem such as how to move a heavy object (by means of a lever), whereas a dull child might need to resort to trial and error. Thus, we have seen that a number of factors affect the level at which we approach and solve a problem. Trial and error and insight are *both* characteristic of learning.

Stimulus-response and Cognitive Theories of Learning. Underlying our discussion of instrumental learning are two broadly different conceptions of the learning process. One we shall call the *stimulus-response* theory; the other, the *cognitive* theory. In this book we can present only the broad outlines of each theory and show how they compare with one another.

The stimulus-response theory, of which Thorndike's is an example, regards learning as the formation of habits, that is, of associations between stimuli and responses. A typical (simplified) stimulus-response principle is that whenever a stimulus is followed by a response which is rewarded, there is an increment (an increase) in the strength of the habit. That is to say, the next time the stimulus occurs, the response is more probable, occurs sooner, is greater in amount, or some combination of these. Thus if a child sees his aunt, approaches her, and gets candy, the next time he sees her he will have a stronger tendency to approach her. The more often the response occurs and is rewarded, the stronger becomes the habit of approaching the aunt.

From the point of view of the stimulus-response theory, the task of the investigator is to identify the stimuli leading to the response in question and to determine the conditions which affect the strength of these stimulus-response associations. The

Figure 12.6. Transfer of training in a testing situation. The examiner (after lining up a row of blocks) asks the child to "build a 'train' with just as many 'cars' as mine." The child has no adult concept of "just as many" and makes his train "just as long" as the examiner's; but since his "cars" touch each other, his train has more cars than the examiner's. If the boy had been able to count, or to match his "cars" one-to-one with the examiner's, he would have solved the problem. Instead he transferred, inappropriately, the notion of "just as long." (Photographs courtesy of Dr. David Elkind, Austen Riggs Center.)

psychologist usually approaches this task objectively (with emphasis upon measurement) and tends not to speculate about the perceptions and thoughts of the learner. In most versions of stimulus-response theory, reinforcement (usually in the sense of reward) is given a central place in the strengthening of responses.

Stimulus-response theorists generally hold that motives are necessary before reward, which strengthens responses, can occur. Motives also foster persistent and variable behavior, so that eventually an effective response is likely to occur. After a habit is formed, motivation is necessary to bring about response. For example, the sight of the food dish does not cause a cat to approach it unless he is hungry.

Cognitive theories (Tolman [5] is the leading exponent) regard learning as a change in the way of perceiving a situation. For example, Köhler's apes at first perceived the out-of-reach bananas as something to be jumped for and later as something to be reached by means of stacking boxes. Such a change in the way of perceiving the parts of a situation in new relationships is called *perceptual reorganization,* which is learning. There are now new expectations as to what events (stimuli, responses) will lead to what further events. Thus the child who approaches his aunt and receives candy is more likely in the future to perceive that she has candy and to expect that he can get it from her by going to her.

Cognitive theorists seek to determine the conditions under which insight is most likely to occur. For example, they hold that learning is more likely to occur if the essential parts of a problem situation are open to view and manipulation than if they are not. Thus Köhler's apes learned more readily to stack boxes when the boxes were

directly in the field of view as they tried to get the banana than when the boxes were off to one side. According to cognitive theorists, the essential process in learning is perceptual reorganization—seeing things in new relationships—rather than the strengthening of associations between stimuli and responses as a result of reinforcement.

Cognitive theorists contend that motivation is not essential for learning to occur. Motivation, if not too intense, may be helpful in making certain parts of the situation (such as rewards) stand out, so that they may more readily be perceived as related. Motivation is also necessary for performing what has been learned. For example, if we have learned to expect that pushing a switch will turn on the light, then we shall push the switch if we want to have light. Cognitive theorists usually feel that responding is not essential for learning to take place, except in so far as responding leads to further information. For instance, a child might need to open a cooky jar in order to learn that it contained cookies.

Table 12.1 shows further comparisons between the stimulus-response and cognitive theories. It should be emphasized that each theory has advantages for dealing with certain kinds of problems. For example, stimulus-response theory is useful in explaining processes like animal learning, especially in trial-and-error situations; the learning of skills, such as typewriting; and verbal learning, such as of lists of words. Cognitive theory is useful in explaining processes such as human (and animal) problem solving and thinking.

A second point is that at least some of the differences in the two theories may be merely in the words which are used. For example, "learning a fear response to a stimulus situation" (or object) may not be very different from "learning to *perceive* or *expect* that this object leads to possible injury" (and therefore fear of it).

Third, these two theories are influencing each other's development. For in-

[5] E. C. Tolman, *Purposive Behavior in Animals and Men,* Appleton-Century-Crofts, New York, 1932. See also E. C. Tolman, "There is More than One Kind of Learning," *Psychological Review,* 56:144–155, 1949.

Table 12.1   Comparison of Stimulus-response and Cognitive Theories of Learning

	Stimulus-response theories	*Cognitive theories*
Preferred type of learning task	Tasks requiring primarily a trial-and-error approach	Tasks which may be solved by means of perceiving a relationship or principle
What is learned	Stimulus-response associations (habits)	Understandings of relationships (cognitive reorganization)
Role of motivation	Motives are necessary for learning to take place and for performing what has been learned	Motives are necessary for performing or utilizing what has been learned, but not essential for learning itself
Role of reward	Reward strengthens habits (in most varieties of stimulus-response theories)	Reward is not essential for learning unless it provides a basis for perceiving relationships which would otherwise not be clear
Role of responding	Responses must occur and be reinforced if learning is to occur	Responses are not essential for learning except in so far as they permit the learner to perceive the effects of the responses
Role of repetition	Repetition of a response strengthens a habit only if reinforcements (rewards) occur	Repetition may be effective by virtue of providing more opportunities to perceive the essential relationships

stance, stimulus-response theorists are coming to pay more attention to symbolic processes (thoughts, expectations) which come between stimuli and responses. Likewise cognitive theorists are coming to formulate their principles somewhat more rigorously (in the manner of stimulus-response theories) so that more definite predictions can be made. As these trends continue, it is probable that the two theories will become more and more unified.

LEARNING OF SKILLS

What happens when we try to acquire a skill, such as reading, public speaking, dancing, or group discussion? Although the content of such skills will vary, there appear to be many features common to learning all of them. In each case, the course of improvement tends to be gradual. In each, moreover, there are some more or less defined standards of proficiency which the learner attempts to reach. Finally, in each, a lot of practice appears to be necessary in order to acquire and to maintain the skill.

Typical Course of Learning a Skill. The changes which take place in learning to typewrite will illustrate the typical course of learning a skill. If we are beginners, we must learn the location of the keys, where

Figure 12.7. A training device for giving driving instruction in the classroom. The device is equipped with an automatic shift as well as with a standard conventional shift. There is evidence of considerable positive transfer of training from such a device to actual road driving. (Aetna Life Affiliated Companies.)

our fingers go, and how to strike the keys. We must also learn to use the space bar, carriage return, and other controls. At first we make a lot of errors. We are physically tense, and we work slowly and irregularly, being somewhat erratic in how well we do. Distractions are likely to bother us, and we may feel that we are working pretty hard. Gradually, however, we improve, although the course of improvement tends to be irregular. Indeed, we may even get worse for a time and show little or no apparent improvement for several days. After a long time, we reach a point beyond which practice results in no further improvement.

For convenience, the changes which typically accompany increasing skill may be listed:

Reduction in errors or improvement in accuracy
Improvement in rate
Reduction in over-all physical tension
Smoothness and regularity of performance
Greater uniformity of performance
Greater freedom from the effects of distractions
Decreased feelings of effort

A device that has been frequently used in the study of motor learning and performance is known as the pursuit rotor.

This requires the subject to keep a metal stylus in contact with a metal plug on a rotating turntable. An electric clock measures the amount of time that the stylus is in contact with the target plug during each period of practice. As the subject makes progress in mastering the task, he becomes more accurate, experiences less physical tension, varies less in his performance, is less subject to distractions and interference, and has less feeling of effort.

Learning Curves. The rate of learning, as measured by performance, can be represented graphically and is depicted in the curves of Figure 12.8. The base line shows units of practice, such as the number of trials or the amount of time spent in practice. The vertical axis indicates degree of learning as measured by some index of performance, such as percentage of correct responses, amount of time on target, or score in points. Curve A illustrates rapid initial improvement, followed by decreasing gains from practice. This is a curve of *decreasing returns.* Curve C indicates little or no improvement initially, after which there is a period of rapid improvement, which in turn is followed by little further improvement. This curve is called an *S-shaped* curve because it looks somewhat like an S lying on its side. Curve B, which has not been smoothed like A and C, indicates the irregular nature of most learning curves, that is, how performance fluctuates during learning. This curve also shows a *plateau*, which is a period during which there is little or no measurable improvement in performance, although learning may still be going on during this period.

The rate of improvement in acquiring skills varies from person to person and also from time to time for any given person. In learning a sport such as bowling, for example, one beginner shows rapid improvement, while another needs to practice for a long time before his score improves appreciably. Sometimes a bowler reaches a certain level (a plateau) and remains there

for several weeks, then again shows improvement. After a great deal of practice, each bowler tends to reach some level and stay there. Similar characteristics in performance curves have been noted in learning many other skills, such as typewriting, telegraphy, reading, writing, target shooting, and playing a musical instrument.

Why do we differ in our learning curves? What accounts for plateaus in these curves? For temporary drops in score? For improvement after years of no improvement?

One reason why we acquire skill at different rates (and to different limits) is that we differ in our heredity; that is, hereditary factors influence the rate and degree to which we benefit from practice. Some of us, for example, have a much greater apti-

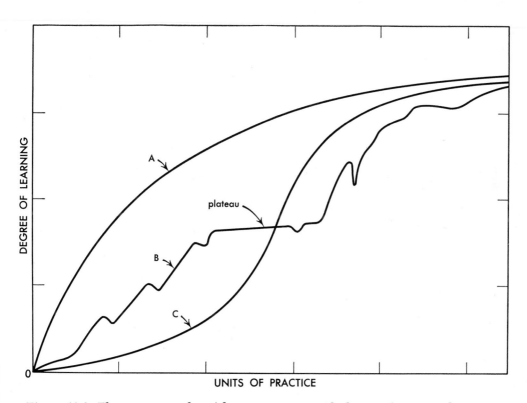

Figure 12.8. These are examples of learning curves. Which one shows rapid improvement at first with smaller gains later on? Which one pictures slow initial improvement? How would you describe the remaining learning curve?

tude for acquiring certain athletic skills than do others.

A second reason why we improve at different rates is that we differ in the amount and kind of previous learning which we can bring to a new task. As we have seen, this transfer of training may be either positive or negative. A lot of motor skills, such as bowling and throwing a baseball underhand, probably have a lot in common, so that practice on one helps in learning the other. It sometimes happens, however, that previous learning may interfere with new learning, in which event improvement is delayed.

Another reason why we improve in skill at different rates is that we differ in motivation. If we really want to learn a skill, we practice harder. Also, if we are highly motivated, we set higher goals, pay more attention to ways of improving our performance, and persist longer in the face of discouragement.

Still another reason why we do not all improve at the same rate is the fact that we may use different methods of practice. Some methods may permanently block important improvement. Others, such as a hunt-and-peck system of typing, may yield rapid gains at first but keep us from ever becoming expert. Other methods, involving thorough grounding in fundamentals, may not result in much improvement at first, but later on help a great deal.

Someone who has been working for years at a certain level of performance (as in typing, bookkeeping, or public speaking) may improve very much with the help of changed methods of working. Setting higher goals often helps, too. One of the most vital tasks of a trainer is to get us to want to improve and to accept new methods. There must be willingness to learn.

One of the puzzling features of learning curves is the plateaus that sometimes appear in them. These are periods during which little or no improvement in performance occurs, although afterward there may be further improvement. Possibly learning is going on while there is a plateau, although it is not at the moment apparent in improved scores. In typing, for example, a plateau may occur while we are learning to respond to words and even phrases instead of single letters. Some plateaus are caused by a temporary loss of motivation when there has been initial improvement because of transfer from past learning, but hard work is necessary for further improvement to occur.

Finally, what accounts for irregularity in performance, particularly temporary drops in the learning curve? Such irregularities are more typical of the early stages in learning, but sometimes they happen even after long practice, as when a batter goes into a slump. The causes are not fully known, but a change in motivation (distraction, worry, fear of failure) or a change in method may have damaging effects. Even skilled performers may need coaching assistance in identifying the source of the difficulty. Unfortunately most of our evidence on the point is anecdotal, such as a report by a major-league batter that a change in stance unconsciously developed and resulted in a batting slump. When the cause was recognized, the difficulty was removed and performance again improved.

Training in Skills. Some methods of acquiring skills are more effective than others. The person who teaches others or trains them in skills needs to know and understand the factors that are important in acquiring skills.

One thing a trainer ought to do is to provide clear standards of performance. It is difficult—if not impossible—to learn a skill if we do not know what we are aiming for. We need to know when we are doing well, and when we are doing poorly. Indeed, we should know in what *particular ways* we are doing well or poorly.

There are a number of ways for a trainer to go about pointing out standards of performance. He can tell us, as when a super-

Dr. and Mrs. Keith Hayes tried the noble experiment * of keeping a female chimpanzee, Viki, in their home over a number of years beginning with her earliest infancy. Viki was given the same care and attention as would be given a child. She was cuddled, diapered, fondled, given toys, talked to, and in other ways exposed to the experiences typical of human childhood. By the time she was three, Viki handled such problems as form boards, peg boards, picture puzzles, block piling, and buttoning with the skill appropriate to a child of that age. After reaching the age of six, she was able to equal many six-year-old children in solving a variety of problems. For example, she could switch on an electric fan, when it failed to go on, she checked the wall socket and plugged in the wire.

The main area in which Viki was inferior to human children was that of language ability. With considerable difficulty Viki learned to say a few words acceptably and to use them purposefully, although she understood many more words than she could say. It is interesting to note that Viki babbled less than most children do, and this fact may have had something to do with her limited linguistic development. The whole experiment was an important demonstration of the effect of heredity on learning when nearly ideal conditions are provided for such learning.

* George W. Gray, "The Yerkes Laboratories," *Scientific American,* 192:67–77, 1955.

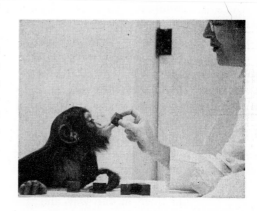

The tendency of the chimpanzee to explore and manipulate with lips and tongue rather than with hands appears to be significant in explaining why it falls progressively behind human infants in the development of manipulative abilities. (*Courtesy of* Scientific American.)

visor describes our job responsibilities. He can have an expert demonstrate. It does not help, of course, to know that we are not as good as the expert. Rather, we need to know specifically what he does that is so effective and what we do that does not work so well. It is one of a trainer's responsibilities to make just these points clear. Sometimes it is hard to say what are appropriate standards of performance. This is true to a large extent in education, which has no simple tests of how well training has equipped us for life outside the classroom.

A second thing that a trainer should do, if he can, is to improve our motivation. One way of enhancing motivation is to clarify the goals and objectives of the training. A training course for salesmen, for example, is more effective if the salesmen are led to feel a need for the training. A training program which is superior in all other ways will fail if we do not want to learn, or if we are resentful about participating in it.

Sometimes learning curves are used to help motivate learning. Seeing progress is encouraging to most of us. We frequently

Figure 12.9. Ballet dancing is a skill requiring much practice and careful direction from a trainer. The trainer acts as a model, points out particular errors and correct responses on the part of the student, and endeavors to foster high levels of aspiration. A mirror is provided so that the students may observe their performance and correct their mistakes. Motivation on the part of the students is, of course, essential. (Courtesy of Ballet Theater Foundation.)

compete against ourselves, trying to better our previous scores.

Some trainers instill rivalry to increase motivation. The competition may be arranged so that it is between individuals or between groups, with prizes or honors for superiority. Such methods often work well, but some of us do not do our best under conditions of rivalry.

Praise and reproof are widely used to motivate learning, but a trainer needs to be careful in using them. Some of us react to them in one way and some in another. Many educators feel that *general* praise and reproof are ineffective. What is needed instead is to identify specific accomplishments to praise and specific mistakes to criticize. A general *atmosphere* of approval is something different, however. A trainer can approve of our efforts while still pointing out shortcomings that need correction.

Some of the other responsibilities of the trainer are to (1) arrange for practice of the skills; (2) make use of training aids of various kinds, such as films, charts, tape recordings, and demonstrations; (3) evaluate and keep records of performance; and (4) give the training in such a way that it can be applied later under practical or field conditions.

HOW TO STUDY EFFECTIVELY

At one time or another all of us have had to face the problem of developing effective methods of study. Certainly this is a problem for most students in school. As industry provides more and more training programs, the problem becomes important there, too. How can we study most effectively?

Improving Motivation and Attitudes. To begin with, why do we wish to study? What is our underlying motivation? What attitudes do we have toward the task? Studying needs to be related to important goals and objectives in life. A college student who finds it "difficult to concentrate" will find it helpful to consider what are his purposes in going to college and how the material to be learned fits in with his goals. In some cases, counseling may be needed.

Many attitudes may interfere with effective study. One is a feeling that studying and learning have no long-run practical value. In some cases, this belief is a pure rationalization. Trainees have many stereotypes, often false, as to what learning is important. Trainers may try to correct these beliefs by presenting the views of former trainees who are professionally important and experienced.

Immature attitudes toward teachers may also interfere with effective study. Many students carry over to their teachers an adolescent rebellion against their families. Studying is something required by authority; therefore, they feel, it is to be avoided. Unfortunately, authoritarian behavior by some teachers intensifies the tensions behind this rejection of the student role.

"Inability to concentrate" in studying may be due to emotional distractions. Some students are worried about finances, or are anxious about their abilities, or are having conflicts with their parents. Such feelings interfere with effective study.

Specific Methods for Effective Study. Although proper motivation and attitudes are probably the most important factors in effective study, there are a number of specific methods which may be helpful.

Self-recitation has been found to be effective. In self-recitation we try to state the main ideas in the material in our own words. For example, as we look at a section heading, we ask ourselves, "What is the point?" Looking away from the book, we state the point in our own words, and then check ourselves if necessary.

A famous study by Gates [6] illustrates the value of self-recitation as compared with straight reading. Large numbers of children from different school grades learned nonsense syllables (meaningless "words" which are widely used in studies of verbal learning) and biographies. With a fixed amount of time available for study, the *least* efficient method was to spend all the time in reading. The efficiency of learning

[6] A. I. Gates, "Recitation as a Factor in Memorizing," *Archives of Psychology*, no. 40, 1917.

increased as proportionally more time was spent in recitation. In the case of the biographies, which are somewhat like the meaningful material of most textbooks, 40 per cent of the time, and even more, spent in self-recitation proved to be most effective. In the case of nonsense materials, the effect of self-recitation was even more marked, the maximum advantage occurring with 90 per cent of the time spent in self-recitation. Similar results have been obtained in other more recent studies. Recitation is believed to be of value largely because it helps us to *organize* the material, to make it more meaningful.

Another method of improving study habits is to *distribute practice*, i.e., to devote a number of brief study periods to the material rather than to spend the same total amount of time in a single long study period. There is some evidence that distribution of practice is relatively more important with materials to be learned by rote, such as vocabulary lists and numerous separate factual details, than with materials that are more meaningful and better organized.

Review at various intervals after learning has also proved to be valuable. Such review should be done carefully, for a superficial review may even interfere with remembering. A review should help to organize the material so as to make it more meaningful. Deficiencies in information should be recognized and corrected during the review.

It is often a good practice to look over the material as a whole first. We may do this by looking at section headings in order to see how the material is organized. Sometimes we prefer to read the summary and conclusions first. We may find it useful to read a chapter rapidly, perhaps making marginal notes and underlining. Then we can move on to a detailed study of the material.

The material may be made more meaningful by deliberately and habitually looking for relationships to other things already

**DISTRIBUTION
OF PRACTICE
IN LEARNING
A MOTOR SKILL**

▶ A piece of apparatus often used for the study of perceptual-motor skills is the mirror-drawing apparatus (see Figure 12.4). Mirror drawing is a difficult task to learn, because what appears visually to be farther away is actually nearer, and what is seen as closer actually is farther away. The subject must learn to reinterpret visual stimuli and move his hand appropriately. The accompanying figure shows learning curves under three different conditions of practice in this task.* In this graph, the lower the score, the better the performance. In the massed practice condition, 20 trials were given in immediate succession, without any provision for rest. Under the other two conditions 20 trials were given with either 1-minute or 1-day intervals between trials. The above results and other later experiments suggest that more important than the length of the *rest* period (beyond some minimum) is the length of the *work* period. That is to say, there was little or no difference between the value of a 1-minute and a 1-day rest period, but a short work period was preferable to a continuous work period. Later investigations have yielded similar results.

* I. Lorge, "The Influence of Regularly Interpolated Time Intervals upon Subsequent Learning," *Teachers College Contributions to Education*, no. 438, 1930.

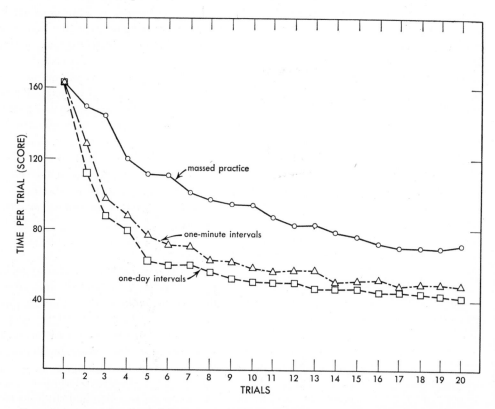

Learning curves for three different conditions of practice on a mirror-drawing task. The lower the score, the better the performance. The results show that 1-minute rest intervals between trials and 1-day intervals were of nearly equal value, and that both were better than massed practice (no rest at all).

known. In studying a psychology textbook, for example, we should actively think about examples from our own experience. We should relate what is said in the text to what we have found in our other books, such as personalities in literature. With an active, reflective attitude, we can consider a book (or a lecture) as a mere starting point for our own thinking.

Finally, we should arrange for a good setting in which to study. Factors which are well known, but frequently not controlled, include freedom from distractions and interruptions; a comfortable, well-lighted work place; and adequate reference books, papers, etc. Although these factors are conducive to effective study, they are not sufficient in themselves. Motivation and attitudes are probably the most important factors in effective study.

REMEMBERING AND FORGETTING

All of us have had the experience of trying unsuccessfully to remember something which we once knew quite well. Educators have found that only a fraction of what is learned in school is remembered afterward. Forgetting is a common everyday experience, but why does it occur? What conditions affect the rate at which we forget? Or, to look at the question another way, what happens in remembering? How do our memories of past experiences change over time? These are some of the questions which we shall try to answer in this section.

Measuring Retention and Forgetting. How much does a person remember after an interval without practice? In order to answer this question, we must consider ways of measuring retention and forgetting. Three principal methods have frequently been used in psychological studies of retention: (1) the recall method, (2) the recognition method, and (3) the relearning method.

In the *recall* method, performance after

Figure 12.10. A memory drum, which is a device for the controlled presentation of verbal (or other) materials, is widely used in the study of verbal learning and retention. The memory drum presents the items of a list at a controlled rate—for example, one item every two seconds. Nonsense syllables are often used as the learning materials in order to control the differences among subjects in prior familiarity with the materials. Many of the results which have been found in the case of nonsense materials also hold for meaningful materials. (Courtesy of Ralph Gerbrands.)

an interval without practice is compared with that at the end of training. For example, if we can name the capitals of the 48 states without error after training, but make 12 errors after an interval without practice, then the number of errors indicates the amount of forgetting. The number of capitals named correctly expresses the degree of retention. In terms of recall as a measure of retention, we remember 75 per cent of what we had originally learned.

Another measure of retention is *recognition.* Suppose, for example, that we met 10 people at a party. If later we pick some of these 10 out of a larger group at a better-than-chance level, we have some retention. In order to recognize members of the original 10, we must have learned enough about their appearance to discriminate them from

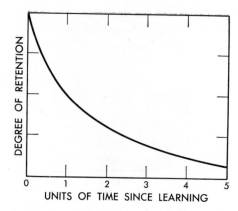

Figure 12.11. *This is an example of a retention curve. How would you interpret this curve? For explanation, see text.*

centage of the originally learned items which are recalled. The curve shows a rapid initial drop in retention, followed by progressively smaller losses as time passes.

There is no one true form of retention curve. Although curves similar to the one we have discussed are often obtained, the course of retention varies with many conditions. For example, the form of the curve varies with the method of measuring retention. Other factors which affect the form of retention curves include the degree of original learning, the type of task or material, and the method of learning the material. Let us look at some of the results of research on these factors.

First, the higher the level to which a task is learned, the more slowly it is forgotten. Suppose we have learned a poem so well that we can recite it without error. Now if we were to study it some more (to *overlearn* it), we should remember it better and for a longer time than if we had not done so. Overlearning is consequently an excellent way of improving retention, a point relevant to how to study effectively.

Second, under a wide range of conditions, retention is better after distributed practice than after massed practice. That is, if we have only a certain amount of time in which to study material or to practice a skill, it is usually better to divide our practice into a number of short sessions than to mass it in one long session.

Third, material which is meaningful tends to be remembered better than material which is less meaningful, such as lists of isolated facts. Meaningful material is material which can be perceived in an organized way, the different parts fitting into a structure. Remembering a part of such material helps us to remember other parts which are meaningfully related to it.

Some Questionable Beliefs about Remembering. There are some questionable popular beliefs about factors affecting retention and forgetting. For example, many people believe, without adequate evidence, that

others. It is apparent that the more similar the learned objects are to others from which they are to be discriminated, and the more other such objects there are, the more difficult such recognition would be.

In the *relearning* method (sometimes called the *savings* method), we are required to learn the task once again to the original level of performance. If we need less than the original amount of practice (as measured by errors, time, etc.) for relearning, then this is evidence of retention. If, for example, we originally needed 40 trials to reach a certain level of proficiency, and 10 trials afterward to relearn to the same level, then 30 trials (or 75 per cent of the original 40 trials) were saved in relearning. The relearning method is a very sensitive measure of retention.

Retention and Forgetting Curves. A retention curve (see Figure 12.11) shows graphically how much is remembered as a function of time since learning. Figure 12.11 is only one example, for there are many other forms of retention curves. On the base line are units of time since learning, the number 0 representing the time of completing the original learning. The vertical axis indicates the degree of retention in terms of some unit such as number or per-

In a study by Cain and Willey,* subjects learned lists of 12 nonsense syllables. One group (massed-practice condition) learned the syllables in a single session, while the other group (spaced-practice condition) learned the same material to the same criterion level of performance in three sessions. Each of these groups was then divided into three subgroups which were tested 1 day, 2 days, and 7 days after training. In each case, the spaced-practice group showed the greater retention. Many other studies have also demonstrated greater retention when the material was learned under distributed-practice conditions, although with highly organized and meaningful materials the difference may be small or even in the other direction.

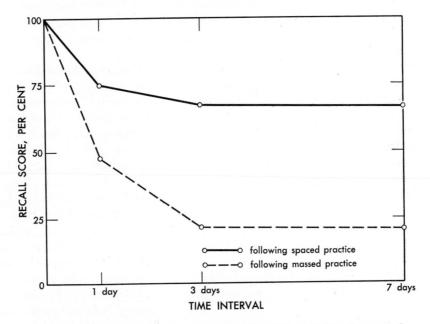

These are retention curves for verbal material learned under spaced (distributed) conditions of practice and under massed conditions of practice. Although the material was learned to the same standard of proficiency under each method, retention was better for the material learned through distributed practice. (Courtesy of the American Psychological Association.)

* L. F. Cain and R. deV. Willey, "The Effect of Spaced Learning on the Curve of Retention," Journal of Experimental Psychology, 25:209–214, 1939.

a person who is slow in learning a task will remember it better than one who learns it more rapidly. When this is the case, as it sometimes is, it is usually because the slow learners overlearned certain parts of the task which were learned early in practice.

In controlled experiments in which materials, such as nonsense syllables, are dropped out of the task as they are mastered, the faster learners on the average remember somewhat better than do the slower ones.

Although it has often been asserted that motor tasks, such as swimming, are remembered better than verbal ones, the evidence is inadequate. It really is difficult to compare how well we remember, say, swimming with how well we remember Lincoln's Gettysburg Address. In the first place, there is no way of determining whether the two tasks were originally learned to the same degree. Aside from the typical difference in amount of practice in the meantime, there are no common units for comparing the present levels of retention.

It is often said that we remember what we see better than what we hear. But in controlled tests when the same material is learned by reading it and by hearing it, no consistent differences are found in either how rapidly we learn it or how well we remember it. A lesson taught by aid of a film might—and probably would—have somewhat different content and interest value from that of a lesson taught by a lecture method. It is easy to see that more than just a difference in the sense organ —eye versus ear—is involved in this question.

Is Forgetting Ever Complete? When we hear very old people give accounts (often unreliable) of their early childhood experiences, they may remember things that for practical purposes had been long "forgotten." The relearning method for measuring retention, which is an extremely sensitive measure, has been used to demonstrate retention of even nonsense material over a number of years. All these considerations strongly suggest that our learning experiences have enduring effects. As a matter of fact, it is impossible to *prove* that forgetting is ever complete, because a more sensitive test, if devised, might reveal retention.

Causes of Forgetting. Why is it that we tend to forget when we do not continue to practice? A "common-sense" answer is that we forget because of the passage of time. In theory, however, it is not the passage of time *as such*, but processes which go on *in* time which cause forgetting. Such an explanation, moreover, does not account for the fact that some materials are forgotten faster than others. The explanation that we forget knowledge or a skill because we do not use it assumes that memories normally deteriorate (in the absence of practice) but does not explain *why* they deteriorate.

Why, then, do we forget? The most widely held theory of forgetting is the interference theory. According to this theory, we forget because new learning interferes with what we are trying to remember. Many experiments show that under certain conditions learning a second task after learning a first one interferes with retention

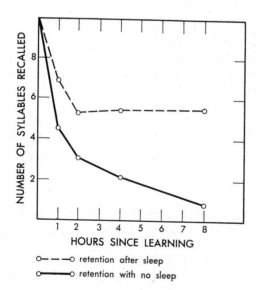

Figure 12.12. According to a well-known experiment, human subjects show better retention during sleep than during the same number of hours while awake, as the curves show. How might you use this knowledge? (J. G. Jenkins and K. M. Dallenbach, "Oblivescence during Sleep and Waking," American Journal of Psychology, 35:610, 1924. Courtesy of the publisher.)

of the first. For example, learning French after studying German tends to interfere with remembering German. Another line of evidence is research showing that very little forgetting occurs during sleep, when, of course, little or no learning is going on.[7] Verbal materials learned just before going to sleep are partially forgotten during the first two hours (as determined by the recall method), but during the next six hours of sleep the loss is negligible. Some of the loss during the first two hours may not be forgetting but rather a result of being awakened from deep sleep. Although the interference theory has a lot of support, it is often difficult, of course, to identify just exactly *what* further learning, for example, interferes with the retention of an algebra lesson during the course of the day.

There is a second cause of forgetting. At least some of our forgetting is the result of the process of repression, which is discussed in Chapter 6, in connection with self-defense. When the emotional difficulty underlying repression is relieved, such material may be recalled. Hypnosis and certain drug conditions sometimes may induce recall of repressed material. The Freudian technique of free association, in which the subject tells everything that an experience makes him think of, sometimes aids the recall of repressed material. The most convincing evidence on repression comes from clinical cases in which long-forgotten memories, usually quite threatening to the self, have been recalled. It has sometimes been asserted that pleasant events are remembered better than unpleasant ones, with the suggestion that the latter tend to be repressed. The evidence from research studies, however, is hard to interpret. For instance, experiences without strong feelings attached often are remembered *less* well than the supposedly repressed un-

pleasant materials. Actually, it is hard to create in the laboratory threats to self which are sufficient to cause repression.

We also forget because of a change in *set*. The concept of set has quite a variety of meanings. Here the word is being used in the sense of our frame of reference, as discussed in the preceding chapter. That is, the stimulus situation and our expectations at the time of trying to remember may be somewhat different from what they were during learning. There is even experimental evidence that verbal materials learned in one room tend to be less well remembered in a different room. A person whom we know on our college campus may not even be recognized in a faraway city—the setting, the context, is different. We say, "I didn't *expect* to see him here." Often when a few items of information are given to provide the proper set, recall may be remarkably detailed. A little warm-up on a task may have a very favorable effect on retention.[8]

A final reason for forgetting is that the item either was not learned in the first place or else was learned very inadequately. If we say, "I can't remember names," we probably never did learn the names. We cannot remember what we have not learned, and inaccurate initial learning is likely to result in inaccurate recall.

Qualitative Changes in Remembering. The main emphasis thus far has been on how *much* is remembered, not on *what* is remembered. The changes which occur in the content of memories are called *qualitative* changes. F. C. Bartlett,[9] among others, reports experiments on such qualitative changes in remembering. Bartlett regards remembering as an active process in which past experiences are reconstructed according to an over-all interpretation (called a *schema*). For example, if we are trying to

[7] J. G. Jenkins and K. M. Dallenbach, "Oblivescence during Sleep and Waking," *American Journal of Psychology*, 35:605–612, 1924.

[8] A. L. Irion, "The Relation of 'Set' to Retention," *Psychological Review*, 55:336–341, 1948.

[9] F. C. Bartlett, *Remembering*, Cambridge, New York, 1932.

remember an automobile accident in which we were involved, our over-all interpretation (schema) might be that our car was hit from the rear after we had stopped on a traffic signal. In trying to remember the accident, we tend to remember or invent details that fit in with this schema and forget those which do not.

Remembering is not so much a matter of looking at the screen of the past through clouded glasses as it is an active process of reconstruction. This is apparent when we try to recall any extensive set of experiences, such as our first day at school. Such memories tend to be *selective*. Certain events are remembered because they fit in with an over-all interpertation of the experience. Other events were scarcely noted in the first place and have little relevance, on recall, to the over-all interpretation of the situation. On the whole, the recollection tends to be simplified in accordance with this over-all view.

We often fill in the gaps where our memories are incomplete. The gaps are filled in such a way as to *make sense* of the total experience. This is not to say that remembering is pure rationalization, but within

limits rationalizing certainly plays a part.

There is also evidence that aspects in the original experience tend to be sharpened. What was perceived originally as a small difference of opinion may be remembered as a quarrel. Sometimes, of course, these incidents become progressively exaggerated in retelling, especially when such sharpening makes a better story.

Although there is good evidence of qualitative changes in remembering, we need more information about the processes involved. For example, the way in which we remember something can be strongly influenced by how we originally perceived it. It is also very likely that further distortions may occur as we reconstruct the experience according to our over-all interpretation of it and as we are influenced by our motives at the time. Whether or not systematic changes take place in memory in the interval between the original perception and the time of remembering is still another question— one that is difficult to answer.

Finally, regarding memory of experiences, all the mechanisms of self-defense and self-enhancement are free to operate at the time of remembering, just as at the

Figure 12.13. Artist's sketch based on another person's description of a suspected criminal. Compare the actual photograph of the suspect with the sketch. Notice that certain "landmark" features (dark, unruly hair, light windbreaker, and light, baggy trousers) were definitely remembered and exaggerated. (International News Photos.)

time of perception of the original situation. We may, for example, rationalize when we describe a failure experience.

Qualitative Changes in Skills. Most theory and research on qualitative changes in memory have dealt either with objects that have been perceived or else with verbal materials, such as stories. Qualitative changes, however, also take place in skills. Changes in one part of a skill can cause changes in other parts. Everyone who has participated in sports has had this happen to him. The batter becomes careless and shifts his stance, thus standing somewhat off balance. This affects his swing, perhaps even the way he follows the ball visually as it comes toward him. One wrong move leads to another in an attempt to compensate for the initial error. Gradually these bad habits are learned and interfere with the better ones which are required for peak performance.

CONCLUSION

Let us see how the material in this chapter ties in with what has gone before. The process of learning and remembering is something that the whole *person* does; it does not happen in a vacuum. Our learning is at the service of our motives. These motives affect what we learn and how we use it. In this respect, learning is like perception. Our needs affect what and how we perceive, and perceiving is necessary in responding so as to satisfy our needs.

Another relationship between learning and motivation lies in the fact that we can learn to want or not want certain things. Our goals, which are a part of our motives, are learned. Learning also plays a part in functional autonomy (Chapter 3), although some aspects of the process are not fully understood.

We recognize, too, that learning plays an important part in the development of the self, our particular ways of enhancing the self, and the development of our personality. Furthermore, our roles, attitudes, and beliefs are learned.

Finally, learning ties in very closely with perception. Most, if not all, the meanings (expectations, frames of reference) that go into perceiving are learned. It is also clear that perception has much to do with learning. We could not learn if we could not perceive objects and the effects of our responses. It will be remembered that when we solve problems through insight we are perceiving relationships and principles.

SUMMARY

Learning is defined as a change in behavior as a result of experience. Many different kinds of behavior are learned, and learning is necessary for individual adjustment and social living.

One variety of learning is conditioning. Reinforcement is necessary for learning conditioned responses. Nonreinforced conditioned responses become extinguished, although partially reinforced responses are markedly resistant to extinction. Conditioned responses generalize to similar stimuli. Stimuli come to be discriminated as a result of the reinforcement of responses to one of the stimuli but not to the other.

The learning of instrumental responses, which have to do with goal-oriented behavior, has been described as a trial-and-error process and also as a process of obtaining insight. Each of these descriptions has some merit, their applicability depending on factors such as availability or relevant past experiences, the nature of the task, and the capacities of the learner.

Stimulus-response theories of learning look upon learning as the formation of stimuli and response associations, usually as a result of reinforcement. Cognitive theories of learning regard learning as a change in the perception of relationships. Both theories are useful in explaining learning processes.

In acquiring skills, the following changes typically occur: reduction in errors or improvement in accuracy; improvement in rate; reduction in over-all physical tension; greater uniformity of performance; greater freedom from the effects of distractions; and decreasing feelings of effort.

Learning curves represent changes in performance as a function of practice. They vary in form. Individual differences depend on hereditary factors, past learning, motivation, and methods of practice.

Trainers may encourage learning by providing standards of performance and by fostering motivation.

The main factors in effective study are motivation and attitudes. In addition, self-recitation, distribution of practice, review, getting a meaningful overview, and having an appropriate setting are important.

The main ways of measuring retention are the methods of recall, recognition, and relearning. Quantitative changes in retention (and forgetting) depend on a variety of factors, such as degree of original learning, distribution of practice, and meaningfulness of the material.

Forgetting occurs because new learning interferes with the retention of previous learning, because of repression of anxiety-arousing experiences, and because of change in set.

Qualitative as well as quantitative changes in remembering take place; remembering is an active process which is affected by the over-all interpretation of the situation (schema) and by factors such as set and motivation at the time of remembering. The remembering of skills shows analogous qualitative changes.

QUESTIONS

1. What is meant by "learning"? What are some of the different kinds of behavior which can be learned?

2. Define each of the following: conditioning, extinction, partial reinforcement, generalization, discrimination. Give an example of each.

3. Compare and contrast trial and error and insight as descriptions of goal-oriented learning. Which of these descriptions seems most applicable in each of the following cases: (*a*) learning to play tennis; (*b*) learning a poem; (*c*) learning the meanings of a list of French words; and (*d*) solving a problem in engineering?

4. State the essentials of the stimulus-response theory of learning. What appear to be its strengths and weaknesses?

5. State the essentials of the cognitive theory of learning. What appear to be its strengths and weaknesses?

6. What are the typical changes that occur as a skill is learned?

7. What are the main responsibilities of a trainer? What is meant by setting standards of performance?

8. What are the important factors in effective study?

9. Describe the following methods of measuring retention: recall method, recognition method, and relearning method.

10. Evaluate each of the following explanations of forgetting: (*a*) lack of use or passage of time; (*b*) interference from new learning; (*c*) repression; and (*d*) change in set.

11. What is meant by qualitative changes in remembering? What causes these qualitative changes?

12. What are some of the probable causes of variations and irregularities in learning curves?

SUGGESTED READINGS

Bartlett, F. C.: *Remembering*, Cambridge, New York, 1932.

(A stimulating treatment of remembering as an active process influenced by personality and social factors.)

Deese, J.: *The Psychology of Learning*, McGraw-Hill, New York, 1952.

(A standard textbook on learning covering both animal and human learning.)

Guthrie, E. R.: *The Psychology of Human Learning*, Harper, New York, 1935.

(A stimulus-response theory of learning applied to numerous everyday-life situations.)

Hilgard, E. R.: *Theories of Learning*, Appleton-Century-Crofts, New York, 1956.

(A survey of the major theories of learning.)

Hull, C. L.: *Principles of Behavior*, Appleton-Century-Crofts, New York, 1943.

(A technical statement of a stimulus-response theory of learning.)

McGeoch, J. A., and A. L. Irion: *Psychology of Human Learning*, rev. ed., Longmans, New York, 1952.

(A survey of the major findings and theories regarding human learning.)

Tolman, E. C.: *Purposive Behavior in Animals and Men, Appleton-Century-Crofts*, New York, 1932.

(A fundamental statement of the cognitive theory of learning.)

13 THINKING AND PROBLEM SOLVING

A truck driver came to a low underpass. It was even lower than he thought it was, and when he tried to drive his truck through, it got stuck. A heavy wrecker was sent for, and everybody huffed and puffed to get the truck loose, but to no avail. After a while, a boy standing by said, "Hey, mister, why don't you let some of the air out of the tires?"

This story illustrates the practical importance of thinking and problem solving. In this chapter we shall discuss the nature of these processes.

Thinking may be studied in two main ways. One of these is by the introspective method—by observing and reporting our own thought processes. This might appear to be a good method, but it has actually been less valuable than the second method, that of objective observation of other people. In other words, we can learn about thinking by observing how people solve problems and react to other situations which require thinking.

THE NATURE OF THINKING

Our purpose in this section is to clarify the nature of the process that we call *thinking.*

Definition of Thinking. In thinking we use symbols which stand for or represent our world of experience. When we think of a car, for example, we have an image of an automobile or we think of the word "car" or respond in some other way which represents the physical object. In a later part of this chapter we shall consider different kinds of symbols and their properties. For

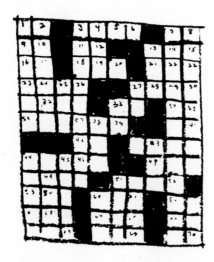

the present it is sufficient to say that *thinking is the manipulation of symbols.*

Function of Thinking. Just what functions does thinking have? One reason we think is in order to solve a problem. Thinking, like all other behavior, is motivated. This fact of motivation is, of course, quite apparent when we have a problem to solve, as our truck driver did. Not only do we think as a way of trying to solve problems, but we may think for the enjoyment of the process itself (admitting that other motives may also be present). Many times we get enjoyment out of trying to solve a puzzle or explain an unusual event. Some of us get real satisfaction from putting order into our experiences, even where such order has no obvious utility. In other words, thinking itself may be enjoyable.

Some of our thinking, instead of being directed, as in the above examples, is of a more undirected and autistic nature. Thus we might review in thought the pleasant or unpleasant features of past experiences, or daydream about what we are going to do next summer. A large amount of thinking is of a wish-fulfilling character, and much of it, such as daydreaming, is unrealistic. Such thinking often serves the purposes of self-enhancement and self-defense, discussed in Chapter 6.

Thinking and Feeling. Traditional conceptions of thinking have tended to emphasize its rational and logical aspects. Thinking, in this view, is a normally rational process, and feeling and emotions are regarded as disturbing and distorting it. (In this sense thinking is also considered an essentially conscious process.) A more adequate conception regards thinking and feeling as normally going together. The affective (emotional) nature of most thinking is easy to understand if it is granted that all thinking is motivated. Many of our words, of course, are highly emotionally toned, such as "dirty," "loyal," "democratic," and "moral." We have seen earlier how many of our explanations are motivated

rationalizations. When we think about things that are meaningful to us, our feelings are bound to be a part of such thoughts. Instead of regarding emotions and feelings as unusual in thinking, it would be more correct to regard thinking as *normally* affective in character, acknowledging, of course, that some thinking, such as mathematical reasoning, may have very little affective tone.

Where Thinking Takes Place. Thinking goes on within the body. If someone asks *where* in the body thinking goes on, we shall have to say that thinking is done with the whole body, although some parts, such as the brain, are more centrally concerned in the process. (This same problem is also discussed in Chapter 9.) When we think, we react to sensory stimulation and make a variety of responses. Although the amount of bodily involvement may be small in some cases of thinking, some activity still is present (as is brought out later in this chapter). In other cases of thinking, we may be extremely active in going about getting information and manipulating tools and other objects in our environment. We may conclude that thinking involves the whole person in interaction with his environment.

Thinking and Consciousness. Conscious thinking is the only kind that we can introspectively observe. By definition, if a thought process is unconscious, we are not aware of it at the time. To hold, however, that *all* thought processes are conscious is highly questionable. Thought processes are not always sharply defined or at a high level of awareness. Suddenly we may become aware of the fact that we have been thinking all along about something. Our thought processes may vary all the way from those which are well defined in awareness to those of which we are not aware at all. Indeed, it is likely that acute awareness of thoughts is unusual and that normally we think at a barely conscious or even unconscious level.

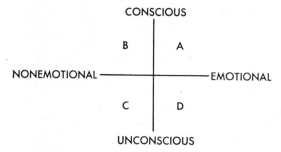

CONSCIOUS

B | A

NONEMOTIONAL —————+————— EMOTIONAL

C | D

UNCONSCIOUS

Figure 13.1. This scheme shows two ways in which thinking may vary. Thinking varies in the degree to which it is conscious and also the degree to which it has emotional components. Probably most thought processes fall in quadrant D; that is, they are relatively unconscious and affective. The thinking represented in quadrant B, by contrast, is affectively neutral (nonemotional) and conscious. See whether you can interpret quadrants A and C and think of examples of this type of thinking from your own experience.

There are other indications that there is such a thing as unconscious thinking, or at least, unconscious factors in thinking. Inventors, for instance, sometimes report that the solution of a problem suddenly occurred during a period when they were not consciously thinking about it. It is quite possible, however, that they were unconsciously working on (thinking about) the problem. We have seen in Chapter 3 that posthypnotic suggestions may operate at an unconscious level and may influence behavior, including rationalizations at a conscious level. The process of free association also suggests the existence of unconscious factors in thinking. Suppose we associate freely, letting the words come to mind as they will, as follows: house, fire, insurance, money, work, retirement. The gaps between these words might readily be filled by unconscious symbols which connect the words of which we are aware.

SYMBOLS

Earlier in this chapter thinking was defined as behavior involving a series of symbolic processes—words, images, and certain muscular movements. The purpose of this section is to clarify the nature of symbols and to describe the different kinds of symbols and their properties.

Nature of Symbols. We shall define a symbol as something (an object, an event, or a response) which stands for something else. For example, a policeman has been assigned to count the cars which cross at a certain intersection. He makes a mark each time a car passes by. Each mark is a symbol of one car. By adding up marks he can add up cars.

The thing a symbol stands for is called its *referent*. Not all referents are as easy to describe as are cars. The referents of words like "stock market," "personality," and "language" are quite complex and abstract.

Anything can be a symbol, as long as it means (refers to) something other than itself. For example, the symbol may be a word (*any* word) which is either spoken, written, or thought about. Or it may be a picture or an image (such as visual image of a car). It may even be a movement, such as the gesture of steering a car, or something so arbitrary as snapping our fingers if to us this means a car.

Some symbols are *external;* that is, they are outside us. Examples of external symbols are maps, flags, and printed and written language. In order to function as symbols, however, they must be perceived as referring to something, as when a map is perceived as referring to a certain territory. Obviously, external symbols may be useful for record purposes and mass communication.

Our words, images, and gestures are often called *internal* symbols. Essentially they are responses which stand for something else. They may be, and often are, quite individual in meaning. Obviously such responses must be produced (for example, remembered) before they can function as symbols.

A symbol, of course, is not the same as its referent; indeed, it may be, and usually is, quite different. The word "car" is not at all like an actual car, nor is the word "pig" anything like the animal with the pink snout and the curly tail. Someone is said to have commented that the word "pig" fits the animal in question, since the word itself has a dirty, unflattering character. He was, of course, confusing his feelings about pigs with the word, which in itself is neutral.

Some people make the mistake of thinking that symbols have meanings in themselves, apart from what people think they mean. The meaning of a symbol, however, exists only in the person or persons for whom it has that meaning. Of course, if we

Figure 13.2. A map is a set of symbols which represents the territory to which it refers. The map is useful to the extent that it is an accurate guide (for our purpose) to the territory. In the same way, other symbols such as the words of our language may orient (or mislead) us with regard to reality.

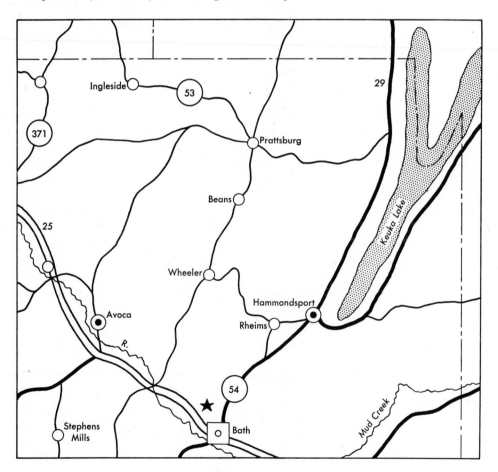

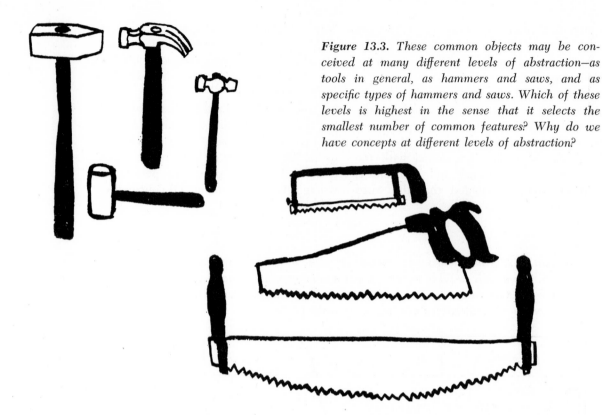

Figure 13.3. These common objects may be conceived at many different levels of abstraction—as tools in general, as hammers and saws, and as specific types of hammers and saws. Which of these levels is highest in the sense that it selects the smallest number of common features? Why do we have concepts at different levels of abstraction?

are going to communicate with somebody else, we and the other person need to have similar meanings for the symbols we use.

An important characteristic of symbols is that their referents may not be physically present. By means of thinking, we may represent past events; these memories may yield satisfactions or act to influence future conduct. The referents may also be purely imaginary—ghosts, the square root of minus one, what our room would look like with the desk over by the window, what would happen if we waited a few days to pay the rent, what effect an increased degree of tension would have on tolerance of frustrations, and the like. By means of symbols we may explore various possibilities and anticipate their consequences. Obviously, the ability to anticipate reality with the aid of symbols may be of great value.

Symbols and Concepts. We have symbols for many different *concepts.* When a

person reacts to a set of objects—dogs, bank statements, or something else—as equivalent to one another in certain ways, he is said to have a *concept.* Our concept of dogs is the set of characteristics by which we identify something as being a dog. It also includes our *feelings* about dogs and our expectations about dogs— that dogs bark, chase cats, and are subject to rabies. This whole set of reactions is the meaning of a dog for us. In general, our concepts help us to identify objects and prepare us to react to them.

Concepts are learned. On the basis of our experience with different objects and the names other people give them, we learn to group them into certain classes and to distinguish them from objects of other classes.

Some symbols are more abstract in reference than are others. To abstract is to respond to only a part of a stimulus pattern. For example, here is a dog whom we shall call Rover. Rover has an unlimited number of characteristics—color, weight, manner of barking, bodily movements, etc. —which make him uniquely different from any other dog. Now, when we classify Rover as a collie, we are referring only to certain characteristics that Rover has in common with other dogs in this breed, but leaving out those in which he differs from them. So we have abstracted still more. When we call Rover a "dog" we are including only those characteristics which are common to all dogs, but leaving out those which are specific to his breed. When we classify Rover as a mammal, then as a vertebrate, and finally as an animal, we are abstracting still more, that is, leaving out more and more characteristics. The more characteristics are left out, the more abstract is the concept, and (in the main) the broader is the range of objects to which it may be applied.

Abstractions may be enormously useful in enabling us to generalize (or transfer) our knowledge. For example, when a chemist classifies something as an organic compound, he can bring to bear a considerable fund of knowledge about such compounds.

Images as Symbols. As has been said before, images may function as symbols; that is, images may represent various objects of experience or else be reorganizations of such experiences. Visual images are already familiar—an image of the furniture in your room, of a baseball pitcher winding up, or of a parade. So familiar are visual images that we tend to underestimate the frequency and importance of other kinds of imagery. It is true, however, that most of us also have auditory images, such as that of a melody, and also images corresponding to some of the other senses, such as touch, pressure, and temperature. We can imagine a feather brushing our cheek, or pressure on our chest, or shivering in a cold wind.

Many of our images are actually blends or composites of images in various sensory modalities. For example, if we imagine ourselves eating an apple, we shall probably have some kind of visual image of an apple. But in addition we may imagine its fruity odor, its flavor, its crisp texture, the crunching sounds which accompany chewing, the smooth, waxy texture of the skin, and many other qualities. Many, if not most, of our images are just such composites.

People differ a great deal in the content, vividness, and variety of their imagery. For example, a moment ago, some of us may have had a vivid image of eating an apple, while others had only the faintest kind of an image. Some of us may have been able

IS IT A CONBOL?

Figure 13.4. What are the essential characteristics of a "conbol"? What is the concept that includes the positive instances and excludes the negative instances? Materials such as these may be used in investigating how we learn concepts and the symbols which refer to them by experiencing a series of positive and negative instances (see next page for solution).

Figure 13.5. A picture for testing eidetic imagery. After looking at the picture for a brief time, children with eidetic imagery can visualize and remember most of the details. Some can even spell backwards the long German word in the upper left. (Courtesy of Dr. G. W. Allport.)

to imagine vividly a number of different sensory aspects of the experience, whereas others were limited to one or a few at most.

Some people have an extremely vivid kind of visual imagery known as *eidetic* imagery. After a person with eidetic imagery has been shown a picture for a few seconds, he can name and draw most of the details. He is said to have "photographic memory," since his memory image has detail something like that of a photograph. Such a person may be able to study a page of technical material for a few moments and then recite it simply by reading from a visual image of the page. As in all other extremes of performance, persons with eidetic imagery simply differ in de-

Solution to Figure 13.4: A conbol is a figure with two rectangles and a dark inner part.

gree from other people in the vividness of their visual imagery. At the other extreme are people who have only the faintest of visual images. Incidentally, contrary to what many might think, some very able mathematicians (who may make extensive use of spatial representations of mathematical relationships) do not depend particularly on visual imagery. The symbols of mathematical notation, which have restricted and exact meanings, seem to play a more important role for them than do visual images.

It is sometimes said that so-and-so is of the "visual type" while someone else is of the "motor type." However, it is difficult, and perhaps impossible, to classify people into visual, motor, or other imagery types. In the first place, most of us employ various kinds of images to some degree. In the second place, if we have vivid images of one type, we do not necessarily have weak ones of another type. In the third place, the relative vividness of different types of imagery seems to vary more directly with whether visual or other aspects are prominent in the stimulus situation than it does with the person.

Since imagery tends to be so important in thinking, the question arises as to whether *all* thinking involves images. For a long time it was thought that it did. About 1900, however, certain psychologists in Germany discovered in their research what they termed *imageless thought*. For example, when they asked a subject to name an animal and he said "dog," the response usually occurred before there was any image of that animal. These psychologists also found that judgments often were made without the subjects' being able to report any image. For example, if we close our eyes and first pick up one weight and then after a few seconds another weight, most likely we shall be able to compare them without having an image of the weight of the first. These psychologists

▶ Children learn the meaning of the words that they use in thinking in a variety of ways. One of these ways is by experiencing the words in a variety of verbal contexts, that is, in the context of the other words in sentences. The purpose of the study to be reported here * was to determine how children at different age levels learn the meanings of words from verbal contexts.

The subjects were five groups of children, with twenty-five children in each group. The age groups were nine, ten, eleven, twelve, and thirteen years. The child's task was to find the meaning of twelve artificial words, each of which appeared in six different sentences. For example, the artificial word in the first set of six sentences was CORPLUM, which meant "stick" or "piece of wood." The verbal contexts for CORPLUM were as follows:

A CORPLUM may be used for support.
CORPLUMS may be used to close off an open place.
A CORPLUM may be long or short, thick or thin, strong or weak.
A wet CORPLUM does not burn.
You can make a CORPLUM smooth with sandpaper.
The painter used a CORPLUM to smooth his paints.

After each sentence, the child was asked to give a meaning for the word and then how and why the meaning given fit the sentence.

As might be expected, the older children more quickly and more frequently arrived at correct word meanings than did the younger ones. The children's responses were classified by three different judges, and the various types of errors were analyzed. One type of error was *pluralization*: the child found a meaning for a word in one sentence and simply added different elements of meaning to this core concept in order to make it fit different contexts. For example, one child decided that the artificial word *LIDBER* meant "collect." This meaning was altered to "collect ribbons" in the sentence, "All children will *LIDBER* at Mary's party." In the sentence, "People *LIDBER* quickly when there is an accident," the meaning given for the artificial word was "collect information." In still another sentence it was given the meaning "collected autographs."

There were many other attempts to arrive at solutions which were equally inventive. The study as a whole certainly points up the complexity of the thought processes that children utilize in learning the meanings of words.

* Heinz Werner and Edith Kaplan, "Development of Word Meaning Through Verbal Context: An Experimental Study," 1950, 29:251–257, *Journal of Psychology*.

came to the conclusion that most acts of judgment take place without the mediation of an image. In addition, many people report that they often think without being aware of images of the objects about which they are thinking. Our conclusion is that, while images are often important in thinking, they are not *all*-important.

Verbal Symbols. A great deal of our thinking is in words, which are also symbols. These words are drawn from language, which is a social product. The word symbols, or groupings of such symbols, have more or less standardized meanings in a given population of persons. These meanings represent the abstract similarities

Forming concepts of different classes of objects is important as a basis for thinking. In order to study the process of forming concepts, psychologists usually construct stimulus materials that fall into several classes, each defined by a particular concept. The task of a subject in the experiment is to learn to give a distinctive response, such as the same name, to each member of a class, that is, to each instance of the concept in question.

The problem of the study to be reported here * was as follows: "Are there differences in the readiness with which human adults attain concepts of three different sorts—concepts of concrete objects, concepts of spatial forms, and concepts of numbers?"

Nine concepts were to be learned, and a nonsense syllable name was to be learned for each concept. The concepts, classified as to type, and their names are shown in the accompanying table.

Concepts and Names Used in the Experiment

Concrete objects		Spatial forms		Numerical quantities	
Concept	Names	Concept	Names	Concept	Names
Face	Relk	O	Fard	2	Ling
Building	Leth		Stod	5	Dilt
Tree	Mulp		Pran	6	Mank

Sixteen series of drawings were prepared. In each series, there were nine drawings, one for each concept. So in each series there were three drawings of concrete objects, three of spatial forms, and three representing numbers. The first three series of the 16 are illustrated in the figure. You will note that the instances of each concept differ from series to series, but are alike in the essential respect defined by the concept. For example, the number concept of five is pictured by glasses, diamonds, and spoons, and in still other ways in the other series.

The experimenter began with series I, presenting each drawing followed by its concept name. Each subject was instructed in advance to learn the name of each drawing so that on repetition of the series he could say the name before the experimenter said it. The series was repeated until the subject was able to anticipate the name of each drawing on two successive presentations of the list. The same procedure was repeated with series II and so on through the entire sixteen series.

As the subjects mastered the concepts, they became able to give the right names for the drawings the first time through a new series; that is, they recognized instances of the concepts. The results clearly showed that concepts of concrete objects were most readily learned, those of spatial forms were of intermediate difficulty, and those of number were most difficult.

* Edna Heidbreder, "The Attainment of Concepts: I. Terminology and Methodology," *Journal of General Psychology*, 35:173–189, 1946. Also, Edna Heidbreder, "The Attainment of Concepts: II. The Problem," *ibid.*, 35:191–223, 1946.

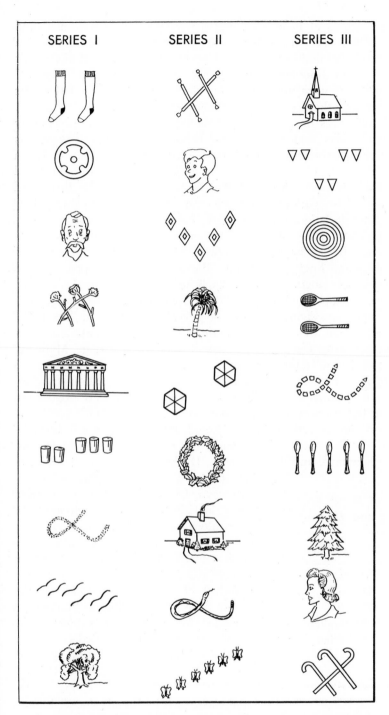

Three of the sixteen series of stimulus figures used in Heidbreder's study of concept formation. (Reproduced by permission of the American Psychological Association.)

and differences which are significant in a given society. If we share these meanings with other people, we can communicate with them. Furthermore, in our thinking (and perception), we tend to organize the world of experience much as others do. Recognizing these social influences on individual thought, we should also realize that each of us is unique in his experience and outlook.

Another aspect of language is shown in its grammatical structure. The various parts of speech in the English language and the many and complicated rules of grammar are familiar to us. It has been argued by some philosophers and linguists that the grammatical aspect of language has important consequences for our thinking. For example, the word "perceiving" tends to suggest a process, one that is changing and dependent on many conditions, whereas the word "perception" might suggest a static entity. In this chapter, we have used the word "thinking" rather than "thought" in the title for the purpose of emphasizing the process rather than "frozen hunks of thought."

Of great importance in language, and in thinking, are the words which do not stand for objects or events but which function to organize thinking. For example, words such as "because," "and," and "whereas" symbolize important logical relationships in our language.

What do we know about the psychology of verbal behavior? One line of study has been conducted with *free association,* in which the subject is given a stimulus word and told to respond with the first word that he can think of. These responses may vary in many ways. Some responses to a particular word are more probable than others, at least in a given group of people. For example, the word "hot" is more likely to be followed by "cold" than by "daisy." Someone who responds "rod" might be revealing interest in "hot rods."

Sometimes the responses have a similarity in sound, such as "dog–log." More significant are meaningful similarities such as "fast–rapid" and "generalization–transfer" or antonyms (words which are opposite in meaning) such as "up–down" and "hot–cold." Freud, the founder of psychoanalysis, made use of the technique of free association. He had his patients freely associate (often giving whole phrases or sentences as responses) about many different things, including incidents in dreams. His observations, and those of others who have studied free association, show that we have a rich network of relationships among our symbols and their meanings.

Studies of *controlled association* also give us some understanding of thinking. In controlled association, the subject is instructed to give response words bearing a specified relationship to the stimulus word. It may be specified, for example, that the words stand for objects that are in the same class, such as "bond–stock." In such an experiment, the subject may improve in his ability to give associations of a given type. After practicing a certain type, he may show improvement on new stimulus-

Table 13.1   Frequency of Word Associations in 1,000 Men and Women

Stimulus: "long" *		Stimulus: "chair" *	
413	short	191	table
81	distance	127	seat
50	length	107	sit
32	road	83	furniture
26	tall	56	sitting

* The subjects were told to give the first word that occurred to them other than the stimulus word. Only the five most frequent responses are shown for the two stimulus words.

SOURCE: From Kent, G. H., and A. J. Rosanoff, "A Study of Association in Insanity," American Journal of Insanity, 67:37–96, 317–390, 1910.

Figure 13.6. This record shows the correspondence between imagined activity and action currents. Jacobsen recorded electrical activity by placing electrodes over the right biceps muscle. The subjects, who had been trained to relax, were instructed in one part of the experiment to "imagine some rhythmical activity such as climbing a rope." At regular intervals there was a burst of electrical activity. (From E. Jacobsen, "The Electrophysiology of Mental Activities," American Journal of Psychology, vol. 44, fig. 1–4, opposite p. 682. 1932. Courtesy of the publisher.)

response pairs even though the particular pairs have not been practiced. Furthermore the process of selection is not usually at a deliberate, conscious level. The instruction appears to act as a directive influence and largely at an unconscious level. We may say that the subject becomes *set* to give a certain type of response and that this set may improve with practice.

Our thought processes have an organized character, that is, the symbols we use are related to each other. The words of a phrase, clause, sentence, or other unit together determine the meaning of the whole. The meaning of particular words depends on the context furnished by the other words.

Muscular Movements as Symbols. Muscular movements (and bodily postures) may function as symbols. We know already that gestures and other bodily postures may be used as symbols in communicating with others. They may also function as symbols in our own thinking. For example, we may rehearse in anticipation the gestures of signaling in traffic. Or we may symbolically brace ourselves for facing a difficult situation by assuming an erect and alert posture.

A muscular movement may act as a stimulus for further reactions. For example, there is the case of the recruit who had difficulty in drill because he could not respond quickly to the words "right" and "left." After a while he learned to tense his *writing* hand for turning *right* and his other hand for turning left. The muscular movement mediated between the verbal command and the final response.

When muscular movements function symbolically, they tend to be *implicit;* that is, they are reduced to such an extent that they are no longer obvious. Indeed, symbolic muscular movements may become so reduced in size that they can be detected only by sensitive electronic devices which measure action currents (changes in electrical potential) in muscles. When we think of clenching our fist, there usually are very small changes in the appropriate muscles, even though we are trying to be relaxed. It is of course difficult to demonstrate experimentally that there is a perfect one-to-one correspondence between the awareness of images of movements and the occurrence of implicit muscular movements, but the evidence thus far shows a relationship between the two.[1]

Psychologists have also recorded changes in the speech apparatus (tongue, vocal cords, etc.) when a person thinks in words. The movements correspond to those which would be made in actually speaking the

[1] E. Jacobsen, "The Electrophysiology of Mental Activities," *American Journal of Psychology,* 44:677–694, 1932.

words out loud, except that they are very much reduced in scale. These movements in turn give rise to stimuli which may act as cues for further behavior, including further speech movements.

The observation that speech movements occur when we think with words led some psychologists to say that verbal thinking is the same as subvocal talking. That is, they said that thinking is nothing but implicit speech movements. At present, most psychologists believe that such a view is too narrow. In the first place, the fact that implicit speech movements and introspections about words are correlated does not prove that these two events are identical—they may simply be interrelated aspects of the same underlying process. In the second place, there is considerable evidence that other processes, especially in the central nervous system, are critically important in verbal thinking. Indeed, paralysis of the speech apparatus (by means of anesthetics) does not eliminate verbal thinking, whereas certain types of brain injuries may impair one or another aspect of verbal thinking (without impairing the vocal apparatus as such). So we may conclude that, while speech movements are important in verbal thinking, they are only part of the total process.

PROBLEM SOLVING

In this section we shall be interested in the use of thinking to solve problems. Problem solving is discussed in connection with learning in Chapter 12. In human beings it is very likely that thinking plays a considerable role in much of our learning. For instance, the conditioning of reactions in us can be affected by our thoughts—how we interpret the situation, our self-instructions, and our attitudes. In the learning of a maze or a motor skill, we may give ourselves instructions and verbalize the steps in the process. These verbal or other symbols may help us master tasks requiring responses to signals and a series of responses in a particular order. In the solution of more complicated problems, thinking usually plays an even more prominent part.

What a Problem Is. It is difficult to say what a problem is except from the point of view of the person who has one. Subjectively a problem is felt as a gap, as an unclear relationship, as something which needs completion. For example, the truck driver mentioned earlier had the problem of how to free his truck and get through the underpass, which meant that he had a goal and no clear way of reaching it.

The direction of thinking in problem solving is given by the problem itself. We vary a great deal in what we see as problems. Our problem might be so specific as how to find a parking place for our car or as broad as the nature of man. But in every case there is some goal to be reached or something to be understood, without any clear or immediate way of attaining this objective.

Some Factors Affecting Problem Solving. The likelihood of solving a problem de-

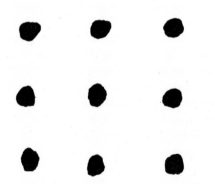

Figure 13.7. The nine-dot problem. Try to draw four straight lines (without removing the pencil from the paper and without retracing any part of the line) so that all nine dots are on the lines. See Figure 13.9 for solution.

Figure 13.8. In Maier's string problem, the task was to tie the ends of two strings together. The strings were so short and far apart that it was not possible to hold one and walk over to seize the other. Very few subjects solved the problem. Why were most people unsuccessful? (From N. R. F. Maier, "Reasoning in Humans: III, The Mechanisms of Equivalent Stimuli and of Reasoning," Journal of Experimental Psychology, 35:351, 1945. Courtesy of the American Psychological Association.)

pends on a number of factors. Some of them are touched upon in discussing insight in Chapter 12.

How the problem is conceived. One factor is how the problem is conceived. It is characteristic of problem solving that the way in which we define a problem, that is, what we think the problem is, has a great effect on whether or not we can solve it. So long as chemists looked for the nonexistent substance known as "phlogiston," which was supposed to be given up by substance in burning, there was little prospect for an understanding of the nature of combustion.

An experiment by Maier [2] is helpful in understanding the influence of the person's conception of the problem. In one of his experiments the task, called the *string problem,* was to tie together the ends of two widely separated strings suspended from the ceiling. The strings were so far apart that it was impossible to hold the end of one string and, while holding it, to walk over to seize the end of the other string. Some subjects perceived the difficulty as being that the strings just were

[2] N. R. F. Maier, "Reasoning in Humans: I. On Direction," *Journal of Comparative Psychology,* 10:115–143, 1930.

not long enough. Having defined the problem in this way, the next step naturally would be how to lengthen the strings, which would have worked had the appropriate materials been available. Other subjects perceived that they were simply not tall enough to bring the two strings together. With appropriate materials one might have made a platform on which to walk so as to be "tall enough." The solution, which was comparatively infrequent, was to tie a pair of pliers (which was lying nearby) to one string and then to swing it as a pendulum, catching it on the backswing while holding the other string. This solution appeared more often when the experimenter, as if by accident, brushed against a string, setting it in motion. How we conceive our problems, this illustration shows, has a great deal to do with their solution.

Intensity of motivation. A second factor in problem solving is the degree of motivation. Although moderate motivation is helpful, intense motivation may be harmful. If we are in danger, for example, we may be so badly frightened that we blindly and repetitively try the same ineffective method of escape when all we need to do is trip a latch. Or our attempts may be

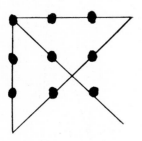

Figure 13.9. Solution of the nine-dot problem. If you solved the problem, how did you do so? So long as one is "set" to solve the problem by staying within the bounds of the figure, no solution is possible. In other problems, too, an inappropriate set may block solution.

scattered and erratic. Thinking in an orderly way is difficult when there is pressure to rush into action. Under extreme conditions of tension, our thought processes tend to become so disorganized or perseverative (stuck in a rut) that we are less likely to reach a solution.

On the other hand, if motivation is too weak, we may not persist long enough in our attempts at solution. In the history of science, some problems have been solved only after years of effort. In such cases, the motivation was strong but well directed.

Transfer of learned responses. Another factor affecting problem solving is the transfer of previously learned responses. Any problem situation has at least some similarities to previously experienced situations. As a result, previously learned responses are likely to generalize (see Chapter 12) to the new situation. Some of these responses, including ways of perceiving the problem, may aid solution while others may actually hinder it. As an example of the latter, a belt is usually perceived as an article of clothing. In Maier's string problem, would the subject be likely to perceive his belt as stringlike, so that it could be used as a way of lengthening one of the strings? It would probably be easier for him to perceive it in this way if it were hanging from a hook than if it were around his waist.

Having solved a whole series of problems of the same kind as the new problem may be helpful. In such a case, it is sometimes difficult to identify exactly what transfers. Methods of approaching the problem, principles, and the like are possibilities. Sometimes, however, we may become *set* to solve a problem in a certain way as a result of previously solving others like it; then we mechanically apply this method when a simpler way might work better.

A critical element necessary for solution may be hidden or masked from view, or it may be so emphasized that it becomes readily available for solution. In the string problem, setting a string in motion helped, even when subjects reported afterward that they had not noticed its motion or used this motion as a hint. In some of Köhler's experiments with chimpanzees, insight was more likely when the critical materials, such as a stick for raking in an article of food, were near the subject and the goal. Solving a problem when the means of solution, such as a tool, is absent is even more difficult. The properties of absent objects are not available perceptually but must be thought of. Exploring the materials at hand may enable us to perceive properties which may be helpful in solution. Verbalizing what would be needed for solution may set us to searching for objects with the required characteristics. It should be clear that our past experience may play a vital role in this solution.

Theories of Problem Solving. There are three main approaches to understanding problem-solving behavior: (1) the approach of logic, (2) the stimulus-response theory, and (3) the cognitive theory. We shall discuss these views in turn.

Logical view of problem solving. First, there is the view that problem solving is a matter of applying the laws of logic, or that thinking can be described in terms of logical concepts such as abstraction, classification, rational inference, and the like.

According to this notion, the more fully we follow the procedures of logic, the more effectively we shall solve our problems.

Most traditional texts in logic distinguish between deductive and inductive logic, and some people try to fit thinking and problem solving into these two pigeonholes. Deductive logic deals with rules for drawing valid conclusions from assumptions. A classical example of a syllogism, which is used in deductive logic, is the following:

> All men are mortal.
> Socrates is a man.
> Therefore Socrates is mortal.

As many people have noted, deductive logic is not so much a matter of discovering new knowledge as it is a method of proof. As a matter of fact, formal reasoning, whether by means of syllogisms or by means of more modern forms of logic, is actually quite rare in real-life problem solving.

Inductive logic, which is not formal, is a matter of reasoning from particular facts to generalizations (from which these and other facts may be deduced). J. S. Mill's famous Canons (rules, principles) for inductive reasoning [3] provide some standards for inductive reasoning, but they are not especially useful in *guiding* inquiry. Here again we find that a *psychological* approach to understanding problem solving is more likely to explain how we actually solve problems.

Some have argued that training in formal logic and mathematics somehow "strengthens the mind," as though the mind were like a muscle which could be strengthened by appropriate exercises. There is little evidence for such a view.

[3] For an account of Mill's Canons and logic generally, see M. R. Cohen and E. Nagel, *An Introduction to Logic and Scientific Method*, Harcourt, Brace, New York, 1934.

Figure 13.10. *A child (four years, eleven months) is asked to pour beads from the narrow jar (in his hand) into the wide one. His finger pointing at the wide jar indicates that he expects the beads there to reach the same level as they did in the narrow one. What knowledge is he transferring to this problem? What facts is he not taking into account? What factors might account for his behavior? (Courtesy of Dr. David Elkind, Austen Riggs Center.)*

Formal logic may sometimes serve as a useful tool in checking the validity of reasoning processes, just as mathematics (which is a kind of formal logic) may be a tool which is both convenient and essential for solving certain problems. It is highly doubtful, however, that such training helps us better to solve problems in general.

Stimulus-response theory. Stimulus-response (or association) theory also endeavors to explain problem solving. As is pointed out in Chapter 12, stimulus-response theorists view all learning as the formation of habits. Problem solving is transfer of learned responses to the stimulus conditions of the problem situation. Further learning—in the sense of forming new habits—may also be involved. Applying the theory to Maier's string-tying experiment, the motive is to tie the ends of

Many people are not aware of the distinction between logical validity and factual (or empirical) truth. A conclusion is valid if it necessarily follows (by the rules of logic) from the premises (the first two statements of the syllogism). A conclusion is true if it "corresponds" to factual observations. As shown below, there are all possible combinations of truth and validity.

If all wood burns, and if all crates are made of wood, then all crates burn.	Logically valid and factually true
If all materials burn, and if water is a material, then water burns.	Logically valid but factually false
If water is not wood, and if wood burns, then water does not burn.	Logically invalid but factually true
If wood burns, and if rubber burns, then rubber is wood.	Logically invalid and factually false

If the premises are true *and* the logic is valid, then the conclusion will be true. On the other hand, if the conclusion is true and the logic is valid, this does not guarantee that the premises are true (although our confidence in them may be increased). If the conclusion is *false* while the logic is valid, we know that one or both of the premises are false. To make our point in another way, the factual confirmation of many deductions from a theory increases our confidence in the theory, but even a single deduction which is false teaches us that there is a flaw in the theory. (Incidentally, there are various forms of formal reasoning in addition to syllogistic reasoning, e.g., mathematical reasoning.)

the string together. At the outset, on the basis of past learning, certain responses—such as trying to grasp the end of one string and bring it to the other—are more probable than others. From moment to moment the subject is making symbolic responses such as "The strings are too short," and "If I were taller, I could reach both strings." Each of these sentences acts as a stimulus for further symbols, such as "Make the strings longer somehow" and "Stand up on something so that I will be taller." These responses in turn act as stimuli orienting the subject to find objects or means of meeting these requirements.

We shall not try to carry this example further, but merely say that stimulus-response theory does not regard problem

solving as an "automatic, rote, mechanical" transfer of elementary habits, but as a complex and flexible process involving thinking. In predicting problem-solving behavior, the stimulus-response theorist tries to analyze the stimuli in the problem situation, the learned responses which are likely to follow from these stimuli, and the symbolic habits of the subject. He recognizes that the transfer which occurs may be either positive or negative, or some combination of these.

Cognitive theory. Another approach to an understanding of problem solving is cognitive theory.[4] According to this view,

[4] Probably the best exposition of the cognitive approach is that of K. Duncker, "On Problem Solving," *Psychological Monographs*, no. 270, 1945.

problem solving (and learning) is a matter of perceptual reorganization. In a problem situation, a person usually has some goal, such as tying the ends of the strings together in Maier's experiments. He perceives a region (or more than one) of difficulty—the strings are too short, he is not tall enough, etc. These perceptions further influence the way in which he perceives the rest of the situation. Thinking, whether by means of words or images, is influenced by the perceptual organization of the moment, which may lead to changes in perceiving. Whether or not these changed ways of perceiving lead to solution depends on many factors in the particular problem.

Cognitive theory places little emphasis on past experience, but a great deal on how the parts of the problem situation are arranged. For example, in Maier's string-tying problem the perceptions of "strings too short" and "need to be taller" were very stable—but unfruitful—perceptions. On the other hand, if the strings had been weighted and set swinging, the perception necessary for solution probably would have emerged readily.

Evaluation of these theories. We have already evaluated the logical theory, which is not really a theory of behavior but a set of standards for validating reasoning. The stimulus-response theory and the cognitive theory are not so different as they might seem at first sight. Each theory begins with a person who has a goal that he is unable to reach immediately. Furthermore, each theory holds that the person perceives the stimulus situation or some parts of it. Cognitive theorists emphasize the view that the perception of any part of the situation is influenced by all the other parts. On the other hand, stimulus-response theorists have a tendency to regard certain elements as stimuli, without taking the whole into account. The difference, then, is in the size of the stimulus or perceptual unit which is considered to be influential. Here stimulus-response theorists

may have erred by having too "atomistic" a notion of the stimulus. On the other hand, cognitive theorists may have erred by neglecting to analyze the stimulus situation, while continually repeating that "the whole is greater than the sum of its parts."

Both theories allow for the influence of thinking processes, with stimulus-response theory going somewhat further to explain the arousal and sequence of symbols. Finally, cognitive theory seems to provide an easier language in which to describe thinking. Actually, both theories are of value in trying to explain problem solving and thinking. Rather than trying to choose between them, it would be better to use the insights of each.

EFFICIENCY IN THINKING AND PROBLEM SOLVING

All of us would like to make more efficient use of our thought processes in order better to solve problems. Although there is no simple formula for improving thinking, it will be worthwhile to look at some of the conditions of effective (and ineffective) thinking. Many of the points we shall make must be tentative, for research in the field of thinking has not yet provided definitive answers.

Proper Formulation of the Problem. The way we formulate the problem determines how readily it may be solved—or, for that matter, whether it can be solved at all. In scientific work, for example, it is necessary to ask the right questions of nature. One suggestion is to avoid a too narrow or prematurely rigid definition of the problem. For example, it probably would be inappropriate to define the problem of the control of juvenile delinquency by asking, "How can we punish delinquents so severely that they will avoid future acts of delinquency?"

Previous experience with an area of knowledge is usually of help in formulating problems which are important and capable of being solved. Thus when scien-

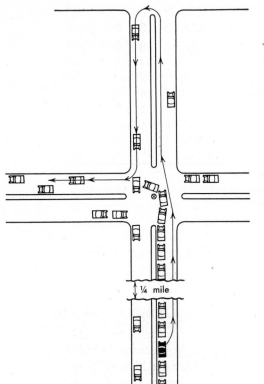

Figure 13.11. "An example in reasoning. The driver in the black car is blocked from making a left turn by the traffic jam in the left lane. In the distance he sees the cars in the much lighter traffic coming from the opposite direction making the right turn easily on the road he wants to take. He thinks, 'If I were only going the other way.' This stimulates him to think of how he could be going the other way. He pulls out into the right lane, passes the cars ahead, turns around, comes back the other way, and makes a right turn onto the highway. (The small circle at the center intersection indicates a traffic light.)" (*Figures and caption from J. Dollard and N. E. Miller,* Personality and Psychotherapy, *McGraw-Hill, New York, 1950, p. 112. Courtesy of the publisher.*)

¼ mile

tists have developed an area of knowledge it generally becomes easier to formulate properly further problems in the same area.

Getting Adequate Information. We are more likely to think effectively about something if we have abundant relevant information. Some people propose to teach students "how to think." While there may be some general methods of value, we need to have at least some facts in order to think well. How ineffective it would be to plan an insurance and investment program if we had little or no information, and if, moreover, what little we had was inaccurate! Not only is it important to have adequate information, but it is also important to know what needed information we do *not* have. Many plans during wartime or in the business world must take into account the important information that is lacking.

Using Clearly Defined Concepts. Concepts should be clearly defined. It is diffi-

cult to think effectively with hazy, ill-defined concepts. Abstractions may be powerful tools in thinking, but there is the ever-present risk that they may become grandiose and divorced from the world of reality. Most people, for example, find it difficult to think carefully about such omnibus abstractions as "human nature," "personal integration," "liberal education," and the "universal nature of man." Simply defining something in a definite way, of course, does not guarantee that such a definition will be useful. Nor, so far as we know, can science get along without at least some terms called *constructs* (such as matter, energy, motive, and the like) which are not directly definable by reference to objects.

Controlling Emotional Factors. As was pointed out earlier in this chapter, our feelings play a big part in our thinking, often leading us to rationalize and distort reality. Furthermore, strong anxiety or guilt often leads not only to avoiding the problem area and possible solutions, but also to repression. How can we control these emotional factors? Here are a few practical recommendations:

First, we should seek to identify some of our emotional biases regarding the problem in question. If we know that we have a prejudice against a minority group, for example, we can be on our guard against the influence of this feeling on our thinking. We realize, however, that many unconscious biases may continue to operate.

Second, if we are emotionally disturbed, we should wait (if there is an opportunity to do so) until later when we are calmer to think about the problem. After we have a solution, we should regard it as tentative and reconsider it again after an interval.

Third, we should check our views against those of disinterested persons. Often, after having worked out a solution, we can reevaluate it by talking it over with other people who do not have strong feelings about it and thus can be more objective.

Fourth, we should avoid the use of emotionally loaded (either positively or negatively) words or other symbols. It is difficult to think objectively in terms of labels such as "communist agitator," "capitalist overlord," "right to work," and "progress." Such terms as these, with their strong affective reactions, inevitably influence us to make evaluations which are similar in emotional tone.

Other Conditions of Effective Thinking. Our thinking will be more effective if we critically examine our assumptions; something that we are taking for granted may not be true.

We should be cautious in thinking in "either-or" terms, as if everything were either black or white. We should also be cautious about making sweeping generalizations; there may be exceptions.

It will be helpful to look for alternative solutions, instead of pouncing on the first plausible possibility, and to look for general principles, instead of using a rote rule of procedure.

Finally, we should be careful about trying to explain anything in terms of a single cause or factor; usually there are many factors involved.

CONCLUSION

It is worthwhile to point out that psychologists have as yet made only limited progress in the investigation of thinking and problem solving. For a long time they were seriously handicapped by popular and philosophical preconceptions. The prospects, however, are very encouraging for a genuinely psychological approach to the subject and the rapid development of experimental methods for its study.

SUMMARY

Thinking is behavior characterized by the manipulation of symbols—words, images, and certain muscular movements—which represent aspects of our world of experience. There are various motivations behind thinking, such as the desire to solve a problem and the desire to enhance or defend the self. Thinking and feeling usually go together, and much of thinking involves unconscious processes. We study thinking by observing our own thoughts and the behavior of others.

A symbol is something which stands for something else. We use both external and internal symbols. Concepts, which are meanings that are common to a class of objects, help us to identify objects and prepare to react to them in certain ways. Some concepts are more abstract than others in the sense that fewer characteristics are used in identifying members of a class (and the classes are more inclusive). Abstractions permit wide generalization of knowledge. The meanings of symbols are learned. The fact that symbols can have referents that are not physically present helps us to solve problems.

Images, which are one type of symbol,

occur in different sensory modalities, and people differ in their imagery. Although images are important, it is doubtful that *all* thinking involves images.

Certain muscular movements, especially in the speech apparatus, may function as symbols. While speech movements are important in verbal thinking, they are only part of the total process.

Words are part of language, a cultural product. The categories (abstract similarities and differences) embodied in language influence thinking, although we differ in what words mean to us. Studies of free and controlled association and of word contexts all show the many and complex associations among words.

Problem solving, which involves thinking, begins with a problem as perceived. The way in which a problem is formulated has an influence on how it is attacked.

Various factors, such as intensity of motivation and transfer of expectations and habitual reactions, affect problem solving.

Approaching problem solving from the point of view of logic fails to explain actual problem-solving behavior, although standards of validity of reasoning may at times be helpful. Stimulus-response theory endeavors to explain problem solving mainly on the basis of transfer of learned reactions, with symbolic habits playing an important part. Cognitive theory emphasizes perceptual reorganization. Both the stimulus-response and cognitive theories contribute to our understanding of problem solving.

Efficient thinking in problem solving depends on various factors: correct problem formulation, adequate information, use of clearly defined concepts, control of emotional factors, and others.

QUESTIONS

1. What is meant by thinking? How is thinking related to feeling?

2. What is the significance of unconscious factors in thinking? What is the evidence that they exist?

3. What are the relative advantages and disadvantages of images, words, and muscular movements as symbols?

4. Evaluate introspective observation and objective studies of behavior as ways of studying thinking.

5. What factors influence the likelihood of solving a problem?

6. What is the relation of logic to thinking? Can thinking be illogical and yet solve problems?

7. How does stimulus-response theory try to explain problem solving? Evaluate the strengths and weaknesses of this approach.

8. How does cognitive theory try to explain thinking? Evaluate the strengths and weaknesses of this approach.

9. What influences do emotional factors have on problem solving and thinking? How may the influence of emotional factors be controlled?

10. What do studies of free and controlled association teach us about thinking?

11. What recommendations would you make for improving the efficiency of problem solving and thinking?

12. Think of a problem which you have solved recently in an inventive way. How did you arrive at the solution? What part did previous experience play in the process of solution?

SUGGESTED READINGS

Dollard, J., and N. E. Miller: *Personality and Psychotherapy*, McGraw-Hill, New York, 1950.
> (A stimulus-response analysis of learning and thinking.)

Dunker, K.: *On Problem Solving*, Psychological Monographs, no. 270, 1945.
> (An account of some valuable experiments on human problem solving.)

Hayakawa, S. I.: *Language in Thought and Action*, Harcourt, Brace, New York, 1949.
> (A treatment of thinking and communication from a viewpoint of general semantics; interestingly and simply written.)

Katona, G.: *Organizing and Memorizing*, Columbia University Press, New York, 1940.
> (Compares rote and meaningful methods of problem solving.)

Korzybski, Alfred: *Science and Sanity*, 2d ed., International Non-Aristotelian Library Publishing Co., Lancaster, 1941.
> (Thinking and language from the point of view of general semantics.)

Leeper, Robert: "Cognitive Processes," in S. S. Stevens (ed.), *Handbook of Experimental Psychology*, Wiley, New York, 1951, pp. 730–757.
> (A technical discussion of the methodology and results of research regarding thinking.)

Thouless, R. H.: *How to Think Straight*, Simon and Schuster, New York, 1939.
> (A popular treatment of the subject of effective thinking.)

Vinacke, W. E.: *The Psychology of Thinking*, McGraw-Hill, New York, 1952.
> (A text covering a wide range of topics related to thinking.)

Wertheimer, M.: *Productive Thinking*, Harper, New York, 1945.
> (A stimulating treatment of thinking and problem solving.)

14 ATTITUDES
AND BELIEFS

In order to understand a person's behavior, it is helpful to know what his attitudes and beliefs are. Knowledge of attitudes and beliefs is also of great practical importance. Politicians need to know the attitudes and beliefs of the public they serve. So do advertisers. Religion is largely a matter of attitude and belief. In this chapter, we shall consider the nature of attitudes and beliefs, how they are formed, why they tend to be stable, and how they may be changed.

NATURE OF ATTITUDES AND BELIEFS

What do we mean by the terms *attitude* and *belief?* How are attitudes and beliefs different from one another, and how are they related? What is the function of attitudes and beliefs? And how do we identify and measure them? If we can answer these questions, we shall be in a better position to understand the nature of these factors in human behavior.

Meaning of Attitude. An attitude may be regarded as the way a person feels about something. This is not a very technical-sounding definition, but if we examine its meaning we shall obtain a clearer understanding of the concept involved. As a feeling about something, an attitude has an *object*. The object toward which the attitude is directed may be anything—a person, a material object, a situation, a policy, etc. It may be as concrete as a building or as abstract as existentialism. It may be as real as the Democratic party or as unreal as ghosts. In other words, the object of an attitude may be anything that we can perceive or think about.

This feeling can be any motivational (or emotional) state, and like all motives, it must be inferred from behavior. Consider, for example, our attitude toward the church. If it is a favorable one, we feel reverent when we are in church. If our church needs money or services, we are ready to help out. We will defend it against those who would attack it. Its goals are our goals. We should like to see its educational program furthered. In many other respects, we are favorably disposed toward the church.

To have an attitude toward something does not mean that we continuously experience a feeling regarding it. We may have a favorable attitude toward the church, but we are not continually in a state of tension regarding it. We do, however, have a readiness to become motivated in ways which are favorable to its welfare. An attitude, in other words, is a *readiness to become motivated with respect to an object.* Under certain conditions, such as when we are in the presence of the object, or when the values which it has for us can be enhanced or defended, we are likely to become appropriately motivated.

A course of action or a statement of opinion is usually determined by a whole *set* of attitudes and beliefs. Our decision about how much money to give to the church may be influenced by many factors. Some of these factors, such as our liking for Jimmy's Sunday-school teacher, may influence us to give more; other factors, such as the unexpectedly heavy income tax we may have paid, may influence us to give less. Our decision will be determined by these various opposing forces.

Dimensions of Attitudes. Attitudes may be regarded as varying in several ways; that is, they have various dimensions. One of these is *direction;* we can be for or against something. A second way attitudes may vary is in *degree*—the degree of favorableness may vary all the way from be-ing extremely favorable through neutrality to being extremely unfavorable. To be neutral in attitude is to be indifferent to the object. In practice, though, it is difficult to determine the point on an attitude-measuring scale which represents true neutrality. Attitudes also vary, thirdly, in the *intensity* with which they are held. We may say, for example, that we feel the church is necessary for the existence of law and order. This statement indicates a favorable attitude; the degree of *confidence* with which we assert it indicates the intensity of our attitude. As might be expected, our most intense attitudes tend to be the more extreme ones—either favorable or unfavorable.

Another way in which attitudes vary is in how ready we are to react in terms of the attitude. A person who is prejudiced against all Englishmen, for example, needs very little provocation to find undesirable things in the behavior of Englishmen. Nearly *anything* Englishmen do may irritate him.

Attitudes may also vary in the *degree* in which the object of the attitudes is *common* to a number of people or *unique* to a particular individual. Of course an object must be a common object if we are to compare people as to the degree, intensity, and other aspects of the attitude. It would, for example, be impossible to devise a scale to measure attitudes toward the church, that is, to *compare* people in their attitudes, unless the church were a common object for them. Being socialized in the same culture, we tend to have attitudes toward many of the same significant social objects—the church, marriage, free enterprise, etc.

Attitudes also vary in the extent to which they are conscious. By now the notion of unconscious processes is quite familiar, so it should come as no surprise to discover that attitudes may be unconsciously held. Indeed, it is likely that most of our attitudes are ones of which we are not clearly

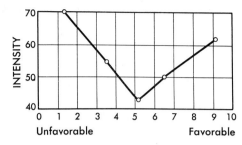

Figure 14.1. This figure shows how the intensity of an attitude varies in relation to the degree to which that attitude is favorable or unfavorable. The more favorable or unfavorable the attitude, the greater its intensity (the confidence with which it is held). The graph is based on opinions expressed about government control of business. Can you be intensely "neutral" on an issue? (From H. Cantril, "The Intensity of an Attitude," Journal of Abnormal and Social Psychology, *41:129–136, 1946. Courtesy of American Psychological Association.*)

aware. Prejudice furnishes a good example. On an intellectual level, we may have unprejudiced beliefs. Yet in certain circumstances deeper hostile feelings emerge, or projective tests may reveal their existence. Some of our most important attitudes and beliefs are simply taken for granted. We do not ordinarily talk about them or even think about them. But let a crisis situation arise in which such taken-for-granted attitudes and beliefs are challenged—then their strength and importance will be dramatically revealed.

A person can simultaneously hold inconsistent attitudes toward the same object, or at least toward aspects which are not clearly discriminated from one another. For example, he can have both favorable and negative attitudes toward the church, in which event he is *ambivalent* in attitude. These different attitudes may be maintained through repression, dissociation, or other devices for enhancing and defending the self (see Chapter 6).

Meaning of Belief. A belief may be defined as the acceptance or rejection of a proposition about reality. For example, our belief that the world is round is an assertion which we accept about reality. The truth or falsity of this belief and of many, but not all, other beliefs can be determined by an appeal to factual data. But some of our beliefs cannot be thus verified, or else their verification is difficult or impossible at this time. Many of our beliefs in the realm of religion are of this type. Indeed, we have systems of beliefs (ideologies) about all the important institutions of our society, such as the family, free enterprise, and democratic government, which are difficult to verify, although we have great confidence in them. Such beliefs are matters of faith. It is an interesting thing about human behavior that some of the beliefs that we hold to most tenaciously—and with the strongest feelings—are matters of faith and not readily subject to proof or disproof.

In this chapter, we shall not emphasize a distinction between attitudes and beliefs. Most, if not all, attitudes involve related beliefs. For example, a favorable attitude toward the church may involve beliefs that the church helps to curb delinquency, that it makes people happier, that there is a God, and so on. Likewise, many of our beliefs involve attitudes. For example, a belief that the government of another nation intends to harm us usually goes along with the attitudes of fear and hatred. Indeed, it is difficult to know which—attitudes or beliefs—comes first, for the two are highly interrelated. The closeness of the relationship is apparent from the fact that a change in beliefs is usually followed by a change in related attitudes. When workers come to believe that management has their interests at heart, their attitudes toward management become more favorable. It works the other way, too: attitudes seem to influence beliefs. An antagonistic attitude toward a minority group tends to support beliefs which define such a group as inferior, vicious, and the like. Let attitudes become more favorable, and the unfavorable beliefs tend to change too. Furthermore, both attitudes and beliefs involve a readiness to be motivated with respect to an object.

It seems reasonable to hold that attitudes and beliefs go together, although in a particular instance the motivational or the cognitive aspect may be more apparent. The interdependence of attitudes and beliefs will be even clearer when we consider the function of attitudes and beliefs.

Function of Attitudes and Beliefs. Of what value are attitudes and beliefs? What function do they serve for us? Of course, this subject is discussed in Chapter 11, in connection with perception. The function of attitudes and beliefs is to orient us toward reality (or what we take to be reality). They help us to prepare for action, to anticipate what will happen next, and in other ways to attain our goals and avoid threats. A belief or a system of beliefs that fails to meet human needs usually crumbles in the long run. We have discussed how autism and defense and enhancement of the self influence human behavior. They also characterize beliefs and attitudes.

Inferring Attitudes and Beliefs. How do we identify other people's attitudes and beliefs—or, for that matter, our own? We have to *infer* other people's attitudes and beliefs from what they do and say, whether in informal situations or in formal tests. Typically, we look for consistencies in a person's behavior, and from these consistencies we infer what must be his beliefs and attitudes. In the case of attitude toward the church, for example, if a man gives freely of his time and money to the church, seeks new members, speaks often of religious matters both in and outside the church, carries on family worship, and so on, it is likely that he has a favorable attitude toward the church. The various behaviors form a consistent picture. Like

all other appraisals and evaluations of personality (see Chapter 18) conclusions about a person's attitudes and beliefs are subject to error and should always be based on all available information.

As we have said, a person does not fully know his *own* attitudes and beliefs. It is a familiar experience in psychotherapy, for example, for a person to find that he has attitudes toward himself and others that he had been unaware of. In everyday life, we may have beliefs and attitudes which are largely at an unconscious level—some repressed, and others simply unverbalized and taken for granted. The earlier chapters of this book should have made it clear that we usually have only limited insight into our own motives and ways of enhancing and defending the self. In other words, it is no easy matter to know our own attitudes and beliefs.

Measuring Attitudes and Beliefs. There are various methods for measuring attitudes and beliefs. One of these is the attitude questionnaire, which is a paper-and-pencil test consisting of a series of statements of opinion.

One example appears in Table 14.1, which exhibits selected items from a scale for measuring attitude toward war. This type of scale is known as a *Thurstone*-type scale, since the technique of scaling employed was developed by Thurstone. The statements, which in this case numbered twenty-two, vary from those which are highly favorable to those which are highly unfavorable. The person who completes the form is instructed to check the statements with which he agrees. Each statement has a scale value determined by an extensive and technical procedure. A person's score is the median, which is a special kind of average (see Chapter 16), of the scale values of the items which he has checked. In this case, the scale values of the items (determined by a technical procedure) vary from 0.0, which is at the antiwar extreme, to 11.0, which is at the pro-

Table 14.1   Selected Items from a Droba Scale for Measuring Attitudes toward War

Scale value	Item
1.3	1. A country cannot amount to much without a national honor, and war is the only means of preserving it.
2.5	2. When war is declared, we must enlist.
5.2	3. Wars are justified only when waged in defense of weaker nations.
5.4	4. Peace and war are both essential to progress.
5.6	5. The most that we can hope to accomplish is the partial elimination of war.
8.4	6. The disrespect for human life and rights involved in war is a cause of crime waves.
10.6	7. All nations should disarm immediately.

SOURCE: *From D. D. Droba, A Scale for Measuring Attitude toward War, University of Chicago Press, Chicago, 1930.*

war extreme. Similar scales have been devised to measure attitudes toward other subjects, such as church, capitalism, and various nationality groups.

A second kind of attitude questionnaire is a Likert-type scale. An example is shown in Table 14.2, which has selected items from a scale for measuring attitudes toward Negroes. The respondent is told to indicate one of five degrees of agreement or disagreement with each item. In this case, the number 1 indicates the anti-Negro extreme while 5 indicates the pro-Negro extreme. His score is the sum of the scale values of the degrees of agreement or disagreement that he checks.

There are many other varieties of attitude questionnaires similar to the ones we have discussed. In nearly all of them, the person taking the test has a rather clear idea of whether his responses are favorable or unfavorable. Consequently he can deliberately falsify or unconsciously distort his responses so that they enhance or defend the self. Knowing, for example, that prejudice toward minority groups is disapproved by many people, and perhaps feelings a little guilty about his own prejudice, he may respond in a way that gives an erroneous impression that he is unprejudiced. What a person writes on such a test, or what he says in response to opinion-poll questions, must always be interpreted and usually cannot be taken at face value.

Other methods are therefore sometimes required to obtain a truer picture of attitudes. One such method is the projective test (see Chapter 18), which requires a person to respond to an indefinite (unstructured) stimulus situation. The rationale behind such tests is that, when the stimulus situation is unstructured, the individual's responses are determined mainly by his needs, frames of reference, and other personal factors. For example, Figure 14.2 shows some kind of streetcar or subway scene.[1] The subject is instructed to tell what this picture is about, the feelings

[1] G. W. Allport and L. Postman, *The Psychology of Rumor,* Holt, New York, 1947.

of the people, what led up to this situation, and how it is going to turn out. Suppose our subject said something like this:

The Negro (the dark-skinned fellow) is a bit drunk. He has been abusive to one of the women passengers, and one of the white men has objected. The Negro is quarreling violently with the white man, who is trying to be restrained and polite. In a moment the Negro will become violent and slash the white man with the razor that he is holding in his hand.

Actually the dark-skinned man is not holding anything in his hand; it is the white man who seems to be holding a razor. In fact, the whole story is a projection of the respondent's attitudes and beliefs, and it strongly indicates a prejudiced attitude.

Projective tests of attitude are particularly valuable in the study of prejudice, since so many of our prejudices operate at an unconscious level or are deliberately disguised to conform with prevailing taboos against the expression of overt prejudice.

In addition to attitude questionnaires and projective tests of attitudes, there are also rating methods for measuring attitudes. Like all ratings, these are essentially judgments. The more clearly the attitude in question is defined and the larger the number of independent judges doing the rating, the more likely the ratings are to be reliable (consistent) and valid (measure what they are supposed to measure). The subject of rating methods for the appraisal

---

Table 14.2   Selected Items from Likert's Scale for Measuring Attitude toward Negroes

No Negro should be deprived of the franchise except for reasons which would also disfranchise a white man.

Strongly approve (5)	Approve (4)	Undecided (3)	Disapprove (2)	Strongly disapprove (1)

Negro homes should be segregated from those of white people.

Strongly approve (1)	Approve (2)	Undecided (3)	Disapprove (4)	Strongly disapprove (5)

If the same preparation is required, the Negro teacher should receive the same salary as the white.

Strongly approve (5)	Approve (4)	Undecided (3)	Disapprove (2)	Strongly disapprove (1)

All Negroes belong in one class and should be treated in about the same way.

Strongly approve (1)	Approve (2)	Undecided (3)	Disapprove (4)	Strongly disapprove (5)

SOURCE: *From R. Likert, "A Technique for the Measurement of Attitudes."* Archives of Psychology, no. 140, 1932.

Figure 14.2. This picture illustrates an unstructured stimulus situation suitable for a projective test of attitudes and beliefs. What is happening in this situation? How do the main characters feel? What led up to the situation, and how will it turn out? (G. W. Allport and L. Postman, The Psychology of Rumor, *Holt, New York, 1947, p. 71. Courtesy of the publisher.)*

and evaluation of personality is further discussed in Chapter 18.

FORMING OUR BELIEFS AND ATTITUDES

How do we form our beliefs and attitudes? Generally speaking, we learn them. The process of learning is discussed in Chapter 12. The principles discussed there apply generally to *all* learning. Our interest here, however, is in learning that has a social setting. In other words, we shall discuss the *social learning* of attitudes and beliefs—recognizing, of course, that such

learning obeys the same principles as does learning in general.

Sources of Attitudes and Beliefs. *Specific experiences.* One way we learn our attitudes and beliefs is through specific experiences with the object of the attitude. For example, after a series of rewarding experiences in dealing with a person we usually come to like him. By contrast, a series of frustrating, punishing, or otherwise negative experiences will usually engender an unfavorable attitude. Sometimes, even a single experience produces a strongly favorable or unfavorable attitude.

For example, a man who has lost heavily on an investment in stocks may learn in a single experience to have an unfavorable attitude toward the buying of stocks. He is, of course, transferring (see Chapter 12) his reaction, based on a specific experience, to the buying of stocks in general.

Instruction. In part, our beliefs and attitudes are formed by the instruction, either formal or informal, we receive from others. There are many agencies to instruct us, such as the home, the school, the church, and various mass media (magazines, newspapers, etc.). Through them we are continually exposed to the views which are widely shared in our society and some which are not.

Probably most of our beliefs and attitudes are learned from other people. Consider some of the beliefs which we hold. We may believe that the Republican party is best, probably because our parents felt that way. Most of us believe that the world is round, yet few of us have gone around the world ourselves. Many of us think that public utilities should be privately owned, yet most of us have not ourselves made a direct study of this question. It is easy to see that many of our beliefs are based on other people's views. We should recognize, of course, that we modify these shared beliefs and attitudes in the light of our own particular experience. As a result of reflection we can qualify or otherwise change these beliefs which we have learned from others.

Of particular interest is the informal instruction which children are given in the family. From a very early age, a child may hear his parents say things such as the following:

"It isn't good manners to lick your fingers at the dinner table."

"People who steal other people's things are bad."

"Doctors know a lot of things; they are important people."

"People who are careless of other people's rights ought to be punished."

"Jews are good businessmen."

Statements such as these, made by those with whom a child identifies, tend to have a profound influence on his beliefs and attitudes.

We know, of course, that not all indoctrination is successful. For it to be effective the individual who is being influenced must have a favorable and respectful attitude toward whoever is trying to influence him. In the home situation the child is very likely to feel positively inclined toward his mother and father. In the school situation, his teachers may carry a lot of prestige in his eyes.

Models. Not all our beliefs and attitudes are formed through instruction from others. Some are developed through imitation of models. The process is something like this: In a particular situation, we see how another person behaves. We interpret his behavior in terms of the attitudes and beliefs his action implies. If we identify with him and respect his judgment, we accept this (inferred) way of perceiving and feeling about the situation.

For example, suppose that Jimmy and his mother are experiencing a thunder storm. Jimmy sees that his mother is afraid. She closes the door to her room, puts her fingers in her ears to shut out the noises, and trembles every time there is a loud peal of thunder. This behavior on his mother's part defines the storm as a dangerous thing. Remember that Jimmy believes that his mother is far more powerful than he is and that her way of interpreting things is often correct. By being led to perceive the situation as dangerous, Jimmy can acquire an attitude of fear toward storms just like that of his mother.

Jimmy also sees that his father watches sports of all kinds on television. In this way he may come to believe that sports are interesting and important things to watch.

Figure 14.3. What different attitudes toward religion are embodied in these two churches? Such physical settings provide only part of the institutional supports for beliefs and attitudes. What are some of the other factors that influence religious attitudes?

He notes that his mother and father are careful with the furniture in the living room and less careful with the furniture in the back yard. He may therefore come to believe that some possessions should be treated more carefully than others. All this learning can take place without his parents saying anything explicitly about these matters.

Children are often quite vigilant in noticing how their parents react to different people. They learn by observing whom their parents respect, whom they treat with condescension, whom they regard as friends, and whom they dislike. Such evaluations may be acquired without the child's directly interacting with such people.

Institutional factors. Many institutional factors (see Chapter 8) function as sources and supports of our attitudes and beliefs. For example, consider the description of a certain church. When the people come into this church, they kneel down to pray.

They then walk very quietly to the plain, bare pews where they sit with heads bowed. Their clothes are quite plain, but of good quality. When the minister enters, they all rise to attention while he faces the highly ornate altar and chants. The entire service is devoted to ritual. At the end of the service, the minister leaves from the front of the church, and then the members of the congregation file out quietly.

From this description we can make some rather good guesses as to the general character of the religious attitudes and beliefs in this church. There is *implicitly* an attitude of reverence, an orientation toward a deity, a ritualized rather than a spontaneous expression of feeling, a sharp differentiation between the minister and the congregation, and so on. The different parts of the institution—the architecture, furnishings, people's clothing and behavior—have a meaning which fit in with certain beliefs and attitudes. There are many other institutions in our society—schools, military organizations, and the like—which also function as sources and supports of attitudes and beliefs.

Interaction of Influences. There is a tendency for the various sources of attitudes and beliefs to be mutually supporting. For example, a child's specific experiences, instructions from other people, the behavior of models, and institutional factors may all work together to develop his attitudes toward other groups.

When a recruit joins the military service, he is thoroughly indoctrinated in military courtesy. He learns how he should act in relationship to officers. He is to salute them, to obey their commands, and to show other signs of respect and obedience. Likewise, he sees about him the existence of a rank hierarchy. There are higher-ranking officers, lower-ranking officers, noncommissioned officers, and privates. They are distinguished from each other by various insignia and by different privileges, duties, and powers. So the way in which he is instructed and what he sees in the behavior of others tend to reinforce each other. He will come to accept as normal the difference in the power and prestige of the different ranks.

Sometimes, however, the different sources of influence may *not* be mutually supporting; in this event, a person is subjected to incompatible influences. An example would be the situation of a child whose parents preached tolerance but were very intolerant in their behavior. This incompatibility in turn can lead to a variety of consequences—personal conflict, rejection of part or all of these influences, etc.

Our attitudes and beliefs are determined by both individual and social factors. For example, one person may be prejudiced toward a minority group because of beliefs and attitudes current in his own group. His prejudice simply is socially learned. Another person's prejudice may be due to individual factors; his personality may be

such that he needs to enhance his self-esteem by degrading and attacking weaker groups. It is likely that personal and social factors interact in most prejudiced persons.

Conditions Affecting the Formation of Beliefs and Attitudes. A number of conditions have rather important effects on how we form our beliefs and attitudes.

First of all, it is important whether or not we identify with other people who have certain beliefs and attitudes or who express them in their behavior. A child who identifies with his mother and father is far more likely to learn and to accept their beliefs and attitudes. At school or at work if we identify with our teacher or supervisor, we shall probably come to interpret and evaluate situations much as he does. On the other hand, if we reject other people to whose attitudes and beliefs we are exposed, it is unlikely that we shall accept their beliefs.

Another condition which is very important in the formation of our beliefs and attitudes is the degree to which other people's attitudes and beliefs are uniform. If

Figure 14.4. What are some of the many factors that might influence the attitudes of each of these two children toward members of the other race? (Courtesy of Henry Leighton.)

Figure 14.5. This Bari maiden enjoys the distinction of being the beauty queen in her native village. Do you think she would be so considered in Hollywood? Would your opinion be different if you were a Bari resident? (Courtesy of British Information Services.)

more and more variation in opinion. Our beliefs and attitudes, ideally, became less absolute, and we came to regard evidence, rather than mere agreement, as the criterion for validity. In the world of politics and business, too, we experience some differences in opinions. Because we have a degree of freedom in the selection of our group memberships, our adult attitudes and beliefs are less absolutely determined by others.

It is probably true that those beliefs and attitudes which we acquire first tend to be the most stable. We did not come into the world with ready-made beliefs and attitudes about it. The views which we first learned from others, especially in the family, gave an order and meaning to our world. They constituted a frame of reference, helping to shape our experiences. They may be modified in particular details in the light of new indoctrination and personal experience, but rarely will they be supplanted by an entirely new set of attitudes and beliefs.

Transferring our Beliefs and Attitudes to New Situations. Beliefs and attitudes acquired in one situation tend to transfer to other similar situations. Transfer of training and generalization are discussed in Chapter 12. For our present purposes, the point is that attitudes and beliefs learned in one situation may be applied to other situations which we perceive as similar. In a new situation, these transferred views may be appropriate or inappropriate.

For example, a child may generalize to other people an attitude toward one of his parents. Suppose the child has learned to perceive his father as a harsh, authoritarian person and has developed an attitude of hostility toward him. Then he is likely to carry over this attitude to other men whom he encounters in leadership situations. This illustrates how an attitude acquired in a specific situation may generalize to other situations.

everyone else we know has about the same beliefs and attitudes regarding some situation, we are more likely to agree with their views. There probably are a number of reasons for this influence of uniformity. First, if we have not been exposed to certain beliefs, our opportunity to acquire such beliefs is limited. Second, if we disagree with a unanimous or nearly unanimous majority, we are likely to suffer social disapproval and even outright rejection. Third, we find it easier to communicate with others if we talk in terms of their attitudes and beliefs.

As we grow from childhood to adulthood we typically experience an increasing range of variation in beliefs and attitudes. The greatest degree of uniformity was probably experienced in the family, but as we played with other children, we found that they and their parents had somewhat different views. In school, especially at higher levels of education, we encountered

CHANGING PREJUDICED ATTITUDES OF GROUPS

▶ It has often been held that if groups that are antagonistic to one another are brought into contact, their prejudiced attitudes will disappear. A considerable amount of research, however, has demonstrated that the outcome of such contact depends on many conditions. One of the most valuable studies in this area was performed in the summer of 1954.* In the first stage of the experiment (stage of in-group formation) two carefully selected groups of eleven boys were placed in separate camp sites in Robbers Cave State Park, about 150 miles southeast of Oklahoma City. During this phase the boys developed strong in-group feelings, and definite leaders emerged. In stage II (intergroup friction and conflict) the boys were brought into numerous competitive situations. One group, which called itself the Eagles, generally had the advantage in sports events over the other group, the Rattlers. The Eagles and the Rattlers became quite antagonistic toward each other, and incidents such as name calling, burning the other group's flag, accusing each other of cheating, and the like became quite common. At the same time the solidarity of each group increased. Members chose each other as friends, tended to overvalue each other's performance in contests, and in general viewed their own group as superior.

In stage III (reduction of intergroup friction) the two groups were brought together in a number of situations in which they had to solve their problems by joint action. They were placed in situations in which they worked for what the researchers called *superordinate* goals. For example, the experimenters arranged for the supply truck to stall. The boys of both groups pitched in to get the truck moving, pulling together on a rope. On another occasion the experimenters arranged for an interruption of the water supply. Facing this common problem, the boys of both groups worked together in inspecting the pipeline so as to locate the difficulty and correct it.

As a result of having to depend on each other to solve common problems, that is, working for superordinate goals, the intergroup prejudice gradually broke down. Boys in each group began to choose friends from the other group, and fewer activities were organized along their original group lines.

* M. Sherif, O. J. Harvey, B. J. White, W. R. Hood, and C. W. Sherif, *Experimental Study of Positive and Negative Intergroup Attitudes between Experimentally Produced Groups: Robbers Cave Study*, Intergroup Relations Project, University of Oklahoma, Norman, Okla., 1954. (Multilithed.)

We also see a tendency for a person to generalize an attitude from a part of a situation to a whole situation. Suppose an employee has had an unfavorable experience with his foreman. Since the average employee feels that his foreman *is* the company, this employee may transfer this unfavorable attitude toward the company as a whole, even though the company's higher-level administrators may have policies altogether different from those of this particular foreman.

Existing beliefs and attitudes can color our further learning. In the example of the employee who had an unfavorable attitude toward his foreman, this feeling of antagonism on his part led him to perceive unfavorably many things which the company did. But if he had a favorable attitude toward his foreman, he might have excused what appeared to be some shortcomings on the part of the company. Sometimes a soldier who has had an unfavorable experience in a military setting generalizes this unfavorable attitude toward all aspects of the military service. He expects to have unfavorable experiences; he tends selectively to perceive the unfavorable and to remember those things which are in line with his unfavorable attitude.

WHY BELIEFS AND ATTITUDES TEND TO BE STABLE

Many of our attitudes are remarkably stable. Prejudice learned in early childhood often persists throughout life, sometimes in the face of favorable experiences with persons who are the object of the prejudice. Political, religious, and other attitudes and beliefs often show a remarkable degree of persistence.

Adequacy as Guides to Adjustment. Beliefs and attitudes generally remain stable as long as they continue to work. They help to make sense out of our social experience, and they make more understandable the institutions we find in our society. As long as our existing beliefs and attitudes play this role successfully, they are likely to remain unchanged. However, when a crisis arises for which our attitudes and beliefs are inappropriate, we are very likely to change them. For example, during the Great Depression, many people's attitudes and beliefs about government and business underwent remarkable changes. Many people who previously objected violently to government help became more and more willing to accept it. As long as the beliefs and attitudes were adequate guides to adjustment they remained stable, but when they were inadequate to deal with a threatening situation, they quickly changed.

Selective Perception. Many of our beliefs and attitudes tend to remain stable because we do not notice the exceptions or pay attention to them. This is the process of selective perception. For example, a person may have a stereotype regarding Jews. He regards Jews as sly, grasping, unethical in business practices, and clannish as a social group. Suppose now that a Jew moves into the house next door and that this particular Jew is a very friendly, sociable person who is helpful and a good neighbor. The person with a stereotype unfavorable to Jews can simply explain this case as an exception. All Jews are so-and-so, according to his stereotype; *this* one is simply an exception. On the other hand, even a few examples of Jewish behavior fitting in with the stereotype will tend further to reinforce the stereotype.

Similarly, a person who believes that the government should keep out of business selectively perceives instances in which the government's participation in business has had an unfavorable outcome. He also sees many instances in which private enterprise, free from government control, has been strikingly effective. In fact, not only does he *perceive* more readily experiences which are in line with his existing beliefs and attitudes, but he also remembers them better.

Loyalty to a Reference Group. Our beliefs and attitudes are stable, too, because we tend to be loyal to groups with which we identify. Such groups are called *reference groups.* Sometimes they are groups in which we are currently active. At other times, they may be groups in which we formerly participated or in which we should like to be members.

For example, let us consider the case of a young woman who will not play cards, dance, or smoke, even though most of her present acquaintances do so. Having been trained in a family with rigid standards, she feels that she would be disloyal to her father and her mother if she were to do things of which they disapproved. A deeper understanding of her personality would be necessary to account for her continuing dependence on her parents, particularly if her

Figure 14.6. "*All Wallonians have square heads.*" *With a "picture in his head," the individual often sees what he expects (and needs) to see, dismissing as exceptions the cases that do not fit. If most of the other people who are important to him say that all Wallonians have square heads, it must be so. Both selective perception and loyalty to a reference group work in the same direction in such a situation.*

nonconformity prevents her from being accepted by the group.

Another example would be that of an American who has been captured by Communist soldiers. Because of his strong identification with his country, he strongly resists communistic indoctrination. In addition to other reasons he has for resisting, he feels that it would be disloyal for him to agree with their beliefs and attitudes. In other words, a person does not want to be disloyal to those with whom he identifies. Indeed, he does not want to be disloyal to what is a part of the self. Identification as an expansion of the self is discussed in Chapter 5.

Need for Self-defense. A person may resist change in his beliefs and attitudes simply because he feels that a change would imply weakness or inadequacy on his own part. Such behavior is motivated by a need for self-defense, discussed in an earlier chapter. Suppose, for example, that an employee proposes to his supervisor a new sales technique. The supervisor may perceive this proposal as a threat, as a sign of his own personal inadequacy in carrying out his role. If so, he is likely to feel unfavorable to the proposal.

As another example, take George Jackson, who was in charge of the repair shop of a large garage. Included in the repair shop was a large parts department. One day his supervisor proposed that the parts department be separated from the repair shop and showed how this would have some advantages for the operation of the company. Mr. Jackson, however, was resistant. He argued that it was more efficient to have the parts department under the control of the repair shop, so that the repair shop could keep the parts department continually informed of the need for parts. But underlying Mr. Jackson's resistance was a deeper concern. He felt that, if the parts department were made separate from the repair shop, then his own job would become less important. His need for self-defense created resistance to a change in his beliefs and attitudes.

When our self-esteem is threatened we are very likely to resist vigorously any change in our beliefs and attitudes. Indeed, we may reject another's evaluation simply because agreeing would appear to admit his superiority. Sometimes, however, after the threat has been removed, we can consider proposals more objectively and change our opinion.

Continuing Social Support. Probably the most important reason why our individual attitudes and beliefs tend to be stable is that they are continually reinforced by others who hold similar views. So long as group opinions are stable, we are subject to the same expressed and implied views. Moreover, if we conform, we are more likely to be accepted by the others, and we can communicate more readily if we share group opinions.

HOW BELIEFS AND ATTITUDES CHANGE

Thus far we have considered the factors or conditions which make for stability or lack of change in beliefs and attitudes. Under certain conditions, however, our opinions do change. Let us consider some of these conditions.

Group Pressure. Group pressure sometimes causes us to change our opinions. By controlling important rewards and punishments a group may exert a powerful influence in a particular direction. Positive incentives such as popularity, promotions, and symbols of recognition function as rewards for conformity. The penalties for continued nonconformity may be unpopularity, loss of prestige, ostracism, and the like.

The more we deviate from the group-shared attitudes and beliefs, the greater pressure the group will tend to exert to bring us into line. Smaller deviations in opinion, however, may be tolerated.

The more we want to belong to a group, the more pressure the group can put on us to get us to conform to group norms. If, on the other hand, our desire to belong is weak, we react to strong pressure by rejecting and leaving the group, providing we are free to choose.

The more the group wants us as members, the more it attempts to influence us to agree with group norms. A person who has low prestige in a group may be allowed to deviate simply because the group has more important concerns. But a person of high prestige who deviates is likely to become the object of strong pressures to bring him into line.

A condition affecting the degree to which group pressure can influence our attitudes is the amount of ambiguity in the situation. The fewer the objective standards according to which a person can judge and evaluate, the more he is subject to pressure from others. Suppose, for instance, the issue arises as to whether or not to support a par-

Figure 14.7. Cartoons may embody complex attitudes and ideas. What different views do these cartoons imply regarding the reality of communistic influences in American government? Which view do you feel is the more accurate? (*Courtesy Bruce Shanks, Buffalo Evening News, and Herblock.*)

"Hurry Up With That Dragon. The Audience Is Getting Impatient," Herblock's *Here and Now,* Simon and Schuster, 1955.

ticular political candidate. Often we do not have much reliable or objective information about the qualifications of a candidate. Under these circumstances, if others in our group hold rather strong opinions favoring a candidate, we can be greatly swayed by group pressure. If we have objective standards for holding our own opinions, however, we are better able to resist group pressure.

A person is more likely to change his attitudes if a group with which he identifies changes. Suppose that in the past the employees of a company have opposed unionization, but as a result of an intensive campaign aimed at organization, a majority votes to organize. An antiunion employee who finds that his fellows have approved unionization is then likely to change his mind. But the process of changing attitudes and beliefs is not purely automatic. Being uncomfortable in his deviation, our employee will rethink the facts and issues. He may talk again with others to see why they feel as they do. Gradually he may arrive at interpretations consistent with his existing values and also in line with the group's decision. The change is motivated, and it involves a gradual process in which his perception of the situation is changed while his values probably remain stable. For this change he is rewarded by a relief from tension and greater acceptance from others. We should acknowledge, of course, that a person does not always go along with the group, and that he may become even more fixed in his opinion as a result of group pressure.

The greater the uniformity in a group, the greater the pressure the group can exert on the individual. It makes a difference, when we disagree, whether *everyone* in our group feels different from us. Unanimous agreement is difficult to resist. This is true even if the matter at issue is an objective matter of fact, although the group influence is more effective when the situa-

▶ A study * was undertaken to test the hypothesis that attitudes toward an object, or situation, may be changed by altering a person's perception of the object relative to valued goals. The basic idea was that, if an object becomes perceived as a means to attaining goals that a person values, then his attitude toward this object will become more favorable.

Two groups of college students were used as subjects—an experimental and a control group. Both were given an attitude test designed to measure their attitude toward allowing Negroes to move into previously white neighborhoods. The subjects varied in attitude all the way from those who were opposed to those who were favorable to Negroes in this regard. In addition, the subjects were given a questionnaire consisting of twenty-five value items, such as "America having high prestige in other countries," "Security of the value of one's real estate," "All persons having the chance to realize their potentialities," and "Being a person who is experienced, broadminded, and worldly-wise."

In this set of twenty-five items were eight critical items, which described four values in terms of which the experimenter subsequently attempted to influence attitudes toward Negroes moving into white neighborhoods. Each subject rated each value item in different ways, as to (1) how much satisfaction he would get from the goal indicated in the item, and (2) to what degree he perceived allowing Negroes to move into white neighborhoods would realize the goal stated by the item. The first of these ratings pro-

* E. R. Carlson, "Attitude Change through Modification of Attitude Structure," *Journal of Abnormal and Social Psychology,* 52:256–261, 1956.

tion is ambiguous. Suppose that one morning all our friends said it was Thursday, even though we thought it was Tuesday. Such a discrepancy probably would disturb us. We should try to account for the disagreement, perhaps checking the date on the newspaper. Suppose the newspaper said Tuesday, but other people still insisted that it was Thursday. In this conflict situation, most of us would try very hard to find an interpretation which would rationalize the discrepancy. We might even accept the group opinion as fact, even though we could not satisfactorily explain away our own experience. There is, of course, a difference between simply conforming to group opinion while privately disagreeing and actually distorting our perception so as to fit group interpretations.

It is of interest to note, however, that when even one member of a group agrees

with us it is easier to resist group influence. Suppose we have participated in a group discussion in which only ourselves and one other held a view opposed to the majority. Such a supporter may help us to resist changing our view. It makes a difference, of course, whether or not our supporter has prestige with us and with the group.

Regarding changes in beliefs and attitudes, we should distinguish among four possibilities:

1. We may reject the group's norms (group-shared beliefs and attitudes) while holding rigidly to our own beliefs and attitudes. Indeed, we may even aggressively defend our own beliefs and attitudes. Probably the group will not affect us much if we are indifferent to it, or if we feel intensely loyal to another group with different norms.

2. We may not really change our beliefs and attitudes at all but may simply conform

vided a measure of the strength of the values described by the critical items. The second provided an index of the degree to which a person perceived the proposed action as leading to realization of the values he had come to accept.

The next phase required the subjects in the experimental group to write an essay showing how allowing Negroes to move into white neighborhoods would lead to the four values previously mentioned.

The experimenter expected that this written exercise would cause the experimental subjects to perceive more fully than before that the policy in question would lead to realization of values which they held. In addition, the instructor subsequently led a discussion designed to achieve the above change. The control group, on the other hand, did not write an essay, nor did it participate in the discussion.

In the third phase of the experiment, both groups once again took the attitude test, and rated the items as before.

The results showed that the written exercise and discussion led to an increased perception that allowing Negroes to move into white neighborhoods would achieve the four values previously mentioned. Those having the greatest change in attitude in the favorable direction were not unusually prejudiced or nonprejudiced initially.

This experiment lends support to the view that attitudes toward an object may be changed by getting people to perceive that this object leads to realization of values which they hold. As in other studies, the greatest changes in attitudes were found in those who did not hold extreme attitudes, whether favorable or unfavorable.

to group norms because of outside pressure or other reasons. At the same time we are aware of the fact that privately we disagree with the group's standards.

3. We may accept the group's norms at a superficial level, but without any deep-level changes in our beliefs and attitudes. We conform not only in our actions, but also in our thinking and feeling (at least at a conscious level), but the superficial character of the change is shown when we move to a new group, where we take on new beliefs and attitudes, like putting on another mask.

4. We may relate the group's norms to our own set of beliefs and attitudes, accepting some and perhaps rejecting others. The changes which do take place will be relatively enduring ones and will carry over to new situations.

In the fourth case, we are being flexible and discriminating. We do not wholly ac-

cept group norms, nor do we reject them completely, nor do we adopt them as a convenient pattern only to cast them aside later, nor are we indifferent to them. Rather we are self-determining and yet sensitive to the beliefs and values of others.

Favorable or Unfavorable Experiences. Thus far we have considered changes in attitudes and beliefs brought about by social influences. This source of change is important because so many of our attitudes and beliefs are formed, not through direct experience with the situation itself, but through communication with others. We can, however, also change our attitudes and beliefs because of favorable or unfavorable experiences with a situation.

Let us take the case of a man who through his personal experiences changes his attitude from an initially favorable attitude to an unfavorable one. Mike Harwick

▶ We have all heard that "if a person says a thing often enough, he will begin to believe it." The purpose of the experiment to be reported here * was to determine whether a person's publicly defending a view different from his own opinion results in a change in his opinion.

The subjects were ninety college students. They were given a questionnaire containing, among others, three key items, as follows:

Item A: During the past year a number of movie theaters were forced to go out of business as a result of television competition and other recent developments. At the present time there are about 18,000 movie theaters remaining. How many commercial movie theaters do you think will be in business three years from now?

Item B: What is your personal estimate about the *total supply of meat that will be available for the civilian* population of the United States during the year 1953? (..... per cent of what it is at present.)

Item C: How many years do you think it will be before a *completely effective* cure for the common cold is discovered?

About a month later the subjects, who had been divided into three-man groups, were asked to give an informal talk based on a written outline that

* Irving L. Janis and Bert T. King, "The Influence of Role Playing on Opinion Change," *Journal of Abnormal and Social Psychology,* 49:211–218, 1954.

joined a company because of what he believed were excellent chances of promotion. He found, however, that his superior was very jealous of his authority. When Mike made any suggestions for changes, his superior tended to interpret these suggestions as a personal threat. Furthermore, Mike found that his fellow employees were very competitive. Stories came to him that they were saying unfavorable things about him to the supervisor. He noticed, too, that many of these employees were not really loyal to the company. Gradually Mike's opinion of the company became quite negative. His originally favorable opinion had become very unfavorable because of his experiences with the company.

Of course, experience may also change an unfavorable opinion into a favorable one. Mrs. Jones, because of economic cir-

Figure 14.8. These players have a high regard for their teammate because he contributes to goals which are important to the team. The picture shows Robinson scoring on a homer in the fourteenth inning of the final game of the season with Philadelphia in 1951. (International News Photos.)

the experimenter had prepared. This outline stated a conclusion about one of the three key items and listed supporting arguments that, though relevant, were biased and one-sided. Each person actively advocated the conclusion pertaining to one of the three items while the other two members passively listened and read the outline. Then the second and third members took their turns relative to the remaining items. After the talks, the members were given an "after" questionnaire that asked for a variety of ratings and another expression of their opinion on the three key items, among others.

The results showed that in the case of the first two items the speakers changed their opinions in the direction of the outline more than did the listeners. On item C, however, there was no significant difference between speakers and listeners in the amount of change, but self-ratings indicated that speakers had more *confidence* in their changed opinions than did listeners, a result that also held in the case of the other two items.

The experiments suggest that two factors may have accounted for the results:

First, the speakers, who frequently improvised arguments in defense of the conclusion they were to advocate, became convinced by their own "cogent" arguments, clarifying illustrations, and appeals in trying to "sell" the idea. Second, the speakers probably experienced feelings of achievement and self-satisfaction in presenting their case.

cumstances, was forced to sell her home in a desirable neighborhood and move into what she considered to be a poor residential area. She did not like the way in which the houses were maintained in this poorer neighborhood, and she felt that many of the people there had attitudes and beliefs which were different from hers. However, a number of these neighbors called on Mrs. Jones soon after she had arrived and made her feel quite at home. They invited her to their homes. To her surprise, she found that she had much in common with them. Gradually she came to feel more and more attached to her new neighborhood. As a result of her experiences, her attitude became more favorable.

Now, whether or not experiences will change our attitudes depends partly upon the strength of our initial attitudes and beliefs and partly upon how strongly favorable or unfavorable the experiences may be. If we do not have any particular attitudes

and beliefs about a thing, then favorable or unfavorable experiences can have rather marked effect on the formation of our attitudes. On the other hand, if we already have strong beliefs and attitudes, we are likely to resist changing them. Indeed, as we have seen, we can be so strongly prejudiced that we interpret what would otherwise be favorable experiences as exceptions. Moreover, we may be especially sensitive to any experiences which are unfavorable. Nevertheless a prolonged series of strikingly favorable or unfavorable experiences can effect a change.

Influence of Prestigeful Persons. It has often been held that we can be influenced to change our attitudes to agree with those who have prestige in our eyes. Now, who are prestigeful persons? A prestigeful person may be a friend whose judgment we value. Over a period of time we have learned that this person's evaluation of situations tends to be realistic and accurate.

A prestigeful person may be an expert. Experts are believed to be competent judges in their specialty. Many of us, however, have mixed feelings toward experts. We may feel that the expert is different from ourselves and even remote. It sometimes is easier to identify with someone more like ourselves, such as a friend.

The prestige of a person, and his influence, may generalize from the field in which he is expert to others in which he has no special competence. Advertisers often make use of the prestige of motion-picture stars or sports figures in endorsing their products. We all know, however, that such persons are no better judges of toothpaste, for example, than the rest of us. In every community there are persons who have high prestige and whose opinions outside their specialty are given much weight.

How do we react when a *positively val-*ued person has an opinion different from our own? We may try to find out why he thinks as he does. Arguments which we may have discounted earlier may be considered anew. Supporting facts which we may not have questioned previously may be subjected to more critical scrutiny. This process does not guarantee that we shall come to agree with the other person, but the likelihood of such a change is increased. If the other person is a friend, mutual influence is likely.

But how do we feel when a *negatively valued* person has an opinion different from our own? His disagreement is likely to add support to our view. Agreement from a disliked person or group may lead us to question our own views. For example, a prominent gambler who comes out in support of the political candidate of our choice may induce us to reevaluate the candidate.

SUMMARY

An attitude is a readiness to become motivated with respect to an object. Attitudes vary in a number of ways, such as direction and degree, intensity, the extent to which they are common or unique, and the degree to which we are aware of them. A belief is an acceptance or rejection of a proposition about reality. Some beliefs are verifiable, whereas others are mainly matters of faith. A course of action or a statement of opinion is usually determined by a whole set of attitudes and beliefs. A decision may be influenced by opposing forces.

Attitudes and beliefs are interrelated. They serve a function in enabling people to satisfy their needs. Beliefs and attitudes are not directly observable but must be inferred. Ratings, attitude questionnaires, and projective tests are some of the useful ways of assessing individual attitudes and beliefs.

Attitudes and beliefs are formed as a result of specific experiences, formal and informal instruction, the influence of models, and institutional factors. These various influences tend to supplement one another. Various conditions affect the acquisition of attitudes and beliefs and their transfer to new situations.

Beliefs and attitudes tend to be stable because they continue to work, because of selective perception, because of loyalty to a reference group, because of a need for self-defense, and because of continuing social support.

Attitudes and beliefs change because of group pressure, because of favorable or unfavorable experiences, and because of the influence of prestigeful persons.

QUESTIONS

1. What is meant by the term "attitude"? How are attitudes related to beliefs?

2. What are the functions of attitudes and beliefs?

3. To what extent are your attitudes and beliefs determined by those of other people?

4. Why do people resist changing their attitudes and beliefs?

5. How would you go about trying to change a person's political attitudes and beliefs?

6. Show how a decision—such as a choice of vocation or whom to vote for—is influenced by a whole set of attitudes and beliefs.

7. What are some of the factors which influence attitudes toward a minority group (such as the Jews or the Indians)?

8. What are the sources of your attitudes and beliefs about Russia? To what extent have your evaluations been arrived at independently?

9. What is meant by a reference group? What are some of your reference groups, and how do they influence you?

10. To what extent is it possible for a person to evaluate situations without being influenced by the attitudes and beliefs of others? What factors do you think would affect a person's susceptibility to such influence?

11. What is the relationship of frames of reference to attitudes?

12. Discuss the consistency of attitudes. Can one have conflicting attitudes toward the same object?

SUGGESTED READINGS

Allport, G. W.: *The Nature of Prejudice*, Addison-Wesley, Cambridge, Mass., 1954.
> (A balanced and readable account of individual and social factors in prejudiced attitudes and beliefs.)

Allport, G. W., and L. Postman: *The Psychology of Rumor*, Holt, New York, 1947.
> (An analysis of the influence of rumor on attitudes and beliefs.)

Doob, L. W.: *Public Opinion and Propaganda*, Holt, New York, 1948.
> (A text on the formation, measurement, and change of attitudes, with emphasis upon the role of mass communication.)

Hovland, C. I., A. A. Lumsdaine, and F. D. Sheffield: *Experiments in Mass Communication*, Princeton University Press, Princeton, N.J., 1949.
> (An account of methods and findings regarding the influencing of attitudes and beliefs in World War II.)

Krech, D., and R. S. Crutchfield: *Theory and Problems of Social Psychology*, McGraw-Hill, New York, 1948, chaps. 5–9.
> (A discussion of attitudes and beliefs, in Chapters 5, 6, and 7; of prejudice, in Chapters 8 and 9.)

Newcomb, T. M.: *Social Psychology*, Dryden, New York, 1950.
> (A textbook with informative chapters on attitudes.)

Sherif, M., and C. W. Sherif: *An Outline of Social Psychology*, rev. ed., Harper, New York, 1956.
> (A textbook with consistent theoretical treatment of attitudes and beliefs.)

15 ROLES AND SOCIAL BEHAVIOR

Most of us have no doubt been, on occasion, in a situation in which we did not know how to act, where we were not quite sure of what other people expected of us. It might have been because we were not clear as to our *position*, that is, our place, function, or office in an organization. Perhaps we have been in a group, without being entirely sure whether or not the others in the group regarded us as a member. Even if we knew how actual members should act, we may still have been confused in this situation. It has been said that adolescents in our society are often confused because they are not sure whether they are in the position of adult or child. Probably other people's inconsistent treatment of adolescents adds to their difficulties.

Not only is it important for us to know our position or positions, but it is also necessary for us to know the *role* that goes along with the position. That is, we need to know what behavior is expected of us in this position and to have the skills necessary for carrying out this behavior. For example, when a student goes to college, he knows very well that he is in the position of a student. But he may be quite unclear as to what is expected of him by his teachers, his family, his fraternity, and his fellow students. In addition, his skills (or lack of them) and many other factors determine how he carries out his role of student.

Anthropologists and sociologists study positions and roles as parts of culture. From a psychological point of view, however, we are interested in roles and positions because they influence our individual behavior and personality.

NATURE OF POSITIONS AND ROLES

In the next few pages we shall consider the nature of positions and roles from the point of view of their significance for understanding the person.

Meaning of Position. First, however, we need to be clear as to the meaning of the term "position." A *position* is a place, function, or office in a social organization of any size. The notion may be illustrated in terms of certain positions which in one form or another occur in nearly every society. In our culture, we classify people according to age and sex, in addition to many other ways. Each of us is either male or female, and each of us falls in some age category, whether that of child, adolescent, young adult, middle-aged, aged, or some other. In addition, each adult is married or single, in some more or less defined social class, and in some occupational category (even if not "gainfully employed"). With each of these broadly defined positions go various rights and duties; each position is characterized by certain behaviors which are typical of it.

The kinds of positions we have considered thus far are occupied over long periods of time, and they play a part in determining our behavior in a wide variety of situations. For example, the fact that we are male or female has an important bearing on how we act—or how we are expected to act— under many different circumstances. Many other positions—indeed, most of them—are relatively specific and temporary. For example, we may be the chairman of a committee, a week-end guest in a friend's home, or a substitute Sunday-school teacher. These positions, unlike those such as sex and age, are relatively limited in their influence. So long as we are in one of these positions, certain rules of behavior apply; as soon as we leave that position and get into another, new rules apply. As we move from position to position, we are in an ever-changing psychological environment with varying influences acting upon us.

We should distinguish between *ascribed* and *achieved* positions. Some of our positions are ascribed by society on the basis of characteristics which lie outside our individual efforts. Positions such as male or female, adult or child, and Negro or white are ascribed by our society and carry with them certain nearly inescapable requirements for behavior.

Other positions are achieved by virtue of our actions. We can achieve such positions as being a college graduate, being in a higher social class, being a criminal, and being married. As compared to other cultures, our own has relatively few ascribed positions and permits or influences a person to move to a wide variety of possible achieved positions. That is, we have a great deal of freedom of choice as to positions. Since the various positions involve many different rights and duties, degrees of prestige, and demands upon us, they are vitally important parts of our lives.

Another point is that each of us has a number of different positions, either at the same time or successively. This fact is illustrated in Figure 15.1. Ordinarily these different positions, each of which has various behavior requirements, tend to be congruent; that is, they fit together. Usually we are able to choose positions which are not incompatible in their requirements and to schedule our activities so as to discharge satisfactorily the responsibilities involved. Sometimes, however, the behaviors required in our various positions are in conflict, a fact which can cause some rather serious personal problems. This problem will be discussed at greater length later in this chapter.

Positions and Prestige. One of the important things about positions is that they have prestige. The prestige may be high, as in the case of a Supreme Court judge, or relatively low, as in the case of a person

Figure 15.1. Which of these is the real John Smith? What needs do his various statuses (or positions) satisfy? What conception does Mr. Smith have of himself in these different roles? How much of his behavior is determined by the several statuses and roles that he occupies?

dependent on public charity—or it may be anywhere in between these two. Our social-class position is determined on the basis of various criteria (see Chapter 8), and membership in each class has a prestige value, whether high or low. Almost all organizations have some kind of a prestige hierarchy which is tied to the positions in it. Generally a foreman is higher than a worker, a division manager higher than a foreman, and the president of the company at the top of the heap.

The prestige of different occupations has been studied. Table 15.1 (page 306) shows prestige value of five occupations highest in prestige (or status) and the five lowest

in prestige in 1925 and in 1946.[1] Although there were some changes in prestige over this twenty-one-year period, the stability of the prestige values is remarkably high.

Along with the various positions usually go various *symbols* of prestige, such as insignia, titles, uniforms, office furnishings, and the like.

Of what significance for us are these facts about the prestige of positions? They are usually very important. In the first place, the prestige of our positions tends to have a lot to do with how other people evaluate

[1] M. E. Deeg and D. G. Paterson, "Changes in Social Status of Occupations," *Occupations*, 25: 205–208, 1947.

us and with the privileges they allow us. Of course after people have an opportunity to know us at first hand, their evaluation of us may change—either upward or downward.

The prestige of our position (whether high or low) may also have a great deal to do with our self-esteem. Indeed, status usually has a considerable bearing on the enhancement and defense of the self. This point is discussed in Chapter 6.

Meaning of Role. Along with each position goes a certain more or less defined role. A *role* is the set of behaviors which is typical of the occupants of a particular position. If we want to know the role of foreman in a particular company, we need to observe what foremen do. We could tabulate the frequency with which they perform various actions—such as requisitioning of materials and instructing employees—under particular circumstances. Although individual foremen, just like individual students, would vary somewhat in their behaviors, those actions which most of them usually perform comprise the role of the foreman, at least in this company. In order to describe a role, we may also find it useful to interview people who are in the position or people who work closely with them. This is the way in which one housewife described her role:

Shop for food and clothing
Prepare and serve meals
Supervise homework and music practice of the children
Supervise maid (who comes three days a week)
Drive children to parties, music lessons, school, etc.
Schedule social engagements of the family
Act as hostess
Do sewing of dresses, slipcovers, etc.
Keep family financial records and make regular payments
Answer telephone
Arrange for visits of playmates for her children
Participate in PTA and Sunday-school work
Referee conflicts among children
Discuss family affairs with husband
Counsel husband regarding his problems in connection with his work
Etc.

Of course the way in which this housewife takes her role (or role *pattern*) may differ somewhat from the way that other housewives of her social level take theirs. The ways in which they are most often alike comprise the role. The partial listing given above should also serve to illustrate

Figure 15.2. These men hold and/or held high positions in the Russian government and in the Communist Party. The place each one has in the reviewing stand (who is in the center and who stands next to whom) often provides clues to the status of his political position in the U.S.S.R. at a given time. (Sovfoto.)

Table 15.1 The Five Occupations Ranking Highest in Prestige and the Five Ranking Lowest in Prestige

Occupation	Rank in 1925	Rank in 1946
Banker	1	2.5
Physician	2	1
Lawyer	3	2.5
Superintendent of schools	4	4
Civil engineer	5	5
Teamster (truck driver)	21	21.5
Coal miner	22	21.5
Janitor	23	23
Hod carrier	24	24
Ditch digger	25	25

SOURCE: *Based on data from Deeg and Paterson.*

how much a person finds it necessary to learn in order to carry out the requirements of a position.

Some of the behaviors of a role pattern are more typical than others. They are the more central features of the role. For example, practically all housewives prepare and serve meals, but not all supervise music practice.

Another point—and one that might not be apparent at first sight—is that the occupants of a position usually carry out a role with a characteristic style or emotional tone. These features of the role, while not so obvious as specific actions, are also vital parts of the role. For example, dignity is a part of the role of diplomat on state occasions. Sometimes when the appropriate emotional tone is lacking—as when a mother cares for a child without showing any warmth—the person just is not fulfilling the role, and others will usually recognize this fact.

The term "role" should not be construed in the sense of an actor's role. A role is simply a pattern of behavior that is typical in a given position or situation. A person can behave in this typical way without even being aware of the fact that he is doing so. Often the members of a group are not aware of these group-shared ways of acting. So long as people carry out these roles we are not usually aware of the roles, but if someone fails or neglects to carry out an important role, then the fact that we have roles becomes obvious.

Norms for Roles. Corresponding to every position and role are group-shared standards as to how people in the particular position *ought* to act; that is, there are *norms for the roles.* What are our standards for the role of student in a university? That is, what do we think a student should do? What are his rights and duties? We might say something as follows: "A student attends classes, takes lecture notes, studies textbook assignments, prepares assigned reports, and takes examinations." Should we also include such things as "attends public lectures and concerts," "does suggested outside reading," and "participates in scholarly organizations"? What do we regard as central in the student's role, and what do we regard as unessential or even harmful to this role?

Although each person has his individual

standards for the roles which are significant for him, generally there will have to be some degree of agreement among the members of an organization as to their standards for the roles. Such group-shared standards are norms for the roles, but all role norms allow for some variation in how people carry out the roles. In other words, there are tolerance limits for a role in the same way that a machinist might have tolerance limits for error in the machining of a part. Not only is there ordinarily some latitude in the prescriptions for a role, but different groups of people may actually differ in their standards for the role. Again the role of student furnishes a good example. Teachers and students may have a somewhat different conception of the rights and duties of students, while the parents and other members of the community may have still other conceptions. The role itself, however, is what people in that position of student *do,* not the conceptions about and standards for the role.

The norms for roles are important for each of us. They are important because they are standards by which *other* people evaluate and otherwise react to our behavior when we are in some situation to which the standards could apply. In addition, the norms for roles, *in so far as these are accepted as standards,* are important as frames of reference for self-perception. In other words, norms for roles may be related to the self. This subject will be discussed in greater detail later in this chapter.

Role Expectations. There may on occasion be a difference between what we think persons in a position *ought* to do and what we *expect* them to do. A foreman, for example, might think that employees *ought* to get to work on time, but he might *expect* them to be somewhat late. If they habitually *are* late, then this lateness of arrival is a part of their role—the behavior characteristic of the position.

It is important that role expectations be valid, that is, conform to reality. In this way, people will be able to predict how others will act, even if these actions do not square with norms for the role.

A discrepancy between role norms and role expectations is usually a source of tension. The standards can be modified in the direction of expectations. For example, the foreman may decide to accept late arrival as being all right.

HOW ROLES ARE LEARNED

Obviously we all have to *learn* our roles. When a child goes to school he has to learn what is expected of him as a school child. When a person joins an office force he has to learn the office routines and how his own particular position fits into those routines. Sometimes we learn our roles intentionally, as when we take a training course in how to drive a car. More frequently, however, we learn our roles in-

Figure 15.3. Mother's little helpers copy her in many ways. Moreover, the older child often serves as a model for the younger. (Standard Oil Company, New Jersey.)

cidentally without either formal instruction or deliberate intention to learn.

Ways of Learning Roles. There are a number of different, though related, ways in which we learn roles. These ways include learning from models, learning through instruction, and learning in the practical situation.

Learning from models. It has often been said that we learn by example—through imitation—and there is some truth in this statement, particularly in the case of learning roles. All of us have undoubtedly seen a little girl copying the behavior and dress of her mother. Parents are sometimes amazed—and dismayed—by the minute detail in which their child may copy their mannerisms and other aspects of their behavior.

Children's play usually includes a variety of roles—cowboy, milkman, doctor, policeman, etc. Sometimes their play indicates a remarkable keenness of observation, whereas in other instances it shows a complete lack of understanding. It is very likely true that such play develops skill not only in enacting the roles, but also—and this is important—in perceiving others in these roles.

One of the most important models for a child is the parent of the same sex. A boy whose father is absent from the home by reason of death, desertion, or some other cause lacks an important model—one from whom boys (and girls) learn about the masculine role. Often such boys tend to be effeminate in behavior, having taken the mother as a model, although they may later react against these tendencies in themselves. Identifying with men outside the family and with other boys may help to overcome the lack of a masculine role in the home.

The learning of roles from models is not limited to childhood. Indeed, models become increasingly available as we approach adulthood. This fact—which has important consequences—is illustrated in Figure 15.4. Whereas the child has relatively few models, an adult has potentially many models. In adulthood, however, we are not likely to find that any one model meets all our personal needs. Indeed, when we observe someone who slavishly models himself after a particular person we may rightfully have doubts about his personal adjustment. Typically we model ourselves after some persons in particular ways, after others in other ways, according to our own needs.

Copying the behavior of models is often a very rapid way of learning how to respond appropriately to situations. The models are already familiar with such situations and usually know how to act. When we copy such a model we may not know precisely the standards by which he decides what to do, but we find that many of his behaviors obtain a satisfactory response from other people and get tasks done. By and by, we may learn for ourselves under what conditions certain behavior is appropriate so that we no longer have to depend upon a model.

One of the most important factors in learning from models is identification with the model. A child who identifies with his mother and father wants to be like them. Being like them—or perceiving that he is like them—in their behavior and standards is gratifying to him. Students who identify with their teachers and employees who identify with their supervisors usually are able to learn quite rapidly from these models. On the other hand, a *negative* attitude toward a person may interfere with such learning or even induce one to act quite differently.

Learning through instruction. A second way in which we learn roles is through instruction. Probably the most thoroughgoing instruction in roles takes place in the home. For example, the mother tells the child how he is supposed to act when he

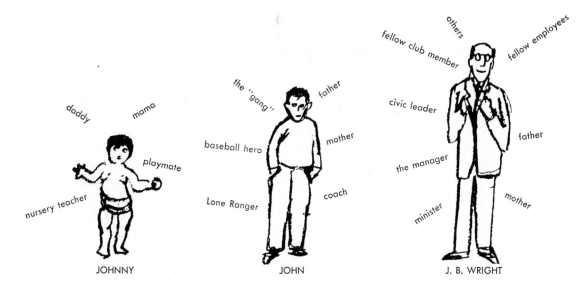

Figure labels:

JOHNNY — daddy, mama, playmate, nursery teacher

JOHN — the "gang", baseball hero, Lone Ranger, father, mother, coach

J. B. WRIGHT — others, fellow club member, fellow employees, civic leader, the manager, father, minister, mother

Figure 15.4. As you grew up, did you, like Johnny, acquire an ever-larger number of role models? Which of these models once influenced you strongly but no longer do so? What people are your current models? Why?

goes to church, to the store, or to a party, or when he visits in another home. The schools, too, play an important part in role instruction. Whole books have been written on what are the right ways to act in certain situations. A book on etiquette describes literally hundreds of different social situations and what behavior is appropriate in each. When a new employee joins an organization, he typically is told about the routines of the company. Many factories have provided supervisory training programs in which foremen and other supervisors are instructed in how to carry out their duties.

One of our favorite ways of getting instruction about our roles is to ask other people who have been, or are now, in the same situation as ourselves. This reflects our knowledge that formal instruction is not always realistic. We like to hear first-hand from another person exactly what is expected and how things work in practice.

Although instruction may be helpful in learning a role, there are many instances

in which it is not sufficient by itself. The niceties of the role, the stylistic and emotional features of it, are difficult, often impossible, to learn merely by being told about them. Many of the instructions that seem so clear beforehand turn out to be ambiguous in the practical situation. Furthermore, we may find that we do not necessarily have all the skills that the role calls for.

Learning in the practical situation. Another way in which we learn our roles is in the practical situation, that is, on the job. When an employee joins a company, say as a secretary, she has to learn from the practical situation what is expected of her. Of course, there will be instructions and models, but still she must actually try out different behaviors to see which ones will work for her in concrete situations. For example, in a trial-and-error manner, the secretary may discover that there are certain favorite ways for filing material in this organization. She also learns the exceptions to the rules and how to take her role with different persons with whom she works.

When we are learning our roles on the job, we are getting actual practice in the real situation in which the roles have to be performed. It is to our advantage if others are permissive when we begin to take our roles and if they recognize that we shall make errors. One of the most difficult of all social situations in which to learn roles is that in which the consequence of making errors is severe punishment.

Probably this is one of the reasons why *role playing* is such a successful technique in retraining people in their roles. In role-playing training a person is put in a hypothetical situation, one in which there are no practical risks involved, and he is expected to play a particular part as though he were in the actual situation. For example, a foreman may practice in a role-playing situation ways of dealing with a difficult employee. He is free to try a variety of different behaviors without any of the practical consequences which real failures would entail.

Transferring Old Learning. Typically in a social situation we have at the outset some expectation of the right ways to act. A lot of this knowledge is transferred from other situations in which we have taken similar roles or have observed others taking the roles. When an employee is promoted to the position of foreman he is very likely to act as he has seen foremen act. In other words, he is transferring to the situation role behavior that he has already learned about. Likewise, someone who has functioned as a leader in one organization is very likely to carry the same skills over into leading another organization.

Sometimes, however, the learning we transfer to another situation may not be appropriate, for the situations may be different in very important ways. Suppose, for example, that a man has been a manager of his own business and that he has used very permissive, democratic techniques. During active military duty he may need to carry out the duties of a company commander. If he attempts to transfer unchanged his democratic techniques of leadership, he may find that this behavior is confusing both to his subordinates and to his superiors. It will be necessary for him to discriminate between the back-home situation and the military situation in order to behave appropriately.

It is often valuable to be able to carry over into a new situation the learning which one has obtained in other situations. Ideally, however, a person ought to have available many different ways of acting that he can bring to bear upon a particular situation according to its demands. There clearly are individual differences in the ease with which people adapt to new role situations. Some tend to be rather rigid and inflexible in carrying over to a new situation old patterns of behavior which are not appropriate. Others learn very rapidly which are the successful ways of acting and which are the unsuccessful ones. It is likely that appropriate transfer will be facilitated by a knowledge of *principles* in addition to knowledge of detailed *facts* about the new situation.

We have seen, then, that roles are learned in a number of different ways. We learn our roles from models, particularly from those models with whom we are identified. We also learn our roles through instructions, although instructions usually need to be supplemented by actual practice. Further, we learn roles in the practical situation, such as on the job. Finally, we transfer old roles over into new situations more or less appropriately.

Conditions Making Learning of Roles Difficult. Certain conditions tend to make the learning of roles difficult.[2] One condi-

[2] L. S. Cottrell, Jr., "The Adjustment of the Individual to his Age and Sex Roles," *American Sociological Review*, 7:617–620, 1942.

▶ An experiment by Bishop * was designed to investigate mother-child inter-action (these are mutually dependent roles) and transfer (generalization) of the child's behavior to a "neutral" adult woman.

The subjects were 34 mother-child pairs. The children, who attended the Preschool Laboratories of the Iowa Child Welfare Research Station, varied from 3 years 4 months to 5 years 7 months in age. Half of them were boys and half were girls.

Each child was observed for two half-hour sessions (on different days) with his mother and for two other half-hour sessions with a "neutral" adult, a woman who was a stranger to the child. Half the children were observed with the mother first and the neutral adult second; the other half were in the opposite order.

The behavior of the adults was scored in terms of eleven main categories: lack of contact, interactive play, teaching, helping, praising, structurizing, directing, interfering, criticizing, cooperation, and noncooperation. Child behavior was scored in terms of these categories: bid for attention, bid for physical proximity, directing, interfering, criticizing, indications of anxiety, cooperation, noncooperation, bid for praise, affection, asking for information, asking for permission, and asking for help.

The part of the study we are concerned with here demonstrates that children tended to transfer to the neutral adult the same patterns of behavior which they had in relation to their mothers. "As the child became more familiar with the neutral adult his behavior approached that displayed toward the mother" (page 33). The experiment shows that role behaviors tend to be transferred to similar situations.

* B. M. Bishop, "Mother-Child Interaction and the Social Behavior of Children," *Psychological Monographs*, no. 328, 1951.

tion is vagueness or ambiguity in the role itself. Such is the case when there is a lack of definition of the role. When there are no clear-cut patterns of the behavior that is expected of us, it is more difficult to know exactly how to act.

A second condition making the learning of roles difficult is disagreement among people as to what the role ought to be. Sometimes we may be caught in the middle between conflicting expectations of others as to how we ought to act.

Another condition which may make the learning of roles difficult is inconsistency of reward and punishment on the part of others. For example, a student is confused when his teacher sometimes rewards him for originality and later punishes such be-havior without clarifying his grounds for doing so.

Another condition which makes for difficulty in the learning of roles is having previously learned an incompatible role. A person who for years has led people in an authoritarian fashion—requiring immediate and unquestioned obedience, inflicting severe penalties for failure, and the like—may find it very difficult to overcome his old habits (with all their emotional supports) and learn new and more permissive techniques of leadership.

Still another unfavorable condition is the presence of threat. When we feel that the risks of failure are very serious, we are much less flexible in trying out different forms of behavior.

Finally, it is possible that the requirements of the role may be incompatible with our own personality. A role such as acting, which calls for a lot of expressiveness, may prove to be very difficult for someone who tends to be timid before others. Likewise having to take the role of a leader in a dangerous combat situation may be hard for someone who has very limited self-confidence. Again having to carry out a rather solitary type of job may be trying for someone who loves to be with other people.

CARRYING OUT ROLES

As we have already said, no two people in the same position act in quite the same manner. We all carry out our roles in somewhat individual ways. Although norms for roles place some limits on how we act as students, military officers, husbands, and foremen, still these norms allow for at least some variation. Other, and perhaps

Figure 15.5. What are some of the factors that might influence the way in which the supervisor and the employee carry out their roles? (Standard Oil Company, New Jersey.)

deeper, reasons for individual differences in role taking are the varying needs and personalities of people and the varying circumstances in which the roles are to be carried out.

Influence of Many Interacting Factors. The way in which we take our roles is influenced by many factors. Some of these factors, such as formal company policy, are external; others, such as personal ambition for advancement, are internal. Relationships with other people—both those present and those in the background—influence our actions. Our needs play a vital part in the process. Just how these different factors—and more that we might analyze—would be weighted would depend on the specific situation. A rebellious employee might well bring into play both the foreman's need to dominate others and his need to fulfill the expectations of a hard-driving supervisor. At the same time he might be concerned with maintaining a satisfactory relationship with the union steward, and so on. In another situation, his rivalry with other foremen and his personal ambition for advancement may be relatively more important. In other words, in taking our roles we are influenced by many factors over and above the norms for the role itself.

Levels of Role Taking. There are various degrees of ego-involvement in the taking of a role.

1. We may reject the role, which is really *not* taking it. The student rejects the role of student if he neglects to attend classes, to study, to do any reading on his own, or to be interested in his courses.

2. We may accept the role, but only at a minimum level, doing only what is required, and that only because of external pressure. A student who does only the bare minimum necessary for getting by, when he could do more, has not really accepted the role as a part of the self.

3. We may accept the role in the sense

that we identify with it. It then becomes a part of the self and we evaluate ourselves by how well we carry it out. A student who identifies with his role not only satisfies formal requirements but goes far beyond them. He is interested in learning and thinking, and he pursues his intellectual interests independently and creatively.[3]

Of the many roles we are called upon to perform, we identify with some and we treat others as more or less external to ourselves. For example, a man may devote a lot of time and put much energy into his role as owner of his business. Many of his important needs and values are related to this role, and it becomes a part of the self. This same man may have various other roles, such as his role as member of a club, which are of less importance to him. He is less ego-involved in such roles. Although he may carry them out reasonably well, they have less to do with enhancement and defense of the self.

It makes a practical difference whether or not we identify with our role. If we do, we are likely to evaluate ourselves according to the standards of the role. A workman who identifies with his role is inclined to evaluate himself according to standards of good workmanship. A professional person who identifies with his role is very likely to perceive himself as adequate or inadequate according to the standards of his profession. A lawyer who has identified with the code of ethics of lawyers can feel genuine guilt if he violates such a code and genuine satisfaction if he carries out its requirements. A businessman who identifies with his executive role can feel genuine gratification in carrying out efficiently the task which he has chosen.

[3] There is an excellent treatment of levels of role taking in an article by A. Curle and E. L. Trist, "Transitional Communities and Social Reconnection," *Human Relations*, 1:240–288, 1947.

When we identify with a role, it becomes an integral part of ourselves and our personality. We carry out its expectations because they are a part of our own needs. In fulfilling them we obtain genuine satisfaction, and if we fail to realize them we feel guilt and shame. We place a genuine value upon serving the functions of the role, and we feel anxiety if we do not succeed in doing so.

On the other hand, if we do not identify with a role, then we are not likely to carry it out in an effective manner. We may simply abandon the role whenever it becomes inconvenient or when too much pressure is exerted upon us. Or we may carry out the requirements of the role in a very mechanical manner. That is, not identifying with the role, we simply do the minimum which is required. We assume no responsibility beyond that which is demanded by others. All organizations in which there is work or responsibility would like their members to identify with their roles

Sometimes we can help a person identify with a role by seeing that he has favorable experiences with it. We may also try to get him to appreciate the value of the role and how it is relevant to his needs.

Evaluating Our Own Roles. Most of us feel that our major roles, such as our jobs, are important. It is easier, of course, to value our role if others also consider it valuable. Physicians, for example, can readily value their own roles, but garbage collectors, having low prestige, find it more difficult to have positive self-esteem in their jobs, even though their jobs are necessary. Certain roles, such as those of clergymen and teachers, are generally considered to be highly valuable.

It is of interest that various occupational groups tend toward professionalization. That is, they may establish ideals of service, set up standards of competence, and evolve codes of ethics together with some way of enforcing the codes. The medical and legal professions are good examples. More recently, psychologists have been working toward the goal of professionalization. Why does this process take place? Part of the answer, of course, is a need to foster good public relations and to control competition; another reason has to do with the enhancement and defense of the self. Having a worthy set of standards—and living up to them—is an important way of feeling worthwhile as a person.

The way in which we evaluate our roles depends a great deal on how we perceive them in relation to our needs and values. The position and role of banker may satisfy prestige needs, among others. Or a role such as that of minister in a church may satisfy a need to serve others. Unless we can see such a relationship, the role does not mean much to us; it tends to be rejected, or carried out in a routine and perfunctory manner.

Sometimes we are struck by the fact that a person does not evaluate his role by the usual standards. For example, a businessman may be unscrupulous in business matters and yet avow the most ethical and idealistic sentiments on Sunday. Somehow he is keeping his business behavior separate from his moral code through rationalization, repression, dissociation, and the other devices of self-defense. But notice that this same businessman may be proud of his shrewdness in transactions, which implies self-evaluation in terms other than ethical standards.

Flexibility in Taking Roles. Sometimes we carry out our roles in rather rigid ways irrespective of the circumstances. Probably one reason for this is that there is a certain amount of protection in the rules. If we react to every situation according to the rules, we can point to the rules as the justification for our behavior. Such rigidity may be a sign of personal insecurity in the role. When we are beginners in a role, with limited knowledge of what we are to do, most of us are quite likely to rely heavily

Figure 15.6.

upon some limited set of rules. But as we become better acquainted with the situations which arise, we learn how to vary our behavior as circumstances may require. Administrators frequently are worried lest deviation from rules result in precedents which will give them difficulty in the future. In some cases, this worry is realistic. In others, the administrator is simply dodging the responsibility of taking a variety of factors into account.

Figure 15.6 caricatures rigidity in carrying out a role—that of teacher. We find this particular teacher instructing people in all kinds of inappropriate settings. Of course, most examples of role rigidity are not this extreme, but occasionally a person may carry some aspect of his behavior into settings in which the behavior is not fully relevant. For example, a businessman may appraise everything in terms of costs.

When we are in a particular position, such as that of member of a discussion group, we may enact our role narrowly or broadly and flexibly—or anywhere in between. We may even take different roles at different times. As an example, in a discussion group we may initiate proposals, contribute information, ask for or give opinions, summarize, or recognize agreement. It is possible to tabulate for each of us the frequency with which we take each of these roles. Ideally, the various members of a discussion group ought to become adept at a variety of roles and to enact them at appropriate times.

Personal Conflict about the Role. Sometimes we have a conflict about our role. For example, a college professor is expected, on the one hand, to be a good teacher. On the other hand, in many universities, he is expected to be a productive research worker. Frequently these two requirements get in each other's way. He may take a deep interest in the instruction of his students, but in order to get research done, it may be necessary to slight teaching. Yet, if he devotes most of his time to teaching,

Figure 15.7. *Seldom do our roles, however important and demanding, satisfy all our needs.* (*Wide World Photos.*)

he may find that his research suffers. As a consequence, many persons in this role feel a certain amount of guilt about their failure to meet both requirements fully.

Sometimes a role may not be entirely compatible with our personality. For example, a person who takes a position as a salesman must make many face-to-face contacts with people in an attempt to influence their attitudes in favor of buying. However, if he is timid and lacks self-confidence, he is likely to find that such contacts are quite difficult for him. Moreover, being a salesman might require that he be away from home for long periods of time. If he places a great deal of value on family life and enjoys the stability which a regular routine provides, he may find a selling career unsatisfying. Also, if the product he sells is one that he regards as shoddy and inferior, he is likely to feel some personal conflict about trying to sell it to others He may know the role requirements perfectly, but not find them at all gratifying.

▶ Six college women were specially selected to enact the role of a daughter in the following situation: * "You have just been informed by the dean that your grade average does not warrant your remaining in the University. You have returned home and are about to tell your father about it. Mr. P. will take the role of father." These six subjects had been selected so as to vary widely in role-taking aptitude, as measured by a special "As If" test in which they answered the questions: (1) "How would your life have been different if you had been born a member of the opposite sex?" and (2) "How would your life have been different if you had been born a Russian?" For purposes of control, these six subjects had been equated with respect to age, agreement with the expectations of others as to the attributes of the daughter role, and agreement between the self-concept and the daughter role.

After the six women had enacted the daughter role in the experimental situation, twenty-nine other college women, who had observed the enactment, rated each of the six subjects on a 200-adjective check list characterizing her enactment of the role. Examples of the adjectives were "informal," "poised," "pleasure seeking," and "sensitive." In addition they ranked the six subjects in order of *adequacy of enactment* of the daughter role. Each of the six subjects rated herself on the 200-adjective check list. Finally, a measure of social adjustment was obtained.

The results were that the girls who had the best role-playing aptitude, as shown on the "As If" test, most validly performed the daughter role. That is, their enactment was closest to that regarded as characteristic of the daughter role. Also, those who had the best role-taking aptitude showed the greatest changes in self-picture as a result of having taken the daughter role. In addition, there was a positive relationship between role-taking aptitude and a measure of social adjustment; that is, the girls who had the greatest ability to take the point of view of a person in a different position also had the best personal-social adjustment.

* T. R. Sarbin and D. S. Jones, "An Experimental Analysis of Role Behavior," *Journal of Abnormal and Social Behavior*, 51:236–241, 1955.

During wartime, many persons came from civilian life into positions of military responsibility. In these positions they often were required to make decisions of great importance, affecting the welfare of many people. Usually it was necessary to exercise rather arbitrary authority in order to carry out their responsibility. Frequently they were obliged to deal with people as a group instead of studying each individual case on its merits. Each of these requirements may have proved to be in conflict with a person's values. Some officers felt anxious and guilty about exercising such authority.[4]

Changing Other People's Perception of Our Own Role. Sometimes we want other people to change the way they perceive us in our roles. For example, when a worker is promoted to the position of foreman, his former fellow workers are likely to regard him as a worker like themselves.

[4] An interesting treatment of role conflict and personality will be found in an article by S. A. Stouffer, "An Analysis of Conflicting Social Norms," *American Sociological Review*, 14:707–717, 1949.

In order to do his job properly, however, the foreman needs to have his former co-workers perceive him in his new position. Frequently this involves a conflict. If the new foreman begins by giving exacting orders and being coldly distant, then his former fellow workers resent it. On the other hand, if he attempts to act like a fellow worker and be as familiar as before, it is difficult for them to see him in his supervisory role. As a consequence, many companies switch a promoted employee to a different group. The same practice is often followed in military organizations. An enlisted man who has been promoted to the rank of officer usually, except in combat situations, is not likely to continue to work with his former fellow soldiers. Instead, he is transferred to another unit in which the men have never associated with him in the lesser status.

So one of the most effective ways to get others to perceive our role in a different way is simply to move into a different group, a setting where the others have not known us in our former status.

SUMMARY

The positions and roles of our culture are important determinants of behavior. A position is a place, function, or office in a social organization. Some positions—such as age category—are very general, whereas others are more specific and temporary. Some positions are ascribed, while others are achieved. Positions also vary in prestige.

A role is the set of behaviors that is typical of the occupants of a position. People have norms—standards of behavior —for roles and also expectations regarding how people in a position will behave.

People learn their roles from models, through instructions, and in practical situations. They transfer elements of learned roles to new settings. Some conditions (such as that of ambiguity in the role) often makes the learning of roles rather difficult.

People carry out their roles in more or less individual ways. Many interacting factors influence the ways in which roles are carried out. Roles are carried out—or not carried out—at various levels. When people identify with roles, they generally carry them out well. In addition, the norms for the roles become standards for self-evaluation. How a person evaluates a role depends on how he perceives it in relation to his needs and values. Flexibility in carrying out roles involves adapting behavior to specific and changing conditions. People sometimes have personal conflicts about their roles.

QUESTIONS

1. What is meant by each of the following terms: position, prestige, status, role norms, and role expectations?

2. What is your conception of what you consider to be your most important role? How closely does your conception agree with that of others?

3. What are the main ways in which we learn roles? What are some of the principal difficulties in learning roles?

4. What are some of the factors which account for individual differences in the taking of roles?

5. Distinguish among the different levels of carrying out our roles.

6. How would you try to get someone, such as an employee, to identify with his role?

7. Are you subject to any conflicting role requirements? If so, how do you handle these conflicts?

8. What are some possible courses of action when a person finds that a role is unsatisfying to him? What can he do if circumstances compel him to take the role?

9. What relation is there between roles and the self? With which roles do you identify most highly?

10. What differences are there between achieved and ascribed roles?

11. What are the most important roles for a person of your particular age and sex groups?

12. What is meant by identifying with a role? Illustrate.

SUGGESTED READINGS

Hartley, E. L., and R. E. Hartley: *Fundamentals of Social Psychology,* Knopf, New York, 1952, chaps. 16, 17, 18.

(A treatment of roles, adjustment to roles, and status.)

McClelland, D. C.: *Personality,* Sloane, New York, 1951.

(A textbook in which roles are regarded as one of the main factors in personality.)

Miller, N. E., and J. Dollard: *Social Learning and Imitation,* Yale University Press, New Haven, Conn., 1941.

(A theoretical and experimental analysis of learning from models.)

Newcomb, T. M.: *Social Psychology,* Dryden, New York, 1950.

(A textbook with selected chapters on roles and their relationship to personality.)

Sarbin, T. R.: "Role Theory," in G. Lindzey (ed.), *Handbook of Social Psychology,* Addison-Wesley, Cambridge, Mass., 1954, vol. I, pp. 223–258.

(A theoretical analysis of research on roles in relationship to personality.)

16 MEASUREMENT AND INDIVIDUAL DIFFERENCES

In every phase of our living we face the problem of assessing the differences between people. Some are selected for employment and some are rejected on the basis of differences. Some go to college and some do not because of individual differences. Acceptance or rejection for graduate study or professional training is based upon differences among those applying. People differ in all measurable traits and characteristics, although in some of these they are more alike than in others. This is a problem of special importance to the psychologist.

The statistical treatment of the observations of these differences is a topic of considerable interest in the understanding of human behavior. To some extent this topic is relevant to the first chapters of this book, but it is even more important in connection with the appraisal of intelligence and psychological testing, discussed in the chapters that follow.

Why do psychologists find statistics an important aspect of their subject? The reason is simply that, for many facts, a single observation is either meaningless or—what may be worse—misleading. In other words, until an observation is evaluated in the light of many other observations it is easily misinterpreted. Statistics is a tool for the evaluation of observations.

HISTORY OF THE STUDY OF INDIVIDUAL DIFFERENCES

Like any other subject of current interest, that of how and to what extent people are unlike in their various physical and psychological characteristics has a history. In this case the history goes far back into the

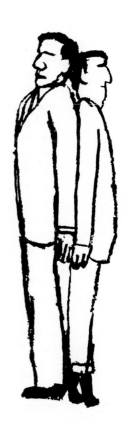

past. Let us look briefly at some instances of early recognition of these facts and then at some more modern findings.

Early Interest in Individual Differences. Since the beginnings of the human race, man has evidently been interested in and recognized differences among people. Among the earliest records of ways of differentiating between people are those found in the Bible. One example is this: [1]

And the Gileadites took the fords of the Jordan against the Ephraimites. And when any of the fugitives of Ephraim said "Let us go over," the men of Gilead said to him, "Are you an Ephraimite?" When he said, "No," they said to him, "Then say Shibboleth," and he said "Sibboleth," for he could not pronounce it right; then they seized him and slew him at the fords of the Jordan. And there fell at that time forty-two thousand of the Ephraimites.

Thus it can be seen not only that differences were recognized but that they were recognized as being important. Many other examples could be cited from history. Though these differences have been recognized through the centuries, their systematic and scientific measurement has been confined to relatively recent times.

Modern Recognition of Individual Differences. The year 1796 is often looked upon as the beginning of the systematic and scientific recognition of individual differences. It was in this year that Maskelyne, the Astronomer Royal at the Greenwich Astronomical Observatory, dismissed Kinnebrook, his assistant, because he erred, by nearly 1 second, in recording the time that certain bodies passed an observation point. According to the "look-and-listen" method used at this time, the observer had to look at the star as it crossed his field of vision and at the same time count the seconds by listening to the tick of the clock. From the notations of these observations an estimate was made of the exact time (in tenths of a second) at which

[1] *Judges* 12:5–6 (Revised Standard Version).

the star crossed the observation point. Naturally, people differed considerably in their judgments, though Maskelyne was unaware of this.

Twenty years after the Kinnebrook incident, Bessel, the astronomer at the Königsberg Observatory, became interested in the report and began to study what he called the "personal equation" of different astronomers. He collected data from several trained persons and studied the errors made in their reports. He also studied the variations of the same individual from time to time. From these data Bessel concluded that each astronomer did indeed have his "personal equation" and that real differences between astronomers were usually found. His work showed—too late to be of help to the unfortunate Kinnebrook—that discrepancies as large as those between Maskelyne and Kinnebrook were the rule rather than the exception. These differences in the estimates of observers came to be known as differences in *reaction time*.

The latter part of the nineteenth century saw a considerable amount of research being done on this and related problems. In 1884 Sir Francis Galton established his anthropometric laboratory at South Kensington Museum in London. Here he gave certain tests to people who came into his laboratory. Most of these tests were concerned with sensory-motor abilities, visual discrimination of length, the highest audible pitch, strength, and simple reaction time. Some of the instruments he invented (such as the Galton bar and the Galton whistle) are still in use. Galton confirmed and extended the findings of Bessel. The beginnings of the psychological testing movement around the turn of the century gave great impetus to the study of differences among people.

THE NATURE OF THE DIFFERENCES BETWEEN PEOPLE

If people are different, it becomes necessary to evaluate these differences and to relate them to any general principles which we may be able to formulate.

Extent of Differences between People. The truth is that no two of us are exactly alike, and at the same time we are not completely different. In many respects, most of us are similar enough to enable us to make use of uniform standards. Take the matter of clothing, for example. Manufacturers make up patterns which, with a minimum of change or alteration, will fit a great number of us. Many of us could exchange articles of clothing without loss of fit. Anyone who lives in a college dormitory, as either borrower or lender, probably realizes how true this is.

All this suggests that there may be some uniformity even in the way we differ. We do not, in other words, merely differ haphazardly, but rather *we differ in a predictable manner* in many situations. Several facts should be noted about how we differ.

In the first place, a great deal of our variability *is one of degree rather than of kind.* For example, there are not two (or more) kinds of height, so far as humans are concerned. Rather, some people are very tall, others are a little less tall (or are a little shorter), others still more so, etc. Thus we can say that, so far as height is concerned, the tallest of us differs from the shortest only by degrees.

In the second place, in most situations, when we go from one extreme to the other (in a large, unselected group), there are few if any gaps. Thus if we find a person in a large group who is just 5 feet tall the chances are that we can also find one who is about 5 feet 1 inch tall and one who is about 4 feet 11 inches tall. This same principle will hold for most measurements, though it must be admitted that the farther we get out toward the extremes the more likely we are to find some gaps.

In the third place, in most groups, most people are not at the extremes of the distribution but rather near "the mean between the two extremes." Again height

Figure 16.1. As a baseball player Babe Ruth showed exceptional ability. After thirty years some of the records he set still stand. (Culver Service.)

makes a good illustration. Most of us are of moderate height. Needless to say, there are many other illustrations of this fact.

Finally, in any large, unselected group, there is usually someone about as far below the average as someone else is above it. Thus, as we have just seen, there are only a very few people who are extremely tall. But the interesting thing is that at the same time there is about the same number who are extremely short. The same point can be made with regard to other characteristics.

To understand these facts, it is necessary to know about statistics. Indeed, in this chapter, the statistics of individual differences will be among the items considered. Before we get to that topic, however, let us look at some of the characteristics in which people vary and examine the extent of these variations.

Differences in intelligence. Since intelligence is dealt with at some length in Chapter 17, we shall not spend much time with

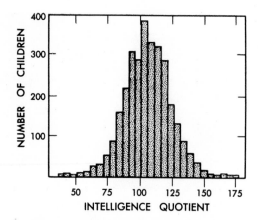

Figure 16.2. Most people fall in the middle range of intelligence, as shown in this frequency distribution of the intelligence quotients of 2,970 school children. The distribution approximates the normal curve. Notice the preponderance of scores in the middle ranges. See how closely the number of scores on the lower side approximates those on the higher side of the distribution. What is true of intelligence has been found to be true of many, if indeed not of most, psychological characteristics. (Morgan, Introduction to Psychology, McGraw-Hill, New York, 1956, p. 196. Courtesy of the publisher.)

Figure 16.3. This distribution of scores on the Otis Self-administering Test of Mental Ability (Higher Exam, Form A) shows the wide range over which the scores of 117 applicants for electrical apprenticeships are spread. (Arthur S. Otis, Otis Self-administering Tests of Mental Ability, World, Yonkers, N.Y., 1922. Copyright by the publisher.)

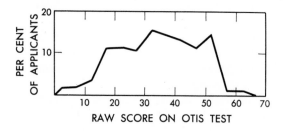

it here. It is worth noting, perhaps, that the four points made above about how we vary also apply to variations in intelligence. Figure 16.2 shows how the IQs of 2,970 school children were found to vary.

As might be expected, the variations represented in Figure 16.2 are not restricted to school children. Figure 16.3 gives the same sort of information for a smaller, more restricted group.

Differences in physical ability. In the field of athletics, two individuals may start out very nearly even so far as certain abilities are concerned. But when they are subjected to similar periods of training, we usually find that one excels the other. There must, then, have been some basic differences in potential or capacity in addition to other factors.

Take, for example, a track and field meet. As we observe these well-conditioned men, we may feel that they are all superior to the average of those in their age groups, and they probably are. There are nevertheless differences among them. As they start the race, they are grouped close together, but as the race progresses the individual differences in their ability become increasingly apparent, particularly if the race is a long one. In this case the distance between the leader and the one running last becomes greater as the race progresses. The ones in between may be scattered all along the distance between the first and last. The differences between them may be slight, but there is usually a winner, even though he breaks the tape only a small fraction of a second before the next man reaches the finish line.

Table 16.1 illustrates this point well. The persons involved were 214 ten-year-old girls, and the task was to run the 50-yard dash. As can be seen from the table, the time of the slowest was almost twice that of the fastest, and the points made earlier about individual differences apply here also.

Differences in efficiency of work. The same principles have been found to apply to the output of employees in a factory. Again we find, upon investigation, that some people perform quite poorly and others quite well, with the majority of the group usually fairly close to the middle. Figures 16.4 and 16.5 illustrate these points.

Differences in other aspects. It is probably obvious by now that the same points can be made with regard to all—or at least nearly all—of the many ways in which people differ. Thus we could talk about the interests of people (as is done in Chapter 18), and we should find similar differences there. Or we could consider the various personality traits of the individual, and we should find again the same situation. Similarly in aptitudes, attitudes, values, and other aspects of personality, we are alike, but we are also different.

Significance of Individual Differences. Since it has been found that human beings vary in so many of their traits and characteristics, this variation becomes a matter of concern to scientists. If they were to study only the general principles that apply to everyone, they would neglect many significant aspects of human behavior. Scientists want also to know how and to what extent people are not alike.

It should be noted, incidentally, that some of the early work in this field was undertaken, as is frequently true in science (see Chapter 1), not for the sake of its usefulness, but simply for the sake of knowing. Certainly Galton's work was principally of this sort, and the same can be said of several other investigators whose research we have not described.

Not only do people differ, but these differences are *great enough to be significant.* In other words, regardless of any strictly scientific interest we might have in human variation, most of us inevitably also develop a practical interest in the subject. In

Table 16.1   Achievement of Girls on 50-yard Dash

(N = 214 ten-year-olds)

Percentage of girls doing as well as, or better than, time shown	Time, seconds
99	11.5
98	11.1
95	10.5
90	10.1
75	9.6
50	8.8
25	8.4
10	7.9
5	7.7
2	7.5
1	6.9

With a range of almost five seconds from the fastest to the slowest in such a short space of time, the difference becomes quite significant.

SOURCE: *Courtesy of Research Committee of Texas Association for Health, Physical Education, and Recreation.*

Figure 16.4. People differ in productivity. This chart shows the distribution of quantity of productivity among thirty-six electrical fixture assemblers. (Reproduced by permission from Industrial Psychology, 3d ed., Joseph Tiffin, p. 11. Copyright, 1942, 1947, 1951, by Prentice-Hall, Englewood Cliffs, N.J.)

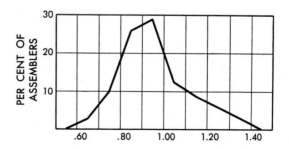

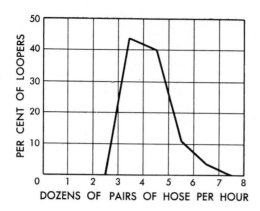

Figure 16.5. Ordinarily only a few people are found at the extremes of a distribution. This curve shows the production records of ninety-nine experienced employees in a hosiery mill. (Reproduced by permission from Industrial Psychology, *3d ed., by Joseph Tiffin, p. 13. Copyright, 1942, 1947, 1951, by Prentice-Hall, Englewood Cliffs, N.J.)*

every phase of our daily living in which we come in contact with other people we make choices, appraisals, and evaluations based on these differences. This holds true in our choice of friends and associates as well as in business, industry, and school situations. It is not surprising, therefore, that much time and energy have been spent in studying individual differences and that a number of statistical techniques have been developed for dealing with them.

The scientific study of individual differences demanded the use of suitable tools and techniques. To meet these needs psychologists have made use of psychological tests and statistical techniques.

The Testing Movement. The psychological testing movement is young as such movements go, the first real psychological test having appeared in 1905. During World War I the urgent need to appraise people resulted in rapid growth and expansion of the use of psychological tests. The experiences of World War II added impetus to the movement.

Psychological tests have come to have an important place in the appraisal of people in our present-day society. Tests are now used in schools and colleges, in business and industry, in mental health clinics and mental hospitals, in vocational counseling centers, and in many other places. They are used to select people, to evaluate their present status, and to predict their future behavior. Sometimes, of course, they serve as a basis for comparing groups, but typically they are employed to appraise the single individual.

Naturally, the psychological testing movement has had its problems. The nature of psychological tests is not generally well understood, and considerable misunderstanding about the use of tests is widespread. In particular, we find many instances of two extreme and erroneous attitudes toward testing. On the one hand, some people sometimes reject tests as having no real value at all. They feel that their own opinion of people is usually more accurate than the result of a test. Furthermore, they feel that tests are impractical and out of touch with the realities of the everyday world. On the other hand, some people have become overenthusiastic about tests. They seem to feel that test scores afford the most accurate possible appraisal of a person. Tests are sometimes surrounded with an air of mystery, as if the test were infallible.[2]

The General Nature of a Psychological Test. A psychological test typically consists of some items, questions, or problems to be solved or tasks to be completed. Such a test is used to discriminate between people. Ordinarily the answer is indicated by a check, a number, or some similar device. Usually, psychological tests contain problems such as true-false or multiple-choice questions or short-answer questions that have only one correct answer, though this is not always true.

[2] This point is well evaluated by Milton R. Blum, *Industrial Psychology and Its Social Foundations,* Harper, New York, 1949, pp. 363–366.

> **DIFFERENCES IN
> PREMEDICAL
> STUDENTS**

▶ At the University of Minnesota, Richard S. Melton * selected 102 non-veteran premedical students for study. These students had enrolled at the university during the summer and fall of 1949 and were studied over a period of three years. The study was aimed at the discovery of differences between the successful and unsuccessful premedical student.

The criterion of success used was honor-point ratio achieved over the three-year period. The ultimate criterion of success, however, was acceptance by a medical school.

Predictive measures used were the 1947 ACE test, Cooperative English test, high school rank, and the Physician scale on the Strong Vocational Interest Blank.

Of the 102 men studied, 45 were admitted to medical school. These 45 had higher mean scores on all measures used except the Physician scale. High school ranks, ACE scores, and Cooperative English scores were all found to be useful predictors for discriminating between the successful and unsuccessful.

* Richard S. Melton, "Differentiation of Successful and Unsuccessful Premedical Students," *Journal of Applied Psychology*, 39:397–400, 1955.

One fact which must constantly be borne in mind is that before a test is really a psychological test it must be *standardized*. An ordinary test or other examination is simply written down and given, but a psychological test is subject to careful analysis, item by item and as a whole, before it is adopted. What do we mean when we say that a test has been standardized? We simply mean that its validity and reliability have been determined and norms have been established. These procedures, basic to effective testing, are to be discussed in the following paragraphs.

Test Validity. In the process of standardizing a test, a number of things must be taken into account. The first of these is the *validity* of the test. A test is valid if it *measures what it purports to measure.* That is to say, it is valid if it measures what it is used to measure. For example, a valid intelligence test measures intelligence.

On the face of it this appears to be a simple matter, but actually it is not simple at all, for before we can determine the validity of a test we must have something with which to compare the results obtained from its use. Thus, before we can say that

an intelligence test is valid—i.e., that it really measures intelligence—we must be able to show that very intelligent people actually make high scores on it, that people who are average in intelligence make average scores, and that the dull and the feeble-minded make low scores. This implies, of course, that we have a group of people whose intelligence is already known.

This brings us to what we call the *criterion problem*.[3] A criterion is simply a standard for comparison, an accepted measure of the particular aptitude or achievement in which we are interested. Perhaps it is sufficient here to say that before we can validate a test we must have a criterion group, a representative group of known ability, capacity, or the like. Validity refers to the extent to which test scores correspond to the known capacities of the people in this group. The comparison is made by means of a statistical technique called *correlation*, which is discussed later in this chapter.

[3] For a discussion of this problem in business and industry, see C. H. Lawshe, Jr., *Principles of Personnel Testing*, McGraw-Hill, New York, 1948.

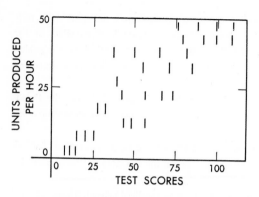
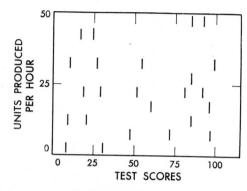

Figure 16.6. Assuming that units of output per hour is an adequate criterion of successful performance by a worker and that each of the marks in diagrams above represents the performance (as to output and test score) of a worker, the test on the left would have considerable validity. This is true because, generally speaking, the higher the score on the test, the higher the production of the worker. However, making the same assumptions as for the test on the left, the one on the right has no validity, simply because the output of a worker cannot be predicted from his test score with any more than chance accuracy.

Test Reliability. In the second place, if we are to standardize a test we must determine whether or not it is *reliable*. By reliability of a test we mean its *consistency in measurement*. If a reliable test is given a second time under approximately the same circumstances, it will yield approximately the same results. In other words, it yields comparable results each time it is administered under the same conditions.

There are several methods of determin-

ing reliability. One of these, as is indicated above, is the *test-retest method*. In this method, the test is given a second or third time, usually after a lapse of time, to the same people, and the results of the two (or three) testings are correlated. Another is the *split-half method*. In this method, the performance on half the items is compared with the performance on the other half. Specifically, we ordinarily use the *odd-even method*. Here the scores on the odd-num-

Table 16.2   Illustration of Item Analysis

Item no.	Percentage getting item		Interpretation *
	In top quarter of group	*In bottom quarter of group*	
1	80	20	Discriminates
2	55	49	To be rejected
3	20	2	Discriminates
4	100	95	To be rejected
Etc.			

* To be sure how to interpret an item requires a consideration of the number of people in each subgroup. Interpretation listed is the probable one, therefore.

> Women, more than men, seem to manifest an interest in clerical work. Are there differences in ability between the sexes that might account for these differences in interest?

DIFFERENCES IN CLERICAL ABILITY BETWEEN SEXES

The Minnesota Clerical Test is widely used in business and industry as an aid in selecting clerical employees. Also, this test is used extensively in vocational counseling programs. Speed and accuracy in checking numbers and names are the factors measured by this test.

Engelhardt * in a study of the clerical aptitude of 512 men and women found that the women had significantly higher mean scores on both parts of the Minnesota Clerical Test than did the men. The results of this study indicate real differences between the sexes in this ability.

* Olga E. de Cillis Engelhardt, "The Minnesota Clerical Test: Sex Differences and Norms for College Groups," *Journal of Applied Psychology*, 34:412–414, 1950.

bered items (Nos. 1, 3, 5, 7, 9, etc.) are compared with scores on even-numbered items (Nos. 2, 4, 6, 8, 10, etc.). For all these methods the comparisons are made by use of the correlation technique, and the result obtained from this statistical procedure is called a *coefficient of reliability*.

When we check the reliability of a test, one of the things we determine is the degree to which each of the items on the test correlates with the test as a whole. In other words, it is not sufficient for items merely to have the same form and involve the same general ideas. Scores on the individual items must correspond, at least in general, to scores on the test as a whole. Thus, if an item is difficult and only 25 per cent of those taking the test get the correct answer, for the item to be a satisfactory one most of that 25 per cent must come from those who do well *on the test as a whole* and not from those who do poorly. Item analysis is an important part of standardization and may be regarded as essentially one method of checking the reliability of the test.

Compared with validity, reliability is relatively easy to determine. Hence, it is not surprising that, in the development of tests, a great deal of attention has been paid to reliability and considerably less to validity. It is obvious, however, that the determination of reliability is essential also to the satisfactory use of a test.

Norms. Finally, so far as standardization is concerned, it is necessary to establish *norms* for a test. These norms must consist, as a minimum, of two things. In the first place, we must have some idea of the average score for the group on which the test is standardized, so that when we tell a person his score on a test we can also tell him whether his score is above or below the average. In other words, there must be some measure of what we call *central tendency*, explained later in this chapter.

In the second place, it is necessary to know the *range* of the scores and how the scores are distributed over this range. Thus the scores may be closely bunched and a few points of deviation from the average may represent quite a high or quite a low score. Or they may be spread out a great deal, in which case a few points of variation from the average would indicate that for all practical purposes the person has made an average score. Determining the spread of the scores may be as important, therefore, as determining the average score. An example will help make this clear.

Suppose someone makes 105 on a test, and the average or mean is 100. He is therefore five points above the mean. Now it makes a great deal of difference whether the top score on that test was 107 or 200. If the top score is 107 in an unselected sample of the population and he has made

Table 16.3 A Set of Scores Used to Illustrate How Scores Are Interpreted

Scores	f	cf
160–169	10	1,000
150–159	21	990
140–149	69	969
130–139	150	900
120–129	250	750
110–119	250	500
100–109	150	250
90–99	72	100
80–89	18	28
70–79	10	10
	1,000	

105, he would be close to the top. On the other hand, if people make as high as 200 and he makes 105, it would be accurate to say that he made about an average score.

STATISTICS IN PSYCHOLOGY

Results obtained from the administration of psychological tests are usually expressed in numerical terms. These data must be compiled and ordered in such a way as to make them meaningful if they are to become useful. It is through the use of statistical methods that this is done. An understanding of some of the elementary statistical concepts therefore becomes necessary. Let us then turn our attention to some of these techniques.

Frequency Distribution. If we have only a few numbers, scores, or measurements, it is usually easy to get a good impression of their characteristics—how much they vary, how they average out, where they form clusters, and where there are gaps in the series. But when we have a large number of measurements, the characteristics of the set of data are harder to perceive through mere inspection. For this reason, we often find it useful to organize the data in the form of tables and to picture them in the form of graphs.

Two terms which we shall be using often in this section are *distribution* and *frequency*. A distribution is simply a set of data (scores or measurements) which vary. Frequency refers to *how many* numbers there are of a certain size (or how many numbers fall within a certain category).

Unordered Distributions. Suppose that we have a set of measurements such as those in Table 16.4. These numbers are arranged in columns for convenience, but they are not in any particular order. They form an *unordered distribution*. From looking at this table we can readily conclude that most of the scores are over 100. We can also pick out the highest score (157) and the lowest (56), which tell us the *range* over which these scores vary. From such a table, however, it is difficult to get a very good idea of the performance of any individual in relation to the group and of the group as a whole.

Ranked Distribution. It improves our understanding of the data to arrange the

Table 16.4 Total Scores of Ninety-four Freshmen on ACE Psychological Examination

117	116	115	89	97	102	94	114	121	95	120	116	120	84
91	56	117	100	103	135	106	132	99	104	114	119	126	120
125	132	129	124	100	90	107	124	126	123	105	117	102	121
100	128	110	109	140	127	126	99	132	115	138	90	136	120
80	94	82	103	108	144	98	56	101	110	61	123	136	132
97	133	107	116	137	91	144	119	98	101	93	152	110	151
157	105	131	145	116	118	93	73	83	102				

Table 16.5 Simple Frequency Distribution of Scores in Table 16.4

S	f	S	f	S	f	S	f
157	1	131	1	105	2	79	
156		130		104	1	78	
155		129	1	103	2	77	
154		128	1	102	3	76	
153		127	1	101	2	75	
152	1	126	3	100	3	74	
151	1	125	1	99	2	73	1
150		124	2	98	2	72	
149		123	2	97	2	71	
148		122		96		70	
147		121	2	95	1	69	
146		120	4	94	2	68	
145	1	119	2	93	2	67	
144	2	118	1	92		66	
143		117	3	91	2	65	
142		116	4	90	2	64	
141		115	2	89	1	63	
140	1	114	2	88		62	
139		113		87		61	1
138	1	112		86		60	
137	1	111		85		59	
136	2	110	3	84	1	58	
135	1	109	1	83	1	57	
134		108	1	82	1	56	2
133	1	107	2	81			
132	4	106	1	80	1		

scores in order from the highest to the lowest, i.e., as a *ranked distribution*. Now at a glance we can see the highest and lowest scores. We can readily compare any particular score with the other scores by counting how many it exceeds. In addition, we can make a rough estimate of the average of these scores by noting the size of the scores in the middle of the list.

Simple Frequency Distribution. A further simplification is to prepare a *simple frequency distribution*. In Table 16.5 we have made such a distribution using the data of Table 16.4. In the column marked S (scores) are listed in decreasing order all the possible scores between 157 and 56 inclusive. In the *f* (frequency) column is shown the frequency of each score. For example, there are two 144s and no 143s. In looking at this table, we can immediately pick out the highest and the lowest scores. It is also apparent where there are gaps in the distribution of scores, where the scores tend to "bunch up," and how few scores there are toward either the higher or lower extreme.

Grouped Frequency Distribution. We can further simplify these data by placing them in the form of a *grouped frequency distribution* (see Table 16.6). Here the

Table 16.6 Grouped Frequency Distribution of the Test Scores in Table 16.4

Class intervals	Tabulation	f
151–157	///	3
144–150	///	3
137–143	///	3
130–136	ֿ/////	9
123–129	ֿ/	11
116–122	ֿ/	16
109–115	///	8
102–108	//	12
95–101	//	12
88–94	/////	9
81–87	///	3
74–80	/	1
67–73	/	1
60–66	/	1
53–59	//	2

scores have been placed in a limited number of categories (or *class intervals*). That is, the quantitative data are arranged in order of magnitude and divided into a number of natural or arbitrary classes. Although there is no definite rule for how many class intervals to use, usually from ten to twenty is satisfactory. Each of the class intervals should be of the same width, that is, include the same range of possible scores. In our table, each class interval has a width of seven units. Next, we tabulate the scores by making a tally mark for each score according to the class interval in which it falls. Finally we record the frequency of scores in each class interval.

By grouping the scores, we have lost some information about the exact value of individual scores; the coarser the intervals, the more information is lost. On the other hand, we now have a simple table showing the distribution of the scores. We can easily see where they bunch up and where they are thinly scattered. We also can estimate the average fairly well and judge the magnitude of any particular score in relation to the others. Placing data in the form of a grouped frequency distribution simplifies further statistical analysis.

Graphic Representation of Measures. We may picture a frequency distribution by

Figure 16.7. A frequency polygon.

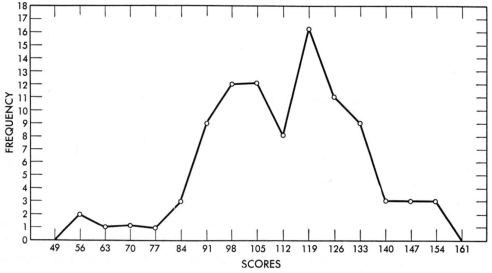

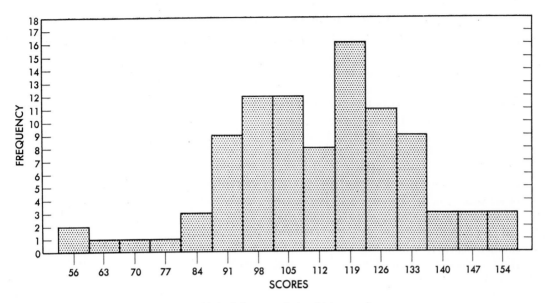

Figure 16.8. A bar graph (or histogram).

means of a graph. Figure 16.7 presents the data of the grouped frequency distribution in the form of a graph called a *frequency polygon*. The horizontal axis of the graph represents the scale of scores. Here the mid-points of the class intervals are indicated. For example, 91 is the mid-point of the class interval 88–94. The vertical axis represents frequencies; note that there are two scores in the class interval 53–59. We locate the mid-point of this class interval and go up to two on the frequency scale. We also record the frequency for each interval in the distribution, and then connect these points by means of straight lines. We now have a picture of our frequency distribution—one that is easy to perceive.

Frequency graphs are often seen in the form of bars or rectangles, as shown in Figure 16.8. Such a bar graph simply shows the frequency of scores in each class interval. The area of each bar or rectangle is proportional to its contribution to the total frequency.

Forms of Distributions. Frequency distributions vary in their forms. One of the

most important forms is the *normal curve*. The normal curve (see Figure 16.9) is derived from a mathematical formula. It is a theoretical distribution and a mathematical ideal. Many actual frequency distributions, however, have a form that is almost normal. The normal curve is bell-shaped, and its right and left halves are alike. The scores occur most frequently in the middle of the distribution, and they taper off in frequency toward each extreme.

Various kinds of data tend to be normally distributed. Numerous physical measures, such as height and weight, and the results of psychological tests tend to be normally distributed. (In some cases, the tests are

Figure 16.9. A normal frequency distribution.

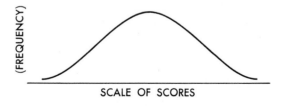

rescaled so as to *make* the distributions normal.) In experimental work, and in studies of human judgment too, errors of measurement usually are normally distributed.

Although many distributions of measures approach the normal form, there are many others that do not. For example, some distributions are *skewed;* that is, they have a tail ("skew") pointing off in one direction while the scores are bunched up in the other direction. In Figure 16.10 the curve on the left is *negatively* skewed, since the tail points in the negative direction (toward smaller scores), while the curve on the right is *positively* skewed. Sometimes a test may be easy (or the students unusually good), so that the scores tend to pile up at the high end of the distribution (negative skewness). On the other hand, if the test is quite difficult (or the students unusually poor) then the scores tend to pile up at the lower end of the distribution (positive skewness). Even though the scores of a group as a whole may be normally distributed, selectively eliminating those at one extreme or the other will cause skewness. For example, the intelligence-test scores of college students are positively skewed because those below average in intelligence are not generally admitted to college.

The normal curve has many uses in statistics, so we shall have occasion to refer to it again.

Measures of Central Tendency. In most distributions, the scores are concentrated near the center of the distribution. This tendency is referred to as the *central tendency* or average of the series. In describing a group of scores, it would be useful to have a single number that would stand for the central tendency of the distribution. It would also be useful to have measures of central tendency in order to compare the scores of two groups.

Although there are numerous measures of central tendency, we shall consider only three: the mean, the median, and the mode. These three are used more often than are the other averages.

The mean. The most important and frequently used measure of central tendency is the mean (represented as M). It is the measure which is popularly known as the "average," although statisticians use the term "average" generally to refer to any of the measures of central tendency. The mean is obtained by adding the scores and by dividing this sum by the number of scores. This is the formula for the mean:

$$M = \frac{\Sigma X}{N}$$

where M is the mean

Σ is the Greek capital letter sigma, meaning the operation of summing (adding)

X is any score

N is the number of scores

The formula is read as "the mean equals the sum of the scores divided by the number of scores." The application of this formula to an ungrouped set of scores is very

Figure 16.10. Examples of skewed distributions.

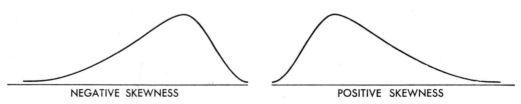

NEGATIVE SKEWNESS   POSITIVE SKEWNESS

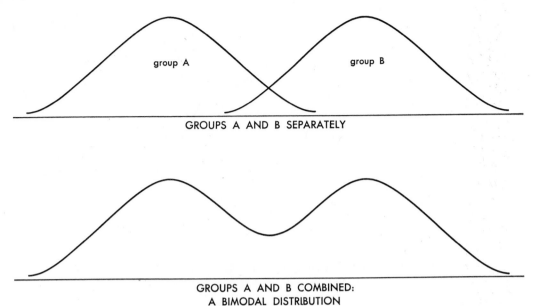

group A

group B

GROUPS A AND B SEPARATELY

GROUPS A AND B COMBINED:
A BIMODAL DISTRIBUTION

Figure 16.11. Combining two groups with different central tendencies yields a bimodal distribution.

simple: we merely add up the scores and divide by their number. The mean of a grouped frequency distribution may also be calculated, although we shall not discuss the method here.

One of the characteristics of the mean will illustrate its nature as a measure of central tendency. If we subtract the mean from every score (some of these differences will be positive while others will be negative) and then add up these differences, they will sum to zero. This is always true; try it and see. Hence the mean may be thought of as a point about which positive and negative deviations are balanced—a real point of central tendency.

The median. A second measure of central tendency is the median (represented by *Mdn*). The median is the *point* in a distribution of measures below which one-half of the scores fall; the other half of the scores, of course, are found above it. It will be referred to later as the 50th centile. If we are working with an ungrouped series, we arrange the scores in decreasing order of size. For example: 17, 15, 14, 11, 9, 8, and 6. The median of this uneven number of scores is the middle score, 11. If the number of scores is even, the median lies halfway between the two middle scores. The median may also be computed in the case of grouped frequency distributions.

The important thing about the median is that it is a measure of position—the middle of a ranked series of scores, not influenced by the presence of extreme scores (unusually high or low scores); whereas the mean *is* markedly influenced by such scores.

The mode. Another measure of central tendency is the *mode* (represented by *Mo*). The mode is defined as the measure which occurs most frequently. (In a grouped frequency distribution the mode is considered to be the mid-point of the class interval containing the greatest number of scores.) When the data are graphically represented, the mode is the point on the scale of scores where the frequency curve is highest.

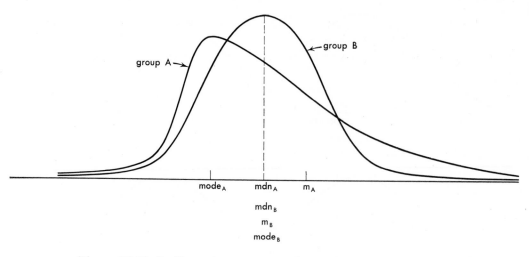

Figure 16.12. Problems in comparing the averages of two groups. Which measure of central tendency is most appropriate?

Most distributions have a single mode. Sometimes, however, distributions may have two or more modes. For example, the lower curve in Figure 16.11 is bimodal, since it has two humps. As is shown in this figure, a *bimodal distribution* may result from combining the data of two groups which have different central tendencies.

Relationships among mean, median, and mode. In a normal distribution the mean, median, and mode are the same. The mean is the most widely used measure of central tendency. It ordinarily permits more exact comparisons than the median or mode, and provides estimates that are of greater utility. It is generally a good policy to use the mean unless there is a special reason for using one of the other measures of central tendency.

When comparing groups with respect to central tendency, it is especially important not to use a measure which is misleading. Figure 16.12 illustrates a situation in which comparison in terms of means might lead to misunderstanding about the differences among the groups. The mean of group A is greater than the mean of group B, but on the whole group A scores are no higher

than those of group B. In fact, the two groups have the same median, and the difference in the modes is actually opposite in direction to the difference in means.

Measures of Variability. Not only is it important to know the central tendency of a set of scores, but it is also valuable to know about their variability. That is, we need a measure of the scatter or dispersion of these scores. This fact is important, for example, in comparing groups. Two groups may have the same mean, but they may still differ in variability. Two classes might have the same average intelligence, but in one class the students' scores might cluster closely together (be *homogeneous*) whereas in the other they might vary to either extreme (be *heterogeneous*). As another illustration, suppose that two groups take an examination, one under conditions of anxiety and the other under relatively non-anxious conditions. The averages of the two groups may be the same, but the anxious subjects are likely to differ from one another by a greater amount than do the non-anxious subjects. Measures of variability may also be used to tell us whether the same group becomes more or less variable over a period of time; that is, whether individual differences increase or decrease.

There are various measures of variability, but for the purposes of this chapter we shall discuss only three: the range, the standard deviation, and centile scores.

The range. The range is simply the difference between the highest and the lowest score. If the highest score is 157 and the lowest is 56, the range is 101.

The range has the advantage of being a simple, easily obtainable measure of variability. But it has the disadvantage of giving relatively little information about the variability of the numbers between the two extremes. In our above example, the numbers might be bunched up near the lower extreme or they might be scattered over the entire range. The danger of using the range without furnishing other information should be apparent when groups are compared. Two groups might have the same range, but in one group almost all the measures might cluster closely together, while in the other they might be distributed over the entire range.

The standard deviation. By far the most important measure of variability is the standard deviation. It is important not only as a measure of variability but as a step in many other statistical operations. To explain the nature of the standard deviation, we shall give its formula and show in a very simple illustration how it may be calculated. The formula for the standard deviation is as follows:

$$\text{S.D.} = \sqrt{\frac{\Sigma x^2}{N}}$$

where S.D. is the standard deviation (another symbol is the small Greek letter sigma, σ)

Σ is the sum of (a sign indicating the operation of adding)

x is the deviation of each score from the mean $(X - M)$

N is the number of scores

The formula can be read like a recipe. It says to do these things, which are illustrated in Table 16.7:

1. Find the mean (M).
2. Subtract the mean from each score $(X - M)$ to get a deviation or difference (x).
3. Square each deviation (these squares will always be positive in sign, though the x may be either positive or negative).
4. Sum the squared deviations.
5. Divide the sum of squared deviations by N (the number of scores).
6. Take the square root of this ratio to get the standard deviation.

Table 16.7   Calculation of the Standard Deviation

X	x	x^2
8	2	4
10	4	16
2	−4	16
4	−2	4
6	0	0
$\Sigma X = 30$		$\Sigma x^2 = 40$

$$M = \frac{\Sigma X}{N} = \frac{30}{5} = 6 \qquad \text{S.D.} = \sqrt{\frac{\Sigma x^2}{N}} = \sqrt{\frac{40}{5}} = \sqrt{8} = 2.8$$

▶ The purpose of this study * was to devise an objective test that would help in selecting people to do graduate work in psychology. The test questions were in the form of analogies, one example of which is

Orchestra:Violinist::Test (1. Battery   2. Stem analysis   3. Item 4. Validity   .) In this example, choice 3 is the correct answer.

After some preliminary work, including the elimination of items not found suitable, the test consisted of two virtually equivalent forms of 75 items each.

The test was then given to graduating seniors, first-year graduate students, second-year graduate students, and third-year graduate students. As the first table clearly brings out, the average scores increased in the expected direc-

Results of Administering Psycho-Analogies Test to Various Groups of Students

Group	Number	Mean	Standard deviation
Graduating seniors	33	51.7	7.37
First-year graduate students	50	57.7	6.91
Second-year graduate students	44	61.6	6.46
Third-year graduate students	31	66.6	4.25

tion, and the variability also decreased somewhat in the same direction. That is, third-year graduate students on the average did best on the test—and also varied less among themselves; then came second-year graduate students, then first-year graduate students, and finally seniors. This argues, of course, that the test does have some usefulness in selecting persons who will do well in graduate study.

An interesting fact about these results, however, is the overlapping between the groups. Thus, there was one graduating senior who did better than the average third-year graduate student, and there was one third-year graduate student who barely exceeded the average for graduating seniors. The same kind of remarks can be made about the other two groups.

Incidentally, the above results are based on one form of the test alone. Both forms were given to these groups, half of each group receiving form A first and then form B, and the other half taking them in reverse order.

* Abraham S. Levine, "Minnesota Psycho-Analogies Test," *Journal of Applied Psychology,* 34:300–305, 1950.

Another way in which to get an impression of the meaning of the standard deviation is to look at its relation to the normal distribution (see Figure 16.13). Taking the mean as a point of origin, we can lay off a scale in standard-deviation units in both the positive and the negative direction. Right where the curve changes direction (stops bending one way and begins bending in another) is one standard deviation unit away from the mean. In a normal distribution, about two-thirds of the scores fall within one standard deviation on each side of the mean, about 95 per cent within two standard deviations, and over 99 per cent within three standard deviations. Any score

Scores on form A correlated with those on form B to the extent of .89. And scores on a preliminary form of the test correlated with final-examination grades in various courses to the extent of .41 to .74.

Frequency Distributions of Psycho-Analogy Test Results

		Group					Group		
Score	Seniors	1st-yr. grad.	2d-yr. grad.	3d-yr. grad.	Score	Seniors	1st-yr. grad.	2d-yr. grad.	3d-yr. grad.
74				1	53	3	1	3	
73			1	1	52		2	2	1
72				1	51	1	2		
71			2	1	50		2		
70		1	1	4	49	1	1		
69		1	2	3	48	2		1	
68		2	2	2	47				
67			3	4	46	1			
66		1	4	3	45	1	1		
65	1	2	1	4	44	2			
64		1	4		43	1			
63		3	3	2	42	1			
62	2	4	2	2	41				
61	1	3	3	2	40		1		
60	1	4			39				
59		2	1		38	1			
58	2	5			37	1			
57	1	3	2		36	1			
56	1	2	2		35				
55	6	3	3		34	1			
54	2	2	2						

in a distribution may be expressed in standard deviation units; it is then called a *standard score* or a *z-score*.

Unlike the range, the standard deviation is based on *all* the scores. It is generally an excellent measure for comparing the variability of two groups or of the same group at different times. Its only important disadvantage is that it is sensitive to extreme measures; a few scores that differ greatly from the others can markedly inflate the size of the standard deviation.

Centile scores. One of the most commonly used methods of expressing a person's place on a distribution scale is by means of centile scores (sometimes called *percentile* scores). It may be desirable to have a more precise measure than to say that a person placed in the upper half or the lower half of his class or even to say that he placed in the upper or lower quarter.

The centile score indicates a point in the distribution below which and above which

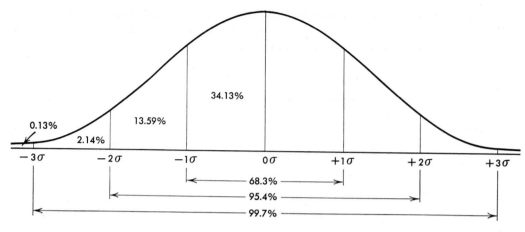

Figure 16.13. Relation of standard deviation units to a normal curve. The figure shows the per cent of scores falling between selected standard deviation limits.

a given percentage of the group falls. For example, the median is the 50th centile point and indicates that one-half of the group scored lower than this point and, of course, one-half scored higher. If, on the other hand, a person scored at the 10th centile point, that would mean that only 10 per cent of the group scored below him while 90 per cent scored above him. In a like manner any other score can be expressed as a centile point.

Measures of Relationship. There are many situations in psychology in which we are interested in knowing the direction and degree of relationship between two variables. For example, we might want to know the extent to which two traits such as intelligence and physical size go together. In selecting students by means of college entrance tests, we may wish to know how well the tests predict college success as measured by grade-point averages. The user of a test may wish to know also how reliable the test is. These are a few of the many situations where the technique of *correlation* is useful as a way of measuring relationships among variables.

Correlation diagrams. One of the best ways to approach the subject of correlation

is to consider correlation diagrams, which are graphs of relationship between two variables. Figure 16.14 shows three kinds of relationship between variables. The graph, or correlation diagram, on the left pictures a *positive* relationship: The higher the college-entrance-examination scores, the higher on the average are grade-point averages. As one variable increases, so does the other, which means that the relationship is positive. At the same time, the relationship is not perfect in the sense that the order of scores agrees perfectly with the order of grade-points. If the relationship were perfectly positive, all the points would lie on the same line beginning in the lower left and slanting to the upper right of the graph.

The graph in the middle pictures a *negative* relationship between two variables; that is, as one variable increases, the other decreases. For example, the correlation between scores on an intelligence test and time to complete a test depending on knowledge of word meanings might be negative, since those who are more intelligent require less time on the average.

Whether a relationship is positive or negative has nothing to do with its degree

—a negative relationship may be just as great as a positive one. For instance, knowledge of a subject as measured by ratings on an oral examination may be correlated positively with the number of correct items on an objective test and negatively with the number of errors. On many personality tests the choice as to which end of the scale is the high end and which is the low is arbitrary. A negative correlation is just as useful as a positive one.

The graph on the right shows a zero relationship, or no relationship at all. As one variable changes, the other shows no systematic change. For example, intelligence and physical size have little or no relationship in adults. (Some investigators have reported a slightly positive relationship.) Bright people are about as likely to be tall as to be short, and tall people are about as likely to be bright as dull. The two variables simply are unrelated.

Ways of measuring correlation. There are a number of different ways of measuring correlation. We shall discuss briefly two of these. One method is to compute what is termed the *product-moment correlation coefficient,* the symbol for which is *r.* This measure, *r,* varies between $+1.00$, which indicates a perfect positive correlation, through .00, which indicates no rela-

tionship at all, to -1.00, which indicates a perfect negative relationship. In practice, perfect positive or negative relationships are not obtained. Reliability coefficients, which are correlations usually between equivalent parts of a test or successive administrations of a test, over .90 are frequently obtained. Correlations between independent measures, as between intelligence test scores and grade-point averages, generally run much lower, from zero to about .80, with values around .50 being very common.

Another way of measuring the degree of relationship is to compute the *rank-difference correlation coefficient,* the symbol for which is *rho* (ρ). It is proper to compute rho when data are in the form of ranks. For example, two supervisors may each rank six employees in order from the most to the least efficient. Rho, which is really only a special case of product-moment correlation, is calculated directly from these ranks, or from scores which have been put in ranked form. Rho varies from $+1.00$ through .00 to -1.00 and has an interpretation like that of *r* as discussed above.

Correlation and causation. The fact that two measures are correlated is not to be interpreted as meaning one causes the other. This is sometimes the case, but we

Figure 16.14. Examples of correlation diagrams. Each dot represents a pair of scores—one on one variable and the other on the other variable.

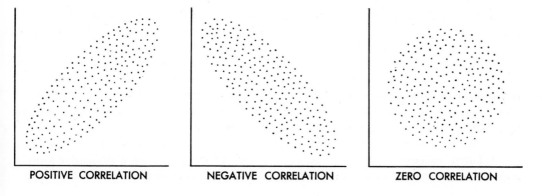

POSITIVE CORRELATION   NEGATIVE CORRELATION   ZERO CORRELATION

should be careful in making any such inference. Let us take height and weight as an example. In general the taller the person the greater his weight, though there are many exceptions. This being true we should expect to get, and do get, a positive correlation between the two measures. It is quite different, however, to assume that greater height *causes* greater weight or that greater weight *causes* greater height. Correlation means, then, that the measures tend to vary together, that as height increases weight tends to increase.

Sampling. In our discussion of statistics thus far we have considered what statisticians call *descriptive statistics*. Our purpose was to find simple and informative ways for describing the quantitative characteristics of a set of data. But the data which we obtain are almost always only a sample from a larger population about which we wish to generalize. For example, in a public-opinion poll, we sample only a part of the total population about which we desire information. When a test is standardized, we typically select what we hope is a representative sample from the population to which the test is to be applied in order to get norms in terms of which we can evaluate individual scores. When we do an experiment, such as one involving two groups, our subjects are only a sample of the larger population from which the sample was selected. In view of these considerations, we should take a brief look at *sampling statistics*, the kind of statistics that has to do with statistical reasoning.

Representative sampling. A sample should be representative of the population about which we are going to generalize. If we wish to generalize about a population of voters, we should sample from those who have a high probability of voting. If we wish to make statements about the relative success of arts-and-sciences and business-school students in the business world, we need to get a representative sample of each of these populations. It is not always easy to get a representative sample, and in nearly any study we must make some compromise with what would be ideal. But we should always be prepared to evaluate the risks in such departures from ideal conditions and to be properly cautious in drawing conclusions from such data.

One technique of sampling is *random sampling*. In random sampling every member of the population is given an equal chance of being selected. We could, for example, get a random sample of the students in a university by putting each student's name on a tag, mixing these tags thoroughly, and then, without looking, taking out as many tags as we wanted students in our sample. A second method of sampling is what is termed *quota sampling*. This method is named from the fact that the subjects are selected so that a certain percentage falls into each category. For example, in a political poll we may want the sample to have the same proportions as does the population of voters in regard to matters such as sex, political affiliation, and socioeconomic class. When properly done, quota sampling yields reliable results with smaller samples than does random sampling.

Sampling variability. Suppose that we were to take a sample from a population and compute its mean. Then suppose that we took a second sample, and a third, and so on, each time computing the mean. These sample means would differ from one another. The statistic in question, the mean, would vary from sample to sample, i.e., it would show sampling variability. All statistics—means, correlation coefficients, standard deviations, etc.—have sampling variability.

If so, then how much confidence can we have in the results of a particular sample, even if it was selected by a method which *in the long run* is representative? What guarantee is there that the correlation between an aptitude test and later achievement as reported in a particular study is not too high or too low as compared with the correlation in the population? What assurance is there, when we compare two groups in an experiment, that the difference between their means is not simply a matter of chance, of sampling variability? We shall not discuss here the statistical methods for dealing with these questions beyond saying that the mathematics of probability is employed. A good research report will indicate the reliability and significance of its results in terms of such probability statements.

SUMMARY

We are alike, yet we are all different, and these differences are great enough to be significant.

The earliest scientific interest in the way people vary from each other appeared in astronomy, where differences in the so-called "personal equation" had an important bearing on the accuracy of observation. This interest then spread to other branches of science, largely as a result of the work of Sir Francis Galton.

Though people do differ from each other, they usually differ in a predictable manner. Such differences are ordinarily in degree rather than in kind, are generally more or less continuous from the smallest to the largest measurement, tend to pile up near the center of the distribution, and usually contain about as many high measurements as low ones. Few, if any, physical or behavioral aspects of the individual are exempt from these general rules about individual differences.

Since people do vary so greatly, to understand and deal effectively with these differences requires the use of statistics. One of the most useful concepts of statistics is the frequency distribution, which enables us to order a great variety of measurements. Frequency distributions are often represented graphically. Such a distribution may appear in the form of the normal curve, a skewed curve, or a bimodal curve (among others). The frequency polygon and the bar graph are two ways of presenting data in the form of a graph.

The principal measures of central tendency are the mean, which is the arithmetical average; the median, which is the point above and below which 50 per cent of the measurements lie; and the mode, the most frequent measurement or score. The chief measures of variability are the range, which is the difference between the highest and the lowest measurement; the standard deviation, which is the square root of the sum of the squares of the individual deviations from the mean; and centile scores, which give the percentage falling below a given score.

Another important idea is that of correlation, the relationship between two variables. Two well-known coefficients of correlation are the product-moment coefficient, calculated directly from the measurements themselves; and the rank-difference coefficient, calculated from the ranks of the data in each distribution. We must always be on our guard against interpreting correlation as cause. It may sometimes be, but it often is not.

In sampling, the problem is the extent to which a relatively small number of measurements are representative of all possible measurements of this same sort. We can never be sure that ideal representation has been achieved, but we attempt to achieve it through methods such as random sampling and quota sampling. Sampling techniques such as these are at the heart of determining the reliability of a mean or of the significance of differences between two such measures.

QUESTIONS

1. Discuss briefly the history of our interest in individual differences.

2. Why do we need to use statistics in psychology?

3. How would you attempt to prove that differences between people are great enough to be significant?

4. What is meant by saying that people vary in a predictable manner? What would you usually expect to be true of a set of measurements representing variation in people?

5. What is meant by "item analysis" in connection with the development of a psychological test?

6. Compare and contrast validity and reliability as they apply to testing.

7. How do you determine (a) the validity of a test, (b) the reliability of a test?

8. What is a frequency distribution? Why are frequency distributions used extensively?

9. Compare and contrast (a) the frequency polygon and a bar graph; (b) the normal curve and a skewed curve.

10. Distinguish among (a) the mean, (b) the median, and (c) the mode as measures of central tendency.

11. What is (a) the range; (b) the standard deviation? How is each calculated, and what is its usefulness?

12. Discuss the concept of correlation, including positive and negative correlation.

13. Compare and contrast (a) the product-moment coefficient of correlation, and (b) the rank-order coefficient.

14. What are some of the problems we encounter when we treat a sample as representative of an entire population?

15. Compare and contrast (a) random sampling, and (b) quota sampling.

SUGGESTED READINGS

Anastasi, A., and J. P. Foley, Jr.: *Differential Psychology,* Macmillan, New York, 1949.
> (A comprehensive text on psychological differences among groups, with chapters on subnormal and genius and on sexual, racial, and socioeconomic differences.)

Cox, C. M.: *Genetic Studies of Genius,* Stanford University Press, Stanford, Calif., 1926, vol. II.
> (Reports on study of 300 mentally gifted.)

Cronbach, Lee J.: *Essentials of Psychological Testing,* Harper, New York, 1949.
> (An introductory text in the field of psychological testing.)

Edwards, Allen L.: *Statistical Methods for the Behavioral Sciences,* Rinehart, New York, 1954.
> (A description of the application of statistical methods to the data of the behavioral sciences.)

Guilford, J. P.: *Fundamental Statistics in Psychology and Education,* 3d ed., McGraw-Hill, New York, 1956.
> (A standard text in statistics.)

Underwood, B. J., C. P. Duncan, J. A. Taylor, and J. W. Cotton: *Elementary Statistics,* Appleton-Century-Crofts, New York, 1954.
> (An elementary treatment of statistical methods in psychology.)

17 INTELLIGENCE AND APTITUDES

One of the purposes of this book is to lead to a better understanding of ourselves and other people. The behavior of anyone bears some relationship to his intelligence. Therefore, if we are to understand his behavior, it becomes necessary to have some appreciation of the level at which he is functioning intellectually. In this chapter we shall try to explain what intelligence is and, to some extent, the part it plays in behavior.

THE NATURE OF INTELLIGENCE

We usually think of intelligence in terms of how an individual behaves. This is, actually, a very practical consideration, for it is usually more defensible to say that a person has behaved intelligently (or stupidly) than it is to say that this person has (or lacks) intelligence. This point of view has been presented in the following words: [1]

We may first refute any assumption that mental tests have any mysterious power of detecting intelligence as an entity apart from life performance. There is no such measure at present, and the probability is that there will never be any direct measure of intelligence. In fact, it is very doubtful if there is any such entity as intelligence. It is much more defensible to say that a person *acts intelligently* than to say that he has *intelligence*. The term "intelligent behavior" is a description of behavior under certain conditions. We can generally agree on what behavior is intelligent even though we might never agree about the mysterious "intelligence" within the individual. By analogy we apply the term intelligent to

[1] Carroll A. Whitmer, "Has Man Measured His Intelligence?" *Pitt, University of Pittsburgh Quarterly*, 1941, No. 9, pp. 38–39.

Figure 17.1. Beauty is no deterrent to intelligence or vocational accomplishments. This young woman achieved top scholastic honors in civil engineering and then became a college instructor in this field. (Courtesy of Columbia University.)

the following paragraphs we shall discuss some of the ways in which people differ as to intelligence.

One indication of intelligence is how a person learns. But to grasp the meaning of intelligence we must also concern ourselves with *what* he learns as well as with *how* he learns it. Even this does not tell the whole story. Some people learn well, rapidly, and very much in certain areas of behavior, while others do quite poorly in these areas but at the same time do well in others.

We think of intelligence as being composed of many abilities—or factors, as psychologists choose to call them. Or to speak in more general terms, we might say that the layman frequently, and perhaps usually, thinks of intelligence as the ability to learn—particularly in school situations. But intelligence involves the ability to solve problems of many kinds. It also involves the ability to recognize relationships, to recall, to evaluate, to choose wisely or effectively, and to apply parts of past experiences to present behavioral situations. Thus, in the application of the knowledge and skills which a person has acquired, we see evidence of his intelligence. When a person faces a novel situation or problem and must make some adjustment to it, the adjustment is made in keeping with his level of intellectual functioning. Though he has never faced a similar situation before, the intelligent person is able to deal with it more effectively than is the person who is lacking in intelligence.

the person who acts intelligently. People are considered more or less intelligent on the basis of their behavior and in the practical world past behavior is considered to be the best basis for predicting future behavior.

Intelligence is not a "thing" which one can see, hold, touch, etc. Instead, intelligence is a way of behaving. As such, then, we may expect, and do find, that people differ widely in this respect. They differ not only in the degree of intelligence they possess but also in the kind, i.e., the different mental abilities they have. These abilities are discussed later in this chapter. The typical behavior of some people is consistently at a high level, and they are said to be intelligent. Likewise, the typical behavior of others is consistently at a much lower level and they are said to be dull, stupid, or significantly lacking in intelligence.

Two people may function intellectually at about the same level and still vary greatly in the kind of intelligence they possess. In

INTELLIGENCE TESTING

The term "mental tests" first appeared in the psychological literature in 1890. In that year James McKeen Cattell published an article in *Mind* in which he described some tests which he had devised for use with his students at the University of Pennsylvania. In these tests he attempted to measure keenness of vision and hearing, color vision, color preferences, sensitivity to pain, rote memory, mental imagery, and reaction time. Cattell was attempting to find a practical way of measuring these abilities in the hope that he could determine any given student's chances of success in college.

"Mental test" is a term which was once used as a synonym for—or in place of—"psychological test." Indeed, a few years ago the term "mental test" was the popular term for tests in general, having appeared in the title of texts in the field.[2] Today, however, we prefer "psychological test."

There is a thoroughly sound reason for this particular preference. The term "mental" suggests the intellectual and thus makes us think of intelligence tests or at least of tests of mental ability. Now, as we have already seen, psychological tests deal with such things but are by no means restricted to them. The term "mental" is appropriate enough if we are attempting to find how well a freshman will probably do in college or how quickly an apprentice will master his classroom training. But suppose we are measuring hand-eye coordination or dexterity in assembling a relay or even capacity to learn to be a stenographer. It is obvious that the term "mental test" does not fit these tests well. On the other hand, any or all of them may appropriately be called "psychological tests."

The Binet Scale. The first really usable scale for the measurement of intelligence was that introduced by the French psychologist Alfred Binet in 1905. For a number of years, Binet had been working with problems of placing children in school. In 1904 the Minister of Education assigned him the task of devising some means of distinguishing between the children who could profitably attend the regular school and the ones who could not. Binet was seeking a means of measuring the ability to *acquire* knowledge rather than of determining what had already been learned.

Binet, in collaboration with Simon, devised a scale consisting of thirty items. These items ranged in difficulty from those suited to low-grade idiots to those suited to children in the upper elementary grades. The following examples give an idea of the type of items employed by Binet:

1. Coordination of movements of head and eyes in following a lighted match.
6. Execution of simple orders and imitation of gestures.
9. Enumerating objects shown in pictures.
20. Stating similarities of two familiar objects.
30. Distinguishing between abstract terms.

Items for the test were selected for the various age levels by trying the items out on children in these age groups. In order to be acceptable for six-year-olds, an item had to be too easy for seven-year-olds and too difficult for five-year-olds. The same procedure was used for the other age levels.

With the revision of the scale in 1908, Binet introduced the concept of mental age (MA). Average scores were determined for each age level. Then later, when the scale was administered to other people, the scores would be compared with the table of norms. If, for example, a person made a score comparable to that made by the average seven-year-old child, then this person, regardless of his chronological age, was said to have a mental age of seven. This whole concept, of course, is based on the assumption that on an *average* a person matures mentally at the same rate that he does chronologically.

There is some fallacy in saying that a person older or younger has the intelligence of a seven-year-old child even though he may get the same score on a test. While it is true that the intelligence possessed by this person, in terms of score achieved, compares with that of the seven-year-old, it is still not quite the same. Despite this, however, this person still scores a mental age of seven on the test.

The Stanford-Binet Scale. Since the first intelligence scale was developed by a

[2] See, for example, Frank N. Freeman, *Mental Tests,* rev. ed., Houghton Mifflin, Boston, 1939.

Ability to count four objects shows her concept of that number

Three oral directions are to be executed in proper sequence

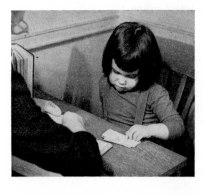

Perception of likenesses and differences measures discriminating reactions

Building a bridge with three blocks measures motor coordination

Choosing the prettiest picture measures cultural patterns and esthetic judgment

Frenchman, it did not lend itself to use with American children without revision. There were revisions by several American psychologists, but none was so well received as the one by Terman at Stanford University. This scale was introduced in 1916 and for the following twenty years was the most widely used test of its kind in this country. Several factors contributed to the widespread use of this test. One of the principal ones was the introduction of the intelligence quotient (which will be explained a little further on) as the basic way of expressing test results. Users of the intelligence test—"mental test," as it was then called—had for some time recognized the inadequacy of the mental age as an indication of the child's intelligence.

Despite the wide use made of this scale it had certain obvious weaknesses. It provided tests from age three to superior adult, but its effectiveness at the extremes of this age range was much less than in the middle range. Another serious limitation was the fact that it provided only one form, so there was no provision for immediate or early retesting.

The New Revised Stanford-Binet Scale made its appearance in 1937 after ten years of intensive research, study, and work. In this scale the attempt had been made to correct the limitations of the first scale. The standardization group was increased to nearly 3,000 cases selected from many areas of the United States both urban and rural. Two comparable forms, L and M, were made available, and the range was extended from an age of two years through four levels of adult intelligence. Six subtests are available at most age levels, and two months of mental growth is allowed for each subtest passed.

Intelligence Quotient. It was about 1912 that William Stern suggested that a term to express the ratio between mental age and chronological age would be both meaningful and convenient. The suggestion seemingly passed unnoticed until Terman made use of it in the Stanford-Binet Scale. This term has come to be known as the *intelligence quotient* or IQ. It is derived from the following formula:

$$IQ = \frac{MA}{CA} \times 100$$

in which MA is the mental age as determined by the subject's performance on a test of intelligence, and CA is his "real age" or the length of time that has passed from the time of his birth to the time of testing. This ratio is then multiplied by 100 simply to move the decimal point two places to the right and express the IQ in terms of a whole number. The usual procedure is to express both MA and CA in months. For example, if a child aged six years eight months (80 months) has an MA

Figure 17.2. This series of pictures illustrates the administration of the Stanford-Binet intelligence test for children. The child is shown taking various subtests ranging in level from three to six years. (Courtesy of New York University Testing and Advisement Center.)

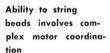
Ability to string beads involves complex motor coordination

Folding a paper triangle demonstrates coordination and spatial visualization

Telling what is wrong in distorted pictures shows analytical sense

of eight years (96 months), what is his IQ? We substitute in the formula and

$$IQ = \frac{96}{80} \times 100 = 120$$

Since the introduction of the Stanford-Binet Scale in 1916, a number of tests have been developed for the purpose of measuring intelligence. Many of these tests yield a single score or IQ. When we have only one such score, we actually know very little about the intelligence of the person tested. All the tests do not tap or measure the same abilities, and therefore, though the score totals may be the same, they do not carry the same meaning. When we use the term "IQ" it is a good idea to indicate its source, that is, the test from which it was obtained. Unless we are familiar with the test used, even this does not have much meaning. However, those using the test, if not already familiar with it, can find a good deal about it from the test manual or other sources.

The IQ, as shown here, is a very convenient way of expressing a person's level of intelligence, but we should exercise caution in interpreting its meaning. It is so easy to think that a person "actually has" a certain IQ and that once it has been determined he will always have it. Furthermore, we sometimes think of the IQ as a sort of ceiling or limit on the intellectual achievement of a person, a ceiling or limit which he cannot influence materially.

The intelligence quotient of a person simply represents his score on a certain intelligence test. If he were to take another test, he might—indeed, he probably would—obtain a somewhat different score. In unusual cases, the score might be very different, though ordinarily it would be close to the first.

The point is that, though tests are useful, we need to be careful in interpreting their results. There are circumstances, in other words, where they can be helpful in the appraisal of people, but since they are only human instruments, made by human beings, they can be in error. We cannot assume that two people who have the same IQ have identical intelligence. Psychologists have demonstrated that intelligence is made up of many abilities or factors. In many cases the totals may be the same but the value of the several components may vary widely. This is just one difficulty that has arisen from use of the IQ.

The Wechsler Scales. In 1939 David Wechsler, chief clinical psychologist at Bellevue Psychiatric Hospital, introduced the Wechsler-Bellevue Intelligence Scale. He believed that the whole concept of IQ based on mental age, as it had been used for two decades, was not truly representative of adult intelligence. The MA is only a score obtained on a test.

One of the significant differences between the Wechsler scale and the Stanford-Binet is that the former is a point scale on which the IQ is derived by comparing the performance of the subject with the average performance of those in his particular age group. The authors of the Stanford-Binet assume mental maturity to be reached, on an average, at fifteen years. In test-retest situations a point is reached beyond which there is no further increase in MA score, and the authors have, therefore, accepted fifteen as being the maximum. The result is, then, that an adult's performance is not compared with that of other adults but instead with that of a fifteen-year-old. To Wechsler this was unrealistic and inadequate.

The Wechsler scale yields three separate measures of intelligence: (1) the Verbal Scale, (2) the Performance Scale, and (3) the Full Scale. The Full Scale is a composite of the other two. The Performance Scale is designed to get at a measure of intellectual functioning in which a minimum of verbal ability is required. The inclusion of such a scale helps to avoid one of the frequent criticisms of the Stanford-Binet—that

Figure 17.3. A performance test used in measuring intelligence. Here the subject is (A) assembling the parts of a jigsaw puzzle, and (B) arranging blocks to form a design like the pattern in the booklet before him.

it is too heavily loaded with the verbal factor.

In the Verbal Scale there are six separate subtests:

1. The *Information* test consists of questions concerning factual data. To be able to answer all these questions correctly requires a background of rather broad general information. Questions similar to these are used: "Where is Argentina?" "How many quarts make a gallon?" The arrangement of the questions roughly approximates the order of difficulty.

2. The *Comprehension* test is made up of questions which call for an understanding and explanation of commonplace situations. The quality of the response given is important in determining the number of points allowed.

3. The *Digit Span* subtest calls for the subject to repeat after the examiner a series of numbers progressing from three to nine digits. The second part of this test requires the subject to repeat the numbers in reverse order. For example, if the number given by the examiner is 6-4-7, the subject repeats it as 7-4-6. Wechsler found this to be a rather poor test for measuring intelligence generally but an extremely good measure for discriminating at the lower levels. This is his justification for keeping the test in the list.

4. The *Similarities* test calls for the identi-

fication of similarities between certain objects or concepts. This has proved to be one of the best measures on the scale and includes such items as "What is the difference between 'idleness' and 'laziness'?"

5. In the *Arithmetic* test simple verbal reasoning problems are used. These ten problems are arranged in order of difficulty.

6. *Vocabulary* includes a list of words beginning with simple, commonly used words and becoming progressively difficult. In the original scale the vocabulary test was used as an alternate, but it proved to be a very useful measure. In the later edition it was included as one of the regular tests.

The Performance Scale consists of five subtests:

1. The *Picture Arrangement* test consists of several groups of pictures similar to comic-strip drawings. These are presented to the subject, each on a separate card, in a disarranged sequence and the subject is required to rearrange them in such a way as to make the best story.

2. The *Picture Completion* test is made up of a number of drawings in each of

which some important part is missing. The subject is asked to name the missing part.

3. In the *Block Design* test the task is to arrange four, nine, and then sixteen colored blocks in such a way as to reproduce a series of designs which are given the subject one at a time.

4. The *Object Assembly* test is similar to a jig-saw puzzle. The task is to arrange the pieces so as to make a manikin, profile, and hand.

5. The *Digit Symbol* test is one in which the subject is required to substitute a given symbol for each digit from 0 to 9, the digits being given in an unordered series. It yields a measure of speed of learning.

The scale is individually administered and requires considerable skill on the part of the examiner to administer, score, and interpret. Points are scored for accuracy of response, and in some instances bonus points are allowed on the basis of time of response. These points are totaled and then converted to scaled scores, after which they are compared with the norm for the age group of the subject to obtain the IQ.

In 1945 the Wechsler Intelligence Scale for Children was introduced. This scale is commonly referred to as the WISC and in structure is very similar to the scale described above.

A recent revision (1955) of the scale, the Wechsler Adult Intelligence Scale, has been made available. After using the earlier scale for nearly fifteen years its author sought to correct some of its limitations by extending the norms upward to include an older age group and enlarging the standardization group to make it more representative of the entire population.

Group Tests of Intelligence. With the introduction of the Stanford-Binet Scale in 1916 came the focusing of much attention on the subject of measuring intelligence. This and other tests held promise of being valuable aids in selection, classifying, and assignment of people in many fields. Level of intelligence seemed to offer a useful basis for the selection of men for officer training in World War I. Since the instruments available were designed for individual testing, however, they posed a serious problem for the testing of large groups of men. This led to the selection of a group of psychologists who were assigned the task of constructing a test suitable for administration to whole groups of individuals.

The Army Alpha test. Many of the psychologists of the day had been working independently on their own ideas for a test of intelligence. In the interest of the war effort these men made the results of their work available to the group. This resulted in the development of the first group test for the measurement of intelligence—the Army Alpha. Scores obtained from the Alpha were compared with results obtained from the same subjects by use of the Stanford-Binet, and a significant correlation was found.

The Alpha was found to have some limitations. It was a verbal test and as such required some skill in reading. It was thus found to be unsuitable for use with illiterates. This resulted in the development of the Army Beta, which attempted to minimize the influence of reading and writing. The real purpose was to test for the individual's intelligence and not the extent to which he had developed skill in these areas. It consisted of a series of pencil mazes, groups of figures in which the one that did not belong was to be indicated, etc. Since the Beta correlated significantly with the Alpha, the two to a certain extent were measuring the same factors.

As indicated earlier, the Alpha was the test that pioneered the field of group testing of intelligence. There is little question but that it was administered to more people than any other test up to the time of World War II. By that time many changes had taken place in our culture, and the Alpha was no longer believed to be adequate to do the job of testing inductees in this second conflict.

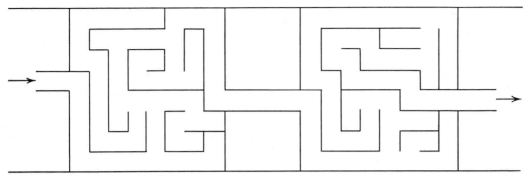

Which is the shortest path through the maze?

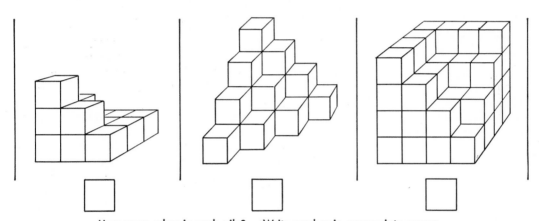

How many cubes in each pile?   Write number in appropriate square.

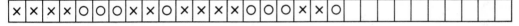

Complete the series.

Figure 17.4. The Army Beta test used during World War I was made up of tests such as those shown here. Performance of these tests required a minimum of verbal ability. (Courtesy of the Psychological Corporation, New York.)

The Otis Self-Administering Tests of Mental Ability. The Otis S-A, introduced in 1922, was among the earliest group tests. One form was designed for use with senior high school and college students and adults. Another, the intermediate form, is suitable for use with elementary and junior high school students. These tests have been revised and made into a second series known as the Otis Quick-Scoring Tests of Mental Ability. These, at three levels are Alpha, for grades 1 to 4; Beta, for grades 4 to 9; and Gamma, for grade 9 to adult. The S-A series, known as the higher examination, consists of seventy-five mixed items arranged in order of difficulty. Involved are vocabulary, sentence meaning, analogies, proverbs, and number series items designed to measure verbal, arithmetical, and spatial abilities.

Norms have been determined for thirty-minute and twenty-minute time limits. A revision by Wonderlic, which he called the Personnel Test, has a twelve-minute time limit and is essentially the same as the S-A.

The Army General Classification Test (*AGCT*). Because of the highly technical nature of the jobs to be done in the armed services by the time of World War II, there was a great need for an instrument to measure general learning ability. The result was the development of the AGCT by a group of Army psychologists in the Personnel Research Section, Classification and Replacement Branch, the Adjutant General's Office. There were four comparable forms of the test, and between 1940 and 1945 it was administered to every literate soldier who was inducted. In all, this test was administered to more than 12 million men and women. It is quite unlikely that any other test has ever been administered to such a large sample of the population. The test is in three parts and was designed to measure general learning ability in three separate areas. These areas are (1) vocabulary, which gives a measure of verbal ability; (2) arithmetic word problems, to measure number and reasoning abilities; and (3) block counting, designed to measure ability at spatial perception.

The AGCT was revised, and in 1945 this revision replaced the first edition for Army use. The original test was then released for civilian use and as such has been widely employed.

Thurstone's Primary Mental Abilities. Until about 1930 most of the theorists had thought of intelligence as a unitary trait. In 1932 L. L. Thurstone and his wife, Thelma Gwinn Thurstone, began a series of research studies at the Psychometric Laboratory of the University of Chicago. Through use of factor analysis, they came to the conclusion that intelligence can best be thought of as several different abilities.

In their work the Thurstones were able to isolate eight primary mental abilities, and they indicated that there may be more to add to the list as the research continues.

Science Research Associates of Chicago publish the Primary Mental Abilities Tests, and from the manual we get the following descriptions of the eight abilities which have been isolated:

1. *Verbal Meaning* (V) is the ability to understand ideas expressed in words. It is used in any activities in which information is obtained by reading or listening to words.

2. *Space* (S) is the ability to think about objects in two or three dimensions. It is difficult to describe verbally, for it has nothing to do with words. It is perhaps best described as the ability to imagine how an object or figure will look when it is rotated, to visualize objects in two or three dimensions, and to see the relations of an arrangement of objects in space.

3. *Reasoning* (R) is the ability to solve logical problems—to foresee and plan. It is probably the most important of the mental abilities. The person with good reasoning ability can solve problems, foresee consequences, analyze a situation on the basis of past experience, and make and carry out plans according to recognizable facts.

4. *Number* (N) is the ability to work with figures—to handle simple quantitative problems rapidly and accurately. It is one of the abilities easiest to explain and demonstrate, since it involves primarily speed and accuracy in handling numbers.

5. *Word Fluency* (W) is the ability to write and talk easily. It differs from verbal meaning because it concerns the speed and ease with which words can be used, rather than the degree of understanding of verbal concepts.

6. *Memory* (M) is the ability to recall past experiences.

7. *Perceptual Speed* (P) is the ability to locate visual details rapidly and accurately. Activities requiring recognition of likenesses and differences bring out this ability.

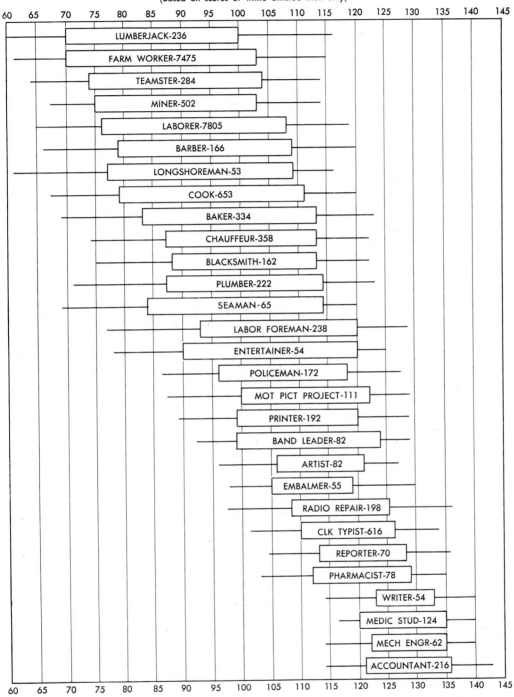

Figure 17.5. *Army General Classification Test scores of men in various civilian occupational groups. (Courtesy of Science Research Associates, Chicago.)*

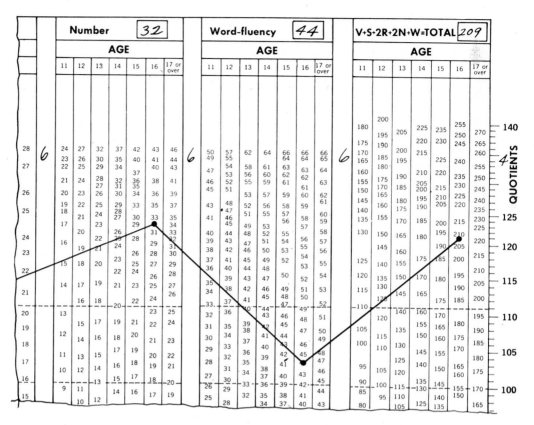

Figure 17.6. Performance of a student on the Primary Mental Abilities Test. Do you see how a wide difference in the various abilities could still result in the same general average? (Courtesy of Science Research Associates, Chicago.)

8. *Motor* (Mo) is the ability to coordinate eye and hand movements.

When we measure these primary mental abilities, a wide range of individual differences is found. Some people consistently score high in each area; others consistently score low in all areas. Then there are those who are extremely high in some and extremely low in others. It is just this sort of problem, then, that one faces in trying to give real meaning to a single score as a measure of intelligence. The single score, as for example, an IQ of 114, tells us nothing about the differences in the various abilities which go to make up this total.

The profile chart, Figure 17.6, shows the performance of one subject when tested

on five of the primary mental abilities. Just a brief look at this profile tells us that this person could have had many other combinations of mental ability and still have the same general level of performance.

Many other instruments have been developed for group testing of intelligence which will be treated in later courses.

LEVELS OF INTELLIGENCE

Growth in Intelligence. Test scores, taken as indications of intelligence, for the most part increase from early childhood to some point approaching the adult level. A point is reached beyond which these scores do not increase. The average age at which this is reached is not agreed upon. Some say it is as early as thirteen years and others as late as the early twenties. Whatever this point is, it is taken to mean that mental maturity has been reached. The first Stanford-Binet took sixteen years as the maximum chronological age to be used in the formula. From later research the authors of the revised scale concluded that this was too old, and therefore in the revision the maximum was placed at fifteen years.

There are individual differences in rate of growth as well as the point at which the maximum growth is reached. In using a constant denominator for the CA at adult levels there is an implicit assumption that IQ remains constant beyond the maximum point reached. When the MA is used as a basis for IQ, this assumption is fallacious. The fallacy of such an assumption is borne out in the research done by Wechsler.[3]

[3] David Wechsler, *Measurement of Adult Intelligence*, 3d ed., Williams & Wilkins, Baltimore, 1944, pp. 19–35.

Intelligence-test scores gradually increase as the child grows older. At about age thirteen this yearly increment begins to decrease for the average child and reaches a limit at age fifteen (Stanford-Binet). However, for the superior child the increment, though reduced, continues to about age twenty and in some cases even beyond.

At some age, from about fifteen to twenty-two years, intelligence-test scores begin to fall off. This decline is shown in Figure 17.7. If MA scores remained constant, the line of growth after reaching maturity would continue parallel to the base line. This, of course, applies to groups. In some instances, however, older people may show a high degree of test ability.

The interacting influence of heredity *and* environment has been stressed throughout this book. This combination of factors is no less influential in the area of intelligence than in other areas. That a potential for intellectual growth and devel-

Figure 17.7. Mental growth continues until the late teen years, after which, according to this scale, there is a gradual decline. (After David Wechsler, Measurement of Adult Intelligence, Williams & Wilkins, Baltimore, 1944.)

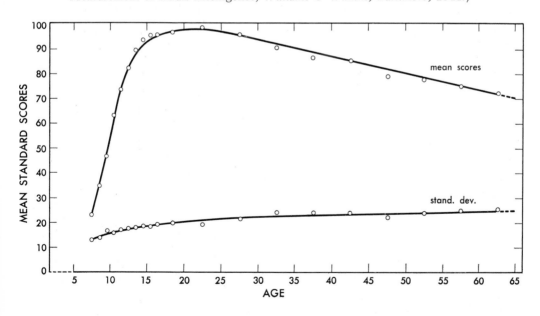

opment is within the child at birth (a product of both heredity and environment) is admitted. However, the postnatal environment exerts a great influence upon the degree of intelligence developed. Not only the richness or barrenness of the environment but also the constancy of the environment within which the child lives is a very important factor.

Range of Intelligence. The range in intelligence extends all the way from zero (theoretical) to an IQ of about 200. The average, however, is thought of as being 100. The distribution of intelligence in the general population approaches that of the normal curve of probability (see Chapter 16). That is to say, there are a few individuals in the extremely high and low ranges of the scale, but the great majority fall in the middle ranges.

In establishing norms for the 1937 Stanford-Binet Scale, Terman and Merrill show the distribution of scores of 2,904 subjects ranging in age from two and one-half to eighteen years. The curve of this distribution is reproduced in Figure 17.8.

The IQ is designed to tell how much above or below the average a given individual is. The average must be obtained from some group. This may be the average of the general population inferred from the measurement of a sample, or it may be the average of an actual group not presumed to be representative of the whole population. Wechsler's classification of intelligence according to IQ and based on the actual measurements (actual ages ten to sixty) is reproduced in Table 17.1.

No one really knows what average intelligence represents. However, on a scale such as the Wechsler it is expressed as some numerical score. On an age scale such as the Stanford-Binet, it is represented by an MA score. Because of their conven-

Figure 17.8. Distribution of IQ in the group on which the Revised Stanford-Binet Scale was standardized. (After Terman and Merrill, Measurement of Intelligence, *Houghton Mifflin, Boston, 1937.)*

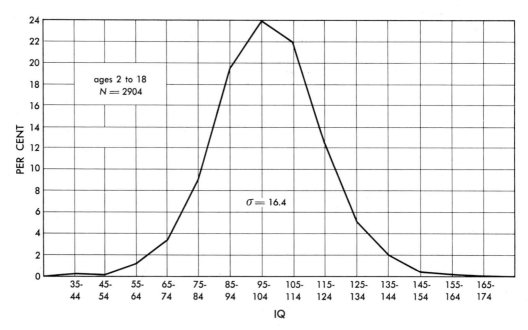

Table 17.1   Intelligence Classification According to IQ—Ages 10–60 (Actual)

Classification	IQ limits	Percentage included
Defective	65 and below	2.2
Borderline	66–79	6.7
Dull normal	80–90	16.1
Average	91–110	50.0
Bright normal	111–119	16.1
Superior	120–127	6.7
Very superior	128 and over	2.2

SOURCE: *David Wechsler*, Measurement of Adult Intelligence, *3d ed., Williams & Wilkins, Baltimore, 1944, p. 40.*

ience the classifications listed in Table 17.1 have come to be widely accepted, but there is considerable difference of opinion as to the range of IQs for each category.

There are some practical considerations that may be given to the range of intelligence. There is some evidence that an optimum level of intelligence is required for success in many jobs. Those who fall below the minimum level find it difficult, or even impossible, to perform the tasks necessary for the job. Those who fall in the categories above the required limits tend to find the job uninteresting and become bored, while those in the optimum range are most likely to succeed. Table 17.2 from Cronbach gives an idea of the intelligence needed to perform successfully on certain jobs.

Degrees of Intelligence. Table 17.1 contains the broad classifications in terms of level of intelligence. It must be borne in mind, however, that the lines separating the various groups are not clearly defined and firmly fixed. Instead of individuals' falling neatly into these groups, the progression is gradual from the very lowest to the highest without clear lines of demarcation. Perhaps it will be helpful to discuss the various classifications in a little more detail.

The feeble-minded. Certainly there can be no single criterion of feeble-mindedness or mental deficiency. However, our chief concern here is with the part that intelligence plays. A widely accepted view is that, so far as intelligence is concerned, anyone who consistently scores 70 or lower in IQ is to be classed as mentally deficient or feeble-minded. These are generally classed into four groups.

1. The idiot. This is the lowest classification on the scale, and in terms of IQ it falls within the range of 0 to 24 points. With this group mental growth is arrested at a very early age and seldom exceeds two years of mental age at maturity. These people are unable to care for their own bodily needs. They cannot even dress themselves, and care of their own physical hygiene is impossible. In an earlier age they were often kept at home, where sometimes people in the community generally did not know of their existence. Now they are usually institutionalized. They rarely learn to speak, and capacity for memory and imagination is almost wholly lacking.

2. The imbecile. This is the next higher level. In terms of IQ the range is usually accepted as being from about 25 to ap-

Table 17.2 Reference Points for Establishing the Meaning of an IQ

IQ	
120	Needed to do acceptable work in a first-class college with normal effort.
114	Mean IQ of children in Middle Western city, from white-collar, skilled-labor families.
107	Mean IQ of high school seniors.
104	Minimum IQ for satisfactory (i.e., average) work in high school, in academic curriculum.
100	Average IQ in unselected population (theoretical).
93	Median IQ of children in eight one-teacher rural schools in Texas.
91	Mean IQ of children in Middle Western city, from low-income, socially depressed homes.
90	Adult of IQ 90 can assemble some parts requiring some judgment, can operate sewing machine where threading and adjusting machine is required. Child of IQ 90 can progress through eight grades with some retardation. With persistence may complete high school with some difficulty.
70	Adult of IQ 70 can set and sort type, do farm work. Child of IQ 70 will be able to attain fifth grade and may do average work there.
60	Adult of IQ 60 can repair furniture, paint toys, harvest vegetables.
50	Adult can do rough painting, simple carpentry, domestic work.
40	Adult can mow lawn, handle freight, do simple laundry work.

SOURCE: *Lee J. Cronbach*, Essentials of Psychological Testing, *Harper, New York, 1949, p. 124.*

proximately 50. Imbeciles do not ordinarily develop beyond the mental level of the average child from 3 to 7 years of age. They may learn to speak, using a very limited vocabulary. They can learn to protect themselves from some of the common physical dangers. They may learn to perform simple tasks but are usually unable to carry them out independently. They are incapable of self-support and remain dependent. How well they are able to adjust to the environment depends upon where they live. In a rural environment, where conditions are less complex than in an urban area, they have a better chance of making a more adequate adjustment. In a situation like this they are usually known, understood, and tolerated more than in a less protected environment where they are not known.

3. The moron. Those in this classification make up the highest level of the mental defectives. In terms of IQ the range usually accepted is from 50 to 70. They make some progress in school and may get as far as the seventh or eighth grade, with two or more years of retardation. They are lacking in creativeness and imagination, and their reasoning powers are very poor. They may learn to perform simple household tasks or unskilled or semiskilled labor. In an environment that is not too complex and demanding they often become self-supporting, marry, and sometimes rear a family.

4. The idiot savant. This is a special classification for a few feeble-minded people who hardly fit into any of the above categories. Although their general level of intellectual functioning is usually about that

of the imbecile, there is one rather strange and unusual difference. The idiot savant shows a level of ability, usually in a single area, that is entirely out of keeping with his general level. This may be, for example, in the field of music. Some such individuals have been reported who, though unable to learn to read the music, played instruments with a degree of skill far above their general level of ability. Such abilities are not limited to the field of music, for they may be in any one of a great number of fields. However, they are ordinarily limited to a single area.

The borderline. Above the mentally defective group and below the normal is another group sometimes referred to as borderline. Obviously these people are rather low in intelligence, but they are generally able to be self-sustaining. They may with a very considerable effort and some retardation do a small amount of high school work, but they are hardly capable of performing at a sufficiently high level to enable them to complete the work of a first-class high school.

The dull normal. This group, with IQs ranging from about 80 to 90, consists of those who are not quite able to measure up to the capabilities of even those in the lower limits of the average range. They are rather dull and slow mentally, and learning does not come easily with them. They may be able to complete high school, but only with a great deal of effort and usually some retardation.

The average. From Table 17.1 we see that this group includes about 50 per cent of the tested population. To the extent that we can generalize from this, it can be said that about half the people in the general population fall into this range.

The bright normal. This group, ranging in IQ from about 110 to 120, is also sometimes referred to as the superior group. Probably most of the college-student population falls within this range. Some who are highly motivated and possess very superior abilities in specific areas may achieve at a high level.

The superior. People in this classification, with IQ range from approximately 120 to 140, are sometimes classed as the very superior. About 6 to 8 per cent of the population would fall in this range. In finding their level of work they often become managers, business executives, and professional people.

The genius. When we take the whole population into consideration we find very few, actually 1 per cent or less, in this group. People in this classification show very unusual ability. Attempts have been made to list some of the people who, on the basis of their accomplishments at an early age, would fall into this grouping. Among those usually included are John Stuart Mill, Goethe, and Einstein.

Group Differences in Intelligence. It is commonly recognized that there are some differences in intelligence between certain groups of people—differences between men and women, between rural and urban populations, between workers in various occupations, and so forth. There have been many conflicting views, feelings, and opinions concerning these group differences. In fact, the differences between these views are probably as great as, if not greater than, the measured differences in intelligence between the groups. If a person has a great need to feel that one group is intellectually superior or inferior, he can probably find some evidence to support his view. This evidence may be greatly distorted, but he may not be aware of the distortion.

Sex differences. There seem to be no significant differences between the sexes in general intelligence. However, when we break down the factors making up intelligence some differences are noted.

As a group, girls generally excel in memory, vocabulary, and linguistic abilities. The average age for beginning to talk favors the girls over boys. Boys usually excel in numerical or mathematical ability and skills involving mechanical abilities. Environmental expectancies account in large part for these differences as children are growing up. Boys are expected to excel in mechanical and mathematical abilities, girls are expected to excel in the social skills.

Total test performance, however, usually shows no significant differences between the sexes.

Rural-urban differences. Children living in the rural regions of this country, as a rule, make lower scores on intelligence tests than do those living in the urban areas. There are at least two factors which may contribute to this difference. First, many intelligence tests have been criticized for being *loaded* with test items which favor the urban child. Some con-

tend that if rural and urban children were tested on knowledge of and adjustment to their respective environments, the rural child's performance would compare more favorably.

Secondly, for a number of years there has been a movement of the population from rural to urban areas. If, as some contend, the more intelligent and ambitious of the rural group move away and leave those largely on the lower levels of the intelligence scale, then we could only expect a lower average intelligence for the rural child. In Figure 17.9 we note the measured differences in a group of 1,964 urban and 940 rural cases. The mean IQ of the urban group is given as 105.7 and that of the rural group as 99.2.

Figure 17.9. Two groups, rural and urban, were tested for intelligence. This distribution of IQs shows the rural group to rate generally a little lower than the urban group. (After Terman and Merrill, Measuring Intelligence, *Houghton Mifflin, Boston, 1937.)*

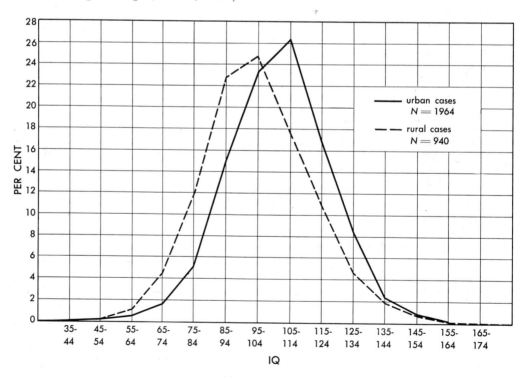

Table 17.3 Mean IQs of 2,757 Children Classified According to Their Fathers' Occupations

Fathers' occupational level	Children's mean IQ
I. Professional	116.2
II. Semiprofessional and managerial	111.9
III. Clerical, skilled trades, retail business	107.5
IV. Semiskilled, minor clerical and business	105.0
V. Slightly skilled and unskilled	97.2
VI. Rural owners	95.1

SOURCE: *Data from L. M. Terman and M. A. Merrill,* Measuring Intelligence, *Houghton Mifflin, Boston, 1937, pp. 14, 48. Compiled by Henry E. Garrett, Great Experiments in Psychology, Appleton-Century-Crofts, New York, 1941, p. 44.*

Occupational differences. Figure 17.5 shows the distribution of AGCT scores according to occupation. A wide range of individual differences is found within the groups, but when we consider the mean scores, occupational level and intelligence scores are more closely related.

These differences extend also to children of the men in the various occupational groups. Garrett has compiled the data in Table 17.3 from the data of Terman and Merrill which show these differences.

The Mentally Gifted. The intellectual superiority of the mentally gifted is apparent early in life. They develop the usual motor skills at an earlier age than the average. As a group they reveal many signs of precocity. Adeptness, at an early age, in learning to read, reading the classics, and solving mathematical problems requiring ability far beyond the capability of the average child their age is not uncommon.

The superior groups as a whole achieve at a superior level, but it should be noted that all the gifted do not have a history of success. The gifted child faces many difficulties in his relationships with others. Because of his superior mental ability, he sometimes becomes bored with the activi-

ties of the average in his age group. Public school programs, designed for the average, are not sufficiently challenging. The fact that he excels the other children, and often even the teacher, in mental ability sometimes makes his social adjustment difficult.

APTITUDES

"Aptitude" is used here to refer to a special ability. It is more specific than intelligence. In our use of the term we are also thinking of the potential for developing a specific ability. In other words, does a person show sufficient *promise, trainability,* or *aptitude* for a particular line of work to justify a period of training for that work? Therefore, measurement of aptitude comes to be of practical importance when a person is about to undergo training or enter a particular vocational field. In general, aptitudes may be broken into two major classifications: (1) scholastic aptitude and (2) vocational aptitude. We shall discuss these separately and mention some of the tests used for their measurement.

Scholastic Aptitude. It is a generally accepted fact that all people do not have the same level of ability to do school work at

▶ About 1921 Terman * selected more than 1,000 elementary school children who showed a measured IQ of 140 or more. The average IQ was about 150, and they were regarded as children of superior mental ability, since much less than 1 per cent of children in the population generally would be expected to score in this range. These children were selected from a group of about 250,000 and came mostly from homes of the professional and higher business groups. Only a very small percentage of them came from the lower occupational groups. Both the heredity and richness of the environmental background contributed to the mental superiority of the group.

Some differences were noted in the early life of these children. Their birth weight was more than the average. They walked and talked earlier than the average, and at the time of their selection they were more than an inch taller than the average child their age.

Terman kept in contact with these children and made progress reports for nearly thirty years. His findings have added much evidence to discount the views that so many people have held about the mentally superior.

* From L. M. Terman et al., *Genetic Studies of Genius*, vol. I, *Mental and Physical Traits of a Thousand Gifted Children*, Stanford University Press, Stanford, Calif., 1925.

the secondary, college, or professional level. Admittedly intelligence is a factor in scholastic success, but this alone is not enough.

In order to predict success in scholastic undertakings, tests have been administered to those just entering various levels of education, and the results have been correlated with their later achievement, usually measured in terms of grades. One of the most widely used tests of this sort is the American Council on Education Psychological Examination, commonly referred to simply as the ACE. This test, with annual revisions, has been used since 1924 for the purpose of measuring the probable success of college freshmen. In 1955 there was begun a gradual replacement of the ACE by the School and College Ability Test. Each of these tests yields *quantitative* and *linguistic* scores. Both these measures, as well as the total score, have value in predicting scholastic achievement. Though these are not perfect predictors, experience with them has shown that those scoring high on the tests tend to do well, while those scoring low tend to do poorly.

In recent years many schools have had more applicants for graduate study than they are able to take. Tests have been employed in selecting those believed most likely to succeed. In the fields of liberal arts and the natural sciences the Graduate Record Examination has been widely used as a selective device. This examination is in two parts: (1) the aptitude test, which gives a measure of a person's general fitness for graduate study; and (2) the advanced examination, which covers sixteen different fields such as French, history, psychology, and physics, and gives a measure of the applicant's present knowledge of the particular field in which he proposes to study.

Many professional schools have come to make use of tests as a part of their selection program or for guidance and counseling purposes. The Medical College Admission Test is required of applicants to most, if not all, of the medical schools in the country. Examination and use of this test is restricted to those who have applied for and are taking the test, but it is designed to measure the capability of the candidate

A summary of some of the findings indicate that:

1. The death rate for this group is lower than for the general population.

2. Cases of suicide and insanity were found less frequently than in the population generally.

3. College entrance was about 40 times higher than the average and a much greater percentage of them graduated.

4. Even during the depression years their income was twice the national average and a much higher percentage of them were in the higher income brackets.

5. Family adjustment appeared to be better than average, for they had a much lower divorce rate.

It must not be assumed that all in the group made an outstanding success. Some of them failed to complete their college work, some failed to achieve vocational success, and some had their difficulty with the law. However, as a group, in achievement, adjustment, and leadership they were superior to the average.

for successfully doing the work required of a medical student.

The American Dental Association sponsors a test designed to measure the fitness of students for study in a college of dentistry.

Tests designed to measure the suitability of students applying for admission to schools of law have been developed at a number of universities such as California, Columbia, Iowa, Michigan, Minnesota, and Yale. Educational Testing Service has more recently developed a test used in selecting law students. These tests are used to measure abilities such as reading comprehension, verbal reasoning, interpretation of legal material, etc.

The Psychological Corporation has developed a battery of tests which they use to aid in the selection of students for schools of nursing.

Since World War II there has been a notable increase in the use of tests in an effort to predict the suitability or aptitude of applicants for all kinds of study. The perfect instrument for measuring scholastic aptitude has not yet been devised; how-

ever, a point has been reached that indicates such tests are of value in the selection program.

Vocational Aptitude. Knowledge of a person's vocational aptitude is helpful to the employer selecting workers for a particular job and to the individual who is trying to select the vocation for which he is best suited. In the first instance the employer wants to know, as accurately as can reasonably be determined, the extent to which applicants can profitably be trained to use the skills required by the job in question. In order to make such a determination it is first necessary to know what abilities are required for doing the job. This calls for a careful analysis of the job. The next task is to find those individuals, from the ones available, who best meet these requirements. In this case, then, tests of specific ability would be required.

For the person who is interested in a general vocational evaluation as a further aid in selecting a vocational area for study, a more general sort of test would probably be used. There are factors other than aptitude that are important in selection of per-

The purpose of this study * was to devise aptitude tests for predicting success in engineering school during the first and second years.

There were thirteen tests in all, grouped under four headings: general scholastic ability, mathematical reasoning, understanding scientific relationships, and spatial visualization. The tests were given to all applicants for the fall, 1951, semester and later to 1,168 applicants for classes beginning after that time. The schools involved were the University of California at Berkeley and the University of California at Los Angeles.

The items to be used in the test were first tried out on small groups of students in order to get some idea of the difficulty level and the time required. They were then given to a larger group and analyzed from the standpoint of item difficulty, item discrimination, and distribution of wrong choices. The tests used in this study resulted from these investigations.

One important question is the reliability of each of the thirteen tests. This was calculated by the odd-even method on the results obtained from all or part of the applicant groups mentioned above. Generally speaking, the reliability coefficients were found to be satisfactory, although in three of the tests the reliability coefficients were low enough that they were dropped from the battery. The coefficients ranged from .61 to .95.

The other important question concerns the validity of the battery. For this purpose test scores were correlated with the grade-point averages of 533 students who had (by July 1, 1954) completed the freshman year, and of 199 students who had completed the sophomore year. Here the coefficients were, of course, smaller, ranging from .03 to .39 for the freshmen and from .02 to .36 for the sophomores. Incidentally high school grade-point averages correlated with college grades to the extent of .39 for the freshmen and .38 for the sophomores. By use of statistical techniques it was determined that a combination of high school grade-point average and the three subtests predicting best would yield a coefficient of about .50 with college grades, a point that the authors of this study feel is about as high as can be reached in view of the facts that (1) college grades are far from fully reliable, the reliability coefficient being about .70 in this study; and (2) the lower part of the high school graduating class is excluded from admission to the college, thus lowering the *range* of ability and hence the coefficients of correlation involved.

* Margaret Hubbard Jones and Harry W. Case, "The Validation of a New Aptitude Examination for Engineering Students," *Educational and Psychological Measurement*, 15: 502–508, 1955.

sonnel or in the choice of a vocation. Intelligence, discussed in the preceding chapter, is one of them. Also of importance are vocational interest and personality, and tests relating to these factors are discussed in the following chapter.

Many tests are available for testing vocational aptitude. While some of them are probably more valuable than others, all have been used rather extensively.

Differential aptitude tests. This battery provides specific measures of eight abili-

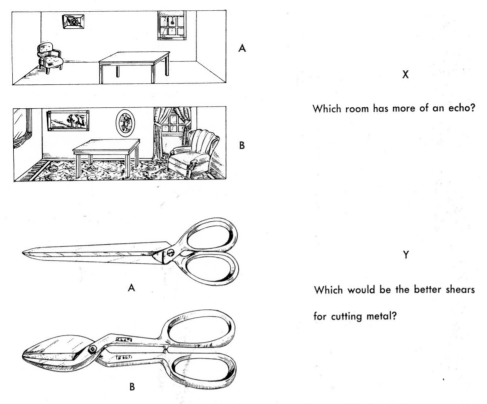

X

Which room has more of an echo?

Y

Which would be the better shears

for cutting metal?

Figure 17.10. Items such as these are used in the Bennett Test of Mechanical Comprehension. (Courtesy of the Psychological Corporation, New York.)

ties found useful in educational and vocational guidance at the junior and senior high school levels: (1) verbal reasoning, (2) numerical ability, (3) abstract reasoning, (4) space relations, (5) mechanical reasoning, (6) clerical speed and accuracy, and (7) language usage in two parts: (a) spelling, and (b) sentences.

Musical aptitude. Seashore pioneered measurement in this field with the introduction of his *Measures of Musical Talents* in 1919 and its revision in 1939. They are recorded on phonograph records and measure six aspects of auditory discrimination: (1) pitch, (2) loudness, (3) time, (4) timbre, (5) rhythm, and (6) tonal memory. The tests cover a wide range of diffi-

culty and have been found suitable for use with children from the fifth-grade through the adult levels.

Mechanical ability. Spatial visualization and mechanical information are two factors that seem of great importance in mechanical aptitude. The Bennett Test of Mechanical Comprehension is designed to measure these factors. This test, of which several forms are available, is designed for use with high school students, engineering school applicants, candidates for technical courses, applicants for mechanical employment, and women mechanical workers.

The Revised Minnesota Paper Form Board, a spatial-relations test, has been found useful for counseling concerning the

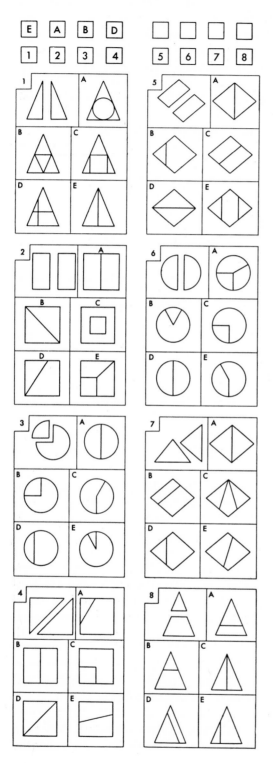

choice of courses in several areas such as trade courses, engineering, dentistry, and art. Correlations between this test and tests of mechanical comprehension are low enough to indicate that they are measuring separate factors. Presence of a high degree of spatial visualization may not be a good predictor, but its absence can be considered as an unfavorable sign for those considering training or employment in the mechanical field.

The performance of some jobs requires manipulation of the hands and fingers. Certain of these jobs, such as watchmaking, require a high degree of finger dexterity. Tweezer and pinboard tests have been designed to measure this ability. The Minnesota Rate of Manipulation Test is one test used to determine manual dexterity, which is an ability required for mechanical work involving certain types of machine operation.

Clerical aptitude. We should expect speed and accuracy in the checking of numerical and verbal symbols to be an indication of the ability necessary to become a successful clerical worker. The Minnesota Clerical Test is one which is extensively employed for checking these abilities. Norms are available for high school boys and girls, adult clerical applicants, and adult clerical workers.

Figure 17.11. Ability to perceive spatial relationships is an important factor in determining aptitude. For example, it is often thought to be important in determining mechanical ability or aptitude. (Courtesy of the Psychological Corporation, New York.)

During World War II men who went into pilot training were often given an extensive battery of tests. This study * reports on the results for 185,367 men given a combination of six apparatus tests and fourteen printed ones. The tests were scored in terms of *stanines*, with 1 being the lowest and 9 the highest. Shown below are (1) the stanine, or score on the test battery; (2) the number of men making that score; and (3) the percentage of the men who did not complete primary pilot training.

Test Scores and Success in Primary Pilot Training

Stanine	Number of men	Eliminated in primary pilot training, %
9	21,474	4
8	19,440	10
7	32,129	14
6	39,398	22
5	34,975	30
4	23,699	40
3	11,209	53
2	2,139	67
1	904	77

As a check on these results in 1943 almost a thousand men were admitted to the program, tested with this battery of tests, and put into training regardless of their scores. These scores, however, were not made known to anyone responsible for their training. The men went to various training centers and, if they finished flying training, completed it in 1944 or 1945. A comparison of scores made on the battery of tests and those not completing training is as follows:

Relation between Test Scores and Completion of Flying Training

Stanine	Number of men	Eliminated from flying training, %
7, 8, or 9	158	34.8
4, 5, or 6	368	69.7
1, 2, or 3	391	95.7

Of the 125 men in the above sample making a stanine of 1, not one completed flight training in the Army Air Force.

These results indicate that psychological tests can be quite useful in predicting future behavior, if the reliability and especially the validity are sufficiently high.

* John C. Flanagan, "Scientific Development of the Use of Human Resources: Progress in the Army Air Forces," *Science*, 105:57–60, 1947.

Figure 17.12. Speed and accuracy in checking names and numbers have been found useful in evaluating clerical aptitude. (Courtesy of the Psychological Corporation, New York.)

Instructions

On the inside pages there are two tests. One of the tests consists of pairs of names and the other of pairs of numbers. If the two names or the two numbers of a pair are *exactly the same* make a check mark (√) on the line between them; if they are *different*, make no mark on that line. When the examiner says "Stop!" draw a line under the last pair at which you have looked.

Samples done correctly of pairs of *Numbers*

79542	79524
───	
5794367 √	5794367
───	

Samples done correctly of pairs of *Names*

John C. Linder	John C. Lender
───	
Investors Syndicate √	Investors Syndicate
───	

Now try the samples below.

66273894	66273984
───	
527384578	527384578
───	
New York World	New York World
───	
Cargill Grain Co.	Cargil Grain Co.
───	

This is a test for Speed and Accuracy. Work as fast as you can without making mistakes. Do not turn this page until you are told to begin.

SUMMARY

Intelligence is a way of behaving. A person may behave intelligently or stupidly. Two very important factors are instrumental in determining this behavior: (1) the kind of nervous system, particularly the brain, that he is born with; and (2) the extent to which the potential has grown or developed. In other words, intelligence consists of the knowledge and skills he has acquired and the use to which he puts them. There is no way of describing intelligence apart from the performance of a person.

There is no instrument available that will enable us to measure intelligence directly. It is made up of a number of factors, not all of which are yet known. A number, known as primary mental abilities, have been factored out. Measures of such abilities as verbal meaning, number ability, word fluency, memory, reasoning, and spatial relations give results which are indicative of the level of intelligence. Since many of these factors or abilities enter into the total intelligence, two people may have the same total or general level and still vary widely in individual abilities.

The first intelligence tests were developed in 1905 by the French psychologists Binet and Simon. Since that time these original scales have been revised many times and adapted to use with people, particularly children, in many other countries. The revisions most widely used in this country are those done at Stanford University in 1916 and 1937. These tests have been used mostly with school children. Norms or averages have been computed for each age level. Test performances tend to increase up to about twenty years of age. Some psychologists believe this increase ceases, on an average, at about fifteen or sixteen. From test performance we get a score called *mental age*. If a child's mental age and chronological age are the same, he has an IQ of 100. If his MA is higher than his CA, his IQ is above 100. Similarly if his MA is lower than his CA, his IQ is less than 100. Hence the IQ of the average person is 100. For the child whose endowment is average and who has average educational opportunities, the IQ remains relatively constant.

Feeling the need for more adequate measures of adult intelligence, Wechsler developed scales for use at this level. These scales give separate, as well as combined, measures for verbal and performance.

An important limitation of individual tests, such as the Stanford-Binet and Wechsler scales, is that they are not suited to group administration. The Army Alpha and the Army General Classification tests, developed in World Wars I and II respectively, have been the most widely used tests of the group type.

The Primary Mental Ability Tests yield an over-all intelligence score but in addition they give measures of several different mental abilities.

Intelligence in the general population is spread over a wide range from the mentally defective to the genius. In a large unselected sample this distribution closely approximates the normal curve. One interesting observation about the behavior of people is that those low on the scale tend to remain low, the average tend to remain average, and the superior tend to remain superior. The low, average, and superior groups remain so but individuals within these groups are subject to greater variation.

Aptitude is trainability, or potential for developing specific ability. Many tests have been designed to measure aptitudes. Widely used are the School and College Ability Tests for high school students and college freshmen. The Graduate Record Examination is used for selection of students for graduate study. These tests attempt to measure scholastic aptitude as a means of predicting success in school.

In the vocational field, tests are used to measure the potential a person has for various jobs in such areas as mechanical, clerical, music, and art.

QUESTIONS

1. Does your everyday observation of people indicate that they differ? List some of the differences you have observed.

2. What are some of the limitations placed upon the interpretation of a person's intelligence when it is indicated by a single score such as IQ of 115?

3. Why is MA inappropriate when used as an indication of adult intelligence?

4. If we know a person's IQ, can we accurately predict his academic achievement at the college level? Why?

5. Does your observation suggest any relationship between a child's intelligence and his father's occupation?

6. How would you validate a test for selection of students for graduate study in psychology?

7. Air Force personnel psychologists are doing research on the selection of pilots. What might they use as a criterion measure of success as a pilot?

8. The psychological literature contains more research reports on test reliability than on test validity. Why is this so?

9. What are the advantages and disadvantages of (*a*) a verbal test of intelligence, (*b*) a performance test of intelligence?

10. "The best measure of aptitude in any field is a measure of achievement in that field." Can you defend this statement? How?

11. What types of tests might be used in selecting students for a school of engineering?

12. What does "aptitude" mean to you?

SUGGESTED READINGS

Hollingsworth, L. S.: *Children above 180 I.Q.,* World, Yonkers, N.Y., 1942.
> (A treatment of some of the problems of the mentally gifted child.)

Super, Donald E.: *Appraising Vocational Fitness by Means of Psychological Tests,* Harper, New York, 1949.
> (The use of psychological tests in counseling and selection.)

Terman, L. M., and Maud A. Merrill: *Measuring Intelligence,* Houghton Mifflin, Boston, 1937.
> (Information about the Stanford-Binet test.)

Terman, L. M., and M. H. Oden: *The Gifted Child Grows Up,* Stanford University Press, Stanford, Calif., 1947.
> (Summary of a twenty-five-year follow-up study of a large group of gifted persons chosen as children.)

Tiffin, J.: *Industrial Psychology,* 3d ed., Prentice-Hall, Englewood Cliffs, N.J., 1952.
> (Summary of the extent and importance of individual differences in business and industry.)

Wechsler, David: *Measurement of Adult Intelligence,* 3d ed., Williams & Wilkins, Baltimore, 1944.
> (Information about the Wechsler-Bellevue scales.)

18 EVALUATION AND APPRAISAL

The proper appraisal or evaluation of our fellow human beings is a constant and continuing task for all of us. Regardless of our job, our present situation, or our background we are likely to spend much of our time in this activity.

One area in which appraisals are important, of course, is schools and colleges, where grades are generally used. However, we all know that grades often do not reflect correctly the ability or effort of a student, especially if he has more than the usual number of emotional or other problems. In politics also we are faced with an evaluation problem: we must appraise those who run for office and choose the individual who best fits the purposes we have in mind. In the psychological clinic and the mental hospital, to mention a third area, the problem of appraising another human being is a most important one. Here the primary concern is to understand his difficulties and help him solve them.

In business and industry appraising and evaluating people becomes one of the most important questions facing management. People must be selected for positions of leadership. Unquestionably, successful leaders go a long way toward making a business profitable, and unsuccessful leaders can spell disaster to it. It is also necessary to evaluate people when any job is filled or any assignment is made, whether or not leadership responsibilities are involved.

This list of areas in which appraisals are important could be extended considerably. Whoever we are and whatever we do, from

Figure 18.1. A problem in evaluation—selecting the candidate for whom we wish to vote.

time to time we shall be called upon to evaluate people. And often we do a good deal of this evaluation even when we are not required to.

ORDINARY OBSERVATION AND THE APPRAISAL OF OTHERS

A great deal of this evaluation depends on what we usually refer to as *ordinary observation*. This means simply observing people wherever they are, without any attempt to set up special situations or use special devices for observation or evaluation, and drawing conclusions from these observations.

There are some advantages to ordinary observation, especially if the observation occurs over a long period of time, if the contacts with the individual are relatively close, and if we see him in many situations.

But ordinary observation also has many limitations.

Difficulties of Ordinary Observation. One of the difficulties of ordinary observation is that we usually see only a few aspects of the individual. We may know him on the job or at home or in the club, but often we do not get a chance to know him under a wide variety of circumstances.

Another limitation of ordinary observation is that the person we are observing usually "keeps his guard up," so that we see only a part of him. Every individual wears a sort of "front" or "veneer," and usually it is difficult to see behind this to the real individual, to know what he really thinks and feels.

A third difficulty with ordinary observation is that we are frequently not objective about the person to be evaluated. It is very easy to become ego-involved in other people: our children, our teachers, our subordinates, or our friends. We come to know them well, and, at least in many instances, we develop high regard or even affection for them. This undoubtedly influences our judgments and conclusions about them, even if we have situations otherwise perfect for observation. Having definite feelings about another person, in other words, is very likely to interfere with correct conclusions about him.

Importance of Ordinary Observation. In spite of its weaknesses, however, we must depend on ordinary observation for many of our important evaluations of other people. Other methods may be used to supplement it and even in some cases to take its place. But in many situations there is no practicable substitute for it.

However, as we use ordinary observation in appraising people, there are two things we must always keep in mind. In the first place, we must come to know the individual whom we are appraising as fully as is practicable. We must watch him under as many circumstances as we can and see him in as many different kinds of situations as possible. In the second place, we must strive for objectivity. We must remember the distortions introduced by ego-involvement and do our best to see the individual as he is, not as we hope or need to believe he is. Incidentally, one of the best ways to improve our judgment in these situations is to confer with another person who is in a position to know this individual. Naturally, comparing notes with two or more people is better than checking with only one.

PSYCHOLOGICAL TESTS IN APPRAISAL AND EVALUATION

Another method for getting information about an individual is through the use of psychological tests. As is pointed out in Chapter 16, it is possible to put too much faith in test results, just as it is possible to neglect or undervalue them. But they have their place nevertheless. In this section we shall describe some psychological tests not covered in the two previous chapters and discuss the use of tests in evaluation and appraisal.

Kinds of Psychological Tests. In the chapter just preceding this, intelligence and aptitude tests are described. Let us now look at several other sorts of psychological tests.

Achievement tests. Just as there are tests designed to discover what a person *can learn,* so there are tests designed to discover what he *has learned,* the latter being known as *achievement tests.* Such tests may be broad in coverage, as, for example, one which attempts to discover what he has learned from four years in high school, or the Graduate Record Examination,

which samples four years of college training and covers more closely his field of specialization. On the other hand, they may be very specific, such as an oral test designed to see whether an applicant for a job has acquired the basic knowledge required in that occupation. Most achievement tests are in between, so far as degree of specialization is concerned.

The majority of achievement tests relate to school subjects. Thus, many grade schools periodically give achievement tests designed to measure progress in relation to national norms for the test, as well as progress in particular school subjects. As

Figure 18.2. It is hard to tell what a person is really like, especially when he tries to keep us from knowing.

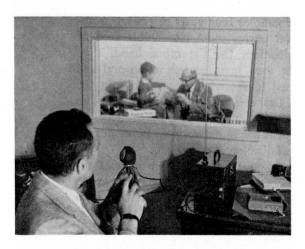

Figure 18.3. This is an example of observation, but because it involves special planning and a number of mechanical aids, including a "one-way" screen, it goes considerably beyond ordinary observation. (Photo by Cal Bernstein, Black Star.)

has been indicated, there are similar tests at other levels of the educational system. In addition, there are achievement tests covering a single subject of grade school, high school, or college.

There are also achievement tests for areas not directly connected with schools. Ability to read blueprints or to use certain measuring devices would be one example. Skill in typing or in taking shorthand would be another.

It is interesting to note that achievement in a certain area may very well represent aptitude for a more advanced area. Thus, an *arithmetic achievement* test may be a good *algebra aptitude* test. Incidentally, the form of achievement-test items is similar to that of aptitude-test and intelligence-test items, discussed earlier, and scores are reported and interpreted in much the same way.

Dexterity tests. There are also tests that attempt to measure manual dexterity, eye-hand coordination, and, in general, skill in the use of the various parts of the body.

These are varied in nature, since they cover many different sorts of activity. There are times when they can be quite useful in the evaluation of an individual, especially in certain work situations. Scores on these tests are usually reported in terms of percentiles.

Trade tests. Trade tests are usually developed in a business for the uses of a particular firm and relate to certain jobs in that firm. Trade tests may be either of the aptitude type or of the achievement type. The former is used to pick employees who can learn to do a certain job well, whereas the latter is used to select people already skilled in their jobs. Thus, if someone is hiring a man to go into an apprentice training program in an aircraft maintenance shop, he should use the aptitude type. On the other hand, if he is hiring carpenters for a construction job that is already under way and he plans to use tests for this purpose, he should use the achievement type. In this case his problem is not which men can *learn to be* carpenters, but rather which men *are* good carpenters already.

Naturally, trade tests, like all other psychological tests, must be standardized. It is not sufficient simply to make up a list of questions and ask people to answer them. Norms must be established, item analyses must be run, and the reliability and validity of the test must be determined.

Interest scales. One kind of test that has become quite popular is that which attempts to determine the principal interests or preferences of the individual. One of the first of these was the Strong Vocational Interest Blank. This test was standardized on a great many people. Strong, a professor in Stanford University, secured a fairly large number of successful men in various occupations or fields, such as lawyers, salesmen, and farmers. He prepared a large number of items for which a person might express liking or disliking (for example, algebra, or being chairman of the social

▶ This is an experiment * on what in this chapter is called ordinary observation. The experimenters set up 11 discussion groups of 3 people each and had them work at a task for fifteen minutes. Then 11 other groups were constituted in such a way that no person worked in the second group with anyone who was in his first group. For each group a trained observer was present, and in no case did he observe the same individual in successive groups. The subjects were 33 undergraduate students who did not know each other at the beginning of the experiment. Of these, 24 were men and 9 were women, but in all cases men worked only with men and women worked only with women.

The first task for each group was to carry on a discussion on the question, "Should college grades be abolished?" and the second was to construct a meaningful sentence using the words "to," "too," and "two." Each group was stopped after fifteen minutes and each member was asked to fill out a questionnaire on both his own performance and that of his two associates. The trained observers also filled out the questionnaire for each of the group members.

The judgments showed considerable consistency on certain items but much less on others. Thus, "leadership," "contribution to group decision," and "dominance" were judged quite reliably, whereas "satisfied with group decision," "wanted to do a good job," and "yielded to others" were lower in this regard. Judgments of a person about his own behavior and judgments by the trained observer followed about the same pattern as judgments of a person by the other two people in his group.

Thus we see that this sort of observation may yield useful information, at least on certain characteristics, especially when no better means of obtaining this knowledge is available.

* Robert R. Blake, Jane Syrgley Mouton, and Benjamin Fruchter, "The Consistency of Interpersonal Behavior Judgments Made on the Basis of Short-term Interactions in Three-man Groups," *Journal of Abnormal and Social Psychology*, 49:573–578, 1954.

committee in a club). On these items, he found the typical interest pattern of the successful lawyer or salesman or farmer—and so on for more than forty occupations. When a person takes the Strong Vocational Interest Blank his interests are compared with the interest patterns of successful men in all these various occupations. There is also a form of this blank for women, covering twenty-eight occupations.

The second type of interest test that has been widely used is the Kuder Preference Record. This record measures preferences in ten broad areas, such as *outdoor, me-chanical, computational,* and *social service.* The items of the test are arranged in groups of three. There are 168 of these groups. In each group the subject is asked to indicate the one he would *most like* to do and the one he would *least like* to do. The method of standardizing this scale differs considerably from that used by Strong, and the scoring is relatively simple. This latter fact largely accounts for the widespread use of the scale. Incidentally and contrary to what many people seem to think, it is not an aptitude test. Rather it is an *interest schedule.*

How effective are interest tests? In the first place, answers to items on interest scales can be deliberately faked. There is some question as to their usefulness, therefore, in situations where the individual knows what sort of person is required and has a great desire to appear to be that sort of person.

In the second place, the results of interest tests may be *unconsciously* distorted. The desire to defend and enhance the self may operate here just as it may in any aspect of our lives. If we want to appear to ourselves as interested in people or in engineering problems, we can unconsciously change some of our answers to fulfill that desire.

Interest tests are particularly helpful in serving as a starting point in counseling interviews, especially those involving educational or vocational counseling.

Personality questionnaires. Another instrument for appraising people came out of World War I. During this period, emphasis was placed on testing intelligence, but it became apparent that a highly intelligent person may still lack many qualities of a good soldier. Among the other factors that are important, the adjustment or maladjustment of the individual, his emotional stability, and similar characteristics must be included.

The personality questionnaire is an at-tempt to get at such factors. It asks a great many questions about the personal life of the individual, particularly as to how he feels about many things. Fears, ups and downs in mood, miserable feelings, feelings of loneliness—these are examples of the kinds of things asked about. The person taking the test is instructed to check "Yes," "No," or "?" according to how he feels about the matter under consideration. The questionnaire usually yields a score—sometimes several scores—usually expressed in terms of percentiles. The assumption is that the person giving the largest number of unfavorable answers is the most maladjusted.

Personality questionnaires have a number of rather serious limitations.[1] In the first place, as is true of interest tests, the answers to the questions can be faked. A person may give what he thinks will be the most successful answer, without regard for the actual truth. Some personality questionnaires have built into them devices for detecting this sort of thing. Certain questions are so phrased that the answer must, by the nature of the case, go in a certain direction, though the "favorable" answer would be in another direction, and if the individual gives the "favorable" answer to many of these items his score is discounted. Many tests, however, do not contain these devices for detecting faking, and even when they do, there is considerable question as to whether all important instances of faking can be uncovered.

In the second place, personality questionnaires are also subject to unconscious

[1] Albert Ellis, "Validity of Personality Questionnaires," *Psychological Bulletin*, 43:385–440, 1946.

Figure 18.4. The Purdue Pegboard Test, used to measure the speed and accuracy with which one can use his hands. (Courtesy of New York University, Testing and Advisement Center.)

Report on Vocational Interest Test for Men

(See other side for explanation)

Name .... Age .... Date .... Agency or school .... Case no. ....

Group	Occupation	Raw Score	Standard Score	C						B—	B	B+	A				
				0	5	10	15	20	25	30	35	40	45	50	55	60	65
I	Artist																
	Psychologist (rev.)																
	Architect																
	Physician (rev.)																
	Psychiatrist																
	Osteopath																
	Dentist																
	Veterinarian																
II	Physicist																
	Chemist																
	Mathematician																
	Engineer																
III	Production Manager																
IV	Farmer																
	Carpenter																
	Printer																
	Math. Sci. Teacher																
	Policeman																
	Forest Service																
	Army Officer																
	Aviator																

Figure 18.5. A portion of the report sheet for the Strong Vocational Interest Test for Men. The test enables one to compare his interests with those of successful men in forty-five different occupations (of which twenty-one are shown above). The subject receives an interest score on each of the occupations. Scores falling to the right of the shaded area for each occupation indicate that the person has the interests of men in that occupation (and the farther to the right the more certain the finding becomes). In the same manner scores to the left indicate that the subject does not have the interests in question. (Reprinted from Vocational Interest Blank for Men *by Edward K. Strong, Jr., with the permission of the publishers, Stanford University Press. Copyright 1952 by the Board of Trustees of Leland Stanford Junior University.)*

distortion of the results. After all, nearly all of us want to be as worthy as we can be, and we tend to create a picture of ourselves that is acceptable or even praiseworthy. In taking a personality questionnaire, we may answer questions, not in accordance with the reality of the situation, but in accordance with our own needs for self-defense and self-enhancement. Actually, this is probably a more serious objection to personality questionnaires than outright faking. Studies of deliberate faking reveal that it occurs less frequently than might be expected. Unconscious dis-

tortion is more difficult to detect and has been less frequently studied.

A third limitation of personality questionnaires concerns the validity of the questionnaire itself. The questionnaires are especially vulnerable on this count. For many of them the indication is that their validity is slight or altogether lacking. In other words, there is serious question as to whether they really measure the traits that they are often used to measure.

In the light of all this, our conclusion is not surprising: personality questionnaires are to be used with caution and then only

EVALUATION AND APPRAISAL *377*

by someone trained in their use and familiar with their limitations. They are certainly not the fine devices that they may appear to be or that we might like them to be.

Projective techniques. A testing method that is relatively new in psychology and has received considerable attention is the projective technique.[2] The important feature of this technique is that it presents to the subject material that is ambiguous, that he can see as almost anything that he wants it to be. Such *unstructured material*

[2] Harold H. Anderson and Gladys L. Anderson, *An Introduction to Projective Techniques,* Prentice-Hall, Englewood Cliffs, N.J., 1951.

permits him to give his interpretation of what he sees. We all know, for example, that different people see many different things in clouds floating overhead, and even the same person may interpret them differently from moment to moment.

How can a person's responses to unstructured material be meaningful or useful in appraising him? The theory underlying the use of projective techniques is quite simple: when a person deals with such material, he tends to interpret it in accordance with his motives, his needs, his repressions, and the like. Thus, his responses to a projective device may reveal a great deal about him. Some of what is

Figure 18.6. Could these drawings be properly considered as projections of the thoughts and, especially, of the feelings of the artist? What sort of a person do you think the artist is?

The drawings are the work of a twenty-one-year-old female mental patient in St. Elizabeth's Hospital in Washington, and they doubtless help those who are treating her to understand something of her attitudes, wishes, fears, etc. (Wide World Photo.)

uncovered he may be unwilling to reveal directly, and some that he reveals he may not know himself, at least at the conscious level. This latter position may seem questionable, but the evidence for it is indeed impressive.

One of the best-known projective devices was introduced in 1921 by the Swiss psychiatrist Hermann Rorschach. This technique is known as the Rorschach Ink Blot Test. It consists of ten ink blots of rather large size and irregular shape. These ten blots were selected by Rorschach after he had experimented with many times that number. Interpreting the subject's response to the blots is a complicated procedure, one for which a great deal of professional preparation is required. In scoring the responses to the ink blots, attention is paid to whether the person sees a human, a lower animal, or something else; how much and what sort of detail is given; whether the card is interpreted as a whole or on a part-by-part basis; and whether there is a definite response to color. (Five of the ten blots use color, the other five are black on a white background.) Several other aspects of the responses are also considered.

A second projective device is the Thematic Apperception Test, frequently abbreviated as the TAT. The TAT is like the Ink Blot Test except that pictures instead of ink blots are presented to the subject. These pictures are of human beings, but the human beings are in neutral situations; that is, they are not obviously sad or happy, afraid or secure. The subject is then asked to tell a story about each picture. The assumption is that the story told will be determined largely by his drives, motives, needs, and other phases of the personality, especially the unconscious ones. Incidentally, there are a number of other projective devices.

Projective devices are not only relatively new and to some people rather strange, but they have caused a good many people to ask serious questions as to their useful-

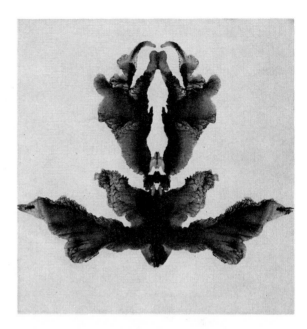

Figure 18.7. An ink blot similar to those used in the Rorschach Ink Blot Test. What do you see in this ink blot?

ness in personality appraisal. How adequate are they for this sort of task?

In the first place, it is obvious that projective devices are to be used only by trained individuals. It is generally accepted at the present time that the minimum training needed for the use of one of these devices is a master's degree in psychology plus additional special training in the administration, scoring, and interpretation of the instrument itself. There is more and more of a tendency to require that anyone using the Rorschach, TAT, or similar projective device have a Ph.D. in psychology.

In the second place, the adequacy of the projective devices is less than it might be because projective devices so far have been used largely with groups of abnormal people, that is, people who are emotionally disturbed, neurotic, or even psychotic. As a result, not only are the standards for comparison based on the abnormal, but even the terminology used in the test is

Figure 18.8. What do you see in this picture? Why is this woman in this position? What has happened to her and how does she feel about it? What sort of people live in the house?

This picture can be used as a projective device because the observer is able to answer these and other questions in many different ways, since there is no way to be sure what the answers are. The inner needs of the observer have a great deal to do with what he sees in the picture. (The Museum of Modern Art, New York, Purchase.)

slanted in that direction. In the literature on the projective devices, we read a great deal about symptoms of mental illness. These may be appropriate for the clinic, but they fit rather poorly many cases of the school psychologist or the problems of business and industry.

A third question about the adequacy of the projective devices is this most persistent question of validity. Theoretically, projective devices *should* get at the unconscious impulses, motives, and drives of the individual. They *should* bring into the open conflicts which he has within himself. But do they? That is, do they really get at what

they purport to get at? A great deal of work has been done along this line, and the evidence indicates that there is considerable validity in the projective devices. Yet much is still to be done. As has already been indicated, this is especially true as relates to the normal individual.

We are concluding, then, that projective devices, properly employed by a person skilled in their use, may be quite helpful in appraising the personality of an individual, especially if he is in emotional conflict.

Using Psychological Tests. Psychological tests have proved to be valuable in appraising and evaluating people. In a test, the conditions are the same for everyone, and tests are scored in an objective, unbiased manner. For most other methods of appraisal, personal opinion has a large influence, and thus the liking or disliking of the person to be evaluated may make a great deal of difference in the results obtained. In the case of tests, however, these factors are reduced to the minimum.

Situations in which tests are used. Tests are used in a great many situations. The achievement of grade school children is frequently checked in this objective fashion, as we have already pointed out, and the results are usually beneficial both to the individuals tested and to the instructional program. This same process is often continued through high school.

In addition, in high schools and colleges tests are frequently used to get information for the choice of various courses of study and for vocational guidance. It is well known that the student's preference and even his scholastic achievement do not provide a complete basis for decisions in these important areas, and tests prove to be valuable supplements.[3] Tests are also used as one of the bases for admission into many colleges and universities.

Business and industry have also found tests to be valuable aids in the selection of employees and, to some extent, in their promotion. Again the matter of objectivity enters in. Otherwise selection and promotion are often matters of personal opinion. When tests were first introduced into business and industry they were used uncritically, more being expected of them than they were designed to accomplish. Even today, many problems occur in the use of tests in such situations, but their use is well established and often profitable for all concerned.[4]

A third place where tests are employed in large numbers is in the armed services. To an extent, the armed services have the problems of both education and industry, for they must provide vocational guidance and also be efficient in placement and promotion. It is significant that the Army Alpha was given to almost 2 million men during World War I and the Army General Classification Test to almost ten times that number in World War II. These mass testings—the largest in the history of our country, and perhaps anywhere in the world—have helped to make Americans test-wise, as well as providing valuable information about tests and testing. Every branch of the armed services uses many tests, for a variety of purposes.

Finally, there are the psychological clinic and the mental hospital. One of the contributions of the psychologist to the clinic team (discussed in Chapter 1) is his skill in the selection, administration, and interpretation of tests. Individual intelligence tests and the projective devices have been used most extensively here, but many other sorts of tests have also been included.

There are other places where tests are used: government agencies, group work projects, research, etc. However, enough has been said to show that the testing movement of today is extensive and important.

Some precautions about tests. In view of these facts, it is easy to see how people can become overenthusiastic about tests and what tests can do. Let us look at some of the limitations they have in actual use.

[3] Many studies have been made of the usefulness of tests in predicting success in school subjects. For an example of such research in a school of medicine, see Robert I. Watson, "Predicting Academic Success through Aptitude and Achievement Tests," *Journal of Medical Education,* 30:383–390, 1955.

[4] A great deal of research has been done on the use of tests in business and industry. A recent nontechnical summary of findings along this line is J. P. Guilford, "Is Personnel Testing Worth the Money?" American Management Association, General Management Series, no. 176, New York, 1955, pp. 52–64.

One limitation is that tests never tell the whole story about any individual. No matter how extensive the test or how carefully it is administered and interpreted, every human being is more complex than any set of test results. We must always realize that we are dealing with a person and not merely some test scores.

In the second place, there are many situations where the use of tests is inappropriate. Students can hardly select their teachers for next semester by means of tests, nor are tests appropriate in deciding whom to date or marry. Even in some situations involving vocational guidance in school and selection or promotion in business and industry, tests may be inadvisable.

In the third place, it is easy to be uncritical in the interpretation and use of test scores. Here is the big danger for anyone who has only slight training in testing. It is easy to learn what a mean and a standard deviation are and to look up the definition of intelligence or mechanical aptitude, and then proceed to make an interpretation that seems sensible enough but may be filled with error. To use a test effectively we must be trained in testing. We must know the particular test well—its norms and how they were determined, its reliability and especially its validity, what others than the author have found about it, etc. In addition, we need a knowledge of the dynamics of human motivation and reactions, and as much knowledge as we can get by other means about the individual in question. Testing may appear to be simple, and many a novice is led to believe he can do it successfully. But it is technical, complicated work and should be left to those with the proper training and experience.

The test battery. So far we have spoken as though only one test were being employed and interpreted. Actually, in many (perhaps in most) cases a battery of tests is selected or devised, and used. Thus, for educational or vocational guidance a battery would be likely to include one or more intelligence tests or perhaps the Primary Mental Abilities Tests; achievement tests in various areas; an interest scale; aptitude tests along several lines; a personality questionnaire; and perhaps a number of others. Ideally, such a battery should be set up only after careful selection and validation of each of the tests, but that is not always practicable. It is important, however, to evaluate the individual in the light of all the results. This point is dealt with in the accompanying study of the test battery used to predict success in trade school.

One point hard to overemphasize is the importance of supplementing test results, wherever practicable, with information from other sources. Ordinary observation has already been mentioned. *Pooled judgments* (opinions of a number of observers) are often useful. *Rating methods,* discussed in the next section of this chapter, may be helpful, and the *interview,* dealt with in the last section, is a valuable and frequently useful device. It must always be kept in mind that we are striving for a fair and accurate evaluation of the whole individual, and any practical means to that end should be employed.

RATING METHODS OF APPRAISAL

One appraisal method, developed principally in the last forty years, is that of *rating* the person to be evaluated. For all practical purposes, this method had its beginning in the Army in World War I. Since that time it has had increasing use in government service and in business and industry. It is only fair to say, however, that many problems attended its use and that there probably is not as much enthusiasm for it as there once was.

Kinds of Rating Scales. Any rating system, of course, must involve a rating scale or a form. Let us look at three of the possible ways of constructing and using such a form.

A TEST BATTERY AND SUCCESS IN TRADE SCHOOL

▶ The Bennett Test of Mechanical Comprehension, the Revised Minnesota Paper Form Board, and the Army General Classification Test were given to 350 men entering a trade school in the Middle West.* These men were given training in air conditioning, automobile repair, drafting, carpentry, printing, welding, or other occupation. After six months, 126 had dropped out of school and 224 remained. The question is, "Do scores on these three tests accurately predict who will drop out and who will remain?"

In order to check as thoroughly as practicable on the test results, the total group was broken up into two subgroups, and this was done entirely by chance. When scores on the tests were correlated against the pass-fail (or remain-in-school versus dropout) criterion, each test showed a positive and significant relationship to the criterion. However, the relationship was higher in one subgroup than it was in the other.

Later it was possible to apply the same battery of tests to 298 other entering students. Results again indicated a significant relationship between test scores and pass-fail.

The authors point out, however, that while the relationship is significant, accuracy of prediction is far from high. Thus, if we should set a combined score on the three tests sufficiently high to eliminate 50 per cent of the dropouts, 30 per cent of the successful students would also be eliminated, and if we eliminated 29 per cent of the dropouts by means of the tests we should also eliminate 9 per cent of those who stay in school for six months or longer.

Thus, we conclude that, while under these circumstances these tests enable us to predict with accuracy considerably better than chance, they still leave a great deal to be desired.

* C. H. Patterson, "The Prediction of Attrition in Trade School Courses," *Journal of Applied Psychology*, 40:154–158, 1956.

Descriptive adjective. One form of rating scale simply presents the rater with perhaps seventy-five or one hundred descriptive adjectives (or phrases that function as adjectives). To the left of each adjective is a box, and a check mark made in this box indicates that the rater believes the adjective applies to the ratee. Those not thought to apply are, of course, left blank. These adjectives may describe the individual in any number of ways. Some will be favorable, some unfavorable, and some neutral or indifferent.

This scale has its limitations. One problem is the choice of the adjectives to be used. Which should be included in the scale and which omitted? If the scale is to yield a total score, how should each adjective be weighted so as to provide the most accurate picture of the person? Then there is the question of validity: does the scale really measure what it is being used to measure? For these and other reasons this scale is not used as extensively at present as one might expect.

Graphic. The most popular rating form is probably the graphic scale. Here the name of a quality is printed on the page; just underneath it a line is drawn across the page from left to right, and underneath the line some phrases or even sentences are written describing the ratee in terms of that quality. Thus at the extreme left (or right) of the line he is described in a very complimentary fashion; in the middle of the line, a phrase indicating an average amount of the quality is expressed; and at the other end there is an uncompli-

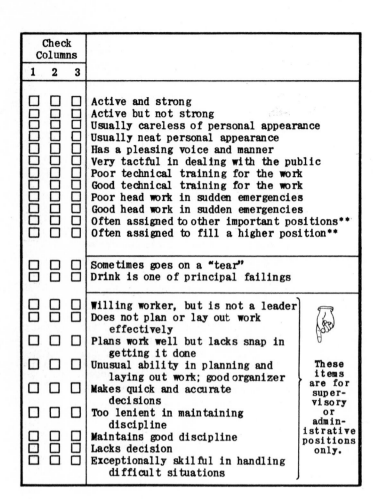

Check Columns			
1	2	3	
☐	☐	☐	Active and strong
☐	☐	☐	Active but not strong
☐	☐	☐	Usually careless of personal appearance
☐	☐	☐	Usually neat personal appearance
☐	☐	☐	Has a pleasing voice and manner
☐	☐	☐	Very tactful in dealing with the public
☐	☐	☐	Poor technical training for the work
☐	☐	☐	Good technical training for the work
☐	☐	☐	Poor head work in sudden emergencies
☐	☐	☐	Good head work in sudden emergencies
☐	☐	☐	Often assigned to other important positions**
☐	☐	☐	Often assigned to fill a higher position**
☐	☐	☐	Sometimes goes on a "tear"
☐	☐	☐	Drink is one of principal failings
☐	☐	☐	Willing worker, but is not a leader
☐	☐	☐	Does not plan or lay out work effectively
☐	☐	☐	Plans work well but lacks snap in getting it done
☐	☐	☐	Unusual ability in planning and laying out work; good organizer
☐	☐	☐	Makes quick and accurate decisions
☐	☐	☐	Too lenient in maintaining discipline
☐	☐	☐	Maintains good discipline
☐	☐	☐	Lacks decision
☐	☐	☐	Exceptionally skilful in handling difficult situations

These items are for supervisory or administrative positions only.

Figure 18.9. A portion of a descriptive-adjective rating scale. The columns marked 1, 2, and 3 are for three different raters, e.g., a supervisor and the two people immediately above him. [From John Bernard Probst, Service Ratings (Technical Bulletin No. 4 of the Bureau of Public Personal Administration), 1931. By permission of Public Personnel Association, Chicago.]

mentary phrase. A couple of other phrases could be added between the center and the extremes. The rater simply makes a check at the position on the line that he thinks to be the appropriate one for the ratee. A total of perhaps five or ten qualities, each with its own descriptive phrases, is ordinarily used.

This form provides for fine discriminations on the part of the rater and also is easily converted to a total score, thus making possible comparisons among a number of people. But, like the descriptive-adjective form, it has its shortcomings. There are the questions of what qualities should be included, how they should be described,

and what phrases should be put underneath the line for any particular quality. There is also the question of whether the various qualities should have different weights and the problem of how accurately a score can reflect the actual qualities of the individual. Behind all these questions, of course, is the validity of the judgments of the rater.

Forced-choice. Among the most recent developments in methods of appraisal is the forced-choice rating scale. This scale differs from the others in two important particulars. In the first place, it presents to the rater twenty-five to forty groups of four (or sometimes more) statements each about the individual. Generally, half the statements in each group are favorable and half are unfavorable. The rater is instructed to pick the one phrase that he thinks best describes the ratee by checking it in a "most like" column, and to pick the one least like the ratee by checking it in a "least like" column.

Figure 18.10. This is a rating scale much like the graphic, the only difference being that the rater is to check the appropriate descriptive phrase for each quality rather than checking elsewhere on the line.

EMPLOYEE PERFORMANCE AND WORK APPRAISAL FORM

Date...................................19

Judge the employee on the basis of the work now being done. Be sure that each characteristic is considered separately, regardless of where the appraisal falls on any of the other characteristics. Place a check (√) in the box below the group of words which best describes the individual, but only one check for each line. However, it is essential that every line be checked.

NAME............................. JOB TITLE............................. DEPT. ....

How long under your supervision? .... Date of Employment? ....

1. **KNOWLEDGE OF JOB:** Consider knowledge essential to person's job.	Has an Exceptionally thorough knowledge of work ☐	Has good knowledge of work ☐	Requires Considerable coaching ☐	Has inadequate knowledge of work ☐
2. **QUALITY OF WORK:** Consider the ability to turn out work which meets quality standards.	Highest Quality ☐	Well Done ☐	Passable ☐	Poor ☐
3. **QUANTITY OF WORK:** Consider the volume of work produced under normal conditions.	Large Volume ☐	Good Volume ☐	Slightly Below Average Volume ☐	Unsatisfactory Volume ☐
4. **ATTENDANCE & PUNCTUALITY:** Consider frequency of absences as well as latenesses.	Record is Excellent ☐	Occasionally Absent or Late ☐	Frequently Absent or Late ☐	Undependable: Absent or Late Without Notice ☐
5. **ATTITUDE:** Consider his attitude toward his work, company and associates, and his willingness to work with and for others.	Usually Fine Attitude ☐	Good Attitude ☐	Passable ☐	Poor Attitude ☐
6. **JUDGMENT:** Consider his ability to make decisions and to utilize working time to best advantage.	Justifies Utmost Confidence ☐	Applies Himself Well; Needs Little Supervision ☐	Needs Frequent Checking ☐	Cannot be relied upon; Needs constant Supervision ☐
7. **RELIABILITY:** Consider the ability of the person to get the work out under pressure, and to follow job through to completion.	Can always be counted upon ☐	Generally can be counted on ☐	Unpredictable under Pressure ☐	"Cracks up" under pressure ☐
8. **FLEXIBILITY — ADAPTABILITY:** Consider the speed with which he learns and the amount of instruction required to teach him new duties.	Learns Fast ☐	Learns Reasonably Fast ☐	Slow to Learn ☐	Unable to Learn ☐
9. **PERSONAL CHARACTERISTICS:** Consider Appearance, Personality, Integrity, "Housekeeping".	Decidedly Favorable ☐	Good ☐	Passable ☐	Generally Unsatisfactory ☐

Appraised by.............................Date..................Reviewed by.............................Date.............

(See other side)

Here is an example from a scale designed to measure the contributions of a man to his fraternity.[5] Twenty-five groups of four statements each were selected; Table 18.1 presents one group.

Table 18.1   A Set of Statements from a Forced-choice Scale

Most like	Least like	
————	—————	Well-rounded
————	—————	Seems to think he is self-sufficient in all things he endeavors to do
————	—————	Enjoys just being with the brothers
————	—————	Is not a strong influence in chapter meetings

It is easy to see that the first and third of the above statements are favorable, whereas the second and fourth are not. But the rater is restricted to *one* "most like" and *one* "least like" out of the four statements. Why may he not choose all of them if he wishes? This brings us to the second difference between this and conventional rating methods.

The forced-choice method differs from earlier methods in that each of these phrases has been previously evaluated. That is, of the two favorable statements it has been determined that each is about equally *popular* (that is, each is chosen with about the same frequency) but that only one of these discriminates good fraternity men (for example) from poor ones. The same thing in reverse is true of the unfavorable statements: each is about

[5] John R. Greenstreet, "An Application of the Forced-choice Rating Technique to a College Fraternity Situation," M.A. thesis, Southern Methodist University, Dallas, 1952.

equally popular, but only one of the two actually discriminates poor fraternity men from good ones.

In the example above, which of the two favorable statements really discriminates, *in this particular chapter of the fraternity,* between a superior and inferior fraternity man? It would be hard to say, but investigation (by means of a technique into which we do not have time to go here) revealed it was the first statement and not the third. Likewise, of the two unfavorable statements it was the last (and not the second) that actually was shown to discriminate.

Here is the real point of the forced-choice method. If we are trying deliberately to rate a person higher than we think he deserves, we have about a fifty-fifty chance of checking (in the "most like" column) the third statement. Likewise, in trying to rate the person higher than he deserves, we have a fifty-fifty chance of checking (in the "least like" column) the second statement. But the logic of the forced-choice method is that if he *really is superior we have better than an even chance* of checking (in the "most like" column) the first statement. This is true because in this particular situation it has been found that superior fraternity members actually are, as a general rule, well-rounded men. The same logic works in reverse for the inferior fraternity man, where ordinarily the rater would check "most like" an unfavorable statement and "least like" a favorable one.

Figure 18.11 is an example of a part of a forced-choice form.

One difficulty with the forced-choice system, of course, is its length. Even if there are only twenty-five groups of statements, the process obviously becomes time-consuming if the rater has a number of people to rate. Another difficulty is that the key showing which statements actually discriminate must be *a closely guarded secret,*

Figure 18.11. *Part of a forced-choice rating form once used by the U.S. Army in evaluating the efficiency of officers. (By permission from* Introduction to Psychology *by C. T. Morgan, Mc-Graw-Hill, New York, 1956, p. 423.)*

INSTRUCTIONS: Read carefully each group of four phrases, then check the one that is most descriptive of the person being rated and also the one that is least descriptive of him.

	Most	Least
A. A go-getter who always does a good job	☐	☐
B. Cool under all circumstances	☐	☐
C. Doesn't listen to suggestions	☐	☐
D. Drives instead of leads	☐	☐
A. Always criticizes, never praises	☐	☐
B. Carries out order by "passing the buck"	☐	☐
C. Knows his job and performs it well	☐	☐
D. Plays no favorites	☐	☐
A. Constantly striving for new knowledge and ideas	☐	☐
B. Businesslike	☐	☐
C. Apparently not physically fit	☐	☐
D. Fails to use good judgment	☐	☐

and the reasons for this secrecy may be difficult to explain to both raters and ratees.

Finally, there are the same questions we have raised about the other sorts of rating scales. What does the total score mean? Does the form actually yield valid measures of the individuals appraised?

Some Problems of Rating. Accurate rating is by no means the simple process that it appears to many people to be. There are many problems to be solved before rating can be made accurate and useful.

Adequacy of the form used. Several questions can be asked about any form which is used in a rating situation. In the first place, are the qualities to be rated clearly defined? In the second place, are the directions definite and unambiguous? In the third place, does the form cover all the significant traits, or as many as need to be covered? Next, does the form actually describe well the traits to be rated? There is serious question as to whether it is advisable to give a different weight to each of the traits to be rated, but if we decide to do so, do all the traits receive their proper weights? Does the rating give an accurate picture of the various traits of the individual—and of the whole individual?

This last point deserves further consideration. It is easy to believe that, when we

▶ A question which has had some interest for industrial psychologists is whether there is any advantage, in connection with the use of a rating scale, in assigning different weights to the qualities on the scale or to the degrees of the quality in question. Thus, it might seem, to take an example, that "dependability" is worth twice as much as "promptness," though in some situations there might be disagreement with these weights. Likewise it might seem, to take another example, that, in answer to the question, "Is he dependable?" the reply "Definitely yes" would be worth twice as much as "Probably yes."

In a study * that throws some light on this question, the rating scale involved six qualities with descriptive phrases under each. Weights were given to these phrases in two different ways. First, a statistical technique was used to determine the best weight for each. Second, weights were assigned on the basis of convenience. Thus, one question was, "Would you hire this employee over again if you could make the decision?" and the following weights were assigned, on the two different bases, to the four possible answers to the question:

Ordinary weight	Answer	Statistical weight
4	Definitely yes	6
3	Probably yes	4
2	Probably no	2
1	Definitely no	1

The other five qualities were dealt with similarly.

When the results obtained from the use of the ordinary weights were compared with those derived statistically, on three groups of over 200 employees each, almost perfect correlation was obtained, the smallest r being .994. This was true whether probationary or permanent employees were being considered. Furthermore, the reliability of the scales did not vary significantly when the two different sets of weights were used.

The conclusion is that under these circumstances statistical weighting of the rating responses is not worth the time and effort involved.

* C. E. Jurgensen, "Item Weights in Employee Rating Scales," Journal of Applied Psychology, 39:305–307, 1955.

have rated a person on ten qualities and summed the ratings on them, we have an accurate picture of the individual. But a poor score on a certain trait can very well outweigh all the good scores that he might make on all the other traits. For instance, take the trait of dishonesty. If the person is being considered for a position involving the handling of a great deal of money, this single undesirable characteristic might more than outweigh all his other qualities.

Then too we come again to the question raised in Chapter 7 as to whether the whole is simply the sum of its parts. Can we assume that the total score (based on any number of qualities) actually represents accurately the individual? Or is a person in the last analysis more than such a sum?

Thus it is easy to see that there are problems connected with the practice of taking various traits, arriving at a sum of the scores on each, and then saying that this represents an appraisal of the total personality.

Adequacy of raters. Again a number of questions can be raised with regard to the adequacy with which the raters do their job. In the first place, do they understand the real purpose that the rating form is to serve? Do they understand clearly the qualities described and the meaning and use of the terms? The chances are, unless they have been trained in rating and more specifically in the use of this particular rating form, that they do not fully understand either of these.

In the second place, are they in a position to rate as they really feel? What use is to be made of the rating? Will they later have to face the ratee and justify these ratings? It is obvious that the circumstances under which ratings are done will influence their accuracy.

In the third place, what about the *halo effect*—the tendency of an over-all judgment about the individual to influence the ratings on particular traits or qualities? If a supervisor has a good over-all opinion of a particular subordinate, then unless he is careful, he will rate that subordinate high in nearly all qualities, including some in which he should be rated average or even low. Likewise, an unfavorable over-all opinion is likely to lower the rating of a person in all qualities, including those in which his rating should be average or

above. In both these cases, we speak of the halo effect.

Then, what about the *generosity error,* the tendency to give the individual the benefit of the doubt—to rate him higher than he should be rated? What about the *average error,* the tendency to rate the individual toward the middle or average when in doubt?

It is obvious that no rating system is better than its raters and that the effective use of ratings involves careful training of those who do the rating.

Use of results. What is really done with the results when the ratings are completed? There is a tendency in some quarters to make the results of rating scales the sole or principal basis for judgment about the ratee. An example is the practice of tying the results of a rating system very closely to promotion or to salary increases in a business. This policy is usually unwise. There can be no objection to considering

Figure 18.12. Something closely related to the "halo" effect. Even poorly prepared food may taste good under some circumstances.

the ratings of an individual before promoting or upgrading him, but there is serious question as to whether the rating should be the only, or even the principal, factor to be considered.

Another aspect of this problem, so far as the use of results is concerned, is whether the rating actually helps the ratee. Are the results of the rating discussed with him? Is the form so designed that it might be helpful to a person who wants to counsel with him with a view to his improvement? Are the raters who presumably have been trained in rating also trained in counseling? If they have not, then there will be considerable difficulty in making the system work effectively.

Incidentally, a limitation of the forced-choice system is that, even after the rating has been done, we do not know exactly how we have rated a person, since we never see the key. This, along with some other features of this system, makes it difficult to use the forced-choice rating scale as a basis for discussion with the ratee or as a basis for helping him improve in the future.

The early enthusiasm for rating methods has been tempered as we have had additional experience with them. Rating is used effectively in certain places, including some industrial and business establishments, but it is far from being *the* answer to the problem of the evaluation of people.

THE INTERVIEW IN APPRAISAL

The interview is, of course, a device which is used extensively in evaluating people. In schools and colleges, business and industry, the armed services, the psychological clinic, and many other situations we find people attempting to understand and appraise other people on the basis of one or many conversations with them. The interview is an essential part of many appraisals under such circumstances, and it deserves our careful scrutiny.

Kinds of Interviews. A number of different kinds of interviews can be distinguished. They can be classified on the basis of the use to which they are put, in which case we might talk about selection interviews, selling interviews, counseling interviews, interviews for review of performance, etc. Another classification might emphasize the form that the interview takes or the strategy that is used in it. Thus, an interview might consist mostly of direct questions, or the purpose might be to get the interviewee to select the subjects to be discussed and to talk about them.

So far as the question-and-answer type of interview is concerned, attention must, of course, be given to the choice of questions, the way they are phrased, the stress under which the interviewee is placed, his probable willingness or unwillingness to discuss critical subjects, and the like. Comments could be made about most other kinds of interviews, but let us select for discussion two somewhat unusual kinds.

The standardized interview. In a good many situations the standardized interview is used. Here the interviewer has a prepared list of questions, and his purpose is to get the answers to these questions. In employment situations, for example, several such forms have been prepared. Not only are the answers recorded but in some cases keys have been prepared for scoring the responses, so that each candidate for employment is given a total score, which becomes an essential part of evaluation and selection.

Such forms have the obvious advantage of objectivity and extensive coverage, but they have the disadvantage of allowing for little individuality on the part of the interviewer and the interviewee. Some interviewers make considerable use of these forms, but most interviewing is done on a more informal basis.

The depth interview. At several points in this book we have talked about the unconscious feelings, motives, and needs of the individual. These, we have said, are very important to understanding the individual, and hence there has been much interest in them and how they are discovered. Tests, especially the projective devices, are helpful along this line. In addition psychologists have become interested in using the interview for this purpose. Such an interview is often referred to as a *depth interview.*

Needless to say, to use the depth interview well requires a great deal of skill and training on the part of the one who uses it. He must know how and when to listen. He must know how to bring the other person to say what he wants to say but cannot—or even what he needs to say but does not want to. Gestures, pauses, facial expression, etc., must be interpreted, and all the findings brought together in a significant interpretation of the dynamics of the individual.

These methods have been applied most frequently in counseling and in the clinic. A well-known method along this line is *nondirective interviewing,* developed chiefly by Carl Rogers.[6] Another, earlier method is known as *psychoanalysis,* developed largely by Sigmund Freud.[7] In marketing activities in business and industry a somewhat similar procedure has been worked out by Ernest Dichter[8] and others, and is frequently referred to as *motivation research.* All three of these, of course, are complicated subjects and involve more time and space than we have available here, but depth interviewing has a bright future.

[6] Carl Rogers, *Client-centered Therapy,* Houghton Mifflin, Boston, 1951.

[7] There are a number of references to Freud at other points in this book. Freud described his method in many writings, among them *A General Introduction to Psychoanalysis.* One edition of this book was published by Perma Giants, New York, in 1949.

[8] As an example of this approach, see Ernest Dichter, "Psychology in Market Research," *Harvard Business Review,* 25:432–443, 1947.

Limitations of the Interview. The interview has many obvious limitations as an appraisal device. Indeed, many of the questions raised about raters and ratings could be repeated here. Personal opinion always enters into such situations, and bias may play a part also. Interviews are often held in a haphazard fashion, with no clear purpose in mind and no definite procedure being followed. The amount of time available for some interviews is much less than is needed, and the conditions under which they are held often leave much to be desired. Finally, the great majority of interviewers have had no training in interviewing skills or techniques.

It is not surprising under the circumstances that the reliability and validity of interview judgments are often found to be quite low. One study,[9] for example, involved a dozen experienced interviewers evaluating between fifty and sixty applicants for a certain position. So great were the differences in evaluation that one applicant was actually placed first by one interviewer and last by another. The interviewers also disagreed about many of the other applicants.

Regardless of its shortcomings, the interview, like ordinary observation, will always be with us. The day may come when we no longer use tests to evaluate people, though that is most unlikely, but we can hardly imagine a time when we no longer evaluate people by observing and talking with them. Let us therefore consider some ways in which we may increase our efficiency as interviewers.

Improving Interviewing Techniques. There are a number of ways in which we can improve our interviewing skills. In the first place, reading in general and, in particular, reading about interviewing will help. We do not maintain, of course, that we can become good interviewers simply by reading, or even by reading about in-

[9] H. L. Hollingsworth, *Judging Human Character,* Appleton-Century-Crofts, New York, 1922.

terviewing, any more than we can become good baseball players simply by reading about baseball. However, in an interview any subject may come up, and the ability, fostered by wide reading, to respond to many different subjects and to talk about them intelligently may be very helpful. The benefits to be gained by reading about various kinds of interviewing should, of course, be quite obvious.

A second suggestion is to have the purpose of the interview clearly in mind. This is usually not difficult if only the general or over-all purpose is considered, but what we are discussing here is something more specific. Just what kinds of questions do we expect to have answered? What sorts of information are we trying to get through the interview? What definite objectives do we have in mind? What is the best way to accomplish them? Such questions as these need careful consideration.

Another point, and one that certainly must not be overlooked, is the importance of *planning*. It is impracticable, of course, to plan every interview in which we engage, but we can plan the *important* interviews. There is far too much tendency in the field of interviewing to "fly blind," that is, to depend on ability to handle developments as they occur. But at times *what* we say to another person may be less important than *how* we say it. If we are to do a good job in a crucial interview, we need to make the same sort of careful preparation that we would make if we were getting ready to deliver a public speech. Surely we should plan carefully if we were called on to appear before a large audience, and sometimes the outcome of an interview, es-

pecially one involving issues and decisions that the other person feels strongly about, is more important than that of a speech. Even though we have to be flexible in using a plan, the need for planning an interview is apparent to anyone who gives the matter careful consideration.

In the fourth place, if we expect to improve our interviewing skill, we should develop techniques for getting below the surface, for going behind what the person says to why he says it. As we have already made clear, to become really proficient in this requires much training and experience, but all of us can improve our ability to observe another person as a means of coming to understand him. One of the best ways to do so is to develop *skill in listening*, or in drawing the other person out. Most of us do too much talking and not enough intelligent listening. Drawing the other person out through effective listening is one of the best ways of learning to understand him.

CONCLUSION

Ordinary observation, psychological testing, rating, and interviewing all contribute to our understanding of other people, though all may mislead us. Our appraisal of others is often inaccurate, sometimes as concerns what they do, but if anything, even more frequently in regard to *why* they do it. Our goal, in every evaluation, is to use each method wisely to whatever extent it is practicable to do so, and to combine the results from all of them, or from as many as we can use, to get an accurate picture of the individual.

SUMMARY

From time to time all of us must appraise and evaluate other people. Sometimes this appraisal is a part of our daily work, e.g.,

as a foreman, a physician, or a clinical psychologist. Sometimes it involves activities not directly related to work, e.g., rearing children, selecting friends, or choosing between candidates for an office.

Ordinary observation must frequently be used, but as a method of appraisal it is limited. It is hard to observe a person in a sufficiently large number of situations and also to get at the real causes of his behavior. Besides, our feelings about other people often interfere with our judgments about them.

Psychological tests also represent a means of evaluating people. In addition to the tests of intelligence and aptitude discussed in Chapter 17 there are achievement tests, tests of dexterity and sensory acuity, trade tests, interest scales, personality questionnaires, and projective techniques. Tests are largely objective in interpretation and often provide valuable information. However, they cannot reveal all the facts about a person, and their reliability and especially their validity are sometimes low. They are ordinarily grouped together in batteries and should be used and interpreted only by those who are trained in their use. They are extensively employed in schools, industry, the armed services, and the psychological clinic.

Another way to evaluate people is by means of rating scales. There are at least three kinds: descriptive-adjective, graphic, and forced-choice. Each of these has its limitations, and no one of them is *the* answer to effective evaluation. Besides, untrained raters make a good many errors regardless of the form which they use.

We also evaluate people by means of the interview. Like the other methods of appraisal, the interview may lead to many erroneous conclusions, especially for those who are not trained in its use. One special kind of interviewing, the depth interview, is used in market research and in dealing with people who need counseling or therapy. Another special kind is the standardized interview. We can improve our interviewing skills by reading about interviewing, determining the specific purpose of the interview, planning it carefully, and developing skills in listening.

QUESTIONS

1. What are the advantages and disadvantages of ordinary observation as a means of evaluating another person?

2. What is the nature of an achievement test? Where and for what purposes are achievement tests used?

3. What is (*a*) a dexterity test, (*b*) a sensory acuity test, (*c*) a trade test? How might each of these be used in evaluating an individual?

4. Discuss the nature of (*a*) the interest scale, (*b*) the personality questionnaire, and (*c*) the projective technique. In what ways do these differ from the other kinds of tests?

5. What is the theory on which projective devices are based? How successful are they in accomplishing the objective for which they are used?

6. Discuss the use of psychological tests (including intelligence and aptitude tests) in appraising people.

7. Describe and evaluate (*a*) the descriptive-adjective rating scale, (*b*) the graphic rating scale.

8. What are the distinctive features of the forced-choice plan of rating? What are the advantages and the disadvantages of this kind of rating?

9. What are the advantages of using rating scales as a means of appraising people? What are the limitations of such scales for this purpose?

10. Discuss the principal weaknesses of the interview as a method of evaluation and appraisal. Why do we continue to use it?

11. How may we improve our interviewing techniques? What is (*a*) a depth interview, (*b*) a standardized one?

12. Suppose you were a supervisor and were called upon to select one of your several sub-ordinates for promotion. How would you proceed to carry out this assignment? (Be sure to consider practical as well as theoretical aspects of the situation.)

SUGGESTED READINGS

Bellows, Roger M., and M. Frances Estep: *Employment Psychology: The Interview,* Rinehart, New York, 1954.

> (The interview in the selection process; errors in interviewing; improving interviewers' judgments; supplementing the interview with other devices.)

Cronbach, Lee J.: *Essentials of Psychological Testing,* Harper, New York, 1949.

> (Survey of the most important psychological tests, with material on both construction and interpretation of tests.)

Drake, Frances: *Manual of Employment Interviewing,* American Management Association, New York, 1946.

> (A short treatment of what companies are doing and should do about the interview and other methods of evaluation for employee selection.)

Hepner, Harry Walker: *Psychology Applied to Life and Work,* 2d ed., Prentice-Hall, Englewood Cliffs, N. J., 1950, chap. 17.

> (The use of psychology in industry, including that having to do with the evaluation of employees.)

Lawshe, C. H., Jr.: *Principles of Personnel Testing,* McGraw-Hill, New York, 1948.

> (The problems that arise in connection with devising tests for industrial situations and the application of these tests to such situations.)

Maier, Norman R. F.: *Psychology in Industry,* 2d ed., Houghton Mifflin, Boston, 1955.

> (Problems of evaluation and especially of interviewing and counseling in business and industry.)

Super, Donald R.: *Appraising Vocational Fitness by Means of Psychological Tests,* Harper, New York, 1949.

> (The use of tests in vocational counseling and placement.)

Tiffin, Joseph: *Industrial Psychology,* 3d ed., Prentice-Hall, Englewood Cliffs, N. J., 1952, chaps. 4–8.

> (An extensive discussion of tests in business and industry; especial attention to tests for vision and visual skills.)

Yoder, Dale: *Personnel Management and Industrial Relations,* 4th ed., Prentice-Hall, Englewood Cliffs, N. J., 1956, chaps. 8, 16.

> (A widely used text in personnel administration; tests, merit rating, and interviewing in the work situation.)

19 SOCIAL RELATIONSHIPS

Most of us at one time or another are likely to ask ourselves questions such as the following:

"Am I as attractive as the others in my crowd?"

"If Johnny can buy a house in Riverdale, why can't I?"

"Why don't people pay any attention to me?"

"What can I do to make more friends?"

"How can we train people so as to make them more effective leaders?"

"What can I do to get my subordinates to take responsibility?"

Every one of these questions has to do with relationships with other people—a vital part of our lives. By exploring this important subject, we can hope to better our understanding of human behavior.

PERCEIVING OURSELVES IN RELATION TO OTHERS

Comparisons with other people are important factors in our personalities. How do we perceive ourselves in relation to others? Are we tall or short? Attractive or unattractive? Clever or dull? High or low in prestige? These questions cannot be answered without comparing *ourselves with others*. We have defined the self as the individual as known to and felt about by the individual. A great deal of this self-knowing and feeling is a matter of perceiving and evaluating ourselves in relation to other people. Although it would be an exaggeration to say that our interpersonal relationships are *all* that determines self-perception, it is nevertheless true that these relationships are the most important factors in self-perception.

Figure 19.1. In what ways do you compare yourself with others?

Feeling Privileged or Deprived in Comparison with Others. Typically we compare our privileges and our deprivations with those of other people; that is, we compare ourselves with others who are in the same boat. Often the absolute amount of privilege or hardship is not so important as the *relative* amount. Parents have often noticed how their children are acutely aware of their relative privileges. Children in a family often want to be equal in very exacting ways: going to bed at the same time, getting the same amount of attention, and even having their food served in identical dishes. Why this concern with equal treatment? Most likely, the children are interested in equal treatment because of what it signifies with respect to the parents' love and affection.

In the adult world, too, we find great concern with relative privileges. For example, officers in the military services usually expect and receive greater privileges than do those below them in rank. An officer's privileges in a combat area may actually be below those of an enlisted man in a rear area, but if the officer feels relatively privileged, he may be quite content. As another illustration, a person usually evaluates his salary in relationship to the salaries of those whom he feels are his equals in seniority, experience, job, etc. In other words, we compare our lot with that of others who are in the same boat.

How we evaluate our status depends on the people with whom we compare ourselves. A bank clerk may be quite pleased with the prestige involved in his job and the conditions of his work as compared with those of a day laborer, but when he compares himself with people in professional groups he may feel relatively underprivileged. By and large, however, there is usually some particular group, typically one close at hand, with which we most frequently compare ourselves.

Setting Goals by Comparing Ourselves with Others. Not only do we compare our privileges and deprivations with those of others; we also set our goals in relation to others' performance. In other words, we expect to do at least as well as other people who are in a comparable status. We aspire to excel those whom we consider inferior in capabilities as compared with ourselves. On the other hand, we do not expect to do as well as others whom we perceive to be superior to ourselves.

There are many examples of this process of setting goals by comparing ourselves with others. A boy who sees a *younger* one outrun him will then muster greater effort in order to surpass his younger rival. In our achievement-oriented culture, it is very easy to stimulate an older child to attempt to outdo a younger one.

Another example is a scientist who feels that his own work is progressing reasonably well but one day finds that a former classmate has published a significant piece of research. This scientist then becomes motivated to emulate this standard.

The same tendency is shown in the world of business. Suppose a businessman finds that a competing firm has set up a new branch in an exclusive business district. He may feel that, since his business rivals have been so enterprising, he too ought to show some initiative in setting up branch offices.

In the previous examples, a person sees how others whom he regards as his equals or inferiors have achieved, and he tends to set his standards according to their achievement. Now let us consider the case of the person who sees someone else whom he regards as superior to him achieve or not achieve, and how this affects his own motivation. A small-town boy is a reasonably good student in the junior class in high school. He has a friend in the senior class whom he regards as being a considerably better student. The next year, this friend goes to a big university and finds it extremely difficult to make his grades. In fact, after the first semester, he drops out of the big university and goes to a smaller school, where the courses are easier and where he receives more individual help and attention. Under these circumstances the younger boy feels that if his friend, who is even more able in his estimation, is unable to succeed in the large university, perhaps he too would fail there. He therefore decides that on graduation from high school he will enter a small college.

The conclusion from this example and the ones before it is that comparisons with others play an important part in determining our goals.

MALADJUSTED RELATIONSHIPS

We have discussed our social relationships in the sense of how we perceive ourselves relative to other people. Let us now examine such relationships from the point of view of how satisfactory they are as forms of adjustment. A survey of some of the different patterns of *maladjusted* relationships will help us to understand difficulties in social relationships and prepare us to discuss how such relationships can be improved.

There are a number of inadequate ways of trying to get along with other people.

Among those we shall discuss are being dependent on others, dominating others, rebelling against others, and avoiding others.[1]

Being Dependent on Others. A person may try to get along with other people by assuming a dependent relationship with them. He may seek the support of influential people and try to ally himself with those who are in positions of power or prestige. Indeed, he may even assume a fawning manner around important people.

A dependent person is likely to show a self-effacing type of conformity. He may conform rather rigidly to rules of proper behavior. But his conformity is not necessarily inspired by a real acceptance of the values underlying such behavior. Rather he is attempting to protect himself from punishment and is seeking the love of others.

When we look at the personality of someone who assumes a dependent relationship with others, we usually see a person who wants love. It is possible that as a child he felt strongly rejected. In adulthood, he wishes to secure the affection of other people. Possibly he fears others and does not want to do anything which will risk rejection. Also he is likely to be anxious about expressing hostility toward others. If he is aware of such hostility, his consequent anxiety may induce him to act in ways not evoking hostility. A dependent person may even repress his hostility, so that he is not aware of the fact that he feels it. In the clinical treatment of such dependent persons, however, the repressed hostility is likely to be uncovered. Insight into these hostile tendencies helps the person to adjust.

[1] The discussion which follows is based in part on the ideas of Karen Horney, a psychoanalyst who has emphasized the influence of learning in personality development, both abnormal and normal. The reference is K. Horney, *Neurosis and Human Growth*, Norton, New York, 1950. See also K. Horney, *Our Inner Conflicts*, Norton, New York, 1945.

Although a dependent person may receive many benefits as a result of his dependency, he frequently resents his dependency. His sense of worth is threatened, and at least some of his needs are frustrated.

Dominating Others. Instead of trying to get along with others by being dependent on them, a person may try to dominate them. That is, he may seek to be so powerful that he can bend other people to his will. Often he exploits them to his own ends. A supervisor, for example, may be hard-driving in his treatment of his subordinates in order to obtain his own advancement. Or a dominating person may try to excel others in any type of competitive situation. If he is a student, he may try to be the best in various sports or in his school work. If he is a businessman, he may attempt to be the most powerful and successful in his field. A person who assumes a dominating relationship with others tends to perceive a wide variety of situations as competitive. It appears that he easily becomes threatened by other people's achievements.

The pattern of dominating others is sometimes found in business organizations. A supervisor may attempt to carry out a paternalistic pattern; that is, he may adopt the role of a benevolent autocrat. He may ask his employees to come in to see him whenever they have personal problems, and he may even direct their personal affairs. Such a role enhances his self-esteem by making him feel important and generous. As long as his employees assume a properly dependent role in relationship to him, this supervisor can operate smoothly, and his employees will often receive many favors. As was pointed out in our discussion of being dependent on others, however, employees frequently resent their dependent status.

In contrast to a paternalistic pattern of dominating others is an authoritarian pattern. As an example, let us consider a harshly competitive executive. He drives his employees. When decisions are made, *he* makes them. *He* is the one who determines all policies. His employees are expected to obey him. Here there is no pretense of benevolence—at most, only a stern "justice."

What are some of the needs and attitudes of a person who seeks to dominate others? It is quite possible that he has strong hostility toward other people. In a sense, winning over others, excelling them, forcing them to do what he wants, can be used as devices for punishing, destroying, and degrading them. It is true that this hostility may be masked in the guise of efficiency, but often it is still there.

Often a person who seeks to dominate others has a need to be important to others and important in his own eyes. Very likely he has some considerable sense of inferiority. If he is in a position of superiority and power, it is easier for him to have a

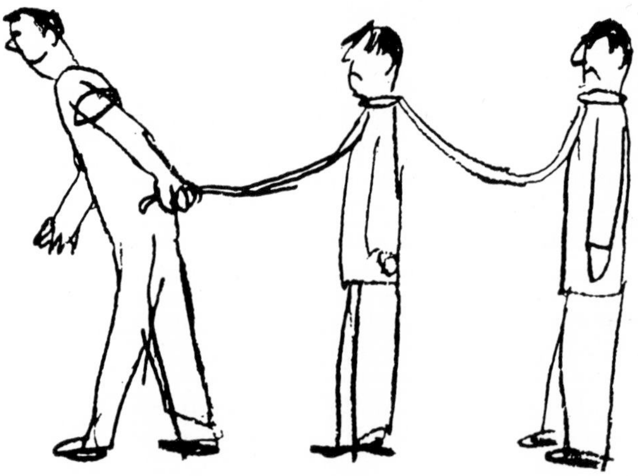

Figure 19.2. One *way to get people to* "string along" *with you.*

favorable self-picture. Yet underneath there may be a feeling that he is somehow not good enough, somehow not really important. He may wish to be so strong that he cannot be hurt by others.

There is the strong likelihood that a dominating person deeply needs love from people. Usually he will deny that he has such a need, because his dependency needs have become repressed. He may say that such feelings are mere sentimentality. When a hard-driving executive goes to a hospital with a gastric ulcer, he may have his repressed dependency needs satisfied without serious threat to self-esteem. After all, he did not ask for love—he is simply sick and needs help.

Rebelling against Others. Still another pattern of relationships with other people is rebelling against them. Here the person is fighting against others. He resents supervision and authority in all forms. He resists conforming to rules, and he takes any requirements as a personal affront. Frequently he attacks those in authority, or gives only grudging compliance to rules.

Let us look at the example of Jerry Harper, who was convicted of assault on his foreman. It appears that Jerry's foreman called him down for being late one day. Before Jerry knew what had happened, he attacked his foreman and badly injured him. Jerry was committed to prison for this offense. In prison Jerry taunted his guards. One day when he was called into the warden's office to discuss his plans after leaving prison, he offended the warden—told him to "mind his own business."

All his life Jerry had been fighting with those in authority—his father, his teachers, and policemen. He knew that his reaction led him into trouble, but he just could not help himself. Whenever Jerry dealt with a person having authority, he became irrationally angry.

Why is it that a person rebels against others? What sort of needs does such behavior serve? For the explanation of this behavior, we usually must go back to childhood experiences as the source of the difficulty. Jerry Harper's father was harsh and domineering. Jerry felt rejected by his father, whose arbitrary demands were irksome and damaging to Jerry's self-esteem. Gradually he built up a pattern of bitter rejection of authority in his father. When Jerry went to school he carried over this same pattern, with the result that he antagonized some of his teachers. Their antagonism only made him more resentful. Understanding teachers attempted to deal permissively with Jerry, but he was highly suspicious and misinterpreted their intentions—considered them weak. Soon Jerry found himself allied with other boys who also felt somewhat hostile to authority. Acts of vandalism followed. Soon the breaking of laws was both an assault on hated authority and a way of winning acclaim from his fellows. When Jerry left school and went to work, he encountered authority again in the person of his foreman.

A person who rebels against people tends not to identify with them; that is, he is not genuinely concerned with their welfare. Not feeling loved himself, he cannot love others. Such a person's rebelliousness is aggravated by anyone who assumes an unusually dominating or authoritarian role in attempting to control him.

Avoiding Others. Another inadequate way of dealing with people is to avoid them. One way to avoid others is to do so physically. A solitary job, for example, permits a person to avoid others physically, so that he does not really have to adjust to them. As long as he can be alone, he does not have to face the problems of getting along with people.

A person may also avoid others psychologically. This is, he may keep all his personal contacts on a superficial level.

Figure 19.3. Why might a person avoid the company of others? What effect do you think his behavior has on others? Does a person who has limited interaction with others necessarily have a disturbed personality?

Although he may be around other people most of the time, his contacts exclude all intimacy. He does not form any deep friendships. His personal life is kept purely private. When people ask him about his own affairs his answers are likely to be evasive, formal, or casual.

How can anyone be around many people and still avoid them? Let us look at an example. Mike Hannah works as a salesperson in a downtown store. In the course of his work, he meets many people during the day, but all his contacts with people are on a strictly routine level. He sticks strictly to business. At coffee breaks, Mike is likely to busy himself with his records instead of going out with the others. For his noon lunch, Mike prefers to bring a sandwich from home. Occasionally he goes to the drugstore down the street and has a snack at the counter—again, all by himself. After work he walks through the crowds and experiences a loneliness which is hard to satisfy. Perhaps he spends the evening alone at a motion picture. He has no girl friends. In all these ways Mike

keeps his relationships with other people on a formal and superficial level.

Why does a person choose to avoid other people? Why does he take this particular way of getting along with them—or, really, *not* getting along with them? Probably underlying this pattern is a fear of others. Fearing rejection, such a person maintains all his personal relationships on a formal plane. By not asking anything of anyone else, he knows that he cannot be refused. If he does not interact with others on a personal level, he feels less likely to be hurt.

Another feeling that a person who avoids others might have is a hatred of people. His hostility may cause him to avoid others. The feelings of anxiety and guilt that sometimes accompany hostility may also be alleviated by avoiding people.

It is probably true that fear of others and hostility toward them tend to go together. One who both fears and avoids others is not likely to get love from them. This very frustration of a need for love is likely to be deeply resented. A self-defense is to deny both the need for love and the aggressive feelings.

Other Aspects of Unsatisfying Relationships. Although we have discussed four kinds of maladjusted relationships with people, it should be emphasized that this classification is merely a matter of convenience. A person may—and often does—show tendencies in more than one of these directions. For example, a person might both seek to dominate others and yet rebel against authority. In utilizing the insights we have discussed, we should keep in mind the fact that this typology—like others—does not include all the significant factors in personality and does not do full justice to individual differences.

It is worth noticing that most of our discussion has centered on attitudes acquired in early childhood. Attitudes of insecurity learned in childhood may render a person more vulnerable to further threats. Moreover, his ways of behaving may result in further experiences which add to his difficulties. To some degree, however, the influence of unfavorable experiences in childhood may be counteracted by other factors. As the child matures he may acquire skills that help him to achieve self-esteem. Other people may be supportive and permissive, so that the negative feelings remain in the background. In other words, unfavorable early childhood experiences do not necessarily doom a person to lifelong misery in his relationships with others.

IMPROVING SOCIAL RELATIONSHIPS

Thus far we have discussed some kinds of maladjusted relationships with others. We should, however, also consider what satisfying relationships are like and how they may be cultivated.

Nature of Satisfying Relationships. Let us recognize in advance that probably no one has uniformly smooth and pleasant relations with other people. There are almost certain to be some points of strain and conflict in getting along with others, although in a well-adjusted person such difficulties are usually only temporary. Furthermore, there are many different ways of dealing successfully with people, not just one way.

With these cautions in mind, here is a portrait of a person who has satisfying personal relationships. He enjoys being with other people and working with them. Different status relationships do not bother him. He is comfortable with a superior, a subordinate, or an equal. Having convictions of his own, he still is willing to consider without ego-defensiveness the evaluations of others. He is tolerant (accepting) both of others and of himself. He identifies readily with other people and is interested in them. Basically, he feels that others are trustworthy and friendly—or at least neutral—until he has grounds for believing otherwise. Needless to say, he does not fear or hate others; nor does he anxiously crave their love and approval, although he finds these things satisfying.

In other words, having satisfying relationships with others is fundamentally a matter of having appropriate attitudes toward the self and others.

Cultivating Satisfying Relationships. There are no certain methods for improving our social relationships. Each of the following suggestions (and others that might have been included) may be effective in certain cases. To evaluate them, we must consider their relevance to our own situation.

Working with others for group-shared goals. We usually find it helpful to work with others for group-shared goals—a better product, an improved training program, better service to clients, building a new hospital or church. If the goals of a group are worthwhile and consistent with our values, we usually do not find it very difficult to identify with the group. In contributing to their objectives, which we share, we tend to receive their approval and earn our self-respect. In focusing upon group objectives, we are not so likely to experience negative feelings of hostility, fear, and rivalry.

Mastering popular recreational skills. Many of us find it helpful to master some of the popular recreational skills such as bowling, dancing, and bridge. It is true that skill in these and other pursuits does not guarantee satisfying personal relationships, and some people may be able to establish such relationships without them. Nevertheless, a moderate degree of proficiency often aids us in getting to know others and so may lead to relationships on a deeper level.

Communicating with others. Many of us benefit from sharing ideas and feelings with others. People who keep their thoughts and evaluations to themselves are keeping an important part of themselves away from other people. Whether they do so because of fear or hostility, or for some other reason, they block themselves from interacting with others in ways that are significant. Our best friends are usually people with whom we enjoy talking about things that matter. But communication is a two-way street. We also need to listen to the other fellow—how he feels and how he thinks. This helps us to understand him, and this in turn may improve our relationships.

Some problems may be solved more readily by discussing them with people who are of importance to us—close friends or members of our family. Of course we should use some discretion about topics, times, and places. Husbands and wives may need to discuss frankly some of their conflicts, but it may be unwise for them to rush

Figure 19.4. Working and playing with other people are two of the best ways to develop satisfying personal relationships.

headlong into the most threatening material. The emphasis should be on the problems and their solution, not merely on expression of sympathy and reassurance.

Observing well-adjusted people. It may be helpful to observe well-adjusted people. Most of us know a few people who are very effective in relationships with others, but the choice of suitable models is no easy matter, and no one model may fully satisfy our needs. The best model is not necessarily the most colorful or dominant person.

The thing to look for is how such people *evaluate and perceive* their relationships. Probably it is more important to understand a model on this level than to know some of the specific skills that he uses in getting along with people.

Other ways of improving relationships. There are a number of other ways of improving human relationships which are related to the ones that we have discussed. One of these is to take up a hobby that may be shared with others. Interests in common activities tend to make our relationships with others more satisfying. Doing things for other people may have the effect of achieving values that we consider worthwhile and of winning the friendship of others. It may even be helpful to move to an environment in which our relationships with others are subject to less strain.

In more serious cases, counseling and psychotherapy may be necessary. Practically all treatment of this kind involves getting insight into and reevaluating our relationships with others. Usually it also is necessary to try out new ways of adjusting to other people until more satisfying ways are found. Generally these ways are discussed with the therapist, further insight is gained, and still other ways of acting are explored.

Although the personal relationship between a disturbed person and his therapist is always a vital part of the treatment process, the role of other people is even more apparent in group therapy. Under skilled leadership a very permissive group situation is set up. Each member is encouraged to express his feelings regarding himself and others—without fear of punishment or rejection. In the give-and-take of group discussion, each person can check his evaluations against those of others. Generally he discovers that other people too have problems, often like his own. In the therapy group he can freely try out new ways of interacting with other people Gradually he may carry over some of the more successful ways of behaving to situations outside the group. Such methods have been used both with adults and children, although with children the emphasis usually is less on discussion and more on shared activities and play.

Ordinarily the process of changing our ways of adjusting to other people is a gradual one. After all, the ways we have been using have been thoroughly learned, and they have powerful motivational supports. To a considerable degree, they are self-enhancing and self-defending. Often we find ourselves resisting change, and the changes which do occur usually are limited. Nevertheless, it is possible for relearning to take place. Ideally, satisfying interpersonal relationships amount to more than the avoidance of anxieties; they involve positive enjoyments.

EFFECTIVE LEADERSHIP

Whenever there is a group of people, there will usually be one or a few individuals who are more influential than are others. These individuals play a larger part in directing, initiating, and controlling activity than do others. This function of directing the activity of a group may be termed *leadership*, a subject which has both interest and importance. Let us consider further the nature of leadership, the

Figure 19.5. Almost all groups have at least one member who acts as a leader. Think of the groups to which you belong. Who are the leaders, and why have they become leaders? Why have certain other people not *become leaders? Why are some people consistently followers?*

determinants of leadership, and some techniques of effective leadership.

Nature of Leadership. Leadership should be regarded as a process—the process of directing, initiating, regulating, and coordinating group activity. A particular individual, the leader, may do most of the directing, or the direction may come from more than one person. In the latter case, various people initiate proposals, provide information, give directions to others, summarize, and perform various other roles in the total process. More typically, however, there is someone who is more influential than anyone else, although the margin of his power over other members of the group may be greater in some groups than in others.

We should distinguish leadership in a voluntary group from leadership in a formal organization. The leader of a voluntary group, such as a fraternity or a club, emerges from the group itself. He becomes a leader by virtue of his resourcefulness, popular appeal, and the like. On the other

hand, the leader of a formal organization, such as a company or a governmental agency, is appointed from above, or has created the organization with himself at the head. He is known as a *formal leader.*

In order to carry out his role, a formal leader must obtain from the group acceptance of his influence (there may, of course, be mixed feelings about him). In addition to formal leaders, *informal leaders* often develop in formal organizations. These informal leaders have no status in the formal organization, but nevertheless they usually exert considerable influence. In order to exercise effective leadership a formal leader must work through these informal leaders. If they are against him, he has little chance of success.

It will be helpful to look at some of the different forms of the leadership role. No one system of classification will fully cover the many styles of leadership, but the following division into *authoritarian, laissez-faire,* and *democratic* types of leadership may be useful.[2]

In authoritarian leadership, the leader exercises arbitrary power. He gives orders, with or without explanation. He makes the decisions without consulting the group, evaluates performance according to his own standards, which he may keep to himself, and controls the rewards and punishments.

The authoritarian pattern of leadership is encouraged and expected in some forms of organization, such as the military services. Skilled authoritarian direction may sometimes result in very great accomplishment, which may be gratifying to the members of the group. Taking the role of an au-

[2] A fuller discussion of these styles of leadership and a report of research in this area may be found in R. Lippitt and R. K. White, "An Experimental Study of Leadership and Group Life," in G. E. Swanson, T. M. Newcomb, and E. L. Hartley (eds.), *Readings in Social Psychology,* rev. ed., Holt, New York, 1952, pp. 340–355.

**EMERGENT LEADERS
IN CONFERENCES**

During the years 1948 through 1950, a research team observed conferences in seventy-two business, government, and industrial organizations. The problems of the study * had to do with the conditions under which leaders other than the designated leader of a conference emerge. Such unofficial leaders were called *emergent* leaders.

Observers obtained a number of different measures for the purpose of this study. The frequency with which each conference participant performed the following functions was tabulated: goal setting, problem proposing, information seeking, information giving, solution proposing, development seeking (e.g., asking for clarification), development giving, opposing, supporting, summarizing, and non-problem-directed (irrelevancies). On a postconference rating sheet the observers indicated who was the designated leader of a group and who were the "real" leaders (those who most often performed what the research team considered central leadership functions). In addition the observers rated each group for the extent of divergence or similarity of opinions of the members and also for the presence or absence of cliques. Motivation to take the leader's role was measured by rating methods. Acceptance of leadership by other members was ascertained by having each member rank all others in terms of their "neededness" in the conference.

The results showed that (1) emergent leaders tended to be present when the designated leaders performed relatively few of the acts central in the leader role, (2) emergent leaders were present in conferences where there were cliques and differences of opinion, (3) emergent leaders had high personal motivation (ego-involvement), and (4) emergent leaders were highly rated as "needed" by the group.

The results of this study are in line with the conclusion that being a leader depends on performing the acts which the group expects and requires of a leader.

* Walter H. Crockett, "Emergent Leadership in Small, Decision-making Groups," *Journal of Abnormal and Social Psychology,* 51:378–383, 1955.

thoritarian leader is easier for some people than for others. The members of a group do not always *want* responsibility, and they may be confused if it is thrust upon them.

In laissez-faire ("hands-off") leadership —which is not really leadership, but the absence of leadership—the leader exercises no positive influence. The members may agree that he has the position of leader, but he plays a very inactive part in initiating and coordinating activity.

The laissez-faire pattern of leadership usually is quite ineffective. The person in the leadership position may be afraid to try to exercise influence or may have been frustrated in his attempts. Essentially he is not carrying out a leadership function. For the members of the group, this situation usually results in frustration. In order to endure, the group must evolve some leadership structure (formal or informal).

In democratic leadership, the leader assists the group in the making of decisions. He encourages the group to formulate goals and procedures and standards of performance. It would be a mistake to regard a democratic leader as a sort of nondirective therapist who reflects the feelings and thoughts of the members. He may do

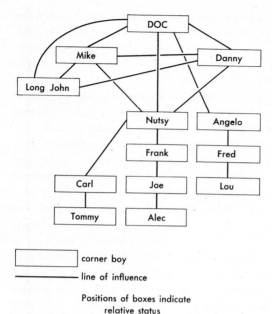

DOC

Mike   Danny

Long John

Nutsy   Angelo

Frank   Fred

Carl   Joe   Lou

Tommy   Alec

☐ corner boy

── line of influence

Positions of boxes indicate
relative status

Figure 19.6. Diagram of leader-follower relations in a voluntary group. Doc Norton's gang of "corner boys." Street-corner society is made up mainly of single young men who have no regular employment and who tend, as the name suggests, to hang around street corners. Doc, who is the leader, has lines of influence reaching down to the lower-ranked members. (After W. H. Whyte, Street Corner Society, *University of Chicago Press, Chicago, 1943. Used by permission of the publishers.)*

some of this, but he also exerts a positive influence.

Democratic leadership requires appropriate attitudes and skills on the part of both leaders and followers. People with poor personal adjustment—such as those who need to dominate, rebel against, or avoid others—usually find it difficult to exercise democratic leadership. The followers in the group must be willing to assume responsibility for goal setting, decision making, and carrying out decisions.

Our description of democratic leadership has been most relevant to voluntary groups, such as clubs, rather than to groups that are parts of formal organizations. For example, a department in a factory or a class in a school is a part of a larger organization. This larger organization has goals—or the people who control it have—which may or may not be those of the people in one of its divisions. A factory, for example, must produce at a profit. A university seeks to educate and add to human knowledge (among other objectives). The leader, appointed from above, thus has responsibilities both to the organization and to the group of which he has charge. The organizational objectives place limitations on the decision-making power of any group which is part of the organization. A history class, for example, cannot be empowered to decide to study chemistry, get a different instructor, and do away with grades. One of the functions of the leader of such a group is to clarify the over-all objectives of the organization, to try to get the group to identify with these objectives, and to help the group to understand its relation to the organization as a whole. As a representative of the organization, he has a responsibility to evaluate performance and hold up standards. There is a great deal of interest in the industrial world today in developing methods which will take into account the functional requirements of the organization and the personalities of the people—on whatever level—who make it up.

In the past, many treatments of leadership have focused on the *traits* of leaders rather than on the *process* of leadership. Most psychologists now feel that there is no single pattern of leadership traits and that leadership depends on many factors in the total situation. Although, on the average, leaders tend to be more intelligent, better adjusted, and physically larger and stronger than their followers, there are many exceptions. Increasingly, investigators have shifted their attenton to the

Table 19.1 Comparison of Authoritarian, Laissez-faire, and Democratic Leadership

	Authoritarian	*Laissez-faire*	*Democratic*
Source of leader's authority	From above, or based on his own power to control rewards and punishments	(Authority not exercised)	From group; delegated by leader (with limitations)
Objectives of leader	To get task done; to attain his personal ends	To avoid conflict with members or the effort of assuming responsibility, while hoping task will somehow get done	To help group formulate and attain its goals; to help group develop
Distribution of leadership functions	Concentrated in leader, or delegated by him in part	Scattered and irregularly assumed	Relatively widely distributed, although on the whole leader has more influence than any other member
Efficiency	May vary from high to low	Generally low and variable	Usually moderate or very high (especially in the long run)

nature of the *situation* in which leadership occurs.[3] Given the goals of a group, what knowledge, skills, and other characteristics are required of a leader? A person who meets the particular needs of the group very effectively has an excellent chance of gravitating to a position of leadership. The attributes which qualify a person for leadership in one group—for example, being the only person on a camping trip who knows about camping—do not necessarily qualify him for leadership in another group. Certain groups, however, may require the same *class* of skills, such as those in directing discussion and planning, so that the same person might very well perform a leadership role in any of these groups. Of course, whether a person who can perform a leader's role *will* do so depends on his motives, on whether or not

[3] C. A. Gibb, "Leadership," in G. Lindzey (ed.), *Handbook of Social Psychology*, Addison-Wesley, Cambridge, Mass., 1954, vol. 2.

others are already acting as leaders, and on many other factors.

Cultivating Leadership Skills. From what has been said thus far about the nature of leadership and the personality factors in interpersonal relations, it should be apparent that developing effective leadership is a very complicated process. No one can give us a set of rules which will make us effective leaders. On the other hand, training in leadership may have some beneficial results.

Many of these leadership-training programs seek to inform leaders. The conception here is that a leader needs to know the technical aspects of his job and how the activities of his group fit into those of the larger organization. A second aim of most leadership-training programs is to educate the leader in a philosophy of leadership—generally a democratic one. Trainees are influenced to believe that the function of a leader is *not* to manipulate the mem-

Figure 19.7. The key to leadership is having the personal characteristics which fit the requirements of the situation. Each type of group situation calls for some distinctive pattern of interests, skills, and other characteristics on the part of the potential leader.

bers of the group but to help them to develop to a level where they can set worthwhile goals, plan effectively, and take responsibility for carrying out their plans. A third goal which leadership-training programs may seek is to educate people in the nature of group process. This involves an understanding of how personality factors influence people in groups, the nature and operation of groups, and the relation of a group to factors outside the group such as the organization as a whole, other groups, the community, and the like. A balanced program of training does not rely solely on lectures but seeks also to use workshop and laboratory methods in which the trainees actually participate in group activities and observe, analyze, and discuss their experiences.

We shall make a number of suggestions for ways of cultivating effective leadership.

Paying attention to both the people and the task. One of the traps into which we, as leaders, can fall is to become so highly absorbed in the task that we forget the people who carry out the task. Some foremen see their job solely as "getting out the production," just as some teachers focus on the task of "putting across the subject matter." But we must also take into account the personalities of the people who

make up the group—their goals, their attitudes toward one another, their feelings about themselves and their leader, and the like. It has been said that the most effective leaders tend to be *person-centered* in the sense that they are interested in people first and the task second.

In order for a group to function effectively, two broad classes of requirements need to be satisfied.[4] One class is *task requirements*—getting the job done, reaching the task objectives of the group. The second class has to do with *group maintenance requirements*—building and maintaining suitable attitudes of the members toward one another and toward the leader. Different leaders and different groups vary in how adequately they handle one or both of these requirements.

As leaders, we need to cultivate sensitivity to other people's attitudes and needs. In part, this skill depends on good personal adjustment, which permits objectivity. It also depends on the knowledge of human behavior in general and on information about the particular individuals and groups which are involved. If we succeed in making others feel secure and worthwhile, they

[4] K. D. Benne and P. Sheats, "Functional Roles of Group Members," *Journal of Social Issues,* 4:41–49, 1948.

THE RELATIVE
INFLUENCE OF
LEADERS AND
MEMBERS

Merei * studied the relative influence of leaders and members in a group. Children from two nurseries were observed over a period of time, after which they were divided into a number of groups. Each group was made up of children of the same sex and within a two-year age range, who were average in influence (by certain criteria), and who had neither strong likes nor strong dislikes for one another. Within three to six meetings each group had formed certain "traditions" regarding who sat where, who played with what, ceremonies, order of games, and jargon. At this point a child who was judged to have leadership potential (older, domineering, frequently imitated, aggressive, and tending to initiate activity) was put in each group.

The problem was whether the group follows the leader or whether it forces its traditions upon him. Which influence is the greater, that of the leader or of the group?

The results show that the influence of the group tended to be greater than that of the leader. "In the overwhelming majority of our cases the leader was forced to accept the group's traditions—that is, he proved weaker than the group but still managed to play the leader's role." Different leaders asserted leadership in different ways—by ordering members to do things already in accordance with their traditions; by becoming proprietor of the objects of play; by diplomatically accepting group traditions and then gradually transforming them.

We should recognize, of course, that any conclusions from this experiment must be restricted to the conditions under which the results were obtained. But the study is a fine attempt to study the dynamics of the leadership process.

* F. Merei, "Group Leadership and Institutionalization," in G. E. Swanson, T. M. Newcomb, and E. L. Hartley (eds.), *Readings in Social Psychology*, rev. ed., Holt, New York, 1952, pp. 318–328.

work more effectively and are more cooperative. Being less defensive, they are more objective and task-oriented. How can we make others feel more secure and worthwhile? We must obtain their trust through honest, sincere, nonthreatening actions. We must impress them with our concern for their welfare and our respect for their potentialities. Incidentally, it is easier to communicate such an impression if we actually feel that way. In fact, it is nearly impossible if we do not!

Getting the members to work for the group. A second way to cultivate effective leadership is to get the members to work for the group; in other words, to get them to identify with the group and its objectives. In a voluntary group which is not part of a larger organization, the members, assisted by the leader, are free to set their own goals. Our main function as leaders in this regard is to see that as many of the members as possible participate in the process of setting the goals. In addition we can encourage the members to take responsibility for working out ways of attaining these goals and for carrying out their plans.

The problem is somewhat more complicated when the group is part of a larger organization. As was stated earlier, such a group is subject to requirements from above, although in some organizations groups may have a voice in deciding policies and objectives at the organizational level. As leaders, we must clarify for the members the nature and reasons for these

**ROLES IN A
DISCUSSION GROUP**

Benne and Sheats * have made an interesting analysis of the roles people take when they may participate in a discussion group. They classify these roles as (1) group task roles, which further the carrying out of the task; (2) group building and maintenance roles, which foster good personal relations within the group; and (3) individual-centered roles, which are disruptive in that they tend to satisfy narrow personal needs. These roles are described below:

Group Task Roles

The *initiator-contributor* suggests or proposes to the group new ideas or a changed way of regarding the group problem or goal.

The *coordinator* shows or clarifies the relationships among various ideas and suggestions, tries to pull ideas and suggestions together or tries to coordinate the activities of various members or sub-groups.

The *orienter* defines the position of the group with respect to its goals by summarizing what has occurred, points to departures from agreed-upon directions or goals, or raises questions about the direction which the group discussion is taking.

Other task roles are those of *evaluator-critic, information seeker, information giver, elaborator, energizer, procedural technician,* and *recorder.*

Group Building and Maintenance Roles

The *encourager* praises, agrees with and accepts the contributions of others. He indicates warmth and solidarity in his attitude toward other group members, offers commendation and praise and in various ways indicates understanding and acceptance of other points of view, ideas and suggestions.

* K. D. Benne and P. Sheats, "Functional Roles of Group Members," *Journal of Social Issues,* 4:41–49, 1948.

END-OF-MEETING EVALUATION FORM

Please give your reactions to today's meeting.
Your evaluations will be considered carefully
so that we may improve future meetings.

1. How do you feel about today's meeting? (check)

   Poor   Mediocre   All right   Good   Excellent

2. What did you like least about today's meeting?

3. What did you like best about today's meeting?

4. What suggestions do you have regarding future meetings?

Figure 19.8. An end-of-meeting form. Such a form is usually unsigned, so that members will feel free to express their views. The leader, sometimes with the aid of a committee, may use this information in order to plan activities which will fit the needs and interests of the group.

The *harmonizer* mediates the differences between other members, attempts to reconcile disagreements, relieves tension in conflict situations through jesting or pouring oil on the troubled waters, etc.

The *compromiser* operates from within a conflict in which his idea or position is involved. He may offer compromise by yielding status, admitting his error, by disciplining himself to maintain group harmony, or by "coming half-way" in moving along with the group.

Other group maintenance roles are those of *standard setter*, *group-observer*, *follower*, and *gate keeper* (who attempts to keep communication channels open by encouraging or facilitating the participation of others).

Individual-centered Roles

The *aggressor* may work in many ways—deflating the status of others, expressing disapproval of the values, acts or feelings of others, attacking the group or the problem it is working on, joking aggressively, showing envy toward another's contribution by trying to take credit for it, etc.

The *blocker* tends to be negativistic and stubbornly resistant, disagreeing and opposing without or beyond "reason" and attempting to maintain or bring back an issue after the group has rejected or by-passed it.

The *playboy* makes a display of his lack of involvement in the group's processes. This may take the form of cynicism, nonchalance, horseplay and other more or less studied forms of "out of field" behavior.

Other individual-centered roles are those of *recognition-seeker*, *self-confessor*, *dominator*, *help-seeker*, and *special-interest pleader*. All such roles disrupt group discussion.

organizational objectives. For example, an executive in a business organization must make clear to his subordinates why costs must be kept down, why quality must be kept up, why certain decisions and actions are necessary, and the like. One way in which we can foster identification with these objectives is to encourage individual and group planning as to how these objectives may be reached. Within the limits imposed by organizational requirements from above, we may permit and encourage a group to set goals and make other kinds of decisions. In other words, we should encourage members to "get into the act."

Other methods. There are a number of other ways in which we can cultivate effective leadership. One of these is to ask for suggestions from members of the group. Some of these suggestions, of course, will be useful. Others, not so practical, should also be treated with respect.

It is also a good idea to keep the members of the group informed, especially about the matters that most directly concern them. In this way, unexpected changes may usually be avoided, and the reasons for policies and actions are more likely to be understood.

As leaders we should strive to be as permissive as practicable. That is, we should allow members to exercise freedom in setting their goals and in expressing their feeling within the limits imposed by the larger objectives of the organization.

At all times we should try to set a good

example in our attitudes and values. People usually find it easy to identify with a leader whom they can respect and admire.

We should have a regard for the dignity and worth of people. Most people resent being treated as a means to an end. They appreciate an attitude of concern for their welfare and are more likely to cooperate with us if we offer that kind of leadership.[5]

[5] A relevant research study of the effects of factors in leadership is D. E. Katz et al., *Productivity, Supervision, and Morale in an Office Situation,* University of Michigan Press, Ann Arbor, Mich., 1950.

SUMMARY

In order to understand human behavior it is necessary to consider a person's relationships with others. We compare our privileges with those of others and set our goals in relation to other people as standards.

There are a number of maladjusted ways of relating ourselves to others—dominating, rebelling, being dependent, and being submissive. In each case, the behavior serves as a way of handling feelings such as fear, hostility, frustrated needs for love, and the like. More satisfying relationships may be cultivated, although in extreme cases psychotherapy may be required.

Leadership is the process of directing, initiating, regulating, and coordinating group activity. This function, which is necessary for all groups, may be concentrated in one person or be more widely distributed. Authoritarian, laissez-faire, and democratic leadership vary in a number of important respects, such as amount of the leader's influence and ego-involvement of members.

Leadership depends both on the requirements of the situation and on the characteristics of the person who is leader. Different people are suited for leadership in different types of situations.

Leadership skills may be cultivated, and leadership-training courses endeavor to develop these skills. To be effective as leaders, we must (among other things) pay attention to both the people and the task and get the members to work for the group.

QUESTIONS

1. With what individuals or groups do you most often compare yourself? Are your goals influenced by such comparisons? In what way?

2. What are the four types of maladjusted social relationships that were discussed? Is this an adequate classification? Evaluate its strengths and weaknesses.

3. Which of the mechanisms of enhancement and defense of the self do you think is characteristic of each of the four kinds of maladjusted relations that were discussed?

4. What recommendations would you make for cultivating more satisfying relationships with others? What factors might affect the relearning of existing ways of adjusting to other people?

5. What is leadership? Why do groups have leaders?

6. Compare the position of leader in a formal organization with that of leader in a voluntary group.

7. Compare and contrast authoritarian, laissez-faire, and democratic leadership. What problems does a leader have in trying to be democratic when his group is subject to controls from above?

8. Give some illustrations of the point that leadership depends both on the requirements

of the situation and on the characteristics of the person (as potential leader). Can people with different personalities function equally well as leaders in a given situation?

9. To what extent does the leader influence the group, and to what extent does the group influence the leader? With what factors might the relative influence of leader and the group vary?

10. If you were setting up a leadership-training program for a particular group of your ac-

quaintance, what methods of training would you employ?

11. Why is it necessary for a leader to be concerned with the attitudes of the members toward him and toward each other? What can he do to encourage the development of favorable attitudes?

12. What functions may the so-called "followers" in a group perform, and what satisfactions may they obtain?

SUGGESTED READINGS

Bradford, L. P., and J. R. P. French, Jr. (eds.): "The Dynamics of the Discussion Group," *Journal of Social Issues*, 1948, vol. 4, no. 2.

(A series of articles dealing with the fascinating subject of group dynamics—the personal and social forces determining group behavior.)

Gibb, C. A.: "Leadership," in G. Lindzey (ed.), *Handbook of Social Psychology*, Addison-Wesley, Cambridge, Mass., 1954, vol. 2.

(A summary of theory and research regarding leadership.)

Horney, K.: *Neurosis and Human Growth*, Norton, New York, 1950.

(A psychoanalyst's approach to understanding personality, with emphasis on the influence of early childhood experiences and of cultural factors.)

Lindzey, G. (ed.): *Handbook of Social Psychology*, Addison-Wesley, Cambridge, Mass., 1954, vols. I and II.

(Essays and summaries of research in the major areas of social psychology.)

Shaffer, L. F., and E. J. Shoben, Jr.: *The Psychology of Adjustment*, 2d ed., Houghton Mifflin, Boston, 1956.

(A revision of a well-known text on personal adjustment, with chapters on mental hygiene and related topics.)

Swanson, G. E., T. M. Newcomb, and E. L. Hartley (eds.): *Readings in Social Psychology*, rev. ed., Holt, New York, 1952.

(A text with many articles bearing on the influence of other people on a person's behavior, various articles having to do with leadership being included.)

GLOSSARY

Absolute threshold. The smallest amount of stimulus energy capable of arousing an impulse in a receptor or nerve cell, resulting in a sensation.

Abstraction. A selected aspect of a totality. For example, shape is an abstraction from a physical object, which has many aspects in addition to shape.

Achieved position. Any position which is assigned to an individual by society by virtue of his actions and accomplishments. Being a husband and a college graduate are examples of achieved positions.

Achievement test. A standardized psychological test designed to discover what an individual has learned. This should be distinguished from what he *can* learn and also from his general mental ability. *See* Aptitude test, Intelligence test.

Activation theory. The view that emotions and motives are high levels of neural activation, especially of the cerebral cortex.

Adaptation. The process by which a sense organ gradually ceases to respond to a constant stimulus. Olfaction and the cutaneous senses adapt very quickly.

Adrenalin. A hormone secreted during emotion by the inner portion of the adrenal glands. It stimulates the sympathetic nervous system, constricts blood vessels, reduces muscular fatigue, and is generally useful in times of stress. (Same as *adrenin*.)

Adrenals. Endocrine glands located on both kidneys. They secrete adrenalin and a number of other hormones. *See* Adrenalin, Cortisone.

Adrenosympathetic reaction. The mutual stimulation, during emotion, of the adrenal gland and the sympathetic nervous system. Nerve impulses cause the secretion of adrenalin, which in turn causes more outpouring of impulses by the sympathetic system.

Affective. Pertaining to emotional or feeling tone in an organism.

Age scale. Test for which age norms have been determined. The Stanford-Binet is one example of an age scale.

Ambivalence. Mixed or conflicting attitudes regarding an object. Some of the conflicting positive or negative attitudes may be unconscious.

Anomalous color-weak. Partially color-blind individuals who see all hues but who have difficulty with pinks, greens, tans, and browns.

Anthropology. The science studying various peoples and putting particular emphasis on culture. *Physical* anthropology emphasizes the physical features of various peoples, while *cultural* anthropology studies their achievements, values, habits of reaction, etc.

Approach-approach conflict. A conflict situation in which either two incompatible goals attract an organism (divergent type) or two incompatible motives direct an organism to a common goal (convergent type).

Approach-avoidance conflict. A conflict situation in which a goal object both attracts and repels the organism.

A priori. Not dependent on experience or observation but arising from the conjectures of the individual. *A priori* reasoning is about the same as "armchair" theorizing.

Aptitude. Potential for learning; trainability or capacity for learning certain skills, e.g., typing or sales.

Aptitude test. A standardized psychological test measuring trainability or capacity for learning a certain skill. *See* Achievement test, Intelligence test.

"Armchair" theorizing. Reasoning from assumptions which are not questioned and which the individual would often be unwilling to question. It may lead to correct conclusions, but usually it does not. It is the opposite in many ways of the scientific method. *See A priori.*

Ascribed position. Any position which is assigned by society on the basis of characteristics beyond control of the individual. Age and sex are examples of ascribed positions.

Aspect of personality. Any phase or part of personality. "Aspect" is a broader term than "trait." Thus emotional instability is both a trait and an aspect of personality. Mental alertness, on the other hand, is an aspect of personality but is not usually thought of as a trait. No hard and fast line, however, can be drawn between trait and aspect. *See* Trait of personality.

Astrology. The pseudo science alleging that there is a connection between personality and the stars under which a person is born, under which he starts a new venture or undertaking.

Attack. A way of defending or enhancing the self in which a person engages in hostile or aggressive behavior. This hostility may be an actual physical attack, it may be only verbal, or it may even be confined to his imagination. It may be directed against the real cause of the frustration, or it may be taken out on something else. *See* Displaced aggression, Scapegoat.

Attention. Selectivity in perception; the direction of perception to certain stimuli rather than others.

Attitude. Readiness to become motivated favorably or unfavorably toward a person, policy, or other object; a motivational state which accounts for a certain amount of consistency in behavior relative to an object.

Audiometer. An instrument for determining the absolute thresholds of loudness for tones of various frequencies.

It is used in the diagnosis of deafness.

Authoritarian leadership. A leader pattern in which the leader exercises authority not derived from the group to direct the activities of members toward goals not evolved by the group.

Autism. The tendency for an individual's needs (motives, drives, etc.) to influence his perceptions, his judgment, and other intellectual processes.

Autokinetic phenomenon. Apparent movement of a stationary light source when viewed in the dark.

Autonomic nervous system. A division that serves the smooth (involuntary) muscles of the body and most of the glands and visceral organs. It is important in both emotion and motivation.

Average error. The tendency of a rater to avoid very favorable or very unfavorable descriptive phrases and to choose those nearer to the average; especially likely to occur when the rater has little information about the ratee. The term is also used in statistics to signify the average of the deviations of individual measurements from the mean.

Avoidance-avoidance conflict. A conflict situation in which an organism must choose one of two goals, both of which repel the organism.

Axons. Fibers of a neuron that conduct the nerve impulse away from the cell body toward a synapse or a muscle or gland.

Basilar membrane. A membrane stretched the length of the cochlea, containing the organ of Corti.

Behavior. All the responses and reactions of an individual. His behavior includes his thoughts, needs, feelings, etc., as well as his muscular responses and glandular secretions.

Belief. Acceptance or rejection of a proposition about reality. Beliefs are related to attitudes but are not identical with them.

Binocular cues. Cues arising from the use of both eyes at once that allow the seeing of depth and the third dimension. The main cue is retinal disparity.

Catalyst. Any chemical that has the property of speeding up or slowing down a chemical reaction without itself being used up in the reaction. Hormones, vitamins, and enzymes are organic catalysts.

Cell division. A means of reproduction in a single cell, in which the cell splits into two equal parts. In *ordinary* cell division, as the cell divides, replicas of all chromosomes go to each half. In *reductive* cell division, one member of each pair of chromosomes goes to each half as the cell divides.

Centile. A value which, for a given score, gives the percentage of cases below that score in a given distribution; also called percentile.

Central nervous system. All the neurons composing the brain and spinal cord. All other neurons, along with motor fibers from the central nervous system, compose the peripheral nervous system.

Central tendency. Any typical or representative value of a set of data such as arithmetical mean, median, and mode.

Central theory. The view that both the conscious awareness and the bodily changes and expressions of emotion go on simultaneously, controlled by the brain. Also called the *hypothalamic* theory of emotion.

Cerebellum. A part of the hindbrain, containing many centers for control and coordination of muscular activity.

Cerebral hemispheres. The uppermost part of the forebrain or telencephalon. In man these hemispheres are the largest and most highly developed part of the brain. The cerebral cortex contains a vast number of neurons.

Cerebral lobes. The four parts of the cerebral hemispheres: frontal lobes, parietal lobes, temporal lobes, and occipital lobes.

Cerebrotonia. One of Sheldon's types of temperament. According to Sheldon, cerebrotonia means being restrained and inhibited, overintense, and sensitive. The corresponding body build is ectomorphy. *See also* Ectomorphy.

Character. That aspect of personality having to do with ethics, with judgments about right and wrong, and with ethical or unethical behavior on the part of the individual.

Chromosomes. Threadlike bodies in the nucleus of cells. The genes are carried by the chromosomes.

Chronological age. The period of time from birth to date in question or under consideration.

Clinic team. A psychiatrist, a clinical psychologist, and a psychiatric social worker. While each of these brings a certain specialized background of training and experience to the aid of any particular case, there is also much cooperative work involved in the team approach.

Clinical psychology. That branch of psychology which attempts to understand people who have emotional or other similar difficulties and to help them with these difficulties.

Cochlea. The spiral bony structure of the inner ear. Within the cochlea are the receptor cells for hearing.

Coefficient of correlation. A number which indicates the closeness with which two variables (measures) tend to vary together.

Coefficient of reliability. A number indicating the self-consistency of a test. It is obtained by correlating two halves of test or measures obtained on same test at different times.

Coefficient of validity. A measure used to indicate the degree to which a test measures what it is designed to measure.

Cognitive theory. A theory of learning and problem solving which views learning as a process of perceptual reorganization, perceiving relationships and principles.

Color blindness. The total or partial inability of the eye to distinguish hues. Some hues are correctly seen by certain types of color-weak eyes, while other hues are confused.

Common sense. As used in this book, the opinion of the majority of people, who do not have expert knowledge or training for the problem at hand. It sometimes implies the wisdom of folklore, which may be old and respected but which may also be in error.

Common-sense theory. The view of emotion holding that conscious awareness precedes the bodily changes and expressions in emotion. "We weep because we are sad." *Cf.* James-Lange theory.

Compensation. A defense mechanism in which, when a person finds his first choice unavailable, he chooses a second best, but continues to feel unconsciously that it is a second best.

Complementary colors. Hues opposite each other on the color circle. When mixed on a color wheel, complementaries result in the appearance of gray; for example, yellow and blue give gray when so mixed.

Compulsion. An irrational or apparently meaningless impulse to engage in a certain activity. A person may compulsively count the steps in a flight of stairs or steal things he does not need or even want. Compulsive stealing is known as *kleptomania*.

Concept. The set of characteristics common to a class of objects; for example, the concept of triangularity includes all three-sided figures.

Conditioned response. A response that becomes associated with a previously ineffective stimulus as a result of pairing this stimulus with an adequate stimulus for the response.

Conditioned stimulus. A stimulus that acquires a capacity to evoke a (conditioned) response as a result of having been paired with an unconditioned stimulus.

Conditioning. Learning as a result of pairing a previously ineffective stimulus with an effective (unconditioned) stimulus.

Cones. Retinal cells that are differentially sensitive to the various wavelengths of light. By use of the cones the organism is able to distinguish color (hue).

"Conquering hero." A form of fantasy in which the individual imagines that his wonderful achievements lead those who have mistreated him to feel and express deep regret for what they have done.

Control of variables. Holding constant or balancing out the influence of factors other than the independent variable. The effects of the latter on the dependent variable are the real concern of the experiment.

Controlled association. A procedure in which the subject is required to give responses having specified relationships to the stimulus word. For example, a response word may be required to be opposite in meaning to the stimulus word. *Cf.* Free association.

Conversion. A process by means of which emotional disturbance is converted into or shows itself as physical symptoms. Thus a functional appendicitis may be caused by serious emotional difficulty. *See* Functional illness, Hysteria

Cortisone. A hormone secreted by the outer rind of the adrenals. It is used in medicine to relieve the symptoms of rheumatoid arthritis.

Counseling psychology. That branch or field of psychology especially interested in understanding and helping people solve the more or less ordinary but nevertheless important questions they face (e.g., vocational guidance). Counseling psychology is to be distinguished from clinical psychology in that the latter deals with people who are emotionally maladjusted or perhaps mentally ill.

Cretinism. A type of feeble-mindedness resulting from an undersecretion of the thyroid gland that occurs from birth onward. Some amelioration of this condition can be obtained by the early and continued administration of thyroxin.

Criterion. A standard by which something is judged. A criterion of validity is a measure of behavior which serves as a standard for evaluating a test which purports to measure or predict this behavior.

Culture. The principal ways of behaving, values, and material possessions of a people.

Cutaneous senses. The skin senses: pressure, pain, coolness, and warmth. The cutaneous senses are commonly called the sense of touch; however, touch correctly refers only to pressure.

Cytoplasm. The material or protoplasm of a living cell, exclusive of the membrane and nucleus.

Defense mechanism. A more or less specific behavior pattern in which an individual engages so as to keep his own self-respect or self-esteem. Defense mechanisms are not deliberately chosen by the individual who uses them, nor is their full meaning known to him.

Delusion. A system of false beliefs which is defensively maintained despite evidence to the contrary; for example, delusions of grandeur.

Democratic leadership. A leader pattern in which the leader's authority derives from the group and the leader functions mainly to coordinate and mobilize the skills, interests, and resources of the group.

Dendrites. Fibers of a neuron that conduct the nerve impulse toward the cell body from a synapse or a receptor.

Dependent variable. The factor or force in an experiment which changes as a result of changes in the independent variable. For example, if we try to determine the effect of loss of brain tissue on the learning ability of a white rat, the various amounts of brain tissue removed would be the independent variable and the changes in learning ability would be the dependent one. *See* Independent variable, Experiment.

Depth interview. An interview in which an attempt is made to get behind the superficial or stereotyped responses of the interviewee and discover his hidden or unconscious motives. *See* Nondirective interview, Psychoanalysis.

Descriptive-adjective rating form. A rating form which consists of many adjectives (and adjectival phrases), some complimentary and some uncomplimentary, which may be applied to an individual. The rater checks those that he thinks most correctly describe the ratee.

Dexterity test. A standardized psychological test measuring skill in the use of particular parts of the body, e.g., quickness of reaction and hand-eye coordination.

Dichromats. Color-weak individuals limited to two hues, usually blue and yellow. Most often they tend to confuse certain reds and greens.

Differential threshold. The smallest amount of difference between two stimuli that can be detected by use of a receptor or sense organ.

Differentiation. The process by which specific details of behavior are gradually separated and distinguished. For example, all emotions are thought to be differentiated from the newborn child's sole emotion (excitement).

Discrimination. Reacting differently to two stimuli. In conditioning, discrimination training involves reinforcing the response to one stimulus and nonreinforcing the response to a second stimulus.

Disorientation. Inability of an individual to locate himself in time or place. Disorientation is frequent in the psychoses of old age.

Displaced aggression. A defense mechanism in which a person takes out his feelings of hostility on an innocent bystander. For example, a teacher may deal harshly with her pupils not because of the way in which they have behaved but because of how other people have caused her to feel.

Dissociation. A splitting off or splitting apart. When used defensively, as it usually is, it means to keep separate, at the conscious level, inconsistent trends or tendencies within the individual.

Distributed practice. Practice in which the work periods are separated by rest periods; similar in meaning to "spaced practice."

Dominant gene. A gene whose influence is observable in the organism possessing the gene.

Drive. A complex state within an organism that directs behavior toward a goal or incentive; often used in the sense of "physiological drive." *See* Motive.

Drosophila. A type of fruit fly used in experiments in genetics because of its giant-sized chromosomes.

Dual personality. A form of dissociation in which a person develops two different self-pictures and alternately accepts first one and then the other. These two self-pictures usually involve quite different if not inconsistent tendencies and motivations. *See* Dissociation.

Dynamics. The underlying causes or motivations of behavior. They are often unconscious.

Ectomorphy. One of Sheldon's types of body build. According to Sheldon, ectomorphy means being relatively weak and thin. The corresponding temperament type is cerebrotonia. *See also* Cerebrotonia.

Ego-involvement. Making someone or something outside the self a part of the self. *See* Identification.

Emergency theory. The view that emotions evolved to serve the organism in time of emergency and stress. This theory was originated by Charles Darwin.

Endocrine gland. A gland of internal secretion (ductless). These glands secrete hormones directly into the blood.

Endomorphy. One of Sheldon's types of body build. According to Sheldon, endomorphy means being relatively broad or thick in proportion to height, with prominence of the deeper abdominal tissue. The corresponding temperament type is viscerotonia. *See also* Viscerotonia.

Environment. All the factors (except the genes) that influence an organism in any way. *See* Internal environment.

Enzyme. An organic catalyst that regulates one step in metabolism. An organism has many different enzymes.

Essence. As used in this book, a concept not based on observation but rather on "armchair" theorizing or *a priori* reasoning. It refers to something not observable and not directly inferred from observations.

Experiment. A method of observation involving control of all variables except the independent one (and the dependent one in so far as it is affected by changes in the independent one). Experiments are seldom if ever perfect; the term is therefore applied to situations where reasonably good control is exercised. *See* Independent variable, Dependent variable, Control of variables.

Experimental neurosis. Disturbed, anxious behavior resulting from gradually reducing the difference between discriminated stimuli until the subject no longer can distinguish them.

Extinction. Reduction in the strength of a conditioned response as a result of repeatedly eliciting it without reinforcement. For example, a conditioned salivary response to a tone may be extinguished by repeatedly presenting the tone without giving food.

Extrovert. One of Jung's psychological types. According to Jung, an extrovert is an individual whose chief concern, at the conscious level, is in things outside himself. He is much influenced by external facts and by the opinions and values of others. A person who is extroverted at the conscious level is introverted at the unconscious level. *See* Introvert.

Fantasy. A defense mechanism in which the person retreats from the world as it is and gains satisfaction through daydreams or imagination.

Feeble-minded. Mentally defective. Those scoring below 70 IQ are generally regarded as feeble-minded.

Figure. In perception, the part of a stimulus pattern which stands out from the background; the most vivid, sharply defined, and organized part of the stimulus field.

Folkways. Expected or "correct" ways of behaving in a society; customs not so mandatory as mores.

Forced-choice rating form. A rating form consisting of twenty-five to forty groups of four (or more) statements each, with half the statements in each group favorable and half unfavorable. Only one of the favorable and one of the unfavorable statements discriminates between superior and inferior performance or characteristics. Checking statements that discriminate counts for or against the ratee, while checking those

that do not discriminate has no effect on his total score.

Formal leader. The leader of a formal organization, or of one of its divisions, who either is appointed, or who controls the organization through ownership or by other means. Examples of formal leaders are a foreman in a factory, the dean of a university, and the owner and manager of a business.

Formal organization. A group of people having a definite social structure usually consisting of one or more departments and levels of management. Examples are schools, factories, corporations, and military organizations.

Fovea. The point of focus on the retina. It is closely packed with cones and contains no rods.

Frame of reference. A system of scales and standards of comparison that influences perception.

Free association. A procedure in which the subject gives his immediate responses to a stimulus such as a word or picture. *Cf.* Controlled association.

Functional autonomy. The condition in which a motive continues in strength after the original set of circumstances in which it was learned has ceased to exist.

Functional illness. An illness with no known physical derangement or bodily disturbance. Functional illness is closely related to unwise defensive behavior.

Future-orientation. Emphasis on future objectives; evaluating the present with respect to long-term goals.

Galvanic skin response (GSR). A change in the resistance of the skin to the passage of a weak electric current, caused by emotion and certain other body conditions. Sometimes it is called *psychogalvanic reflex* (PGR).

Ganglion. A group of nerve-cell bodies lying outside the central nervous system, for example, the sympathetic ganglia (plural) of the autonomic nervous system.

Generalization. The tendency of a stimulus similar to the conditioned stimulus to evoke the conditioned response.

Generosity error. The tendency of a rater to give the ratee the benefit of the doubt and hence to rate him more highly than he should be rated.

Genes. Submicroscopic particles in the chromosomes. The genes are the unit carriers of heredity.

Gestalt psychology. A systematic viewpoint in psychology that emphasizes the organized character of perception, learning, etc.

Glycogen. A substance secreted by the liver during strong emotion or strenuous exercise. As soon as it enters the blood stream, it becomes usable sugar.

Goal. Any object which is sought by an organism and which is capable of satisfying a motive.

Goiter. A swollen condition of the thyroid gland. It often results from a diet poor in iodine. The thyroid is unable to secrete enough thyroxin and grows excessively; thus the goiter or swelling in the neck is formed.

Gonads. The sex glands, the

ovaries in the female and the testes in the male. Their primary function is the production of eggs and sperm cells. Secondarily, they secrete hormones that help effect the secondary sexual characteristics.

Graphic rating form. A rating form involving a number of different qualities, with the name of each quality followed by a line, above or below which are descriptive phrases indicating various degrees or amounts of the quality. The rater indicates his judgment of the ratee by putting one check on each line.

Gray matter. A collection of nerve-cell bodies in the nervous system, as in ganglia, nerve centers, etc. The cerebral cortex is such a collection and actually has a gray appearance.

Gregarious drive. The tendency of certain animals (including the human) to seek out and live in groups of their own kind.

Group-maintenance requirements. Functions which need to be performed in a group so as to preserve and develop favorable attitudes of the members toward one another and the leader.

Group pressure. Influences toward conformity which a group exerts on its members by virtue of its control over rewards and punishments.

Group test. A test, usually of paper-and-pencil variety, so constructed that it may be administered to a large group simultaneously.

Gustation. The sense of taste. The receptors for gustation are located mainly on the tongue.

Hair cells. The receptor cells for hearing, located on the organ of Corti. Hair cells are also found in some other sense organs.

Hallucination. An experience of sounds, visual objects, etc., which are not really present but which the experiencer regards as real. Hallucinations occur in some abnormal personalities and in normal people under unusual conditions such as certain drug states.

"Halo effect." The tendency of a rater's over-all judgment about a ratee to influence the rating (favorably or unfavorably) on a particular characteristic or quality.

Hedonistic paradox. The belief that if a person strives to get pleasure he usually misses it or fails to enjoy it when he gets it. The way to be happy, according to this view, is to identify with something challenging and worthwhile and to work hard for it. Happiness comes as a by-product of this endeavor.

Heredity. The influence on the organism of the genes received from the parents.

Heterogeneous. Different in quality, kind, or sort; members of a heterogeneous group vary widely on some measure.

Homeostasis. The tendency of the body to maintain an internal physiological and biochemical balance.

Homogeneous. Close in kind or quality. Members of a homogeneous group tend to be alike on a certain measure.

Hormone. An organic catalyst that helps control metabolism and other vital bodily reactions. Hormones are secreted by the endocrine glands.

Hue. The distinctive quality of color, as red, blue, green, or yellow.

Human engineering. That branch or field of psychology concerned with the human problems of design of instruments, machines, tools, etc. Its purpose is to design the device (or combination of devices) so that it may be used most easily and efficiently by the human beings concerned. Psychologists in this area work closely with various sorts of professional engineers.

Hybrid. An offspring of parents who differ in their dominant and recessive genes.

Hypnosis. A state of increased suggestibility, in which the subject is intensely motivated to follow the directions of the hypnotist.

Hypothalamus. A part of the diencephalon or lower part of the forebrain that is adjacent to the thalamus. It contains centers for emotion, sleep, activity, temperature, etc. The pituitary gland is located just beneath the hypothalamus. *See* Central theory.

Hypothyroidism. The condition resulting from an undersecretion of the thyroid gland. The affected person is mentally and physically sluggish because of a low rate of metabolism.

Hysteria. A form of psychoneurosis in which a prominent symptom is the conversion of emotional difficulties into the symptoms of organic illness. This is sometimes called *conversion hysteria*. *See* Conversion.

Identification. Making someone or something outside the self a part of the self. It is used in two related senses: (1) coming to care for another person or object to such extent that we defend and enhance it; and (2) making another a part of the self and getting our joys and satisfactions through his accomplishments. In the first sense it means the same as "ego-involvement"; in the second sense it is one of the defense mechanisms. *See* Ego-involvement.

Ideology. A system of beliefs associated with an institution; for example, capitalist ideology.

Idiot. Lowest-grade mental defective, having IQ below 25.

Idiot savant. An individual of any grade of feeble-mindedness who has special talents or skills in one or more lines, such as music or rapid calculating.

Illusion. An error in perception which depends on stimulus conditions and is experienced by all normal observers.

Image. A perceptionlike experience that does not depend on stimulation of a sense receptor and is not confused with reality by the person who experiences it. Images usually are less vivid than perceptions. They may be visual, auditory, olfactory, etc.

Imageless thought. The theory that thinking may take place without the mediation of images.

Imbecile. Middle-grade mental defective, having IQ within range 25 to 50.

Implicit speech movements: Very small movements of the speech apparatus; subvocal talking. Sensitive electronic apparatus may be required to detect these movements.

Incentive. A goal, with emphasis on the fact that this goal-object attracts or repels the organism. Except for this emphasis, "incentive" is synonymous with "goal."

Independent variable. The factor or force operating on a situation which is allowed, encouraged, or forced to change while all other forces are controlled or allowed for. The record made of changes in or by the independent variable is the heart of an experiment. *See* Experiment, Dependent variable, Control of variables.

Individual test. A test so designed that it can only be administered to one individual at a time. Stanford-Binet and Wechsler scales are examples.

Individualism. A cluster of beliefs and values emphasizing excellence and power of the individual.

Industrial psychology. That branch or field of psychology primarily interested in understanding and helping to solve the human-relations problems of business and industry. It is to be distinguished from human engineering in that the latter is especially concerned with adapting the machine to the capacities of the human being who operates it. *See* Human engineering.

Informal leader. A leader in a formal organization who has emerged from the group and is not recognized as such in formal tables of organization; leader in function, but not in title.

Insanity. Serious mental illness; a legal term also used in everyday speech. Insane individuals are usually treated in mental hospitals. *See* Psychosis.

Insight. A learning process characterized by perception of a principle or relationship. Criteria of insight include sudden improvement, ability to reproduce solution on future occasions, and ability to perform the task under widely varying conditions.

Institution. A system of social practices; for example, the family institution.

Instrumental learning. Learning responses which lead to goals; for example, learning to solve a puzzle, solve a problem, master a skill.

Insulin. A hormone secreted by the pancreas. Insulin is essential in the metabolism of sugar.

Intelligence. A way of behaving, measured in terms of learning ability, problem solving, visualization, etc.

Intelligence quotient. Intelligence-test score; ratio between mental age and chronological age times 100.

Intelligence test. A standardized psychological test of general mental ability. *See* Achievement test, Aptitude test.

Interaction. Mutual or joint determination of variables; for example, interaction of heredity and environment, or interaction of social influences.

Interference theory of forgetting. The theory that forgetting is attributable to learning new responses that conflict (or interfere) with previously learned responses.

Internal environment. The blood and lymph fluids of the body and all the chemical substances they contain.

Introjection. Adopting as our own the attitudes that others show toward us or the standards they impose upon us. When used defensively, it usually leads to our imposing upon ourselves standards of conduct which those in authority insist we must follow.

Introspection. A method of observation by means of which we discover our own thoughts, feelings, emotions, etc. Introspective observation is often contrasted with *objective* observation, in which we observe external things by means of the sense organs.

Introvert. One of Jung's psychological types. According to Jung, an introvert is a person whose values and concerns rotate around his own experiences and reactions. Thus he tends to be determined by his own subjective values. An individual who is introverted consciously is extroverted in his unconscious experiences. *See* Extrovert.

James-Lange theory. The view of emotion holding that bodily changes and expressions of emotion precede the conscious awareness of it. "We are sad because we weep." *Cf.* Common-sense theory.

J.n.d. The just noticeable difference between two stimuli, also known as the *differential threshold*.

Kinesthesis. The movement sense. The receptors for this sense are in the muscles and joints.

Kleptomania. *See* Compulsion.

Laissez-faire leadership. A leader pattern characterized by lack of direction or control; passive leadership; really, lack of leadership.

Law of effect. The principle that learning depends on the effects of responses, that is,

on their consequences. In different versions of the law, these consequences are variously classified as rewarding, nonrewarding, punishing, confirming, etc.

Law of parsimony. A principle which holds that when we have two equally adequate explanations for a set of observations, we should always choose the one which makes the fewer assumptions ("stays closer to the facts").

Law of Prägnanz. The principle that a person tends to perceive a stimulus pattern in as "good form" as stimulus conditions permit.

Law of proximity. The principle that stimuli that are close together in time or space tend to be perceived as forming a pattern.

Law of similarity. The principle that similar stimuli tend to be perceived as forming a pattern.

Leadership. The process of directing, initiating, regulating, and coordinating group activity.

Learning. A change in behavior as a result of experience; to be distinguished from changes attributable to factors such as fatigue and drugs.

Learning curve. A graph which shows change in performance as a function of amount of practice.

Logic. A system of formal rules for manipulating symbols so as to derive the implications from a set of assumptions.

Loudness. The auditory sensation that varies mainly with intensity, although the frequency of the sound waves plays some part.

Massed practice. Practice in which there are no rest peri-

ods during learning or at least a minimum of rest. When the practice period is divided into trials, the trials occur in close succession.

Maturation. The process by which an organism completes its growth and development. Both heredity and environment are involved in maturation.

Mean. Arithmetical average. The sum of the measures divided by the number of measures.

Mechanism of self-defense. *See* Defense mechanism.

Median. The 50th centile; point above which and below which 50 per cent of scores of a distribution fall.

Medulla (oblongata). The lowest part of the brain. It connects the spinal cord and the rest of the brain. It is often called the "bulb"; the adjective "bulbar" is widely used in "bulbar poliomyelitis." Many vital functions (breathing, heartbeat, etc.) are controlled by the medulla, hence its common name "the vital knot."

Mental age. A unit for measuring intelligence. It is the level of performance on an intelligence test that is typical of persons of given chronological age.

Mental illness. A condition in which the individual shows serious emotional disturbance and often considerable intellectual disturbance as well. A mental illness may be *organic* (due to known physical malfunctioning) or *functional* (relating to the overuse of the defense mechanisms). *See* Psychosis, Psychoneurosis.

Mesomorphy. One of Sheldon's types of body build. According to Sheldon, mesomorphy means being relatively strong and well built, with a prominence of bones, muscles, and connective tissue. The corresponding type of temperament is somatotonia. *See also* Somatotonia.

Millimicron. A length or distance equal to a billionth of a meter.

Mode. The most frequently made score or measure in a distribution.

Model. A person who serves as a standard against which to match our behavior; an object of imitation.

Mongolian feeble-mindedness. Idiocy or imbecility in an individual with peculiar-appearing eyes, a long pointed tongue, and certain other distinctive physical characteristics.

Monocular cues. The cues that allow a single eye to perceive some depth, such as linear perspective, overlap, and shadows.

Mores. Required ways of behaving in a society; mandatory customs, such as those required by the law.

Moron. Highest-level mental defective, having IQ within range about 50 to 70.

Motivation research. A kind of depth interview in which, through the use of general (or "open-end") questions and related devices, an attempt is made to get at the real feelings (as opposed to the expected or stereotyped responses) of the interviewee about the subject under investigation. It has been used most extensively in market research. *See* Depth interview.

Motive. A complex state within an organism that directs behavior toward a goal or incentive. Some psychologists differentiate among the terms "need," "drive," "motive," etc. This book makes very little differentiation.

Myelin. A white, fatty substance which covers and insulates nerve fibers and bundles of nerve fibers (nerves).

Naturalistic observation. Observation of events as they occur, without any attempt at control of variables. Naturalistic observation involves careful attention to events, note-taking, checking results with those of others, repeated observations under similar conditions, etc. *See* Control of variables, Experiment.

Need. A certain lack within an organism. An animal that needs something is one that lacks something. The term is similar in meaning to "motive."

Nerve. A bundle of nerve fibers, covered with myelin. Axons and/or dendrites from a number of neurons form a nerve. The sciatic nerve in the leg is a good example.

Nerve impulse. An electrochemical reaction in the nerve cell and its fibers. The impulse corresponds to a depolarization of the membrane of the cell.

Neuron. A nerve cell, consisting of dendrites, a cell body, and an axon. It is the basic structural unit of the nervous system.

Neurosis. *See* Psychoneurosis.

Nondirective interview. A kind of depth interview in which the fundamental purpose is to bring the interviewee to talk freely about his needs, hopes, aspirations, frustrations, etc., with the purpose of giving him emotional release and helping him to develop self-understanding. *See* Depth interview.

Numerology. The pseudo science holding that the personality of an individual is closely related to numbers connected with him (e.g., his street address, letters in his name, his birth date, etc.)

Objectivity. The characteristic of an individual which leads him to interpret, evaluate, and respond on the basis of what he actually discovers rather than as a result of his feelings, emotions, needs, and the like.

Obstruction box. A piece of apparatus used to measure the strength of the several physiological drives in the rat. The "obstruction" is an electric grid which a motivated rat must cross to obtain the goal.

Olfaction. The sense of smell. The receptors for smell are located in the bony structure of the nose in the olfactory epithelium.

Organic illness. An illness based on the malfunctioning of or a disturbance in some part, organ, or system of the body.

Ossicles. The three bones (malleus or hammer, incus or anvil, and stapes or stirrup) of the middle ear. These ossicles pick up sound waves at the tympanum and carry them to the inner ear.

Overcompensation. A form of compensation in which the person carries a certain activity to such an extreme that it becomes obvious to observers that the activity is a second choice or a second best. The individual himself does not realize that people see this in his behavior, and he may even deny to himself that the activity is not that which he most desires. *See* Compensation.

Overlearning. Carrying practice beyond the point required for meeting some criterion of learning. For example, 50 per cent overlearning is giving 50 per cent additional trials beyond the number required for learning the material to the criterion of two successive errorless repetitions.

Palmistry. The pseudo science alleging a connection between personality and the lines on the palm.

Parasympathetic nervous system. A subdivision of the autonomic nervous system that tends to conserve the organism's energy. It controls such processes as digestion.

Parathyroids. Endocrine glands located on the thyroid gland in the neck. They secrete a substance which controls the calcium and certain other minerals in the blood. *See* Endocrine gland.

Partial reinforcement. A conditioning procedure in which reinforcement occurs on only a fraction of the trials.

Percentile. *See* Centile.

Perception. The process of interpreting stimuli so as to make them meaningful.

Perceptual constancy. The tendency of a stimulus object or attribute to be perceived in the same way under various conditions; for example, brightness constancy.

Perceptual reorganization. A changed perception of the relationship between elements of a problem; the process by which insightful learning occurs.

Performance test. A test in which the subject is required to perform some task, e.g., making designs with colored blocks (Wechsler).

Permissiveness. Acceptance and tolerance of another person; a nonevaluative and nonjudgmental attitude toward another person, such as a subordinate or a patient in psychotherapy; encouraging in others the expression of their real feelings, including negative ones.

Personal worth. A cluster of beliefs and values emphasizing the dignity, value, and potentiality of persons.

Personality. The individual's characteristic ways of reacting and the dynamics which cause them. "Personality is the dynamic organization within the individual of those psychophysical systems which determine his unique adjustments to his environment."— Gordon Allport.

Personality questionnaire. A large group of questions asking the individual about his feelings, emotions, irritations, and the like. The test is standardized; that is, norms are established, and validity and reliability are determined.

Phenylpyruvic oligophrenia. A type of feeble-mindedness. It results from one defective gene. In this condition, phenylpyruvic acid is not metabolized by the brain but rather thrown off in the urine.

Phi phenomenon. The apparent movement which is perceived when one light is turned off and another nearby is turned on; perception of motion when a visual stimulus appears successively in two different places.

Phobia. An irrational fear. For example, to be afraid of falling when one is high off the ground and in a precarious position is rational and to be expected, but to be afraid to look out the screened or barred windows of a high, well-constructed building would indicate a phobia of high places (acrophobia).

Phrenology. The pseudo science purporting to understand and deal with a person effectively from a knowledge of the contours of his skull ("the bumps on his head").

Physiognomy. The pseudo science holding that there is a definite relationship between the personality of an individual and the size and shape of his body (or perhaps of certain parts of the body).

Physiological drive. A drive or motive thought to be connected in some way with the homeostatic regulatory mechanisms of the body. Such drives are thought to grow out of physiological needs.

Physiological psychology. That branch of psychology and of physiology which studies the effect of the individual's body and its structure and functioning on his behavior.

Physiology. A biological science which studies the functioning of the various parts of the body and how they work together to comprise the organism.

Pitch. The auditory sensation that varies mainly with the frequency of the sound waves, although intensity plays some part.

Pituitary. Endocrine gland located at the base of the brain; also called *hypophysis*. It secretes a host of hormones that control growth and affect all the other glands. It is often called the "master gland."

Plateau. The part of a learning curve in which there is no over-all improvement in performance and which is preceded and followed by improvement.

Point scale. A form of arranging material and scoring a test so that points are given for passing part or all of the test. Wechsler scales are point scales.

Polygraph. An instrument that records a number of bodily changes such as heartbeat, blood pressure, breathing, and GSR. It is often used to detect emotion. In police work it is called a "lie detector."

Population. The entire group under study. Samples representative of the population are often taken for study.

Position. Place, function, or office in an organization or institution; similar in meaning to "status." Examples of positions are student in a university, president of a corporation, and member of the middle class.

Posthypnotic suggestion. A suggestion given during the hypnotic trance which is to be carried out after the subject is no longer hypnotized.

Prejudice. An attitude, usually unfavorable, based on inadequate or biased information. Generally the person has a stereotyped conception of the object of prejudice.

Premise. An assumption which is made for purposes of syllogistic reasoning.

Prestige. The value or worth assigned to an individual, organization, or position. Prestige varies from positive to negative.

Prestige hierarchy. Graded scale of value assigned to different persons, positions, organizations, etc.

Problem. A state characterized by a goal without, however, any clear or effective means of reaching it. Subjectively, a problem is experienced as a state of tension, a feeling of incompleteness or even of frustration.

Profession. An occupation that requires extensive training (including college) for entry, has a well-developed and self-enforced code of ethics, and develops in its members a considerable sense of obligation for the correct practice and continued improvement of its skills and knowledge.

Projection. Seeing others as possessing the feelings, desires, fears, etc., that we find in ourselves. We may project pleasant, admirable feelings onto others. Projection is a defense mechanism, however, when our own unworthy or undesirable feelings are seen in others.

Projective technique. A device for appraisal of personality that presents the individual with ambiguous or unstructured material and encourages him to give his interpretation of what he sees or tell a story about it.

Prolactin. A pituitary-gland hormone. Its primary function is the stimulation of milk secretion. It also influences certain other aspects of maternal behavior.

Pseudo science. An endeavor purporting to be scientific but actually being far from it. The conclusions reached by the pseudo sciences are usually in error; more important, their spirit and method of procedure are contrary to those of science.

Psychiatric social worker. A member of a clinic team for the diagnosis and treatment of emotional and other difficulties. The team also includes a clinical psychologist and a psychiatrist. The social worker specializes in developing the background of the case and the social factors influencing it. *See* Clinic team.

Psychiatrist. A medical doctor who specializes in the treatment of the mentally ill, i.e., those with serious emotional disturbances, as well as those with less severe emotional disturbances. The psychiatrist may practice independently or as one member of the clinic team, which also includes a clinical psychologist and a psychiatric social worker. *See* Clinic team.

Psychoanalysis. Both the system of psychology and the method of psychotherapy formulated by Sigmund Freud.

Psychological hedonism. The view that man always strives to increase his own pleasure or to avoid his own discomfort.

Psychology. The science which studies the behavior of living organisms. It emphasizes the reactions of the whole individual as opposed to the reactions of one of the bodily systems and is concerned with the individual human being as a person. It also studies the behavior of lower animals, especially of the more complex sort (e.g., rats and apes).

Psychoneurosis. A form of emotional and intellectual disturbance less severe than psychosis. Psychoneurotics are often treated successfully outside a mental hospital, while psychotics usually require hospitalization. "Neurosis" is a synonym. *See* Psychosis, Mental illness.

Psychophysical. Pertaining to the whole organism; a term emphasizing the unity of personality. Organic and behavioral functions are regarded as interdependent parts of a whole.

Psychosis. The most severe form of emotional and intellectual disturbance. Psychosis is the major or most severe kind of mental illness, and psychoneurosis is the less severe sort. Psychotics usually require treatment in a mental hospital. The popular term with the nearest to equivalent meaning is "insanity." *See also* Insanity, Mental illness, Psychoneurosis.

Range. The interval between the highest and lowest values of any set of data.

Rating. A process by which one person's judgments concerning the fitness, competence, appearance, etc., of another individual are indicated on a previously prepared form.

Rationalization. A defense mechanism in which the individual gives reasons for his conduct that are partly or completely false, without being aware of the false nature of the reasons.

Reaction formation. A defense mechanism in which the individual exhibits (and, at the conscious level, believes he possesses) the opposite sort of feelings from those he possesses at the unconscious level.

Recall. A method for measuring retention in which the subject attempts to reproduce the material without outside assistance such as prompting, samples of the material, etc.

Receptor. Any organ or structure by means of which an organism receives stimulation (stimuli), such as the eye, the ear, or the pain receptors in the skin.

Recessive gene. A gene whose influence is not observable when it is paired with a dominant gene. If, however, two recessive genes are paired, the organism then shows their influence.

Recognition. A method of measuring retention in which the subject is required to identify the items originally learned when they are mixed in with other items.

Reduced cues. A situation in which part of a stimulus pattern is sufficient for identifying the complete pattern.

Reference group. Group with which a person identifies and by whose standards he evaluates and judges situations and himself.

Referent. The object to which a symbol refers. The object may be concrete, such as a house, or abstract, such as democracy.

Reflex arc. A functioning neural unit made up of at least one sensory, one central, and one motor neuron.

Regression. A defense mechanism in which, as a retreat from a present, unpleasant situation, a person adopts the ways of thinking, feeling, and reacting which were satisfactory in an earlier period of his life.

Reinforcement. Strengthening the association between a conditioned stimulus and a conditioned response as a result of pairing the unconditioned stimulus with the conditioned stimulus.

Reliability. The self-consistency of a test or other measuring instrument. The degree to which a test measures consistently whatever it measures.

Repression. A defense mechanism in which threatening memories and motives are kept from conscious awareness.

Restructuring. Making over or making more satisfactory to the purpose at hand. In self-defense we may restructure either the self or things outside the self. Autism is usually present in this process. *See* Autism, Unstructured material.

Retention curve. A graph showing the amount of material remembered as a function of time since learning.

Retina. The sensitive back wall of the eyeball, containing the rods and cones.

Rods. Light-sensitive cells located in the retina. The rods are very sensitive and are used for dim-light vision. They cannot be used by the organism to differentiate colors (hues).

Role. A set of behaviors characteristic of the occupants of a particular position.

Role conflict. Personal conflict attributable either to conflicting role requirements or to the presence of personal motives incompatible with the role.

Role enactment. The behavior of an individual with reference to a role; similar in meaning to "carrying out role" or "role taking."

Role expectations. Predictions or assumptions of a group as to how the occupants of a position *will* act, as distinct from how they *should* act.

Role norms. Group standards of behavior for the occupant of a particular position; how the person ought to act in carrying out the role.

Role playing. A training method in which a person acts a role in a contrived situation.

Sampling. Selection of limited number of cases taken at random from an entire group or population.

Saturation. The amount of the color or hue present in proportion to the amount of gray or white.

Scapegoat. The victim of displaced aggression. *See* Displaced aggression.

Schema. A person's over-all interpretation of a situation which influences both perception and remembering, leading to reconstructions in line with this global view.

School psychology. That branch or field of psychology primarily concerned with understanding the problems of the school system and the applications of psychology to these problems. It deals with teacher-administration relationships as well as with teacher-pupil relationiships.

Science. Primarily a method of investigation which depends on observation and on careful, conservative interpretations of observations. It is characterized by objectivity and a willingness to question any assumptions. "Science" is also used at times to mean the conclusions arrived at through the use of the scientific method.

Selective perception. Perceiving those aspects of a situa-

tion which fit in with our attitudes and beliefs while excluding incongruent aspects.

Self. The individual as he knows himself and feels about himself. Some aspects of the self are conscious and others are unconscious; however, there is no hard and fast distinction between conscious and unconscious aspects. *See* Self-picture, Unconscious aspects of the self.

Self-acceptance. The willingness to take ourselves as we are and to recognize ourselves for what we are. This does not necessarily mean lack of ambition, for we may still want to improve, but it means that we recognize where and how we are at present.

Self-defense. Attempts to keep our own good opinion of ourselves, to keep our self-picture (and our self) from becoming less admirable or worthy.

Self-enhancement. Attempts to improve our opinion of ourselves, to make our self-picture (and our self) more admirable and worthy.

Self-picture. The conscious aspects of the self; what a person knows (or thinks he knows) about himself and how he evaluates himself. *See* Unconscious aspects of the self.

Self-recitation. A method of study in which a person recites to himself the essential points in the material which he is learning.

Self-rejection. An individual's feeling that he is unworthy and of no consequence. This leads to an unwillingness to defend or enchance the self.

Semicircular canals. The sense organ for the rotation sense,

located in the same bone as the inner ear. Stimulation occurs when the head is rotated.

Sensations. The lights, sounds, odors, etc., experienced by the organism during the stimulation of its receptors or sense organs.

Sensory acuity test. A standardized psychological test of how efficiently a person is able to use one or more of his senses. Most sensory acuity tests deal with seeing or hearing, although there are others.

Set. A system of expectations, purposes, standards, assumptions, and the like; frame of reference.

Sibling. A brother or sister. All children of a given man and woman are siblings.

Social class. A set of people having a position in a status hierarchy; for example, upper, middle, and lower classes.

Social learning. Learning that occurs under the special conditions of social influence. Learning from models is an example.

Social motives. Motives learned in relationships with other people; often contrasted with the physiological drives.

Social norm. A group-shared standard for evaluating and judging situations. Behavioral norms prescribe some actions and prohibit others.

Social psychology. That branch of both psychology and sociology which studies the individual in the group, including the effect of the individual on the group and its effect on him.

Sociology. The science of the group. It differs from anthropology in its emphasis on all sorts of groups (and not primarily cultural ones) and from psychology in its emphasis on the group rather than on the individual.

Somatotonia. One of Sheldon's types of temperament. According to Sheldon, somatotonia means being assertive and aggressive, loving exercise and adventure, and being courageous and unrestrained. The corresponding type of body build is mesomorphy. *See also* Mesomorphy.

Somesthetic. Referring to the cutaneous and kinesthetic senses. Sometimes somesthesis is called the "body sense."

Sound localization. The ability of a person to tell the direction from which a sound comes.

"Sour-grapes" mechanism. A form of rationalization in which a person convinces himself that something he wanted very much but could not get was actually undesirable and unworthy. *See* Rationalization.

Specific hunger. A hunger for some food for which the organism has a specific need.

Standard deviation. The most useful measure of spread or variability of the individual measurements about the mean.

Standardized interview. An interview which follows a form prepared in advance. This form indicates the questions that should be asked, provides space for notes on the answers given, and often suggests a method of placing a score on each answer.

Static sense. The gravity sense, which responds to the position or angle of the head; located in a bone of the skull near the inner ear.

Status. The position which a person occupies in society as a whole or any part of it. Examples of statuses are male, child, president of a corporation, and husband.

Status hierarchy. Any series of social positions that form a graded scale of power, privilege, and/or prestige.

Stereotype. A concept that erroneously characterizes a set of objects without adequate recognition of individual differences; for example, racial stereotypes often assign traits not characteristic of all members.

Stimulus. Any physical energy in the environment capable of exciting or arousing a receptor or sense organ.

Stimulus-response theory. A theory of learning which regards learning as a change in stimulus-response relationships.

Subculture. The culture of a definable part of a people; for example, the Hopi subculture.

Sublimation. A defense mechanism in which the motivation toward an unworthy or antisocial goal is redirected toward a socially approved one. Thus a person may sublimate aggressive tendencies to vigorous activity for a worthy cause.

"Suffering hero." A form of fantasy in which the individual imagines that his suffering and even his death lead those who have mistreated him to feel and express deep regret for the way they treated him. *See* "Conquering hero."

"Sweet-lemon" mechanism. A form of rationalization in which the individual convinces himself that something

which he does not like or has to take as a second choice is fine and desirable. *See* Rationalization.

Symbol. Any event, such as word, image, or muscular movement, which stands for something else.

Sympathetic nervous system. A subdivision of the autonomic nervous system. It is concerned in strong emotion and in times of emergency and stress. It mobilizes the body for strenuous action.

Synapse. The place where the dendrite of one neuron and the axon of another form a functional connection which makes it possible for a nerve impulse in one neuron to set off a nerve impulse in another.

Task requirements. Functions which need to be performed in a group in order to achieve its work objectives, whether these objectives be to produce a product, educate students, or the like.

Temperament. That aspect of an individual's personality having to do with his prevailing or usual emotional state. Thus, he might be optimistic or moody "by temperament."

Test battery. A number of psychological tests, each designed to appraise different aspects, given at approximately the same time and used to get a more complete picture of the individual than would be possible otherwise.

Thalamus. A part of the diencephalon or lower part of the forebrain. It is a great relay center for the many fibers going from the lower brain and spinal cord to the cerebral hemispheres.

Thinking. Behavior in which symbols are manipulated.

Thyroid. An endocrine gland located in the neck. It secretes thyroxin, essential in the regulation of metabolism.

Trade test. A psychological test devised and standardized in a particular organization for a certain job or family of jobs in the organization. It may be of the aptitude variety (picking those who can *learn* the job easily) or of the achievement variety (picking those who can *do* the job well). *See* Achievement test, Aptitude test.

Trait of personality. A characteristic like agreeableness, introversion, objectivity, sociability, and the like. It refers to the usual ways of evaluating particularly an individual's social relationships and his subsequent behavior.

Transfer of training. Effect of having learned one task on the learning of a second task. Transfer is classified as *positive* if the effect is facilitating, *negative* if the effect is interfering, and *zero* if the over-all effect is neither positive nor negative.

Trial and error. Learning characterized by variation in response, gradual reduction in errors, and increase in probability of correct responses.

Twins. Two offspring from a single birth. *Identical* twins are two siblings with the same heredity, resulting from the union of a single egg and a single sperm cell. *Fraternal* twins are the results of two different fertilized eggs and are no more alike in heredity than ordinary siblings.

Tympanum. The membrane which separates the external

ear from the middle ear, commonly known as the eardrum.

Type of personality. A fundamental kind of personality. Types of personality were once thought to be inherited. Now we know that, if there are any, they are the result of both heredity and environment.

Unconditioned response. An unlearned or a previously learned response to a stimulus.

Unconditioned stimulus. A stimulus which is adequate to evoke the response in question, and which if paired with neutral stimulus results in the response's becoming associated with this previously neutral stimulus.

Unconscious. As an adjective, unaware; as a noun, that of which we are unaware. The difference between conscious and unconscious is not primarily one of kind but one of degree of awareness.

Unconscious aspects of the self. The feelings which a person has about himself but of which he is unaware. There are also conscious aspects of the self. The distinction between conscious and unconscious aspects is one of degree and not one involving two entirely different sorts of things. *See* Self-picture.

Unstructured material. An ink blot, a picture, or similar device which is ambiguous or unstructured so far as definite meaning is concerned. It is the basis for projective technique. *See also* Projective technique.

Validity. The extent to which a test measures what it purports to measure.

Variability. Scatter of scores of many individuals on a given test. An indication of the scatter or dispersion of a set of measures.

Verbal test. A test whose items depend upon understanding of words.

Vestibular sense. The sense of balance, which includes the rotation and static senses. *See* Semicircular canals.

Viscerotonia. One of Sheldon's types of temperament. According to Sheldon, viscerotonia means love of physical comfort and of social contacts, evenness of emotion, and complacency. The corresponding type of body build is endomorphy. *See also* Endomorphy.

Vitamin. An organic catalyst that is necessary in the body's manufacture of enzymes. Vitamins must be obtained from the food we eat.

Voluntary group. A group in which people are members through their own choice, not through external compulsion. Examples of voluntary groups are clubs, fraternities, and friendship groups.

Weber-Fechner fraction. The relatively constant ratio (for a given receptor) between the j.n.d. and the level of stimulus intensity.

White matter. A collection of nerve fibers in the nervous system. Their white appearance results from the myelin covering. *See also* Myelin.

Withdrawal. A means of self-defense in which the individual retreats from the trying or threatening situation. He may withdraw physically and yet continue to deal with the situation in his imagination. *See* Fantasy, Regression.

INDEX

Ductless (endocrine) glands, 132, 179–181

"Dull normal," 359

Duncan, C. P., 342

Dunker, K., 275n., 279

Ear, 197–200

Eaton, Joseph W., 168

Ectomorph, 142, 143

Edwards, Allen L., 342

EEG (electroencephalogram), 176

Efficiency, differences in, 323

Egg, fertilization of, 27

Ego-involvement, 95–101

Electric-shock treatment, 123

Electrical potentials in nerve fibers, 174

Ellis, Albert, 376

Ells, K., 168

Emotion, activation theory of, 83–85

   behavioral expressions of, 75–78

     cultural patterning, 77

     facial, 75, 76

      in blind children, 76, 77

     vocal, 77, 78

   bodily changes in, 70–75

     adrenal glands, 72

     breathing, 70

     heart rate and blood pressure, 70, 71

     metabolism, 71

   conditioning and generalizing of, 85

   development of, 79, 80

   differentiation of, 79, 80

   learning of, 231

   as motive, 78, 79

   personal experience of, 69, 70

   theories of, 80, 85

Emotional tone and control in relation to personality, 138

End-of-meeting form, 410

Endocrine (ductless) glands, 132, 179–181

Endomorph, 142, 143

Englehardt, Olga E. de C., 327

English, Horace B., 135

Environment, definition of, 34

   external (physical), 34

   and heredity (see Heredity)

   internal, 34

   social, 35

Enzymes, 179, 181, 182

Eriksen, C. W., 223n.

"Essence" in explanations, 8

Estep, M. Frances, 394

Estrus, 51

Evaluating, 225, 226

Evaluation of others (see Appraisal of others)

Experiment, nature of, 5, 6, 10

   obstruction-box, 53, 54

   use in psychology, 6

Experimental neurosis, 234

Exploratory drive, 52, 53

Externalization of drive, 60

Extinction, 231

Extrovert, nature of, 139, 140

   various subtypes of (Jung), 140

Eye, 190–193

   aqueous and vitreous humors, 190

   retina, 190–192

     fovea, 192

Faking, on interest scales, 376

   on personality questionnaires, 376

Fantasy as defense mechanism, 117, 118

Fatigue, undue, 124

Fear, bodily changes during, 71, 72

   conditioning of, 231

"Feeble minded," 357

   Mongolian, 39

Femininity, 163, 164

Figure, 215

Finlay, W. W., 56

Flanagan, John C., 367

Foley, J. P., Jr., 342

Folkways, meaning of, 150

   relation to mores, 150, 151

Forced-choice rating scale, 384–387

Ford, C. S., 67

Forebrain, 175

Forgetting, change in set, 253

   interference theory of, 252, 253

   (See also Remembering; Retention)

Formal leader, 404

Frames of reference, acquiring of, 225

   and judging and evaluating, 225, 226

   and perception, 224–227

Free association, 268

French, J. R. P., Jr., 413

Frequency distribution, 328

Frequency polygon, 331

Freud, Sigmund, 113, 117, 126, 391

   biographical material, 62

   unconscious hatred, 70

Friendship, personality factors in, 135

Fruchter, Benjamin, 375

Functional autonomy, 58, 59

Hypothalamus, 51, 175, 176
  role in emotion, 82, 83
Hypothyroidism, 180, 181

Identification, as defense mechanism,
    98, 118, 119
  definitions of, 118
  and ego involvement, 95–101
  meaning of, 97–99
  with roles, 313
"Idiot," 345, 357
Idiot savant, 358
Illusions, 213, 219
  distorted room, 221, 222
  imageless thought, 264, 265
Imagery, eidetic, 264
Imagery types, 264
Images, 263–265
"Imbecile," 357
Inbau, F., 87
Incentive, definition of, 46
Independent variable, 5–7
Individual-centered roles, 411
Individual differences, nature of, 321
  prediction of, 321
Individualism, 157, 158
Informal leader, 404
Insanity, 122
  experimentally produced, 184, 185
Insight in learning, 237–239
Institutional factors in attitudes, 288
Institutions, as part of culture, 149, 150
  meaning of, 149
Instrumental learning, 234–241
Insulin, 181
Intelligence, as aspect of personality,
    136
  degrees of, 357
  differences in, 322, 359
    group, 359
    rural-urban, 360
    sex, 359
  group tests of, 350
  growth in, 354
  nature of, 343
  range of, 356
Intelligence quotient (IQ), 347–368
  Full Scale, 348
  limitations of, 348
  nature of, 348
  use of, 348
Interdisciplinary or team approach,
    183, 184
Interest scales, 374–376
  faking on, 376

Interest scales, limitations of, 376
  use of, 376
Interpersonal attractiveness, factors in,
    139
Interview in appraisal, 390–392
  improving techniques of, 391, 392
  limitations of, 391
  nondirective, 391
Introjection, 119, 120
Introspection, 69
Introvert, nature of, 139, 140
  various subtypes of (Jung), 140
Irion, A. L., 253n., 257

Jacobi, Jolande, 140n., 146
James, William, biographical note, 82
James-Lange theory of emotion, 81, 82
Janis, I. L., 299
Jenkins, J. G., 253n.
J.n.d. (just noticeable difference), 193,
    194
Johnson, Louise S., 146
Jones, D. S., 316
Jones, Margaret H., 364
Judging and evaluating, 225, 226
Jung, Carl G., 138–144, 146
Jurgensen, C. E., 388

Kallikak Family, The, 130
Kaplan, E., 265
Katona, G., 279
Katz, D. E., 412n.
Kent, G. H., 269
Kinesthetic sense, 189, 204–206
King, B. T., 299
Kinship, degrees of, 29, 30
Kleptomania, 124
Klineberg, O., 77
Kluckhohn, C., 168
Knowing for the sake of knowing, 9–10
Knowledge, as aspect of personality,
    137
  as part of culture, 148
Köhler, W., 228, 237, 240, 273
Korzybski, A., 279
Krech, D., 301
Kube, Ella, 126
Kuder, G. Frederic, 375, 376
Kuder Preference Record, 375, 376
Kwakiutl Indians, 151, 152

Language, effect of, on thinking, 148,
    149

White, R. K., 404
White, R. W., 127
White matter, 175
Whorf, B. L., 149*n.*
Whyte, W. H., 406
Will, 8
Willey, R. de V., 251
Withdrawal, extreme, 124
Withdrawing, defense by, 108–109
  and retreat into imagination, 109
Witmer, Carroll A., 343
Woodworth, R. S., 87

Woodworth, R. S., on place of psychology among sciences, 169, 170
Worth of a person, 156, 157

Yoder, Dale, 394
Young, P. T., 67, 87

Z-scores (standard scores), 336
Zubec, J. P., 44
Zuñi, 153, 154